After the Dream

CIVIL RIGHTS AND THE STRUGGLE FOR BLACK EQUALITY
IN THE TWENTIETH CENTURY

SERIES EDITORS
Steven F. Lawson, Rutgers University
Cynthia Griggs Fleming, University of Tennessee

*Becoming King: Martin Luther King Jr.
and the Making of a National Leader*
Troy Jackson

*Civil Rights in the Gateway to the South:
Louisville, Kentucky, 1945–1980*
Tracy K'Meyer

*Democracy Rising: South Carolina and the Fight
for Black Equality since 1865*
Peter F. Lau

*Subversive Southerner: Anne Braden and the Struggle
for Racial Justice in the Cold War South*
Catherine Fosl

This Little Light of Mine: The Life of Fannie Lou Hamer
Kay Mills

AFTER
THE
DREAM

*Black and White Southerners
since 1965*

TIMOTHY J. MINCHIN
AND
JOHN A. SALMOND

THE UNIVERSITY PRESS OF KENTUCKY

Copyright © 2011 by The University Press of Kentucky

Scholarly publisher for the Commonwealth,
serving Bellarmine University, Berea College, Centre College of Kentucky,
Eastern Kentucky University, The Filson Historical Society, Georgetown College,
Kentucky Historical Society, Kentucky State University, Morehead State University,
Murray State University, Northern Kentucky University, Transylvania University,
University of Kentucky, University of Louisville, and Western Kentucky University.
All rights reserved.

Editorial and Sales Offices: The University Press of Kentucky
663 South Limestone Street, Lexington, Kentucky 40508-4008
www.kentuckypress.com

15 14 13 12 11   5 4 3 2 1

Library of Congress Cataloging-in-Publication Data

Minchin, Timothy J.
  After the dream : black and white southerners since 1965 / Timothy J. Minchin
and John A. Salmond.
      p. cm. — (Civil rights and the struggle for black equality in the twentieth
century)
  Includes bibliographical references and index.
  ISBN 978-0-8131-2978-5 (hardcover : alk. paper)
  ISBN 978-0-8131-2988-4 (ebook)
  1. African Americans—Civil rights—History—20th century. 2. Civil rights—
Southern States—History—20th century. 3. Southern States—Race relations—
History—20th century. 4. Southern States—Politics and government—20th century.
5. African Americans—Segregation—History—20th century. 6. Segregation in
education—Southern States—History. I. Salmond, John A. II. Title.
  E185.61.M655 2011
  973'.0496073075—dc22   2010053738

This book is printed on acid-free recycled paper meeting
the requirements of the American National Standard
for Permanence in Paper for Printed Library Materials.

∞ ⊛

Manufactured in the United States of America.

  Member of the Association of
American University Presses

This book is for Rhys Isaac,
who has made his mark,
and for Anton Minchin,
who will soon make his.

CONTENTS

PREFACE AND ACKNOWLEDGMENTS

This book begins where many histories of the civil rights movement end—with Martin Luther King's triumphal march from the iconic battleground of Selma, Alabama, to Montgomery, where ten years previously Rosa Parks had refused to yield her seat on the bus. Its focus is on what happened in the South following the passage of the two great pieces of enabling legislation: the 1964 Civil Rights Act and the 1965 Voting Rights Act. It is concerned with their implementation, with resultant social and economic change, with the empowerment of black southerners, with white resistance, accommodation, and acceptance, with national political will and the lack of it. The signal events of the 1960s—the freedom rides, the Birmingham children's crusade, the 1963 March on Washington for Jobs and Freedom, Martin Luther King's dream, the murders in Mississippi—are frequently mentioned, but as precursors to the story we are trying to tell. Increasingly, historians have come to talk of a "long civil rights movement," locating the origins of the modern drive to cleanse the American South of the evils of de jure segregation, of racial discrimination, and of monstrous illegality and violence as early as the 1920s. They have shown that the pace quickened in the post–World War II years, reached its pcak in the multipronged nonviolent revolution of the 1960s, and continued after the civil rights legislation's passage. Indeed, it continues still.

This book surveys the last phase of the movement, the first to do so in any detail. Minchin has told the story of the crucial years between 1965 and 1980, detailing the struggle to make the legislation work and the determination of many white southerners to thwart its implementation. Salmond has surveyed in broader brushstrokes the post-1980 period, the attempt at "counterrevolution" and its effect, and the movement's abiding ledger of great success and business unfinished.

The debts incurred during the making of this book are manifold and can be only inadequately acknowledged here. The study could not have been contemplated, let alone completed, without the generous support of the Australian Research Council (ARC), which gave us a three-year discovery grant for this project. We thank the ARC profoundly. We thank, too, the research committee of the Faculty of Humanities and Social Sciences at La Trobe University for its initial assistance.

Scores of librarians and archivists in Australia and the United States were generous with their help throughout the project. They cannot all be named but are sincerely thanked. We would, however, wish to acknowledge Eva Fisch of La Trobe University's Borchardt Library and Sheryl Vogt and her staff at the Richard B. Russell Library for Political Research and Studies at the University of Georgia for their exceptional support.

Our research assistant, Bronwyn Naismith, was assiduous in digging out important material in a field not her own and in patiently explaining to her less literate colleagues the keys to working with electronic collections. Her work was essential to the book's completion, and we thank her for it. Much of the planning of the book took place over many lunches at the Thai Lantern restaurant in Ivanhoe, Victoria. We thank its owner, Daranee Scarpaci, for her interest and forbearance.

Stephen Wrinn and Anne Dean Watkins at the University Press of Kentucky have been the most encouraging of editors. Anne Dean in particular has been a frequent source of positive thinking and helpful advice. We thank them both as well as other Press staff who worked on this manuscript.

Finally, we thank our colleagues, our friends, and our families. We would like to mention particularly Professors Marilyn Lake, Tim Brown, and Tim Murray. We also thank Warren and Lucy Ellem, Bill and Jo Breen, Doreen Lowe, Jim Hammerton, Gill Cell, Bruce and Carrah Clayton, Rick and Hatsy Nittoli, and Robert and Richard Zieger. Last, but by no means least, we gratefully acknowledge the continued support of our families. Tim especially wants to mention Olga and the latest arrival, Anton Minchin.

INTRODUCTION

On March 25, 1965, Dr. Martin Luther King Jr. addressed a crowd of more than twenty-five thousand onlookers from the imposing steps of the Alabama state capitol. As he returned to the city where Rosa Parks had precipitated the iconic bus boycott, the southern preacher turned national leader celebrated the wider demise of the Jim Crow system. Even in Alabama, where so many of the fiercest battles had been waged, segregation was, King proclaimed, "on its deathbed." Building to a rousing climax, he declared that southern blacks were well on the way to achieving a society that was "at peace with itself." "Like an idea whose time has come, not even the marching of mighty armies can stop us. We are moving to the land of freedom."[1]

One of King's most memorable speeches, the Montgomery address has often been viewed as the culmination of the civil rights struggle. King spoke at the conclusion of the Selma–Montgomery march, a protest that would be remembered as one of the most successful of the era. After a decade of direct action, moreover, campaigners had achieved their two main goals—the desegregation of public accommodations and federal protection of black voting rights. Observing these achievements, some standard movement histories even conclude with this rousing speech and the subsequent smooth passage of the 1965 Voting Rights Act.[2]

In many ways, however, King's Montgomery speech was a beginning, not an end. As the black leader noted, southern blacks were "moving" into new territory, yet their journey was far from over. While celebrating how much they had achieved, King was acutely conscious of the work that remained to be done. "The road ahead is not altogether a smooth one," he asserted. "There are no broad highways to lead us easily and inevitably to quick solutions." He urged his supporters to march on "segregated schools until every vestige of segregated and inferior education becomes a thing of the past." In addition, they should "march on poverty" and use their votes to change a political system that was still dominated by segregationists.[3]

After the Dream examines the ongoing civil rights struggle in the years after 1965. In these years, the movement's supporters still had much to do, particularly in the three key areas that King highlighted. In

1964, for example, less than 2 percent of southern schools had offered even token compliance with the 1954 *Brown* decision, which had declared that segregated schools were unconstitutional. Resistance was concentrated in the Deep South; in Mississippi, only 0.2 percent of black children went to school with whites, while, in Georgia, the figure was 0.37 percent.[4] In the mid-1960s, African Americans also lacked political power. In 1964, just 22.5 percent of adult blacks in the Carolinas, Georgia, Alabama, and Mississippi were registered voters, and, in some majority-black counties, the figure was less than 5 percent.[5] In economic terms, southern blacks were still trapped in the lowest-paying, dirtiest jobs, used only as "common labor" by most southern firms. As a consequence, they were much poorer than whites.[6]

While the black struggle continued after 1965, the passage of federal equal rights legislation marked an important shift. As Nick Kotz has recently argued, the Civil Rights Act of 1964 and the Voting Rights Act of 1965 were defining laws that brought about "the end of legal apartheid."[7] From now on, the main task for the movement's supporters was to ensure that these laws were executed effectively. As the U.S. Commission on Civil Rights commented in 1969, "It is not so much new laws that are required today as a strengthened capacity to make existing laws work."[8]

The central task of this book is to examine how these laws were implemented. In telling this story, we focus on the southern states, largely because the civil rights acts of 1964 and 1965 were directed at the region.[9] This was partly because most of the key protests had occurred in Dixie. When he signed the voting rights bill into law, for example, Lyndon Johnson told one black leader, "The struggle has been all about the South."[10]

Historical studies have confirmed Johnson's point. As the late Hugh Davis Graham has documented, public accommodations, de jure school segregation, and racial disenfranchisement were "primarily southern issues." The Voting Rights Act applied only to the seven southern states with the most egregious history of discrimination against black voters, while the Civil Rights Act also focused heavily on the South, the main region where legal segregation had been in place. Title VI of the act empowered federal officials to cut aid from school districts that practiced de jure segregation. By 1968, the federal Department of Health, Education, and Welfare (HEW) had used the provision to carry out more than four hundred reviews of southern school districts, compared to only forty in the North. Throughout this period, the South was also home to at least half the country's African American population.[11]

A southern focus does not mean that broader dimensions are ignored. It was federal officials who were responsible for implementing the provisions of the civil rights legislation, and their efforts provide a central focus here. *After the Dream* explores how eight different presidential administrations sought to implement the legislation. In doing so, it reveals the political pressures that influenced their policies and shows that there were significant differences in how they treated the civil rights issue.

This book reflects a strong trend within civil rights historiography, one of the most vibrant fields in U.S. history. In recent years, many historians have recognized the inadequacy of the traditional "Montgomery-Selma" narrative.[12] In particular, scholars such as Beth Tompkins Bates, Robert Korstad, Nelson Lichtenstein, and Patricia Sullivan have pushed back the start of the modern civil rights era. In a series of influential works, they have shown how black pioneers in the 1930s and 1940s established the foundations for subsequent protests by surging into the National Association for the Advancement of Colored People (NAACP) and by registering to vote in record numbers.[13]

More recently, scholars have also exhibited a growing interest in the era after 1965. In his recent account of the 1968 Memphis garbage workers' strike, Michael K. Honey has urged us to look beyond "the reassuring civil rights legislative victories of 1964 and 1965 to the hard, unresolved issues of racism and poverty that continue to haunt us."[14] Drawing on newly released archival sources, a plethora of case studies have paid close attention to the post-1965 era and have challenged the idea that the black struggle was over. As Joseph Crespino has noted in his study of modern Mississippi, "The civil rights struggle did not end with the dramatic, high-profile victories against hard-line southern segregationists in the 1960s. Important battles over access to schools, jobs, and political power continued into the 1970s and 1980s."[15] Taken as a whole, the new scholarship highlights the importance of studying what Jacquelyn D. Hall has termed the "long civil rights movement." To date, however, there have been few attempts to provide an overview of the post-1965 struggle, especially one that draws on both primary and secondary sources and takes the story into the twenty-first century. The main body of our narrative reaches a logical end in 2007, as the period immediately after this was dominated by Barack Obama's election and subsequent presidency, an unfinished story that future scholars will need to tell in detail. In a brief postscript, however, we do offer some reflections on the significance to our story of the 2008 presidential election.[16]

The 1964 Civil Rights and 1965 Voting Rights acts concentrated on four main areas—public accommodations, employment, education, and voting.[17] As President Johnson declared at Howard University in June 1965, freedom meant "the right to share . . . fully and equally in American society—to vote, to hold a job, to enter a public place, to go to school."[18] The key provisions of the 1964 act included Title VII, which prohibited discrimination in employment, Title VI, which tackled de jure segregation in education, and Title II, which banned discrimination in public accommodations. The act also authorized the Justice Department to file suits in order to enforce the desegregation of public facilities.[19] The Voting Rights Act contained many safeguards to assure black access to the ballot. Crucially, it suspended the use of literacy tests and other voter registration tests in the states of Alabama, Georgia, Louisiana, Mississippi, South Carolina, and Virginia as well as in thirty-nine counties of North Carolina. It empowered the attorney general to send federal examiners into these areas to list persons qualified to vote and to assign federal observers to monitor elections. Under section 5, before applying any new legislation with regards to voting, the covered states and counties were also required to seek court approval or to get the legislation cleared by the attorney general.[20]

There are other reasons for concentrating on these four areas. Between 1955 and 1965, civil rights protesters repeatedly tried to desegregate public facilities. The sit-ins, the freedom rides, and the Birmingham protests were all focused on this key issue. The segregation of public space was one of the most debasing aspects of the Jim Crow system, and blacks were determined to end it. White resistance to the bill's passage also frequently focused on the public accommodations provisions.[21]

Black leaders also saw jobs as central to the civil rights struggle. The 1963 March on Washington was officially termed the March on Washington for Jobs and Freedom. As the historian Nancy MacLean has shown, the black movement continued beyond the battle for legal freedom, as African Americans reasoned that "genuine inclusion" required access to the "economic mainstream." Many blacks certainly viewed access to good jobs as essential, particularly after the mid-1960s. In 1968, for example, Southern Christian Leadership Conference (SCLC) leader the Reverend Ralph Abernathy commented on the shift in the movement's goals by explaining, "We soon discovered that the promise of dignity without money enough to enjoy it was like smelling a T-bone steak broiling over a charcoal flame, and yet not being able to get a bite of it."[22]

Prior to 1965, movement activists had also worked hard to secure the ballot, which many saw as their "ticket to freedom." As the NAACP director Roy Wilkins acknowledged, "free access to the ballot for all people" was at the heart of the association's mission. After 1965, African Americans registered to vote in large numbers and fought any effort to dilute their political rights. Most blacks recognized, in fact, that both jobs and ballots were essential components of citizenship, or "the levers of power," as one group put it.[23]

Education was another central battleground in the civil rights struggle. Reasoning that segregation was anchored in the dual school system, the NAACP invested more than a decade of legal work in the landmark *Brown* case.[24] Both races also placed great faith in the public schools. As the sociologist Gunnar Myrdal wrote in his classic *An American Dilemma,* "Education has always been the great hope for both individual and society. In the American Creed it has been the main ground upon which 'equality of opportunity for the individual' and 'free outlet for ability' could be based." Throughout the 1960s and the 1970s, the schools remained a key battleground. During the Nixon administration, for example, Senator Strom Thurmond wrote the president that school integration was "the overriding issue in most of the South." At this time, many whites were bitterly opposed to the busing of students out of segregated neighborhoods in order to achieve racial balance. Because of its paramount importance, the lengthy battle over busing is explored in detail here.[25]

In the decade and a half after the passage of the Voting Rights Act, some extraordinary racial changes took place in the South. The integration of public facilities happened surprisingly quickly, and soon both races were interacting freely in these spaces. Certainly, progress occurred partly because it was relatively easy to remove *white* and *colored* signs, yet civil rights activists and federal officials also deserve credit because they ensured that Title II was complied with. Once it was clear that the law would be enforced, most southern whites accepted it, although there were some exceptions.[26]

The pace of change was also remarkable in the political sphere. As the U.S. Commission on Civil Rights noted, in the decade after 1965 blacks made "striking" progress in the political arena. By 1976, black registration in the region stood at 63.1 percent, only 5 percent lower than the white level. By this time, there were around two thousand black elected officials in the South, more than the rest of the country put together. When the Voting Rights Act was passed, in contrast, just seventy-two blacks held elected office in the eleven southern states. In a sign of the changing times, the black vote helped consign symbolic figures such as Selma sheriff Jim Clark to the sidelines. By 1979, even Birmingham, once dubbed the most segregated city in America, had a black mayor.[27]

Despite this progress, southern blacks were still grossly underrepresented. By 1980, African Americans held 3 percent of the South's elected offices, yet they made up around 20 percent of the population. The Voting Rights Act, however, was enacted to enforce the Fifteenth Amendment (1870), which had declared, "The right of citizens of the United States to vote shall not be denied or abridged by the United States or by

any State on account of race, color, or previous condition of servitude."
As such, its chief intent was to ensure that blacks could vote freely, and,
on these terms, the act was an undeniable success. In the years after
1980, moreover, the number of black officeholders increased steadily,
closing the gap with whites.[28]

In the education sector, the picture was mixed. On the plus side,
between 1965 and 1975 southern officials were finally forced to dismantle the dual school system. While executive enforcement of Title VI was
important, particularly in the first few years, it was greatly assisted by
the federal courts. In both *Green v. County School Board of New Kent
County, Virginia* (1968) and *Alexander v. Holmes County Board of
Education* (1969), the Supreme Court ordered that southern schools
must desegregate quickly. In the landmark case of *Swann v. Charlotte-
Mecklenburg County Board of Education* (1971), the Court also upheld
the busing of students in order to achieve racial balance.[29] In addition,
pressure from civil rights groups helped ensure that the South's schools
became the most desegregated in the nation. By 1979, a study by the
Institute for Educational Leadership was able to conclude, "Few cases of
de jure segregation are still unknown, and the majority have either been
resolved or await final court action."[30]

The South is a large, diverse region, and white reaction to these
changes did vary. In general, opposition was concentrated in heavily
black areas, especially in the Deep South. As Jack E. Davis's study of
Natchez highlights, whites in these locales viewed black culture as inferior and felt threatened when segregation laws no longer contained the
"reputed immoral nature of blacks." In order to address these fears, officials across the region closed black schools and laid off black teachers
and administrators. Within the unitary schools, black students were also
unfairly disciplined by white teachers and separated into special classes.
By the late 1970s, progress was also being undermined by white flight,
particularly in the bigger cities. As a result, after 1980 the federal courts
continued to engage with complex issues of how to achieve racially balanced schools.[31]

Civil rights groups were much less successful in the economic arena.
When the landmark legislation was passed, the size of the task that faced
black groups was daunting; in 1965, the NAACP calculated that between
41 and 52 percent of African Americans in seven major southern cities
were poor, and this was according to the federal government's "conservative" poverty criteria. Between 1965 and 1980, black income levels
lagged behind those of whites, and their unemployment rate was about
twice as high. Beginning in 1973, a severe economic recession also had a
disproportionate effect on southern blacks, who were often "last hired,
first fired." The downturn lasted for the rest of the 1970s, and, by 1980,

black median income in southern cities was only 55.8 percent of that of whites.[32]

Tackling employment discrimination was difficult, and federal officials did not have the tools to produce quick results. Until 1972, the Equal Employment Opportunity Commission (EEOC), which was set up to enforce Title VII, had no power to compel lawbreakers to change. Even when the agency secured more authority, its officials found that it was much more difficult to meet black economic demands than it had been to grant them access to public accommodations or protect their right to vote. As the black presidential adviser Louis Martin commented in the late 1970s, "In the troubled 60s the paramount concerns of Blacks centered around some basic civil rights issues, notably public accommodations and voting rights. Civil rights issues are still on the Black agenda today but the greatest concern by far revolves around economic issues. Unemployment is the most critical issue today." Martin added that the "economic issue" was the "toughest" aspect of his role as Carter's minority affairs liaison, partly because the president's control over the economy was very limited. In addition, while many whites had accepted the granting of individual rights to blacks, they resisted systematic efforts to address employment bias because they saw them as reverse discrimination. Overall, however, southern blacks did make some important economic advances under the legislation. By 1980, legalized segregation had been dismantled, and the most able blacks had access to a much wider range of jobs.[33]

In examining these changes, it is also important to analyze how black and white southerners reacted to new forms of interaction. Most work on the civil rights era has focused on blacks, and there is still much to learn about how the movement affected whites. This was particularly the case after 1965, when whites had to adjust to new laws that few of them supported. As the historian Jason Sokol has commented, "If any pieces of federal legislation touched the lives of white southerners, they were the 1964 Civil Rights Act and 1965 Voting Rights Act."[34] In the last few years, pathbreaking books by Sokol, Matthew Lassiter, Kevin M. Kruse, and Joseph Crespino have shown that white reaction to the movement was complex and needs to be taken seriously.[35] These works have redrawn the boundaries of the field. "Southern whites," asserted the *New York Times* journalist Patricia Cohen in 2007, "have become the leading edge of academic research."[36]

Building on this work, this study asserts that the white response to the equal rights laws should not be oversimplified. While many chose to fight the legislation, there were others who sought to comply. In the case of the schools, for example, opposition grabbed the headlines, yet many whites quietly cooperated with blacks. They did so because they realized that racial conflict was bad for the economy and would only undermine the public schools and because they saw that change was inevitable. As South Carolina governor Robert McNair commented in 1969, it was a "false hope" to believe that southerners could resist school desegregation any longer. "We have run out of courts and we have run out of time," he admitted.[37]

Even in cases where whites and blacks worked together, however, they remained deeply divided. Throughout this era, whites tended to emphasize that race relations were improving, while blacks stressed ongoing problems. One typical example came from Quincy, Florida, a majority-black community where black protests briefly made the headlines in 1970. As was often the case in the small-town South, Quincy's blacks insisted that whites were in firm control. "People have always tried to paint a picture of good relationships in Gadsden County," commented the NAACP activist Franklin D. Jones. "There never has been a good relationship in Gadsden County. It's not a man versus man relationship here. It's boy versus man." Whites, however, still expressed these views even as blacks rioted and demanded change. "We've been blessed with good race relations here," insisted Pat Thomas, a local resident.[38]

Across the South, this gulf in perception reflected how segregation had scarred blacks more than whites. For whites, Jim Crow had meant order and harmony, but, for blacks, it had represented inequality and humiliation. As legal segregation was abolished, most whites felt that racial problems had been addressed, but blacks disagreed. As the Southern Regional Council (SRC) noted in 1971, "Wide gulfs in perception [are] a part of the legacy of segregation."[39] Because their experiences had been more traumatic, blacks also pushed to remember the civil rights movement, whereas whites generally wanted to ignore it. Throughout the 1970s, for example, African Americans called for a federal holiday to honor Martin Luther King, but most whites resisted the idea. They also opposed other efforts to celebrate the achievements of the civil rights movement and, instead, embraced a conservative backlash against affirmative action and busing. As the closing chapters make clear, the two races remained at odds well into the twenty-first century. "You're always going to have that division," admitted one white Alabamian in 2004, "and when something major happens, it's no big secret, black people look at certain things different than what white people do. I guess it's just culture. I don't know, it's hard to explain."[40]

Another argument of *After the Dream* is that civil rights organizations carried out vital work in the continuing black struggle. While groups that were dependent on direct action did fade, others came to the fore.[41] The NAACP, in particular, played a central role in this story. In recent years, scholars have shown how the NAACP carried on a lonely struggle in the decades prior to 1955. Because of its preference for working through the courts, the association was somewhat eclipsed during the direct action era, but, after this, it reemerged as the most influential civil rights organization. As the historian August Meier has observed, "Over the long view, the importance of the NAACP is hard to overestimate."[42]

In the late 1960s and early 1970s, the NAACP helped enforce the new legislation on the ground. It was particularly suited to this fresh chapter in the movement's history, which revolved around implementing laws rather than agitating for their passage. As early as 1965, NAACP executive secretary Roy Wilkins wrote that the key task was to ensure that "new laws are implemented as to registration and voting, public accommodation, employment and the use of Federal funds." Little changed over the ensuing years. In 1972, for example, NAACP associate director Frank C. Kent called on members to "clog the courts" with suits brought under the legislation. While the cost of lawsuits was considerable, they also yielded real gains.[43]

After 1965, there was no noticeable fall in the NAACP's popularity on the ground. In 1969, for example, the *Race Relations Reporter* noted that the association's membership was heading toward an all-time high of 461,000, while, six years later, the Ford administration estimated that 440,000 people belonged, making the NAACP easily the largest civil rights organization in the country.[44] In the South, the group actually grew as ordinary blacks looked to test the meaning of legal equality. Membership in region 5, which comprised seven Deep South states, increased from 57,450 in 1963 to 69,861 in 1973, and much of the gain occurred in Mississippi, where the new laws gave blacks the confidence to join up for the first time.[45] By 1979, the association's figures indicated that, in region 5, there were 82,618 members scattered across 543 branches. In Alabama, the NAACP had been banned in 1956, but it returned nine years later and promised to "remove the last vestiges of segregation and discrimination in the state." In 1965 alone, more than thirty new branches were chartered in the Heart of Dixie.[46]

While the NAACP was afflicted by financial shortfalls, especially after the mid-1970s, its mass membership allowed branches to work closely with staff lawyers. Following the passage of the Civil Rights Act, for example, many members conducted checks of public facilities and passed on complaints to the association's legal department. In addition, many branches set up labor committees that filed Title VII charges. By 1977, the *New Republic* credited the NAACP with inspiring over ten thousand EEOC charges.[47] Many of these charges turned into lawsuits, and NAACP attorneys led demands for the courts to interpret Title VII more broadly. In addition, they brought suits under the Voting Rights Act and played a vital role in desegregating southern schools.[48]

As the focus of the civil rights struggle shifted, some unheralded groups also came into their own. Generally viewed as a research organization, the Atlanta-based SRC has largely failed to attract historians' attention.[49] After 1965, however, the interracial SRC pressed for school desegregation and funded the Voter Education Project (VEP), an important program that registered thousands of new black voters. Between 1965 and 1975, the VEP played a vital role in educating blacks about their political rights.[50] Established in 1957, the U.S. Commission on Civil Rights was also research focused, but its thorough reports prodded federal officials to take action. In 1971, for example, the conservative presidential adviser Pat Buchanan called the commission "a thorn in the side of the Nixon administration" because it had repeatedly criticized the president's record. At this time, the commission claimed that over 80 percent of its recommendations had passed into federal law.[51]

Other groups also strove to implement the new laws. A separate organization from the NAACP, the NAACP Legal Defense Fund (LDF), formally the Legal Defense and Educational Fund, became involved in several key cases, including *Green* and *Swann*.[52] Established in 1971, the Southern Poverty Law Center (SPLC) also deserves recognition. SPLC suits integrated the Alabama highway patrol, opened up recreational facilities in Montgomery, and allowed blacks to gain a voice within the Alabama state legislature. As the white activist Morris Dees recalled about his reason for establishing the SPLC, "I was ready to . . . speak out for my black friends who were still 'disenfranchised' even after the Voting Rights Act of 1965. Little had changed in the South. Whites held the power and had no intention of voluntarily sharing it." An articulate attorney, Dees was well placed to carry on the civil rights fight, yet he knew that it would not be easy. As King had declared in Dees's hometown, Montgomery, "freedom-loving people" may have been "on the move," but they would have to keep fighting to bring about "a society that can live with its conscience."[53]

1

HISTORIC PROGRESS

*Public Accommodations and Voting Rights
in the Johnson Years*

In the Johnson years, civil rights campaigners faced many challenges. By the summer of 1965, the United States was deeply embroiled in the war in Vietnam, a conflict that drew attention and funding away from racial issues. Just a week after the Voting Rights Act was signed into law, a brutal race riot in the Watts district of Los Angeles left thirty-four people dead and caused millions of dollars in property damage. Smaller riots soon broke out in Chicago, Philadelphia, and other northern cities, and they would be repeated over the next few summers. Reacting to these televised disturbances, many whites associated blacks with uncontrolled lawlessness and unreasonable demands. In August 1966, a *Newsweek* poll related "the spreading white view that enough is enough for now." Reflecting this mood, by early 1967 two congressmen, Mississippi's William Colmer and Florida's William C. Cramer, were leading efforts to pass an antiriot bill. By June 1967, the presidential aide Fred Panzer reported to LBJ that the races were completely polarized. "Whites are uneasy and resistant," he noted. "Negroes are impatient." Panzer cited a Gallup poll showing that 47 percent of southern whites feared racial violence on the streets, up from 44 percent the year before. Although most of the riots had taken place in the North, the southern figure was the highest in the country.[1]

The president had urged them to "close the springs of racial poison," but most southern whites were clearly not listening.[2] Between 1964 and 1968, leading southern politicians were bombarded with letters from white constituents that called for harsh action against the rioters. Writing to Democratic senator Richard Russell in 1967, Walter Hawkins Jr. spoke for many. "In my opinion," he declared, "these niggers riot as a cause to steal and loot. No amount of appeasement . . . will correct the situation." "If I were to do what these negroes are doing," added a correspondent to Senator Herman Talmadge during the Newark riot of 1967, "I would be shot and killed, as I should be, as I would be no better than a mad dog. These black bastards need killing, and I don't mean two or three, but thousands, if it takes this to save our country." While Russell gave a cautious reply to such letters, Talmadge expressed enthusiastic agreement.[3] In sharp contrast, blacks saw the violence as a reflection of economic deprivation and called for far-reaching solutions. As Martin Luther King Jr. put it, "More than half of our people are struggling on an island of poverty in the midst of this ocean of material wealth. . . . In the final analysis this is the reason for the riots and discontent across the nation."[4]

In these years, other problems complicated the task of implementing the new legislation. By 1968, relations between the White House and most civil rights leaders had fallen apart. The causes of the breakdown were complex but included Johnson's commitment to the war in Vietnam and his feeling that black leaders were not sufficiently appreciative of his landmark civil rights legislation. In addition, the successive riots reduced the possibilities for fundamental economic reforms even as they dramatized how necessary such initiatives were. In 1968, Johnson ended up shelving the recommendations of the Kerner Commission, which called for a wholesale commitment of national resources to narrow the economic gap between the races. It was too embarrassing for LBJ to admit that his Vietnam budget was more than three times greater than the amount that the commission wanted to invest in the cities. "By that time," recalled SCLC vice president Andrew Young, "I think we had lost faith in President Johnson altogether."[5]

Civil rights activists confronted other fresh difficulties. Prior to 1965, the leading organizations had worked together to overthrow legal segregation and secure black voting rights. While there had always been tensions, particularly between the hierarchical SCLC and the group-focused Student Nonviolent Coordinating Committee (SNCC), the fight against overt segregation had created what King's former aide Bayard Rustin called "an uncommon unity." Once the civil rights legislation was passed, however, activists differed about the "much more difficult task" of implementing it effectively.[6]

Leading civil rights groups certainly experienced many problems. According to Clayborne Carson, after 1965 SNCC was "severely weakened by police repression, loss of white financial support, and internal dissension and disarray." Many of the difficulties were generated by disputes over black power, which became the group's driving philosophy when Stokely Carmichael replaced John Lewis as chairman in May 1966. SNCC's embrace of black power led to the departure of white staffers and produced negative press from formerly sympathetic journalists. *Newsweek* declared that "SNCC's Stokely Carmichael preaches 'black power' without a program," while the *New Republic* dismissed the doctrine as "racism in reverse." After an ill-fated merger with the Black Panthers, SNCC became a tiny group of warring radicals and no longer engaged in community work. As Carson notes, however, the organization left behind an important legacy, especially in awakening many southern blacks to fight for their political rights.[7]

The Congress of Racial Equality (CORE) did not fare any better. After 1965, factional divisions riddled a group that had initiated the pathbreaking freedom rides just a few years earlier. Advocates of separatism and black power eventually won the day, but, in the process, CORE lost members and influence. In contrast, the SCLC did launch some nonviolent protests in these years, but it struggled to repeat its earlier successes. The group's ill-fated Chicago campaign highlighted Dr. King's awareness that blacks' legal equality had not translated into real economic power. Reflecting this realization, in 1968 King also supported a strike by poorly paid sanitation workers in Memphis.[8]

Despite the increasingly difficult national climate, the key task of implementing civil rights legislation began in earnest, and it would carry on in subsequent years. As David C. Carter has shown in an important recent work, the black struggle "continued even through the years of white backlash and ascendant national conservatism." Reality was far more complex than any neat narrative of decline might suggest, especially when we examine ongoing struggles at the local level. From Virginia to Texas, ordinary blacks were determined to realize the rights granted to them under the law, and they were helped by one organization more than any other. With branches right across the region, the NAACP was uniquely suited to the decentralized nature of the ongoing struggle. While internal divisions over black power damaged other organizations, Roy Wilkins was able to fend off a brief challenge from younger members who were influenced by the doctrine. Under Wilkins's steady leadership, the NAACP brought numerous lawsuits under the new legislation. In an era in which blacks' legal rights had been strengthened, the group's long-standing interest in litigation took on a fresh relevance.[9]

Stressing the necessity of ongoing activism, NAACP leaders set the tone for members. "This is no time to let up in any aspect of the struggle," warned *The Crisis* in November 1965. "The easy part of the struggle is ending and the more difficult part is just beginning." Following this lead, NAACP members tested compliance with Title II of the 1964 Civil Rights Act, filed scores of complaints with the EEOC, and challenged "freedom-of-choice" plans that had failed to integrate the schools. These complaints allowed association lawyers to use the federal judiciary to bring about real change. By the time King was assassinated in

April 1968, southern blacks had clearly made considerable progress, particularly in desegregating public accommodations and securing greater political power. In these areas, federal officials could also take some of the credit for helping address what LBJ had eloquently termed "the crippling legacy of bigotry and injustice."[10]

Substantial Compliance:
Title II on the Ground, 1964–1968

The progress that occurred under the Civil Rights Act was particularly noteworthy because southern politicians had tried so hard to stop the bill's passage. Even more than the Voting Rights Act, the wide-ranging Civil Rights Act promised to transform race relations in the South. As well as demanding the desegregation of public accommodations and schools, the act created the EEOC, a federal agency devoted to tackling job discrimination. As Jason Sokol has noted, "Everything in the law repelled southern politicians, and they made its passage difficult." When John F. Kennedy had introduced the initial legislation, whites in Birmingham had rioted. After Kennedy's assassination, LBJ tried everything he could to push the bill through, but southern Democratic senators still filibustered for three months. The lengthy debate consumed an unprecedented sixty-three hundred pages in the *Congressional Record*. A senator since 1932 and the chairman of the influential Armed Services Committee, Georgia's Richard Russell orchestrated the longest fight in the history of the chamber. Also playing a leading role was Mississippi's John Stennis, who insisted that the "so-called civil rights proposals" were "punitive and oppressive." Taking Title II as an example, Stennis argued that individual business owners should have the right to "select" their own customers and not be told what to do by federal officials.[11]

Southern senators also argued that the Civil Rights Act unfairly picked on the South but allowed discrimination in the North to continue largely untouched. As Russell put it, "The main thrust of this bill is aimed at the Southern states. This is especially true with regard to its harshest and most coercive sections." White southerners added that the bill was a "special privileges bill" that discriminated against them in favor of blacks. Over the coming years, they would constantly repeat both these claims.[12]

Finally recognizing defeat, in June 1964 Russell declared that he and his supporters had "given the last particle of ability and the last iota of physical strength" in an effort to expose the bill's "manifold evils." Outnumbered, they eventually admitted defeat, although the law was not enacted until July 2, 1964, more than seven months after Kennedy's tragic death. Its passage owed much to Johnson, who had worked tirelessly to build support. In signing the law, the president declared, "Those who are equal before God shall now also be equal in the polling booths, in the classrooms, and in hotels, restaurants, movie theatres, and other places that provide service to the public."[13]

Many blacks were delighted with the outcome. As the SCLC worker Willie King recalled, "I was aware, I guess, a few days before President Johnson actually signed it, that the act was going to pass. But when we got the word that it was really going to happen, I think I must have screamed for about five minutes without stopping. We were so elated because a lot of hard work, blood, sweat, and tears, had gone into this act." The act enshrined many of the rights that African Americans had been fighting for since the early twentieth century. As Roy Wilkins put it, "Such an Act has been the goal of the civil rights movement since the modern civil rights crusade began in 1909 with the organization of the NAACP."[14]

In sharp contrast, most southern whites shared Russell's despondency. The experienced senator received hundreds of letters from whites who thanked him for his efforts. "You fought a valiant fight—you gave your all to the cause," wrote H. F. Braselton from Braselton, Georgia. "We are so proud of you. . . . Though our hearts are breaking over that disastrous vote, we are grateful for all you did and thank you." Correspondents insisted that the legislation represented excessive federal interference in state affairs, especially as it restricted business owners' right to refuse service. As the Savannah resident Owen H. Page put it, this was "unprecedented police state legislation." He added, "This law in the hands of one who will abuse it presents a frightening and ominous picture." Several writers blamed Johnson for the outcome and claimed that they would no longer support the Democratic Party. Drawing on these sentiments, Republican Barry Goldwater won five Deep South states in the 1964 presidential election, including Russell's home state.[15] Writers to Alabama governor George Wallace, an outspoken segregationist, expressed great hostility to the "so-called Civil Rights Law," especially the public accommodations provisions. According to the Birmingham restaurateur Jesse T. Todd, "The Civil Rights Bill . . . in its present form will destroy America."[16]

At the same time, however, it is important to realize that the opinions of southern whites were not monolithic. In his files, for example, Russell collected a large stack of letters from whites urging him to support the bill's passage. Bravely written, they came from native Georgians who recognized that the South had to change. Many lived in Atlanta, a city that was widely viewed as a symbol of a New South.[17] Writing from that city, Emmett David Foskey compared the behavior of the southern resisters to an eight-year-old child who had to be dragged to the dentist.

"Integration is coming sooner or later," he wrote, "and you know it as well as I do. Why do we always have to be dragged around by the rest of the country who sneer at the South as being backward? . . . Let us give the colored man the helping hand of friendship." Some correspondents even chided Russell directly. "Not only have you abdicated leadership," charged Atlanta's Marge Manderson, "you lag behind your constituents." While he did not reply to all these letters, Russell insisted that he had opposed the Civil Rights Act on constitutional, not racial, grounds.[18]

These letters show that there was a constituency that was ready to accept reform, particularly in the larger urban areas. Once the law had been passed, moreover, many of its political opponents grudgingly accepted it because they realized that they had little choice. Even Russell counseled that, while the act was a "bitter pill," it was "now the law of the Senate and we must abide by it." Georgia governor Carl Sanders repeated the message; he had testified against Title II, yet, once the bill was passed, he urged citizens to "pull together" and support it. Even in the Deep South, ordinary whites imbibed this message. A lifelong resident of Natchez, Mississippi, Allen Coley later recalled that whites "didn't necessarily like it [the Civil Rights Act] but ninety percent of them, ninety-five percent of them knew it was the law, and knew it was something they had to live by."[19]

As both sides realized, the public accommodations provisions of the Act were far-reaching. Title II of the act prohibited discrimination on government property and in any business that traded in interstate commerce. It meant that nearly every restaurant, cafeteria, sports arena, and motel had to desegregate at once. It was a powerful statement of the principle of equal access, and it quickly secured real results. In April 1966, Johnson proudly reported to Congress that the fruits of Title II were "already impressively apparent." He explained, "Discrimination in places of public accommodation—perhaps the most unbearable insult to Negro citizens—has been made unlawful. The mandate of that law has spread faster and more effectively than its most optimistic supporters believed possible." In the following year, the NAACP broadly agreed with the president's assessment. "Title II may safely be considered the most widely and effectively implemented section of the 1964 Civil Rights Act," it concluded in a key report.[20]

While the provisions of Title II were far-reaching, several other factors help explain why these changes took place. When the act was passed, many cities in the Upper South had already desegregated public facilities, and, thus, the law merely formalized existing arrangements. Elsewhere, it was relatively easy to desegregate public accommodations, as it was often simply a case of removing *white* and *colored* signs. There were few of the complications that occurred when workplaces or schools were integrated. Once the changes started, they generated their own momentum. While many whites were initially hostile, over time their attitudes softened. In 1966, one *Newsweek* poll found that the proportion of southern whites who objected to sitting next to an African American in a restaurant had fallen from 50 percent in 1963 to 42 percent.[21]

Officials from the Johnson administration also worked to encourage voluntary compliance, and this made a difference. Part of the Department of Commerce, the Community Relations Service (CRS) was empowered by the law to assist communities in resolving racial disputes that arose from Title II's provisions.[22] Bound by statute to confidentiality, CRS staff visited many southern communities and quietly encouraged acceptance of the law. In the fall of 1964, for example, two CRS agents visited McComb, Mississippi, and established communications with white and black leaders. Their task was not easy; between June 22 and September 30, 1964, seventeen unsolved bombings had occurred in the town, which had a reputation as one of the most repressive in the state. In November, the CRS's Harold C. Fleming was, consequently, very pleased when several hundred citizens signed an advertisement urging residents to abandon violence and respect the new law. "We were able to give some guidance not only as to the wording of the statement but also as to the general strategy to be followed in the community," he noted in a confidential report. As a result, tests of public accommodations by local blacks went forward "without incident." The case typified the CRS's work; by December 1965, its representatives had worked in more than two hundred communities. Overall, CRS director Calvin Kytle claimed that his agents had "helped bring about a new and expanding consciousness of what it will be to have a genuinely open society."[23]

Other agencies carried out important work. Justice Department officials enlisted the help of the SRC and the Potomac Institute and used them to spread the message that desegregation would not lead to economic losses. In June 1964, for example, the SRC sponsored a gathering in Atlanta that urged local people to support Title II. In meetings with business and community groups, federal officials also stressed the necessity of change. Responsible for coordinating the activity, one government official explained, "We are trying to convince them that putting off compliance is only buying trouble for a town. This isn't like prohibition. The law isn't going to go away." Justice Department officials also promoted voluntary observance because they recognized that it was very difficult to compel southerners to change, especially as the Civil Rights Division did not have the resources to prosecute numerous offenders. When the Civil Rights Act was passed, for example, the Justice Department had just 105 attorneys on staff.[24]

In larger towns and cities, the changes happened quickly. In Georgia, most business owners followed the lead of the Georgia Restaurant Association, which told its members that they had "no alternative but to comply." In Atlanta, civic leaders backed up the association's policy, largely because they feared that defiance could hurt the economy. The chamber of commerce urged all businesses to "adjust promptly and peacefully" to the law, a line that was reinforced by the influential *Atlanta Constitution*. In other major centers, the example of community leaders frequently made a difference. Jackson mayor Allen Thompson, for instance, urged businesses in the Mississippi capital to comply even though he personally disliked the law.[25]

There were still some pockets of resistance, of course. On the whole, hostility was greater in rural areas, particularly in the Deep South, partly because community leaders failed to take a stand. In February 1964, one Johnson administration report captured the mixed picture. "In general, urban areas are making more progress than rural areas," it concluded, "and the more populous states are moving more quickly than states like Mississippi, Louisiana, and Alabama." Once the law was passed, this pattern persisted. In January 1965, for example, an interracial group visited a truck stop in Forrest City, Arkansas, and were eventually served. The two blacks received exactly what they had ordered, but the white customer found that his eggs were overcooked and there was salt in his coffee. "I'll serve niggers, as the law says," commented the manager candidly, "but I don't intend to cater to white integrationists."[26] While there were scattered reports of similar incidents, in much of the rural South blacks remained too intimidated to even seek service at traditionally white establishments. In small towns such as Lexington, Virginia, and Port St. Joe, Florida, signs came down, but little else changed. As late as 1967, the NAACP was still pushing for the desegregation of businesses in some rural areas.[27]

In the Deep South, some political leaders also failed to set a good example. Most notable was the case of George Wallace, who did not respond to CRS advice to urge compliance. Rather, Wallace boasted that the public accommodations provisions would be "universally violated" and that it would require a "police state" to enforce them.[28]

Not surprisingly, some whites followed their governor's lead. In September 1964, three black clergymen were refused service at a gas station located between Birmingham and Anniston. Rather than assisting them, the station's attendants attacked the preachers' car with a "heavy blunt instrument" and subjected them to "vulgar and abusive language." The men protested to Wallace about the incident, but he failed to intervene.[29] The governor was more responsive to complaints from white business owners that black customers were not as clean or trustworthy as whites. From the small town of Guntersville, for example, the restaurateur Mrs.

Beulah Bryson moaned to Wallace about having to serve blacks. "Is there really a law that can do this to people?" she asked. As late as August 1966, the fiery politician was still calling for the Civil Rights Act to be repealed because it destroyed whites' "right to use property as we see fit."[30]

While resistance to Title II was generally concentrated in rural areas, there were exceptions, and one of the most notable ironically occurred in Atlanta. It was true that many Atlanta businesses had desegregated well before July 1964, yet there were a few holdouts.[31] Just one day after the passage of the Civil Rights Act, Lester Maddox refused to serve three black theology students at his Pickrick Cafeteria, a thriving establishment that was known for its chicken specials. When the students returned a second time, they were chased away by Maddox and several white customers. Anticipating these tests, Maddox had been selling ax handles for some time, and the weapons were now used to threaten the black students. Such conduct was not unusual for a man who had founded Georgians Unwilling to Surrender (GUTS) in the wake of the student sit-ins. Harboring political ambitions after two unsuccessful tilts at the mayor's office, Maddox insisted that he would fight the law. "Pickrick will never integrate," he fumed. "They won't ever get any of that chicken."[32]

Maddox's stand won him popularity, and business went up 40 percent after the July 3 incident. Even in other states, whites noticed the former steelworker from the wrong side of the tracks. In a revealing letter, George Wallace congratulated Maddox on what he had done. "I am glad that you have stood and made the test—your action, I am sure, will help alert many people throughout the country," he claimed. "I know that there are many people from my state who stand with you as do those in my administration."[33] The Maddox case also highlighted how difficult it was to effectively resist Title II, however. Because of his actions, attorneys from the NAACP LDF and the Justice Department were able to join together and sue Maddox. By August, the federal courts had ordered the Pickrick to desegregate at once. After another futile attempt to evade the law, Maddox sold his enterprise. Seeing the writing on the wall, most southern business owners were unwilling to follow the Georgian's example. As the presidential aide Lee White reported to LBJ, "The Lester Maddox case in Atlanta highlights how really very few businessmen in the South have been unwilling to comply with the law of the land." The case helped Maddox politically, however, and, in 1966, he won the Georgia governorship on a segregationist platform. Throughout his term, the Atlanta native argued that the federal government was picking on the South but was failing to tackle discriminatory practices in the North.[34]

As the Pickrick case highlights, brave southern blacks were determined to implement Title II. Across the region, African Americans pressed for integrated public accommodations even before the provisions came into effect. In February 1964, for instance, blacks in Chapel Hill, North Carolina, demonstrated to try and force restaurants and hotels to desegregate. In Nashville, Atlanta, Houston, and Memphis, determined blacks also ensured that many public facilities were integrated a few months before the law became effective. Anxious to avoid negative headlines, business leaders often supported these moves. Prior to July 1964, however, any breakthroughs were voluntary, and some business owners went back on their word once demonstrations were called off, usually because of complaints from whites. In May 1963, most of Houston's restaurateurs had agreed to serve blacks, but, by October, many had reneged because of pressure from their white customers. Title II was crucial because it prevented backtracking. When the law was passed, however, there was still a lot of work to be done. In March 1964, a thorough survey of the region by Johnson's staffers found that many cities remained substantially segregated, particularly in the Deep South states of Mississippi, Alabama, and Louisiana. Even outside this area progress was uneven; in Greensboro, North Carolina, for example, lunch counters and restaurants were only "partially desegregated" more than four years after the famous sit-ins.[35]

As soon as the law became effective, blacks sought to test it, and a wide variety of groups were involved. Formed in 1963, the nonprofit Lawyers' Committee for Civil Rights under Law arranged for many early tests and represented plaintiffs in cases that arose from them. In 1965, the Washington, DC–based group also opened an office in Jackson, Mississippi, so that it could redress "discriminatory abuses" in the region. In July, for example, the committee filed actions against ten restaurants in Meridian and Canton that refused to serve blacks.[36]

Across the region, little-known grassroots groups also played an important role. In Bogalusa, Louisiana, members of the Bogalusa Voters League conducted tests of public facilities, while in Vicksburg, Mississippi, the Warren County Improvement League demanded the complete desegregation of all city-owned facilities. National groups sometimes supported these efforts. Assisted by the SCLC, blacks in the Mississippi towns of Grenada and Columbia even marched to demand that all public facilities be desegregated.[37]

Mobile provides a fine illustration of broader trends. In 1956, a bespectacled postal employee called John L. LeFlore had established the Non-Partisan Voters League (NPVL), and he led the group for the next two decades. Initially founded when the NAACP was banned in Alabama, the NPVL carried on the local civil rights struggle in Alabama's second city. Although scholars have largely overlooked it, the NPVL achieved a lot, particularly in the public accommodations area. Between 1964 and 1968, for instance, the league directed desegregation "test-ins" at 225 restaurants, cafés, motels, and other establishments.[38] The tests started as soon as the law became effective and were sometimes led by LeFlore himself. As early as July 5, 1964, four NPVL members asked for service at the Auto Drive-In Theater and were refused. Others had similar experiences; on July 9, the owner of a chicken restaurant told one NPVL member "that no Negroes ever would be served" in his business.[39]

Despite repeated tests by the NPVL, some whites were slow to come to terms with Title II. As late as September 1967, for example, the manager of the Blue Star restaurant in Saraland turned five black customers away and told them never to come back. As they were ejected, the black group noted that white customers "applauded" the manager's statement "in a racist spirit of glee." Because of ongoing white resistance, the NPVL filed more than seventy-five complaints with the Justice Department and initiated seven suits in the federal courts. These efforts secured results; over the course of 1967, six of the cases were settled in the plaintiffs' favor in federal court. By the end of 1968, the group noted proudly that it had helped bring about "extensive integration of lunch counters, restaurants and motels under Title II of the 1964 Civil Rights Act."[40]

Right across the region, the NAACP played a particularly important role in ensuring that the provisions of the Civil Rights Acts of 1964 and 1965 were fully realized. "The NAACP in the Southeast Region pushed and prodded for implementation of all the new laws," noted the region's annual report in 1965. The actions of the North Carolina Conference were typical; it declared 1965 to be the "year of implementation [of the] Civil Rights Act of 1964" and mobilized accordingly. "Every unit of the NAACP in North Carolina must give added meaning to the Civil Rights Act by making the best use of this new law," urged conference president Kelly M. Alexander in February 1965. "The days, weeks and months ahead call for determined, powerful, and dignified efforts to implement the civil rights law of 1964." Once generated on the ground, complaints were passed along either to local attorneys or to the association's legal department in New York City.[41]

Across the region, this vigilance produced results. As soon as Title II became effective, NAACP branches filled in questionnaires that documented reaction at the local level. Passed on to regional and national leaders, these surveys recorded that most southern businesses were accepting the law, especially in urban areas.[42] While pleased with this progress, campaigners still took action against those businesses and organizations that were not in compliance. In Florida, for instance, several branches secured significant breakthroughs. In 1965, seven NAACP members in Fort Myers brought suit to end segregation in the community's recreational facilities. As a result, in the following year the city agreed under pressure to implement "complete desegregation." In the small town of Mulberry, the state field director reported one restaurant to federal agencies because blacks were not being served. As a result, the owners apologized, the restaurant opened its doors to all, and the association's legal action was dropped.[43] In Georgia, NAACP activists carried out successful desegregation tests in a range of cities, including Atlanta, Albany, and Savannah, and led protests in the few locations where they did encounter sustained resistance.[44]

In Mississippi, the state conference responded to Title II by beginning systematic tests to see whether whites in the famously repressive state were obeying the law. On June 22, 1965, for example, Canton's city parks were "successfully integrated" by local members. In the course of 1965, the women of the Biloxi branch also had lunch in a beachfront restaurant, and members were quietly served in Laurel, Hattiesburg, and Clarksdale. Again, the association took action against establishments that flouted the law, securing important results. As a result of a favorable decision in *Hackett v. Kincaid,* for example, all public buildings in Clarksdale were desegregated, including city hall. The NAACP lobbyist Clarence Mitchell explained the philosophy behind these actions. "In the association we have always believed that you confront," he commented in early 1969, "because that's the only way you can get a test."[45]

The actions of these pioneers were crucial, especially as many blacks were afraid to ask boldly for service at establishments that had always barred them. Within a couple of years, however, blacks traveling to the South were noticing that they now had free access to public facilities.[46] The change meant a great deal because all blacks could recall the humiliation they had felt in having to sit at the back of the bus or explain to their children why they could not use white facilities. It was a central theme of Dr. King's "Letter from Birmingham City Jail," one of his most evocative writings.[47] Under segregation, explained the Charlotte native Alfred L. Alexander, "you were mentally kept inferior." Another Charlotte native, Katie Grier, reflected in old age that free access to public accommodations was one of the movement's most significant achievements. "Well, you could feel comfortable sitting on the bus, you know," she explained, "and where there was an empty seat instead of going to the back. I remember those days my dad told me to always go to the seat next to the back if it was empty, otherwise, he said, go all the way to the back, and sit down . . . and you won't have any problems."[48]

While blacks celebrated, whites reacted very differently. Many now sought to avoid contact with African Americans, even if that meant staying away from familiar bars and restaurants. Realizing that Title II covered only public facilities, some even sought to set up all-white private clubs. "Throughout the South," noted *Time* in January 1966, "club-manship has become the most popular way to avoid compliance with the discrimination-banning public accommodations section of the Civil Rights Act of 1964." In 1965, for example, a "private" committee of one thousand took over the movie house in Perry, Georgia, and proceeded to ban blacks. In Jackson, Mississippi, the marble-floored Robert E. Lee Hotel similarly converted itself into a private club rather than accept black guests. Some restaurants also followed suit; in New Orleans, for example, the well-heeled Maylie's Restaurant now became Maylie's Club Restaurant. It claimed three thousand dues-paying members, including local judges, lawyers, and business leaders.[49] In Mobile, the NPVL also found that many blacks were asked for membership cards at restaurants but that whites were usually served straightaway.[50]

Justice Department officials played an important role in tackling these problems. Between July 1964 and January 1966, the department's lawyers sued seventy-five separate establishments, including several so-called private clubs. Of these, thirty-nine desegregated as a result, while many more backed down when threatened with legal action. Overall, in the eighteen months after the law was passed the Justice Department received 1,645 complaints of discrimination in public accommodation, but around half of these were settled out of court. In one particularly important case, the department's lawyers sued the owners of Ollie's Barbecue, a restaurant in Birmingham that refused to seat blacks. Worried that they would lose their white customers if they allowed blacks to sit inside, the restaurant's owners argued that their business was not involved in interstate commerce and should be exempt from the law. In response, federal attorneys demonstrated that the restaurant purchased much of its food from out of state. In December 1964, the U.S. Supreme Court upheld the Justice Department's position, a move that established that Title II was constitutional.[51]

While most change occurred peacefully, occasionally efforts to desegregate public facilities ended in serious violence. A few incidents brought home the bravery of those who tested compliance and reinforced the law's limitations in dealing with the most recalcitrant opponents. In January 1966, the black man Samuel Younge Jr. got into an altercation with Marvin Segrest, the elderly white operator of a gas station in Tuskegee, Alabama. When Younge attempted to use the station's restroom, Segrest drew a gun and ordered him to leave. As an SNCC worker, the twenty-one-year-old student knew how to stand up for his rights. Although he left the premises, Younge later returned and threatened Segrest with a golf club. In return, Segrest shot at Younge, who taunted him as he ran off. His body was later found with a golf club under it. The murder enraged students and faculty at Tuskegee Institute, and their protests helped ensure that Segrest was put on trial within the year. Although the shooting had happened in front of several witnesses, blacks were horrified when a local, all-white jury found Segrest not guilty.[52]

Another serious incident occurred in Orangeburg, South Carolina, where riots erupted in February 1968 after blacks tried to gain access to a bowling alley that still refused to admit them.[53] The owner, Harry Floyd, justified his policy by claiming that he was running a private business. The move rankled students at South Carolina State College, who had to drive thirty-five miles to Columbia to bowl when Floyd's alley was located just two blocks from campus. On the night of February 5, a demonstration against the bowling alley turned violent as black students clashed with local police. Three nights later, police fire killed three students and injured another thirty-seven. While police and the white press asserted that the students had initiated the shooting, a claim that turned out to be errone-ous, blacks argued that they had been the victims of what the SNCC's H. Rap Brown called "the Orangeburg Massacre." The white view held sway, and the black student Cleveland Sellers was the only person con-victed in connection with the event. As Sellers commented, "The South Carolina press and its white public for the most part seemed to accept the official interpretation and justification of events at Orangeburg." The dis-turbances were another indication of how polarized southern whites and blacks were. Visiting the town more than twenty years later, the black writer Tom Dent observed that whites still viewed the protest as "a mod-ern slave rebellion that must be put down as all slave rebellions must be put down, violently and suddenly."[54]

Despite the widespread acceptance of Title II, the Orangeburg violence was a graphic reminder that some businesses were able to evade the law for several years. Shortly after the shooting, however, the Justice Department obtained a restraining order that prevented Floyd from operating the alley on a segregated basis. Many questioned why the federal government had not acted sooner, and the case exposed the existence of staff shortages within the Civil Rights Division. As Attorney General Ramsey Clark admit-ted, "We had a very, very limited enforcement capability because of man-power—just a fraction of what we needed." If Clark's staff had been able to act sooner, three young lives might have been saved.[55]

"A Great Upsurge in Voter Registration": Implementing the Voting Rights Act on the Ground, 1965–1968

On the evening of March 15, 1965, President Lyndon Baines Johnson gave a landmark address to Congress on the issue of black voting rights.

Moved to act by the Selma protests, which he called a "turning point in man's unending search for freedom," Johnson introduced a strong voting rights bill and urged all Americans to support it. In an unusually eloquent speech, the former schoolteacher from Texas declared that it was now time to "extend the rights of citizenship to every citizen of this land." Remarkably, the first southern president in a century openly identified with the civil rights movement and uttered its signature phrase. "Their cause must be our cause too," he declared. "Because it is not just Negroes, but really it's all of us, who must overcome the crippling legacy of bigotry and injustice. And-we-shall-overcome."[56]

A few blocks away, Dr. Martin Luther King was watching Johnson's address on a friend's television. For close to a decade, King's SCLC had tried to secure federal assistance, but the results of its efforts had been mixed. Johnson's speech consequently represented a significant breakthrough; as the SCLC's C. T. Vivian later commented, "It was a victory like none other, it was an affirmation of the movement." As King sat quietly in an armchair, aides saw a tear roll down his cheek, an uncharacteristic burst of emotion from the usually composed leader. Sitting next to King, the Alabama native John Lewis was also moved. The student activist had always viewed Johnson as a "politician," but now he felt that the president was "a man who spoke from his heart, a statesman, a poet." He wrote Johnson to commend him on his speech. "None will soon forget the force and urgency of your message to Congress," he declared, "when you expressed the determination of this Nation that no group of citizens should be denied the basic right to a ballot."[57]

Most of the South's political leaders reacted very differently. As Johnson was applauded, North Carolina senator Sam Ervin sat sulkily with his arms folded. A leading segregationist, Louisiana's Allen Ellender slumped in his chair and looked miserable. These Democratic senators accused Johnson of abandoning his colleagues from the South. A close friend of the president, Richard Russell went so far as to call LBJ "a turncoat if there ever was one."[58] Having already left the Democrats in disgust, South Carolina's Strom Thurmond was free to lambaste the address as a "sickening spectacle" and a "real dictatorial performance." Insisting that it violated states' rights, Thurmond called the Voting Rights Act "a completely unreasonable piece of legislation."[59]

Many ordinary southerners were also appalled by the speech, which was watched by a record audience of seventy million television viewers. Most insisted that blacks were not qualified to vote in large numbers. "This proposed bill is ridiculous!" wrote Mrs. Percy A. Hauglie from Moncks Corner, South Carolina. "By giving the vote to those who are morally, mentally, and educationally unfit, Johnson is cutting his own throat. . . . This bill will not satisfy or pacify the Negro. He isn't interested in his equality—he won't stop until he has supremacy!" A resident of Hartwell, Georgia, Mrs. John Mark Temples felt moved to write the president. Penning her letter on the night of LBJ's speech, she insisted that his actions were misguided. "Many [blacks] cannot write their own names," she claimed. "If they were registered to vote, they have no idea what to vote for. Their votes could be bought by crooked politicians. This is what you're trying to force—unqualified voters registered to vote simply because *they are Negroes!*"[60]

In Washington, however, Johnson's moving rhetoric helped speed the passage of the voting rights bill, which eased through Congress without a hitch. On August 6, 1965, the landmark bill was signed into law in the president's room within the Capitol, the same setting where Abraham Lincoln had freed slaves who had been pressed into military service by the Confederacy. Johnson sat in front of two sculptures of Lincoln as he put pen to paper, telling an audience of more than one hundred that the vote was "the most powerful instrument ever devised by man for breaking down injustice." The significance of the moment was not lost on John Lewis, who had been beaten on the Edmund Pettus Bridge in Selma. "The occasion of the signing into law of the Voting Rights Bill of 1965," he wrote Johnson that night, "is every bit as momentous and significant in the cause of Negro rights as the Emancipation Proclamation or the 1954 Supreme Court decision declaring racial segregation in the Nation's schools illegal." In sharp contrast, the televised ceremony caused more anguish for many southern whites. Writing from Travelers Rest, South Carolina, James B. Bramlett was horrified by LBJ's actions. "It was disgusting," he claimed, "to see him standing beneath the Statue of Lincoln in his arrogance and dictatorial speech."[61]

Not all white southerners shared such views. Out of 106 representatives from the former Confederate states, thirty-one supported the bill, an indication of the diversity of opinion within the region.[62] Most of this backing came from the Upper South, where the black vote had been increasing for some time. When the act was passed, for example, 46.8 percent of adult blacks in North Carolina were registered to vote, compared to just 6.7 percent in Mississippi. After Mississippi, Alabama had the next lowest proportion of black voters (19.3 percent). Even in this state, however, a few brave whites wrote Governor Wallace and urged him to support the new law. "It must be recognized by all that voter requirements have in many instances been so construed in such a manner to keep Negroes off of the registration rolls," noted Mobile's Harry E. Kinnane. Even in Alabama, there was a white constituency that was ready for change.[63]

As Kinnane acknowledged, there were many areas where the law was badly needed. In much of the rural South, whites exerted economic pressure on black sharecroppers and laborers to stop them from becoming politically active, while those who did try to register were blocked by racially discriminatory tests. As the Justice Department's files spotlighted, blacks made up the majority of the population in some Deep South counties, but almost none of them voted. Because discrimination was concentrated in majority-black areas, the Act contained revolutionary political potential. As *Newsweek* noted, in much of the region the Voting Rights Act promised "to change the very face of southern politics."[64]

In the years immediately after its passage, the Voting Rights Act fulfilled much of this potential. In 1968, the U.S. Commission on Civil Rights recorded in its broad-ranging *Political Participation* report, "The Voting Rights Act has resulted in a great upsurge in voter registration, voting, and other forms of political participation by Negroes in the South. In many areas, there has been voluntary compliance." Black registration was now more than 50 percent of the voting-age population in every southern state, whereas before the Act was passed this was the case only in Florida, Tennessee, and Texas. The pace of progress was particularly dramatic in the Deep South. In Mississippi, black registration jumped from 6.7 percent on November 1, 1964, to 59.8 percent on December 31, 1967, while, in neighboring Alabama, it increased from 19.3 to 51.6 percent.[65]

The positive changes were partly due to the efforts of the attorney general, who moved to implement the act "immediately upon its signing into law." Even before the bill was passed, Nicholas deB. Katzenbach worked closely with staff from the Civil Service Commission (CSC). The CSC was given the task of training seventy-five examiners and equipping them with all the materials they needed to register new voters in the South. Examiners were also authorized to assist illiterate applicants in completing registration forms. In addition, Katzenbach's staff conducted an intensive campaign to publicize the law and encourage voluntary compliance. Targeting the worst areas, federal personnel educated southern registrars about the law and promoted acceptance of it.[66]

These efforts produced impressive results. Within a week of the act becoming effective, the Justice Department reported, "There has been widespread and encouraging compliance with the new act in a number of counties in which discrimination against Negro applicants was practiced previously." In many counties, the number of black voters had more than quadrupled in a week. By August 19, over 16,000 new black voters had been registered in Alabama, Louisiana, and Mississippi. While this early pace was not sustained, steady gains still occurred over the following months.[67] By August 1966, Johnson was able to celebrate "twelve months of historic progress." In Mississippi, for example, the president noted that the number of black voters had almost quadrupled, from 35,000 to 150,000. Even here, there was clear evidence of a change in attitude, and Johnson acknowledged that most of the gains had come through voluntary compliance. Responding to the law, the state chamber of commerce had declared that "registration and voting laws should be administered fairly and impartially for all," and other civic and business groups supported this position.[68]

As Johnson pointed out, what was occurring was a truly revolutionary shift. Since the late nineteenth century, most blacks in the Deep South had been denied the most basic of democratic rights. Now, elderly men and women were able to exercise the ballot for the first time in their long lives. In the Alabama primary of 1966, the new voters included Willie Bolden, an eighty-one-year-old who was the grandson of a slave. "It made me think I was sort of Somebody," he commented. As Clarence Mitchell reflected, the 235,000 blacks who voted in the primary represented a watershed. "They turned the corner in the political life of Alabama," he declared. "Because Alabama has been one of the worst states for Negroes, this means that we have turned the corner for the whole South."[69]

Where there was likely to be resistance, the federal examiners stepped in. Crucially, they acted quickly, sending the message that noncompliance would not be tolerated. The first examiners opened offices just four days after the act came into effect, and, by October 30, they had already listed 56,789 black voters in twenty counties. In December 1965, the U.S. Commission on Civil Rights praised the CSC's administration of the examiner program, calling it "imaginatively planned, vigorously executed and closely supervised." By December 31, 1967, examiners had been sent to fifty-eight counties in five southern states and had listed over 158,000 new black voters. The Commission on Civil Right's data also showed that counties in which federal examiners had been present had higher levels of black registration than counties where they had not been. At the end of 1967, for example, examiner counties in South Carolina had a black registration rate of 71.6 percent, but, in nonexaminer counties, the figure was just 50.5 percent. In Alabama, the comparable figures were 59.3 and 45.4 percent, respectively.[70]

The example of a few rural counties illustrates how vital the examiners were. In Holmes County, Mississippi, the pace of change was dramatic, the number of blacks who were registered to vote increasing from 20 to 5,844 in December 1967. "Where the examiners are present," commented the VEP official Marvin Wall, "the registration goes up tremendously almost at once." By March 1968, examiners had also had a dramatic impact in Lowndes County, Alabama, where not one of the 5,122 voting-age blacks had been registered in the 1964 elections. Just over three years later, however, there were 2,792 black voters.[71]

Scene of the climatic struggle that led to the act's passage, Selma also illustrated broader trends well. Mobilized by months of protest, local blacks moved quickly to take advantage of the law; eight days after it became effective, 354 of them had already registered. An examiner stayed in the town for sixty-four days, and, during this time, the percentage of blacks who were registered increased from 9.7 to 60. In the years that followed, the upsurge continued, and the consequences were soon apparent. By February 1968, a black minister was running for mayor, and six blacks were standing for seats on the city council. In the Dallas County sheriff's office, where the brutal segregationist Jim Clark had held sway, there were soon two black deputies working under Wilson Baker, the moderate who had easily ousted Clark in the 1966 election. In a sharp break with the past, city officials were also now meeting with African American leaders.[72]

Between 1965 and 1968, the number of black elected officials also increased sharply right across the South. When the Voting Rights Act was passed, blacks held just seventy-two of the seventy-nine thousand elected offices in the region, but, within a couple of years, that number had grown to over two hundred. In the 1966 elections alone, twenty blacks were elected to southern state legislatures, an increase of nine, and there were many symbolic breakthroughs. In Macon County, Alabama, for example, Lucius Amerson became the first black sheriff in the South since the Reconstruction era. The black vote also decided the outcome of many elections, including Winthrop Rockefeller's successful gubernatorial bid in Arkansas. Receiving more than 90 percent of the black vote, Rockefeller defeated the ardent segregationist Jim Johnson in a close race. In 1967, twenty-two African Americans were also voted into office in Mississippi, including Robert Clark, who desegregated the state legislature after a gap of almost a century.[73]

While federal enforcement was important, black agency also played a vital role in bringing about these gains. In the first three years after the act was passed, NAACP branches conducted voter registration drives right across the South. In the summer of 1965, for example, the association initiated a project in Alabama, Mississippi, and South Carolina that led to over fifty thousand blacks being registered. Branch activists worked alongside the examiners, supplying them with what *The Crisis* termed "scores of applicants to register."[74] In Alabama, where the NAACP had only just reorganized, its efforts were particularly noteworthy. In June 1965, the new state president, Dr. John W. Nixon, pressed Governor Wallace to do more to assist black citizens who wanted to register. "We are entitled to the right to vote," he wrote. "Please help us to get this." Wallace's staff, however, refused Nixon's request for a meeting and insisted that all Alabamians were free to vote "upon making appropriate application."[75]

Such efforts were typical of the NAACP's determined work. In 1968, another election year, the NAACP estimated that it used well over eight million pieces of literature during its voter registration efforts in the region. During May alone, southern branches claimed credit for adding over ninety thousand new voters to the rolls. Members worked closely with the SRC, which provided nearly $80,000 in grants alone. Many southern blacks responded to these efforts because they grasped the importance of the issues involved. As the Charlotte resident Katie McGill recalled, "When we had the right to vote, you know, we encouraged all the black people to go out and vote, because there's so many people had lost their lives for us to have voting rights."[76]

Other groups also carried out essential work. Between 1965 and 1968, the Mobile-based NPVL registered more than fourteen hundred African Americans as voters. Realizing that poor blacks often found it difficult to get to the board of registrars, league staff provided free transportation to and from the board's office.[77] In other major Alabama cities, the SCLC conducted similar campaigns. In January 1966, the group worked with federal examiners in Birmingham and registered 7,108 new black voters, or nearly 10 percent of all potential black voters in Jefferson County. Writing to the president, CSC chairman John W. Macy paid credit to the SCLC for the astonishing progress, which had occurred in spite of very cold weather. "There is strong evidence of interest and the Southern Christian Leadership [Conference] are exerting influence in the Negro community," he noted. In Montgomery, the SCLC also worked with federal examiners and quickly registered 8,000 new voters. Overall, the registration drives clearly reinforced the work of the federal examiners. In 1966, for example, a study by the VEP found that the highest rates of black political participation were in examiner counties where a voter registration campaign had also taken place.[78]

Despite these gains, there was still considerable resistance to the implementation of the Voting Rights Act. Crucially, blacks still were much less likely to vote than were whites. This was partly because federal examiners were simply not present in most counties; the Deep South states of Alabama, Mississippi, and Georgia, for example, together contained 292 counties, and examiners visited only a tiny fraction of these. As early as December 1965, the U.S. Commission on Civil Rights called for examiners to be sent to a broader range of locations. In counties without examiners, blacks complained that they confronted difficulties in registering, especially as offices often had very limited opening hours. Those who worked long hours in manual jobs, in particular, found it impossible to register during the day. Although it was a violation of the act, some counties in Alabama and Mississippi also continued to require proof of literacy.[79]

Because the federal examiners concentrated on the Deep South, there were complaints from activists in other states. In North Carolina, the black leaders Golden A. Frinks and Reginald A. Hawkins called for examiners to be sent to a number of rural counties where few blacks were registered to vote. In June 1968, Hawkins complained to Attorney General Ramsey Clark that eighty-four of the state's one hundred counties lacked a full-time registration system. Concentrating on the eastern part of the state, Hawkins also detailed many cases where white officials were reluctant to register blacks. At this time, whites still held all state political offices in North Carolina.[80]

Across the region, whites also registered in increased numbers so that they could dilute the impact of the black vote. By the spring of 1968, almost 80 percent of whites in the seven covered states were registered voters, compared to 56.5 percent of blacks. White registration was highest in the Deep South; in Mississippi, over 92 percent of whites were listed, while, in Alabama, the figure was 82.5 percent.[81] In these states, some political leaders made a conscious effort to increase white registration levels. Declaring that he would fight the "ridiculous voting rights bill," George Wallace launched a drive to "see that all eligible white people do get out and register to vote." In the summer of 1965, Wallace wrote many letters to drum up support for the campaign, which he termed a "statewide program." He argued that it was essential to register whites because the Voting Rights Act was racially inspired legislation that only sought to help blacks.[82]

White politicians used a wide variety of other techniques to weaken black political involvement. Apart from redrawing the lines of legislative districts in order to dilute the black vote, white officials also increased filing fees for candidates, made many elected offices appointive, and refused to certify nominating petitions from black applicants. As a consequence, the number of blacks who won office was very limited, and gains were largely concentrated in small, majority-black communities. By late 1968, the state legislatures in Alabama and South Carolina remained all white, while those in Louisiana, Mississippi, North Carolina, and Virginia all had just one African American representative. Only in Georgia, where there were twelve black representatives, was the situation substantially different.[83]

Despite the passage of a strong federal law, many blacks remained afraid of becoming politically active, and this fear remained one of the most difficult obstacles for both federal officials and civil rights workers to overcome. As Vice President Hubert Humphrey wrote LBJ in 1966, "Psychological barriers remain a serious deterrent to Negro registration in certain areas." The CSC also blamed fear for its failure to recruit many black examiners. On July 30, 1965, for instance, just two of the new examiners were black, a telling weakness.[84]

In many isolated areas, this fear was justified as whites continued to attack politically active blacks. While such incidents were becoming less frequent, they still occurred with some regularity. In November 1966, for example, local whites wounded Carrie Washington, an NAACP leader in Concordia Parish, Louisiana, who had been encouraging blacks to vote. Around the same time, several other political activists in the parish had their homes bombed. The violence derailed the NAACP's efforts; as the local leader Alberta Whatley admitted, "The people are just afraid; they've been so put down here." In *Political Participation,* the Commission on Civil Rights detailed other similar incidents. In Clay County, Mississippi, the manager of a plantation store declared that he would shoot any black people who tried to vote, while in Dorchester County, South Carolina, the home of a politically active African American was burned to the ground in 1967.[85]

After 1965, however, economic reprisals became more common than physical attacks, partly because whites realized that violence was likely to provoke federal intervention. In rural areas, whites frequently used their economic dominance to intimidate politically active blacks. In late 1965, for example, eight black families in Wilcox County, Alabama, were evicted after becoming active in an SCLC voter registration campaign. All sharecroppers, many had lived in their modest dwellings since slave times. The local unit of the SCLC responded by trying to gain funding to construct low-income housing in the area, but this distracted staff attention away from voting rights work. In other cases, emerging political leaders were targeted. In 1966, Alvin White Jr. found that he was a victim of reprisals after he ran for election to the school board in West Feliciana Parish, Louisiana. White did carpentry work for whites, but, after running for office, his orders dried up. His plight reflected broader problems. As the Commission on Civil Rights explained in one telling passage, "The land and industry in the South are owned almost exclusively by whites. This economic domination of the region together with the history of racial violence previously alluded to, reportedly infects the entire political process in many areas. . . . In many cases a Negro will not go to the polls or cast his vote in a way that he thinks will offend the white persons who own the land and the industry, and upon whom he is absolutely dependent for his livelihood."[86]

By the end of 1968, it was clear that voting rights would remain an important battleground in the civil rights struggle for many years to come. As the Commission on Civil Rights concluded in that year, the South was "still a long way from the goal of full enfranchisement of Negro citizens." While it was mindful of ongoing problems, even the commission acknowledged the ground that had been traveled, however. Given that southern blacks had been politically emasculated since the late nineteenth century, the changes wrought by the Voting Rights Act were remarkable. Johnson and his staff were entitled to take some pride in their achievements, even if it took ongoing black activism to realize many of the changes on the ground. "As an experiment in the role of law and democracy in securing the vote," asserted outgoing attorney general Ramsey Clark in early 1969, "it must be one of the most dramatic of any country at any time." Considering the initial opposition to Title II, the rapid desegregation of public accommodations was also noteworthy. In both areas, change had occurred because federal officials and black activists had acted quickly and because the regulations themselves were effective. When these elements were not present, the outcomes were very different.[87]

2

"Token Beginnings"

The Battle to Desegregate Southern Schools and Workplaces, 1965–1968

The Johnson administration's record was not so impressive when it came to desegregating southern schools and workplaces. In these areas, white resistance was greater, and the civil rights legislation was less effective. Rather than moving quickly, the administration took its time in establishing the new EEOC and drawing up school desegregation guidelines. The lack of progress was also related to weak enforcement; the new EEOC lacked the authority to compel violators to change, while HEW rarely used its powers to cut off funds from recalcitrant southern school districts. The implementation of Title VI proved to be particularly difficult; as the civil rights aide F. Peter Libassi concluded in 1967, "School desegregation is still a highly controversial subject. . . . The more progress made, the more intense becomes the opposition. This nerve-wracking process can be expected to continue." In the end, Johnson's officials recognized that they had done little more than make a start in these areas, and it would be up to others to build on their work. Future policymakers, however, would also have to confront the persistent gap between black and white expectations about how much desegregation there should be in workplaces and schools.[1]

Freedom of Choice? School Desegregation in the Johnson Years

When the Civil Rights Act was passed, the South's schools remained substantially segregated. At the start of the 1964–1965 school year, just 2 percent of black children in the eleven southern states attended desegregated schools, and there were more than fifteen hundred districts that had made no voluntary movement toward complying with *Brown*. The main reason for this situation was that, until 1964, Congress had not given statutory recognition to school desegregation as the law of the land.[2] In both rural and urban areas, only minimal breakthroughs had occurred. As *The Crisis* reported in May 1965, "There has only been meager compliance with the Court's order [in *Brown*]."[3]

As these statistics indicate, resistance to school integration was deep-seated, and the implementation of Title VI was clearly going to be difficult. According to the historian James T. Patterson, the Jim Crow system was "anchored on segregation in schools." Schools aroused strong feelings because both races understood that a good education was vital if their children were to achieve professional success. Parents, moreover, cherished their children so deeply that they were prepared to fight hard if they thought that their education opportunities were being impeded. After 1965, many whites believed that race mixing would undermine the learning process, whereas most blacks felt that desegregated schools offered their best hope of advancement. As a result of these conflicting perspectives, the battle to desegregate schools was long and fierce, and most whites gave way only when decisive federal authority forced their hand.[4]

After the passage of the Civil Rights Act, the pace of school integration did pick up. Title VI banned discrimination in federally assisted programs, and any school district that wanted to receive federal funds had to satisfy HEW's Office of Education that it was no longer maintaining a dual system. Change happened slowly, however. Staff shortages meant that HEW did not publish its first guidelines until May 1965, almost a year after the act's passage. At the start of that year, the agency had only twelve staff devoted to enforcing Title VI, but this increased to seventy-four within twelve months. In subsequent years, the number continued to rise as officials gradually realized that implementing Title VI was a task of "staggering dimensions." Short of personnel, HEW officials decided to issue blanket guidelines, a move that southerners ironically interpreted as a sign of dictatorial behavior. In the first guidelines, Commissioner of Education Francis Keppel specified that school districts had to make a "good faith start" toward desegregation in the 1965–1966 term and to complete the process by the end of 1967. Faculties also had to be desegregated, but, during the first year, districts could prepare for this simply by holding integrated staff meetings.[5]

While the law gave HEW the power to cut off funds, the tactic was used sparingly, partly because the department was anxious not to deprive schools of income. A former schoolteacher, Johnson endorsed this policy. As HEW secretary Joseph A. Califano Jr. explained, "The President wants to make sure that we are doing everything possible so that he does not have to withhold funds from a single school district in this country." Finances could be cut only after lengthy efforts had been made to achieve voluntary compliance. As federal funds constituted only 8 percent of the average school district budget, some noncompliant districts were also willing to forgo federal aid rather than desegregate. There were other limitations; under Title VI, the attorney general could sue to desegregate public schools only after receiving a written complaint from residents and determining that they could not sue on their own behalf. Across the South, however, most blacks were too afraid to complain so publicly.[6]

Defending their guarded approach, federal officials argued that southern school districts had to be allowed time to comply. Aware of the depth of opposition to change, they felt that they had to proceed cautiously. In August 1965, for example, Keppel reported to Califano that he did not anticipate rapid progress. "It would seem wise," he advised, "for the Administration to emphasize whenever possible that we are embarking on a difficult program and that the fall of 1965 is therefore but the first step." Illustrating this, in late September HEW reported that seventy-one southern districts had not submitted compliance documents while 128 had forwarded inadequate plans. Resistance was concentrated in the Deep South states, particularly Mississippi, which Califano described as "a major non-compliance state." At this time, there were twenty-one school districts in the Magnolia State that had failed to submit compliance documents, while many others had filed unacceptable plans. In some of these cases, school board officials had not even appeared at scheduled hearings.[7]

The administration's approach did not satisfy the NAACP, which accused HEW of "vacillation, timidity, and reluctance to act." Association strategists felt that Title VI was a decisive federal mandate and that it should be enforced much more vigorously. Aware of what had happened after *Brown,* they worried that segregationists would seize on the administration's cautious approach and use it to stall. The SRC, the NAACP LDF, and the American Friends Service Committee (AFSC) also called on HEW to be more forceful. "We still have no tangible indication of the vigor with which the Administration will handle defiant school districts," noted one AFSC and LDF memo in November 1965. These complaints had only a minimal impact, however, partly because HEW officials were acutely aware of political opposition to the new guidelines.[8]

HEW files confirm that many school officials were brazenly resisting the new rules. In the case of Hinds County, Mississippi, the agency noted in September 1965: "Inadequate plan rejected in June. No response to subsequent communication." Opposition was often concentrated in majority-black areas, as the notes from Calhoun County, South Carolina, illustrated: "75% of pupils Negro. Reluctant to give desegregated education to those who wish it." While the problems were generally worse in the Deep South, some Upper South districts were also cited. In Northampton County, Virginia, for instance, the plan was described as "seriously deficient," but the superintendent had advised that he was willing to "forego Federal assistance" rather than change it.[9]

Despite these problems, the new legislation did secure some results. School officials were also pushed to change by the Elementary and Secondary Education Act of 1965, which granted nearly $590 million of additional funding to seventeen southern and border states in fiscal year 1966.[10] Over the course of the 1965–1966 school year, the number of southern black children who were attending desegregated schools more than doubled. "We are, at last, beginning to see the practical end of school desegregation," asserted Attorney General Katzenbach in June 1966. There were some notable breakthroughs, particularly in the urban South, where white elites again emphasized compliance. In Atlanta, for example, the first day of the 1965–1966 school year was a memorable one for the family of Dr. Martin Luther King Jr. Seven-year-old Martin Luther King III and nine-year-old Yolanda were part of a small group of African American children who quietly integrated Spring Street School. "Several parents welcomed us and said how happy they were to see us," commented Coretta Scott King. "It went beautifully." Across Georgia's largest city, between two thousand and twenty-five hundred black children now attended school with whites, up from sixteen hundred the year before. In Charlotte, over two thousand blacks also attended integrated schools, a big increase. Backing these moves, moderate whites argued that, while the South could resist a Supreme Court decision, it should not oppose a congressional law.[11]

The King children went to their new school under a "freedom-of-choice" plan. After 1965, such plans were adopted by more than 75 percent of the southern school districts as a way of minimizing progress because they placed the burden of transferring to new schools on the black community. HEW accepted this because the federal courts still viewed such plans as a satisfactory means of desegregating the schools. In most cases, black parents had to obtain transfer forms from white officials and apply to send their children to historically white schools. Only the most confident and articulate parents, like the Kings, were willing to initiate this process. School officials also did their best to uphold the status quo. Black pupils were often advised that white schools were overcrowded or were told that school buses did not run through "colored" areas. Others were informed that they would not be allowed to participate in extracurricular activities, or they were asked to produce complex documentation in order to transfer. In Baker County, Georgia, for instance, 165 black pupils applied for transfers, but only 22 were accepted. Officials used flimsy excuses to reject many students, telling them that signatures on choice forms were forged or that there were too many children from the same family at one school.[12]

All these tactics were underpinned by coercion. In many cases, whites told their black employees that separate schools served both races well. If they did not accept this advice, blacks were warned that they could lose their jobs or homes if they enrolled their children in white schools. By January 1966, the Justice Department had investigated at least eighty alleged instances of intimidation of black families and students in association with desegregation. Such actions took their toll; in 1965–1966, not a single black student had transferred to white schools in more than one hundred districts that had adopted freedom-of-choice plans.[13]

More typically, African Americans did transfer but only in small numbers. By January 1966, the Office of Education claimed that 7.5 percent of black pupils in the South were attending classes with whites, although the SRC argued that the figure was just 5.2 percent. Regardless of who was correct, it was clear that the new law had not produced a rapid breakthrough. As the U.S. Commission on Civil Rights noted in February 1966, "The number of Negro children in the Deep South who are actually attending school with whites is still very low." While most southern whites felt that the law was being implemented too forcefully, however, blacks charged that freedom of choice was a farce. As the NAACP's southeastern conference reported in 1967, "The full weight of responsibility for the most part, remains on the Negro, who has no 'freedom' and no 'choice' to achieve desegregation of Southern schools." According to the association, desegregation was occurring at a "snail's pace" because of the "pussy footing and hypocrisy of HEW."[14]

Whites also harassed black children who did transfer, and these tactics deterred others from trying. In the fall of 1965, for example, forty students enrolled in formerly white schools under a freedom-of-choice plan in Americus, Georgia. Investigating their experience, the Commission on Civil Rights found that "Negro students had been called derogatory names, had had their books thrown on the floor and knocked from their hands, and had been tripped, spat upon and nearly run down by cars in the parking lot." School administrators also disciplined black students much more harshly than they did white students. As a result of these problems, most of the black pioneers decided to move back to their old schools. The commission showed that similar incidents had occurred in several other southern districts, including Webster County, Mississippi, Williamsburg County, South Carolina, and Rowan County, North Carolina.[15]

These problems were prevalent in rural areas, where transferring to the white schools was particularly controversial. The example of Sunflower County, Mississippi, illustrates broader themes well. Although the rural county was majority black, until the school board adopted a supposed freedom-of-choice plan in the summer of 1965 only whites had attended the elementary and high schools in Drew, largely because prominent landowners had intimidated black agricultural workers. In a brave move, however, in August 1965 the local sharecroppers Mae Bertha and Matthew Carter enrolled seven of their thirteen children in the previously all-white schools because they dreamed of getting them out of the cotton fields.[16]

As Constance Curry's moving account has documented, the Sunflower County case highlighted the inadequacies of freedom-of-choice plans. After enrolling in their new schools, the Carter children were spat on, mistreated, and racially abused, with much of the mistreatment being condoned by white teachers. Ten-year-old Pearl was even told by her teacher to go home and take a bath. Other Carter children were not issued public library cards or were told that the facility was "too small" for them to study there. Through all these difficulties, Mae Bertha Carter wisely warned her children not to become bitter. As Connie Carter later reflected, "Mama was right about hate, because you don't feel good about yourself when you hate someone else." Not surprisingly, the children were scarred from their experiences, and Pearl referred to this period as "the years of hell." Because of the family's determination, however, the NAACP LDF was able to win a case based on their experiences. In 1969, the court threw out the county's freedom-of-choice plan and ordered the desegregation of its schools. Helped by this breakthrough, seven of the Carter's children went on to attend the University of Mississippi.[17]

In preparation for the 1966–1967 school year, HEW revised its guidelines to try and address some of these problems. Freedom of choice was still permissible, but the new rules declared that these schemes had to produce significant results. In a similar vein, local communities were now asked to make a "substantial beginning" toward faculty desegregation, and HEW recommended that all-black schools be closed in order to speed up integration. "We are now concluding what some have called the 'paper compliance' phase of our Title VI operations," noted Commissioner of Education Harold Howe II, who had succeeded Keppel. "We can look forward to more emphasis on compliance reviews, field visits, and investigations in order to determine actual performance in making equality of educational opportunity available to all members of our society." Although many did not reply to his entreaties, Howe also reached out to school board officials by offering to discuss the guidelines with them.[18]

The new procedures had little impact on hardcore resisters. Following its promise to take a tougher stance, however, HEW began to bring enforcement actions against districts that had "failed to comply with significant requirements of the guidelines." On August 8, action was initiated against six districts, five in Alabama and one in Tennessee. Only the very worst cases were selected. In Chilton County, Alabama, for example, just 21 black students attended formerly white schools out of a total black enrollment of 4,900. There was no faculty desegregation, and the superintendent openly disagreed with many provisions of the guidelines, including the mailing of choice forms to students' homes. White Alabamians were particularly resistant to HEW guidelines, partly because Governor Wallace urged school officials to defy them. In June 1966, the U.S. Commission on Civil Rights estimated that, in the state as a whole, only 1 black child in every 237 was attending a desegregated school.[19]

In the fall of 1966, enforcement actions were also brought against several districts in Mississippi. Progress in the state remained slow; in Calhoun County, for instance, more than half of the school pupils were black, but none of them attended the white schools, and there was no faculty desegregation. In some communities, whites were willing to use violence in order to uphold the status quo. In the fall of 1966, white men in Grenada used ax handles, pipes, and chains to attack a group of black schoolchildren who had attempted to attend a white school. They also beat two photographers who tried to film the violence. In the same year, black families in Issaquena and Sharkey counties who had enrolled their children in white schools were fired from their jobs and evicted from their houses, while cross burnings were also reported in several communities.[20]

In much of the region as a whole, school board officials deferred to community sentiments and were reluctant to take a stand. In June 1967, the presidential aide Douglass Cater reported to LBJ about the situation. "The major problem here is to persuade local educational officials to assume the responsibility of desegregating their schools," he concluded. "While nearly every school district in the South has made some start on student and faculty desegregation, itself a major accomplishment, the problem will be to encourage movement beyond these token beginnings."[21]

After 1966, HEW continued to take action against the worst offenders, and, by September 1968, Office of Education officials had cut funds to 115 southern school districts.[22] These moves had produced some results, and HEW claimed that 18 percent of southern black pupils were now enrolled in majority-white schools. Compared to the situation in 1965, it certainly represented progress, yet read another way it showed that little had changed for 82 percent of black pupils. This was, indeed, only a beginning. The problem was that most districts kept their funding while carrying out only limited changes. Efforts to tighten the guidelines by requiring greater evidence of "effectiveness" proved largely unsuccessful because the basic mechanisms remained the same. In the fall of 1967, for example, new HEW guidelines encouraged districts to seek alternatives to freedom of choice but added that the emphasis would be on "refining present policies rather than introducing new approaches." Issued in the closing days of the Johnson presidency, an internal HEW analysis summed up the limitations of policy implementation. "Experience has demonstrated," it candidly noted, "that use of the so-called freedom of choice plan simply keeps in effect for the vast majority of Negro students a racially segregated school system with inherently resulting inequities and badges of servitude." Blacks who had tried to transfer to white schools had been subject to "direct intimidation, harassment, and physical force."[23]

Realizing that HEW advocated freedom of choice only because the federal courts allowed it, the NAACP set to work on discrediting the policy. By October 1966, its lawyers had filed cases in 132 public school systems, the bulk of them in the South. The NAACP never wavered in the belief that blacks could achieve a better education only if separate schools were abolished. As the association's 1968 annual meeting declared, "Integration into a system of better schools is inexorably the goal."[24]

These efforts ran into determined resistance, further prolonging cases that the NAACP had already been fighting for many years. In 1968, for example, the NAACP pressed for "more complete integration of students" in Jefferson County, Arkansas. As early as 1959, the group had secured a desegregation order in the county, but subsequent progress had been minimal. "Our position," explained the NAACP attorney Barbara A. Morris in an internal memorandum, "is that the integration of 49 students out of some 1260 in a period of 8 years was a clear indication that additional affirmative action was required of the School Board if they were not to be in contempt of the order of 1959." Board officials disagreed, claiming that they were making progress and that blacks were free to transfer to the white schools. They saw no problem in the fact that the choice forms were kept in the principal's office and had been publicized only once. Almost fourteen years after *Brown*, white officials still asked for more time. "Freedom of choice in this district," asserted the school board attorney Robert V. Light in 1968, "has not been in operation a sufficient period to permit an accurate projection of its probable success as a desegregation procedure."[25]

In Alabama, the NAACP sued the entire state board of education, and the case provided rare insight into the attitudes of school board officials, who generally refused to meet with HEW. These witnesses were apparently oblivious to the bravery that blacks needed in order to apply for transfers. In Walker County, the superintendent defended a plan under which just 82 of 1,400 black students had applied for transfers. "I feel like that they already have freedom of choice," commented Robert Cunningham in November 1966. "They are going where they want to go, there is no problems involved." In a similar vein, the superintendent of Anniston's schools claimed that he was satisfied with a plan that saw 216 of 3,200 black children attending classes with whites. "We have the schools desegregated," he declared.[26]

While resistance to desegregation was widespread, it was particularly prevalent in heavily black, rural areas where fears of race mixing were heightened. Letters written to political representatives provide some insights into these feelings. From majority-black Bertie County, North Carolina, Mrs. Owen Barfield wrote Senator Sam Ervin in early 1968. "My main concern now is the school situation in eastern North Carolina," she explained, "especially in Bertie County. . . . Washington officials say total integration is the answer. In areas where there are about 5% Negroes, total integration may help. In the black belt where there are 75% Negroes, total integration will force the educational status of the white to be lowered." Many parents fumed against HEW, which they felt was implementing Title VI too forcefully. "We are at the mercy of whims of any or all bureaucrats," claimed another rural resident. "Is HEW policy to alienate all WHITES just to get statistical compliance figures?"[27]

Taking their cue from their constituents, Southern political leaders insisted that HEW was moving too fast. They frequently argued that the Civil Rights Act only prohibited discrimination and that it specifically forbade the assignment of pupils on racial grounds. The act did contain language that prevented it from trying to correct "racial imbalances," but this provision was intended to refer to de facto segregation. Southern politicians, however, interpreted the clause to mean that freedom of choice was all that was required under the law and was completely constitutional. They also lambasted the clause as an example of northern liberal "hypocrisy," a readiness to pick on the South but overlook racial segregation in the North.[28]

HEW's desegregation policies were certainly undermined by interference from powerful southern politicians, particularly Democrats. In late 1967, for example, HEW's F. Peter Libassi blamed "political attacks" as one of the factors that had "blunted the program's ability to reach its anticipated goals for this year." From the start, southern politicians tried to destabilize the agency's efforts. As early as May 1965, a group of nine southern governors traveled to Washington to protest against the new school desegregation guidelines. After the meeting, Georgia's Carl E. Sanders embarrassed the administration by claiming that he had secured some favorable concessions. A few days later, moreover, HEW accepted Georgia's state-level desegregation plan.[29]

Democratic congressional representatives also lobbied HEW and the president in an effort to weaken their policies. In September 1966, for example, North Carolina's Harold D. Cooley told LBJ that the guidelines represented "bureaucratic tyranny." The long-serving chairman of the House Committee on Agriculture, Cooley pressured the president to repeal them. In response, Johnson's aides promised to help Cooley get reelected in his district, where he faced a stiff challenge from the Republicans.[30] Aware of their need for support in the South, LBJ's staff took complaints from southern representatives seriously. As the worried aide Henry H. Wilson reported to Califano in 1966, opposition to the guidelines "could be deep enough and strong enough to wreck the very foundation of our relations with the Congress. . . . This is serious business." When HEW revised its guidelines for the 1966–1967 school year, staff consulted many southern representatives in order to undercut their objections. As the attorney general acknowledged, the whole process of implementing the guidelines was "politically painful," especially as concessions to whites further damaged the administration's relationships with black leaders.[31]

Capitalizing on the bonds that they had forged during the fight against the Civil Rights bill, southern senators also undermined HEW. In 1966, for example, seventeen southern senators tried to gut the guidelines, but they were unable to secure sufficient support from their northern colleagues. Led by Georgia's Richard Russell, the southerners also protested to LBJ. The new rules, they insisted, represented a "gross imposition upon local school officials" and should be revoked in favor of freedom of choice. A seasoned political negotiator, the president assured his fellow southerners that many of their fears were unfounded. "In short," wrote Johnson in May, "the guidelines do not abandon freedom of choice, they seek to guarantee it in fact." This reply did not satisfy the senators, who continued to protest.[32]

While they may not have been able to induce a wholesale change of direction, powerful southern senators secured significant concessions at the local level. In the fall of 1966, for example, Senator Russell intervened to stop funds being cut off from the school board in Treutlen County. At the time, 669 of 690 black pupils in the rural county still attended all-black schools, and the board was told that its funds would be deferred unless it improved its performance. Following phone calls by Russell to HEW officials, however, the county was removed from the cutoff list and was allowed to keep its freedom-of-choice plan. Russell also secured a commitment from HEW officials that they would notify his office before taking "any additional action" against the county's board of education. In a revealing letter, the county board's chair ended up thanking Russell for his "splendid work" in the case.[33]

In many areas, however, white parents felt that integration was proceeding too fast, or they reasoned that it was inevitable. As a result, they withdrew their children from the public schools, starting an important trend that would accelerate in subsequent years. In late 1967, a Johnson administration subcommittee concluded that over thirty thousand white students were enrolled in "segregated private schools" in the region. While these numbers were relatively small, in majority-black counties a substantial proportion of whites had already abandoned the public system. As the subcommittee noted, many of the schools were created in "direct response" to desegregation, as the southern states had very few nonsectarian private schools before this time. The growth of these schools was also fueled by state and federal policies. Eight southern states allowed for grants of state or local funds to be awarded directly to the schools or to parents and students. Under federal law, parental contributions to the schools were also tax-deductible, and the schools were exempt from federal taxes. Despite the subcommittee's efforts to close these loopholes, the IRS insisted that they were legitimate. Most whites, however, had not given up on the public schools, instead fighting to keep integration to a minimum within them.[34]

Frustrated with the slow progress of legal cases, some blacks turned to direct action at the local level. Emboldened by the new laws, they demanded fully integrated schools, along with better job opportunities and access to all public facilities. In late 1965, for example, the NAACP branch in Natchez conducted a three-month-long economic boycott that was partly aimed at speeding the pace of school desegregation. In the Mississippi towns of Fayette and Port Gibson, the field secretary Charles Evers also led aggressive boycotts to try to force whites to integrate schools and workplaces. Across the region, the association expected real change on the ground. As *The Crisis* declared in October 1965, "The implementation of the [civil rights] law must not merely crack doors; it must fling them wide open."[35]

Other activists led protests that were entirely focused on the schools. One of the best examples came from Jacksonville, where a vibrant NAACP branch coordinated a series of boycotts to protest against the slow pace of school desegregation. As the historian Abel A. Bartley has shown, the NAACP dominated the civil rights scene in Jacksonville, and the boycotts drew on a long history of activism. By 1966, the branch was able to confidently petition the local school board. "There is still in Duval County a dual system of education," it charged, "which is not only separate, but unequal and inferior for the Negro students of this county." The NAACP claimed that fewer than eight hundred of the thirty-one thousand black students in the county were in "desegregated learning situations" and that there had been no mixing of teachers. After white officials failed to respond to their requests, branch activists decided to take matters into their own hands.[36]

Although they depended heavily on mass participation, the NAACP leaders Wendell Holmes and Rutledge Pearson played key roles in the boycotts. As parents of young children, both men shared a desire to improve education opportunities in local schools. A former star athlete, Pearson was a dynamic speaker at the NAACP's lively weekly meetings.

In all, he helped coordinate four separate boycotts of the school system between 1964 and 1967. They were so effective that the school board ended up suing the NAACP on the grounds that it had lost significant amounts of state funding, which was tied to pupil attendance rates. During a two-day protest on March 7–8, 1966, for example, 47 percent of black children stayed out of school, compared to a normal absenteeism rate of around 12 percent. The NAACP won the case, Judge Roger J. Waybright ruling that the state's compulsory school attendance law was unconstitutional because of a 1959 amendment that declared that no child could be "compelled" to attend an integrated school. He also noted that school board members had refused to listen to black parents' requests. Despite this breakthrough, Jacksonville's schools remained largely segregated until 1971, when a federal court ordered cross-town busing.[37]

Across the South, many African Americans also hoped that their children would go on to college, yet, in the Johnson years, the region's universities remained overwhelmingly segregated. In the late 1950s, several states enacted laws to thwart the desegregation of higher education; South Carolina and Georgia tried to deny state funding to universities that were not segregated, while, in Mississippi, officials closed colleges rather than integrate them. As the historian Peter Wallenstein has documented, white administrators also regarded the few black students who were admitted in these years as "unwelcome visitors." As a result, when Title VI was implemented, 64 percent of traditionally white public universities in the region were still totally segregated. Even after this, universities escaped serious scrutiny. Between 1964 and 1969, HEW's efforts were directed almost entirely at the public schools, and officials admitted that this task overstretched their resources. As Libassi wrote in June 1967, "We have not, to date, seriously undertaken to meet our responsibilities with these institutions [universities]." Not until 1969–1970 did HEW even examine ten states that operated dual systems of higher education, instead relying on voluntary compliance. When they did, they found that most blacks still attended traditionally black colleges, and the few breakthroughs that had occurred had been generated by court cases rather than executive action.[38]

The University of Alabama provides a revealing case study. In February 1956, riots took place after Autherine Lucy became the first African American to successfully enroll at the Tuscaloosa campus. As white crowds shouted "Hey, Hey, Ho, Ho, Autherine Must Go" and "Keep 'Bama White," the university trustees voted to expel Lucy for her own protection. Her reputation smeared, Lucy left her native Birmingham and spent the next two decades living in Texas.[39] Following the Lucy incident, state political leaders fought to uphold the status quo. In June 1963, Governor Wallace even stood in the door of the Foster Audito-

rium to try and stop the enrollment of two black students at the Tuscaloosa campus. Wallace later stepped aside when pressured by federal
troops, and four years later there were three hundred black students
attending the University of Alabama's five campuses. Progress had
occurred partly because of the efforts of the university's president, Frank
Rose, who was described by Douglass Cater as "one of the few strong
leaders in that enfeebled state." Cater explained that Rose had stood up
to the governor when he had attempted to interfere in the university's
business. Despite some important advances, however, African Americans still made up a tiny fraction of the university's 17,621 students. In
Tuscaloosa itself, 93 blacks went to class with 11,000 whites, and
around one-third of the black students were public school teachers doing
advanced work. In May 1967, the journalist Gertrude Samuels also
found that black students were being harassed and that there was a lack
of "significant rapport" between the two races on campus. Anxious to
complete their studies, the black students downplayed these difficulties,
at least in public. "I realize the Negroes at U.A. have problems, but the
experience was worth everything to me," explained Vivian Malone, the
first African American to graduate from the university.[40]

At the University of Mississippi, where whites had rioted in 1962 to
try and prevent the enrollment of James Meredith, progress was also fal-
tering. By June 1967, forty blacks were enrolled, yet they were harassed
by what *Newsweek* termed "a vituperative minority." Many whites
refused even to acknowledge their African American classmates. "It's
the invisible university—the Negroes at Ole Miss," commented one
black student. Although the campus was littered with racist graffiti,
some black students claimed that the situation was improving. "Your
first semester as a freshman you encounter a lot of hostility," commented
a black junior. "The second semester—less. Then the next fall it gets bad
again as new whites come in. But it's not as bad as it used to be." Despite
such optimism, it was clear that more effective enforcement of Title VI
was needed at both the school and the university level.[41]

No More Difficult Question:
Title VII and the Struggle for Economic Equality

In the summer of 1967, Ernest Green went back to Little Rock to address
a labor union conference that commemorated the tenth anniversary of
the city's school integration crisis. One of the original Little Rock Nine,
Green had been the first African American to graduate from Central
High School, and he had gone on to earn a graduate degree from Michigan State University. Now working with minority apprentices in New
York, he noted that Little Rock had changed a lot in a decade, especially

as all hotels and restaurants had desegregated. "This convention itself is integrated," he added, "and we all know that it wasn't too many years ago that integrated facilities for any meeting, including union meetings, were not available." Despite this remarkable progress, Green noted that southern blacks still remained much poorer than whites. "All of these changes," he concluded, "have not altered the basic economic problems of most of the people."[42]

Green's comments capture how it was much easier to integrate public accommodations than to improve the economic conditions of the black community. In the job market, decades of segregation had locked African Americans into the worst jobs, while whites gained significant economic benefits from this system. In contrast, they lost little from desegregating public facilities, especially as few blacks could afford to use expensive hotels or restaurants. After 1965, however, many blacks realized that the issues were linked; they needed better jobs in order to be able to use a wide range of public facilities. As one Louisiana worker put it, "If you've got the dollar, you can go where you want to go." Policymakers also saw that jobs were at the core of the race problem. In January 1966, for example, President Johnson wrote EEOC chairman Franklin D. Roosevelt Jr., "Surely there is no more difficult, nor more important question in the field of civil rights than that of opening up new job opportunities for Negro Americans, helping them to prepare for these opportunities, and assuring them fair treatment at promotion time. Negroes feel, and I think rightly, that full participation in the American promise can never be theirs, until the job question is settled and settled rightly."[43]

Opposition to equal employment legislation had been intense long before Title VII was even conceived. From 1941 to 1963, more than two hundred fair employment practice proposals had failed in the U.S. Congress, often because of filibusters and other delaying tactics by southern senators and representatives. Banning discrimination in private employment, Title VII was the hardest-won section of the bill, passing only after a remarkable 534-hour filibuster by southern senators. During the debate, the Senate watered down the strong equal employment opportunity title that the House Judiciary Subcommittee had added to the administration's bill. The net result was that the new EEOC was empowered only to conciliate with employers who had violated the law. The commission was supposed to use "informal methods" such as "conference, conciliation, and persuasion." It had sixty days to obtain "voluntary compliance"; after this, the complainant was permitted to bring civil action against the respondent named in the charge, but he or she had to do so within thirty days. The Senate also amended Title VII to ensure that the EEOC could not bring suit on behalf of an aggrieved party. Rather, the attorney general had the power to file cases whenever there was "reasonable cause to believe that any person or group of persons is engaged in a pattern or practice of resistance to the full enjoyment of any of the rights secured by this title."[44]

Above all, southern senators felt that the commission should not be given the ability to compel employers to change (so-called cease-and-desist powers). Passing on complaints from their constituents, they argued that even the conciliation process represented undue harassment of legitimate businesses. A Democrat from Arkansas, Senator John L. McClellan typically dismissed the EEOC as "a useless agency, unnecessary, uncalled for." While McClellan insisted that the EEOC would "do a lot of harm," its supporters focused on its limitations. Within the first hundred days of the commission's existence, Chairman Franklin D. Roosevelt Jr. had already asked Congress for "meaningful enforcement" powers, but his calls were ignored. Roosevelt would be the first of several EEOC chairs to demand greater authority. In its early years, the EEOC was plagued with administrative problems, and there were damaging delays in filling key positions and establishing regional offices. Crucially, the commission also confronted ongoing congressional opposition, often receiving only half the funds that the Johnson administration requested. From the beginning, then, federal enforcement of Title VII was plagued by problems.[45]

The EEOC needed ample resources because it faced a huge task. As Title VII banned employment discrimination across the entire United States, enforcement efforts could not target purely the South. In contrast, the Voting Rights Act was so effective partly because it was directed at key southern states. While most of the EEOC's early efforts focused on racial issues, staff were also required to prevent discrimination against women. During debate, Virginia congressman Howard Smith had added the broad-ranging ban on sexual discrimination in an effort to sink the civil rights bill. The eighty-year-old conservative failed to predict that some women would persuade the bill's sponsors to leave it in. While they were a boon to the emerging feminist movement, the gender provisions further increased the commission's workload. In fiscal year 1967, for example, 23.5 percent of charges alleged sexual discrimination.[46]

In the South, the need for a strong commission was especially obvious. Prior to 1964, some progress had been made in integrating schools and in gaining black voting rights, but little had changed in the workplace. Here, a strict system of segregation began to be broken down only with the passage of the 1964 act. As recently as 1962, for example, B. Tartt Bell of the AFSC had told Congress, "In industry after industry and company after company, in town after town, across the Southeast, there is the pattern of vicious discrimination on the basis of race." In the same year, NAACP labor secretary Herbert Hill claimed that employment discrimination in the southern states was the worst in the entire country: "I realize that civil rights represent the great unresolved problem of the whole American society, but there can be no doubt that in the Southern states there currently exists the most extreme, rigid, and systematic pattern of employment discrimination to be found anywhere in the United States."[47]

The South's largest industry, the textile industry, epitomized broader patterns. In November 1966, a special EEOC investigation found that for decades blacks had been "almost wholly excluded" from the mills. In 1960, African Americans made up just 3.9 percent of textile workers in North Carolina, a state that was around one-quarter black. Several factors were blamed, including employer apathy, the "social cohesion" of small mill communities, and the fact that an ample supply of white labor had always been available. After 1964, these practices began to change, but black workers were often unaware of job opportunities because they lacked contacts in the mills. Even when they were hired, moreover, blacks were likely to be placed in low-paying posts that few whites wanted.[48]

In contrast, other industries hired blacks in larger numbers but restricted them to the worst jobs. This was the situation at the big tobacco plants, which were located almost entirely in the South. Reflecting practices that dated back to the late nineteenth century, whites worked in the cleaner fabrication department and blacks in the prefabrication and blending departments, where leaf tobacco was received and processed. Black jobs, acknowledged an American Tobacco Company official, were "dirty" and often involved heavy lifting. At P. Lorillard's plant in Greensboro, North Carolina, the heavily black blending department was the only one that was not air-conditioned. In 1966, a Title VII lawsuit filed against that firm charged, "The departments to which black employees were confined were less desirable in that the pay was lower, the jobs more menial and the promotional opportunities more limited."[49]

Regardless of industry, change came slowly, and federal policy targeted the most obvious problems first. In unionized industries, blacks were kept off the best jobs by being placed in separate lines of progression that were often represented by segregated local unions. In the EEOC's early years, around 18 percent of its charges were filed against unions, and they allowed the commission to start tackling these problems. As early as October 1965, for example, the EEOC decreed that segregated unions were a violation of the law, paving the way for the destruction of separate locals in the oil, paper, and tobacco industries. Within the first year of operation, the EEOC also reached agreements to eliminate segregated facilities; these changes were usually accomplished quickly, yet there were cases where companies simply removed signs and workers continued to use the same amenities.[50]

Despite the law's limitations, the EEOC's southern regional offices were important because they provided black workers with a government body that they could turn to. From the start, the commission received what it called an "unexpected volume of complaints," indicating that it was meeting a vital need. In the first hundred days of the commission's existence, for example, it received 1,383 complaints. Seventy percent of these came from the South, and most covered alleged discrimination in pay, hiring, and promotion. Although the EEOC was required to defer to state antidiscrimination agencies, only one southern state (Tennessee) had such a body, compared to thirty-three states nationwide. By 1968, the New Orleans office, which covered Louisiana, Mississippi, and Arkansas, had received over 1,200 charges, pushing staff to establish legal panels for cases that could not be resolved through conciliation. In 1968, the agency's annual report confirmed the vital role it was playing in the South; over a twelve-month period, the EEOC had received 523 complaints from Alabama and 505 from Louisiana, compared to just 44 from Massachusetts.[51]

The regional offices were able to secure some tangible gains. Employing more staff than any other, the Atlanta office maintained close contact with civil rights groups and regional employers. Following a 1967 forum that focused on the southern textile industry, the office claimed a 27 percent increase in black hiring by the mills. These gains occurred after commission staff visited one hundred southern textile plants and encouraged executives to hire blacks, often establishing early affirmative action programs in the process. By talking with mill owners, the commission also claimed that it was able to point out "subtle forms of discrimination on the lower supervisory levels which management was not aware existed."[52]

The textile gains were not unusual. Within its first three years, the EEOC claimed to have negotiated conciliation agreements worth over $12 million for both claimants and "prospective beneficiaries." While these agreements represented only a start, a lot of barriers were certainly breached. In Richmond, a 1966 agreement with a subsidiary of Federal Paper Board led to blacks being hired as long-distance truck drivers for the first time, while, in Atlanta, officials from the W. T. Grant Company made landmark affirmative action commitments. By 1968, the EEOC had also developed broad guidelines for nondiscriminatory testing procedures, distributing them to thousands of employers, trade associations, and federal agencies.[53]

Across the South, the NAACP played a vital role in generating the "unexpected volume of complaints." Aware that Title VII was not self-enforcing, the group mobilized to use it. As a regional report put it, "NAACP Branches in the Southeast were primed to move immediately that Title VII under the Civil Rights Act became effective on July 2." In

Mobile, branch leaders even met with the local chamber of commerce and received assurances that member firms would comply with the law. Above all, however, branches processed complaints, including many against major employers such as U.S. Steel, Lockheed, Southern Bell, Goodyear, and Kroger Baking Company.[54] In some cities, large branches even set up labor committees specifically to receive and process EEOC complaints. Between May 1965 and May 1966, for example, the Birmingham branch filed five hundred Title VII complaints against nineteen local companies. At association conferences, meanwhile, workshops instructed members on how to utilize the law. In all, the EEOC found that the NAACP generated over one-third of all the charges it received in its first year of operation. Recalling these early years, EEOC director John Rayburn explained, "Obviously, the largest number of cases were in the southeastern United States. Large numbers had been filed through the NAACP. . . . The central office of the NAACP would pull in those cases from throughout the southeast and file those."[55]

The NAACP's files confirm that the setting up of the EEOC helped mobilize local communities around fair employment issues. Once the federal legislation was on the books, southern blacks were unwilling to tolerate job bias any longer. In 1965, the Jacksonville branch led marches to demand better jobs, while, in Griffin, Georgia, activists picketed outside stores that discriminated. Other branches that organized fair employment marches included those in Thomasville, Georgia, and Natchez, Mississippi. Direct action led to a number of breakthroughs, including the hiring of the first black store clerks in Griffin and Thomasville and the first black bus drivers in Jackson, Mississippi.[56]

In subsequent months, the pace did not slacken. By January 1966, the NAACP had already filed one thousand EEOC charges, nearly all of them against southern employers. Crisscrossing the region, labor director Herbert Hill helped many workers prepare complaints. One of the highest-ranking whites in the organization, Hill saw Title VII as a great opportunity to help branch members. By May 1967, the NAACP claimed to have filed sixteen hundred EEOC charges, and the indefatigable Hill showed no signs of slowing down. The volume of complaints also meant, however, that the average case was soon taking sixteen months to investigate.[57]

The commission's increasing workload generated a range of problems, especially as the agency had not anticipated such demand. From the very beginning, overstretched staff were reacting to events rather than setting clear goals. As former EEOC director Ronnie Blumenthal recalled, "In the early days I think they thought a few hundred people would come here and file charges of employment discrimination, and we would work on it and it would get better. . . . We were always overwhelmed by the numbers, even in the early days." Struggling to cope, investigators put in long hours. "We worked all the time," recalled the former employee Hortense Criddell. "After the opening up of the EEOC, [charges] just poured in." The expansion of Title VII's coverage exacerbated the situation; initially, the act applied to employers or unions with one hundred or more staff, but this dropped to seventy-five on July 2, 1966, a change that brought in an extra two million workers.[58]

While around 80 percent of charges were filed against employers, others were levied against companies and unions because they had signed discriminatory contracts together. These cases proved some of the most difficult to address, especially as union leaders defended the seniority rights of their members and refused to accept responsibility. It was employers, they insisted, who were responsible for hiring workers.[59] When it came to changing lines of progression, some employers also dug their heels in, largely because they disliked government interference in their affairs. As early as October 1965, Roosevelt reported to LBJ that his conciliators had met widespread resistance when they tried to change seniority lines. "It became clear that stubborn seniority conflicts might ultimately have to be decided by the courts," he acknowledged.[60]

Labor leaders also argued that they were constrained by the racial attitudes of their members, an excuse that had some validity. This was graphically illustrated in February 1967, when the NAACP activist Wharlest Jackson was murdered after being promoted into a traditionally white job at Armstrong Tire and Rubber Company in Natchez, Mississippi. "My wife and five children should have a chance," explained Jackson at the time. As he left the factory a few days later, a bomb exploded under his pickup, killing him instantly. This was no isolated incident, as another black Armstrong worker was also attacked after he pushed for integration. "Word had spread among the workers that if Negroes were promoted to so-called 'white men's jobs,' the Negroes would not live to enjoy them," noted *The Crisis*. In response, three thousand people marched through Natchez to protest against Mississippi's 304th racist killing in the twentieth century.[61]

Across the region, whites resisted the implementation of Title VII from the start. As scholars of the Jim Crow era have shown, whites derived considerable psychological and material benefits from segregation, and they were not willing to surrender them easily.[62] Some black workers understood the depth of white resistance to change. In 1967, for example, the journalist James P. Gannon interviewed John P. Dykes, a black laborer from El Dorado, Arkansas, who charged that Monsanto's promotion system was unfair to blacks. Dykes had filed his complaint in July 1965, as soon as the law had become effective, but eighteen months later nothing had changed, largely because the EEOC had been unable to conciliate the case. "When you possess something," he explained quietly, "you don't give it up easily even to your own people, much less to someone you consider . . . well, different."[63]

Confronting this resistance, blacks only made limited economic progress overall during the Johnson administration, and Title VII proved more effective as a weapon of protest rather than a weapon of change. In August 1967, for example, a broad-ranging EEOC investigation concluded that blacks were still "largely under-represented in the labor force and generally heavily concentrated in the lowest paying blue collar jobs." The pattern was especially evident in the South; in Atlanta, for example, blacks held 15.2 percent of surveyed jobs but just 2.3 percent of white-collar positions. In addition, over 80 percent of the African Americans who had secured white-collar work in the city were in low-paying sales and clerical posts. The situation was similar in New Orleans, where blacks held just 3 percent of white-collar jobs.[64]

EEOC leaders admitted that they had made only a start. In its 1968 annual report, the commission declared that tackling job bias was a "monumental task" and that the huge backlog of cases was the result of "hundreds of years of discrimination." Lacking effective powers, the federal agency could do little if employers or unions refused to accept its findings. In fiscal year 1967, for example, the EEOC experienced eighty-six unsuccessful conciliations, or cases where "recalcitrant respondents" had refused to resolve complaints voluntarily. A black lawyer, former chair Clifford L. Alexander Jr., blamed the "halting progress" of these years on the fact that employers knew the EEOC lacked power. "We sort of gummed them to death if we could, but we had no enforcement powers," he acknowledged in an interview. "We were successful in some instances, but not nearly as many as were needed."[65]

Observing the situation, civil rights activists grew frustrated. In 1966, delegates at a Johnson administration civil rights conference called for the EEOC to have cease-and-desist powers, and activists on the ground also voiced similar demands. "There is some change but the pace is too slow—Negroes are thus doomed to a marginal chance of employment," complained the NAACP's North Carolina conference in 1967. "North Carolina is not what it should be and all gains will be wiped out unless economic gains keep pace with other gains." With powerful southerners holding sway, however, the U.S. Senate rebuffed efforts to secure these powers; in 1967 and 1968, for example, even President Johnson's backing failed to get cease-and-desist legislation adopted. As the president admitted, the commission was consequently "powerless" when its efforts to conciliate or persuade were unsuccessful.[66]

The legislation's failure was partly due to lobbying from business groups, who insisted that the EEOC was unfairly harassing them. As Robert M. Wood, an attorney for a number of employers, wrote Senator

Richard Russell in 1967, the EEOC was forcing his clients to hire "unqualified" applicants and was conciliating false charges. The agency, he asserted, should not have more authority because its staff were "more advocates than mediators." Calling legislation to grant the EEOC extra powers "unwarranted," Russell agreed with these sentiments.[67]

Unable to secure the economic opportunities that they craved, many southern blacks left the region altogether. This migration dated to World War I, when thousands had traveled north in search of freedom and jobs, and it accelerated in subsequent decades. Between 1940 and 1960, when the economy boomed, more than three million southern blacks moved to northern cities.[68] After 1960, this exodus did slow, yet the North retained an economic pull. In 1968, for example, the Census Bureau reported that half of black families outside the region had incomes of over $5,700 a year but that in Dixie the median income was under $4,000. The cost of living was also higher in the North, however, and many blacks did not prosper there. In early 1968, the Johnson administration estimated that one-third of all black families in the country still lived below the poverty line, a figure that prompted the president to acknowledge, "For most minorities . . . economic and social progress has come slowly."[69]

This slow progress also pushed civil rights groups to launch antipoverty programs, an indication of how economic issues would be a major battleground in the ongoing civil rights struggle. Many of these efforts focused on the perilous condition of rural blacks. Across the South, blacks were being pushed off the land by mechanization but had few alternatives. Unemployment was rife, as few industries located in rural areas and those that did failed to hire many African Americans. Agricultural workers were also vulnerable because they were excluded from the minimum wage standards of the Fair Labor Standards Act.[70]

In the summer of 1967, the NAACP sponsored a detailed investigation of living conditions in Mississippi, the poorest state in the entire country. The effort was led by the social workers Alex Waites and Rollie Eubanks, who spent several weeks on an extensive fact-finding trip. "The condition of the Negro in Mississippi defies adequate description," they concluded. "Everywhere we went evidence of malnutrition, hunger and even starvation were apparent and are supported by pictures we took." The investigators linked the existence of poverty to a lack of good jobs, asserting that rural blacks experienced "omnipresent unemployment and . . . systematic exclusion." Overall, 63 percent of African Americans in Mississippi earned less than the federal poverty level. In order to address the situation, the NAACP obtained federal funding to resettle and retrain some impoverished families, but the size of the problem dwarfed its efforts.[71]

Unfortunately, conditions in Mississippi were not unusual. In 1968, for example, the Southern Rural Research Project conducted an extensive survey of living conditions in Alabama's Black Belt counties. Composed of a variety of organizations, including the SNCC, the SCLC, and the SRC, the project found that widespread poverty in the area was again linked to a lack of good jobs. A quarter of all families could not afford to eat meat, and 14 percent of households contained "children with very noticeably distended stomachs." Low incomes also meant that families could not afford adequate medical care, and a third of all mothers had lost one or more children.[72]

The new federal laws were also ineffective when it came to tackling black poverty. Title VII failed to cover state and local government workers, a crucial weakness. In late 1967, for example, very few blacks worked for the State Cooperative Extension Services in the South. As late as 1967, no blacks had been assigned supervisory responsibility for extension work at a county level, and black extension workers also received lower salaries than comparably qualified whites. The extension services were slow to end segregated service, and this discouraged poor blacks from seeking assistance. In addition, white officials gave more aid to white farmers.[73]

After 1965, the SCLC spent much of its time on programs to tackle black poverty, with limited success. In particular, the group's Operation Breadbasket program pressured employers both to hire and to promote blacks, largely through negotiations and selective buying campaigns. As its name suggested, this initiative was designed to ease what the SCLC termed "the unemployment crisis in the Negro community." While it originated in the North, the program spread to the South after 1964. In July 1965, for example, program director the Reverend Fred C. Bennette Jr. wrote that he wanted to achieve "the up-grading of Negroes in jobs and acquisitions of jobs for Negroes throughout the South Eastern part of the United States." Operating out of Atlanta, Bennette's staff secured some important breakthroughs, particularly in Georgia. Most gains came in urban areas, however, while, in rural areas, the SCLC was overwhelmed by the prevalence of black poverty, a lack of staff, and the reluctance of employers to hire blacks in nontraditional jobs.[74]

Frustrated by the lack of fundamental change, SCLC leaders turned to protest. In particular, the poverty that was uncovered by the NAACP pushed Dr. Martin Luther King to plan a poor people's march from the Mississippi Delta to the nation's capital. Prompted by the NAACP official Marian Wright, in the spring of 1967 four senators had also carried out a highly publicized tour of the Delta and had been shocked by the poverty they had witnessed. As New York's Robert Kennedy observed, the conditions he saw were "a condemnation of all of us . . . that this could exist in a prosperous nation like ours." Hoping to build on this concern, King spent much of the last year of his life planning the campaign, which was one of his most ambitious projects. Although some of his staff worried that poverty was hard to tackle effectively, King pressed ahead with plans to recruit blacks from the Deep South and have them camp in Washington, DC. His aim was to jolt the nation's conscience and push Congress to spend more on antipoverty programs rather than on the costly war in Vietnam. "What we need now," he declared in December 1967, "is a new kind of Selma or Birmingham to dramatize the economic plight of the Negro, and compel the government to act."[75]

In March 1968, King also supported a strike by black sanitation workers in Memphis. Earning less than $70 a week, the workers epitomized black poverty and showed that it was not simply a rural problem. Seeking dignity as well as higher wages, the strikers brought out the best in the eloquent minister. "Now our struggle is for genuine equality, which means economic equality," he told the workers. "We are tired of being at the bottom. . . . We are tired of our men being emasculated so that our wives and our daughters have to go out and work in the white lady's kitchen." The strike allowed King to broaden the meaning of the freedom struggle to include issues of economic justice, yet these demands made whites uncomfortable, especially as many of them viewed all black protesters as dangerous militants. As Michael K. Honey has shown, most white Memphians viewed King's rhetoric as "an affront to supposed racial peace" and claimed that blacks were demanding too much. Reflecting these views, city leaders resisted the workers' demands for better pay and union recognition.[76]

In early 1968, King's calls for economic justice were reinforced by the findings of the president's National Advisory Commission on Civil Disorders. Headed by Illinois governor Otto Kerner, the eleven-member commission investigated the race riots that had occurred in many American cities between 1965 and 1967. In July 1967, for example, riots in Newark and Detroit left seventy people dead and led to over five thousand arrests.[77] The racially mixed commissioners, mostly moderates, blamed "white racism" for helping create the desperate economic conditions that existed in many black ghettos. They called for far-reaching action to address black poverty, including the creation of two million new jobs and federal subsidies to train the hard-core unemployed. The panel warned that, unless such measures were adopted, the end result would be the creation of "two societies, one black, one white—separate and unequal."[78]

Not surprisingly, the two races reacted very differently to the report, and the riots certainly made whites less likely to support federal policies that tackled black poverty, such as reform of the EEOC. Most whites, including the president, were uncomfortable with the white racism charge because they viewed race relations as satisfactory. As the commission member Roy Wilkins explained, "The language was too hard for L.B.J. He could not bring himself to believe it. The churches didn't like the conclusion, either; nor did the clubwomen, the fraternal organizations, and the politicians. They all told us we had done plenty to improve conditions. Millions of whites felt the same way. They couldn't accept the report; they thought things were just fine with the colored: there we were over on our end of town, with our churches, and wasn't a colored boy captain of the basketball team? What were we yelling about?"[79] Across the country, whites responded to the riots by calling for the restoration of law and order, a demand that was championed by southern politicians such as George Wallace and Samuel Ervin. Reaction to the commission's findings was similarly hostile, especially in the South. Speaking for many, Wade Murrah from Blairsville, Georgia, declared, "It is about time to stop devoting 90% of our government's time and attention to 10% of the population." Overall, only a few whites saw any merit in the commission's recommendations.[80]

Polls confirmed that whites rejected the idea that white racism was the main cause of the rioting by a margin of 53 percent to 35 percent, whereas blacks overwhelmingly agreed with the finding. As the commission noted, among blacks there was a mood of increased militancy that reflected "unfulfilled expectations aroused by the great judicial and legislative victories of the civil rights movement." Despite the white backlash, most blacks wanted the new civil rights laws to be forcefully implemented. There were few signs that the gap between the races was being closed, and it was clear that blacks would continue to press their unmet claims for economic justice.[81]

In the midst of this polarized environment, King continued his struggle to secure economic justice for all Americans. On the night of April 3, he returned to Memphis to address the strikers. After his plane was delayed by a bomb threat, he arrived in the city during a tornado watch. Worried about appearing before a small crowd, he agreed to talk at the last moment only in order to avoid disappointing those who had braved the foul weather. With little preparation, he delivered a remarkable address in which he assured listeners, "We as a people will get to the promised land." After the speech, he went back to the Lorraine Motel, a black-owned hotel with exposed balconies. As he checked into room 306, King was unaware of several death threats that had just been made against him, largely because FBI director J. Edgar Hoover had decreed that he should not be informed. The course of the civil rights movement was about to be changed forever.[82]

3

A FRAGMENTED CRUSADE?

The Civil Rights Struggle in the Aftermath of the King Assassination, 1968–1970

In the early evening of April 4, 1968, Martin Luther King Jr. was felled by a single shot as he stood on the balcony of the Lorraine Motel. Traveling at a speed of 2,670 feet per second, the bullet was fired by James Earl Ray, an escaped convict and Klan sympathizer who had rented a room at a local flophouse. Powerful enough to floor a rhinoceros, the 150-grain bullet ripped through the preacher's jugular vein, throwing him onto his back. The thirty-nine-year-old was rushed to St. Joseph's Hospital, where a team of doctors tried desperately to save him. Within an hour of the shooting, however, King was dead. Taylor Rogers, one of the sanitation workers whom King was trying to help, captured the impact of his death well. "It was like losing part of your family. . . . We all just had a hurt feeling," he commented. "The man had done so much good for everybody, black and white."[1]

King's death was a defining moment in the civil rights struggle. Along with the killing of the presidential hopeful Robert Kennedy in June, it snuffed out liberal hopes for racial healing and encouraged a political turn to the right. In the wake of King's assassination, violent riots occurred across the nation, further polarizing blacks and whites. Appalled by the violence, many southern whites rallied behind Richard Nixon, who won the presidency in November by promising to represent the interests of the "silent majority." Relations between the new administration and civil rights groups were poor, and within two years Nixon's aides were engaged in a slanging match with NAACP leaders, who accused them of pandering to southern whites.[2]

Above all, King's death left an enormous vacuum in the civil rights movement, especially as there was no longer a charismatic figurehead for the media to focus on. In 1969, the *New York Times* asserted that, without King, the movement had lost its "mysticism and spiritual quality" and become a "fragmented crusade." It added, "No national leader has been able to replace Dr. King in his ability to express the aspirations of so many Negroes and give them hope." King's quiet understudy, Dr. Ralph Abernathy, was a capable preacher, but he failed to inspire the white media. Abernathy acknowledged that following in his idol's footsteps was daunting. "I am not a Moses and I know it," he told audiences with a resigned air.[3]

The loss of King certainly made it more difficult to launch direct action protests that could mobilize national attention. It was also true that many of the groups that had led the civil rights struggle over the past decade now declined, particularly at the national level. Apart from King's SCLC, this was especially true of the SNCC and CORE. At the same time, however, the national media wrote off the movement too easily. After 1968, organizations that were not dependent on direct action protests worked at the local level to desegregate schools, workplaces, and public accommodations, and they also battled to give blacks greater political power. The NAACP, for example, fought freedom-of-choice plans, filed numerous job discrimination complaints, and conducted countless voter registration drives. Organized by the SRC, the broad-ranging VEP registered thousands of new voters and helped blacks challenge for elected office right across the region. All the while, career lawyers at the Justice Department carried on their work to enforce the law, while millions of ordinary African Americans quietly exercised their newfound rights. As a result of these efforts, southern blacks made important gains, particularly in voting and public accommodations. In 1970, the chair of the U.S. Commission on Civil Rights acknowledged the progress that had occurred in the thirteen years of the agency's existence. "Since 1957," wrote Theodore Hesburgh to the Nixon aide Leonard Garment, "we have largely licked the voting problem for blacks throughout the South. . . . Public accommodations have seen an enormous change since 1957, when blacks could not get a room, a hair cut, a meal, a drink of water, or burial in many places in America."[4]

As Hesburgh also noted, however, it was much more difficult to integrate workplaces and schools, and he pondered whether whites were willing to tackle these problems: "Do we really want to do the difficult task of making equality a reality for all Americans, regardless of race, religion, color, nationality, or sex?" As the next chapter details, the ongoing struggle to desegregate southern schools was a defining issue in these years. The thousands of complaints that poured into the EEOC's offices also indicated that employment discrimination was only beginning to be addressed. As the economy began to slow, moreover, southern blacks complained that their situation was worsening. In 1969, the median income of southern blacks was $4,278, compared to $7,963 for whites. In economic terms, blacks were still better off in the North, where they earned $6,460, compared to whites' $9,318. Although the white press emphasized the pace of change, many blacks saw things differently. "You got the money, you can go anywhere in Atlanta," commented an African American resident in 1970. "They're glad to take it. But making that money—that's your problem."[5]

"There Was So Much Anger among People": Racial Polarization, the King Assassination, and the Changing Political Climate

King's assassination graphically exposed racial divisions. Livid that a peaceful, nonviolent leader had been brutally killed, many blacks took to the streets looking for revenge. By April 11, forty-three people had been killed and more than twenty thousand arrested in racial disturbances in 125 U.S. cities. Over seventy-two thousand army and national guard troops were used to quell the riots, the largest domestic deployment of military forces since the Civil War. As the historian Michael Honey has noted in his fine account of these difficult days, "Something snapped inside many people when King died."[6]

Although the largest disturbances occurred in northern cities such as Chicago, Washington, DC, and Baltimore, southern blacks also took to the streets. In Memphis, rioters looted 275 stores, the vast majority of them white owned. On April 8, police in Nashville reported "hit and run gorilla [sic] warfare" with angry blacks on the streets around Tennessee A&I University.[7] In King's hometown of Atlanta, law enforcement officers worked twelve-hour shifts in order to cope with sporadic acts of vandalism and firebombing. Rioters even bombed the headquarters of the United Klans of America, which was located just a block from where King's body lay in state. In North Carolina, tensions were so acute that Raleigh, Durham, Charlotte, Greensboro, and Wilson were all placed under a curfew. Between April 4 and 8, for example, there were 105 arrests in Raleigh as twelve hundred national guardsmen clashed with black protesters near the Shaw University campus. During April, national guard and federal troops were also mobilized in Montgomery, Durham, Jackson, Memphis, and Tampa, as well as in several smaller southern cities.[8]

Moderate black leaders did their best to contain the violence, with mixed results. In Charlotte, NAACP chief Kelly Alexander Sr. helped avert a riot by venturing into the streets and persuading blacks to go home. "I remember there was so much anger among people," recalled the Charlotte native Robert Albright, who had heard King speak at the March on Washington, "particularly many of the young black students who were not much younger than I was, because they'd all been affected by Dr. King as I personally [had] been affected by Dr. King." In Wilmington, North Carolina, however, community leaders could not quell disturbances that raged for five days after King's death, leading to 198 arrests and over $200,000 in property damage. In an irony that was at the heart of the violence, admirers of King sought to retaliate for his killing, yet, in doing so, they rejected his nonviolent methods. Ultimately, the Wilmington disturbances defied rational explanation and were a reflection of intense pain; as the riot leader Frank "Funny One" Hans later explained, "We did it because we were really hurt." Only the mobilization of 750 national guardsmen eventually put a stop to the violence.[9]

Drawing on the feeling that the fundamental issues raised by the civil rights movement had already been addressed, white reaction to King's death was very different. As one of President Johnson's aides reported to him on April 6, "There is a great gulf of understanding here because the white looks at the great mass of laws that have been written and the Negro looks at the small number of jobs and adequate houses that are available to him. The two races are looking at the world through different colored glasses."[10] In the South, this gulf was particularly apparent. After interviewing three hundred blacks and three hundred whites in Atlanta, one Emory University survey revealed that 78 percent of blacks, compared to 30 percent of whites, described their immediate reaction to King's death as "very shocked, sad." In addition, only 1 percent of blacks were "indifferent" to the slaying, compared to 14 percent of whites. These reactions were illustrated by King's funeral, as local whites stayed away while blacks attended in huge numbers. Although close to 200,000 mourners passed directly by the state capitol, Governor Lester Maddox refused to close the complex and complained that most black cafeteria staff had failed to come to work. He was also angry that the state capitol flag flew at half-mast, although Secretary of State Ben W. Forston Jr. explained that he was following a presidential directive to lower flags on all federal buildings.[11]

Many southern whites shared Maddox's indignation. Three days after King's death, the South Carolinian Lucy T. Davis wrote, "When a hypocritical opportunist such as Martin Luther King dies, as tragic as this is, is it befitting a nation of our history to be dictated a day of mourning and all federal flags flown at half-mast?" Clearly angry, Davis wanted the same honor accorded to American troops who had died in Vietnam. Her letter expressed the prevailing feeling that the rights of blacks counted for more than those of whites. "The White People have no rights, it seems," declared the Columbia resident John B. Halloran. "I guess the only thing left is for the Whites to demonstrate and throw away millions like they have let the Negro do." Viewing King as a radical troublemaker, some insisted that he had invited his own death. The

Georgia residents Frank and Sally Basler, for example, asked Senator Russell, "What is *militant* non-violence which he advocated anyway? Double talk and deception seemed to be his way of life. The results of this are plain enough in the destruction, bloodshed and rioting that has followed in his wake."[12]

Although they were in the minority, some southern whites expressed sadness about King's death and recognized that racial divisions had to be healed. At the University of Georgia, a group of faculty and students called the assassination a "tragedy" and petitioned Senator Russell to avoid "increasing hostility between the races." A few southerners even reported that King's death had caused them to reevaluate their core beliefs. Describing herself as "just a housewife," the South Carolinian Marjorie Langdale was moved to write her first letter to a public official. "I have felt for years the terribleness of the plight of the Negro," she told Strom Thurmond. "Yet, I have been afraid to speak out before now." King, declared Langdale, was "a truly great leader" who had wanted only "the best for all men."[13]

Expressing views that were out of step with those of most southern whites, these letters went unanswered, yet they remind us that white views were not monolithic even at this divisive time. In these years, however, both Russell and Thurmond insisted that southern whites were victims of what the South Carolinian termed "a philosophy of discrimination in reverse." The results of the 1968 presidential election would confirm that most southern whites agreed with them. As the Georgia resident W. B. Outz Jr. wrote in mid-April, "The people I have talked to are fed up with lawlessness, looting, and burning. . . . They are fed up with giving in to the minority and feel like the majority should receive equal treatment."[14]

While hopes of bridging the racial gap were already slim, in early June the assassination of Robert Kennedy removed a leader who might have been able to bring Americans together. Reacting to the killing of King, for example, Kennedy had delivered a remarkable speech in which he advised a black audience that America needed "love and wisdom" rather than "violence or lawlessness." Attending King's funeral, RFK also called for improved dialogue between the races. As the historian John Morton Blum has written, "Kennedy had been the last liberal who could reach both races as well as both generations."[15]

While King's death pushed authorities in Memphis to recognize the sanitation workers' union, the other major SCLC campaign of 1968 ended in defeat. Finally taking place after months of wrangling between staffers, the Poor People's Campaign did little to heal racial divisions. In the course of the troubled crusade, Ralph Abernathy led over three thousand predominantly black volunteers from Memphis to "Resurrection City," a camp near the Washington Monument that was designed to dramatize the plight of America's poor. Demanding jobs and income, many of the volunteers came from Black Belt counties in Mississippi and Alabama.[16] "Men can be made to listen," declared Abernathy, who tried hard to make the project work. Difficulties in mobilizing volunteers, inclement weather, and an unrelenting smear campaign by the FBI all undermined the campaign, however. Most importantly, President Johnson ignored Resurrection City, and Congress was unmoved, reducing federal expenditure on social programs for the third year running. By July, Abernathy acknowledged the "failure" of Congress "to move meaningfully against the problem of poverty this summer."[17]

Rather than generating concern, the Poor People's Campaign angered many southern whites, who insisted that the demonstrators should look after their own welfare rather than demanding assistance from Washington. "Any man physically capable of taking part in such a demonstration is capable of doing a day's work," fumed Mary Neary from Augusta.[18] The Texan Jess F. Heard was also angry. "God Almighty!" he exclaimed in May 1968. "Is there no end to the demands the Negroes will force our nation to meet? Will members of Congress continue to give these Socialists and Communists everything they ask for? Will memories of Martin Luther King dictate the future policy of our Congress?" While some mocked "Insurrection City," others insisted that the police should be granted shoot-to-kill powers to crush the demonstration. The southern press was no more restrained; the *Montgomery Advertiser*, for example, called the protesters "invading hordes" and dismissed Abernathy as "an unprincipled and unspeakable bum without any redeeming qualities whatsoever."[19]

Like Jess Heard, most whites believed that blacks were demanding too much. Reacting to both the race riots and student protests at the 1968 Democratic convention, they wanted a return to law and order rather than more civil rights legislation. Exploiting these concerns, Richard Nixon and George Wallace together won almost 70 percent of the southern vote in the 1968 presidential election. Both promised to represent the ordinary Americans who had, they insisted, been overlooked by Johnson. "I understand the bitter feelings of millions of Americans who live in the South," declared Nixon. Whipping up the crowds, Wallace even promised to run over protesters if they lay in front of his limousine. At this time, Congress also hardened itself against demands for more spending on racial problems. It refused to implement the costly recommendations of the Kerner Commission and opposed Johnson's 1968 civil rights bill, which proposed extensive measures to tackle housing discrimination. In these years, many Americans were also focused on the ongoing conflict in Vietnam, a war that was still backed by most southern whites. As the Nixon aide Harry Dent later reflected, "The South continued to support Nixon on Vietnam when other parts of the country were howling against him." Many southern blacks, however, disliked the war, partly because it drew attention and funding away from racial problems.[20]

From the outset, relations between Nixon and civil rights groups were very poor. Some of the problems reflected his background. The new president had grown up in Whittier, California, where no African Americans lived, and he had little contact with blacks before coming into office. Throughout his life, Nixon also privately doubted black equality. "There has never been an adequate black nation and they are the only race of which this is true," he told one aide. At the same time, however, the historian Dean J. Kotlowski has defended the president, arguing that he opposed racial bias and supported some policies that helped blacks advance.[21]

On balance, however, Nixon's civil rights record left a lot to be desired. Coming into office, the new president failed to establish a rapport with African American leaders, and, within four months, the NAACP had charged that he was trying to slow the desegregation of schools and workplaces.[22] Shortly afterward, the situation deteriorated when the administration sought to weaken the Voting Rights Act by repealing the preclearance provisions. In addition, Nixon angered blacks by nominating Clement F. Haynsworth Jr., a racial conservative from South Carolina, to the Supreme Court. By July, the normally mild-mannered Roy Wilkins told the NAACP's convention that the administration's civil rights policies were "almost enough to make one vomit."[23]

In 1970, following the failure of Haynsworth's nomination, relations deteriorated further when Nixon proposed G. Harrold Carswell instead. Another southern segregationist, Carswell had supported efforts to turn a public golf course in Tallahassee into a private club rather than admit blacks. Civil rights groups united to defeat both nominations, much to Nixon's annoyance. In early 1970, a leaked memo from the presidential adviser Daniel Patrick Moynihan declared, "The time may have come when the issue of race could benefit from a period of 'benign neglect.'" While Nixon insisted that the document was taken "out of context," civil rights groups saw it as conclusive proof of the administration's desire to sideline racial issues. At the NAACP's convention a few months later, Chairman Bishop Stephen Gill Spottswood declared, "For the first time since Woodrow Wilson, we have an administration that can rightly be characterized as anti-Negro." Spottswood charged that the Republicans wanted to weaken the Voting Rights Act and slow the pace of school desegregation, accusations that Leonard Garment called "unfair and disheartening."[24]

In this tough new climate, national civil rights groups experienced many problems. Although it steered some grassroots protests, the SCLC lacked funding and suffered from internal splits. The group focused heavily on economic issues, yet the new president rebuffed their demands for more spending on the black poor. In 1970, a disastrous meeting between Abernathy and Nixon left the SCLC out in the cold. After Nixon had refused to grant a list of SCLC demands, Abernathy responded by calling the meeting "disappointing" and "fruitless." Nixon never forgot Abernathy's public criticisms, noting in his memoirs that the SCLC chief was "a good lieutenant" but "had not developed into a good general."[25] Other groups fared even worse. Weakened by divisions over black power, and heavily infiltrated by the FBI, the SNCC held its last staff meeting in June 1969. Although the organization formally existed for several more years, its national headquarters did not even contain a telephone or full-time personnel. CORE suffered a similar fate, limping into the 1970s under the radical leadership of Roy Innis, a black separatist who declared that integration was "as dead as a doornail." Under Innis, CORE had a tiny staff, few resources, and only a handful of chapters.[26]

Despite the hostile national climate, state studies have revealed that blacks continued to battle for jobs, better schools, and political representation. In Louisiana, Adam Fairclough has established that the NAACP revived in the late 1960s and led a number of campaigns and boycotts. In locations such as Lake Charles, Baton Rouge, and Shreveport, African Americans conducted voter registration projects and pressed for more jobs and access to public accommodations. Similar actions also took place in Georgia. In late 1968, for example, blacks in Twiggs County worked with the SCLC and launched mass marches for integrated schools and jobs. The protests secured a number of concessions from the county commission, including a commitment to hire a black deputy sheriff.[27] In 1969 and 1970, the SCLC also supported striking black hospital workers in Charleston. Part of the SCLC's broader effort to reduce poverty, this major campaign led to nearly one thousand arrests and generated widespread media interest. Backed by white opinion, however, hospital administrators refused to recognize the workers' union.[28]

What is clear is that developments at the national level did not necessarily hinder grassroots civil rights struggles. As the historian J. Mills Thornton III has noted in his monumental *Dividing Lines,* after 1968 the movement remained "as significant as ever" at the local level, where the fight to enforce the law carried on. While southern blacks were assisted by a variety of groups, they frequently worked on their own, and many changes happened quietly. In the sense that the civil rights struggle had switched to the local level, it was indeed, as the *New York Times* noted, "fragmented," yet there is no denying the gains that resulted. By the end of the 1960s, the South was a very different place from the strictly segregated society it had been ten years earlier.[29]

"Oh Man, the South Has Changed":
Big Strides in Voting and Public Accommodations

Everyday race relations changed the most. In the Jim Crow South, African Americans had faced great difficulties when they had wanted to travel; unable to get service at restaurants, and barred from "white" bathrooms, they usually had to pack their own food and search carefully for "colored" restrooms whenever they undertook a long journey. Five or six years after the passage of the Civil Rights Act, the situation had altered dramatically, and returning blacks noticed. "Oh man, the South has changed," noted Robert Gilmore on a trip to his native Charlotte in 1970. "I left here when I was 18—14 years ago—and Negroes couldn't do anything then, couldn't go anyplace. But that's all changed now." In the same year, the Durham native Mary E. Mebane was struck by the "enormousness of the change that has taken place" when she rode a bus from her hometown to Orangeburg, South Carolina. "The used-to-be ubiquitous policeman was no longer on the scene," she noted with some surprise. "Now the bus drivers no longer narrow their eyes to slits as they look with thin lips over the waiting passengers and try to take all the white ones on first." Progress was tempered only by the fact that few whites were now riding the buses, partly because they wanted to avoid integrated public spaces.[30]

Remarkable changes had also taken place in Jackson, Mississippi, where authorities had arrested hundreds of demonstrators who had sought access to public facilities in 1963. Then, Mayor Allen Thompson had asserted that local blacks were "happy and content" and would not follow "outside agitators." Six years later, however, the NAACP held its national convention in the city and was welcomed by white leaders. "Because of the 1964 Civil Rights Act," explained the NAACP leader Clarence Mitchell, "we were able to meet in the hotels of that city on a completely non-discriminatory basis." As Mitchell related, the manager of the Heidelberg Hotel even addressed the convention and personally extended a welcome to the delegates. Realizing that desegregation was good for business, the chamber of commerce worked to ensure that everything went smoothly. Their efforts paid off, as delegates spent at least $300,000 during the six-day gathering.[31]

While blacks celebrated these developments, whites noted that they had not been as disruptive as they had feared. The chairman of the Republican Party in Mississippi, Clarke Reed, provided an excellent example of how attitudes had shifted. In 1964, Reed had disliked the passage of the Civil Rights Act, but, six years later, he felt differently. "Although philosophically I would have opposed the public accommodation section of the 1964 Civil Rights Bill, I must now admit it has done wonders in 'unalienating' the individual black man," he wrote a friend in 1970. "The coffee shops of Greenville, Mississippi are not overrun with Negroes but they know they can now be served without so much as a stare." Across the South, the law had pushed whites to confront their prejudices. Writing to the *Atlanta Constitution* in early 1970, the local man Royce V. Hamrick explained how his views had changed "radically" over the previous decade or so. "When I was raised in rural Georgia, true segregation was a stark reality," he wrote. "Black people were said to be substandard, to say the least. I have since come to realize how drastically wrong the ideas were. My generation has witnessed the abolishment of separate water fountains, eating facilities etc."[32]

Positive changes occurred in many of the movement's former battlegrounds. Ten years after the sit-ins, no sign proclaimed the F. W. Woolworth's store in Greensboro as the site where the protests had started. At the store's lunch counter, however, blacks and whites now sat together and happily munched their meals. Daily events were testament to what the sit-in had achieved; as the *Winston-Salem Journal* acknowledged, the protest had "brought a new way of community life to the dual service and segregated South of the 1960s." The four students who had started it all felt vindicated. "The only way to see a change in the country for the betterment of all mankind is to be the change itself," declared Ezell Blair Jr. on the protest's tenth anniversary.[33]

Previously dubbed the most segregated city in America, Birmingham had also altered a great deal. In 1970, the *New York Times* reported that well-heeled blacks were even able to dine at the plush Parliament House restaurant. While such experiences were somewhat exceptional, it was significant that restaurants and diners across the Magic City were completely desegregated. As the local resident Samuel W. Dart noted in late 1969, "Hotels, restaurants, entertainment facilities, and many businesses are now integrated and it has been accomplished peacefully and is working out well." Dart proudly asserted that southern cities could now claim to be more integrated than big northern centers such as Chicago and New York.[34]

Ninety miles to the south, there had also been rapid progress. By 1970, visitors to Selma reported that blacks could eat freely in restaurants and diners. Most whites also addressed black men as "Mister" and were even willing to shake their hands on the street. "We've learned a lot since 1965," admitted the *Selma Times-Journal* editor, Roswell Falkenberry. "We've learned that the world has changed since 1914, and the black man is going to have a part in it from now on." Even in rural Mississippi, remarkable changes were afoot, and the veteran black leader Aaron Henry linked them directly to the landmark legislation. "Prior to the Civil Rights Act of 1964 the modus operandi of the local police department was to harass whites that visited blacks," he told a white interviewer in 1970. "The law doesn't make you love me, but it stops you from lynching me. It makes you more palatable in terms of your treatment of other human beings."[35]

While white attitudes were improving, the role of the federal government in enforcing the Civil Rights Act was crucial. Operating with little fanfare, the Justice Department's lawyers filed numerous suits that stamped out lingering resistance to Title II. In 1968 and 1969 alone, federal attorneys brought seventy-eight suits to end discrimination by southern restaurants, service stations, hotels, and other places of public accommodation. In the spring of 1969, for instance, lawyers forced Glenn's Frozen Custard, a small restaurant in Burlington, North Carolina, to put up a sign indicating that it complied with the Civil Rights Act. The move angered the owner, Howard Glenn, who insisted that he had the right to refuse service. Such resistance was unusual; by early 1970, the Justice Department was able to report that compliance with Title II was "generally widespread." This was partly because of the agency's intervention in *Daniel v. Paul* (1969), a crucial case in which the U.S. Supreme Court ruled that private recreation areas that were open to the public were covered by the act. The ruling thwarted efforts to establish private clubs that kept out blacks.[36]

On the ground, civil rights activists also played an important role. In 1969, Morris Dees brought a noteworthy case in Montgomery, another movement battleground. Wanting to speed up the pace of change in his hometown, Dees filed *Smith v. Young Men's Christian Association*, which was designed to integrate the all-white Montgomery YMCA. The Y had taken over the city's recreational needs after the authorities had closed swimming pools, parks, and recreational facilities rather than integrate them, and, in 1969, it still refused to admit black children to its summer camp. Although community leaders urged him to drop the case, Dees was undeterred. In the course of his research, the young attorney uncovered a secret agreement in which city officials had given the YMCA control of many of their recreational facilities. He used this to gain a ruling that the association had a "municipal charter" and had to stop discriminating in order to comply with the Civil Rights Act. As a result of this pathbreaking decision, YMCA facilities were soon integrated. In a generous move, Dees gave his fee of $25,000 to the association so that it could be spent on poor black children.[37]

Emboldened by the victory, Dees also established the SPLC with his fellow lawyer Joseph J. Levin Jr. and the former SNCC leader Julian Bond. Starting out with what the Dees termed "some old furniture, one typewriter, a line of bank credit, and no donors," the new organization grew quickly. Over the next decade, its lawyers brought crucial suits that desegregated the Alabama Highway Patrol and reapportioned the all-white Alabama state legislature to give African Americans representation. Building on *Smith,* Dees also brought a separate case that forced the city of Montgomery to upgrade recreational facilities within poor black neighborhoods.[38]

By the end of the 1960s, the Voting Rights Act had also had a remarkable impact. In early 1969, even the circumspect U.S. Commission on Civil Rights was able to declare, "Much progress has been made in eliminating the gap between the proportion of whites and the proportion of Negroes of voting age who are registered." In December of that year, the commission estimated that nearly two million new black voters had registered in the South since the act's passage. "From my perspective of 12 years on the Commission," wrote Theodore Hesburgh, "I think I can say that there has been no more effective piece of civil rights legislation than the Voting Rights Act of 1965."[39]

Increased voting translated into political representation. By December 1969, around five hundred blacks held public office in the South, and many of them were mayors and state legislators. Some had won office in towns where African Americans had only just started to vote. In 1969, for example, Charles Evers was elected Mayor of Fayette, Mississippi. The brother of the slain activist Medgar Evers, he became the first black mayor of a biracial Mississippi town in a century. His victory epitomized the rapid pace of change, as blacks had only just started voting in Fayette. Recognizing the importance of the Voting Rights Act, Evers thanked LBJ. "I'm the mayor because of your pushing the voter rights bill through and because of your concern about getting equal opportunity . . . for those who were left out of the political system," he wrote. The Alcorn College graduate beat five-term incumbent R. J. Allen by effectively mobilizing the town's new black voters. After spearheading the local civil rights movement, Evers was well placed to move into politics.[40]

While most gains occurred in majority-black areas, some southern whites were willing to support moderate black candidates. In 1969, whites helped elect Maynard Jackson as vice mayor of Atlanta, while, in Chapel Hill, Howard Lee became the first black mayor of a predominantly white North Carolina city in the twentieth century. As a liberal college community, Chapel Hill was something of an anomaly, but Lee's victory was still significant. "I'm just so happy I can hardly talk," commented the thirty-four-year-old mayor-elect, who had been born into a sharecropping family in Georgia. A few months earlier, Henry Frye of Greensboro had won a seat in the state legislature, the first African American to do so since Reconstruction.[41]

Federal officials helped southern blacks make these strides. Despite the shift in presidential administrations, under Nixon the Justice Department's career lawyers continued to implement the Voting Rights Act much as they had under Johnson. "During the first five years of the Act," explained Assistant Attorney General for Civil Rights J. Stanley Pottinger, "the Department of Justice concentrated its efforts on law suits to end the forbidden use of literacy tests and devices, on ending the poll tax and, principally on a county-by-county enforcement program of federal examiners and observers wherever voluntary compliance could not be obtained." In particular, the department continued to send federal examiners to counties where registrars were acting in a discriminatory fashion. Between 1965 and 1970, these examiners registered over 160,000 persons, with the biggest increases occurring in Alabama and Mississippi. In this five-year period, black registration in Mississippi increased from 6.7 to 63.3 percent of eligible voters, a remarkable jump. In rural Humphreys County, which had a population of just ten thousand, federal registrars listed 2,067 black voters. Over the same period, department chiefs also dispatched forty-five hundred federal observers to gather evidence at the polling place and launched twenty-one lawsuits against problematic districts. As Pottinger acknowledged, however, most whites voluntarily complied with the law's provisions, largely because they recognized that resistance was futile.[42]

The federal courts bolstered the Justice Department's work. In case after case, judges blocked moves by southern officials who tried to reimpose discriminatory voting requirements. In June 1969, for example, the U.S. Supreme Court upheld a district court ruling against Gaston County, North Carolina, which had sought to use a literacy test to determine who was qualified to vote. In a seven-to-one decision, the Court held that, because county officials had provided better education opportunities to its white citizens, even an "impartial" literacy test would "serve only to perpetuate those inequities in a different form." The case was important because it thwarted efforts to reintroduce unfair literacy tests.[43]

Civil rights groups also deserve credit for the steady increase in the number of black voters. First established in 1962, the SRC's VEP helped register many of the new voters. Between 1965 and 1969, for example, it helped finance nearly five hundred voter registration and citizenship education programs in the region. Initially headed by Vernon Jordan and later by John Lewis, the program was funded largely by outside grants. An admirer of King, Lewis had left the SNCC in 1966 because he disagreed with its embrace of black power. At the VEP, he headed a staff of thirty-eight workers. "We covered eleven Southern states," he recalled in his memoirs, "from Virginia to Texas, spearheading get-out-the-vote drives, presenting seminars for young black people interested in politics, and offering technical and financial assistance to black community groups interested in political education." As part of its work, the VEP issued detailed guidelines that instructed local activists how to organize effectively. "The key to a success-ful registration campaign is good planning and organizing," those guide-lines advised. They also urged blacks to get involved in broader efforts to combat racial injustice within their communities.[44]

Drawing on his experiences in the SNCC, Lewis traveled extensively in the Deep South and pleaded with rural blacks to become politically active. To aid these efforts, he arranged for field visits by black elected officials such as Julian Bond, who was now a Georgia state legislator. On some occasions, Lewis and Bond visited ten counties in one day. Resi-dents were also mobilized with posters that showed two strong black hands, one pulling cotton from a boll, and the other placing a ballot in a box. "HANDS THAT PICKED COTTON CAN PICK OUR ELECTED OFFICIALS," pro-claimed the posters. In small, close-knit communities, these campaigns could secure rapid results. Lewis recalled that, in Waterproof, Louisiana, a tiny community near the Mississippi state line, local blacks began to vote in large numbers for the first time after a visit by VEP staff. Pretty soon, blacks controlled the mayor's office and a majority of the positions on the city council. "That was the basis of the VEP's efforts," observed Lewis, "to allow people who had been left out and left behind to catch up. If you boiled it down, that was the basis of the civil rights movement as well." In this way, the VEP did much to carry on the SNCC's work, especially as the student group had always stressed the importance of organizing at the grassroots level and empowering local people to take control of their own affairs.[45]

Other SNCC veterans became field-workers for the VEP. One of the most effective was Fannie Lou Hamer, the outspoken Mississippi share-cropper who had risen to prominence several years earlier.[46] Although she was now plagued by health problems, Hamer frequently joined Lewis and Bond on field visits. "We continued walking out into the cot-ton fields together," wrote Lewis, "Fannie Lou, Julian, and I, convincing people chopping cotton to vote. We'd move on to an evening meeting, which Fannie Lou would begin by breaking into a song, 'This Little Light of Mine,' the sweat just popping out of her forehead, the people mesmerized by the power of her incredible voice."[47]

In the early years of the Nixon presidency, NAACP branches also registered new voters, and leaders urged that there should be no letting up until all adult blacks in the region were on the rolls. Some larger branches even had political action committees to coordinate voter regis-tration work, while, in other cases, youth units spearheaded these efforts. The results were apparent; in 1969, for example, a vigorous branch-led drive culminated in the election of three blacks to local offices in Clarks-ville, Tennessee. They were the first African Americans to secure political representation in Montgomery County since 1902.[48]

Despite all this progress, problems persisted. At the local level, the political process often remained in the hands of white officials who tried to dilute the impact of the black ballot. As the Nixon adviser Mike Monroe admitted in a memorandum to Daniel Patrick Moynihan in 1969, "There has been a continuing effort on the part of southern officials to keep the black vote to a minimum or eliminate it altogether." As Monroe added, local and state units of the two major parties also continued to tolerate discrimination. While national committees had begun to take steps to tackle bias, it was a different story at the grass roots.[49]

Many southern blacks also remained afraid of becoming politically active because they worked for powerful whites. Darlington County, South Carolina, provided an illuminating example. By 1970, few blacks had registered to vote in the rural area and those who had were reluctant to support black candidates. As the local NAACP leader reported in that year, "The old plantation system still exists and most black people who live on these plantations are treated almost like slaves. They are forced to do their masters' will. A number of these blacks are registered to vote, but when they vote they have to vote the way the white power structure instructs them to vote."[50]

Acutely conscious of these ongoing problems, especially in the rural South, civil rights leaders argued that it was vital to extend the Voting Rights Act. In 1969 and 1970, they exerted much of the pressure to ensure that the law was renewed despite the administration's efforts to expunge the preclearance provisions. At Senate hearings, Clarence Mitchell testified that southern blacks had made political strides only because a strong federal law had been in place. If the federal "policeman" were removed, these gains would be jeopardized. Even with the law in place, there were, Mitchell pointed out, nonexaminer counties in Virginia and North Carolina where registrars worked only on certain days or required blacks to make appointments. "While the 1965 Voting Rights Act opened the door for progress, the battle is by no means over," he concluded. In February 1970, Aaron Henry also advised senators to support renewal. "In my home State of Mississippi today freedom is not yet reality," he asserted, "and I call upon you to help me and thousands of others make Mississippi what it not yet is but what it can be by supporting this simple extension of the Voting Rights Act of 1965." A number of organizations, including the VEP and the U.S. Commission on Civil Rights, conveyed a similar message.[51]

Influential southern whites took a very different view. Chairing the Senate Judiciary Committee, Samuel Ervin argued that the Voting Rights Act represented an abrogation of states' rights. "The concentration of power is what always precedes the destruction of human liberty," asserted the North Carolinian. "That is what we see here." In testimony to Ervin's committee, southern political leaders built on these arguments. Citing the Fifteenth Amendment, Lester Maddox asserted that states had the right to stop unqualified citizens, such as "illiterates," from voting. Maddox concluded his testimony with the assertion that "the South will rise again, Senator," a claim that the chairman did not refute. In a similar vein, Mississippi attorney general A. F. Summer argued that states should control the registration process. "This is in fact rank discrimination practiced by Congress against these six states," he asserted angrily. "By this act Congress has created a protectorate reducing us to the status of provinces."[52]

In letters to their political representatives, white voters also argued that the Voting Rights Act victimized the South and should be applied nationally. Speaking for many, the Georgian Mrs. W. T. Brightwell declared in early 1970, "Any law of Congress should apply to *all* states, not just a few. . . . The Southern *white* man is the most discriminated against minority in the United States."[53] Some writers went further, claiming that the Democrats wanted to punish southerners for supporting Barry Goldwater in the 1964 election. By 1970, however, a few whites did recognize the positive changes generated by the act. As the Atlanta resident Mrs. Sidney Q. Janus put it, "tremendous strides" had been made under the legislation, and it was important not to jeopardize this progress. While such views were unusual, they did create a climate that made it possible to renew the act.[54]

Despite southern opposition, President Nixon renewed the Voting Rights Act on June 22, 1970. In agreeing to the extension, he sought a symbolic gesture that would ease racial tensions. Scrapping his plan to expunge the preclearance provisions, the president also acted pragmatically, as the law was widely regarded as effective. There were other reasons for the act's extension; many policymakers wanted to keep southern blacks working within the political process, and pressure from civil rights organizations made them reluctant to alienate the African American community. The revised statute also suspended literacy tests throughout the country, not just the South, a change that mollified hostile whites. Blacks, meanwhile, were pleased that the crucial measure would stay on the books for at least another five years.[55]

"Labor Committees Are a Must": Black Activism and the Ongoing Problem of Employment Discrimination

In the economic realm, there were no outright victories of this nature. Rather, in the late 1960s the economic problems facing the African American community worsened. Partly, this was due to a general slowing of the economy, but it also reflected ongoing discriminatory barriers.

Between 1968 and 1970, black unemployment rates were almost twice as high as they were for whites, and those blacks who did have jobs faced persistent difficulties in upgrading. "In many industries," concluded a U.S. Commission on Civil Rights study in April 1969, "the jobs held by nonwhites are less desirable, requiring less skill and paying lower wages, than the jobs held by whites."[56]

Observing these developments, civil rights leaders repeatedly stressed that the economic issue was paramount because it was the area where they were making the least progress. Both the Poor People's Campaign and the SCLC's 1969 "Hunger Marches" reflected this concern. In January 1970, Ralph Abernathy also commented on a trip to Europe, "The main task for the Civil Rights Movement in the 1970s is to help poor people." In the same year, a group of black business leaders lobbied Nixon, telling him that "America's most pressing domestic problem is black economic development."[57]

The primacy of the economic issue was also reflected in the actions of blacks at the grassroots level. As part of its "comprehensive legal attack" on job bias, the NAACP continued to help black workers. In January 1969, the group's southern labor director told members that employment discrimination threatened to wipe out precious gains in other areas. "Find an industry not complying with the law and file a complaint," urged Grover Smith. "Labor Committees are a *must*." Heeding this advice, between July 1965 and April 1969 the NAACP and the NAACP LDF generated about half the EEOC's entire racial discrimination caseload. Big branches in Birmingham, Atlanta, and New Orleans had active committees that assisted workers in filing charges.[58] In the Mobile area, the NPVL also helped blacks file charges against the Alabama Dry Dock and Shipbuilding Company, the telephone company, and two major paper manufacturers.[59]

Working together, the EEOC and civil rights groups were most successful at breaking up formal segregation and integrating entry-level jobs. By the end of 1969, the commission had virtually eliminated the word-of-mouth referral systems that had been commonly used by southern employers. Its conciliation agreements had prodded employers to post job openings, helping black workers get a fairer deal. The commission also encouraged employers to begin recruiting within the African American community, and this too produced results. At a steel plant operated by the Continental Can Company in Harvey, Louisiana, for example, all jobs had gone to whites until 1965. By 1971, however, Continental Can had over fifty blacks on its books, and they made up nearly 10 percent of the workforce. The case was illustrative as most firms began to hire more blacks in these years, particularly in lower-paying posts.[60]

The example of the South's biggest industry confirms that Title VII was having a positive impact. At this time, the southern textile plants employed over 600,000 people, providing stable jobs for workers without college degrees. After the Civil Rights Act was passed, African Americans started to hold production jobs in the industry for the first time. By 1970, for example, blacks constituted over 19 percent of the workforce at J. P. Stevens's complex of plants in Roanoke Rapids, North Carolina, whereas, a few years earlier, they had been restricted to nonproduction jobs. Similar improvements occurred across the region. When managers insisted that the law had to be obeyed, they encountered little opposition. As a white textile worker in Gastonia, North Carolina, declared in June 1970, "If it comes between eatin' in the lunchroom with a nigger and losing my job, I'd rather eat with the nigger."[61]

The black breakthrough into textiles was noteworthy. As former NAACP labor secretary Herbert Hill recalled, "The fact that blacks were barred from jobs in the largest source of job opportunities in the South was very significant, . . . so it was important that finally blacks did have some limited access to the southern textile industry." Many black millworkers saw the Civil Rights Act as a watershed. "If they didn't have a law," recalled Alton Collins of Columbus, Georgia, "I don't think it would have changed."[62]

In the economic realm as a whole, however, the negatives continued to outweigh the positives, largely because employment discrimination was so prevalent and so hard to tackle that any achievements were easy to overlook. As EEOC commissioner Elizabeth J. Kuck commented in December 1969, "Some progress has been made in eliminating employment discrimination, but much, *too much* still remains to be done." Even in textiles, gains tended to be concentrated in the lowest-paying production jobs, and many firms used blacks' entry as an excuse for increasing workloads. Seeking to secure better jobs, black millworkers filed numerous lawsuits. Exaggerating only slightly, one textile worker exclaimed in 1970, "No black people have any higher paying jobs."[63]

Federal enforcement was largely to blame. In 1969, the U.S. Commission on Civil Rights claimed that the EEOC's conciliation process had produced "only limited gains" and stressed that the EEOC needed enforcement powers. Although the EEOC found that discrimination had occurred in around 60 percent of its cases, it still had no power to force guilty parties to change their ways. Critics slammed the agency as ineffective. "The Commission," claimed the policy analyst Richard P. Nathan in 1969, "is very new, very weak, and very small." The legal expert Michael Sovern went as far as to dismiss the EEOC as "a poor, enfeebled thing . . . [with] the power to conciliate but not to compel."[64]

Some of Nixon's appointments acknowledged the problems. An

African American lawyer who believed in affirmative action, the new EEOC chairman, William H. Brown III, called the law "seriously deficient" and claimed that Nixon's aides were not supporting him. These criticisms were all the more telling considering that Brown had been handpicked by Nixon to replace Clifford Alexander, an outspoken carryover from the Johnson administration. Like his predecessors, however, Brown soon became frustrated by the commission's lack of authority. In November 1970, he wrote the presidential assistant Robert Brown that Title VII was not being enforced in a "meaningful" way. "Conciliation without the prospect of meaningful enforcement simply does not work," he charged, "any more than traffic regulations would without traffic cops. This Commission must have enforcement powers." Although complainants had the right to bring private suits once the EEOC had found "reasonable cause," such suits eventuated in less than 10 percent of the cases, chiefly because workers lacked the necessary resources. "This is not a healthy condition for any society," concluded Brown. In response, Nixon's staffers accused Brown of poor management and later engineered his resignation.[65]

The EEOC was also underfunded, especially as its workload was increasing. The situation became acute after June 1968, when Title VII was expanded to cover all employers with at least twenty-five workers, rather than fifty as previously. The change brought in six million new employees, a rise of 150 percent. Despite this increase, Congress refused the commission's requests for an expanded budget, with conservative southern representatives arguing that many charges were unfounded.[66]

As a result, the complaint backlog continued to increase. In August 1970, Leonard Garment noted that the EEOC had a buildup of over six thousand cases, but Congress was still rebuffing requests for extra funding. For fiscal year 1971, the administration asked for $19 million to fund the commission, but it was granted only $14.3 million. Regarded as a liberal Republican, Garment tried to push Nixon to intervene. "The situation is such that the effective enforcement of Title VII of the Civil Rights Act may really be in question," he wrote in a memorandum to the president. Nixon, however, favored a restrained EEOC, partly because he was sensitive to complaints from southern employers, whose votes he needed. By the end of 1969, the commission was taking an average of twenty-two months to rule on a case when the Civil Rights Act had intended for this process to take just sixty days. The situation had deteriorated since August 1968, when cases had taken sixteen months to investigate. Rather than grouping charges together and tackling key issues in a systematic fashion, investigators were still proceeding on a painstaking case-by-case basis.[67]

On the ground in the South, the consequences of the EEOC's problems were clear. Even when they provided breakthroughs on paper, conciliation agreements were of restricted value because the commission was unable to enforce their recommendations. At the large Newport News Shipbuilding and Drydock Company in Virginia, for example, the EEOC reached a landmark agreement in 1966. In it, the nation's largest shipbuilder promised to open new job classifications to blacks, to desegregate facilities, and to admit qualified blacks into training programs. The company failed to live up to many of its pledges, however, and disgruntled blacks filed over 150 EEOC charges in the next four years, many of which were upheld by the commission. In an illustration of poor coordination between federal agencies, Washington continued to award lucrative contracts to Newport News, a situation that angered both Chairman Brown and civil rights lawyers. "As things stand," wrote LDF director Jack Greenberg, "it appears that the Office of Federal Contract Compliance and EEOC work without coordination with each other."[68]

As Greenberg highlighted, synchronization between federal agencies was a serious problem. As a corollary to Title VII, in September 1965 President Johnson issued Executive Order 11246; it banned discrimination by federal contractors and stipulated that they had to take "affirmative action to ensure that applicants are employed, and that employees are treated during employment without regard to race, color, or national origin." In January 1966, the Office of Federal Contract Compliance (OFCC) was established within the Department of Labor to ensure that the order was carried out. The federal contract compliance program, however, generally failed to complement the EEOC's work. The OFCC was underfunded, and its officials were reluctant to cancel contracts because they worried about interrupting the procurement process. As the U.S. Commission on Civil Rights concluded in 1969, "The overall implementation of the contract compliance order has been decidedly cautious."[69]

By now, it had become clear to black workers that the EEOC lacked the power to make a decisive difference. Of the many that were written, some letters captured the black mood particularly well. In June 1970, for example, the Little Rock resident Robert Pruitt wrote President Nixon to express his despair about the situation. The letter was especially damning because Pruitt identified himself as a Republican. The EEOC, he complained from personal experience, was "under manned and under financed," and most blacks were "afraid to write the agency because of economy [sic] reprisal." Southern blacks, he asserted, could now get more jobs, but they still found the better-paid positions closed to them. "All southern industry continues to hire black employees but *refuses* to promote blacks to deserved positions," charged Pruitt. "We are 22% of the population ratio of Arkansas, but look at the percentage of blacks to get high paying jobs in industry in the south. This holds true for *all* industry in the south." In reply, a Nixon adviser admitted that the EEOC was underpowered but blamed Congress for the situation. Such claims were unlikely to have satisfied Pruitt, one of many dissatisfied complainants.[70]

Many of these aggrieved workers turned to lawsuits. Across the region, the NAACP encouraged workers to file class actions; by June 1969, for example, the association had filed 154 Title VII cases in the federal courts, the bulk of them in the South. Herbert Hill even viewed the complaints process primarily as a way of securing a legal hearing. Describing the EEOC as "at best a conciliation agency," Hill explained in 1969 that "its major virtue has been that, however awkward and clumsy, it provides a procedure for getting job discrimination cases into the Federal courts." Once there, NAACP strategists hoped to secure landmark rulings that would outlaw discriminatory practices and have a wide-ranging impact. Taken as a whole, this long legal campaign typified the NAACP's staying power in the post-1965 era.[71]

In this fight, members cooperated closely with association attorneys. In 1968, for instance, NAACP general counsel Robert L. Carter brought a suit on behalf of four black workers at the Chrysler Corporation's Space Division in New Orleans. The plant employed 3,200 employees, yet just 187 of them were black, and those blacks all held menial posts. African American employees charged that white workers and managers were cooperating to keep the best positions for themselves. "Let's put promotions this way," explained plaintiff Allison L. Chapital, himself a lifelong NAACP member. "We weren't even given the opportunity to even be interviewed for promotions. . . . We didn't even know about a lot of promotions that were going on until they were filled." Hostile whites also harassed African Americans when they spoke out, yet the all-white supervisory force did nothing to tackle the problem, fearing the reaction of their white employees. As the EEOC concluded, Chrysler had "not provided a working environment free of racial intimidation."[72]

At other major companies, attorneys and workers fought a difficult battle to try and upgrade blacks. In the late 1960s, the largest private employer in the South was Lockheed-Georgia, a division of the California-based aircraft manufacturer. In 1968, the firm's huge Atlanta plant employed twenty-three thousand workers. Just 6 percent of these employees were black, despite the fact that the population of metropolitan Atlanta was around 23 percent black. Plaintiffs in *Banks v. Lockheed-Georgia,* filed by the NAACP, described how they had been channeled to low-paying posts regardless of their qualifications. "They just told me that the only thing available was a wash rack attendant or a utility worker," recalled the college graduate Lincoln Woods. "Although I had my background down, it was irrelevant. So they hired me as a utility worker." After failing to secure promotion, Woods filed charges and then left the company when things failed to improve.[73] White workers and supervisors harassed the *Banks* plaintiffs, and the case highlighted the risks that blacks took when they participated in Title VII actions. Plaintiffs were subjected to "birddogging," where managers constantly watched them in the hope that they would make a mistake or quit, as well as racial epithets and threats. On one occasion, whites even used a doll to enact a fake lynching in the plant.[74]

In the late 1960s, the NAACP's lawyers brought cases on behalf of a wide variety of black plaintiffs, including railroad porters in Arkansas, steel laborers in Alabama, and aluminum workers in Louisiana. The case files show, however, that Title VII litigation was costly and time-consuming and that it usually failed to produce quick results.[75] Many cases required a daunting commitment of resources; *Banks v. Lockheed-Georgia,* for example, generated forty volumes of transcripts and over nine hundred exhibits, yet the NAACP emerged from it with only a compromise settlement. In it, the company promised to post vacancies and eliminate a discriminatory employment test, but, in return, plaintiffs had to promise not to engage in further legal action.[76]

Several settlements were also weakened by the economic demise of manufacturing industries. The *Banks* agreement was undermined by the decline of the giant manufacturer, which was consolidating its operations in California. Between 1968 and 1972, employment at the firm's Atlanta plant tumbled from twenty-three thousand workers to thirteen thousand, and the company promised to upgrade blacks only when there was an upturn in its prospects. The long fight to secure a better deal for black train porters also occurred at a time when the railroads were reducing passenger services. Another large NAACP case, *Norman v. Missouri Pacific Railroad,* began in the mid-1960s, but it was not until December 1973 that a federal court finally granted the porters the right to transfer to other positions without forfeiting their seniority. The decision constituted a symbolic breakthrough, yet, by this time, many porters had been laid off or had retired.[77]

Title VII also applied to trade unions, and historians have documented that the battle to desegregate labor organizations was long and complex. Despite labor leaders' support for civil rights, many members defended the economic privileges they derived from segregation. After 1968, moreover, many saw black demands for greater promotional rights as reverse discrimination.[78] In the North, controversy centered on the building trades unions, exclusive bodies that basically controlled hiring in the construction industry. In the South, black entry into these organizations was not as hotly disputed, largely because unions were much weaker in the region.[79]

In some southern cities, however, the trades also fought efforts to desegregate. In Jacksonville, Atlanta, and Tampa, civil rights groups worked with government agencies to try and tackle the problem. In September 1968, for example, the Tampa Urban League gained $46,000 from the U.S. Labor Department in order to place minority youths in local apprenticeship programs. Working with the Tampa Building Trades Council, around three hundred minority youths were trained to meet the trades' entry requirements, yet the unions accepted only eight apprentices. "None of these have been officially indentured," complained the league, "because of the delaying tactics used by the labor unions and condoned by the local representative of the Bureau of Apprenticeship and Training." The unions argued that the league was failing to send them qualified applicants, yet it was clear that labor resistance to minority participation was a problem. As the *Tampa Tribune* put it, "The unions' traditional reluctance to apprentice blacks has been slow in receding."[80]

In public, union leaders disputed these criticisms, but private records were more revealing. In June 1971, AFL-CIO southern civil rights director E. T. Kehrer noted that the federation's claim to have secured 180 placements for black apprentices in Atlanta was "inaccurate." Certainly, black leaders felt that the unions were dragging their feet. As Lloyd X. Smith of the Atlanta Urban League complained, "No training program in the world can assure minorities they will get work—not if the unions don't want them. And the unions are fighting all the way."[81]

The example of the building trades highlighted how African Americans were still struggling to gain access to the most lucrative parts of the economy. In the early years of the Nixon presidency, aides initiated several programs to stimulate minority enterprise, but the results of these efforts were also meager. Tellingly, as late as 1976 the gross revenue of all the nation's black businesses was less than the annual earnings of the Sears Roebuck Company. Despite the gains that had occurred, civil rights activists had a lot of work ahead of them.[82]

As the 1970s began, many of the problems that remained were interconnected. Across the South, many rural blacks were still afraid to vote because they worked for whites. As Theodore Hesburgh wrote Nixon in March 1969, "Intimidation and economic dependence in many areas of the South continue to prevent Negroes from exercising their franchise or running for office fully and freely." Only greater economic independence could really address this problem, yet blacks could compete for good jobs only if they first received a quality education, and most campaigners realized that this equated to a desegregated education. When Dr. King was killed, most of the region's schools were still segregated, and, over the next five years, the battle to change this situation would be the defining feature of the ongoing civil rights struggle.[83]

4

DEFIANCE AND COMPLIANCE

The Breakdown of Freedom of Choice
in the South's Schools

In February 1970, the mayor of Trussville, Alabama, wrote President Nixon to let him know how local people felt about federal orders to integrate their schools. "In all my experience, in war and in peace," explained Roland Crabbe, "I have never known the people of this section to be so disturbed and upset—all arising out of the unfair, unjust school desegregation policies which are being forced down the throats of the Southerners during this second Reconstruction period." The opposition to the assignment of children to achieve racial balance, added Crabbe, was "fixed, deep seated, and immovable." He urged Nixon to allow southerners to continue with freedom of choice, a policy that was "the only democratic way."[1]

Crabbe's letter was representative of thousands of similar entreaties that Nixon received in his first two years in office. Within the South itself, influential senators such as Strom Thurmond and Samuel Ervin were bombarded with comparable letters. Taken as a whole, this correspondence highlights the depth of white opposition to the complete integration of southern schools. Asserting that their rights were being trampled on, and drawing on a deep-seated southern dislike of federal authority, angry whites promised Nixon a significant fight. "Not since the civil war," declared a group of Florida citizens in 1970, "has more animosity been stirred within the borders of the United States of America by any authority or the orders of our archaic Supreme Court."[2]

The battle to desegregate the South's schools in the early years of the Nixon administration is partly the story of these loud and defiant voices. Faced with demands to abandon freedom of choice, most white southerners hollered and dragged their feet. Many also took their children out of the public schools, initiating a movement that would have grave consequences in future decades.

There was also plenty of violence and bitterness. Over the course of the 1970–1971 school year, the SRC documented nearly one hundred fights related to school desegregation as well as eight bomb explosions and at least a half dozen deaths. Surveying the same year, the National Education Association (NEA) found that, in a sample of 288 southern school districts, there had been over two thousand arrests and eleven thousand pupil suspensions or expulsions. In North Carolina, for example, bomb threats, suspensions, fires, and racial violence affected at least sixty-four schools, with some schools forced to close as a result. The NEA found the "same pattern of suspension, arrests, bomb threats and boycotts" in other states, especially Mississippi, Louisiana, and Alabama.[3]

Despite these incidents, in the space of two years the South made more progress in integrating its schools than ever before. Between 1968 and 1970, HEW documented that the percentage of southern black students attending majority-white schools jumped from 18.4 to 38.1, while the proportion in all-black schools tumbled from 68 to 18.4. While warning that much work remained to be done, in March 1971 the SRC declared, "It would be fair to say that, for the first time, school desegregation in one degree or another is the rule rather than the exception for the children of the South." The following month, the Supreme Court's landmark decision in *Swann v. Charlotte-Mecklenburg County Board of Education* allowed the lower courts to bus students in order to achieve racial balance. As a result, the remains of the dual system would be dismantled in the months that followed.[4]

Behind these statistics lies a story of acceptance as well as resistance, of compliance and defiance. Away from the headlines, community leaders, teachers, parents, and students all worked to desegregate the public schools peacefully. While some supported the changes, others were simply realists who saw further opposition as pointless. As South Carolina governor Robert McNair commented in reaction to *Alexander v. Holmes County,* southerners had "run out of courts" and should now choose "compliance" rather than "defiance." Bearing out this advice, efforts to defy federal orders achieved little, and many white southerners saw the writing on the wall. As the South Carolinian Jack Sanson wrote in response to *Alexander,* "The decision of the Supreme Court is the law of the land and . . . we the people have no recourse but to comply with the law."[5]

Progress was also a reflection of consistent pressure from the African American community. All too familiar with underresourced black schools, the vast majority of black parents saw integration as the only satisfactory option. Interviewed by the journalist Kenneth Danforth in March 1970, an anonymous black mechanic in Gray, Georgia, captured their mood well. "Naw, we're not going to give up," he asserted. "If we had integrated schools just ten years ago, I'd be driving this Riviera instead of bent over the son of a bitch."[6] The NAACP epitomized this belief that good schools were the springboard to a better life. "Education," claimed an NAACP petition to Richard Nixon in 1970, "is that step ladder out of poverty and anarchism into the mainstream of America and democracy. The problem we face is centered on education. Segregated education is wrong legally and morally."[7]

Civil rights groups worked closely with the federal courts. The NAACP LDF brought some of the landmark cases of this era, including *Swann* and large suits in Memphis, Richmond, and Jacksonville. Across the region, NAACP lawyers also filed lesser-known suits and fought for the rights of black teachers and students within the newly desegregated schools. The association's opponents even complained that its lawyers had too much influence over the Supreme Court. "The present court is undoubtedly the weakest we have every [*sic*] had in our history," wrote Senator Richard Russell in 1970, "and they immediately comply with the demands of the NAACP in rendering an immediate decision. This is always against the Southern white man."[8]

Most important of all were two Supreme Court decisions that were generated by the NAACP LDF, although opponents often confused the group with the NAACP. In May 1968, the Court's decree in *Green v. County School Board of New Kent County, Va.* played an important role in striking down freedom of choice. The case involved a plan that had been established in a rural Virginia county in 1965. At the time, blacks made up 57 percent of the school population in Green County, but none of them attended the white school. Little changed under the freedom-of-choice plan, and 85 percent of black students still attended the traditionally black high school when the Court considered the case. Presented with such evidence, the justices sided unambiguously with the plaintiffs. The school board, noted Justice William Brennan, "must be required to formulate a new plan . . . which promises realistically to convert promptly to a system without a 'white' school and a 'Negro' school, but just schools." Frustrated with the lack of progress, the Court explained that freedom of choice was not "an end in itself."[9]

Even after *Green,* white southerners hoped that a new president might intervene and provide some relief. During his campaign, Nixon had encouraged these expectations, and he finished first in the South, with 36 percent of the vote. Another 33 percent voted for George Wallace, who had promised to fight federally driven desegregation. Despite winning the election, the insecure Nixon worried about further challenges from Wallace, who had won five Deep South states.[10] Beholden to southern voters, President Nixon told HEW to delay court orders that would have forced thirty Mississippi school districts to devise desegregation plans for the start of the school year. Outraged by the move, LDF lawyers appealed the case to the Supreme Court. Fearful of turning against *Brown,* in *Alexander* the Court unanimously ordered southern schools "to terminate dual systems at once and to operate now and here-after only unitary schools." As the historian James T. Patterson has noted, *Green* and *Alexander* made it clear that the Supreme Court "would no longer tolerate delay in the implementation of *de jure* school desegregation."[11]

Blacks were delighted with the decision, which was publicized in a short statement on October 29, 1969. The Baton Rouge resident Emmitt Douglas spoke for many when he jubilantly declared, "Deliberate speed is dead, dead, dead." While Georgia governor Lester Maddox denounced *Alexander* as "a criminal act by the Government," for blacks it was the opposite, a validation that their constitutional rights would finally be protected.[12] As *The Crisis* put it, the ruling was "a giant step forward," yet the NAACP also reminded its members to ensure that the judgment was implemented fully.[13]

Arguably the most significant school desegregation decision since *Brown, Alexander* was the crucial breakthrough. From December 2, 1969, to September 24, 1970, the Fifth Circuit issued 166 orders in school cases, and these orders called for comprehensive changes. In other districts, *Alexander* guided the policies of HEW, which now insisted that all school boards had to comply in order to avoid losing federal funds. Working together, the courts and HEW began to trans-form the racial makeup of southern schools.[14]

Most southern whites, however, were not ready for this shift in fed-eral policy. In August 1969, a Gallup poll found that six times as many southern whites felt that school integration was going "too fast" as opposed to those who felt that it was "not fast enough." Now, the Supreme Court said that the pace of desegregation had to be dramati-cally accelerated. Capturing how many felt, the Birmingham resident G. G. W. Hoover wrote Alabama governor Albert Brewer immediately after the *Alexander* ruling. "The decision of the Supreme Court ordering immediate school integration in Mississippi is enough to throw us into a revolution," he declared. Hoover was one of the many who wanted to resist the judgment, even if it meant boycotting the schools, yet others had lost the stomach to fight on. "Needless to say," wrote Billie Ruth Chambless from Montgomery, "at this time I feel quite dejected, rejected, sad and disgusted after Wednesday's ruling by the Supreme Court. . . . I feel public education in the South is doomed. The only answer for us now will be private schools for quality education."[15]

As the process of desegregation got under way, the large gap between the perspective of the two races was a constant theme. Across the region, whites defended freedom of choice and pleaded for more time, whereas blacks responded by pressing for immediate action. As one elderly black Mississippian wrote in March 1970, "Now you're asking for freedom of choice. You have had freedom of choice for a hundred years and did wrong with it."[16]

"A Negro's Sex Life Begins at an Early Age": Whites Fight School Integration, 1968–1970

As school boards abandoned freedom of choice, Southern congressmen from both parties were inundated with thousands of letters from irate constituents. In December 1969, the North Carolina Democrat L. H. Fountain forwarded a typical example to the White House, adding, "We in the Congress have had to answer literally thousands of such letters without being able to give a scintilla of satisfaction." Strom Thurmond wrote in the same year that, although he had been in the Senate for fifteen years, the volume of mail he had received in opposition to desegregation plans had astounded him. Thurmond warned his superiors that the GOP would lose support in the South unless it took decisive action.[17]

The flood of correspondence provides an opportunity to examine white attitudes in detail. In the spring of 1970, a Gallup poll revealed that, while only 17 percent of white southerners objected to sending their child to a school with blacks, 69 percent were opposed to enrolling them in majority-black schools. Whites strongly opposed integration in these circumstances, largely because they stereotyped blacks as highly sexualized predators who would corrupt their children. In 1966, for instance, 94 percent of southern whites declared their opposition to interracial dating. White parents also feared high levels of crime within black neighborhoods, and they questioned the quality of black schools. White opposition guided the policies of board officials, who generally closed black schools and transferred their students to white schools.[18]

Across the South, women expressed their fears more openly than men. As they put pen to paper, most used their husbands' names and spoke as mothers with a special bond with their children. Frequently residents of heavily black areas, they argued that the morality of their children would be destroyed by a mass influx of black students, especially black boys, who were perceived as a sexual threat to white girls. Sexual fears had helped underpin the Jim Crow system, and, now, as the system crumbled, many white women expressed them forcibly.[19]

Writing from Hillsborough, North Carolina, in 1969, Mrs. Percy E. McLamb implored HEW, "*Let us have a freedom of choice in our schools!*" McLamb was concerned by plans to transfer her six-year-old child to a school that was "one-half colored." Recounting a story of a black girl who had "pulled up her dress and pulled down her panties in front of all the children," she claimed that the next school year would be chaos. "It [integration] cannot be done successfully," she asserted. "I see Negro boys making passes at young white girls, looking at them with that lustful, sexual desire in their eyes. Our nation cannot take much more of this." Other writers agreed, adding that blacks were more sexually active than whites and had higher rates of sexually transmitted diseases. "A negro's sex life begins at an early age," wrote Georgia Edwards from Abbeville, South Carolina. "Nine out of every ten have a venereal disease. Will the HEW keep a person on hand at all times with a bottle of disinfectant to be sure the desk seats and toilets are clean?"[20]

Plans to transfer white children to majority-black schools aroused fervent opposition. To some extent, these letters touched on legitimate concerns, the black schools being poorly funded, yet writers frequently concentrated instead on the alleged sexuality and criminality of black students. The Baton Rouge resident Florence P. Gibbens focused on a plan to transfer thirty-three white children to an all-black school in nearby Scotlandville. "This means," she explained, "that these 33 white children are entirely at the mercy of 65 Negro girls and 513 Negro boys, plus an all-Negro staff. We cannot abandon these children. I should say, 'these poor, sick children.'" Gibbens viewed black boys as sexual predators and petty criminals. "I don't know whether you are aware of the dreadful things that are happening in our schools this year," she wrote Thurmond. "One girl in the high school of Port Allen across the river from Baton Rouge was almost raped yesterday. Our white children are being stabbed and spit upon."[21]

Some southerners wrote Harry Dent, a South Carolinian who was an adviser within the Nixon administration. Dent had previously worked for Thurmond, and some whites reasoned that he would help them. As Mrs. Ruel McLeod wrote from Dent's home state, "Being a South Carolinian, you know the two races are not compatible." In support of her assertion, McLeod claimed that blacks had a "high rate of venereal diseases" that was caused by their "immorality and lack of marriage in families." While he did not directly endorse McLeod's views, Dent sympathized with her plight and assured her "that everything possible is being done."[22] Facing pressure from GOP leaders in the region, Dent tried to covertly slow the pace of school integration.[23]

In Georgia, many of Senator Russell's constituents also worried that school integration would lead to miscegenation. While most letters came from women, some husbands and wives expressed their fears together. Mr. and Mrs. Hugh C. Wade from Gainesville, for example, fretted about race "mixing" in the schools, focusing particularly on black male students who insisted on "dancing with white girls, some very intimately." Russell responded to such letters by insisting that federal agencies were unfairly targeting the South and needed to do more to integrate schools in other areas. He vowed to fight for "the justice and fairness to which we are entitled."[24] Keen to secure results, other women took their concerns to national political figures. A leader in the Republican Women's Club in Colleton County, South Carolina, Mrs. G. Carroll Brown Jr. wrote directly to President Nixon, warning him that he was losing support in the region. "The people of the South," she claimed, "just are not going to subject their white girls and teachers to the indignities of the negro male. The negro morality is innately different from the white race as a rule, and no *amount* of education will change this."[25]

As well as writing letters, women took action. In majority-black Bertie County, North Carolina, the Colerain Woman's Club led opposition to plans to transfer whites to black schools. Writing HEW secretary Robert W. Finch, the club leader, Mrs. Franklin McCrery, explained that moves to "totally integrate" the high schools were unworkable, but Finch did not reply. In December 1969, the local women's club in Coral Gables, Florida, also passed a resolution in opposition to the "creation of Artificial School Districts." A group of 350 women, they urged Nixon to save their schools from "social experimentation."[26] On some occasions, women also headed citizens' groups that were opposed to integration plans.[27]

In heavily black areas, whites also opposed integration because they believed that black children learned more slowly than whites. According to this line of reasoning, the greater the proportion of blacks, the less effective the schools would be. A 1969 petition from Denmark, South Carolina, expressed these fears well. Headed by Mrs. Roy Hughes, it was sent to President Nixon and every member of Congress. "Can't you get it in your heads," blasted Hughes, "that a black child (I don't mean any harm by telling the truth, I have many friends that are colored) can not learn as fast as a white child. WHY must our children suffer??????? Because this is a fact." Believing that blacks were less intelligent, many parents also opposed their children being taught by black teachers. "[Only] one of every 6 teachers coming from the colored schools are capable of teaching their assignments," claimed Watt E. Smith, who wrote from Rowesville, South Carolina.[28]

On some occasions, white teachers even refused to work in formerly black schools. In February 1970, the schools in Sandersville, Georgia, were closed for over a week after a group of white teachers failed to transfer to the historically black schools as required. Governor Lester Maddox flew in to the small town and supported the teachers. "The Supreme Court has decided to go along with the Communists," he told around two thousand applauding whites. "Congress has abdicated its responsibility. . . . Our president is running from his commitment to the

American people." As Maddox spoke, police officers held back more than five hundred black demonstrators who wanted to interrogate him.[29]

As the federal courts and HEW demanded change, there were other protests, particularly in the Deep South. On February 5, 1970, for example, racial tensions led to the closure of Lake Providence High School in majority-black East Carroll Parish, Louisiana. School board superintendent B. A. Bayles explained that feelings had been running high since the school had reopened in accordance with a court-ordered plan. "There was a lot of harassment going on," he admitted. A few days later, a combined elementary and high school in Maben, Mississippi, was destroyed by fire on the night before it was due to reopen in accordance with *Alexander*. Located in the northeast of the state, Maben was another majority-black community.[30]

One of the worst incidents, however, occurred in South Carolina. In the Palmetto State, feelings were running particularly high; in January 1970, Governor McNair sent Nixon over 100,000 signatures from residents who were opposed to plans to implement *Alexander* the following month. They insisted that the decision was "unconstitutional" because states should have control over education policies.[31]

Reflecting this mood, whites in the small, majority-black town of Lamar reacted violently when the Fourth Circuit Court ordered their schools to desegregate. In Darlington County, six years of freedom of choice had not achieved much; less than 4 percent of black children attended the formerly white schools, and no whites were enrolled in the black schools. As the local NAACP leader Arthur W. Stanley put it, "The 'freedom-of-choice' plan meant freedom of choice for whites and no choice at all for black children." Bolstered by the *Alexander* ruling, NAACP attorneys were able to secure the contentious order, but angry whites responded by forming the Darlington County Freedom of Choice Committee and promising to boycott the schools.[32]

Beginning on February 18, when the schools opened, the boycott was highly effective. As white parents picketed outside Lamar high school, tensions mounted. On the morning of March 3, three buses set off for the school with seventy-four black children on board. As they approached the building, they were attacked by a mob of about two hundred white adults. The black children were trapped inside, and many were injured by bricks and flying glass. One bus was fired into, and two were tipped over only moments after the children had dashed into the school. Over one hundred state troopers helped the children off the buses before the crowd overturned them.[33] The violence was orchestrated by the forty-two-year-old Jeryl Best, a local restaurant owner who headed the Freedom of Choice Committee. Arrested on March 4, Best described his members as "concerned citizens who lost their right way of thinking for a moment."[34]

The incident made national headlines. Writing in the *New York Times,* Jon Nordheimer described the scene: "Someone in the crowd hollered, 'Stop the buses!' and grim men surged forward with ax handles, broken bottles and rocks. They stood alongside the buses and hammered on them with their long clubs. . . . Not since the bombing in Birmingham had grown men so intimidated children with threats of physical violence."[35] Both state and national political leaders condemned the attack. A shocked Governor McNair called the incident "unspeakable," while Vice President Spiro Agnew declared that the Nixon administration would not allow violence to derail desegregation orders.[36] Even Strom Thurmond called the episode "tragic" and said that it had "sickened South Carolina and the nation." Thurmond, however, claimed that McNair could have averted the violence by requesting federal assistance. On the day of the attacks, Thurmond had described the situation in Lamar as "critical" and had pleaded with Attorney General John Mitchell to relax the court order, but Mitchell refused to do so.[37]

The attack was a terrifying ordeal for those inside the buses, yet only the black press told their story. In *The Crisis,* the black bus driver Woodrow Wilson Jr. described how angry whites had told him, "Boy! If you run over these people, this crowd will kill you!" Wilson's passengers also had vivid memories. Edward Lunn described being attacked by "ridiculously enraged men and women" who shouted "'get them niggers' and 'run, nigger, run.'" Sally Mae Wilds recalled how sticks and bricks had hit the windows of her bus, followed quickly by two shots. "At that time I screamed: 'Oh Lord help us,'" she stated. "I was the only girl on the bus and I was so afraid that I was going to be killed." The students also complained that the white police had done little to protect them.[38]

Visiting Lamar after the incident, Nordheimer reported that even moderate whites were unwilling to condemn the crowd's actions. In private letters to Thurmond, some residents also justified what had occurred. "As for the school problem in Lamar," wrote the local businessman Sammye H. Nance on April 21, "we know some of the individuals who participated in the incident and we know them to be fine God-fearing citizens." Nance blamed federal policies for the outburst, arguing that freedom of choice should not have been abandoned.[39] The local parent James C. Melton also hit out at Washington. "Since the federal government came in and took over our school and forced the white and black children to go to school together, we have had four rape[s] by negro's [*sic*] men on white women," he charged. Even the local minister Ed Duncan defended freedom of choice and tacitly condoned the parents' actions.[40]

For most whites in Lamar, it was blacks who were violent and lawless. While African Americans claimed that the local police had not done enough to defend them, whites implied that blacks did not need or deserve this protection. The recent race riots had clearly hardened their attitudes. "We do not believe in violence," explained the resident Mrs. Clyde C. Dutton in another letter, "but the people are just so upset, and looks like we can get no help from anyone. Yet the Negroes will try to burn down Washington or anywhere else, and the people in Washington or the newsmen will make it look as bad as it was in Lamar yesterday."[41]

In the wake of the violence, the state attorney general filed riot charges against thirty local men, three of whom were later convicted. In order to control tensions, McNair closed the schools for a week and placed state troopers on the ground. When classes restarted, only a small number of students showed up. Most of them were black, and they exhibited a steely determination to secure a better education. "No, sir, I'm not scared," commented ten-year-old Priscilla Green. "I'm going to keep coming as long as they let me." Another noted firmly, "These people around here should realize we're human beings." Calm was gradually restored, yet, over the next few years, many whites took their children out of Lamar High and enrolled them in private schools.[42]

In the fall of 1970, there were more protests when another wave of districts carried out desegregation plans to bring themselves in line with *Alexander.* In Stockbridge, Georgia, for instance, two hundred white parents tried to enroll their children in a white school rather than the formerly black one to which they had been assigned. After administrators refused to admit the pupils, the protest crumbled.[43] In other parts of Georgia, white parents refused to place their children in black schools, instead keeping them at home or educating them elsewhere. In early September, up to five thousand white children in Savannah were boycotting the formerly black schools that they had been assigned to, while, in majority-black Twiggs County, less than half of the nine hundred white pupils had enrolled in their assigned schools.[44]

These were not isolated cases. By early October, the LDF's Jean Fairfax reported that many southern whites were refusing to send their children to the former all-black schools to which they had been assigned. "We can safely say that this problem has reached massive portions in southern cities," she concluded in an internal report.[45] Alabama provided some apt examples. In Montgomery, only 25 of the 359 whites allocated to formerly black George Washington Carver High School showed up on the first day, and they sat in classes with nearly 1000 blacks.[46] In Birmingham, LDF attorneys calculated that 10,000 white students, or about 15 percent of all whites in the system, had failed to report at their allotted schools. This behavior reflected an angry mood in the Magic City, where many parents wanted to defy a recent court order. Writing to Alabama governor Albert Brewer, one Birmingham parent called the Supreme Court justices "old morons" and urged resistance. "There is no justice in their courts," explained John Roche Gould. "Governor Brewer, I say let's fight, if we die it will be for a glorious cause." Unlike his predecessor, however, Brewer refused to endorse such sentiments.[47]

One notable protest occurred in Talladega County, Alabama, where a group of white parents occupied classrooms at three white schools in order to try and stop their children from being sent to formerly black schools. One of the adults even took on the role of principal and began to organize classes. Overall, more than five hundred children were involved in the protest, but it petered out after federal judge H. Hobart Grooms threatened the parents with fines of at least $100 a day if they continued to interfere with the court's plan. The judge also insisted that his integration order was nailed to schoolhouse doors "so that the world will take note." As the *Talladega Daily Home* reported, many of the affected parents responded by organizing a private school instead.[48]

While these protests were going on, whites frantically lobbied their political leaders. Petitions poured in from both rural and urban areas, with concerns about the poor quality of black schools again at the fore. In Manatee County, Florida, citizens objected to a 1970 decree that required white students to transfer to formerly all-black schools. Organized by the local PTA, a petition secured thirty-three thousand signatures in a county where there were just sixty-five thousand eligible voters, and the signatories included local clergy, almost every public official in the county, and Congressman James A. Haley. "We are not rioting, we are not picketing," they informed President Nixon. "We are testing our right to be heard and testing our belief that Americans *do* have a voice in their government."[49] In Atlanta, irate residents organized Help Atlanta's Neighborhood Schools (HANDS across Atlanta). In 1970 over twenty thousand members petitioned the White House and the Supreme Court for relief from a court decision that called for "mathematical racial balance of teachers and students."[50] Many petitions also came in from Mississippi; in August 1970, for instance, Senator John Stennis forwarded one appeal that was "signed by a vast number of Mississippi citizens." In it, residents claimed that *Alexander* was unfair, especially as many northern schools were not racially balanced.[51]

A leading opponent of *Alexander,* Stennis spearheaded efforts to pass a federal amendment to undermine it. On February 18, the Senate passed Stennis's amendment to a $35 billion education bill by a 56–36 margin. In practice, however, the vote to "equalize desegregation enforcement across the country" meant little because Senate liberals changed the amendment to render it meaningless. They did this by stipulating that nothing in the amendment diminished the obligation of officials to enforce Title VI. Although Stennis knew that the amendment was not going to make a decisive difference, it still represented a symbolic victory.[52] The vote certainly reflected the popular mood in Mississippi, where both houses of the state legislature had called for an end to "judicial discrimination . . . against the southern states by the federal courts."[53]

Within the South, several governors also organized opposition. Their efforts peaked in mid-February, when Mississippi's John Bell Williams and Georgia's Lester Maddox had private meetings with three other governors and around fifty southern representatives. As the *Atlanta Constitution* reported, the gatherings were designed to "marshal public support for freedom of choice school desegregation."[54]

Although his bark was worse than his bite, Georgia's eccentric governor perhaps went further than any other southern politician in fighting school integration. In early February, the populist Democrat mailed out more than ten thousand letters on the school issue. Appealing to his supporters' dislike of Washington, Maddox asserted that a "federal police state" was about to "engulf public education" in the South. In a fiery speech on February 6, he also suggested that "somebody should let the air out of all the school bus tires" in order to stall integration and that "they should just do away with the buses."[55] Maddox also tried to suspend Georgia's compulsory school attendance laws as a way of thwarting integration, but the federal courts quickly blocked the move.[56]

Like Maddox, George Wallace also capitalized on white voters' frustrations. In November, Wallace was reelected governor of Alabama after promising to support any teacher or parent who refused to obey federal integration orders. He defeated Albert Brewer, a racial moderate who had tried to encourage calm. In the lead-up to his election, Wallace drew a crowd of more than fifteen thousand when he spoke at a "freedom of choice" rally in Birmingham. Urging the crowd to defy federal authority, the popular politician promised to run for the presidency again "if Nixon doesn't do something about the mess our schools are in."[57]

In these years, an increasing number of southern whites also placed their children in private schools, a move that Wallace himself advocated. "White children by the thousands are fleeing public schools to attend new, hastily organized private schools," reported the *Raleigh News and Observer* in September 1970.[58] On the eve of the academic year, the SRC estimated that over 400,000 youngsters would be attending segregated private schools in the region, a figure that was up sharply from the group's earlier estimate of 300,000. In the Deep South, private schools were particularly popular. Between 1966 and 1970, the number of private schools in Mississippi rose from 121 to 236, and the number of students attending them tripled. At least 61 of these schools were chartered in the year following *Alexander*.[59] In Alabama, the state Private School

Association was formed only in 1966, yet sixty schools soon belonged to it. The group acted as a forerunner to the Southern Independent School Association, which was established in Montgomery in 1971.[60]

While whites publicly defended these schools on academic grounds, blacks saw them as little more than segregated academies. As the civil rights leader John L. LeFlore complained, the new schools had been "established to circumvent court-ordered public school desegregation." Private correspondence between whites highlights the fact that LeFlore's view was largely accurate. In the spring of 1970, for example, Tom Jennings wrote Strom Thurmond from Hartsville, South Carolina, where he had helped organize a private academy. Jennings explained that he was enrolling his children even though he could not really afford it. "It will be hard," he explained, "as we have girl 10, boy 15 to attend. We are sacrificing for [the] White Race." In heavily black Choctaw County, Alabama, W. B. Lindsey was also frank about why white children were leaving the public schools as they were "taken over" by blacks. "The white people of Alabama," he wrote President Nixon, "and the majority of the South are trying to establish private schools to protect and give their dear little ones a decent education. This is an expensive undertaking and many people cannot afford it." Like blacks, working-class whites often bore the greatest burdens of desegregation, and parents frequently made great sacrifices so that they could pay school fees, such as taking extra jobs or working double shifts.[61]

Led by Thurmond, Republican politicians were forceful advocates of the new private schools.[62] As Mississippi's GOP chairman reported to the White House, "Our own party leadership is heavily involved in private schools." Clarke Reed also acknowledged that the schools were a response to racial integration, especially when blacks made up a big proportion of the local population. "Many communities with large black populations have resegregated into private schools at great financial sacrifice," he noted. The Greenville businessman warned his superiors that they must support these initiatives if the party was to prosper in the region.[63]

In some areas, prominent whites even tried to use public facilities to support the new schools. In late 1970, the NAACP LDF reported that there had been a "rapid increase" in the number of private schools and that many of them were using buildings purchased from school boards at "incredibly low cost." In rural Baker County, Georgia, for instance, the board of education auctioned off a public school building at cut price rates to the all-white Baker Academy. It was a similar situation in Warrenton, North Carolina, where the all-white Warren Academy leased public buildings for just $150 a month. The school was one of the newest and best equipped in the majority-black county. Mississippi's authorities also propped up the academies. In Jackson, officials allowed public school buses to be repainted and used by academy schools, while, in Canton, the school board sold desks to the private academy for just fifty cents each.[64]

Professional whites often took the lead in organizing the new schools. As Dr. R. G. Ferrell wrote in 1970, private schools had been formed "all over the South" as a response to federal integration policies. A resident of Macon, Georgia, Ferrell claimed that the schools offered a superior education.[65] Able to afford the costs of private education, middle-class professionals were also well equipped to take leadership roles in the new schools. In Scotland County, North Carolina, for example, Dr. Thomas G. Gibson helped organize Marlboro Academy. Gibson enrolled three of his children in the school and became a member of the board of trustees. In a letter to Congressman Charles Raper Jonas, a family friend, Gibson was open about the motivation for his actions. "Due to the existing situation in our local school system," he explained, "which has been inundated by a better than 50% influx of negro students, a private school was formed and was located last spring approximately four miles south of Gibson in Marlboro County. . . . Thus far, the entire operation has been most satisfactory." After *Alexander,* both Ferrell and Gibson lobbied for financial contributions to private schools to remain tax-deductible.[66]

Worried by these developments, black leaders also mobilized. In 1970, LeFlore urged Governor Brewer to ensure that private academies were not supported by public funds. He pointedly reminded the governor that over five hundred "Alabama black boys" had already died in Vietnam but that "race hatred and segregation" still existed at home.[67] Other black activists pressed for the tax rules to be changed. In January 1970, a group of black parents in Holmes County, Mississippi, secured an injunction that banned the IRS from granting tax-exempt status to private schools unless they agreed not to discriminate. Only a small number of schools proved willing to issue the declarations, and, by March 1971, thirty schools had lost their tax-exempt status. This move outraged many whites, and Nixon was slow to extend the policy because he feared losing support in the South. The U.S. Commission on Civil Rights was critical of the IRS's policies, but the service argued that the tax system should not be used "to enforce civil rights laws." The loophole allowed private schools to flourish in the years ahead, paving the way for resegregation.[68]

Going to a Place Where You're Not Wanted: The Black Experience of School Desegregation

While white opposition did not stop the implementation of the law, it did influence how schools were integrated. Across the region, officials usually created unitary systems by closing black schools and assigning their students to the white schools. In the process, they demoted or dismissed thousands of black teachers and administrators. These policies worried blacks, and they questioned why it was their schools that were invariably chosen for closure. In late 1968, a group of black secondary school principals in Alabama raised their concerns in a "position paper" that they sent to both federal and state officials. In it, they complained that black administrators and parents were being excluded from the decisionmaking process as the schools were merged. Integration, they added, "should be a two way process" and should not lead to the wholesale removal of black teachers and administrators. Despite such entreaties, over the next two years little changed, either in Alabama or elsewhere. As the SRC noted in 1970, the creation of unitary schools usually meant the "preservation of the white school, with its traditions and symbols (and often its old school officers), and obliteration of the distinctive features of the black school."[69]

Within the desegregated schools, many white teachers also treated black students poorly. "When you get a white teacher in the class, he's brought up the same way as most of the whites are—relative to the times," summarized one black student. Even well-intentioned teachers often had little interest in learning about black history or in gaining the perspective of minority students. Blacks also objected to the white assumption that they could automatically learn more if they were taught by whites; the key problem in the black schools, they pointed out, was one of resources. Overall, African Americans perceived that their voices were not being listened to while whites made the decisions. "Many students merely find themselves in a new world with no Black anchors to hang onto, as they try to adjust," noted the Educational Resources Center, a black group from Mississippi. "They are faced with new standards, new teachers, new rules, new curriculums." In February 1970, a Mississippi-based task force from the NEA confirmed these findings, noting that even "successful" desegregation was "being carried out on terms set by whites."[70]

As whites dominated teaching and administrative positions, it is not surprising that black students were much more likely to be disciplined or expelled. In late 1970, the NAACP LDF examined the problem in detail. "Our monitoring is producing evidence that school authorities are tougher in their discipline of black students," it concluded. "Black kids are being suspended at a disproportionate rate." Whites argued that the suspensions reflected the cultural differences that became apparent when poor blacks were transferred into white schools, but blacks asserted that they were being unfairly treated. At Flora High in Columbia, South Carolina, for example, Principal Clinton B. Harvey explained that he had suspended many blacks who came from "the lowest income groups" because "they were uncouth, they were unkind, they were unclean, they were loud and boisterous." Harvey added that the suspensions were "a cultural and class thing, not racial." Black leaders disagreed, insisting that many of the "pushouts" occurred for "very trivial" offenses that white students usually got away with.[71]

In many schools, the playing of songs, especially "Rebel" and "Dixie," also generated tensions. Most whites saw the songs as harmless. As South Carolina's superintendent of education commented in early 1971, "bickering" over the tunes was "essentially trivial." In contrast, blacks felt that the songs were offensive because they recalled the slave era, and they often took action to thwart their use. In October 1970, black students at Butler High School in Huntsville, Alabama, walked out of school when "Dixie" was played at football games. The students also complained that the team was called the Rebels and that the Confederate flag was waved at games. After whites refused to listen to their demands, the black students staged a protest march and fought police outside the school. In all, 113 black pupils were suspended, and several black players left the team, yet the song was still played. Events in Huntsville were replayed elsewhere. In the same month, all the black football players, cheerleaders, and band members at the newly integrated high school in Edgefield, South Carolina, quit their positions until the school stopped playing "Dixie" and flying the Confederate flag at football games. "When two schools merge," explained one black senior, "and whites keep their mascots and songs and the black man loses his, it's as if the black man is being marched over, stepped on again by the white man. That's what we're upset about."[72]

The black students who were chosen to desegregate white schools also met hostility. Events in Selma, where the schools finally merged in 1970, were typical. The small group of black students who were selected to transfer into the white high school never forgot the experience. "My father told me I was to be a part of the integration team," recalled Jo Anne Bland. "It was awful. It was already traumatic enough just to be going to high school for the first time. To go to a place where you're not wanted by the students and teachers because they felt we were forced upon them made everybody unhappy. There were just eight of us, and sixteen hundred and ninety-two of them, dedicated to making our lives miserable. I cried every day. One kid spit on me every day." Bland's persistence paid off, however, and other black students soon followed her example, yet blacks complained that whites stayed in control. The school board remained all white, there were few black teachers, and the new integrated high school got a white principal even though his counterpart from the black school had more seniority. Within the new school, blacks also charged that they were more likely to be channeled into remedial classes. These were all common grievances, and they would continue to be voiced elsewhere in the years that followed.[73]

From the Carolinas to Louisiana, African American students responded to these problems by demanding a voice in the running of the schools. As white administrators refused to listen, tensions increased, and some serious incidents took place. In May 1969, a fifteen-year-old black student in Burlington, North Carolina, was killed in an exchange of gunfire between police and "snipers." Violence had erupted in the small mill town after the failure of students at the newly integrated Williams High School to elect black cheerleaders. According to the *Burlington Times-News*, four black girls had tried to be cheerleaders, but whites had booed them when they made their bids.[74]

While the cheerleader incident sparked the violence, black students at Williams presented broader demands for representation. When Leon Mebane was killed, several hundred pupils were boycotting classes in order to try and secure the appointment of a black school board member and a black student liaison. They also complained about a "lack of respect for black students and black faculty members" at the school. In the aftermath of the shootings, the local chapter of the NAACP pressed these demands before the county's Human Relations Council. It claimed that black students were not represented in the "full life" of the school and were disciplined more harshly than whites. In response, city authorities took a hard line and imposed a strict curfew that was enforced by the national guard.[75]

In the port city of Wilmington, where authorities had closed all-black Williston High and transferred students to two white schools, many blacks were also dissatisfied. Over the course of the 1969–1970 school year, white officials refused to address their demands, fueling tensions between students. As the black student Barnabus Johnson recalled, "Sometimes whites would start fights and say things like: 'What are you niggers up to today?' And almost every time, we ended up chasing them down and kicking their asses. We called them 'search and destroy missions.'"[76]

In December 1970 and January 1971, the situation worsened, and small riots occurred at both New Hanover High and John T. Hoggard High, where black students charged that they were not fairly represented. The pupils also demanded that black studies be recognized in the curriculum and that Martin Luther King's birthday be celebrated. When these requests were not met, they boycotted classes and enlisted the help of Ben Chavis, a young activist who had been a youth coordinator for the SCLC. After the school board still refused to give ground, angry blacks began taking to the streets, triggering outbreaks of serious violence in which two black youths were killed. "The trouble," explained the *Raleigh News and Observer,* "was blamed on tension resulting from Negro teen-agers' demands for change in the public schools."[77]

In Wilmington, one of the biggest problems was that white officials consistently refused to listen to black demands. The hard line was consistent with how city leaders had acted in the past; in 1958 and 1968, for example, authorities had cracked down hard on black protests. The pattern of violence actually dated back even further as in 1898 the city had experienced a brutal riot in which an unknown number of blacks were killed by Democratic militias. Many of the dead were elected officeholders who had opposed the Democratic Party's racist policies. It was, claimed the Wilmington Race Riot Commission, a coup d'état that was "unparalleled in U.S. history." While African Americans saw the 1898 riot as a sign of how whites used force to maintain political control, whites rationalized it as a justified response to black lawlessness. As the black writer Larry Reni Thomas has noted, the incident still haunted Wilmington in the 1970s, its legacy ensuring that many whites were convinced "that violence was the best way to keep blacks at the bottom of the local political, economic and social ladder." Epitomizing the hard line was the police chief, H. E. Williamson, who defended the fatal shooting of a black youngster during the school disturbances. "We are going to stop the trouble, no matter what it takes," he declared.[78]

More than seventy years later, with the legacies of the 1898 riot still apparent, the black community was determined to hit back. Both black and white students carried knives and brass knuckles as they fought one another in the corridors and on the sports fields. At New Hanover High, Principal John J. Scott described the atmosphere as "mob hysteria." Former students never forgot these years. In his gripping *Blood Done Sign My Name,* the southern writer Timothy B. Tyson vividly captures the atmosphere inside the schools. Tyson was a white student who attended the Williston Ninth Grade Center shortly after the implementation of the desegregation plan. "Fistfights at school were common," he recalled. "To go to the bathroom, especially alone, was to risk being beaten up, or worse. . . . Full-scale riots erupted several times a year. . . . We grimly referred to early spring as 'riot season,' as though it were a varsity sport." In the end, the violence was quelled by national guard troops but only after two fatalities and several shootings had occurred. In the years that followed, the white authorities blamed blacks for the disturbances and sought to punish Chavis and his followers severely.[79]

While some of the conditions in Wilmington were unique, significant disturbances occurred in other Tar Heel towns. In the fall of 1970, blacks in the textile town of Henderson protested plans to close a black school and transfer its students to the formerly white school. Again led by Chavis, they demanded the hiring of a black coach and a black assistant principal. Police used tear gas on the protesters, who responded by throwing bricks and bottles. In the melee, one white firefighter died after he accidentally discharged his own weapon. In Warrenton, a heavily black town near the Virginia state line, the local superintendent even claimed that the integration of the schools was "like war." Accounts of who was to blame exposed deep racial divisions. As the *Raleigh News and Observer* reported, "White adults say the blacks have gone on the rampage at the schools. The blacks say the whites are racist." Blacks complained that they were being placed in segregated classes and being disciplined too harshly, yet very few whites were sympathetic. Instead, most white parents reacted to the troubles by enrolling their children in private schools.[80]

North Carolina was not unique; right across the South, blacks launched similar protests against integration plans. In March 1970, the school board in Iberville Parish, Louisiana, desegregated by closing a historic black school, demoting two black principals, and putting black students in separate classes. In response, black students boycotted classes and demonstrated in the streets of Plaquemine, a normally quiet Mississippi River town. Crowds began to clash with local police, who used tear gas to disperse them. Protesters responded by breaking windows, stoning white motorists, and destroying white-owned businesses. As the local leader A. E. Mitchell explained, blacks were no longer prepared to stay quiet and wanted "everything that is rightfully ours." Many of Plaquemine's whites were concerned by such assertiveness. "My gun's loaded," commented one white woman. "But I got nothing to worry about long as we got good law enforce[ment]." Assisted by the NAACP, local campaigners continued the boycott for three months, when a Justice Department injunction forced students back into the classroom.[81]

In the fall of 1970, over three hundred African American students also walked out of class in Earle, Mississippi, to protest the downgrading of black principals and the setting up of segregated classes. After thirty pupils were arrested for violating an antipicketing injunction, black adults organized marches and set up their own private school, which they called Soul Institute. In Eudora, Arkansas, twelve hundred black students similarly walked out to protest the firing of one of their teachers, while, in Butler, Georgia, some six hundred African American pupils boycotted classes after black bus drivers were prohibited from carrying white female pupils.[82] As the Earle protest highlighted, the way in which the schools were integrated did undermine support for the process in the black community, and even committed integrationists acknowledged this. In 1971, the civil rights lawyer Julius Chambers admitted that black students had been "relegated to a segregated status" within mixed schools and that this had led many black parents "to question integration as the policy to follow."[83]

Black principals and teachers were the primary casualties when black schools were closed. In late 1970, a study by the NEA revealed that there had been "massive displacement of black educators" in Mississippi and Louisiana. Civil rights groups were concerned because these teachers had acted as positive role models for youngsters. "Black teachers are being emasculated and stripped of their standing before their own communities," complained Rims Barber of the Delta Ministry, who quipped that so many black principals had been demoted that blacks now claimed that "co-principal" was "short for colored principal." The situation in Mississippi was not unusual. Shortly after the NEA study was released, an investigation by the Race Relations Information Center reached similar conclusions for the South as a whole, while, in 1971, another NEA study found that 69 percent of southern school boards had experienced a decline in their ratio of black teachers over the previous two years.[84]

North Carolina again provided a good illustration of wider trends. In the mid-1960s, the Tar Heel State supported five black higher education institutions, more than any other state, and it was also home to a strong black teachers' organization. Between 1965 and 1969, however, seventy-three black high schools in the state were closed, along with dozens of elementary schools. Within the unitary schools, the new principals were invariably white. In Johnston County, located just south of Raleigh, six black principals were replaced by whites, some with no experience in the post, while qualified black teachers were assigned to work as assistants. By the end of 1969, the North Carolina Teachers Association had filed forty-six legal suits on behalf of its members, while an additional twenty-two cases were under investigation.[85]

Across the South, the NAACP also worked to address these problems. As well as fighting to integrate schools, the association began to represent the interests of blacks within the merged systems. In June 1970, the group opened a Southern Education Office in Tuskegee, and, by the end of the year, its staff had filed over one hundred complaints with federal agencies on behalf of black teachers and students. In 1971, for example, the group challenged the firing of seven black junior college teachers in St. Petersburg, Florida.[86] In one time-consuming case, NAACP attorneys fought a long and unsuccessful battle to secure the reinstatement of Travistine Alexander. A veteran teacher in Warren, Arkansas, Alexander was fired in 1970 after white parents questioned her qualifications and complained that their children could not understand her because of her "poor speech habits."[87]

Because of its representative nature, Alexander's plight warrants further examination. Citing concerns from white parents, during the 1969–

1970 school year officials in Warren had dismissed three black teachers and hired white replacements. In a tense hearing in the summer of 1970, the local lawyer T. E. Patterson accused whites of hypocrisy. "You don't have these complaints when most of the white kids in this town were brought up by uneducated black people until they are about 6 or 7 years old constantly and they are not handicapped at all," he charged. "They are treated better than anybody else, and you trusted them completely with your children. . . . You didn't care very much how she taught in the all black school." Pleading for understanding, Patterson asked that Alexander be given time to retrain.[88]

These pleas fell on deaf ears, and, in November 1971, Judge George Harris upheld Alexander's dismissal on the grounds that school boards had "wide discretion" to hire and fire teachers. In a letter to the NAACP, Alexander thanked lawyers for their efforts, yet she received no compensation for losing her "life's career." Her experience encapsulated how the African American community had to pay a heavy price in order to access better schools. Overall, the U.S. Commission on Civil Rights captured the lesson of these years when it observed, "Racial integration in America has usually taken place on terms dictated by whites."[89]

Making Desegregation Work: White Southerners Comply with School Desegregation

In these years, the schools could not have desegregated as much as they did unless white attitudes were mixed. As we have seen, opponents of change were certainly more likely to put pen to paper than those who quietly implemented controversial plans. Moderate voices were important, however, and they need to be acknowledged and heard.

Initial response to the *Alexander* decision illustrates this as there were mainstream figures who urged acceptance from the start. North Carolina governor Robert W. Scott was one of a growing band of politicians who realized that there was now no chance of upholding freedom of choice. "For the governor to go around the state and say we're not going to do this or that is not unlike a loud-mouthed kid running around the school yard saying he's not going to do what the principal says," he commented in early 1970. In both South Carolina and Virginia, Governors Robert McNair and Linwood Holton took a similar line. As the historian Joseph Crespino has shown, even in Mississippi some politicians recommended "grudging and measured compliance" by this time because they understood that resistance could lead to political and economic isolation. Overall, the reaction of white southerners to *Alexander* was divided. In late 1970, a Harris poll confirmed this; 43 percent disapproved of the decision, but 42 percent agreed with it.[90]

The start of the 1970–1971 school year was a particularly important time. According to the SRC, this school year was "the most crucial one since 1954" as on the first day of classes more integration was set to occur than on any previous day in history. In all, more than 250,000 African American children spent their first day in school alongside whites as nearly two hundred southern school districts complied with federal orders.[91] What was remarkable was that this transformation was accomplished in a generally peaceful manner. As *Newsweek* reported, in much of the region there was "an attitude of resignation . . . and sometimes even a desperate craving to make desegregation work." While "cunning evasions and outright defiance" would continue, most whites now accepted the inevitable.[92]

Generally emphasizing compliance, the southern press was partly responsible for this outcome. In early 1970, for example, the influential *Atlanta Constitution* openly backed the efforts of state school superintendent Jack Nix, who told parents that disobedience was not an option. "If we should elect to defy the courts, . . . the court order to desegregate will remain in full force and effect," he explained. It was a similar story in many other cities; in Winston-Salem, North Carolina, for example, the local paper instructed parents to put children first and support the public schools.[93]

Across the region, the role of school superintendents was also crucial. Title IV of the Civil Rights Act provided technical and financial assistance to help school systems accomplish these difficult changes. In several areas, superintendents used these funds to good effect. Although it was not as well-known as Title VI, the provision played an important and unheralded role in this story. In New Albany, Mississippi, for example, Superintendent J. Bryant Smith used Title IV money to take his teachers to two desegregation-training institutes. As a result of these efforts, the New Albany schools integrated uneventfully, and, within a year, black children in the system had advanced 1.4 grades. In other locations, concluded the U.S. Commission on Civil Rights, the essential ingredients for success were a "firm commitment" by superintendents and "effective use of Title IV funds." In Lauderdale County, Alabama, Superintendent Alan Thornton used the money to educate teachers about the benefits of desegregation, and he also used his authority to drive the process forward. "I did not want to leave the job undone," he reflected.[94]

The role of community leaders was also decisive. In February 1970, the school board in Greenville, South Carolina, was able to carry out a comprehensive desegregation plan largely because of the support of the chamber of commerce, local ministers, and Mayor R. Cooper White Jr. Leading by example, White kept his three children in the public school system. Parents also got involved in the process, even welcoming new black students with banners that declared "We're all one school now."

In addition, they repaired school buildings and acted as volunteers. Anxious to secure a better education, African American pupils also played their part. "I think we'll like it," commented the black student Willie Fuller as he enrolled. "I don't think it's going to be too much different and it will give us an equal chance." While tensions still existed, both sides worked to overcome them.[95]

In February 1970, forceful community leadership also helped ensure that the schools were integrated successfully in the Mississippi cities of McComb and Jackson. In the state capital, local politicians and the press supported the changes, while an interracial PTA countered negative rumors. Even Governor John Bell Williams did little to disrupt the process. As the local black lawyer Ruben Anderson commented of Williams, "He talks a lot but he's been pretty mild." In both cities, young school superintendents oversaw the whole process with quiet determination. Winning over doubters, they stressed that parents should work to preserve the public schools and give their children the best chance. After the first few days of classes, many parents found that their worst fears were unfounded. "It wasn't as bad as I thought," admitted one.[96]

The example of Columbia, Mississippi, spotlights how community leadership could prevent violence from occurring. Columbia was located in traditional Klan country, and its school district was the first to open in the wake of *Alexander*. Prior to the start of classes on January 5, 1970, however, civic leaders set up a biracial committee that worked to build understanding. Over the Christmas holidays, white parents visited the black elementary school and learned that its facilities were not as inadequate as they had feared. In addition, parents were persuaded to help paint and fix up the buildings in preparation for classes, and they soon began to take pride in their work. There were similar efforts at the high school level, where parents attended an open day and were told to support their public schools. "If everybody could just see everybody else as a human being, it might just turn out all right," commented the white high school president Tommy Barber. The president of the black high school was similarly positive. "We can become a lighthouse here in Marion County," asserted Archie Johnson. As a result of forceful civic leadership, parental involvement, and student support, Columbia's schools managed to integrate relatively smoothly.[97]

The desire for outside investment also influenced whites to stress compliance, especially in Mississippi, where business leaders desperately wanted to attract industrial jobs to their poor state. As integration orders loomed, they grasped that a mass exodus from the public schools would undermine their efforts. In the Delta community of Yazoo City, the chamber of commerce consequently set up an education committee that tried to persuade whites to back the public schools. "We need good schools if we're going to attract industry," admitted the chamber official Robert Wheeler. The effort worked, as around three-quarters of white pupils turned up for classes in the majority-black community. After a trip through Mississippi in the spring of 1970, the Nixon aide Louis Patrick Gray reported that most whites recognized that good public schools were essential if their state was to prosper. Gray was an assistant to a cabinet-level committee that itself worked to persuade southerners to support integrated schools. "The public school education system within the State cannot be permitted to languish and die since it is a key attraction for industry considering a decision to locate within the State," he reported. "On this point all those with whom I talked agreed."[98]

In neighboring Alabama, the desire for economic growth was also powerful, and it was not just the chamber of commerce that promoted compliance. In August 1969, for example, the Huntsville resident Edward S. Goode wrote Governor Albert Brewer that the Deep South states with the "stormiest racial images" were failing to attract the same amount of investment as their more moderate counterparts in the Upper South. The way forward was clear; Alabama had to foster "racial peace and harmony" in order to secure "a brighter economic picture." Unlike George Wallace, Brewer agreed and recommended that Alabamians comply with government mandates even if they disliked them.[99] Although he spoke out against specific integration orders, Brewer also kept his own children in the public schools. His stance was praised by some whites, including Birmingham residents who were well placed to judge the costs of continued resistance. In early 1970, for example, Parks Scott applauded the governor's calm approach. "The 'red necks' and the 'hoods' have too long controlled vital parts of our political structure," he wrote from the Magic City.[100]

In Durham, North Carolina, both civic groups and school board officials also exerted real leadership. In July 1970, Judge Edwin Stanley called for the pairing of six schools and the busing of two thousand elementary school pupils, moves that were usually controversial. The Durham school board was determined to implement the plan, however. Helped by an interracial civic group called Women in Action to Prevent Violence and Its Causes, it largely pulled it off. As the *Raleigh News and Observer* noted, the women's group deserved "much of the credit" for the progress that was made. Prior to the start of classes, open house sessions were held at the schools and thousands of queries from concerned parents were answered. As a result, the women were able to convince most adults to keep their children in the public system. "We felt that if we talk about our problems, share them with each other, and try to reduce them, the children will be the definite beneficiaries," explained group president Elna Spaulding.[101]

Durham's schoolchildren also played their part. Unlike some of their elders, they quickly accepted the changes and made friends. "I don't think it makes that much difference to the kids," commented the student Vallerie Stephens. "It's the parents who are worried." While some whites, particularly the better-off, refused to enroll their children in majority-black schools, the two races had still been able to dismantle the dual school system peacefully. Julius Chambers, who handled the desegregation suit against the city, later claimed that Durham had "one of the best implemented plans in the state."[102]

Students played a key role in many other locations too. Many observers insisted that young people were less prejudiced than their parents, partly because many of them could scarcely remember the Jim Crow era. As a black principal in Charlotte commented, "Children are coming up in a brand new world." Some students did more than simply show up for class. At majority-black John F. Kennedy High in Richmond, black students formed a committee to welcome the nervous white arrivals. "We want to make you feel at home here," explained the committee member Gregory Thomas. "This is your school, too." In rural areas, student-led efforts also made a difference. In Hoke County, North Carolina, for example, a conservative community in the eastern part of the state, schools were 50 percent black, 35 percent white, and 15 percent Lumbee Indian. After the county eliminated its triple school system in 1969, the children led the way in building racial understanding. As Superintendent Donald Abernathy explained, "You would see them standing around in clusters on the campus. This was at first. Now you see very little of this. The children have learned to get along with each other. They respect one another. They vote for each other in elections."[103]

In the *Alexander* era, many white southerners certainly refused to accept the inevitable and fought a futile last stand. At this crucial time, the region's political leaders frequently set a poor example. Placing his own children in private schools, Governor Williams urged his constituents to ignore the law. Rather than urging calm, Governor Wallace also advised some parents to violate court orders, while Governor Maddox spent his term fulminating against "Federal control" of education. By their actions, these men encouraged whites to believe that they could still undermine federal laws.[104]

Remarkably, however, many black and white southerners did work together, and they achieved a great deal. Some pertinent examples illustrate the pace of change particularly well. There is the case of Yolanda King, whose articulate father had once struggled to explain why she could not visit an amusement park in Atlanta. Just seven years after he recounted this incident in *Letter from a Birmingham City Jail,* Yolanda was the Junior Class president at a predominantly white Atlanta high school. Also noteworthy was the case of Governor Linwood Holton, who called on all Virginians to obey the law. "No more must the slogan of states' rights sound a recalcitrant and defensive note for the South," he declared in 1970. "The era of defiance is behind us." Backing up his words, Holton sent his four children to local public schools. Although he could have placed them in any Richmond public school because the governor's mansion stood on state land, all four went to mixed or majority-black schools and thrived there. Fifteen-year-old daughter Tayloe even became one of two white cheerleaders (out of a squad of twelve) at John F. Kennedy High School. On the first day of classes, she was one of the white students who were welcomed by blacks.[105]

By the end of 1970, men like Holton and Brewer had helped ensure that the South's schools were becoming the most integrated in the nation. Many problems certainly remained, especially in addressing discrimination within the merged schools, but, where the races had acted in good faith, real progress had occurred. Despite this, the Supreme Court had still to decide whether the busing of students was constitutional. Without busing, the pace of desegregation would slow, especially in large cities where neighborhoods were overwhelmingly segregated. As 1970 came to a close, the Court heard arguments in *Swann v. Charlotte-Mecklenburg County Board of Education,* a case that would do much to determine the pace of school integration over the next few years.[106]

5

THE BUSING YEARS

School Desegregation in the Wake of Swann

On April 20, 1971, the Supreme Court issued its ruling in the landmark *Swann* case. Originally prompted by the efforts of the black missionary Darius Swann to send his six-year-old son to an all-white school, the case went to the Supreme Court after the school board appealed the district court's busing order. At stake were decisive issues about how far the courts could go in devising techniques to dismantle the South's dual school system. After extensive deliberations, the nine justices decided that the city of Charlotte was clearly practicing de jure segregation. Not wanting to contradict *Brown,* they ruled that the federal courts could order busing in order to remove "all vestiges of state-imposed segregation." To achieve their objectives, the courts were also allowed to pair black and white schools and gerrymander attendance zones. "Desegregation plans," asserted the Court, "cannot be limited to the walk-in school." Overall, both federal judges and HEW officials now had broad discretion to integrate the South's schools.[1]

Whites and blacks reacted to the news very differently. Noting that *Swann* applied only to school systems that had practiced de jure segregation, Mississippi senator James O. Eastland termed it "punitive, vindictive and discriminatory." In Charlotte, many whites were also furious. The local businessman L. D. Abernethy Jr. called April 20 "a dark day for America, a nation founded as a republic to be governed by the wishes of the majority of its citizens."[2] Some residents asked their congressman to help, and the Republican Charles Raper Jonas responded by cosponsoring a constitutional amendment that blocked school assignments on the grounds of race. Above all, many whites found it hard to accept that their children might not attend neighborhood schools. "I was heartbroken to hear about the ruling," explained Mrs. B. G. Sanders, whose son was to be bused across town. "It's not that I mind my children going to school with colored children or having colored teachers, but we bought a house in a nice neighborhood so they could go to a nice school."[3]

In the African American community, there was jubilation when the unanimous decision came down. Thirty years later, the teacher Madge Hopkins clearly recalled her feelings when she heard the news. "Alleluia, finally," she exclaimed. "Free at last, free at last. This is what Martin [Luther King] had said." Julius Chambers, the plaintiffs' lawyer, received many congratulatory letters from blacks. "The recent Supreme Court's decision in favor of your school desegregation suit gives us renewed hope and faith," declared the local black leader Mary Nash Jones. Rather than a "dark day," Chambers called April 20 "a great day," adding, "The court has cleared the way for implementing . . . what blacks have been struggling for ages . . . to enjoy the rights most Americans have had for years."[4]

Despite their differences, both races knew that *Swann* was going to lead to further desegregation in Charlotte and elsewhere. As a result of the decision, mandatory busing plans were adopted in more than one hundred southern school districts, including large metropolitan districts in Little Rock, Nashville, and Tampa. In the two years after *Swann,* busing also became a central issue in national politics, but it was southern politicians that led efforts to restrict or prohibit the controversial tactic. "No single word in all the arguments over school integration," declared *Time* in the wake of *Swann,* "has inspired as much fear and anger as *busing.*"[5] By September 1971, forty House members had sponsored twenty-five antibusing bills, all of them designed to amend the Constitution in various ways. The stumbling block was the House Judiciary Committee, which repeatedly refused to hold hearings, while, in the Senate, similar efforts also fell short. In October 1971, for example, Strom Thurmond and Samuel Ervin cosponsored an amendment to ban busing, but it failed to pass. In the spring of 1972, the House Judiciary Committee relented to the popular mood and held hearings, but civil rights supporters blocked efforts to pass hostile legislation. Angered by this, many whites participated in a growing backlash against federal civil rights initiatives.[6]

Because the various antibusing bills failed, the South's dual school system continued to collapse. Credit must be given to the NAACP and other civil rights groups, especially as they overcame their differences and helped defeat the antibusing legislation. Despite the loud voices of defiance, many white southerners also complied with *Swann.* In January 1972, HEW reported that more black pupils attended all-black schools in the North than in the South, the first time that this had occurred. In the eleven southern states, 9.2 percent of black pupils went to all-black schools, compared to 11.2 percent in the North. Between 1970 and 1972, the southern figure had halved, a record of "dramatic improvement" at a time when little had changed in the North.[7]

In 1972, a detailed investigation by a Senate committee confirmed that the South was leading the way. In 1968, 78.8 percent of the region's black students were in 80–100 percent minority schools, but, by 1971, that figure had tumbled to 32.2 percent. "By every standard of measurement," concluded the select committee's report, "there has been pronounced reduction in the isolation of black students in the 11 Southern states during the past 4 years." While there were dramatic strides across a wide range of districts, the gains were particularly noticeable in larger cities. In Nashville, the proportion of black pupils attending all-black schools tumbled from 21.1 percent to none within the space of a year. By the close of 1971, Charlotte's busing plan had also been implemented so effectively that almost 98 percent of all black pupils attended majority-white schools. Soon, the Queen City was being held up as a role model for the rest of the country to emulate. Still, a closer look, especially at local situations, reveals that such gains had not come easily.[8]

"The #1 Question and Concern in the South": *Swann* and the Busing Controversy

After *Swann* was settled, the lower courts moved quickly to force southern school districts to use busing and pairing. Within five months of the decision, federal judges had applied its principles to cases involving forty southern districts, including large urban systems in Dallas, Norfolk, and Jacksonville. The moves brought howls of protest from southern whites, and many wrote President Nixon in the hope that he would help. Nixon had tried to block the ruling; as the justices had deliberated, his attorneys went to the Court and declared that busing was wrong. After the decision, Nixon responded by informing his HEW secretary to "do what the law requires and not *one bit* more." The president had little control over the courts, however, and federal judges soon incorporated busing into their desegregation orders. Their actions worried presidential advisers. "We are heading for political trouble in the South on school busing," reported Harry Dent to Nixon in June 1971. "This is the #1 question and concern in the South. Integration is one thing, but busing goes beyond that. The busing will come in the cities where we won the Southern states in 1968."[9]

White southerners attacked busing for many reasons. Most insisted that they were in favor of desegregation but that busing was not the best way to bring it about. Busing, they argued, would actually undermine the quality of the schools because children would be worn out by long bus rides and would not be able to take part in extracurricular activities. In November 1971, for instance, a group of parents from Norfolk told Nixon that busing represented "educational suicide." As they explained in a petition: "Long bus rides will curtail participation in sports and play time that is essential to the full physical and mental development of children. . . . In addition, long tiring busing will reduce our children's ability to absorb education and instruction that must be accomplished as home work." Even some educators expressed these views. In Dallas, where a 1971 court order mandated widespread busing, school board president John Plath Green insisted that the results had been disastrous. "So, to me, busing is cruel," he explained before Congress in 1972. "Busing is humiliating. To my mind, busing hurts or harms the personal image that a child has of himself, and I think this destroys his motivation and increases the rate of dropout in school."[10]

Because they saw busing as destructive, whites argued that their children should be allowed to attend neighborhood schools instead. In Newport News, Virginia, where the Fourth Circuit Court mandated crosstown trips of up to an hour, Mrs. Henry H. Parish protested to Nixon in March 1972, "It hurts to watch our little children being bused miles from home—passing several [schools] they could attend—for no other reason than to meet an artificial racial ratio in our schools." Whites in the coastal community also asserted that both races supported neighborhood schools.[11]

Many whites also saw busing as inherently undemocratic, asserting that unelected judges and HEW bureaucrats were overstepping their powers and were usurping Congress's right to make laws. Reacting to *Swann*, one Norfolk parent questioned, "When will the Supreme Court tell us which neighborhood to live in[?]" Building on these claims, many saw themselves as the victims of discrimination. "I think when they take away from parents their rights as to where they send their children to school and bus them against their will that this is actually DISCRIMINATION IN REVERSE," wrote a South Carolina businessman to the president. Because they had helped Nixon get elected, some whites felt betrayed. The Dallas mother Stella Claunch even sent the president a concise two-sentence telegram. "I refuse to bus my children. I will never vote for you again," she declared in August 1971. This was exactly the kind of political backlash that Dent had feared.[12]

Southern congressmen took up the fight, pressing for a ban on busing during important hearings in 1972. A powerful figure within the Democratic Party, North Carolina senator Ervin led the charge. According to Ervin, busing represented the culmination of a "dangerous pattern of judicial and bureaucratic tyranny over local school boards which has emerged over the past few years." As a recent biographer has noted, Ervin led a powerful "anti-busing crusade" in these years and was able to mobilize supporters in both the South and the North.[13]

Many Americans certainly agreed with the influential senator. For at least a year after *Swann*, busing was a high-profile political issue. In

March 1972, a Gallup poll found that 74 percent of southern whites were opposed to "compulsory busing" and that 68 percent of Northern whites agreed with them. The *New Republic* captured the mood, noting in early 1972, "Anti-busing fever is running high. . . . Citizens' groups, north and south, are lighting fires under their representatives; there is a lot of support for an anti-busing constitutional amendment in the House." Traditionally a liberal journal, even the *New Republic* now argued that busing was counterproductive and disruptive.[14]

Some whites also tried to disrupt the implementation of busing plans. In February 1972, parents in Augusta, Georgia, protested against a district court order to transport students so that the merged public schools would be 40 percent black. The leader of Citizens for Neighborhood Schools, Richard Anderson, coordinated efforts to keep children in their old schools. "We're going to hold a ceremony, call the roll, have a short prayer, but we're not going to let our children get on the buses," he explained. The protests influenced the Georgia House and Senate to call for a constitutional antibusing amendment, and Citizens for Neighborhood Schools also organized a one-day statewide boycott. As the *Macon News* reported, the boycott was strongly supported in Augusta and Savannah, but it "fell flat" elsewhere. Even in the Augusta area, the movement gradually petered out as whites realized that they would have to live with Judge Alexander A. Lawrence's order.[15]

In Richmond, Virginia, white parents also reacted angrily when Judge Robert R. Merhige ordered that the largely black urban system should merge with two predominantly white suburban districts. Issued in January 1972, Merhige's decree was an effort to break up entrenched segregation. The judge noted that, as late as May 1, 1970, three of seven high schools were 100 percent black and one was 99.26 percent white. "There is little doubt that under freedom of choice Richmond public schools had not achieved a unitary system as required by law," he concluded. Merhige argued that, because whites were fleeing the city and moving to segregated "islands," meaningful progress could be achieved only by transporting students some distance. Brushing aside objections, he noted that busing was not new. "Officials," he blasted, "can hardly assert the compelling nature of obstacles which they overcame earlier in order to perpetuate segregation."[16]

On the ground, Merhige's order was predictably unpopular. In one February demonstration, more than four thousand marchers carried a coffin inscribed "Death of Freedom" to the state capitol building. There, city councilman Howard Carwile denounced Governor Linwood Holton as a "gutless, spineless, [and] no good man." Merhige, who sent his own son to a private school, also came in for some vicious attacks, with one member of the Virginia House even calling for the judge's impeachment as a "judicial pirate." The controversy became a major issue in state politics, and both the House and the Senate called for a constitutional amendment to prohibit busing. Supported by the *Richmond Times-Dispatch*, enraged white parents even organized a motorcade of over thirty-three hundred cars that traveled north to Washington. Taking place in late February, the protest created a twenty-five-mile-long traffic jam along Interstate 95, one of the busiest highways in the country.[17]

Partly influenced by these protests, in June 1972 the court of appeals reversed Merhige's order and argued that suburban counties were not responsible for segregation in the inner city. In May 1973, a divided Supreme Court issued a tied vote that had the effect of upholding the appeal. The stalemate came about after Justice Lewis F. Powell Jr., a former member of the Richmond school board, abstained. The outcome also reflected the efforts of Nixon's aides, who had argued against consolidation in the case. The president had also appointed three conservative justices—Warren Burger, William Rehnquist, and Harry Blackmun—and all of them had supported this position. The decision was a major blow to the NAACP LDF, especially as its lawyers were committed to mergers of suburban and city districts. Although it had been fighting the case for over a decade, the group decided not to appeal because it did not want to establish a damaging precedent.[18]

In Florida, controversial busing plans were adopted in several cities, including Orlando, Gainesville, and Jacksonville. Responding to grassroots pressure, in the spring of 1972 Republican delegates persuaded the state legislature to place an antibusing referendum on the primary ballot. Worried by the move, Democratic governor Reubin Askew was able to attach another question that asked voters whether they supported equal education opportunities for all. When the vote took place, 74 percent of voters said that they favored a ban on busing, while an even greater number (79 percent) claimed that they believed in equal education opportunities. The vote, which had no legal effect, reflected whites' view that busing was not the way forward. Across the state, concerned whites also bombarded their political representatives with letters and petitions. Summing up the mood, one group of Jacksonville parents wrote Richard Nixon that busing was "unconstitutional, unworkable, inhumane, and also disastrous."[19]

Across the region, whites also used ingenious methods to evade busing plans. Some listed phony addresses and proxy residences to stop their children being sent to black schools, while others swapped houses with relatives. In Birmingham, where many whites had violated previous court orders, parents gave false addresses to the Jefferson County School Board. In December 1971, concerned state officials noted that two FBI agents were investigating these actions.[20] In several other cities, parents arranged for suburban families to become legal guardians of their children in order to stop them being sent to heavily black schools. In Little Rock, state representative Art Givens boasted of arranging thirty to forty "guardianships" personally, while, in Hattiesburg, where false guardianships were also common, one white family claimed to be the guardians of twelve children. Sympathizing with parents' plight, school officials often turned a blind eye to these tactics.[21]

While opposition to busing was intense, efforts to restrict or prohibit it faced many difficulties. Nixon's advisers certainly explored every possible route, but they were unable to find a simple solution. In the wake of *Swann,* the Nixon adviser Edward L. Morgan wrote the president, "The busing controversy is a real problem that will not disappear simply by the passage of time." As a result, aides strove for a way to achieve "some immediate, positive anti-busing result" without being perceived as "anti-black." It was a near-impossible task. Advisers concluded that a constitutional amendment was risky because it would be interpreted as retreat from desegregation and would alienate the black community. Passing an amendment would also take time, and even then it would be open to interpretation by the courts and would not affect existing plans that required busing. A moratorium on busing was also problematic because it suspended a remedy for a violation of a constitutional right. As Morgan concluded, any "intervention strategy" was fraught with difficulties because the administration needed to respect both the judiciary's independence and the Constitution. Bombarded with advice, Nixon wavered. In the end, he endorsed a moratorium on busing, but his proposals never passed the Democratic-controlled Congress.[22]

Civil rights groups also ensured that southern school districts were forced to comply with *Swann.* In March 1972, the leaders of seven organizations, including the NAACP, the NAACP LDF, the SCLC, and the National Urban League, came together and urged the president not to abandon the fight for desegregated schools. "What is called for now," they reminded the president, "is strong moral presidential leadership counseling compliance with the law as decreed by the courts of our land rather than defiance and backtracking." Despite some reservations, most African Americans saw busing as necessary if their children were to get a better deal. Bringing together a wide variety of organizations, the Leadership Conference on Civil Rights coordinated this fight.[23]

In the spring of 1972, civil rights activists testified before Congress in order to block a harmful constitutional amendment. Introduced by New York congressman Norman F. Lent, the amendment declared that public school assignments could not be made on the grounds of "race, creed, or color." William Coleman of the NAACP LDF told the hearing that the proposal would have the effect of undermining "meaningful desegregation" even in schools that were not under federal court orders, a position that was powerfully reiterated by black parents. "If Congress were to enact legislation which would, in any way, permit schools to be resegregated or slow the pace of desegregation," explained the Charlotte resident Arthur Lynch, "it would again be telling blacks that they are unworthy of association with whites and telling whites that they occupy a superior position in our society."[24] Also testifying against the amendment were representatives from the U.S. Commission on Civil Rights, the NEA, the American Civil Liberties Union, and the Lawyers Committee for Civil Rights under Law.[25]

Some prominent individuals also took a stand. One striking example was that of Jackie Robinson, the retired baseball player who had integrated the major leagues. Born in Cairo, Georgia, to a poor sharecropping family, Robinson was an immensely talented athlete who also took a keen interest in civil rights. Unable to debut in the major leagues until he was twenty-eight, he knew the true costs of discrimination all too well. "We want busing so our children can compete," he wrote President Nixon in March 1972. "Non-integrated schools, no matter what, are not equal in terms of educational opportunities." Now a business executive, Robinson had initially endorsed Nixon, but he soon became a critic of the administration's civil rights policies.[26]

The NAACP also played a vital role in this struggle, its leaders repeatedly pointing out that whites had accepted busing when it had been used to maintain segregated schools. Since World War I, all the southern states had provided funding for pupil transportation, and they had frequently used it as a way of preserving the dual school system. In some rural areas, black pupils had been transported over forty miles in the Jim Crow era. Reflecting this experience, NAACP activists had little patience with their opponents' claims that they were not racist. "It is not busing of children that arouses hostility," blasted *The Crisis* in 1972. "Rather, it is transporting them from black to white areas or, particularly, from white to black neighborhoods. In other words, race is the sole issue." Testifying before Congress, Roy Wilkins cited the case of a black child in Georgia who had walked six miles to school and had been passed each day by a bus full of white children. "If that isn't demeaning, I would like to know what is," he concluded.[27]

Association leaders carefully monitored political efforts to undermine busing. After President Nixon gave an antibusing speech in March, for instance, the association's Southeast Regional Convention sent a telegram of protest to the White House and Congress. The NAACP also used its extensive branch structure to good effect; in the summer of 1972, for instance, the national office informed all branches that they should pressure Nixon to enforce the law, a call that many members heeded. From Lincolnton, North Carolina, members sent the president a typically unambiguous message: "I want *quality* integrated education for *all* children and I support bus transportation as one of the ways to achieve it." Overall, the force of black agency helped convince Nixon's advisers that it was not politically feasible to ban busing.[28]

On the ground, some blacks also spoke out about the experiences that Wilkins had referred to. In November 1971, for example, the Birmingham resident Sherrell Mitchell wrote a remarkable letter to Governor Wallace. After reminding Wallace that he supported "individual rights and freedom of speech," Mitchell articulated her views. "Recently, the issue of busing became a very important one," she noted. "Why the sudden concern? The poor child who was bused years ago would have welcomed your sympathy. . . . My older relatives, including my parents, were bused all during their school years. They were taken past many schools in order to get to theirs, all because of segregation. Why is it that children cannot be bused now? . . . I have reached the conclusion that you do not want busing because you do not favor intergration [*sic*]." In response, Wallace denied that he was racist but insisted that busing undermined the education process. A few years earlier, however, he had not even responded to hostile letters from blacks.[29]

As southern politicians were acutely aware, busing remained a volatile matter that could be exploited for political gain. The issue helped give birth to the political career of Jesse Helms, a young journalist who eventually became one of the South's most influential politicians. Styling himself as "the Voice of Free Enterprise in Raleigh-Durham," Helms used his slots on WRAL-TV to insist that federal zealots were trampling over the wishes of ordinary, law-abiding southerners. "If the federal masters are so obsessed with busing," he blasted, "let them provide the money and deal directly with the people." In 1972, Helms's editorials helped him win election to the U.S. Senate. North Carolina's first Republican senator in the twentieth century, he would play a key role in opposing future civil rights initiatives.[30]

Despite Dent's worrying, Nixon was, ultimately, able to ride out the busing issue with little political damage, partly because he recognized the potency of white opposition and did enough to placate it. In the run-up to the 1972 election, the president made his feelings clear. "Busing forced by a court to achieve an arbitrary racial balance is wrong," he declared in August 1972. "It adds nothing whatever to the childrens' [*sic*] learning." He also deflected criticism by insisting that it was the courts that generated busing orders. While HEW orders also recommended busing, the pitch seemed to work. As Harry Dent wrote Nixon immediately after *Swann*, "The point has been made on the front pages of most Southern newspapers that the decision is against the position taken by the President last March and also before the Court. There is resentment against the decision, but it seems to fall on the Court."[31]

In the end, Nixon also had some luck, especially when the Democrats nominated the ultraliberal George McGovern as their candidate. With the withdrawal of George Wallace, who was paralyzed during an assassination attempt, Nixon easily carried the South. If a conservative candidate had challenged the president, however, the outcome may have been very different. Before his withdrawal in May, Wallace had pledged to stop busing and was building momentum. In March, he won the Florida Democratic primary by exploiting the busing issue, and his own secret polls showed that well over half the country's voters saw him as an acceptable candidate. Within his home state, he also persuaded the legislature to pass an antibusing law, although a federal judge later deemed it unconstitutional.[32]

While civil rights groups succeeded in influencing public policies, private choices were much more difficult to control. As busing orders were implemented, more and more whites reacted by enrolling their children in private schools. The SRC monitored the growth of the "segregation academies" with characteristic care, concluding in early 1972 that public school enrollment had "dropped so significantly in most Southern states that a large part of the decline can only be attributed to continued white flight from desegregated public schools to private segregation academies." By the 1971–1972 school year, private enrollments were twenty times greater than they had been before the passage of the 1964 Civil Rights Act. The schools continued to have powerful backers, including political leaders and the influential White Citizens' Council, which even ran some schools. Council leader William J. Simmons admitted that these schools were segregated. "No Negroes have applied for admission," he declared, "and we wouldn't admit them if they did."[33]

It is revealing to see just how far some southern politicians went to support private schools. In Alabama, Governor Wallace had extensive correspondence with private school administrators and helped them secure much-needed funds. "We appreciate everything that you are doing to assist private education in the state of Alabama," wrote one principal to the governor in July 1971.[34] The governor worked with his brother, Judge Jack Wallace, in order to raise money. As George Wallace's executive assistant wrote privately, the brothers had "helped raise some several hundred thousand dollars in behalf of setting up private schools." On one occasion, the president of a private school in Camp Hill even thanked the governor for a "most generous" donation that "was recommended by you and Mr. William J. Simmons." The records did not specify where the brothers got the funds from, although George Wallace referred to his brother's contacts with "an anonymous group" that forwarded donations to the schools.[35]

This correspondence also occurred a few months after Wallace had declared that he had "always been a moderate" and no longer believed in segregation. In early 1971, the Barbour County native had also said that the nation "ought to have non-discrimination in public schools." Many doubted whether Wallace had really changed, however, and his main biographer notes that he remained racially insensitive in private. The governor was a product of his times, and it was difficult for him to discard entrenched views.[36]

Other officials also tried to prop up the new private schools. In Wallace's power base of Montgomery, municipal authorities allowed all-white academies to use their grounds for football and baseball games. This saved the schools thousands of dollars and allowed them to offer attractive extracurricular programs. At the games, the schools were also able to raise funds by selling tickets and refreshments. In 1973, however, the SPLC secured a ruling that prohibited the use of public recreational facilities by segregated private schools. The following year, the U.S. Supreme Court agreed that the city's policy was racially discriminatory. Right across the region, it was becoming more difficult for public officials to subsidize private schools.[37]

While proponents stressed the quality of education in the private schools, racial considerations were important, especially as whites felt that the influx of blacks had lowered academic standards. Many white parents admitted their true feelings to sympathetic correspondents, confirming what civil rights leaders suspected.[38] "The level of instruction has been lowered in order that those *bussed* in can compete in a fashion," wrote one South Carolina parent to Strom Thurmond in 1971. "My daughter will be in private school next fall. . . . This will remove her from the dangerous atmosphere which pervades most public schools today." Despite its vigorous support for busing, in 1972 even the U.S. Commission on Civil Rights admitted that the tactic had caused "some white flight."[39]

Looking at the South as a whole, however, the growth of these schools needs to be kept in perspective. At the end of the 1971–1972 school year, the SRC calculated that 535,000 white students attended private schools, an increase of 35,000 over the previous year. While this number was significant, it meant that just 6.2 percent of all elementary and secondary school pupils in the region went to fee-paying schools, a rate that was one of the lowest in the nation (the national average was 10.3 percent). While there were towns, particularly in heavily black areas, where whites had abandoned public schools, overall most white children had stayed in the state system.[40]

While some of these white parents simply could not afford private school fees, others had chosen to support the public schools. Their voices were not always loud or obvious, yet they too deserve to be heard. A resident of Laurinburg, North Carolina, Mrs. Hugh M. McArn wrote Congressman Charles Raper Jonas in 1971 to explain why she had kept her children in the public schools. "Let's remember that parents who send their children off to private schools simply to avoid integration and busing are cheating their children out of the experience of learning to get along with all races etc. now, when they are young and it is easier for them to adjust," she explained. "Don't you feel that it is every citizen's duty to support and upgrade the public schools as hard as it may be on our children and on us?" There was no record of a reply from Jonas, an outspoken opponent of busing.[41]

"Let's All Work to Keep Our Public Schools in Good Shape"

Across the region, many whites did come to accept busing plans. "Here in the South," wrote the visiting journalist James T. Wooten in 1972, "most families have complied, however reluctantly, with court-ordered plans for busing, pairing, zoning and other techniques." By September 1973, when another writer traveled to the region, he found that the public schools were operating largely peacefully.[42] On the tenth anniversary of Martin Luther King's "Dream" speech, the *New York Times* noted that the South's schools had made "enormous" progress. "Despite the rancor that accompanied many of the changes," added Jon Nordheimer, "and the bleak failures in school districts where the white parents withdrew their children from the system, the institution of segregated schools in the South collapsed." While there was a great deal of resistance, this should not obscure how many whites and blacks had worked together through trying circumstances. As the U.S. Commission on Civil Rights observed in 1972, conditions at the grassroots level often contradicted the headlines, which concentrated on protests and conflict. In reality, most schools were relatively peaceful.[43]

The example of several communities helps throw light on this process and shows that support from white leaders and interracial dialogue were key elements. In Memphis, moderate whites strove to implement a busing plan that was drawn up by district judge Robert M. McRae Jr. Designed in 1972, McRae's order called for the transportation of thirteen thousand elementary and junior high students. A few months before it was enacted, the chamber of commerce and school board formed Involved Memphis Parents Assisting Children and Teachers. The group conducted a major public relations campaign, telling parents, "Let's all work to keep our public schools in good shape." Although some whites enrolled their children in private schools, the plan was enacted without major incidents. Overall, the SRC considered Memphis to be a "success story," especially as there was no repeat of the major racial disturbances that had occurred there in 1968. In the tenth largest public school system in the country, this was a notable achievement.[44]

Elsewhere, whites also gradually adjusted to busing plans. A city of around 130,000 people, Winston-Salem, North Carolina, still had separate schools in the late 1960s. In 1968, the NAACP LDF sued the Forsyth County School Board, setting in motion a case that produced dramatic changes. In June 1970, the district court paired several black elementary schools with white schools and pushed the school board to increase the pace of desegregation. Inspired by Nixon's rhetoric, white parents formed a group called the Silent Majority and vigorously fought these efforts. Silent Majority members attended school board meetings in large numbers, wrote numerous letters to the media, and coordinated student boycotts of the schools. Using the language of freedom of choice, they also petitioned the president. "We ask your help," they wrote, "in keeping this a free country and in so doing, allowing us to keep the freedom we now have of sending our children to the schools of our choice." When the school board began to require busing in the 1971–1972 school year, opposition intensified, with objections again focusing on the transportation of white youngsters to formerly black schools.[45]

When staff from the U.S. Commission on Civil Rights visited Winston-Salem's schools in early 1972, however, they found that opposition was fading. While many whites still disliked busing, they saw the benefits of desegregated schools, and they also recognized that there were few alternatives to the court's plan. "I hate the busing, I really hate it. But to return at this point to all white or black schools would be a disaster," acknowledged one white mother. Again, strong leadership helped ease tensions. Crucially, the school board hired a human relations specialist who worked with students and parents, school principals were taught conflict resolution techniques, and seminars were held throughout the year to help students and teachers adjust. The school board also headed off black protests by ensuring that all student organizations were racially mixed. The local press played its part; reacting to *Swann*, the *Winston-Salem Journal* declared that "uncertainties" had been removed and urged compliance. Crucially, students played a key role. While initially reluctant to transfer, many soon took pride in their schools and were keen to resolve disputes. While some tensions still existed, Winston-Salem had clearly weathered the storm. Again, however, some middle-class whites opted out, and two new private schools were set up in the wake of court-ordered integration.[46]

Tampa provides another illustration of how skeptical whites could adjust to busing, especially when school administrators and civic officials exerted effective leadership. Rather than appeal a May 1971 order that required both pairing and busing, the school board appointed an interracial committee that was composed of about 150 community representatives. Using Title IV funds, the school board also hired specialists to work out racial problems, while, within every school, biracial student committees tried to build understanding. Even with these mechanisms in place, incidents still occurred. In September 1971, two students at a formerly white high school painted a large sign in the school yard that said "Niggers Go Home." When black students saw the message, about fifty of them rampaged through the school and seriously injured nine whites. Once tensions subsided, however, the schools got back to business, and most parents learned to accept the changes. While some spoke of the benefits of the new order, others were more philosophical. As the commission concluded, "While not stating that they favor integrated schools, many white parents are resigned to integration, as required by law, and are not attempting to thwart it."[47]

These examples show that many of the fears that white parents harbored were unfounded, a conclusion borne out by broader examinations. In 1973, a federally sponsored study of 555 recently desegregated southern schools found "no evidence that busing per se has any negative consequences." More important, according to the research, was the way in which desegregation was handled. As case studies indicate, it was the commitment of administrators and parents to the process that was crucial, not the method used to bring it about. Similar results were noted by the U.S. Commission on Civil Rights, which concluded that "standards had not been lowered in any way" because of busing.[48]

The city that started it all, Charlotte, illustrates well how genuine progress was made in these years, although it also shows how the African American community ended up paying a heavy physical and emotional price. As was the case elsewhere, transporting students across town was a last resort for a city that was residentially segregated. As early as September 1957, Dorothy Counts had been one of the first black students to attend an all-white school in the city, but she was harassed and withdrew after just four days. Three years later, the city and county schools were consolidated, a crucial move that later made busing more tenable. In the short term, however, officials were slow to accept more than a few blacks into white schools. During the 1959–1960 school year, only one African American attended a white school, three fewer than two years earlier.[49]

Some brave parents sought to change this. They were led by Darius and Vera Swann, who in 1964 sought to enroll their six-year-old son, James, into the all-white Seversville school. Former missionaries who had moved to Charlotte from India, the Swanns were unwilling to accept the existence of segregated schools. "We believe that an integrated school will best prepare young people for responsibility in an integrated society," they wrote the local board of education. "Having lived practically all of his life in India, James has never known the meaning of racial segregation." Despite these efforts, Seversville principal Scott Thrower turned down James's application on the grounds that the Swanns did not live in the school's "attendance area." Angered by not being able to enroll their son in his local school, the Swanns headed a broad school desegregation suit.[50]

Although Judge J. Braxton Craven Jr. upheld the school board's position and an appeal was unsuccessful, the plaintiffs continued to press for further desegregation. In late 1968, the case was reheard at a more favorable time, just as the courts were rejecting freedom-of-choice plans because of their failure to produce meaningful results. The following April, the newly appointed federal judge James McMillan issued a pathbreaking order that required the local school board to use busing to eliminate racially identifiable schools. A native North Carolinian, McMillan recognized that the dual school system still existed and that it was upheld by a variety of means, including gerrymandered district lines and freedom-of-choice policies. In a bold move, he told the school board to come up with a plan that eliminated the racial identifiability of all the district's schools.[51]

At the time, McMillan was considered an establishment lawyer, and many were surprised that he had boldly called for the desegregation of one of the largest school systems in the country. The breakthrough was partly due to Julius Chambers, the gifted LDF attorney who had brought the case. Chambers showed that children in Charlotte's all-black schools were underperforming on standard achievement tests, results that surprised McMillan. "I lived here for 24 years without knowing what was going on," he acknowledged. "I really didn't know." Confronted with such compelling evidence, the judge felt that he had to take decisive action. As he wrote another lawyer at the time, "My respect for the judicial process is high enough that when I find it leads down unpopular roads I think the process rather than comfortable prejudice or avoidance of a tough issue is what should merit respect and what should guide my actions."[52]

McMillan's decree was strongly opposed, especially by middle-class whites. "If anyone thinks they're going to bus my children across town to make room for someone else's child from across town, without a fight, they're dreaming," fumed Mrs. Charles Warren. Warren explained that she had worked hard to buy her brick house in the suburbs and felt that she should be able to send her children to local schools.[53] Informed by what the historian Matthew D. Lassiter has termed "the suburban ethos of middle-class entitlement," similar letters poured in from affluent districts on the eastern side of the city. "I think it is a disgrace to pick my child up and take her across town to put her in another school in the interest of the minority group when I bought my home because it was near the school," wrote Mrs. Geraldine T. Barris in June 1969. Some residents feared that busing would lead to a fall in house prices, undermining the value of their most precious asset. Stirred by Nixon's oratory, many threatened action if their concerns were not heeded. "We have no further recourse in the courts," seethed the local doctor G. Don Roberson in a letter to Congressman Jonas. "Every legal channel has been to no avail. The unorganized silent majority is about ready to take to the streets with tactics that have seemed to work so effectively for the vocal minority groups."[54]

As Roberson's letter indicates, the climate in Charlotte was extremely tense at this time. After issuing his order, McMillan received death threats and had to confront picketers outside his home. Fearing for his life, he even carried a pistol for self-protection. Chambers also received hate mail. "There's going to be more blood shed in Charlotte because of busing," blasted one anonymous writer in 1971. "Why don't you Niggers go home to Africa. Martin Luther King was warned to leave for Africa or die here, he got it."[55] These were not empty threats; during the 1970–1971 school year, arsonists destroyed Chambers's legal offices and attacked the service station run by his father in Mount Gilead, the small town where Julius had himself attended segregated schools. The tension also spilled over into Charlotte's schools, where white and black students fought one another. "It really was not a pleasant experience during integration," admitted the black teacher Daisy S. Stroud.[56]

Other whites sought to overthrow McMillan's order through legal means. Insisting that the judge had gone too far, school board chair William Poe called the decision "utter folly." An influential member of the Charlotte bar, Poe urged the board to appeal. Mobilized by the order, the newly chartered Concerned Parents Association (CPA) also organized rallies that drew crowds of up to ten thousand people. In the spring of 1970, three CPA members were elected to six-year terms on the school board, which now had a conservative majority. The CPA was most concerned about the busing of elementary school children in and out of the main black section, which was located northwest of downtown. Members objected vehemently to the pairing of thirty-four elementary schools in order to integrate 15,301 white children with 7,077 black ones.[57]

The CPA did not represent all whites in Charlotte, however. Led by its editor, C. A. "Pete" McKnight, who had spoken out against segregation as early as 1950, the influential *Charlotte Observer* supported the busing plan. McKnight grasped that racial disturbances could hurt the thriving local economy, and growth-obsessed civic leaders desperately wanted to avoid this. In April 1963, for instance, city officials had agreed to voluntarily desegregate hotels during a trade fair.[58] Even at the height of the school crisis, Chambers received support from whites, particularly business owners. As the attorney acknowledged in 1970, "I have felt all along that notwithstanding the loud noises there were still, at least, many responsible people residing in the city."[59]

Students also played a crucial role in implementing the plan. Following the interracial fights of early 1970, pupils at several high schools conducted "love-ins" in order to build understanding. "It was like old-time religion," commented the high school principal Dr. Laird Lewis. "There were white and black, rich and poor, expressing mutual respect and love for one another." By making friendships across the color line, children nudged their parents to reconsider their views. Even before the Supreme Court had upheld McMillan's order, the SRC was optimistic about the city's future. "Given half a chance," it noted in a detailed study, "Charlotte could achieve real integration, and that would mean real education."[60]

The resolution of *Swann* also helped racial moderates. With no more courts to appeal to, many white leaders insisted that it was now time to accept the inevitable. Often, residents were ready to listen to such advice. As the local stockbroker Jerry Hoogenaker commented, "Busing is probably inequitable, but if that's what it takes to achieve equality it's just got to be done." Proud of their state's progressive image, many citizens also wanted to prove that they could implement the ruling successfully.[61]

By the time that the Supreme Court made its decision, many whites had also had time to get used to busing. As Daisy Stroud recalled, as the plan was implemented white parents' views gradually softened. "I found out that the white parents were most supportive if you helped their child," she explained. "And so if they got the idea that you were helping their children, there was no problem." Some local parents were even prepared to admit that they had been wrong. "It [busing] hasn't upset my child like I expected," commented Mrs. Leroy Spoon in 1971, "and though I'm surprised to hear myself say this, I think in years to come we'll see that it's something that had to be done. Desegregation would never have happened if it had been left to the people." While some whites had clearly moderated their views, others had simply become weary of the controversy. "I wouldn't care if they bused my children to South Carolina, I'm so tired of it all," admitted another parent at the time.[62]

School administrators also took steps to ease tensions, particularly within the white community. At West Charlotte High, a formerly black school, an additional guidance counselor was added for the 1971–1972 session, and the school also appointed a principal from a white school. Across the city, teachers also tried to listen to parents' concerns. Because they believed in public education, few teachers quit during these difficult years; in 1972, the turnover rate among faculty members was actually lower than it had been several years earlier. Administrators also arranged for a group of interracial ministers to patrol campuses when there were signs of racial problems, while more than four thousand citizens worked as volunteers during the integration process.[63]

Under the capable leadership of Kelly Alexander Sr., the local NAACP also helped create a constructive climate. An independent funeral director, Alexander had founded the Charlotte branch in 1940, and he went on to become the association's statewide president, a position he held for thirty-six years. By the early 1970s, he used his considerable influence to sell busing to the African American community. Aware of how blacks were often sidelined when they moved to white schools, he also tried to make the process as equitable as possible. At two large high schools, for instance, the NAACP organized youth councils. Helped by Kelly M. Alexander Jr., young activists overcame opposition from white principals and secured a number of concrete improvements, including the introduction of black history into the curriculum and the provision of bus transportation so that poor parents could attend PTA meetings. "It is simply not enough to integrate a building," explained Alexander Jr. "We must take care that within that building our children receive a quality education."[64]

While its views were diverse, Charlotte's African American community generally recognized the benefits that busing could deliver. Transported across town in the early years of the plan, Timothy Gibbs felt that the sacrifices he made were essential. Because neighborhoods were segregated, residents needed a "motivation . . . to venture out and mix and mingle amongst people that aren't like them." Another student at the time, Madelyn Wilson, recalled that most black pupils "were a little anxious" about changing schools but that they helped motivate one another. "We said, 'OK, if we've got to go, we're going together,'" she recalled. Overall, Wilson was more ambivalent about her experiences than Gibbs. "In the long run, I know there was some good that came out of it," she stated, "[but] I know that there were some people who were damaged and scarred."[65]

As Wilson's remarks indicate, African Americans had some negative memories of these years, partly because most black schools were closed. Black students were often proud of these schools, where they had forged close relationships with particular teachers and administrators. In their new schools, in contrast, black pupils were harassed by white students and often ignored by teachers. When interracial violence occurred, it was also black students that were harshly punished. During the 1970–1971 school year, for example, the Charlotte-Mecklenburg system suspended four thousand students, 90 percent of them black.[66]

In November 1972, black students at six high schools convened a special mass meeting to discuss these problems. "We, the Youth of Charlotte," they declared, "feel that we can no longer sit idly by while Black students suffer injustices at the hands of the Charlotte-Mecklenburg school system." Although the meeting helped voice grievances, tensions still existed. In March 1973, the schools were hit by a new wave of disorders as black pupils pressed for more representation. Investigating the disturbances, the NAACP LDF again blamed the attitudes of white teachers and administrators. "Black students generally feel that white students planned the trouble and at the same time these students refused to be dominated by the white students or the white administration without being heard," concluded the staffer Reginald Smith.[67]

These problems tested the resolve of the African American community. Many adults worried about the closure of historic black schools and the consequences this would have for their communities. In addition, parents were concerned about the safety of their children and the time they spent on the buses. Unlike many of their white counterparts, however, blacks generally reasoned that such sacrifices were worth it. "I was kind of bothered about tiny little black children standing in the dark," recalled the teacher Patsy Rice Camp. "Bothered me a great deal. [I] thought it was unfair that the little ones had to get up so early and go so far. At the same time I knew that at that particular time that was the only equity we were going to be able to get." In the final analysis, most citizens agreed with Camp. As the janitor Sam Brooks told the press, "Busing is the only way to get things the way they should be and we'll manage."[68]

As the busing plan was implemented, other problems emerged. While most whites tried to carry out the order, a minority sought to evade it, chiefly by supporting private schools. "To be sure," notes the scholar Davison Douglas, "white enrollments in the public schools did decline following implementation of the busing plan." Between 1970 and 1972, the U.S. Commission on Civil Rights estimated that up to eight thousand students, or around 10 percent of total enrollment, had left the school system as a result of desegregation. In this time, at least five new private schools were established in the Charlotte area. As they took their children out of the public schools, some parents admitted the importance of racial fears. Reacting to *Swann*, Mrs. Grace J. Broskie wrote, "I shall move from Charlotte, to another county, where the taxes aren't so high, so I can afford to put my child in a private school. . . . The forcing of integration is causing cities across our Nation to become another Washington, D.C."[69]

In addition, some well-heeled whites used proxy addresses to ensure that their children were not bused. In 1972, one anonymous businessman admitted that he rented a small apartment near the downtown and still made payments on his suburban house. The apartment stood empty, but, because it was listed as his official residence, his teenage daughter was spared a lengthy ride to an all-black school. "She has a right not to be carted thirty miles a day for an education," asserted the man. This experience was not unusual; Chambers received many reports of parents who rented apartments in other districts or used relatives' addresses on their school forms. Overburdened school officials accepted that they could not investigate every case. "As long as there are those who make up their minds to get around the plan, we are going to have these schemes," acknowledged William Self, the superintendent of the Charlotte schools.[70]

Some whites never reconciled themselves to the changes and, instead, claimed that McMillan and Chambers had ruined the public schools. Writing to Chambers in March 1973, the local man John E. Cobb encapsulated this mood perfectly. Cobb explained that his son wanted a professional career but insisted that the public schools were not up to the task of preparing him for it. "Thanks to Judge McMillan and you," he charged, "it appears that I am going to have to place my son in a private school. . . . We used to have a very fine educational system in Charlotte and it was something to be proud of. I am sorry to say that this is no longer true. . . . I hope that you are satisfied in what you have helped to create." A forthright man, Chambers responded by telling Cobb to support the public schools rather than "trying to perpetuate a haven that should long ago have passed."[71]

Despite these problems, the overall picture was encouraging. As early as January 1972, Chambers reported that the plan was "working well and students and parents are adjusting." After two years, some white parents were proud of the changes that had occurred. As one wrote McMillan in May 1973, "I think real good has been accomplished in changing attitudes toward the blacks bused in. . . . Our junior high school even has a black principal now."[72] In late 1974, McMillan deactivated the *Swann* litigation because he was satisfied that every school remained within the court-ordered racial ratios. Impressively, the formerly black West Charlotte High School now had a 61 percent white enrollment. While they remained concerned about discriminatory practices within the schools, the plaintiffs' lawyers did not contest McMillan's decision.[73] In the years that followed, Charlotte's schools were held up as a role model; in 1978, for example, *U.S. News and World Report* declared that the Queen City had "probably the most thoroughly integrated school system in the entire United States." While most metropolitan school districts had become heavily black, Charlotte had managed to avoid this fate, although only by constantly moving pupils around. Between 1970 and 1974, McMillan carefully adjusted busing routes to maintain white majorities.[74]

Not all the changes can be attributed to human endeavor as Charlotte-Mecklenburg had several natural advantages. The school system was predominantly white, avoiding the need to bus large numbers of whites to majority-black schools. In general, such assignments were the most unpopular. In addition, it was crucial that Mecklenburg County contained only one school district; this ensured that white parents who wanted to avoid desegregation had to leave the county altogether. The size of the county (forty miles by twenty) made this very difficult, especially as Charlotte was located in the center. As a result, white parents could not easily work in Charlotte and live outside the school district. An African American teacher and administrator, Elizabeth Schmoke Randolph, acknowledged these advantages. "We would never have satisfactorily . . . desegregated the schools if we had not yet consolidated the city and the county into one school system," she asserted in 1993. After a lifetime in education, Randolph was in no doubt that the battle had been worth it. "I would never go back to the segregated schools, never go back," she concluded.[75]

Although a case study of Charlotte illustrates that southern blacks and whites could find common ground, it also reminds us that the two races had very different experiences and memories. Once they decided to accept the ruling, whites emphasized that there were few problems, whereas blacks were a lot more conscious of continuing difficulties. Looking back, whites pushed the view that Charlotte had desegregated smoothly and was a city characterized by its "progressiveness." Keen to attract outside investment, civic leaders were soon pitching Charlotte as "The City That Made It Work," a view that African Americans disputed. Assigned to teach in a part of town that she had never even visited, Daisy S. Stroud repeatedly described her experience as "very traumatic." When questioned by an interviewer from the University of North Carolina at Charlotte, Stroud rejected the idea that the city's experience with integration had been uneventful. "I don't think it was smooth at all," she stated. "It was a rough, rough road. . . . It was not peaceful at all." In the early 1970s, southern blacks made many other gains, but this disparity in experience would be constantly apparent.[76]

6

HOME HAS CHANGED

Southern Race Relations in the Early 1970s

Away from the classroom, black southerners made some significant gains in the early 1970s. The rapid integration of public facilities prompted many to move to the region, reversing a pattern of out-migration that dated back to World War I. In these years, African Americans also emerged as a decisive political force; in 1971, for instance, the Harvard psychologist Thomas Pettigrew went as far as to call the black surge into southern politics "a miracle, literally a miracle." While the economic picture was mixed, southern blacks certainly made some progress, and the media asserted that a black middle class was emerging. Much remained to be achieved, however, and blacks refuted suggestions that they were making dramatic economic strides. The national economy slowed in these years, developing into a lasting recession that had a devastating impact on the African American community.[1]

"I Don't Mind Seeing Them in Restaurants"

In the early 1970s, the most dramatic changes occurred in everyday race relations. In August 1973, the journalist B. Drummond Ayres Jr. visited Jackson, Mississippi, and found that blacks were using public facilities freely. Breaking deeply held taboos, the two races even swam together in hotel pools. It was a rapid transformation; as recently as 1963, Jackson police had arrested hundreds of civil rights demonstrators and hauled them away in dirty garbage trucks. At that time, the local resident Medgar Evers had been assassinated because he had sought an end to the Jim Crow system. The pace of change surprised many locals, yet both races were becoming accustomed to the new order. Even the Ku Klux Klan leader Joe Denver Hawkins acknowledged, "I've come to where I don't mind seeing them [blacks] in restaurants."[2]

In smaller communities, remarkable changes were also under way. Anxious to attract outside investment, most white leaders wanted to avoid racial strife, and their example was helping forge a new society. While white visitors to the South often commented on this transformation, blacks also noticed it. "Home had changed," noted the African American writer J. K. Obatala, who took a trip back to Tifton, Georgia, in 1973. Obatala was surprised to find that whites were now willing to converse freely with blacks, who were served courteously in the downtown stores. One store that had once refused to serve blacks while whites "sat in what appeared to be the greatest comfort" now even had a black saleswoman.[3]

Crucially, the fear that had held segregation in place was disappearing, largely because violent attacks on blacks were becoming unusual. As the New York Times's Paul Delaney declared in September 1973, "Perhaps the most remarkable change in recent times in this fast-growing region [is] the virtual disappearance of random violence against blacks that went unpunished." Delaney linked the shift to the growth in black political power, including the election of black law enforcement officers. At the local level, many blacks noticed the differences. "Black people are not afraid of whites any more," asserted the Alabamian Mattie Powell. "Maybe a few older people are, but younger blacks are not."[4]

Beneath the surface, of course, there was continuity. Whites still held the best jobs and monopolized key political positions, particularly on school boards. Even in Tifton, the white-dominated school board was opposed to busing, and most blacks toiled in low-paying jobs. In Jackson, too, blacks remained much poorer than whites, and the crumbling black neighborhoods were unchanged.[5] In the public accommodations area as a whole, there were some restaurants and bars that continued to deny service to blacks, particularly in the rural Deep South. In December 1971, for example, staff at the Three Way Truck Stop in Bude, Mississippi, turned the black truck driver Jessie Kyles away. "We ain't never served any colored people in here, and we ain't about to start doing that now," they told him. The treatment stunned Kyles, a proud provider for a wife and ten children. "The dehumanizing incident almost destroyed my appetite," he wrote in a complaint.[6]

While they were shocking, such incidents were now exceptional; as LDF director Jack Greenberg wrote in 1971, his group was no longer filing Title II cases because there was "a very substantial degree of compliance." Over the South as a whole, enough change had occurred to cause many blacks to migrate back. Given that African Americans had been fleeing the region for decades, this was a notable shift. "After more than 100 years of migration by black Americans from the South to the North, a trend toward a turnaround seems to be developing," declared U.S. News and World Report in 1973. Between 1965 and 1970, census data showed that 162,000 blacks moved to the South, a 32 percent increase over the period 1955–1960. Although some blacks left northern cities because they were tired of crime and cold weather, they were also pulled south by the improved racial situation. As the African American writer Mary Mebane noted in 1972, "The primary reason for the influx of blacks into the South is the Civil Rights Acts of 1964–65. Once the overt signs of racial discrimination were removed—'White Only' and 'Colored Only'—and some of the most vicious racist practices discontinued, either because of Government action or black political muscle, the North lost much of its allure."[7]

Individual stories support Mebane's point. The druggists Andrea and Mack Harris, for example, moved from Chicago to Gulfport, Mississippi, in order to open their own business. "The civil rights legislation of the 1960s changed the South to such an extent I can't believe it is the same place," commented Andrea, who had been raised in the Gulfport area. Others had similar experiences. A former Marine major, J. Gary Cooper, returned to Mobile in the early 1970s to sell insurance, and he was one of many to benefit from the NPVL's efforts to desegregate public accommodations. "I remember days as a young Marine lieutenant when I returned to Mobile and was told to sit in the back of the bus," he explained. "Little incidents like that told me Mobile was not the place for me. But today, I find a completely different climate. There are still problems, but a lot of progress has been made." Returning migrants even asserted that northern racism was now more insidious and troubling. "It is harder to deal with hidden prejudices," claimed one.[8]

One prominent returnee was James Meredith, who had precipitated a riot when he had tried to enroll at the University of Mississippi. When Meredith started classes in 1962, federal troops had to be mobilized to control the tense situation.[9] After graduating, the Kosciusko native lived in New York City for six years, but, in the early 1970s, he began to visit his home state and decided to move back. The atmosphere, he asserted, was "significantly better" as blacks could use public facilities without experiencing "embarrassment" and "humiliation." Now a lawyer, Meredith also hoped to develop black economic power because he saw this as the most effective way to help local people.[10]

Hope and Despair: Southern Blacks and Politics in the Early 1970s

In the early 1970s, more and more southern blacks took advantage of the Voting Rights Act. In 1972, even a critical report by the Washington Research Project (WRP), an independent civil rights group, acknowledged the changes. "The past seven years have been ones of progress for black political participation in the South," it concluded. "A significant proportion and number of blacks are now registered to vote in all states of the South." Thanks largely to the legislation, black registration had almost trebled, rising from 1.3 to 3.4 million in the course of a decade. Across the region, white candidates now recognized the black electorate, and the race-baiting campaigns of the past were almost unheard of. Some candidates were also realizing that, rather than being a liability, the black vote could actually help them.[11]

By the early 1970s, African Americans also held many elected offices, particularly in majority-black counties. In June 1973, there were 1,144 black elected officials in the South, around half the national total. This was an impressive advance on the 72 offices blacks had held when the act was passed. Once strongholds of segregation, Alabama and Mississippi led the way. By 1971, Alabama had 105 black elected officials, more than any other state except Michigan and New York. In Greene County, blacks controlled the administrative apparatus after securing the election of a new probate judge and a new sheriff as well as a county clerk and two school board members. As the *New Republic* noted, these victories were "a direct outgrowth of the Voting Rights Act of 1965." Greene County was now the only biracial community in the country where both the administrative and the educational apparatuses were directed by blacks. A black man also sat in the sheriff's office in Lowndes County, where no African Americans had even been registered to vote when the Montgomery-bound marchers had passed through the area six years earlier. Helped by the SNCC, which had set up the original Black Panther Party in the county, local blacks had become a political force.[12]

Many southern blacks now saw political activism as the best way of carrying on the civil rights struggle. With strong laws on the books, they believed that this was more effective than direct action protests, which were becoming rare. "Anyone looking for the civil rights movement in the streets is fooling himself," declared the new Atlanta mayor, Maynard Jackson, in 1973. "Politics is the civil rights movement of the 1970s. Politics is the last non-violent hurrah."[13] Shortly after Dr. King's funeral, Jackson decided to enter politics because he saw it as "the best available non-violent means of changing how we live." Other movement activists made the same choice. By the end of 1973, the black leaders Mrs. Amelia Boynton and the Reverend F. D. Reese sat on the city council in Selma, while former SCLC staffers had been elected to council positions in Atlanta and Sandersville, Georgia. In Mobile, John L. LeFlore also won a seat in the Alabama state legislature by drawing on his long record as a civil rights leader. Noting these changes, SCLC president Ralph Abernathy asserted, "The Movement is far from dead—no matter what you read or hear."[14]

Jackson's election was emblematic of broader changes. A towering man who weighed close to three hundred pounds, he became the first black mayor of a major southern city. The capital of a key southern state and a burgeoning metropolis, Atlanta had tremendous economic and cultural importance. Jackson's election inspired hope among African Americans, but it also created tremendous expectations. "All of a sudden," recalled Jackson, "I became the mayor not just of Atlanta, but of black people in Georgia and even some neighboring states. That was an extraordinary burden."[15]

Jackson won a hard-fought election in which his opponent appealed to the fears of the city's dwindling white population. Sam Massell's campaign slogan was "Atlanta's Too Young to Die," which many whites interpreted as a warning that a black mayor would ruin the city. By 1973, the city's population was predominantly black, and Jackson owed his victory to the mobilization of these voters. He received an impressive 95 percent of black votes, while Massell got 83 percent of white votes.[16] In his inaugural address, Jackson asked "all Atlantans" to "work together for the good of our City." It was easier said than done; the white business community fought Jackson's plans to give a greater share of city contracts to black businesses, and he received negative press from the influential *Atlanta Constitution*. Looking back, Jackson recalled that he had to confront an "exaggerated anxiety" in the white community. "That anxiety," he added, "was, 'Oh, my God, what are we going to do? We've got a black mayor! What does this mean? Is this the end of Atlanta?'" Jackson was unable to allay these fears, and whites fled the city in record numbers while he was in office. Even in the Sun Belt South, the two races were deeply polarized.[17]

In these years, civil rights groups carried out essential work to make political breakthroughs possible. In particular, lawyers from both the SPLC and the NAACP thwarted white efforts to dilute black political power. In 1970, for example, the two organizations brought a class action suit on behalf of black voters in Alabama's three major cities. In Montgomery, the key plaintiff was E. D. Nixon, the veteran activist who had helped initiate the 1955–1956 bus boycott. Assisted by the retired Pullman train porter, the plaintiffs argued that the all-white Alabama state legislature was "racist" because it had deliberately diluted the black "ghetto" vote. As Dees later wrote, "The state had been gerrymandered into large, white-majority, multi-member districts to prevent blacks from getting elected." Citing the Voting Rights Act, the plaintiffs argued that black votes should be "meaningful."[18]

Despite opposition from white politicians, in 1972 a panel of three federal judges sided with the plaintiffs and ordered the House to reapportion itself into new districts. "Further delay is inappropriate," declared the court. Later in the year, the U.S. Supreme Court affirmed this decision. As a result, Alabama now had the only court-ordered single-member district plan in the nation, ensuring that blocs of minority votes could not be offset or split by white majorities. The landmark ruling produced a rapid increase in black political representation. In the 1974 elections alone, seventeen black legislators won office, an increase of fourteen.[19]

Both groups also won smaller cases that increased black political power in Alabama. After a lengthy battle, the SPLC secured a ruling that the government of Montgomery County was unconstitutionally elected under an at-large system. In 1972, the NAACP also proved in federal court that city officials in Uniontown, Alabama, were disqualifying registered black voters. The court ordered that the names of all eligible voters be placed on the lists, a move that paved the way for the election of a black mayor and three black council members. In a small Black Belt community, this represented a huge transformation.[20]

In South Carolina, the NAACP also fought to stop the state legislature from being elected on an at-large basis. Brought in 1972, this case was typical of the association's efforts to prevent voters in a jurisdiction at-large from voting for all the contested seats on a government body such as a city council or a county commission. As black voting increased steadily, at-large elections became increasingly common, and some localities used the system to try and negate the impact of the Voting Rights Act. Many studies have shown that at-large elections disadvantage ethnic minorities, especially when there was a history of opposition to minority participation in politics. Under the district system, in contrast, blacks fared better because they usually lived in well-defined, segregated neighborhoods. Because few whites were willing to support black candidates, it was vital for blacks to get single-member districts if they were to be fairly represented.[21]

Working with the Columbia attorney Matthew J. Perry, the South Carolina plaintiffs argued that the at-large system worked to "dilute and cancel out" black voting strength because most African Americans voted "as a bloc." They explained that, as few southern whites would vote for black candidates, majority-black districts were essential. "Race is an ever present issue in South Carolina elections," argued Perry in a polished and persuasive brief. "The testimony is clear in showing that progress has been made toward eliminating race as an issue, but that there is a long way to go.... Substantial numbers of white voters ... simply will not vote for a candidate who is black or is identified with the interests of black voters." Under pressure from the NAACP, the state revised its reapportionment plans.[22] Again, similar victories also occurred at the local level. As the historian Orville Vernon Burton has documented, the shift to single-member districts "substantially increased" black representation on county councils right across the Palmetto State.[23]

In Georgia, the NAACP also fought for black political rights. In October 1971, the General Assembly reapportioned the state's ten congressional districts so that each contained around 460,000 residents. Under the law, the heavily black parts of Atlanta were divided up into three separate districts. It was an obvious effort to exclude blacks from the congressional delegation, especially as the homes of potential African American candidates were deliberately barred from the boundaries of the new fifth district. Appealing the plan, NAACP attorneys argued that the move violated both the Fifteenth Amendment and the Voting Rights Act. It was designed, they asserted, to "undermine and destroy the present and potential effectiveness of Black urban voters . . . and to benefit White Atlanta suburban voters." In 1972, the Justice Department backed the NAACP and forced the state to enact a new plan that increased the number of black voters in the main Atlanta district.[24]

The move cleared the way for the election of Andrew Young, the former SCLC leader who had also moved into political life. In 1972, the talented activist became Georgia's first black congressional representative since Reconstruction. Young's election was a powerful symbol of how the black vote had transformed the South's political landscape. In a state where the General Assembly had passed a restrictive literacy test as recently as 1958, it was a remarkable turnaround. "Andy's ascension was cause for us all to celebrate," noted John Lewis, "something to hold up to the people we were working with through the VEP—the Deep South's first black U.S. congressman of the century."[25]

On the eve of the 1972 congressional elections, Young was predicted to lose by 4 percentage points to the liberal Republican Rodney Cook, but he turned the situation around by mobilizing white voters concerned about environmental issues and the high cost of the Vietnam War. Young's victory was also a reflection of his extensive efforts to get out the black vote; on a rainy election day, his staff transported over six thousand blacks to the polls. As a trained Congregational minister, Young was also adept at inspiring black voters. The New Orleans native viewed his success as representative of what the civil rights movement had achieved in a short space of time. "Walking the halls of Gilbert Academy and later the lonely Highway 80 from Selma to Montgomery," he wrote in his memoirs, "I could never have imagined myself in the halls of the United States Congress."[26]

As the Georgia redistricting suit highlighted, the Justice Department was also responsible for important political breakthroughs. After 1970, the department's efforts shifted from registering black voters to objecting to changes that diluted the black vote. As Assistant Attorney General J. Stanley Pottinger explained, this switch came about because resistance to black registration had "significantly dissipated." Concentrating on what Pottinger termed the "second phase" of implementation, between 1971 and 1973 department attorneys disallowed 160 changes in voting rules because they would have violated section 5 of the Voting Rights Act. In one typical case, federal lawyers forced officials in Petersburg, Virginia, to adopt single-member districts, a change that facilitated the election of four African Americans to the city council.[27] Some of the agency's work had a broad impact. In 1971, Attorney General John Mitchell objected to the reapportionment of both houses of Louisiana's state legislature on the grounds that the plan was designed to reduce black voting strength. These actions paved the way for the creation of single-member districts in the Pelican State, a crucial shift. Over the course of the 1970s, the number of African Americans in Louisiana's legislature jumped from one to ten.[28]

In these years, the black vote also had an impact on white politicians, and even the movement's former enemies were affected. By 1971, for instance, Laurie Pritchett was the police chief of High Point, North Carolina, a furnituremaking center located over four hundred miles north of Albany, Georgia, where Pritchett had made his name for arresting over fifteen hundred black demonstrators in 1961–1962. Then, Pritchett had closed municipal facilities rather than desegregate, but a decade later he was keen to put these events behind him.[29] "Albany has been an embarrassment to me over the years," he claimed. "The power structure in Albany made the law, and I had to enforce it or quit. I enforced their law, but not their philosophy. I didn't agree with their philosophy." After starting a new life in High Point, Pritchett reached out to the African American community. Although he hired several black police officers, some were not convinced that he had really changed. "If the power structure here wanted him to act as he did in Albany, there's no question that he would," asserted the local black lawyer John Langford. Backed by both races, however, Pritchett served as High Point's police chief until his retirement in 1974.[30]

The truth was that elected officials had to moderate their views if they wanted to stay in office; the alternative was isolation. During the Birmingham demonstrations of 1963, Commissioner of Public Safety Eugene "Bull" Connor achieved national notoriety when he turned firehouses and police dogs on peaceful black demonstrators. As he snapped out orders and toured the city in his white tank, Connor became a potent symbol of the segregationist power structure. The veteran official lost his post after the demonstrations, however, and, by 1972, he was an insignificant figure who had been unable to get reelected to the Alabama Public Service Commission. The following year, the seventy-five-year-old suffered a massive stroke and died in an integrated Birmingham hospital.[31]

Another symbol of Jim Crow, Sheriff Jim Clark, also lost his post soon after the Selma protests. In 1966, public safety director Wilson Baker reached out to the city's new black voters and defeated Clark quite easily. There was no way back for a man who sported a lapel button that read "Never." By the early 1970s, Clark was an obscure businessman and had little hope of a return to public life. Later in the decade, his credibility was completely destroyed when he was convicted of smuggling $4.3 million of marijuana into the United States.[32] With Clark on the sidelines, Selma's blacks continued to make political strides; in August 1972, for example, five African Americans were elected to the ten-member city council, which had been all white. While Mayor Joseph Smitherman was still in formal control, he had reached out to black voters in order to keep his position.[33]

As their political power increased, African Americans were able to press for important civil rights leaders to be recognized. Responding to this pressure, on June 12, 1973, Mississippi governor William Waller called for a statewide observance of Medgar Evers Memorial Festival Day. The day marked the tenth anniversary of the night that the NAACP's field secretary had been assassinated on the porch of his Jackson home. Mississippi's first official recognition of a civil rights leader, the move came after lobbying from Charles Evers, who was now a powerful political figure in his own right. As they remembered Medgar Evers, activists also demanded that his killing be reexamined. In 1964, two all-white juries had failed to convict the Klansman Byron de la Beckwith, despite the fact that his fingerprints were identified on a rifle that was found near the scene. Although many years would pass before de la Beckwith was convicted, the increasing awareness of the case created pressure for it to be reopened.[34]

In general, southern whites wanted to forget the civil rights movement, and they resisted calls to commemorate its leaders, particularly Dr. King. In the black community, however, the moves to memorialize King started almost as soon as he was killed, and, by 1971, his birthday was recognized by several northern states. It was a different situation in the South. In Dallas, for example, school board officials refused to acknowledge the significance of January 15. "If you let school out for one person, you will have to do it for others who have done as much until eventually there will be more school holidays than regular school days," commented one civic leader. Undeterred, King's supporters built a powerful movement. In January 1971, for example, Coretta Scott King and Ralph Abernathy presented Congress with eight million signatures that called for January 15 to be declared a national holiday.[35]

At this time, whites were able to rebuff such pleas because black political power was still quite limited. In 1972, the Washington Research

Project explored registration patterns in meticulous detail, finding that southern blacks were still not voting as much as whites. A forerunner of the Children's Defense Fund, the WRP was a nonprofit organization that monitored federal civil rights programs. In both organizations, the black activist Marian Wright Edelman played a leading role. A native of Bennettsville, South Carolina, Edelman was determined to expose the discrimination that still confronted blacks in the rural South. *The Shameful Blight: The Survival of Racial Discrimination in Voting in the South* was a good illustration of the WRP's work. In the 214-page study, researchers documented that, in much of the rural South, black registration rates were 20–30 percent lower than those of whites. As a result, there were some majority-black counties where whites still monopolized the political process. In eastern North Carolina, for instance, Bertie County was 63 percent black, but all its elected officials were white.[36]

Above all, *The Shameful Blight* showed that many blacks were still afraid to vote because they worked for powerful whites. "The greatest barrier to equal political rights for blacks in the South is probably their economically depressed and dependent position," concluded the report. As case studies highlighted, factory workers, maids, and agricultural laborers were particularly affected. "We found," explained VEP workers in Leflore County, Mississippi, "that in order for most of the rural people to go to register it has to be a rainy day because their 'boss' will not let them off work to go and register." The registration process also worked against rural blacks. The limited opening hours aside, the offices were usually located within the county courthouse, a building that remained a compelling symbol of white power. In some cases, registrars also treated black applicants in a demeaning and insulting manner. In 1970–1971, for instance, registrars in at least two Georgia counties continued to use white cards for the registration of whites and brown cards for blacks.[37]

In general, however, open intimidation of black voters was now unusual. More commonly, African Americans hung back because they feared the consequences if they did become politically active. As a black voting rights organization reported from eastern Georgia, "In Warren County we find vast number of poor blacks most expressing fear of registering to vote. Fear that the White landlord will put them in the street (out of his house) and that their welfare check will be cut off or they will be dropped from the food stamp program."[38]

In the early 1970s, whites in many areas also required all voters to reregister, a tactic that had a clear racial impact. By the end of 1971, about thirty counties in Mississippi had been through the reregistration process, which officials justified as a response to redistricting. Civil rights groups, however, felt that the moves were designed to deter black voting, especially as whites generally found it easier to register. "Well, you see, in reregistration, particularly in the rural areas," explained the NAACP's Aaron Henry in 1971, "it is difficult, No. 1, to get a person who lives on plantations to defy his employer or take a position that they are going down to register in the first place, because of fears which in some instances might not be well-founded. But in a man's mind there is that fear and as far as he is concerned, he is afraid." In congressional testimony, Henry added that some politically active blacks had, indeed, been beaten or threatened by whites.[39]

Even when blacks gained political office, moreover, they usually did so in very poor areas. Greene County, Alabama, again provided a revealing example; with an average annual per capita income of just $900, it was the fifth poorest county in the entire country. The population was 80 percent black, and most residents lived in crumbling shacks that lacked indoor plumbing. Rather than joining with blacks to tackle the area's problems, most whites fled once blacks gained political control. "The county is broke anyway, so we ought to let them have it," observed one. Even after they had moved out, however, whites still owned most of the businesses and land in the area.[40]

African American mayors faced similar problems. In 1972, seventy of the new officeholders created the Southern Conference of Black Mayors in order to help them address common problems. Members noted that they had "inherited" poor communities with "monumental problems in the areas of housing, water and sewerage, health, education, employment and community and industrial development." In Uniontown, Alabama, Mayor A. M. Hayden's election was cause for celebration, but the new officeholder presided over a community where most houses still relied on outdoor privies. The community of Prichard, Alabama, epitomized many of the difficulties. Located just north of Mobile, Prichard's population was declining as whites moved out. By the early 1970s, over a quarter of its residents lived below the poverty line, and the black mayor lacked the tax base that he needed in order to provide essential services.[41]

In addition to these difficulties, new black mayors lacked political experience and struggled to meet heightened expectations among their constituents. The ongoing racial divide also ensured that it was often impossible to help blacks without alienating whites. "It's a very fine line to walk," commented the Georgia legislator Julian Bond. "You can't afford to let Group A know you're helping Group B—but you've got to help them." Most mayors also struggled to secure the support of the local business community, which was invariably white and conservative.[42]

Overall, then, the political picture was somewhat mixed. As VEP director John Lewis testified in June 1971, black attitudes of "hope and optimism" coexisted alongside "a lack of hope" and "a climate of despair." There was every reason to feel encouraged; in less than a decade, southern blacks had made remarkable strides, yet, at the same time, over two million of them were still unregistered. As Lewis made clear, many of these people remained afraid of economic reprisals, a situation that would improve only if they could secure financial independence.[43]

"The Presiding Obstacle in the Struggle for Black Equality"

On the tenth anniversary of the historic March on Washington, black leaders paused to reflect on how much the movement had achieved. In a special edition of *Newsweek* published in September 1973, they agreed that progress had been greatest in the political sphere and that these gains had partly fulfilled King's dream. "He said that we'd never be free as long as people in Mississippi couldn't vote," recalled Andrew Young, who had worked alongside King in the early 1960s. "Political progress over the last ten years has been miraculous. Mississippi has more black elected officials than any state in the country. You can go almost all the way across Alabama on Highway 80, the road where Viola Liuzzo was killed for advocating our right to vote, and be under the jurisdiction of a black sheriff in more than half the districts." As Young acknowledged, the new generation of southern blacks also had much better education opportunities than their parents or grandparents.[44]

In sharp contrast, economic progress had been paltry. Another of King's former aides, Jesse Jackson, charged that whites were unwilling to fund the programs that were needed to tackle poverty. "Dr. King had often told us that yielding certain civil rights—public accommodations and voting rights, for instance—didn't cost America anything except a bit of racial arrogance," he related. "But the struggle for a civilized economic system is quite another matter." Even Young, no racial militant, asserted that African Americans had yet to cash the "promissory note" that King had spoken of a decade earlier. "The black minority is still holding a bad check," he declared.[45]

On the ground, employment discrimination remained a major problem because its effects were so long lasting and because the federal machinery to tackle it was inadequate. In November 1972, the U.S. Commission on Civil Rights documented the scale of the predicament in a thorough analysis of federal employment data. The commission concluded, "The employment picture for our society indicates that the groups victimized by discriminatory employment practices still carry the burden of that wrongdoing." Black workers faced a range of "discriminatory barriers," including employers' reliance on word-of-mouth contacts for recruitment, job qualifications that were not related to actual requirements, and managers' reluctance to address the effects of their past actions. "Intentional discrimination, such as job assignment by race, is but the tip of the iceberg," it noted.[46]

These problems were particularly severe in the South, the region that still generated the bulk of the EEOC's charges. Blacks were struggling to secure their fair share of good jobs, and they were more likely to be laid off when they secured them. Overall, the unemployment rate of southern blacks was immobile, sitting at about twice that of their white counterparts. In 1970, black families in the South also earned just 57 percent as much as their white counterparts.[47]

In the early 1970s, charges of discrimination continued to pour into the EEOC's offices; during the first seven and a half months of 1972 alone, the commission received close to fifteen thousand complaints, upholding 60 percent of them. Employment discrimination, acknowledged Commissioner Raymond L. Telles, was not a problem restricted to a "few malcontents and troublemakers" but reflected "the frustrations and despair of people who are capable and willing workers but who see their best efforts constantly shortchanged." The NAACP remained active in helping workers file charges. In 1972, for example, the Memphis branch filed complaints against several major employers, including International Harvester, the Kellogg Company, and the Memphis Fire Department.[48]

On the ground, black workers were frustrated that they confronted so much racism. In the early 1970s, some of them formed little-known grassroots groups that demanded better enforcement of Title VII. At the Southern Bell Telephone Company in Columbia, South Carolina, blacks chartered the Black Caucus of Telephone Workers and demanded an end to racist practices. In September 1972, the group submitted a list of twenty-five demands to management. It complained that blacks were locked out of white-collar jobs, were harshly disciplined by white supervisors, and had to endure "hollering and belittling comments" on the job. Clearly inspired by the black power movement, the caucus demanded more access to management posts and better treatment from white union representatives.[49]

There were similar moves elsewhere. In the early 1970s, blacks at a Mead Packaging plant in Atlanta organized Black Employees against Discrimination, an assertive group that petitioned company officials. "There should be an elimination of all 'black' jobs made by Mead and affirmative action should be taken to prevent such jobs from reoccurring in the future," it declared confidently. Again, the workers charged that they were frozen out of white-collar jobs and that they had to endure racist treatment on the job. "Compulsory seminars are needed for plant foremen on how to talk to and supervise blacks," they declared.[50]

Others also drew on the rhetoric of black power to demand a better deal. In the early 1970s, African American employees in the southern paper industry organized the Black Association of Millworkers (BAM), a self-assured group that pressured both management and unions. Showing an awareness of affirmative action, BAM petitioned companies to "actively recruit within the Black community" until all jobs reflected "the racial make-up of the labor pool in the hiring area," while unions were pressed to hire more black staff and represent black workers more forcefully. With branches along the Gulf and Atlantic coasts, BAM allowed blacks to voice their complaints collectively, reducing the risk of individual harassment.[51] Black frustration with unions was also evident in the 1972 foundation of the Coalition of Black Trade Unionists (CBTU), a national group that lobbied the AFL-CIO to do more to assist its black members. By early 1974, CBTU had over a million members in thirty-three separate unions, and they charged that unions privileged the interests of the white majority. While AFL-CIO leaders listened to CBTU demands, they resisted quotas, which they viewed as unfair to whites' accrued seniority rights. Union leaders also claimed that discrimination was a reflection of the "wrongs of management."[52]

While employment discrimination was clearly prevalent, the EEOC still lacked the power to deal with it effectively. As the Commission on Civil Rights summarized, "The mechanisms created by Title VII alone cannot handle the dimensions of the problem." Some EEOC leaders continued to press for change, and civil rights groups also increased the pressure on Congress. Testifying on behalf of both the Leadership Conference on Civil Rights and the NAACP, Clarence Mitchell told a Senate hearing in 1971 that federal officials needed to be more committed to enforcing Title VII: "I am fed up and disgusted with those entrusted with the task of enforcing non-discrimination laws who tell us what they can't do rather than what we know they can and ought to be doing." Other activists portrayed the title as the weak link in the federal enforcement effort. The EEOC, claimed the conference's Joseph L. Rauh, had "no powers" and had achieved only "very limited success." Representing a coalition of 125 progressive organizations, the conference argued that the commission needed cease-and-desist powers in order for employers to respect it.[53]

Finally recognizing the need to strengthen the EEOC, in 1972 Congress passed the Equal Employment Opportunity Act. Backed by liberal representatives and civil rights groups, this legislation had been introduced in 1969 but had encountered fierce opposition. The version that was passed extended coverage of Title VII to state and local governments as well as businesses and unions with fifteen or more employees (rather than the previous twenty-five). The EEOC could now bring litigation on its own, yet it still lacked cease-and-desist powers. Brushing aside the concerns of civil rights groups, President Nixon opposed giving the commission this authority. The president was responsive to business leaders who insisted that cease-and-desist remedies would turn the EEOC into a court with arbitrary powers. As the Atlanta chapter of the American Society for Personnel Administration put it, the EEOC could not be "both advocate and impartial judge." Led by Senator Ervin, powerful southern politicians also argued that it was wrong to give quasi-judicial powers to bureaucrats who were "responsible to nobody on the face of the earth." The outcome greatly disappointed liberal activists, who felt that intransigent employers could still violate the law, especially as most lawsuits took years to settle.[54]

The 1972 act was an improvement, however. Because of it, African Americans began to get more jobs in state and local governments, a significant advance, although many gains came only after litigation. In Mobile, the NPVL used the new powers to sue the Mobile City and County governments, forcing officials to address discriminatory practices. As late as June 1970, blacks made up about 35 percent of Mobile's population, yet all the city's firefighters were white. A believer in negotiation, John L. LeFlore repeatedly pressed officials to hire more blacks, but little changed until he filed suit. As the veteran activist wrote to Mobile mayor Joe A. Bailey, "It is a sad commentary that black citizens almost invariably have to institute court proceedings or follow a harsh and unwelcomed method of protest if they hope to achieve a semblance of fairness and justice from those who represent the power structure." League efforts led to the integration of Mobile's police and fire departments and won more jobs for blacks throughout the county and city government.[55]

Bolstered by their new powers, EEOC officials began to recommend remedies that fostered racial balance and promoted "affirmative action" in the recruitment and advancement of employees. As the economic historian Robert H. Zieger has pointed out, affirmative action "could mean anything from informing African Americans that historically discriminatory companies were now in compliance with the Civil Rights Act to establishing numerical targets for the hiring and upgrading of black workers." While African Americans charged that the commission still lacked authority, whites claimed that its officials had gone too far and were misconstruing the straightforward language of the Civil Rights Act, which simply prohibited discrimination. Prodded by the EEOC, some well-intentioned employers certainly took positive steps to diversify their workforces. At Sears Roebuck in Atlanta, a stringent affirmative action program helped ensure that the number of black sales employees increased from 8.2 percent in 1970 to 13.9 percent in 1972. The proportion of blacks in the company's workforce was also higher than it was in metropolitan Atlanta as a whole.[56]

In a wide range of industries, African Americans made gains, and some increases occurred even in places where there had been no formal EEOC or OFCC proceedings. In these cases, the threat of legal action and pressure from national corporate officials led to improvements. Litigation also continued to yield important breakthroughs. In 1971, the Supreme Court ruled in *Griggs v. Duke Power* that the North Carolina company's standardized preemployment tests were unrelated to work content and had a "disparate impact" on black applicants. The landmark ruling helped strike down such tests, which had been widely used to screen out African Americans.[57]

The region's largest industry, cotton textiles continued to illustrate broader trends particularly well. While some of the gains came through litigation, others were the result of mill owners beginning to hire more blacks without being first taken to court. Over the course of the 1960s, black employment in textiles increased four times faster than the national average for all manufacturing. In some areas, a labor shortage also helped as vacancies were created when whites left the mills for better jobs. Across the region, there were particularly notable gains for black women, who had been shut out of most textile jobs. In South Carolina, the number of black women employed in the mills jumped from just 240 in 1960 to over 8,000 a decade later.[58]

While acknowledging that blacks were making some progress, civil rights leaders were cautious. The black professor James E. Jones Jr. told the NAACP's conference in 1971, "The presiding obstacle in the struggle for black equality is economic. The continuing disparity between black and white incomes despite educational gains of blacks gives a hollow ring to the progress reports to which we are treated annually."[59] In the summer of 1973, the NAACP took issue with a well-circulated article by the economists Ben J. Wattenberg and Richard M. Scammon. Published in *Commentary,* the organ of the American Jewish Committee, the essay insisted that blacks were making major economic strides. Using census data, Wattenberg and Scammon claimed that black family income had jumped from 53 percent of the white level in 1961 to 63 percent in 1971. "Enormous progress has been made by American blacks in the past decade," they concluded. Refuting these claims, the NAACP argued that the authors had underestimated the level of black unemployment, especially as many of the jobless evaded the census takers.[60]

NAACP leaders also worried that positive reports would encourage whites to believe that all racial problems had been addressed. As a result, *The Crisis* constantly stressed the tenuous nature of any black gains. The small improvements that blacks were making, they pointed out, reflected the high rate of labor force participation by married women. In the early 1970s, about 49 percent of black mothers with preschool children were in the labor market, compared to 32 percent of their white counterparts. Black women were coming into the workforce in order to supplement their husbands' incomes, yet they lacked job experience and were vulnerable to layoffs. The unemployment rate for black women, claimed Texas congresswoman Barbara Jordan, was about twice as high as it was for white women.[61]

Despite closing the gap slightly in percentage terms, blacks also insisted that they were falling behind in terms of the actual monetary gap between black and white incomes. As the Atlanta-based economist Vivian Henderson put it, "People spend and save dollars. It is this dollar difference that counts." Henderson insisted that the dollar disparity between black and white annual incomes had increased from $2,500 in 1947 to $3,600 in 1969. Blacks also had larger families than whites, and this contributed to their high poverty rate, particularly in the South. In 1973, the black educator R. D. Morrison calculated that there were 5.17 million black youngsters in the South and that over 50 percent of them came from families earning less than $6,000 a year.[62]

The controversy over the *Commentary* article again illustrated the gap between white and black perceptions. In these years, whites frequently argued that racial issues were no longer relevant because equal rights had been assured by federal legislation. They tended to emphasize the considerable progress that southerners had made in eradicating racism. As early as 1971, the Alabama journalist H. Brandt Ayers proclaimed a "postracial South," while the writer Willie Morris asserted that the region could offer "more than a few crucial lessons to other Americans." Some felt that the civil rights movement was over because legislation now guaranteed black equality. Acutely aware of what Floyd McKissick termed the "failures of the civil rights movement," black leaders disagreed. According to the North Carolina native, blacks were still "at the bottom of the economic ladder," and "final emancipation" could come only when they possessed real economic power. During the presidency of Gerald R. Ford, black activists continued to struggle to reach this elusive goal.[63]

7

PAVING THE WAY FOR FULL PARTICIPATION

Civil Rights in the Ford Years

At 10 A.M. on July 1, 1975, President Gerald R. Ford rose to address the NAACP's sixty-sixth annual convention in Washington, DC. The new president received hearty applause as he praised America's oldest civil rights group as a "unique organization" with a "distinguished" history. "The NAACP," he declared, "has a proud record that spans 65 years with markers of achievement in racial equality unmatched by any other organization." Terming himself president of "all the people," Ford assured delegates that he was keen to establish a dialogue with the African American community. While stressing that great progress had been made in the civil rights field, he accepted that much remained to be done. "The end of racial discrimination by law has paved the way to the beginning of full participation," he declared.[1]

Ford's address to the NAACP encapsulated some of the differences between the new president and his predecessor. Coming into office in the wake of the divisive Watergate scandal, the Michigan Republican worked hard to restore confidence in the presidency. Personable and gregarious, Ford reached out to groups that Nixon had alienated, and his efforts quickly secured results. At the 1974 NAACP convention, delegates had called for Nixon's impeachment, but, just a year later, *The Crisis* noted that Ford had been "warmly received."[2]

Ever willing to meet with blacks, Ford was the second president in history to address the NAACP; only Harry Truman, a Democrat, had previously done so.[3] While not agreeing with most of Ford's political beliefs, association leaders established a sound personal relationship with the new president, who was known for his decency. Roy Wilkins praised Ford's "high moral character," while Clarence Mitchell claimed that the Michigan native had a "wholesome and straight-forward image." Not content with rhetoric, these officials also lobbied the new president to enforce civil rights laws vigorously, and their efforts yielded some gains. When the Voting Rights Act came up for renewal in 1975, Ford backed its extension.[4]

In other respects, however, there were a lot of similarities between Ford and Nixon. During Nixon's first term, Ford had championed the administration's cause in the House, and these actions secured him the vice presidency when Spiro Agnew resigned. On taking over the presidency, Ford was, ultimately, beholden to the Southern whites who had elected his predecessor, and he was soon searching for a way to stop busing. A product of neighborhood schools in Grand Rapids, Ford felt that the courts had gone "far too far" in ordering a remedy that had "torn up" numerous communities.[5] The issue was close to his heart; Ford even wrote "Excellent—we should use" on one antibusing letter that he read. In it, a teacher claimed that busing hurt weak students by making it harder for parents to come to school to discuss their child's problems. Ultimately, while Ford's style of leadership was different than that of his predecessor, his civil rights policies were very similar. "Mr. Ford does listen and he does pay attention," concluded Roy Wilkins in late 1974. "The question is what does he do about it and the answer is that he does little about it."[6]

The Ford years were dominated by an economic recession that hit the African American community hard. While complex in nature, the downturn was related to rising government deficits primarily caused by the cost of financing the Vietnam War, which weakened the dollar and increased prices. In 1973 and 1974, inflation hit double digits, and, from 1975 to 1980, the nation experienced stagflation, where unemployment and inflation increased simultaneously. Beginning in 1973, an Arab oil embargo also contributed to skyrocketing oil and gas prices.[7]

The slump had what the NAACP termed "a devastating effect" on blacks. "What was described as a recession for white workers was, in fact, a full-scale depression for black wage-earners and their families," asserted the association in 1974. "Many of the gains made in the past decade were rapidly being wiped out through the combined effects of unemployment and inflation." As the economy tightened, blacks found that they were once more "last hired, first fired." Inflation also hurt low-paid workers more because they spent a higher portion of their income on necessities such as groceries and gasoline. In addition, blacks were concentrated in sectors of the economy that were vulnerable to layoffs, particularly manufacturing industries.[8]

As the recession worsened, African American leaders became preoccupied with economic issues and demanded action. Ford, however, refused to implement full employment legislation, instead focusing on the fight against inflation, an issue that he saw as defining his presidency. Claiming that he was the president of all Americans, he was also opposed to introducing a bill to alleviate the black plight. "I would like as many supporters in the black community as possible," he declared in Texas in

April 1976. "But, to go out and offer a particular piece of legislation for any segment of our society in order to get them to vote for me I think is the wrong approach for a Presidential candidate."[9]

Despite Ford's stance, opposition to busing did subside during his presidency. A crucial change occurred in July 1974, when the Supreme Court overturned a lower court order calling for the amalgamation of city and suburban districts in Detroit. After this, the courts backed away from recommending similar plans in other cities. Where busing orders had already been implemented, many whites had adjusted to them. Violence often grabbed the headlines, but the lesser-known story of a society coming to terms with desegregation often went unreported. "For every case of violence, there are many examples of successful, responsible integration plans which include busing," acknowledged the presidential advisers Art Quern and Allen Moore in 1976.[10]

African Americans made other gains in these years, especially in the South. Attorneys from the Justice Department stamped out lingering resistance to Title II, encouraging more blacks to move back to the region. With the courts behind them, HEW staff continued to dismantle the dual school system, and they also made some progress in desegregating southern universities. Helped by the landmark Voting Rights Act, southern blacks made political strides as well. "It is in politics that blacks have made some of their most visible and most significant gains," concluded *U.S. News and World Report* in 1974. Increasingly, however, stubborn economic disparities overshadowed these positive developments. Employment discrimination did not evaporate, and many whites guarded the best jobs as fiercely as ever. As the *New York Times* noted in 1974, "Job discrimination is perhaps the most frustrating racial problem Negroes face these days, particularly Southern Negroes."[11]

By the mid-1970s, however, southern blacks were a political force to be reckoned with, and they were able to express their dissatisfaction with Ford's economic policies en masse. In a landmark presidential election, the black vote swung behind the Georgian Jimmy Carter and provided him with his margin of victory in several key states. Receiving more than 90 percent of the southern black vote, Carter was able to carry every former Confederate state except Virginia. Commenting on the symbolism of Carter's victory, Andrew Young was eloquent. "The hands that picked cotton finally picked the president," he declared.[12]

"I Feel Free": Public Accommodations and the Strengthening Tide of Reverse Migration

Regardless of who occupied the Oval Office, much of the progress occurring was impossible to reverse. By the mid-1970s, the vast majority of southern whites had become used to blacks having equal access to public facilities. Both races were putting the Jim Crow era behind them, and a new generation was emerging that took the changes for granted.[13] It was a highly significant shift, particularly in psychological terms. A native of Georgia, the black writer Jack White had vivid memories of the humiliations that he and his parents had endured before the Civil Rights Act was passed. "Because of the civil rights movement," he wrote in 1976, "I will never have to explain to my four-year-old son that he can't go to an amusement park or swim in a public swimming pool just because he is black. He will never see me diminish in his eyes because some white man can lord it over me and make me seem like a child."[14]

Other blacks described the mental lift they received from these changes. As the Atlanta resident Lonnie King put it, "It did something to a person to know he could not drink from a particular water fountain because it was a 'white' fountain. It was debilitating." Overall, Title II had completely transformed everyday race relations. "To native Southerners," summarized *U.S. News and World Report* in 1974, "the progress of blacks is nowhere more striking than in the area of public accommodations. Here desegregation has come about principally because of the Civil Rights Act of 1964, which not only struck down all the old legal barriers but also threw the powers of the Federal government into enforcing the new code."[15]

Any lingering resistance was tackled by the Justice Department, whose cadre of attorneys carefully monitored compliance. Ten years after the passage of the Civil Rights Act, the department had filed more than four hundred suits against hotels, restaurants, gas stations, truck stops, bars, and other businesses that served the public. As Assistant Attorney General J. Stanley Pottinger reported, thousands of other businesses had achieved voluntary compliance following investigations by his staff. Under Pottinger's watchful eye, federal attorneys also oversaw the desegregation of southern prisons.[16]

Remaining opposition came mainly from small, family-owned restaurants or bars, especially in rural areas. The owners of these facilities either feared that they would lose white customers if they served blacks or believed that they could avoid federal regulations, yet, in reality, there was no escape. In September 1974, for example, the department sued a bar in Houma, Louisiana, that still brazenly declared that it was for "White Only." Federal lawyers told the tavern's owners to remove the offending sign and replace it with a notice of compliance with the Civil Rights Act. The case was typical; around the same time, Justice Department attorneys also filed suit against a bar in Sanford, Florida, that refused to seat blacks and a drive-in restaurant in Gulfport, Mississippi, that served them only at a separate side window. In urban areas, however, there were now only a tiny number of cases.[17]

The Justice Department's agents quickly dealt with most of the cases that came across their desks. Through brief field visits, it was not hard to prove that businesses were violating the law, and the remedy was also easy to carry out. At the bar in Sanford, Florida, the owner admitted that he refused to seat blacks, and, following negotiations with federal attorneys, he reluctantly agreed to a consent decree that prohibited further discrimination. Still, there were a few cases of ongoing defiance. Some business owners refused to post compliance notices and were threatened with further legal action, while others tried to dodge the law by making up their own notices. One Macon bar even posted a notice that declared, "We Welcome All People Who Conduct Themselves as Ladies and Gentlemen." After complaints from Pottinger, bar staff removed the notice and replaced it with the official one.[18]

With nowhere to hide, even recalcitrant opponents were forced to give ground. In December 1974, the movement achieved a symbolic victory when Lester Maddox reopened the Pickrick Cafeteria on a desegregated basis. While claiming that he still believed in segregation, Maddox agreed to serve blacks in order to pay off a $200,000 debt that he had incurred in an unsuccessful gubernatorial campaign. Running in 1974, he lost in the Democratic primary to George Busbee. In a region where blacks were a considerable political force, Maddox was never able to win elected office again.[19]

The continuing influx of black migrants was testament to how much race relations had improved. From small beginnings, this movement gathered force; between 1970 and 1973, for example, census data showed that, while 166,000 blacks had left the South, 247,000 had moved in. "After generations in which Southern blacks streamed northward almost as soon as they were able, the tide is turning," declared *Newsweek* in 1974.[20]

Most migrants were young professionals who settled in the region's cities, where compliance with Title II was most pronounced. Although they had spent most of their lives in the North, they felt a strong attachment to the South, especially as many relatives still lived there. "Everywhere I go I find folks who have come back home," commented John Lewis in 1974. "There's absolutely no doubt that the return flow is increasing all the time and that the flow North is decreasing. Why should that be so surprising now that the South has an open society? This is, after all, the place of our birth. It is home." Lewis's point was supported by the example of Willie Joseph Woods, who was born in Georgia but raised in New York and Los Angeles. In 1974, the thirty-five-year-old college graduate was happy to take a job in Atlanta. "I tried it all up there," he explained to a journalist. "It just wasn't home."[21]

Not all the migrants were young professionals; some were older African Americans who had gone north in search of more freedom. The return of these émigrés, especially to the rural South, was particularly significant. In the mid-1950s, for example, Howard Spence escaped the terror of rural Mississippi, where blacks were frequently killed if they violated racial norms. After two decades in Chicago, he moved back to his home state and felt that he had come to a different world. "I'm not afraid about anything happening now," he declared. "When I was here before, I was afraid. The big difference is I feel free. I'm much more in control. I can make a decision without being afraid. I can go downtown, anywhere I want to. I can talk to anybody."[22]

"Their Children Are Right in the Middle of It Now": The South Adjusts to School Desegregation

When Ford took office in August 1974, the implementation of Title VI remained controversial, especially when busing was used. That fall, for example, a tense busing crisis in Boston generated a huge amount of media coverage. Federal judge W. Arthur Garrity Jr. became a hated figure after he ordered Boston's schools to desegregate immediately. The city was rocked by protests and student boycotts, and schools had to be regularly patrolled by state troopers. Like their counterparts in the South, most white parents in Boston claimed to support desegregated schools but insisted that "forced busing" was unfair and counterproductive.[23] As they watched the Boston protests on national television, some southerners felt that northern hypocrisy had been exposed. As Alabama's superintendent of education wrote a Birmingham resident, "The people of Alabama have borne this cross with commendable dignity and constraint compared with the violent display of emotion which the people of Boston showed on the national news media in recent days." Now that northern children were being bused, added LeRoy Brown, southerners might finally secure "relief from these ridiculous court orders."[24]

In the South, the busing issue remained contentious in some places. In Corpus Christi, for example, a group of white activists were engaged in an ongoing fight to stop the "crime" of "forced busing," which had been ordered by the district court. Many southerners were also mobilized by events in Louisville, a border city that was ordered to adopt metropolitanwide busing in 1975. In October, Ford received a petition against the Louisville plan that contained almost five thousand signatures. Many of the signers lived in southern states, particularly North Carolina and Tennessee. They declared that "*Forced* Busing" was "not the way to achieve Quality Education" and asked for a constitutional amendment to outlaw the practice.[25]

As the United States celebrated its bicentennial, antibusing activists added a new twist to their arguments. Contending that the public was

Civil rights activists carry an American flag during their March 1965 march from Selma to Montgomery to protest denial of voting rights to African Americans. (© Steve Schapiro/Corbis.)

Kelly M. Alexander, president of the North Carolina State Conference of the NAACP, 1948–1984. (University of North Carolina at Charlotte.)

April 9, 1968: The mule-drawn caisson carrying the casket of Dr. Martin Luther King Jr. is followed by dignitaries and aides as it moves toward the campus of Morehead College in Atlanta, GA, for a memorial service. (© Bettman/ CORBIS.)

Coretta Scott King at her husband's funeral at the Ebenezer Baptist Church, Atlanta, GA, April 9, 1968, wearing a mourning veil with her daughter Bernice sitting on her lap. (Photo by CBS Photo Archive/Getty Images.)

At the 1973 presidential inauguration in the House Chamber of the U.S. Capitol, December 6, 1973, Gerald R. Ford shakes hands with President Richard M. Nixon (*right*) as James Eastland (*rear*), president pro tempore of the Senate, looks on. The oath was administered by Chief Justice Warren Burger of the Supreme Court. (Photo by David Hume Kennerly/Getty Images.)

Jimmy Carter, the thirty-ninth president of the United States, and former president Gerald Ford (*right*) at the White House, Washington, DC, May 20, 1977. (Photo by Gene Forte/Keystone/CNP/Getty Images.)

President Ronald Reagan signing the Martin Luther King Jr. Day holiday proclamation with (*left to right*) Dr. King's sister, Christine Farris, his son Dexter, and his widow, Coretta Scott King, January 12, 1988. (Photo by Diana Walker/Time Life Pictures/Getty Images.)

The January 1990 Ku Klux Klan march against the Martin Luther King Jr. holiday in Pulaski, TN. (Photo by Mark Peterson/Corbis SABA Credit © Mark Peterson/Corbis.)

Left to right: Gloria Ray Karlmark of the Little Rock Nine, Fatima McKindra, student body president, Carlotta Walls Lanier of the Little Rock Nine, and President William J. Clinton at the September 1997 ceremony marking the return of the first black students to attend Central High in 1957. (Photo by Cynthia Johnson/Time Life Pictures/Getty Images.)

Congressman John Lewis (D-GA) (*right*) stands near Senator Barack Obama (D-IL) (*left*) and other members of Congress during a media conference on Capitol Hill, May 2, 2006, in Washington, DC. The bipartisan House and Senate officials met to voice support for legislation to reauthorize the Voting Rights Act for an additional twenty-five years. (Photo by Mark Wilson/Getty Images.)

President George W. Bush speaks at the funeral ceremony for Coretta Scott King on February 7, 2006, at the New Birth Missionary Baptist Church in Lithonia, GA. *At rear (from left):* First Lady Laura Bush, former president Bill Clinton, Senator Hillary Clinton (D-NY), former president George H. W. Bush, and former president Jimmy Carter. (Photo by Pool/Getty Images.)

Rita Schwerner Bender, the widow of the slain civil rights activist Michael Schwerner, leaves Neshoba County Courthouse after a jury convicted Edgar Ray Killen in the 1964 slayings of Schwerner, Andrew Goodman, and James Chaney, June 21, 2005, in Philadelphia, MS. The guilty verdict came on the forty-first anniversary of the Klan killings. (Marianne Todd/Getty Images.)

Taking part in the groundbreaking ceremony for the Martin Luther King Jr. Memorial on the National Mall on Monday, November 13, 2006, in Washington, DC, are (*front, left to right*) King's daughter Yolanda King, the civil rights leader Congressman John Lewis (D-GA), former labor secretary Alexis Herman, King's sister Christine King Farris, and Darryl R. Matthews, president of the Alpha Phi Alpha fraternity, (*top left*) Bill Walton, and the Reverend Marvin Winans (*center*) consoling the Reverend Jesse Jackson (*top right*). (AP Photo/Evan Vucci.)

The Reverend Jesse Jackson leads hundreds of supporters to the La Salle Parish Courthouse in Jena, Louisiana, on September 20, 2007. This was the second march of the day. (© Vernon Bryant/Dallas Morning News/Corbis.)

Andrew Jackson Young Jr. is an American civil rights activist, a former U.S. congressman and mayor of Atlanta, and the first African American ambassador from the United States to the United Nations. Young was with Martin Luther King, with whom he worked closely, when King was assassinated in 1968. He is currently the chairman of Goodworks International, a company specializing in business development in Africa. Young was photographed in Atlanta in 2008. (© Brooks Kraft/Corbis.)

"being forced by all three branches of our government to accept a policy propounded by a minority," the resident Kathleen M. Troth pondered the meaning of the American Revolution. "I guess if you're going to go ahead and ignore the pleas of the majority of Americans, you may as well get it done in this, the year of our 200th anniversary of freedom," she concluded ironically. Troth wrote from Dallas, where around seventeen thousand students were being transported across town.[26] Conscious of the historic anniversary, other writers made sure that their elected representatives were aware of their feelings. Reminding Ford that 1976 was also an election year, concerned citizens called on the president to take a "firm stand" against busing.[27]

Under pressure to act, Ford toyed with proposals to restrict the use of busing. Like Nixon, however, he discovered that obvious alternatives, such as a constitutional amendment or the development of specific legislation, were all deeply problematic. In particular, executive interference with judicial decisions was fraught with constitutional difficulties. After an eight-month-long review of his options, Ford drafted legislation that busing could be used only for short periods to remedy "proven unlawful acts of discrimination." Although it was drawn up in June 1976, the legislation was never presented to the Democratic-controlled Congress, partly because Ford became consumed by trying to secure the Republican nomination and then win the presidential election.[28]

In these years, leading southern politicians continued to try and undermine the school desegregation process. Frequent correspondents with one another, Strom Thurmond and Jesse Helms still received some letters from whites who felt that the schools were integrating too quickly.[29] In response, both men took action. In late 1974, Helms sponsored an amendment that sought to undermine Title VI by prohibiting HEW from cutting off funds from school systems that refused to "classify teachers or students by race, religion, sex, or national origin." The Senate Appropriations Committee eventually defeated the amendment, which had threatened to cripple the Civil Rights Act. The setback did not deter Helms; in early 1976, for instance, both he and Thurmond backed fresh antibusing bills.[30] While Helms was still a relative newcomer in the Senate, the elder statesman Thurmond was used to lobbying the GOP on this issue. As he complained to President Ford, HEW was "over-stepping its lawful mandate enacted by Congress, and attempting to legislate itself into the position of overlord in all our nation's school systems."[31]

Despite some ongoing opposition, by the mid-1970s many southern whites had got used to racially mixed schools, even in places where federal officials had insisted on stringent plans. In October 1975, a Harris poll even revealed that southerners were slightly more likely to support desegregated schools than northerners were. Feeling that they had no choice, some whites had reluctantly concluded that change was inevitable. As LeRoy Brown wrote a concerned pupil in 1974, he and Governor Wallace still opposed busing but were "powerless to overrule or go against the conditions specified in . . . court orders." Others, however, had renounced their old views and embraced the new order. Georgia governor Jimmy Carter spoke for many when he explained in the mid-1970s, "Once we had to confront the fact that we were right or wrong in the eyes of God, we said we're wrong, and if we can find a way to make this change without losing face, we'll do it. And the Supreme Court and other court orders were the things that permitted us to do it without losing face. And in many instances we did it with a great sense of relief."[32]

Other forces also generated these changes. On a practical level, many southern whites put their children first and decided not to upset their education once they were enrolled in merged schools. In 1974, a state official in Mississippi commented on this reality: "Their children are going to school with blacks. They don't want any more explosive situations because their children are right in the middle of it now." Across the South, business and community leaders continued to play a crucial role. In 1976, the U.S. Commission on Civil Rights found that it made a real difference when civic leaders backed desegregation orders. In 411 districts that had not witnessed any serious disturbances, at least two-thirds of the business and political leaders and over 90 percent of religious heads had backed desegregation or had not taken a stance against it. In 95 communities where violence had erupted, however, less than one-third of the political and business leaders had supported desegregation or had stayed silent.[33]

By the mid-1970s, many whites had also reconciled themselves to busing, often because it had not produced the dire consequences that they had feared. In the course of their detailed investigations, Ford's aides uncovered evidence to support this conclusion. In March 1976, for example, HEW secretary David Matthews wrote privately to the president, "There are a great many cases where transportation by buses is working well according to the research reports we have."[34]

Announced in July 1974, the Supreme Court's decision in the Detroit case also defused the busing issue. In a 5–4 judgment, the Court overturned a lower court mandate that the predominantly white suburbs and overwhelmingly black city should be consolidated into one school district. Chief Justice Warren Burger ruled that the proposed interdistrict remedy was "wholly impermissible" because officials in the suburban communities had not intentionally discriminated. As a result, Burger told the lower courts to devise remedies to improve districting within city limits. The ruling made it harder for federal officials to order the busing of children across metropolitan lines, the strategy that civil rights lawyers advocated. According to the dissenting justice Thurgood Marshall, this was "a giant step backward." While it did not affect existing plans, *Milliken v. Bradley* undermined the most controversial form of busing.[35]

Working with the courts, the Justice Department also kept up the pressure on southern school boards. Between 1964 and 1974, the department's lawyers sued more than five hundred southern school districts, and their efforts led to many breakthroughs. According to federal data, the proportion of southern black pupils who attended all-black schools fell from 68 percent in 1968 to just 8.7 percent in 1974, and progress continued in the Ford years. Headed by Pottinger, the department's Civil Rights Division intervened in a number of important cases. In the fall of 1974, for example, the school board in Gibson County, Tennessee, claimed that it could not implement a comprehensive desegregation plan until the 1976–1977 school year because it needed time to construct new facilities. Federal lawyers rejected these pleas. As the division's executive officer reported to Pottinger, "Our expert testified that the desegregation plan in question could be implemented 'overnight' if necessary, as few changes within the schools will be required and noted that existing constitutional standards require that school plans have the promise of immediate implementation."[36]

Reviewing the gains that had occurred, some white journalists claimed that the South's schools set an example for the rest of the country. Shortly after the twentieth anniversary of *Brown,* John Caughey wrote in *The Nation* that 44.4 percent of southern black schoolchildren attended majority-white schools. "That is far better than the report card for the North and West," he declared. Such optimism was not so evident at the NAACP, where leaders stressed ongoing difficulties. As General Counsel Nathaniel R. Jones wrote in the same year, "Not only have the attacks on the *Brown* decision been frontal, but there have been subtle attempts to circumvent it." Even Jones accepted that there had been a "gain" in the South, yet the situation was not as pleasing in large northern cities. The Ohio native picked out the case of Cleveland, where 91.2 percent of black children attended schools that were from 90 to 100 percent black.[37]

Positive reports also glossed over the problems that remained within the desegregated schools. As the NAACP put it, black students and teachers continued to endure a "heavy and disparate burden" when schools were integrated. Across the South, black students complained that they were placed in separate classes and were much more likely to be disciplined or expelled. In 1975, a thorough study of 505 southern school districts by HEW's Office for Civil Rights confirmed that black children were twice as likely as whites to end up in special classes. In Emporia, Virginia, for example, black students were routinely assigned to occupational training classes, but whites were placed in traditional academic subjects. Across the South, data also indicated that black children were two to three times more likely to be suspended than their white counterparts, and many of these suspensions were highly arbitrary. In Macon, Georgia, one sixteen-year-old was expelled because he could not pay five dollars to replace a broken ruler, while, in Mobile, another student was ejected after she became pregnant. Unlike white mothers, the student was not allowed to make up work that she had missed during her pregnancy.[38] Concerned by these problems, in May 1974 the House Education and Labor Committee investigated black "pushouts." The committee heard that expulsions were most common in the South and that assertive black males were the most likely to be targeted. As NEA leader Samuel Etheridge commented, "The Martin Luther Kings and other leaders of tomorrow are not being allowed to graduate."[39]

Even federal officials admitted that they needed to do a lot more to tackle these problems. As Office for Civil Rights director Peter Holmes acknowledged, "The physical desegregation of a school system does not necessarily mean the end of discrimination." The widespread use of ability groupings and tracking—the practice of assigning middle or high school students to certain self-contained curricula such as vocational studies—was particularly troubling. In particular, it undermined the prospects of students who were left behind and often resulted in continued racial segregation. As an SRC study concluded, students placed in these classes felt that they were "second-class persons."[40]

The long battle to desegregate the schools also meant that HEW neglected the higher education sector. As late as May 1970, the agency had never cut off funds from any state for failing to desegregate its universities or colleges, even though similar action had been taken against numerous school districts. Following its first major review of the college sector, HEW told ten southern states to submit desegregation plans, but five of them—Florida, Louisiana, Mississippi, North Carolina, and Oklahoma—failed to comply, and the other five entered schemes that were unacceptable. Despite this, federal officials were consumed by the battle with the schools, and they failed to take decisive action. Frustrated by the situation, the NAACP LDF sued HEW, but the case proceeded slowly, and, it was not until late 1973 that the agency finalized its desegregation guidelines.[41]

By the fall of 1974 HEW's own data highlighted that just 4 percent of the students at ten major southern state universities were black. Ironically, the best-performing institution was the University of Alabama, where Governor Wallace had staged his "stand in the schoolhouse door" in 1963. At the main Tuscaloosa campus, 6.4 percent of students were now black, a gain that was largely credited to the actions of top university administrators. In contrast, just thirty-one of almost eight thousand students (or 0.4 percent) at the University of Arkansas in Fayetteville were African American. All the universities had a lot of work to do, especially as African Americans constituted over 20 percent of the population in the ten states. Pottinger acknowledged that federal efforts in this area were still in their infancy. "There has been," he wrote in late 1974, "no co-ordinated federal effort to deal with the dual structure of many State university systems."[42]

In accordance with the court's order in the LDF case, in June 1974 HEW finally accepted desegregation plans from eight of the ten affected states. Louisiana failed to submit a plan, however, and Mississippi's plan was deemed unacceptable. As a result, the Justice Department sued both states, adding its weight to private suits that were already before the courts. In the other states, progress was slow, and the plaintiffs pressed for relief, yet university officials were far from obliging. In September 1975, the presidential adviser James Cannon reported that efforts to enforce Title VI in higher education had received "sharp criticism" from university officials, who disliked federal interference in their affairs. HEW secretary Caspar W. Weinberger was sympathetic to their arguments, advising Ford not to push affirmative action in university recruitment policies.[43]

The outcome of this situation was that most southern blacks who went to university still attended black colleges. Nearly one hundred black colleges had been created in the Jim Crow era, and they had never been provided with sufficient resources. After 1965, the black colleges also faced new challenges, especially as they lost some of their best students to traditionally white universities. In a new era, many questioned whether they could even survive.[44]

A graduate of a black college, the presidential adviser Stanley Scott lobbied the black colleges' cause within the Nixon and Ford administrations. Like Scott, many black leaders felt that these institutions performed a valuable role, especially in providing black role models for students. Scott's correspondence with college administrators highlighted that these institutions were desperately short of funds. In October 1973, the president of Natchez Junior College wrote that his institution's needs were "so numerous that it is very difficult to make any preference over another." The ninety-year-old college had no sports facilities, and much of its student housing was "not conducive to human habitation." In addition, admitted M. K. Nelson, "many of our books in the library are out-dated and irrelevant to our curriculum requirements." Elsewhere, the situation was similar. The president of Alabama A&M University, R. D. Morrison, related that, in the 1973–1974 academic year, 64 percent of his twenty-six hundred students required full financial assistance but that the university was able to help only a third of them. "The need for every kind of aid by our students is of critical importance," he pleaded.[45]

Overall, the Congressional Black Caucus estimated that 70 percent of black college students could not continue without financial aid. The black colleges struggled to attract federal funding, and they were unable to meet the shortfall by relying on affluent alumni, a vital source of income for many white institutions. Scott's efforts did help to alleviate the situation. Personally ambivalent about integration, President Nixon respected the black colleges, which were the largest minority-run enterprises in the country. Nixon increased aid to them, and Ford continued these policies. In 1970, state-assisted black colleges received 9.7 percent of their income from federal grants, but, by 1975, this had jumped to 13 percent. While it was not enough to meet all their needs, the extra funding ensured that black colleges would survive, at least in the short term.[46]

"Front-Line Victims": Economic Recession and the Ongoing Struggle for Equality in the Workplace

Even before Ford took over, African Americans were more concerned about the slowing economy that they were the constitutional drama of Watergate. Between World War II and the early 1970s, the U.S. economy grew, and average family income increased steadily. Although blacks shared in some of these gains, their economic status was precarious. In 1973, moreover, both inflation and unemployment rose sharply for the first time in over three decades. As recent arrivals in industrial jobs, blacks were the first to be laid off, while as low-wage earners they were hit hard by high rates of inflation. As a result, it was soon clear that black income levels were stagnating. In 1975, the Congressional Budget Office found that black families earned only 61.5 percent as much as whites, compared to 61.3 percent six years earlier, and that 27 percent of African American families lived in poverty.[47]

Although the region was now viewed as a booming Sun Belt, the recession also had an impact on the South, especially in rural areas.[48] Right across the country, traditional manufacturing industries were hit hard by the downturn, and southern plants were not immune. In unionized industries such as steel and chemicals, the application of seniority rules had a harsh impact on African Americans. The number of black workers at Continental Can Company in Harvey, Louisiana, had increased from two in 1964 to over fifty a decade later, but, when two hundred workers were laid off in 1975, all but two of the black workers were let go. Although the layoff occurred in accordance with a union contract, the affected workers viewed it as discriminatory and challenged it in the courts. Even in nonunionized industries, new employees were usually shown the door first. In 1976, a report by the U.S. comptroller general concluded, "Minorities and women hired in recent years were among the groups hardest hit by the downturn since employers generally followed the practice of last hired, first fired."[49]

Observing these developments, black leaders began to attack union seniority systems as discriminatory, straining the alliance between organized labor and civil rights groups. Union leaders fiercely defended their members' accrued rights. "Bona fide seniority systems protect every worker, black or white," asserted AFL-CIO civil rights director William E. Pollard in 1976. "To destroy seniority systems would not create a single job, but would permit management to pick and choose workers without regard to date of hire." Union staffers worked behind the scenes to blunt criticism from civil rights activists over what they termed "the seniority question." By calling for full employment, labor leaders also sidestepped the seniority issue and found common ground with black leaders. In an economy that was failing to produce enough jobs, however, seniority provisions undoubtedly hurt blacks.[50]

The economic downturn also undermined the work of civil rights groups in the South. Organizations such as the SRC, the VEP, and the SCLC depended heavily on grants from nonprofit foundations, and these dried up as the economy slumped. In the spring of 1975, the SRC blamed the economic climate for the layoff of thirteen top staff. "The chief difficulty," reported one civil rights official, "is that all social service type agencies are experiencing the same cutback on foundation funds simultaneously."[51]

As the recession worsened, African Americans increasingly focused on economic issues rather than the Watergate scandal. "The Washington Watergate is of little concern to most Blacks," noted the black presidential adviser John Calhoun in June 1974. "Black America sees it this way. Congress is spending $10 million to investigate Watergate—while many needs of the Nation's Blacks and the poor are not being dealt with. Congress has a full year on Watergate and spent little—if any—time on the economic issues, business development, and programs that are needed by the Nation's minorities." Illustrating Calhoun's point, The Crisis gave little coverage to the Watergate debacle, instead stressing the need to continue the civil rights struggle, particularly in the economic area. "The truth is," it declared, "that so much remains that is evil that we cannot slacken the pace of our protest by the merest fraction."[52]

In the fall of 1974, prominent activists organized the national Black Economic Summit in order to analyze the "crisis" from a black perspective. Attended by key leaders such as Maynard Jackson and Roy Wilkins, the gathering declared that the black community was "enmeshed in a depression of the first magnitude." It called for the situation to be alleviated by an emphasis on full employment, including a public works program that would create at least a million jobs. Ford's aides rebuffed these demands, however, largely because they were more concerned with fighting inflation.[53]

After the summit, black groups strove to implement its conclusions. In May 1975, the Congressional Black Caucus declared that full employment was its main priority because the African American community was the "front-line victim" of the recession. Meeting in Atlanta for its 1975 conference, the National Urban League also focused heavily on economic issues. Addressing the gathering, Executive Director Vernon E. Jordan Jr. insisted that the recession was undermining the gains that African Americans had made in other areas. "When a person is ill-fed, ill-clothed, and ill-housed," he asserted, "all other rights become meaningless."[54]

The economic situation also inspired protests. In January 1975, a group of activists marked what would have been Dr. King's forty-sixth birthday by marching around the White House and demanding jobs for poor blacks. Later in the year, Coretta Scott King led a march in Selma that commemorated the tenth anniversary of the original walk to Montgomery. Addressing five thousand people on the Edmund Pettus Bridge, she declared that blacks were still in a "critical state" because "there are no jobs for those who need them and people are hungry."[55]

In the months that followed, King emerged as a forceful leader of the burgeoning full employment movement. In mid-1975, she brought together a wide range of labor, civil rights, and women's organizations into the Full Employment Action Council, an umbrella group that lobbied for job creation programs, especially in the South. In the spring of 1976, she also urged Congress to pass full employment legislation. Cosponsored by former vice president Hubert Humphrey, the proposed Equal Opportunity and Full Employment Act sought to use a variety of initiatives, including public works programs, in order to reduce the unemployment rate to 3 percent within four years. At hearings, the Atlanta resident hit back at claims that the legislation was costly and counterproductive. "It probably takes someone who is black to fully comprehend the helplessness, loneliness, and anxieties of the unemployed," she declared.[56]

By the mid-1970s, Mrs. King also spearheaded a growing campaign to commemorate her husband's legacy. As well as emphasizing the economic focus of Martin's ideas, she devoted much of her energy to building the new Martin Luther King Jr. Memorial Center in Atlanta, which was funded largely by labor and civil rights groups. In the Ford years, considerable progress was made on the construction of the center, which was located next to Dr. King's Ebenezer Baptist Church. An ambitious project, the site included the center's headquarters as well as an entombment area, a memorial park, and a community center. Designated as a national historic site in early 1977, the center was the first institution to be built in memory of an African American leader.[57]

In addition to the recession, ongoing discriminatory practices hurt black workers. Within the public sector, they got a raw deal, especially as Title VII had not even covered state and local governments until 1972. Once the Equal Employment Opportunity Act was passed, federal agencies began to take action, but they were playing catch-up. Between 1972 and 1974, the Justice Department filed twenty-two suits against state and local governments in order to tackle ongoing discriminatory practices.[58] In Mississippi, for example, around 36 percent of the population was African American, but just 6 percent of state employees were black, and most of them were confined to low-paying jobs. "Racism is a sanctioned and accepted practice of Mississippi's government agencies," concluded a 1974 report by the Mississippi Council on Human Relations, an SRC affiliate. The council was appalled by the weak enforcement of Title VII, especially as federal funds continued to flow freely. "Even though the federal government had stringent laws aimed at erasing job discrimination," it noted, "Washington continued to fund much of our state government without the slightest word of caution concerning its racist employment record."[59]

In private employment, discrimination was also prevalent, and frustrated workers continued to turn to the NAACP for answers. "Employment discrimination remains a fact of life for blacks and other minorities," asserted the association in late 1974. "This is attested to by the heavy litigation load carried by the Legal Department." Pointing out that the enforcement of Title VII left "very much to be desired," in November 1975 a leading NAACP attorney directly criticized federal efforts. "In the area of employment," charged J. Francis Polhaus, "we find an Equal Employment Commission with a backlog of 100,000 unresolved charges, an Office [of] Contract Compliance that refuses to impose available sanctions and a growing number of unemployed blacks who are forced out of work under a system that had its roots in a discriminatory history of racial exclusion."[60]

The EEOC was still experiencing many problems. In September 1976, a thorough investigation by the General Accounting Office (GAO) found that the commission had made only "limited progress" in eliminating employment discrimination. "The great promise of Title VII of the Civil Rights Act of 1964," it concluded, "remains essentially unfulfilled." As the study noted, the EEOC was understaffed, and its backlog of charges was rising. On average, charging parties now had to wait two years for their complaints to be resolved, and, even after this, there was a low probability of a negotiated settlement. The report also criticized many of the EEOC's procedures, especially as there was little monitoring of compliance with conciliation agreements and consent decrees. High rates of turnover, especially in top positions, also remained a problem. Since its foundation in 1965, the EEOC had had no fewer than eleven chairmen and twelve executive directors. During Ford's brief presidency alone, the chair's position was held by four different individuals, and the situation was similar in other key posts. Several staff had left because they had not been able to secure the resources they needed.[61]

Responding to the criticisms, EEOC vice chair Ethel Bent Walsh emphasized that commission staff had a very difficult job. "GAO does not appear to have grasped the nature of employment discrimination as a persistent, pervasive, and increasingly complex phenomenon in America," she asserted. Walsh had a point, especially as it was clear that the EEOC's workload was much higher than policymakers had anticipated. In 1965, the commission had received 8,854 charges, but this mushroomed to 80,000 within nine years. While they had given the commission more powers, the 1972 amendments had also increased its workload. Given the size of the task, even the most efficient organization would have struggled to secure quick results, yet it is undeniable that the commission compounded its problems through internal bickering and poor procedures.[62]

In the southern states, the backlog was particularly acute. As of April 30, 1974, the commission's Atlanta and Dallas offices had over thirty-one thousand charges on their books, and EEOC chairman John H. Powell Jr. admitted that many of them had not been assigned to an investigator. Around thirty-nine hundred charges were stalled at the conciliation stage, meaning that the commission had upheld the complaints but had been unable to reach a settlement. Delays were extensive; in all, about 40 percent of the unresolved cases had been on the books for over two years. In seeking to explain the situation, Powell also stressed the scale of the task and pleaded for "greater voluntary compliance."[63]

The EEOC's relationship with employers, however, was poor. Rather than stressing the need for broad initiatives, the lily-white employer groups had a narrowly defined concept of Title VII. They argued that EEOC agents had caused the backlog by using specific charges to investigate unrelated issues. In late 1974, the National Association of Manufacturers (NAM) claimed that the EEOC was launching "fishing expedition investigations." To illustrate, NAM director Michael Markowitz cited a case brought against a utility company in New Orleans. Originally based on a complaint from one black worker, the EEOC encouraged other employees to file charges, and Markowitz claimed that this was typical. In reality, however, black workers had common complaints and were keen to file charges together in order to minimize harassment. Still, southern employers remained suspicious of the EEOC, viewing it as problack. As the Atlanta-based corporate attorney Homer

L. Deakins put it, "[Agents] prejudge[d] respondents because of the investigator's personal bias."[64]

As the GAO report highlighted, the federal agencies responsible for tackling employment discrimination also needed to work together more effectively. Although the EEOC was primarily responsible for enforcing Title VII in private employment, several other agencies were supposed to tackle discrimination in other areas. The CSC, for example, was responsible for federal employees, while the OFCC monitored compliance among federal contractors. In reality, however, these agencies worked at cross-purposes and were slow to take action against violators. To try and address these problems, the U.S. Commission on Civil Rights called for the creation of a national employment rights board to coordinate the federal effort.[65]

As a result of these problems, Title VII was largely enforced through lawsuits. Working together, attorneys from the NAACP and the Justice Department secured some significant breakthroughs. In 1974, for example, a federal judge ordered Georgia Power Company to pay $2.1 million to 360 black plaintiffs. At the time, the settlement was the largest ever awarded in a contested civil rights case, with individual payouts averaging close to $4,000. In addition, the huge power provider was told to drop hiring and promotion requirements, including aptitude tests, when they did not relate to job performance. The decision was a clear victory for the Justice Department, which had filed the original case. It contained a number of pioneering clauses, including a commitment to provide bonuses to black workers when they were refused higher-paying jobs. Executives also agreed to hiring and promotion goals; over the next five years, for example, the number of blacks in clerical jobs was designed to rise from 9.6 to 22 percent.[66]

This was not the only landmark settlement. In 1974, the Justice Department and the NAACP also brought a case against nine steel companies that together employed over 340,000 workers. In their complaint, the plaintiffs alleged that the firms, several of which had plants in Birmingham, were engaged in "a pattern or practice of resistance to the full enjoyment of the right to equal employment opportunities."[67] Following more than eighteen months of legal proceedings, the defendants agreed to settle. In a sweeping consent decree, the employers changed the contentious seniority system, which had locked blacks into dirty jobs. The steel settlements also granted $31 million in back pay and ordered employers to commit to clear goals and timetables. Executives made these changes in order to extract themselves from the "quagmire" of litigation and because they wanted to maintain an industrywide seniority system.[68]

A dogged activist, NAACP labor secretary Herbert Hill criticized the awards as inadequate as the average payout was only $300. Hill was also disappointed that plaintiffs had to waive their rights to participate in further legal action, and he was angry that the NAACP was excluded from the final negotiations. The decree's provisions for upgrading were also predicated on complicated qualification requirements. On balance, however, the agreement helped many black employees. In the years that followed, white steelworkers complained that they were the victims of discrimination, a sign that real change was taking place. Because such rulings were now common, moreover, the massive settlement was not appealed.[69]

As the steel case spotlighted, there were drawbacks to relying on litigation. Above all, the legal process rarely offered quick relief, as many of the large class actions took years to resolve. Delays reflected how Title VII cases raised complex issues about how to prove and redress discriminatory practices. While landmark cases did have a broader impact, most judgments also covered a limited number of workers, the "affected class" who had filed suit. Lawsuits therefore tackled employment bias only in an incremental fashion. Finally, even favorable court rulings could subsequently be diluted by new orders from more conservative justices. This became more apparent in the late 1970s, when many whites argued that affirmative remedies had gone too far. As a former local union leader in Savannah recalled, many white members thought that it was unfair for blacks to be given greater promotional rights. "They felt like they was the victim instead of the blacks," explained Joe McCullough, who observed the implementation of an affirmative action program at the Union Camp paper mill. More than a decade after the Civil Rights Act's passage, a lot of white southerners were deeply opposed to remedies that sought to tackle employment discrimination in a meaningful way.[70]

"An Accepted Reality": Black Voting Rights in the Ford Years

In politics, southern blacks continued to make rapid progress; between 1970 and 1975, for example, the number of black elected officials in the region tripled. After concluding a landmark study of southern politics, the journalists Jack Bass and Walter DeVries encapsulated much of the contrast between the political and the economic spheres. "Although southern blacks basically have won the right to equality in political participation," they noted in 1976, "the ultimate battle for economic justice remains to be won. By the mid-1970s the civil rights movement had moved off the streets and through the ballot box into a slowly growing presence in city halls, legislative chambers, and finally the halls of Congress."[71]

As ever, the U.S. Commission on Civil Rights carefully documented this transformation. In January 1975, the commission reported in *The*

Voting Rights Act: 10 Years After that the law had "contributed substantially" to some remarkable political changes. Black and white observers agreed. At congressional hearings held in 1975, the VEP's John Lewis described the changes in the South as a "quiet revolution." Writing in the following year, the *New York Times*'s Bryant Rollins noted that black political participation was now "an accepted reality," whereas fifteen years earlier attempts by blacks to organize politically had met with "violent resistance."[72]

Even in the Deep South, there had been a sharp increase in the number of black voters. Between 1964 and 1972, the commission recorded that the proportion of black registered voters in the seven covered states jumped from 29 percent to over 56 percent. The rate of increase was particularly high in Mississippi, where over 239,000 new black voters had been registered. While whites were still more likely to be registered than blacks, the gap was narrowing; in the seven states, the disparity between white and black registration rates had tumbled from 44.1 to 11.2 percent. As the 1976 presidential election would highlight, southern blacks had become a potent political force.[73]

Blacks were also securing an unprecedented range of elected offices. By March 1976, there were just over two thousand black elected officials in the South, and the region was home to over half of all black officeholders in the country. At a time when around half of African Americans lived in Dixie, southern blacks had again caught up with their northern counterparts, and no more would they have to move north in order to have a political voice. Scene of the climatic voting rights protests of 1965, Alabama epitomized the rapid changes that had occurred. By January 1975, fifteen blacks sat in the previously all-white state legislature. Some of these gains reflected ongoing black activism; in 1974, for example, the NAACP branch in Bessemer, Alabama, conducted a "massive" voter registration campaign, and this enabled a black candidate to be elected to the state legislature from the area. The pace of change was equally impressive in Georgia, where 101 blacks won elected office in 1974, more than the total number of southern blacks who had held such posts when the act was passed. By April 1974, all seven affected states also had integrated state legislatures, a major shift. "The rapid increase in the number of black elected officials is one of the most significant changes in political life in the seven States since passage of the Voting Rights Act," concluded the commission.[74]

One of the key tasks facing the Ford administration was to decide whether to renew the Voting Rights Act's temporary provisions, which were due to lapse in August 1975. At stake were the crucial stipulations that required any change in local voting laws to be precleared by federal authorities. In December 1974, Attorney General William B. Saxbe argued in a memorandum that, while great progress had been made under the act, some problems remained. Despite the increases in black voter registration, a higher proportion of whites were still on the rolls. The number of black elected officials was also small in relation to their share of the southern population; in Mississippi, African Americans were more than a third of the population but held just 4 percent of elected positions. Saxbe also documented that some southern whites were still fighting the law, resistance that necessitated continued intervention by the Justice Department. "While the Act has thus been very effective and has markedly increased black political participation in covered states," concluded Saxbe, "problems of discrimination have been sufficiently recurrent in the past four years to suggest that S[ection] 5 and the examiner and observer provisions are still needed."[75]

At congressional hearings, Saxbe's conclusions were reiterated by a wide variety of groups. Among those who united to defend a symbolic piece of legislation were the National Urban League, the U.S. Commission on Civil Rights, the Leadership Conference on Civil Rights, and the NAACP. Prominent individuals such as Congressman Andrew Young and John Lewis joined them. "The Voting Rights Act," declared Lewis, "was like an infusion of life to the black struggle for equality in the South. It began to eliminate many barriers that had kept blacks out of the arena of politics. In a real sense, the Voting Rights Act has proved to be the life's blood of the voting rights movement, but we've only received the first infusion."[76]

Like Lewis, most activists stressed that fragile political gains could easily be wiped out if the act was not renewed in full. Speaking on behalf of the NAACP, Clarence Mitchell noted important gains but also cited "appalling evidence" of ongoing problems, including discriminatory redistricting schemes and failure to submit changes in local voting laws for preclearance. The NAACP's president in Mississippi, Aaron Henry, detailed how fourteen counties had recently attempted to authorize at-large elections for county supervisors, a move that would have diluted the black vote. When these moves were blocked by the Justice Department, at least ten counties then tried to alter boundary lines in order to achieve the same result. "I and other blacks would be heavily burdened to even imagine our plight if the Voter Rights Act no longer existed," concluded the veteran activist.[77]

In sharp contrast, whites argued that the legislation victimized the South. Alabama congressman Walter Flowers commented that extending the Voting Rights Act "would amount to punishment and further discrimination against covered jurisdictions." Wary of appearing to oppose black voting rights, whites instead argued that the act was no longer required. As Mississippi attorney general Albioun F. Summer claimed, progress under the legislation had been "astronomical," and Mississippi now treated minority voters better than the northern states. In a similar vein, South Carolina attorney general Daniel R. McLeod argued that the Voting Rights Act had "achieved its purpose" because southern blacks were now a powerful political force.[78]

Acknowledging that he did not represent the views of all South Carolinians, McLeod cited hundreds of letters that he had received from both blacks and whites, and they were completely contradictory. Because they addressed the question of whether the act should be renewed, many of them were included in the record. Writing very brief dispatches, whites insisted that there was "no discrimination," whereas African Americans outlined violations of the law. In a typical case, the Walterboro activist Raleigh R. Williams documented how whites were using intimidation and economic coercion to control the electoral process in Colleton County. "We need the 1965 Voting Rights Act and we need people who are willing to see that it is enforced during elections," he concluded.[79]

As these complaints indicate, black political power was still quite limited. Above all, black candidates found it hard to win higher-level positions because most whites would not support them. In 1974, Andrew Young remained the only black congressional representative from any of the seven southern states covered by the act. When Young resigned at the end of 1976, John Lewis was unable to get elected from the same majority-white congressional district in Atlanta. Across the South, no blacks held statewide office either, and those that had tried had fallen short.[80]

Despite important breakthroughs, African Americans also remained underrepresented in state legislatures. By September 1976, African Americans held just 2.3 percent of all elected posts in the former Confederate states, yet they made up 20.5 percent of the voting-age population. These officeholders were concentrated in places where blacks made up at least 40 percent of the population, yet, even in these areas, whites often remained in complete control. In March 1975, there were still 362 majority-black towns and cities that had yet to elect their first black public official.[81]

At the county level, some white registrars also remained reluctant to register qualified blacks, particularly in rural areas. In Humphreys County, Mississippi, for example, the registrar, G. H. Hood, had been in office since 1960, and blacks complained that he had not moved with the times. As the local activist Lawrence Tardy noted in 1974, Hood's reputation was such that "many people would not register if he came knocking at their door." Similar complaints were heard elsewhere. In one Alabama county, blacks complained that the white registrar greeted them with comments such as "I don't see why you need to vote if you can't even read." In other cases, black applicants complained that the registrars stared at them and discouraged them from applying. Across the region, the black community's lack of economic power also continued to undermine its political effectiveness, especially in rural areas. As one black resident of Talullah, Louisiana, commented in 1974, "When the man controls your paycheck he controls you." By the mid-1970s, however, reports of physical violence against politically active blacks were rare.[82]

In much of the Deep South, the Justice Department's attorneys continued to carry out essential work, particularly in using the preclearance provisions to stop discriminatory changes in voting rules. In October 1974, the department sued the county election board in Lancaster County, South Carolina, arguing that a number of the board's changes, including a move to at-large elections with staggered terms, violated the Voting Rights Act because they had not been cleared in advance, as required under section 5. In sum, these provisions would "dilute minority race voters' potential to elect the candidate of their choice." As a result of the suit, the board dropped the objectionable changes. There were many other similar breakthroughs; in the course of 1974, for instance, federal lawyers also stopped a school board in Kemper County, Mississippi, from switching to at-large elections.[83]

Despite Saxbe's support for renewal, several of Ford's aides worried about maintaining the support of southern whites in the upcoming election. Seizing on this, some southern representatives tried to gut the act by broadening its geographic coverage, thus overwhelming the Justice Department with work. Louisiana congressman David Treen even called the act "one of the most abominable pieces of legislation ever adopted by the U.S. Congress," adding that the South should be removed from "perpetually different standards." Initially favoring a simple extension, the president wavered in the face of southern opposition before reaffirming his original stand. He was influenced by several considerations. As the historian Steven Lawson has noted, by this time the act had "become a mainstay of the American electoral system," and politicians from both sides of the House were reluctant to torpedo it. Building on Saxbe's support, J. Stanley Pottinger threw the weight of the Justice Department behind extension, while the sustained campaign by African Americans for renewal also made a difference.[84]

Aware of the need for political symbolism, Ford extended the Voting Rights Act for another seven years on August 6, 1975, the tenth anniversary of Lyndon Johnson's original signing. At a ceremony that was attended by veteran activists such as John Lewis, Roy Wilkins, and Bayard Rustin, Ford commented, "The right to vote is at the very foundation of our American system of government—and nothing must interfere with this precious right."[85] The extension made the ban on literacy tests permanent and extended the principal features of the legislation, including the preclearance requirements. Ultimately, the act's success ensured that even conservative politicians found it difficult to mount a wholehearted case against it, and the extension passed easily with support from many southern senators. Black groups were delighted. "The vote on the Voting Rights Act," declared the NAACP, "is a story of success feeding on success."[86]

Despite some ongoing problems, overall the Voting Rights Act had transformed the political landscape. As a Ford administration analysis concluded, the act was "perhaps the most successful piece of civil rights legislation ever enacted by the Congress." By the mid-1970s, even vocal segregationists had been affected by the mobilization of black voters. Perhaps the most obvious example was that of George Wallace as the fiery populist had toned down his rhetoric and aides now counted the number of blacks attending his rallies. Some blacks also backed Wallace, either because they hoped that their support would be rewarded or because they genuinely believed that his views had softened, although there were doubters. Just a decade after defiantly declaring "Segregation Now—Segregation Tomorrow—Segregation Forever," however, Wallace crowned a black homecoming queen at the University of Alabama and declared, "We're all God's children. All God's children are equal." In a similar vein, Senator Thurmond boasted about helping his black constituents, yet many questioned whether he had really changed. In these years, Thurmond also quashed rumors that he had fathered a child with a young black household maid, a story that turned out to be true.[87]

The 1976 presidential election confirmed that the Voting Rights Act had transformed the political landscape. In all, the Democratic candidate, Jimmy Carter, received 94 percent of the black vote, an impressive mandate. Southern blacks overwhelmingly backed Carter, aides documenting that the black vote had provided the margin of victory in Alabama, Florida, Louisiana, Maryland, Mississippi, North and South Carolina, and Texas. Without African American support, the former Georgia governor would not have carried the region, yet, with it, he won ten of the eleven former Confederate states. As one internal campaign analysis succinctly concluded, "Blacks elected Carter!"[88]

As Carter came into office, however, over a quarter of all black families lived below the federal poverty line. Many African Americans hoped that the victorious candidate would change this, but meeting these expectations at a time of economic constraint was going to be very difficult. As Carter later admitted to a black audience, "People expected so much from a new Democratic President." After eight years of Republican rule, however, southern blacks believed that they now had a president who would do much more to fulfill King's dream.[89]

8

MIXED OUTCOMES

Civil Rights in the Carter Years

During Carter's presidency, the civil rights movement certainly made some important gains. Known for his integrity, Carter symbolized how some southern whites had become more sympathetic to the black cause. Anxious to try and heal racial divisions, the new president met regularly with African American leaders and identified with their work. "I think," he commented in April 1978, "we have a long way to go to repair the damage that has been done in the past by discrimination." Heading a growing movement to make Martin Luther King's birthday a national holiday, Carter credited King with lifting "the yoke of segregation from around our necks," adding that both races had been "liberated" as a result. While they drew on his born-again Baptist faith, Carter's actions also reflected the growth of black political power, a force that was steadily transforming the behavior of white elected officials. The president also tried to back up his rhetoric with action, appointing an unprecedented number of blacks to administrative posts, and working hard to implement civil rights legislation.[1]

There were, however, also some worrying developments in these years, and most of them were beyond the president's control. Earlier successes in desegregating schools, for instance, were now undermined by white flight and resegregation. Because of past inaction, Title VI was only just beginning to be enforced in the higher education sector, which remained a weak link in federal policy. Even success in desegregating downtown stores and buses was now undercut by the white exodus. As they fled the cities, many whites lost interest in the civil rights issue. Few of them expressed concern about the treatment handed out to the "Wilmington Ten," a group of black activists who received harsh sentences following racial disturbances in the Tar Heel City. In the late 1970s, their case gained international attention, exposing troubling racial divisions in the process.

By the end of the 1970s, African American leaders recognized that much had been achieved but were acutely conscious of the problems that remained. As Coretta Scott King wrote, "We have accomplished so much in the ten years since Martin's death, but there is so much yet to be done." Still carrying on the struggle, the NAACP also saw the glass as half full. "The South has been held high to the world as a symbol of change and progress socially, politically and economically," noted its southern conference in 1980. "With the election of a peanut farmer and former governor from the State of Georgia as President of the USA, the term the New South entered the vocabulary of journalists and politicians. Yet, sixteen years after the enactment of the Civil Rights Act of 1964 and subsequent civil rights laws, Southerners of African descent still find poverty, illiteracy, poor housing, little or no political representation or economic strength, more a fact of life today than ever before."[2]

While the association's report was particularly gloomy, it showed that black expectations were not being addressed. Despite upbeat rhetoric, overall Carter was unable to produce a dramatic improvement in race relations. Between 1977 and 1980, the president's best intentions were undermined by a growing white backlash against civil rights and a persistent economic recession that hit the black community hard.[3]

Realizing King's Dream? Black Political Power in the Carter Years

Entering public life at a time when African Americans were just starting to vote in large numbers, Carter was initially cautious on the racial issue. During his gubernatorial campaign in 1970, for example, he visited segregated private schools and insisted that there would have been "a lot more violence" without them, while, as governor, he expressed sympathy with whites who were protesting against school integration orders. Like many southerners, Carter also attended an all-white church, although he was one of the first members of the congregation to try to integrate it.[4]

On the whole, however, Carter's career illustrated how the Voting Rights Act had quickly changed the political landscape. During his governorship, Carter took a number of steps that marked him out as representative of a new breed of southern politicians. Coming into office in early 1971, he announced that "the time for racial discrimination is over," a brave declaration that attracted national attention. The rhetoric was backed up by deeds; he increased the number of blacks on the state payroll by half, ensuring that, out of fifty thousand state workers, eleven thousand were African American. In addition, he placed portraits of leading black Georgians in the statehouse and organized a biracial civil disorder unit to mediate racial disputes. Although these actions upset many white Georgians, they secured praise from liberals across the country. At this time, Carter also sent his daughter, Amy, to a public school in Plains that was 50 percent black. "She goes there because we want her to be in an integrated school," he explained. "She likes it, her mother likes it, and I like it."[5]

When he ran for president, Carter also reached out to blacks. Rather than seeking to fight or ignore the civil rights movement, the Democratic candidate embraced it. "The civil rights laws are the best thing that happened to the South in my lifetime—they broke down barriers to human understanding and compassion," he commented unequivocally.[6]

Both black and white observers saw Carter's election as symbolic. In an editorial, *The Crisis* noted that his victory had special meaning, especially as the descendants of slaves had now voted for a white southerner. Even political foes paid tribute to the collective power of the new black voters, at least in private. They included Harry Dent, the Republican aide who had worked hard to deliver the region for Gerald Ford. "Sorry 'bout the South," he wrote the Ford staffer Dick Cheney immediately after the election. "We all got caught on the size of the massive—biggest in history—Black vote down South. We set a new record in South Carolina for voter turnout."[7]

Some credit should be given to the VEP, whose staff worked with African American leaders for over six months in order to get out the black vote. The VEP financed over one hundred local organizations, including NAACP branches, and it conducted intensive advertising in the region. While the VEP's work was technically nonpartisan, it was clear that the vast majority of blacks were registering as Democrats. A resident of Atlanta, VEP head John Lewis did not hide his admiration for Carter. "I saw him as a symbol of the New South," he recalled, "progressive, socially sensitive, and racially responsive." Lewis wished Dr. King could have witnessed Carter's election. "He would have been so satisfied," he noted, "to see a candidate from the heart of the Deep South stepping forward to lead the nation, laying down the burden of race—or at least easing it."[8]

Carter realized that he needed to repay this political debt. Once in office, he reached out to black groups and was the first president to be interviewed by a black panel. By March 1977, the administration had also named twelve blacks to secondary positions in cabinet departments. Overall, 12 percent of Carter's appointments were black, compared to 4 percent under his successor, Ronald Reagan.[9]

Several of Carter's choices were particularly significant. In a move that was highly symbolic, Carter selected Andrew Young to be the U.S. ambassador to the United Nations. Little more than a decade earlier, most southern blacks had been unable to vote, but now they had a voice representing their country's interests on the world stage. During his tenure, Young helped negotiate an end to white rule in Rhodesia and was a powerful advocate of human rights in general. Although many blacks were disappointed when Young was forced to resign in 1979 because of an unauthorized meeting with the Palestinian Liberation Organization, he still provided blacks with what the *New York Times* termed "a sense of being represented in the front rank of diplomacy."[10] In 1978, Carter also made Louis Martin his special assistant for minority affairs. Born in Tennessee, Martin had previously been an adviser to Presidents Kennedy and Johnson. A powerful figure within the Democratic Party, he liaised with civil rights groups and gave them a point of contact within the administration. Another Carter appointment was Drew S. Days III as assistant attorney general and head of the Justice Department's Civil Rights Division. A former NAACP lawyer, Days was the first African American to hold this important post.[11]

With Days overseeing enforcement of the Voting Rights Act, black political power continued to grow. Surveying the civil rights field in 1978, the *New Republic* declared that politics was "the area of American life in which blacks have registered their greatest successes." Between 1968 and 1978, the number of black elected officeholders quadrupled, and most of these gains took place in the South. In 1965, hardly any blacks held elected office in the region, but, thirteen years later, 1,568 blacks held elected jobs in the six main states covered by the law. By October 1978, Mississippi had seventeen black mayors, while Alabama and South Carolina had twelve apiece. In 1978, the scholar David J. Garrow concluded in a path-breaking study, "The Voting Rights Act of 1965 revolutionized black access to the ballot throughout most of the Deep South."[12]

Many of these gains reflected the persistence of civil rights lawyers. In 1980, for example, the NAACP settled a reapportionment suit in Mississippi that had been going on for over fifteen years. The agreement led to seventeen new black members being elected to the state legislature, including Aaron E. Henry, the Clarksdale pharmacist who had been active in the NAACP for over three decades.[13] By 1979, the SPLC had also litigated more than forty voting rights cases. Many gains resulted from these efforts; in 1978, for example, the center attorney David Walbert won a suit against McIntosh County, Georgia, whose officials had kept blacks out of local posts by using at-large elections. A year after the settlement, one of the plaintiffs was chairing the county commission. As the NAACP's Mississippi case highlighted, however, voting rights cases could be very time-consuming, and the *Bolden* decision also made it more difficult to win them.[14]

Bolden originated in Mobile, where blacks desperately wanted to be fairly represented. In the mid-1970s, they made up 35 percent of Mobile's population, but no black had ever won an elected city office because all the city's commissioners were voted in on an at-large basis. Assisted by the NPVL, black lawyers challenged this system, but the city fought the case by arguing that it had no duty to ensure proportional representation for any racial group. Defense attorneys also insisted that the switch to at-large voting in 1911 had not been racially discriminatory since blacks had already been disfranchised for some time.[15]

The most high-profile of many similar cases, *Mobile v. Bolden* would eventually be heard by the U.S. Supreme Court in the closing days of the Carter administration. In a crucial decision, the court ruled that plaintiffs must prove that at-large elections were adopted or maintained with a racially discriminatory purpose. While the ruling was a setback, the Voting Rights Act was quickly amended to specify that the courts should outlaw voting systems that were discriminatory in their effects, without requiring proof of intent. The plaintiffs eventually prevailed, and, in 1985, three blacks were elected to the Mobile City Council, the first black officeholders there since Reconstruction.[16]

On old movement battlegrounds, some particularly notable gains had occurred. By 1979, for example, Charles Sherrod was a city commissioner in Albany, Georgia. It had been quite a journey for Sherrod, who had worked with blacks in Albany for more than eighteen years. After the media spotlight had left the city, the former SNCC worker stayed on and helped blacks exercise their rights. His election was testament to the SNCC's philosophy of working at the grassroots level for the long haul.[17]

In October 1979, voters in Birmingham also chose Richard Arrington Jr. to be their first black mayor. A racial moderate, Arrington was endorsed by the city's two main newspapers, and some whites reasoned that a black mayor could attract investment to their declining steel town. Primarily, however, Arrington won solid support from a black community that was enraged by the treatment of Bonita Carter, a twenty-year-old African American who was killed by police after she had stolen a car belonging to a black felon. Blacks were angry with the incumbent mayor, David Vann, who had refused to dismiss the police officer involved. In contrast, Arrington pledged to address the issue of police brutality, which remained an ongoing problem in the Magic City. As a result, Birmingham joined Atlanta, Richmond, and New Orleans in having a black mayor. In his inauguration speech, Arrington pleaded for racial unity. "Although there is still work to be done to improve race relations and to bring about racial justice, we no longer deserve the image of the Birmingham of the early sixties," he declared.[18]

Despite these pleas, many whites felt that Arrington would be soft on crime and would, as one woman put it, "turn the city over to Blacks." In 1979, African Americans composed about half of Birmingham's population, and Arrington's ascendancy encouraged even more whites to flee. Although black votes ensured that Arrington was able to win reelection, he was never able to bridge the persistent racial divide as only about 5 percent of whites supported him. According to Arrington's main biographer, Birmingham in these years was "a city that was struggling to turn its back on the past."[19]

Arrington's experience also demonstrated how the power of black mayors was strictly circumscribed. During his tenure, the city's coffers were drained by the closure of manufacturing plants and rapid white flight. Faced by similar problems elsewhere, black mayors were unable to avoid painful budgetary cuts. Critics charged that blacks managed only bankrupt cities, yet their presence was still significant. As the black political scientist Charles V. Houston pointed out in 1978, when cities had black mayors, expenditures for education and social services were significantly increased. Black mayors also instituted more affirmative action and helped bring about fair law enforcement systems.[20]

Maynard Jackson's career helps illustrate Houston's analysis. When work started on the new Atlanta airport, Jackson decided to allocate a fifth of all the construction contracts to minority firms. Prior to 1973, only 0.5 percent of all municipal contracts had gone to blacks. As Jackson later boasted, his administration "rewrote the books on affirmative action," especially as few other airports were built by minority contractors. While they fueled the emergence of Atlanta's black middle class, these policies alienated local businessmen such as Dillard Munford, who viewed the program as "unfair to white people." As Jackson recalled, most whites felt that "affirmative action means you've got to lower the standard," an opinion the mayor rejected as "a real insult" to African Americans. Jackson was never able to win over most of his critics, and whites fled the city in record numbers while he was in charge.[21]

The same divisions were evident whenever blacks exerted their political muscle. By the late 1970s, the power of the black vote meant that southern authorities were beginning to acknowledge the civil rights movement's importance. In Montgomery, where almost half of all voters were now black, the chamber of commerce had placed King's Dexter Avenue Baptist Church on a tour of historic sites that also included the first White House of the Confederacy and the state capitol. Although a street in a black neighborhood had been named in Rosa Parks's honor, mass petitions demanded that the city council rename Jackson Street, scene of many protests, for Dr. King. Because of white opposition, the state legislature instead chose to name a portion of interstate 85 "Martin Luther King Jr. Expressway." In 1978, the *New York Times* noted that the sign announcing the new freeway was occasionally damaged, but Governor Wallace's workers quickly repaired it.[22]

Taking up an issue that was very important to black voters, President Carter spearheaded the campaign to make Martin Luther King's birthday a federal holiday. As early as 1971, the SCLC and Coretta Scott King had called on lawmakers to authorize the holiday, but their pleas fell on deaf ears. Between 1973 and 1975, however, the movement gathered momentum, and four northern states recognized the holiday.[23] The establishment of the new federal holiday was included in the 1976 Democratic Party platform, and it was strongly supported by Senator Edward M. Kennedy, who was a powerful rival of the president's. For its supporters, the move was an important act of reconciliation. As the Congressional Black Caucus put it, "Recognition of this great leader, who would be the first Black American to be so honored, would be an important symbolic step in progress toward full inclusion of blacks in American society."[24]

Unlike Kennedy, Carter was able to use his southern background to identify with King's ideas. Receiving the Martin Luther King Nonviolent Peace Prize on what would have been the preacher's fiftieth birthday, the president commented, "We are still dedicated to carrying out the purposes espoused by Dr. King." Carter praised King's "dream" of racial brotherhood, claiming that the inclusion of Andrew Young in the cabinet was a step toward its fulfillment. In 1979, he also accompanied Coretta King on an emotional visit to the motel where her husband had been slain.[25]

Back in Georgia, many whites did not share Carter's views. In 1979, the Peach State spent $12 million on commemorations of the birthdays of two Confederate heroes (Jefferson Davis and Robert E. Lee), yet white leaders argued that they could not afford to grant a holiday for King. Another paid vacation, argued Georgia speaker Thomas Murphy, would cost the state about $6 million in salaries. Black Georgians accused their opponents of bigotry. "You cannot expect a rural-dominated Legislature with a racist history and a racially insensitive present to respond to black people when black people are disorganized and are not voting," charged state representative David Scott. Divisions between Coretta King and the SCLC also hurt the holiday movement, as conference leaders felt that Coretta was trying to build a "cult of personality" around her late husband. They stressed that it was more important to perpetuate Dr. King's ideas, particularly his commitment to fighting poverty.[26]

In the late 1970s, other southern states were reluctant to make King's birthday a paid holiday. In Florida, January 15 was an official holiday, but state employees did not get the day off, while, in South Carolina, the day was an "optional" holiday that employees could substitute for one of three Confederate vacations. Following the refusal of the Georgia state legislature to embrace the holiday, Carter instead backed a federal holiday.[27]

Initially, the intensive lobbying by civil groups looked to have paid off. In November 1979, however, the administration-backed bill was killed by a coalition of Republicans and conservative Democrats. Together, they drafted a key amendment that shifted the holiday to a Sunday and provided that federal employees who worked on that day would not get holiday pay. Leading the resistance, Helms and Thurmond mobilized many of their southern colleagues. According to Helms, it was wrong to honor "one man who emphasized discontent" rather than recognizing ordinary Americans who had "built strong families and established communities." Going even further, Georgia congressman Larry P. McDonald asserted that Americans should not sanctify somebody "who deliberately brought violence to American streets."[28] Opponents also argued that the holiday was too costly, but black leaders insisted that it offered modest compensation for centuries of mistreatment. "Given the hundreds of years of economic sacrifice and involuntary servitude of American blacks," asked Coretta King, "is it too much to ask that one paid holiday per year be set aside to honor the contributions of a black man who gave his life in an historic struggle for social decency?"[29]

White views were not monolithic, however, and some Republicans began to see the advantages of supporting the holiday. After the 1976 election, it was clear that the GOP needed black support to win back the White House. One advocate of change was Harry Dent, the South Carolinian who had once championed the "Southern strategy" within the Nixon administration. In the wake of the vote on the King holiday, Dent pleaded with Thurmond to moderate his approach. "I understand your concern," he wrote his former boss, "not only for the cost to the government but also because this fellow had some good and bad motives." Nevertheless, Dent pointed out that King was "a hero to just about all Black people and liberals in this country." He suggested that Thurmond should be able to recognize King without compromising his own integrity. Moreover, if Republicans could make a gesture in favor of civil rights, it could transform their fortunes. "Anything reasonable we can do to improve relations with Black leaders should be done," he advised.[30]

Dent's behavior showed that southern blacks were a political force to be reckoned with, as did Thurmond's reaction. In the late 1970s, the senator publicly opposed the holiday, but he later reversed his position when he grasped its popularity with blacks. In the midterm elections of 1978, Thurmond appointed blacks to his campaign team and openly reached out to African American voters. While admitting that he had made "mistakes," he insisted that he would now represent all his constituents fairly. In a state where African Americans made up 26 percent of all registered voters, no politician could afford to ignore them. During the Carter years, other Republicans began to court the black vote. In one remarkable turnaround, two top officials of the Mississippi Republican Party even attended the NAACP's state convention.[31]

The 1979 defeat did not stop the King holiday movement. Later in the year, the black congressman John Conyers declared that the holiday was "a major civil rights issue" and pledged that supporters would not quit. Bearing this out, in 1980 Coretta King organized mass petitions and testified before Congress in favor of the holiday. Around the same time, the African American singer Stevie Wonder released "Happy Birthday," a hit single that became a rallying cry for the movement. As Wonder eloquently put it, "I just never understood / How a man who died for good / Could not have a day that would / Be set aside for his recognition." Clearly, the fight was far from over.[32]

Mixed Outcomes: Busing and Resegregation

In the Carter years, the movement's mixed fortunes were especially apparent in education. Again, veteran campaigners had much to be proud of, as the South's schools were now the most desegregated in the country. In May 1979, the aide Gordon Stewart noted in a memorandum to the president that there had been a "gradual acceptance [of *Brown*] by the South, which is now in greater compliance than many Northern cities."[33]

Many southern whites had also reconciled themselves to busing. Much of their opposition had been based on fears that the tactic would have negative consequences, but these worries had proved to be largely unfounded. In February 1979, a massive survey of racial attitudes by the National Conference of Christians and Jews found that, while 85 percent of whites still opposed busing, 56 percent of white parents whose children had been bused considered the experience to be "very satisfactory." As the study concluded, "The irony of busing to achieve racial balance is that rarely has there been a case where so many have been opposed to an idea which appears not to work badly at all when put into practice." As a result, the busing issue was no longer the major controversy that it had been. Not surprisingly, supporters of the tactic claimed that they had been vindicated. "It is quite simply the only solution available if there is to be substantial integration in this generation," wrote the political scientist Gary Orfield in 1978. Supporting Orfield's point, in some southern cities busing had destroyed all vestiges of the dual school system.[34]

While opposition to busing had declined, it had not disappeared. As *The Crisis* declared in late 1978, busing was "the issue that will not go away." Showing a capacity to adapt their arguments to the changing political climate, opponents now tried to use the energy crisis to promote neighborhood schools. Fundamentally caused by America's dependency on imported oil, energy shortages were a problem for much of the 1970s. They intensified in 1979, when OPEC price increases and instability in Iran caused the cost of crude oil to almost double. Observing these developments, some whites asserted that local schools offered one solution. In July 1979, the South Carolinian Mrs. Robert Keys wrote Thurmond, "Millions of gallons of fuel per day . . . are wasted by having school buses take children right past their homes to a distant school."[35] Thurmond took up the argument, which drew on long-standing claims that busing was an unnecessary waste of resources. "Forced busing," he wrote in January 1980, "compounds our energy supply problems." In a similar vein, Senator Helms claimed that busing wasted money that should have been spent directly on the schools.[36]

Opposition also subsided because the courts did not order much new busing in these years. "For a variety of reasons," declared *Time* in 1977, "busing is no longer education's most controversial issue." In the wake of *Milliken v. Bradley,* the Supreme Court backed away from endorsing cross-district busing. Ongoing political opposition had also had an effect, especially as Congress was successful in pressuring HEW to turn away from the tactic. In an effort to break up segregation, HEW now sponsored "magnet" schools that offered courses not available elsewhere in the system, as well as state-of-the-art equipment and facilities, in order to attract white students back. Ever the mediator, Carter also worked to calm feelings. Rather than proposing legislation that would stall or halt busing, his advisers urged a "careful, sensitive approach" in what they recognized as a "difficult area."[37]

The turn away from busing also reflected doubts about whether it was an effective means of desegregating the schools. By the late 1970s, many urban school systems were suffering from record levels of white flight. The exodus made busing less relevant because most cities found that they no longer had enough white pupils to transport. In Dallas, where both mandatory and voluntary busing was in effect, rates of flight were indicative. Between 1970 and 1977, over 40,000 white pupils vanished in a system that had enrolled 160,000 students. The school system in the Texan city went from 18 percent black in 1956 to 61.9 percent black in 1976. "We just don't have enough whites to go around any more," admitted a school official in 1978. The situation was even more extreme in Richmond, where whites had been fleeing the city for over a decade. In 1962, the student body was 55 percent white, but, by 1978, it was 82 percent black. "This means," noted *U.S. News and World Report,* "that nearly all black children attend schools that are almost all black."[38]

Across the South, resegregation happened remarkably quickly, and it even affected communities with relatively good race relations. In Durham, North Carolina, for example, the schools had desegregated peacefully, yet many whites still reacted by leaving the city. As Christina Greene has documented, the city's schools soon became dominated by low-income blacks as wealthier residents moved away, highlighting the class biases that were often involved in integration. This flight was not simply related to school desegregation; it was part of a broader shift to the suburbs, particularly by middle-class residents. Its effects, however, were startling. Between 1970 and 1987, the proportion of whites in Durham's public schools fell from 45 to just 13 percent. A similar process was occurring in Birmingham, another sign of that city's troubling racial divisions. A teacher at Greymont Elementary School from 1967 through to the 1980s, Dorothy Craig watched the white exodus affect her classes. "Each year you would see more blacks," she recalled. "The longer I stayed there the blacker it became. . . . I could tell the difference in the flight the next year a little bit more, a few more left—the students."[39]

Atlanta was the preeminent New South city, and it epitomized broader trends. In 1973, the local NAACP had agreed to a limited busing plan that failed to desegregate schools in heavily black areas. Lambasting the deal, the national NAACP suspended the Atlanta branch. In a city that was more racially polarized than its promoters admitted, many whites still disliked the agreement, partly because an African American was named school superintendent and blacks were given half of all administrative positions. They reacted by moving to the burgeoning northern suburbs, a shift that was encouraged by federal highway subsidies. Over the course of the 1970s, the city lost a staggering 40 percent of its white population as more than 100,000 people headed to the suburbs. Critics joked that "The City Too Busy to Hate" had become "The City Too Busy Moving to Hate."[40]

As a result of this exodus, by the end of the decade Atlanta's public schools were about 90 percent black. Some schools, like Southwest Atlanta High, went from being 95 percent white to 99 percent black within a decade. "To what extent can you achieve integration with only 10 percent white enrollment?" asked John A. Minor Jr., an associate superintendent. Most whites now lived in a ring of suburbs that engulfed the overwhelmingly black city, the so-called donut effect. Concerned that the situation might deter investors, the chamber of commerce spearheaded a slick effort to lure whites back. While this public relations campaign failed to substantially increase white enrollments, it reassured investors that civic leaders still cared about the public schools.[41]

In the rural South, resegregation was also a problem. By this time, private academies were a common sight in country areas, particularly where blacks constituted the majority of the population. In Terrell County, Georgia, almost all the county's white pupils attended Terrell Academy, a private school that had opened its doors only in 1971. In the same year, whites in predominantly black Wilcox County, Alabama, also reacted to integration by fleeing en masse to a private academy that was located less than a mile from the formerly all-white high school. As the *New York Times*'s Dan Barry put it, "True integration in the county's public school system lasted about as long as it takes to walk out a door." Across the Mississippi Delta, the picture was the same. As the historian J. Todd Moye has noted, whites in the area essentially "gave up" on the public schools once they realized that freedom of choice was not going to be upheld. By 1985, more than 90 percent of public school students in the Delta town of Indianola were African American.[42]

In Summerton, South Carolina, where part of the *Brown* case had originated, the situation was particularly sobering. Following desegregation in the late 1960s, whites fled to a new private school or to predominantly white public schools in nearby Manning, where parents had bought land so that their children could enroll. By 1979, the Summerton school district was almost totally black. "Actually, the system is 99 and 99/100ths percent black," commented the local NAACP leader William Fleming, pointing out that one white pupil went to school with 2,028 blacks. White parents were again unwilling to send their children to heavily black schools because this would, they insisted, lower academic standards. Despite these developments, the original plaintiff Harry Briggs insisted that his efforts had not been in vain. "The whites they got the private school," he acknowledged in 1979. "But at least the children can ride the buses to school, and they couldn't do that before. You got to take some pride, it's better."[43]

By the late 1970s, however, the resegregation of public school systems was generating concern, even among the NAACP's leaders. "Growing instances of resegregation in the South," declared *The Crisis* in May 1977, "have denied the vast majority of black children their constitutional right [to a desegregated education]." In 1977, the U.S. Commission on Civil Rights also complained about a "pattern of racial isolation" within urban schools. The commission pointed to Georgia, where metropolitan areas now contained "intensely segregated public schools," yet it acknowledged that the problem was much broader. "The continued and rapid migration of whites from cities to suburbs has resulted in heightened racial and economic separation," it concluded.[44]

As some scholars have pointed out, it is simplistic to see white flight purely as a response to busing or desegregation. After all, the exodus from the cities was occurring well before the schools integrated, and it was influenced by the shifting of jobs and services to suburban areas.[45] Busing was used on only a limited basis in Atlanta, but whites still left the city. In New Orleans, where the public schools also became heavily black, officials insisted that many whites had moved for nonracial reasons. "Without question, we have had white flight," admitted school superintendent Gene Geisbert. "The flight to the suburbs was not just racial, however. For many it had to do with economics, seeking the so-called good life."[46]

Nevertheless, racial factors were a significant cause of the exodus. "There is now considerable academic consensus that in large cities a significant linkage exists between white flight and forced busing," declared *Time* in 1978. In the same year, a study of twenty-three cities by the sociologist David Armor concluded that busing had accelerated white flight. Without busing, Armor projected, white student loss would have been between 2 and 4 percent over a six-year period, but busing drove the rate up to 15 percent in the first year in which the tactic was used and 7–9 percent over the next three years.[47]

Other studies confirm that busing accelerated a movement that was already under way. In Nashville, where a comprehensive busing plan was introduced in June 1971, the number of white students in the public schools fell from 66,393 in 1971 to 44,295 eight years later. After a careful analysis of enrollment data, the political scientists Richard A. Pride and J. David Woodard concluded that the public schools "enrolled 15 percent fewer white children than would have been expected in the absence of busing." They also found that middle-class whites were most likely to withdraw their children, largely because they "abhorred" black culture and worried that the presence of blacks would undermine their values of self-discipline, hard work, and politeness. In addition, affluent residents were best placed to enroll their children in private schools. By 1979, white flight was so extensive that a federal judge decided to terminate Nashville's busing plan.[48]

The growth of private schools thwarted Dr. King's dream that white and black children would sit next to each other in the classroom. Realizing this, the Carter administration put pressure on the private schools to accept more black pupils. The IRS code gave tax-exempt status to charitable, religious, and educational institutions, and this allowed the schools to avoid participation in the social security program. More importantly, it allowed whites to make tax-deductible contributions to "segregation academies." Supporters of the schools fought hard to maintain these advantages, and the IRS was slow to change its rules, routinely giving tax-exempt status to new private schools. By 1975, new guidelines meant that schools could maintain this status only if they had a formal policy of nondiscrimination, yet lily-white schools often kept their exemptions by declaring that they did not discriminate. In 1977, Carter's aides sought to clamp down, demanding that schools had to prove that they enrolled at least 20 percent of available black pupils.[49]

The IRS received more than 100,000 letters against this policy, more than it had ever received on a single issue. In them, parents insisted that private schools were necessary to give their children a quality education, claims that did not convince northern liberals. "The fact that many of these schools were founded at the time of desegregation plans is irrelevant, they say," wrote Anne G. Witte in the *New Republic*. "They created their schools as alternatives to the drug abuse, violence and godlessness that took over in the public schools, coincidentally just as they were being integrated." Also viewing the schools as a response to desegregation, most blacks felt that they should not receive public support. "Jim Crow with your own dough," declared one black protester. While race was certainly important, many southern whites also mobilized to defend Christian schools because they believed that the IRS regulations violated the separation of church and state. As the historian Joseph Crespino has shown, the battle to defend Christian schools mobilized evangelical whites into conservative organizations, a development that had lasting consequences for national politics. Taking advantage of new direct mail techniques, groups such as the National Christian Action Coalition organized many of the letters. Their efforts eventually paid off as in 1982 President Reagan decreed that racially exclusive schools should be allowed to receive tax exemptions.[50]

Resegregation was not the only negative consequence of school desegregation; another major problem was the continuing fall in the number of black teachers and principals, a change that demoralized many African American campaigners. By 1978, the Mississippi civil rights leader Alfred "Skip" Robinson went as far as to call desegregation "the worst thing that ever happened to black people." The Magnolia State, he explained, had led the country in its number of black school principals, but very few of these role models now remained in their posts. A dogged supporter of desegregation, even the NAACP acknowledged the problem. In May 1977, *The Crisis* estimated that over six thousand black principals had been dismissed or demoted since *Brown* was handed down. "The price that black children, teachers, and administrators have paid for the constitutional right of equality of educational opportunity has been staggering," it admitted.[51]

In rural areas, whites also retained control of most administrative positions even when the student body was heavily black, and this caused further inequities. By the late 1970s, for example, the vast majority of whites in President Carter's home county sent their children to the private Southland Academy. Among those enrolled at the shining facility were the children of the county school superintendent as well as those of several principals and school board members. In contrast, Sumter County's black pupils attended a high school that had been condemned by the state fire marshal. At the school, pigeons roosted in the rafters, and rain dripped through the ceiling. Longing for a better deal, many blacks were angry. "Integration has not helped the typical black child," commented the local activist Eugene Cooper. "The have completely lost their identity, their sense of community. I think it was designed that way."[52]

Right across the South, NAACP activists continued to fight for a fairer deal within the integrated schools. As a 1980 regional report summarized, "The issue of achieving quality integrated education remained of major concern to units region-wide." Some branches led protests against injustices. In Albany, Georgia, when a white teacher forced a seven-year-old black student to wash her mouth out with soap, the NAACP led mass marches and also filed a complaint with HEW. In many other cases, branches pressed for the reinstatement of displaced black teachers, who were often its members. Right across the region, the association also kept up the pressure to ensure that integration plans were implemented in good faith. In 1979–1980, for instance, the Mississippi field conference filed twenty complaints with HEW to ensure that school districts were brought back into compliance with the provisions of federal court orders.[53]

Despite the problems in the schools, they were much more integrated than the region's universities. For several years, the NAACP LDF had been fighting to get HEW to take stronger action against southern universities, but it was not until 1977 that the federal courts ruled decisively in the plaintiffs' favor. In *Adams v. Richardson,* the District Court for the District of Columbia ordered HEW to devise specific desegregation criteria and required six noncomplying states to adhere to them. Case data highlighted the need for change; at the University of Arkansas in Fayetteville, for example, just 4 percent of students were black. Across the South, young blacks were also much more likely to attend two-year institutions rather than the more prestigious four-year universities.[54]

At the graduate and professional levels, black underrepresentation was striking. In the fall of 1977, 12 percent of the undergraduates in Florida's public universities were black, compared to 7.4 percent of the graduates and 4.7 percent of professional enrollees. Figures were similar in other states, partly because many two-year colleges did not offer master's or doctoral programs. In the late 1970s, for example, none of the five traditionally black colleges in North Carolina awarded the Ph.D. degree. African American students were also more likely to come from poor backgrounds, and this made it harder for them to continue on to graduate study. Because few blacks were enrolled in doctoral programs, the number of black faculty remained small. In 1977, African Americans made up less than 3 percent of the full-time faculty at the traditionally white institutions covered by *Adams.*[55]

While the *Adams* decision represented a breakthrough, it did not bring about a rapid transformation, partly because the universities were given a lot of time to make changes. As the plaintiffs' lawyer John Silard commented, "We were disappointed that HEW has given the States another five to ten years to finish a reform that should have been completed many years ago." The U.S. Commission on Civil Rights also identified flaws in the court's decision, noting that many of the recommendations relied heavily on "good faith intentions" rather than requiring universities to make "specific, affirmative steps." Concerned that little would change, the commission wanted explicit mechanisms for recruiting black faculty and students. Federal officials, however, still deferred to administrators' desires for autonomy from government interference and treated the universities with a softer touch than they had the schools.[56]

The lack of meaningful improvements frustrated some black observers. Speaking at the University of Mississippi in 1979, the African American journalist Lerone Bennett noted, "The admission of a handful of gifted black students and athletes to a white university in which all the lines of authority and power are still controlled by whites is not— repeat—not integration. It is at best desegregation." Supporting Bennett's analysis, the Oxford campus now had eight hundred black students, but there were almost no black administrators, faculty, or decisionmakers. According to Bennett, a native Mississippian, southern blacks had "crossed a river" but still had to "cross a sea."[57] Disillusioned with the lack of progress, some blacks chose, instead, to support traditionally black colleges, yet few whites would enroll at these institutions. In 1978, for instance, 98.8 percent of the enrollment at Alabama State University in Montgomery was black. The following year, the merger of historically black Tennessee State University with the University of Tennessee at Nashville, whose student body was 99 percent white, led to most white students and faculty abandoning the new university. In 1980, a study by the Southern Regional Education Board threw light on this problem, finding that whites still doubted the quality of black universities. "The image which many whites seem to hold of the black institution is one of inferiority," it concluded.[58]

In the Carter years, then, the desegregation of the education sector continued to be bitterly contested. In these years, the controversy over the Wilmington Ten also illustrated that civil rights violations in southern communities could still secure national attention. The case had its origins in the racial violence that had accompanied the desegregation of Wilmington's schools a few years earlier. During bitter clashes, blacks had barricaded one of the city's main streets and posted armed guards because they felt that police would not protect them. Some thirteen months after the violence had subsided, ten black activists were charged with the burning of Mike's Grocery, a small white-owned store that was located in the black neighborhood. Following a lengthy trial, in February 1976 the Reverend Ben Chavis and nine coworkers were convicted of arson and conspiracy and received a combined sentence of 282 years. Over the ensuing months, however, the prosecution's case began to fall apart as three key witnesses, all young blacks, recanted their testimony. In the summer of 1976, for example, one of those witnesses, Allen Hall, admitted that state prosecutors had coerced him into testifying. By 1978, as a growing movement demanded that the defendants be freed, the case had become what *Newsweek* termed "the international cause celebre of the Wilmington Ten."[59]

The prisoners charged that they were victims of old-fashioned southern racism, framed for fighting for racial justice. As Chavis wrote in an open letter to the president, "For six long years, we have suffered from the chronic disease of American racism and Jim Crow injustice of the old 'New South.'"[60] Building on claims that the South had not really changed, they were able to mobilize a great deal of support, particularly from African Americans. In all, the Carter administration received more than forty thousand petitions asking them to free the Wilmington Ten. Rallying to the group's side, black leaders organized a 143-mile march from Charlotte to Raleigh that pressed Governor Jim Hunt to free the defendants, and members of the Congressional Black Caucus and the National Conference of Black Lawyers also demanded the group's release.[61] Criticisms also came from abroad, where Amnesty International called the ten "prisoners of conscience." As London's *Financial Times* noted, "The case has called into question whether racial equality really has been achieved in the new south."[62]

Within the South, however, most whites refused to accept that the defendants had been persecuted for their political views. A native of Wilson who had just come into office, Governor Jim Hunt was responsive to the white majority and initially refused to intervene. For the Carter administration, however, as Louis Martin wrote privately, the case was "an issue that we do not need." Above all, the publicity threatened to undermine Carter's claims to uphold human rights at home and abroad. In the end, Justice Department officials covertly negotiated with Hunt and persuaded him to reduce the group's sentences. Nine of them became eligible for parole by November 1978, although Chavis had to wait until early 1980. In December 1980, the case was finally resolved when the Fourth Circuit Court of Appeals overturned the convictions.[63]

A New Way of Life? White Flight and Public Accommodations

While the Wilmington case raised some troubling questions about race relations in the South, in terms of access to public accommodations there had been enormous progress. By the late 1970s, public facilities were completely desegregated, and the issue no longer occupied the Justice Department's staff. As a group of black lawyers told President Carter in 1979, in many ways the progress made under the Civil Rights Act had been "almost revolutionary." They added, "Some argue today that public accommodations for blacks are better in Mississippi than they are in Maine."[64]

Title II had transformed life in the state that had been dubbed "The Closed Society" a little more than a decade earlier.[65] In 1979, a group of black and white thinkers gathered at the University of Mississippi, the scene of riots when James Meredith had tried to enroll. Now, noted black scholars such as C. Eric Lincoln and Vincent Harding were able to dine with their white colleagues. Reporting from Mississippi's capital in the same year, *U.S. News and World Report* was upbeat about the amount of social interaction that was occurring. "Today," it reported, "blacks and whites mingle in schools and factories, on buses and in places of business. They share tables in restaurants." Overall, segregation was "yielding to a new life that most of its people would have deemed impossible a generation ago."[66]

This new way of life was evident right across the region. When the "Greensboro Four" reenacted their iconic protest in 1980, they were served a meal by the black vice president of Woolworths while the bells of nearby churches rang out in celebration. In a further indication of change, white political leaders now recognized their bravery. To commemorate the twentieth anniversary, Greensboro Mayor E. S. (Jim) Melvin called a weekend of observance, while Governor Hunt declared February 1 as "civil rights and equality day in North Carolina." Now in their late thirties, the four protesters had come a long way since their student days. Franklin McCain, for example, was a midlevel manager at a Charlotte textile company, and Joseph McNeill was a Fayetteville stockbroker. Looking back, however, all of them were proud of the part they had played in striking down Jim Crow.[67]

The South's progress in tackling overt discrimination was highlighted by the 1980 census, which confirmed that blacks continued to return to the region. Between 1970 and 1980, the number of African Americans in the eleven former Confederate states increased by close to two million, topping out at around twelve million. Many of those who moved back were well-qualified professionals. Generally educated in the North, they were a crucial part of the region's growing black middle class.[68]

There was a downside, however, and it was again linked to white flight. Because few whites now rode buses or shopped in downtown stores, the movement's victories in the public accommodations area were undermined. Visiting Montgomery in 1978, the northern journalist John

Herbers found that almost all the passengers on city buses were African Americans. "The bus line that Rosa Parks integrated carries mostly poor blacks who cannot afford automobiles, many of them maids who work on the east side," he wrote. Montgomery's downtown was also deserted as the focus of commercial life shifted to the expanding suburbs on the east side of town. "Dr. King might find it hard to organize a movement here now," concluded Herbers.[69]

The situation was similar in Greensboro. While the former sit-in protesters were now served easily, the broader problem for Greensboro's blacks was finding anywhere to shop or eat downtown. By 1980, there were ten vacant buildings in the two-block area that used to constitute the core of the business district. Even the S. H. Kress store, which had also been a target of the original sit-ins, had closed. Most whites shopped at new malls on the edge of town and had little contact with blacks.[70]

As president, Carter's ability to stall white flight was limited, and many of the developments that blunted his civil rights initiatives were similarly beyond his control. Because he was elected with so many black votes, however, the Georgian was expected to deliver, and many felt that he had not done enough. As Bayard Rustin noted in 1979, "Symbols, even when offered by a decent man like Carter, are simply no substitute for policy." Throughout his presidency, Carter found it very hard to satisfy expectations, and this was particularly decisive in the complex economic area. It would be here that the ongoing limitations of federal civil rights policy would be most apparent.[71]

9

"NO SUBSTANTIAL PROGRESS"

Blacks, the Economy, and Racial Polarization in the Late 1970s

Nowhere were the disappointments of the Carter years more apparent than in the economic arena. Throughout the Carter presidency, the economic downturn had a harsh impact on African Americans, who remained vulnerable to layoffs. As one black leader commented in 1979, "When this economy sneezes, we get pneumonia." Witnessing these developments, civil rights groups focused heavily on economic issues and demanded help. Unlike Ford, Carter was responsive to demands for full employment, yet his efforts to bring it about were largely unsuccessful, frustrating an expectant African American community.[1]

In the South, the economic gap between blacks and whites failed to narrow significantly in these years. By 1980, a detailed report by the SRC concluded, "On basic economic issues the South of the 1970's made no substantial progress in reducing the burden of race which blacks were carrying in the segregated conditions of the 1950's." Council figures showed that black men in the region still earned only fifty-seven cents for every dollar made by their white counterparts, and they were more likely to be unemployed than they had been in the 1950s. Carter certainly recognized the seriousness of these disparities. As he told a group of Atlanta blacks in 1979, "It is not enough to have the right to sit at a lunch counter when you cannot afford the price of a decent meal." On the ground, however, many blacks felt forgotten and frustrated. Some commentators argued that economic inequalities had led to outbreaks of violence, such as the Miami riots of 1980, which resulted in the deaths of eighteen people. As the Atlanta University professor Ed Irons noted, "It is no wonder young black youths are predisposed to riot. Even when the economy is going strong they don't get hired. You can't attribute this to anything but institutional racism."[2]

Pointing to these statistics, black leaders argued that the gains of the civil rights era should not be overstated. On a visit to Mississippi in 1979, Julian Bond asserted, "Movement politics have failed to make any real dent in the economic conditions for blacks in Mississippi and the nation."[3] The Urban League's Vernon E. Jordan even dubbed 1979 a "year of crisis" for African Americans because of the severe economic problems that they faced. Claiming that over half of all black youths were jobless, Jordan criticized the Carter administration for privileging the fight against inflation over job creation. "It is bad economics and bad morality to try to force black and poor people to become cannon fodder in the war on inflation," he asserted. Unable to fulfill expectations, Carter did not receive as much black support in 1980 as he had four years earlier.[4]

Part of the problem was that many whites fiercely opposed efforts to help blacks. In the late 1970s, there were numerous signs that southern whites, in particular, were growing tired of civil rights initiatives. Undermining legal efforts to combat employment discrimination, some were now filing reverse discrimination claims. At the same time, a revival of the Ku Klux Klan also reflected lingering anger over busing and affirmative action. The election of 1980 signaled a sharp turn to the right, and in many ways Reagan's victory was a culmination of a white backlash that Carter was unable to contain. Sensing defeat, on the eve of the vote Carter told the NAACP's conference in Miami, "Our hard-won gains face the most severe counter-attack since the time of *Brown v. Board of Education*. . . . The directions that we choose this year will determine not only what happens in the next few years, but for the rest of this century." Reagan declined an invitation to speak at the convention.[5]

Left Out: Efforts to Address Black Economic Inequality

Of course, some southern blacks did prosper in these years, particularly gifted individuals who could seize the new opportunities. In 1977, the NAACP's Kelly M. Alexander Sr. summed up the mixed picture particularly well. "Some blacks continue to move into higher status jobs as new opportunities are opened to them," observed the North Carolinian. "The problem is, as we see it, progress as to employment mainly has come to the better trained middle class black citizens and the poorer blacks who either have no education or a very poor education are left out."[6]

In inner-city neighborhoods, a black underclass was being left behind as wealthier residents fled to the suburbs. Trumpeted by *Time* as "the black showcase of the nation," Atlanta epitomized the schizophrenic nature of the black economic experience. While a minority of African Americans prospered, many more did not. Residents such as Larry Callahan, a nineteen-year-old interviewed in 1978, spent their days in futile searches for work. "Everywhere I go I see signs saying 'equal opportunity employer,'" he declared, "but they look at some blacks and say that they just ain't got the skill. I just want to have me a good job with decent pay. Everybody keeps saying hang loose, hang loose. But it's hard to hang loose living like this."[7]

In 1977, a failed strike by the city's low-paid sanitation workers highlighted the growing economic divide within the African American community. Confronted by severe budgetary limitations, Maynard Jackson was able to persuade middle-class blacks to back his tough stance against the workers, who demanded substantial pay increases. Jackson quickly replaced the strikers, a move that was endorsed by Martin Luther King Sr. on the ninth anniversary of his son's murder. In view of the strikers' militancy, King declared, Jackson had every right to "fire the hell out of them." On the whole, the city's black elite supported Jackson because they claimed that his economic policies were creating jobs. As a result of the mayor's harsh actions, the sanitation workers had to reapply for their positions, and many ended up earning less than they had before. The Atlanta situation was not unusual; in several other southern cities, tight budgets and public opposition to union demands foiled walkouts by poorly paid municipal workers.[8]

Although the development of a black underclass was a central theme of the Carter years, most white journalists proclaimed that the South was a booming Sun Belt and overlooked the existence of widespread poverty. Most of the Sun Belt prosperity passed blacks by, partly because federal spending tended to go to white businesses. As the southern historian David R. Goldfield has eloquently observed, "The black underclass remained invisible and forgotten; if its members entered white consciousness at all, they could be readily dismissed as beyond hope anyway, considering how many of their brothers and sisters had taken advantage of the new order in the South." Of course, black poverty was not simply a reflection of the weak enforcement of the civil rights laws. The broader causes went much deeper and included the decline of black farms, the demise of traditional manufacturing industries, and the reluctance of new industries to move into heavily black areas. Nevertheless, the implementation of Title VII remained problematic, contributing to the situation.[9]

While the urban poor were more visible, there was also plenty of poverty in the countryside. Across the region, industry failed to move into majority-black counties, partly because executives felt that blacks were poorly skilled and were more prone to join unions. Writing in the New Republic, Nick Kotz was one of the few journalists to explore the problem. "The widely heralded industrial development of the New South has mostly bypassed areas where most blacks live," he noted. "Although hundreds of thousands of new industrial jobs have been created, blacks actually have suffered a net loss of jobs."[10]

The fate of Soul City graphically highlighted the difficulties of attracting industry to heavily black, rural counties. The community was a new town that the activist Floyd McKissick tried to construct in order to address ongoing black inequality. Following his departure from CORE in 1968, McKissick strove to improve blacks' economic plight because he felt that a "strong black economy" would be "the spearhead of racial equality."[11] After winning a $14 million guarantee from Housing and Urban Development (HUD) in 1972, McKissick and his aides worked hard to build their dream community, but it was an enormous task. The town was located in majority-black Warren County, North Carolina, which had one of the lowest per capita income levels in the state and an unemployment rate of over 30 percent. As a freestanding community, Soul City desperately needed to attract industrial jobs if it was to prosper, and planners gave "first priority" to that task. They estimated that the projected population of fifty thousand would need to be supported by eighteen thousand jobs, at least half of them manufacturing positions.[12] In the late 1970s, Soul City's staff met with representatives from major corporations, including carmakers such as General Motors and Volkswagen and giant textile firms such as Burlington Industries and Cone Mills. None of them, however, would commit to building a large plant. Citing a lack of jobs, in 1979 HUD foreclosed on Soul City, a move that effectively killed it.[13]

Industrial executives were partly deterred by the lack of infrastructure in Warren County, but their fears were also racial. As the industrial consultant Billy Carmichael reported in 1978, "Industry appears to have an objection to locating where the ethnic balance does not have some relationship to the national and/or regional ratios. The State feels that this is a major stumbling block to locating industry at Soul City."[14] Many of the companies that did come to the South in these years were also seeking a union-free environment, and Soul City tried to capitalize on this. In 1976, however, over a third of black workers belonged to unions, a higher proportion than among their white counterparts. Mobilized by the civil rights movement, blacks joined unions because they understood the need for collective action to bring about social change. Most executives would not build plants if they thought that workers would organize, and they viewed black workers as a greater risk than whites.[15]

In the rural South as a whole, black poverty was also caused by the decline of the farming sector. These farms had been struggling for some time; in 1978, for example, the U.S. Commission on Civil Rights reported that 94 percent of black-operated farms had gone out of business since 1920. Nearly all these farms were located in the South, and they had often been in the same family for several generations. Between 1969 and 1978 alone, the number of black-owned farms had tumbled from

133,973 to 57,271. While the loss of these farms partly reflected falling employment in the sector and the shift to larger farms, racial discrimination also played a role. As the commission documented, the Department of Agriculture and the Farmers Home Administration (FHA) had "failed to integrate civil rights goals into program objectives and to use enforcement mechanisms to ensure that black farmers are provided equal opportunities in farm credit programs."[16]

As late as 1980, just 4.8 percent of the FHA's loan specialists were black. This was problematic because white agents viewed black farmers as a credit risk and were more likely to give loans to white-owned agribusinesses. The commission concluded that the decline of black farms was "tragic," especially as it robbed blacks of a valuable resource and increased their economic and political dependence on whites. Many blacks who lost their land ended up as migrant or seasonal farm laborers. Poorly paid and rootless, they were some of the most exploited workers in the entire region. Others migrated to the cities but struggled to secure steady work because employers were closing their urban factories, moving instead to the suburbs or to foreign countries. Increasingly, automation was also wiping out the labor-intensive positions that blacks had traditionally performed in these factories.[17]

Unable to secure good jobs in industry or agriculture, rural blacks found it difficult to make ends meet, and their plight was compounded by the weak enforcement of civil rights laws. In state and local government bureaucracies, for example, African Americans were still not securing their fair share of the better positions. A detailed study by the SRC conducted in the late 1970s concluded that, unless blacks controlled county commissions or held powerful city offices, they possessed only a small share of local public sector jobs. "In most kinds of jobs," concluded the report, "time has stood still, frozen since the era when Blacks were unwelcome visitors in the seats of local government." Using a sample of fourteen Black Belt governments, the SRC found that blacks were 40 percent of the population but held their share of jobs only in the "service/maintenance" category. African Americans held just five of 136 jobs as officials or administrators and less than one in twelve professional positions. The underrepresentation was greatest for black women, who were even unable to land their fair share of janitorial posts. In their defense, white officials tried to claim that they could not locate qualified blacks, but the report concluded that these administrators were practicing "affirmative inaction."[18]

At the state level, most law enforcement jobs were also closed to blacks. This was a particularly important area, especially as all-white police forces had been a powerful symbol of white authority in the Jim Crow era. In Alabama, for example, white troopers had stood behind Governor George Wallace when he had promised to maintain segregation "forever," and the state police had also carried out the infamous beating of activists on the Pettus Bridge in Selma. As late as 1972, all Alabama's state troopers were white. Seeing them as a symbol of "systematic oppression in the South," Morris Dees decided to sue the troopers as one of his first acts after establishing the SPLC.[19] "We hoped," he recalled, "not only to win jobs for blacks, but also to use the case to stop the pattern of abuse directed at blacks by the all-white force." His efforts quickly secured a breakthrough. Hearing the case in 1972, district judge Frank Johnson reviewed the patrol's long history of discrimination and ordered it to hire a qualified black trooper for every white trooper until the force was 25 percent black. As the *Poverty Law Report* noted, Johnson's order "marked the first time a federal judge had ever ordered ratio hiring in public employment in the South, and set a precedent for similar suits Southwide."[20]

The landmark ruling, however, was not the end of the case. State officials resisted the order, imposed a virtual ban on hiring, and made it difficult for black officers to finish their training. Although he claimed to have moderated his racial views, Governor Wallace ordered the hard line, partly because he disliked both Johnson and federal interference in state affairs. By late 1977, less than 10 percent of troopers were black, and they complained of a "deliberate campaign of harassment" to force them to quit. As the trooper Billy Ray Jackson explained, "Even though the courts made the department hire blacks, if they mess up in the probationary period they don't have to keep them. And then they can turn around and say to the courts, 'See, we told you they can't do the job.'"[21]

Undeterred, the SPLC's lawyers fought on. In 1977, Dees asked the court to increase black hiring and to appoint an impartial monitor to oversee the implementation of the order. Two years later, state officials agreed to stop discriminating against blacks in hiring, promotion, and disciplinary procedures. After this settlement, more blacks were hired and a black trooper even featured in a recruitment poster. In 1979, moreover, the African American Clara Ziegler became the first female trooper. Her assignment came after the SPLC succeeded in striking down height and weight requirements set for the position. In an ironic twist, Ziegler was assigned to work in Selma, the city that was still widely associated with the movement.[22]

Despite these gains, black troopers complained that they were not promoted into the best positions. By February 1984, African Americans made up over 21 percent of Alabama's troopers, but there was not a single black among the force's six majors, twenty-five captains, thirty-five lieutenants, or sixty-five sergeants. Of sixty-six corporals, one rank above patrol officer, just four were black. The case rumbled on until 1987, when the U.S. Supreme Court finally upheld Judge Johnson's original order, thus forcing the state to make further concessions.[23]

In other southern states, it also proved difficult for blacks to secure law enforcement positions. In the late 1970s, Justice Department attorneys sued the state police in both Arkansas and Texas because they were not hiring enough blacks. As late as April 1977, just 9 of Arkansas's 478 state police were African American, while, in Texas in 1978, only 4.2 percent of highway patrol employees were black. In Arkansas, state officials agreed to a consent decree that resulted in more blacks being taken on, but, in the Lone Star State, the Highway Department refused to settle.[24]

In the private sector, African Americans also struggled to secure better-paying jobs, partly because of ongoing problems at the EEOC. Again, Carter was full of good intentions and tried to tackle the difficulties. One of his most prominent African American appointments, Eleanor Holmes Norton, took over as EEOC chairwoman and initiated much-needed reforms. A gifted and experienced lawyer, Norton cut the EEOC's backlog by culling frivolous charges and by calling early fact-finding conferences. She also tried to improve efficiency by combining charges and increasing the number of industrywide or companywide suits.[25]

Despite Norton's efforts, the EEOC was understaffed, and its agents grumbled that they had to concentrate on reducing the case backlog rather than helping employers develop meaningful plans. "We're not in the affirmative action business," admitted one official. "We're in the complaint processing business." Supporting the point, black leaders complained that, instead of investigating charges, agents needed to engage more with the African American community. In addition, workers who filed charges could still be harassed or even blacklisted by their employers.[26]

In Norton's defense, her task was a very difficult one. In 1977, the U.S. Commission on Civil Rights noted in a thorough study of employment discrimination, "The problems the Government is trying to solve . . . are difficult and persistent." Rather than addressing the issue in a coordinated fashion, however, federal civil rights agencies remained diverse and disparate. Apart from being understaffed, agencies such as the CSC and the OFCC were still struggling to develop procedures to deal with civil rights violations. Norton pressed for the creation of a single, well-funded body that could implement uniform standards, a move that was backed by the Commission on Civil Rights and the Congressional Black Caucus. "The Federal government should immediately begin to speak with one voice on equal employment opportunity matters," asserted one commission report. The proposed national employment rights board was never set up, however, chiefly because of interagency differences about how discrimination should be tackled.[27]

Once Carter was in office, black leaders expected him to address the severe economic problems that afflicted their communities. In the late 1970s, the Congressional Black Caucus listed full employment as its main legislative priority. It spoke out against "the erosion of affirmative action and equal opportunity" and asserted that "special efforts" had to be made to improve the economic position of the black community. The SCLC also concentrated heavily on economic issues. In 1980, for example, the group presented twelve demands to the Carter administration, headed by a call for "faithful implementation of visible, compensatory affirmative action in the context of full employment." Mass unemployment, it added, was as "unacceptable" as slavery.[28]

Coretta Scott King remained a vocal advocate of full employment. As a friend of the president's, King now became one of the most influential black leaders in the country. She also used her position as head of the Martin Luther King Jr. Center for Social Change to organize important initiatives. In January 1977, the newly organized center commemorated the late preacher's birthday by holding a two-mile march for full employment in Atlanta. Despite cold weather, several thousand people took part.[29] The center also supported the Full Employment Action Council and produced the *Full-Employment Newsletter,* both of which pushed for radically different economic policies. "No issue today needs more attention than that of full employment," wrote Mrs. King in 1977. "There never will be full equality of opportunity for all Americans until our society considers it a moral obligation to take whatever steps are necessary to guarantee a decent job to everyone who wants a job." As a resident of inner Atlanta, King could see that unemployment threatened to wipe out many of the gains that she and her late husband had fought so hard to bring about.[30]

The NAACP also focused heavily on economic issues. In 1977, southern labor director Ruby Hurley called on branches to "monitor" discriminatory practices by employers and to resolve complaints from members, especially when they worked in the public sector. Across the region, the association also lobbied for full employment and supported workers' rights to organize into unions. NAACP leaders were especially concerned about the growth of a black underclass in the South's cities. Their research found that 70 percent of young blacks in Nashville and Chattanooga were unemployed, while "chronic unemployment among black youth" was also a severe problem in Memphis, Atlanta, Charlotte, Charleston, Jacksonville, Jackson, and Birmingham. In 1980, the association's southern office helped organize a two-day conference on economic development at which they lobbied government officials for more jobs.[31]

Soon after Carter was elected, black groups united behind the Humphrey-Hawkins "full employment" bill, which proposed that a job guarantee office would provide all "able and willing" adults with work. Many of Carter's advisers warned him against supporting the bill, which they saw as dangerously inflationary. With the president's cautious backing, the legislation passed the House quite comfortably, but, in the Senate, it was gravely weakened by hostile amendments from conservative Republicans. Although it became law in October 1978, the Full Employment and Balanced Growth Act, as the Carter scholar John Dumbrell has noted, "represented little beyond good intentions." Thus, while the act pledged to reduce unemployment to 4 percent by 1983, the president was free to modify the goals in reaction to economic circumstances, and Carter duly submitted an "austerity" budget that disappointed black leaders. The cochair of the Full Employment Action Council, Coretta Scott King, acknowledged, "We did not get all . . . we would have liked." Nevertheless, she added, the legislation was "an important first step in the struggle for full employment." With Carter's defeat in the 1980 election, however, no further ground was made on this key issue.[32]

The bill's fate highlighted Carter's difficulties in meeting black economic demands. By the late 1970s, most African American leaders wanted forceful commitments to affirmative action and full employment, yet granting these requests was financially costly and politically difficult. The administration's task was complicated by the fact that many whites were unsupportive. Although black unemployment was about twice as high as white, 40 percent of white respondents to a 1977 CBS/*New York Times* poll thought the two groups had roughly the same level of unemployment, while only a minority believed that racial discrimination still existed. In marked contrast, a group of black lawyers commented in 1979, "The old civil rights concerns . . . have given way in a large measure to pressing economic concerns. Unemployment is a central issue."[33]

In the second half of the 1970s, black hopes were also undermined by the federal courts, which started to turn away from aggressive enforcement of Title VII. The shift reflected a growing feeling among whites that job bias had been addressed and that affirmative action constituted so-called reverse discrimination. Of particular importance was the Supreme Court's ruling in *Teamsters v. United States*. Dating back to 1974, the case arose out of efforts by the Justice Department to amend the seniority system in the trucking industry so that black workers could transfer to higher-paying jobs without giving up their seniority rights. On May 31, 1977, however, the Supreme Court ruled that "bona fide" seniority systems did not violate Title VII, even when they "perpetuate[d] the effects of an employer's discrimination," as long as they had been designed without discriminatory intent. The decision struck down a major premise adopted by the federal government and civil rights lawyers—that seniority systems that continued the effects of past discrimination were illegal, regardless of intent. With typical understatement, the U.S. Commission on Civil Rights noted that the case was "an additional barrier to equal employment opportunity." In particular, it slowed the progress of class actions because defendants could now appeal earlier judgments.[34]

In Georgia, for example, *Myers et al. v. Gilman Paper Company* (1972) had to be retried following an appeal that cited *Teamsters*. In the case, a group of black employees at a large paper mill in St. Marys, Georgia, sought to change a discriminatory seniority system and secure better opportunities for promotion. As a result of the retrial, the district court's pre-*Teamsters* ruling in favor of the plaintiffs was not upheld until 1982. In the interim, many of the original plaintiffs retired or died.[35]

Russell et al. v. American Tobacco Company also illustrates how Title VII plaintiffs often had to wait a long time to secure justice, especially after *Teamsters*. The case originated in 1966, when Edgar Russell and seven other employees at American Tobacco's plant in Reidsville, North Carolina, filed charges with the EEOC. "The company," complained the plaintiffs, "maintains a practice of keeping Negroes in traditional Negro jobs by denying them the opportunity to train for or be hired in non-traditional Negro jobs except on a token basis."[36]

Following a lengthy investigation by the commission, the plaintiffs filed a joint action in 1968 and were certified as a class twelve months later. In January 1973, the district court upheld their complaints, but the company appealed. Although American Tobacco lost this appeal in 1975, the case was reopened in the wake of *Teamsters,* and it took six years for the district court to find for the plaintiffs again. Then, in 1983, the two sides agreed to a consent decree that granted more than $3 million to the large class of plaintiffs. By this time, the company's stemming operations, where most blacks had worked, were no longer based in North Carolina but had been transferred to Kentucky and Virginia. In the seventeen years since the case was filed, all the U.S. tobacco firms had laid off workers as jobs were automated and demand for tobacco fell. As a result, opportunities for promotion were now very limited.[37]

The fate of the *Russell* plaintiffs was representative as legal victories took time and were undermined by the decline of key southern industries. In Birmingham's ailing steel industry, for example, blacks' promotional opportunities were now restricted primarily by layoffs rather than racism. The NAACP also fought to get better conditions for black train porters just as the railroads were reducing passenger services. A sustained fight against Lockheed-Georgia, previously the South's largest single employer, was also undermined by the decline of the aircraft company's Atlanta plant, while textile breakthroughs meant less as companies contracted. Between 1977 and 1987, for example, the number of workers employed by J. P. Stevens fell from 44,100 to 23,400.[38]

In some landmark legal cases, whites also challenged affirmative action head-on. While they originated outside the South, two lawsuits had a national impact. In the mid-1970s, the law student Marco DeFunis accused the University of Washington of favoring minority students with inferior qualifications. In an influential move, the U.S. Supreme Court decided not to rule on the state supreme court's finding against DeFunis, encouraging others to challenge affirmative action programs. Into the breach stepped Alan Bakke, a mature student who charged that he should have secured a place at the University of California, Davis, medical school. In particular, Bakke asserted that his qualifications were better than those of many African Americans accepted under a special admissions program. *Bakke* was a high-profile case that tackled momentous issues, yet, in the end, the Supreme Court issued an ambiguous decision. Fundamentally divided, in July 1978 the justices forbade rigid quotas based solely on race yet upheld the consideration of race as an element in judging students for university admission. Split 5–4, the Court also affirmed Bakke's right to be accepted into medical school because the admissions program had violated Title VII.[39]

Whatever the outcome of reverse discrimination lawsuits, they popularized the idea that affirmative action was unfair to the white majority and caused employers to question existing plans. As Eleanor Holmes Norton wrote Carter in September 1977, "The mere bringing of lawsuits has deterred these [affirmative action] programs." *Bakke* had its greatest impact in the higher education sector, where many administrators already disliked federal 'interference' in their processes. As the presidential aide Annie Gutierrez wrote before the case was finalized, "The immediate impact of *Bakke* is that schools are beginning to dismantle their minority admission programs. They have seized upon this as an excuse and say that to do otherwise would be illegal. . . . As things now stand, minorities will be losers, even if they should win in the courts."[40]

Encouraged by *Bakke,* some southern whites also began to challenge affirmative action in the workplace. In late 1978, the Supreme Court heard *Weber v. United Steelworkers of America,* a key case that *Time* dubbed the "blue-collar *Bakke.*" *Weber* was the most prominent example of cases where white men charged that they had been victims of reverse discrimination. It threatened to undermine affirmative action on the factory floor, where blacks had slowly made some progress. President Carter wrote in his own notes on the case that *Weber* was "probably more important" than *Bakke.* Most affirmative action occurred in employment, and some thirty-five million workers stood to be affected by the lawsuit's outcome.[41]

In 1974, Brian Weber was a twenty-seven-year-old laboratory analyst who applied to a new training program at Kaiser's plant in Gramercy, Louisiana. Rather than hiring craftworkers from outside, the company and the United Steelworkers Union had adopted a program that offered internal advancement to unskilled production workers. In an effort to upgrade blacks, the two sides agreed that African Americans would get 50 percent of the trainee positions until their representation in the crafts came close to that in the local labor force. Weber sued because he was unable to get into the program, despite the fact that he had more seniority than some blacks who were admitted. Reflecting the mood of the times, Weber claimed that he was being "made to pay for . . . what someone did 150 years ago." Supported by three new conservative legal foundations, this was an important test of reverse discrimination claims.[42]

As well as highlighting Weber's grievances, the case also exposed the other side of the story. It showed that, when the program was instituted, African Americans made up 39 percent of the plant's employees yet held only 1.83 percent of craft positions. Historically excluded from the skilled trades, blacks simply could not acquire the skills that they needed to get access to these jobs, and they were, instead, channeled into low-paying positions. The black worker Jim Nailor, for example, had completed junior college but got hired only as a laborer at Kaiser. "I was depressed all the time," he recalled. "Here I am, I thought, digging a ditch, and I've completed junior college." After the training program was set up, however, Nailor became one of the first black electricians.[43]

Recognizing the need for the program, the Court dismissed Weber's challenge, a move that provoked very different reactions from the two sides. While Weber claimed that the ruling would have "a negative effect on people all over the country toward blacks," Jim Nailor was elated. "The decision," he declared, "means my children will have a chance to do better than I will. That's the American dream." Civil rights leaders were relieved. As the NAACP's Benjamin L. Hooks explained, "Had we lost this case, the cause of affirmative action would have been set back ten years."[44]

As Hooks's cautious tone indicated, whites continued to challenge affirmative action. In 1979, for instance, a white worker at Rock Hill Printing and Finishing Company in Rock Hill, South Carolina, contested a consent decree that had granted black workers greater promotional rights. Alleging reverse discrimination, Norman Youngblood claimed that "the seniority and promotion systems . . . discriminate against whites." Such cases continued to occur because most southern whites saw affirmative action as unfair. In the same month that *Weber* was decided, a South-wide poll found that only 12 percent of whites favored racial quotas in private employment, compared to 44 percent of blacks. Clearly, the issue of affirmative action remained highly contested.[45]

Klan Revival and Ongoing Racial Division

As the 1970s came to a close, there were other signs of a white backlash. After more than a decade out of the news, the Ku Klux Klan reemerged, capitalizing on lingering anger about busing and affirmative action. In February 1979, the *New York Times* reported "stepped-up activity" among Klan groups across the South. In Selma, for example, Klansmen marched through the downtown for the first time in more than a decade. "The white race is rioting again," declared the defiant Klansman Bill Wilkinson, who was confronted by several hundred angry blacks. Now dependent on the black vote, the long-serving Selma mayor, Joseph Smitherman, went red in the face as he confronted Wilkinson's followers. "You will not come into this community with guns and sticks or I will fill the jails with you," he declared. Ignoring this setback, Klan groups continued to organize, marching in Birmingham when blacks protested against the Bonita Carter killing. Birmingham's blacks also refused to back down, even fighting with Klansmen who marched into their neighborhoods. In a fast-changing region, many blacks were no longer afraid of the Klan.[46]

While it is impossible to determine how many members Klan groups had, one major faction was the Louisiana-based Knights of the Ku Klux Klan, which was reorganized by David Duke in the late 1970s. A history graduate from Louisiana State University, Duke strove to make the Klan respectable. As the political scientist Paul Grosser admitted, "[Duke was] giving the Klan a white-shirt-and-tie image. He's appealing to the middle class and tapping their frustrations." In October 1979, Duke even went to the campus of Alfred University in upstate New York and debated the black leader Ralph Abernathy. There, he attacked affirmative action as "racism" and claimed, "We are not reaching toward love and peace through busing." In response, Abernathy asserted that these remedies had produced "magnificent strides in ending discrimination."[47]

Duke's tactics contrasted with Wilkinson's Invisible Empire of the Ku Klux Klan, whose members conducted military training and carried sawn-off shotguns. In May 1979, the Invisible Empire engaged in a gunfight with blacks on the streets of Decatur, Alabama, where the mentally challenged black man Tommy Lee Hines had been charged with raping a white woman. As a result, four people were hospitalized with gunshot wounds. In a city that had risen to fame during the Scottsboro Boys rape case of the 1930s, empire rallies drew up to ten thousand people, and the sheriff admitted to knowing "90 per cent" of the Klansmen involved in the shootings. "I'm alarmed," commented an agent from the Alabama Bureau of Investigation. "We might be on the edge of some new direction in terrorism in this area and we are not prepared for it." Around this time, empire members also beat a black preacher who had protested against Hines's conviction and fired on civil rights workers in Tupelo, Mississippi. Such actions had a broad significance. "Black leaders and informed analysts of civil rights in the South say that the white animosity in Decatur and elsewhere is related to a new 'white backlash,'" wrote the investigative journalist Wayne King, "a growing national resistance to black demands."[48]

In August 1979, Wilkinson's group also led a march from Selma to Montgomery. Ironically, the reenactment highlighted how the original march had become a powerful part of the national memory, and KKK members posed for pictures as they walked across the famous Edmund Pettus Bridge. Fourteen years after the passage of the Voting Rights Act, the Klansmen claimed that white rights now needed to be protected. Observing the protest, local blacks disputed these claims. "What are they out marching for?" commented one. "They've got all the rights. They've got the right to blow away a nigger's a——." Around two hundred Klan members made the walk to Montgomery, where they were promptly arrested for parading without a permit.[49]

The Klan's revival was not confined to the Deep South. Launching a special "Klanwatch" program, the SPLC asserted that extremist factions existed in several other areas. "The Klan poses a real threat in some parts of the country to the lives and security of many black people and other minorities," declared the *Poverty Law Report* in 1980. As a result of these investigations, the SPLC filed suit against forty-six individuals and nine major white supremacist organizations for their roles in hate crimes. Although it took time, the group won judgments that helped put several Klan groups out of business.[50]

Klan groups were particularly active in piedmont North Carolina, where they clashed with left-wing whites who were trying to organize textile and tobacco workers. Early battles in Winston-Salem were a prelude to a fatal confrontation that occurred in nearby Greensboro. On the morning of November 3, 1979, an armed caravan of Klansmen and Nazis drove into the Morningside Homes community, a black public housing project where the Communist Workers Party had organized residents to confront the Klan. The Klansmen faced up to the civil rights marchers; as the Klan member Eddie Dawson asserted, "You asked for the Klan and you got them." In the ensuing gunfight, much of it televised, five marchers were killed and ten others wounded. Despite the footage, two lengthy criminal trials failed to convict the Nazis and Klansmen, who claimed self-defense. Only a subsequent civil trial found that members of the Greensboro Police Department were jointly liable with Klan and Nazi members for the wrongful death of one victim.[51]

In the wake of the slayings, a special advisory committee probed community attitudes for the U.S. Commission on Civil Rights. In particular, the committee commented on the "marked differences" between how white and black residents measured civil rights progress in their "moderate" community. "Greensboro citizens who are white emphasize the progress made," it noted. "They see the Greensboro glass as more than half full. The city's citizens who are black focused on the problems that remain, perceiving the glass to be almost empty." These differences reflected the "lack of meaningful communication" between the two races, especially as they lived and shopped in separate spaces.[52]

An open meeting illustrated these conclusions well. Thus, while Mayor E. S. Melvin praised Greensboro as "a quiet community that allows everyone to have full rights," the NAACP leader Dr. George Simkins saw race relations as "very poor." Whites emphasized that the schools had integrated successfully, but blacks stressed that administrators discriminated against black teachers and students, especially in the application of disciplinary rules. Whites claimed that blacks were advancing in the workplace, but blacks argued that whites still dominated the best jobs. As the committee uncovered, blacks in Greensboro were twice as likely to live below the poverty line as whites. In the ensuing years, moreover, the two races reacted very differently to efforts to investigate the killings.[53]

The experience of Greensboro was representative. In 1979, a thorough survey of racial attitudes by the National Conference of Christians and Jews found that whites were much more optimistic about the state of race relations than blacks. While whites downplayed the race problem, blacks felt that they experienced almost as much discrimination as they had a decade earlier. When it came to economic issues, the "sharp contrast" between the views of the two groups was especially apparent. Over 93 percent of whites said that blacks were getting a "better break" in the workplace than they had a decade earlier, a view that African Americans rejected. As the report concluded, "Whites have obviously missed the depths of both the urgency and despair that blacks feel about their troubles in getting work. The white attitude about black joblessness is one of vague concern, tempered with some heavy doses of indifference." As the decade came to a close, around 43 percent of African Americans listed unemployment as their most urgent concern, compared to just 11 percent of whites.[54]

In May 1979, reaction to the twenty-fifth anniversary of *Brown* was similarly polarized. Recognizing the importance of the occasion, President Carter invited around eight hundred guests, including representatives from all the major civil rights groups, to the East Room of the White House. There, federal officials were generally upbeat in their remarks; HEW secretary Joseph Califano, for instance, insisted that there had been "enormous progress" in the schools, particularly in the South. In his keynote remarks, President Carter celebrated *Brown* as "a watershed in the history of the American people" that had led to momentous changes. "Dismantling the legal apparatus of segregation was a giant stride on freedom's road," he exclaimed.[55]

Black leaders were much gloomier. In a special issue of *The Crisis,* contributors claimed that precious gains were being undermined by resegregation and a white backlash. They also worried about the quality of public schools, especially when most students were black. While Carter had called the period since *Brown* an "era of hope," the black educator Estelle Taylor claimed that early optimism had been replaced by "disillusionment" and "disenchantment." She asserted, "The realist must conclude that the American dream of an integrated education for a *fully* integrated society has, indeed, been deferred."[56]

The *Brown* anniversary highlighted the broad divergence between black and white viewpoints. Fifteen years after the passage of comprehensive equal rights legislation, many whites felt that the civil rights movement was unnecessary. The movement's work, they insisted, was complete; southern blacks had legal equality, could vote freely, and attended desegregated schools. In contrast, many African Americans insisted that ongoing efforts were vital. As the civil rights leader Floyd McKissick wrote in 1978, "People . . . make the statement that the civil rights movement is dead. You mean to tell me that every person I see no longer wants any rights—no longer wants economic success—no longer wants his schooling and housing."[57]

Although activists fought on, they confronted other problems, especially as the recession cut funding to civil rights groups. In 1977, Ralph Abernathy gave up the SCLC presidency, leaving a struggling organization that did not have the money to lead large-scale community projects. Even the NAACP experienced setbacks. In 1979, Carter's aides rebuffed NAACP calls for a full civil rights conference rather than a narrow celebration of *Brown.* Now that de jure segregation had been eliminated, presidential advisers knew how difficult it was to solve the problems that remained. In the wake of *Milliken,* the NAACP was itself unable to break up de facto segregation in the schools. This was a major disappointment for seventy-six-year-old Roy Wilkins, who stepped down as the association's executive director in 1977. Dismissed by critics as too conservative, Wilkins had, nevertheless, guided the NAACP for over twenty years and given it stability. A native of Memphis, the new leader, Dr. Benjamin L. Hooks, addressed financial shortfalls by accepting more funding from corporations, a move that dented the NAACP's social activism.[58]

Some of the NAACP's financial problems were also caused by developments in the South. In August 1976, the association lost a boycotting case against a group of Mississippi merchants and was ordered to pay $1.25 million in damages. The case dated back to 1966–1967, when branch members in Port Gibson, Mississippi, had boycotted businesses in an effort to force compliance with the Civil Rights Act. A group of white businessmen sued the NAACP and argued that its boycott activity was unlawful, a worrying allegation because the NAACP had often used boycotts to put pressure on its opponents. As *The Crisis* warned in 1974, the $3.5 million suit was a "threat to the Association's effective existence in the South."[59]

Together with the high rate of inflation, the ruling compounded the NAACP's financial problems. After the Port Gibson judgment, leaders became wary of endorsing direct action and, instead, fought to overturn the decision. It was more than six years, however, before the U.S. Supreme Court upheld the NAACP's appeal. The delay was damaging; by May 1981, the national NAACP was $1.2 million in the red, and the Mississippi case was largely to blame. Despite these problems, southern blacks continued to turn to the association for help, and, in 1980 alone, the group recruited over eighteen thousand new members in its main southern region.[60]

In May 1980, ongoing racial divisions were brutally exposed by the serious riots that erupted in Miami. The violence resulted in eighteen deaths as well as seven hundred injuries, twelve hundred arrests and over $200 million in property damage. According to the NAACP, this was the "most costly" racial disturbance to have occurred since 1968.[61]

Home to a diverse mix of ethnic groups, Miami was not a traditional southern city. By 1980, there were 600,000 Latinos in Dade County, and they competed with blacks for service sector jobs, leading to accusations that the new arrivals received better treatment. As the *New York Times* explained, "Just as the civil rights movement opened opportunities for blacks to move out of the service industries, the flood of Cuban refugees into Miami, many of them with readily marketable skills, blocked the way for blacks and even took away a large share of the menial jobs. In Miami, blacks began to feel that they had been made third-class citizens, behind whites and Latins."[62]

Many of Miami's blacks were trapped in Liberty City, and the disturbances were concentrated in this troubled neighborhood. The short-term trigger was the acquittal of four white police officers for the fatal beating of the black motorist Arthur McDuffie. "It was just another lynching," claimed the local activist John O. Brown. "So immediately there was a feeling of anger in the entire community." Much of the trouble was concentrated on Martin Luther King Boulevard, a main thoroughfare through Liberty City. Investigating the disturbances for the *Miami Herald,* the black academic Dr. Marvin Dunn recalled riding along the street and seeing a "crazed mob" attacking whites, even kicking them as they lay on the ground.[63]

These actions were also generated by deeper economic problems. "Although the local economy continues to grow at a rate higher than that for the Nation as a whole," noted a detailed investigation of the riots by the U.S. Commission on Civil Rights, "there are few black entrepreneurs, and the black unemployment rate remains high. . . . Blacks in Miami have limited employment opportunities. . . . Local public and private sector employers have a dismal record with regard to hiring blacks." In May 1980, the black unemployment rate was 13.5 percent nationwide, but, in Liberty City, it was almost 40 percent, while, among black teenagers in the neighborhood, it was close to 80 percent.[64]

In the wake of the violence, the Concerned Black Organizations for Justice presented Governor Bob Graham with a list of "collective needs" that concentrated heavily on economic issues. In particular, the group pressed for a "comprehensive job program for blacks over 13 with 'minimum living' salaries of $15,000." In a letter to President Carter, Benjamin L. Hooks also linked the riots to economic hardship. According to an NAACP investigation, nearly 40 percent of all black families in Dade County had incomes below the federal poverty level. "Poverty in a community of wealth and affluence that disproportionately affects blacks is caused in large measure by racial factors," asserted the NAACP.[65]

In 1980, serious racial disturbances also occurred in Wrightsville, Georgia, Orlando, Florida, and Chattanooga, Tennessee. In Wrightsville, for example, angry blacks demanded more job opportunities and an end to police brutality, but whites reacted by riding through the black community and firing shotguns into homes. In all these cases, black leaders reacted by calling for more investment in their communities. As the NAACP asserted at the close of 1980, the wave of violence was a reflection of "underlying conditions of poor housing, little or no political influence and economic power [and] high unemployment, especially among black youth." In sharp contrast, whites stressed the restoration of law and order and insisted that minorities received preferential treatment. In his successful campaign for the presidency, Ronald Reagan was able to capitalize on these sentiments.[66]

Reagan's triumph also reflected a mood of disillusionment within the African American community. Over the course of the 1970s, the black unemployment rate climbed from less than double that of whites to 2.5 times the white figure. In the 1980 election, Carter received about 89 percent of the black vote, compared to 94 percent four years earlier. While he was still strongly supported, the defections contributed to his defeat. As Louis Martin reported, "Blacks appear to have given Ronald Reagan sufficient votes in several closely connected southern states to provide him with a margin of victory." The administration's figures showed that the black vote was particularly important in Tennessee, where Reagan won by only six thousand votes but secured sixteen thousand black votes.[67] Martin also established that some blacks had ditched Carter in reaction to his economic policies, particularly his insistence on fighting inflation rather than reducing unemployment. Reagan himself attacked Carter's economic record and called the recession "the single most dangerous threat to black progress today." The most prominent black leader to abandon Carter was Ralph Abernathy, who accused the president of not living up to his campaign promises.[68]

When he campaigned for the presidency, Reagan also appealed directly to the white backlash against affirmative action and busing. A fierce opponent of the civil rights legislation of the mid-1960s, Reagan understood that the future of the Republican Party lay in appealing to southern whites who felt that these laws had been carried too far. As governor of California, Reagan had also called busing "a vast and dehumanizing manipulation of school populations" and had signed a bill to ban busing without parental consent. In both 1976 and 1980, Reagan met with southern convention delegates and promised to help them more than his GOP opponents would. Immediately after securing the nomination, Reagan traveled to Philadelphia, Mississippi, the tiny town where three civil rights workers had been murdered in 1964. Making no mention of the slain men, he instead declared, "I believe in states' rights, I believe in people doing as much as they can at the private level." As a result, southern whites felt that Reagan's sympathies lay with them rather than the victims of the crime. Many black leaders were incensed, especially as Reagan made the remarks to a virtually all-white audience at the Neshoba County fair. Known for his frankness, Andrew Young claimed that Reagan's use of the term *states' rights* "looks like a code word to me that it's going to be all right to kill niggers when he's President." As Young added, the term had special meaning in Philadelphia, where local officials had been involved in the killings. After the speech, the Invisible Empire of the Ku Klux Klan endorsed Reagan, although he quickly renounced the group's support.[69]

Reagan's tactics worked; he received 60 percent of the votes cast by white southerners, while Carter got just 36 percent. Overall, Reagan secured a decisive victory, and ideological conservatives had a clear mandate to direct national affairs. Most blacks approached the Reagan era with trepidation, worried that the new administration would not just defer the dream of an equal society but reverse the progress they had made under the landmark legislation. As Coretta King saw it, Reagan was a representative of white "exclusiveness" who would bring back the "Nixon-Ford years of benign neglect."[70]

10

THE REAGAN
COUNTERREVOLUTION

"I am still trying to descend from Cloud 9, Strommie Boy [Senator Thurmond], will never descend," wrote an exultant Harry Dent shortly after Ronald Reagan's election triumph. Thurmond's sense of high elation typified the reaction of much of the white South to the victory. It signaled an end to the travails of the years since 1965, a slowing of the pace of unwelcomed social change. Above all, it surely meant an end to busing.[1]

Meanwhile, as the demoralized Carter administration struggled into its final days, those responsible for implementing civil rights policy worked frantically to complete what unfinished business they could. Particularly active was Assistant Secretary of Labor Ernest K. Green, who was responsible for distributing thousands of small job training grants under the Comprehensive Employment and Training Act. In the transition weeks, Green, the first black graduate of Little Rock's Central High and a key figure in the drama that played out there in 1957, used his discretionary power to approve hundreds of such grants, some to such avowedly civil rights bodies as Jesse Jackson's PUSH and the Martin Luther King Center for Social Change. Outraged Republicans demanded their rescission, and Green was eventually investigated by the Senate Committee on Labor for what was a symbolic act of defiance.[2]

HEW also finally moved against segregation in higher education. In early January, it cited four states, Alabama, South Carolina, West Virginia, and Delaware, for maintaining "vestiges of bias" in their colleges and universities, ordering them to take immediate steps to end this. In particular, they were directed to speed up the pace of integration in their traditionally black colleges. This would be, predicted the *Washington Post*, a "political hot potato" for the new administration, given Reagan's clear campaign message to the white South. So concerned was the Reagan transition team by one recent Carter "sweeping affirmative action agreement" guaranteeing more federal jobs to blacks and Hispanics that, on January 16, it filed a brief in the District Court for the District of Columbia arguing for its withdrawal, given the imminent change of administration.[3]

Unnoticed as Washington feverishly prepared for the new president's inaugural festivities, a familiar drama was playing itself out in the small Louisiana community of Buckeye, in Rapides Parish, with the great symbolic issue, court-ordered busing, at its core. There, federal district court judge Nauman Scott, in an effort to settle a school integration suit that had dragged on for fourteen years, had issued a strongly worded desegregation order in 1980 mandating extensive changes to the parish's public school system, including school closings and the imposition of busing. Among those most directly affected were Michelle La Borde and Linda McNeal, both aged thirteen, and twelve-year-old Ramona Carbo. They were currently enrolled at all-white Buckeye High but would henceforth be bused twenty-one miles to Jones Street Junior High in nearby Alexandria, a school described as "mostly black."[4]

Rapides Parish, according to Louis Barry, the African American lawyer who had filed the initial suit against the school board in 1967, had consistently resisted school integration, and its white citizens were hardly likely to comply with Scott's order without a fight. Those parents whose children attended all-white schools marked for closing or had been selected for mandatory busing were particularly incensed. "When Forest Hills High School was shut down," the *Washington Post* reported, "some 700 parents protested, flying the flag at half-staff, parading through the town while a bugler played Taps, and setting out to start their own church schools." One group of parents actually took over the school buildings, establishing what they termed a "squatters school," and left only when threatened with jail. There were similar scenes at Buckeye High, which, though not to be closed, was to have its racial composition decisively altered. Black students were to be bused in, and 106 white seventh and eighth graders were to go to Jones Street Junior High, including Michelle, Linda, and Ramona.[5]

At this stage, Louisiana state judge Richard Earl Lee became part of the action. Described by his admirers as "a burly good ole boy, duck hunter and descendant of Robert E. Lee himself," he persuaded the parents of the three girls to transfer custody of them to friends still residing safely within the Buckeye district. He then made them wards of the state, ordered that they remain at Buckeye High, and personally escorted them to classes. His defiance made him the hero of the hour in Rapides Parish. Soon local radio stations were playing "The Ballad of Judge Lee," with its chorus of "Judge Lee, he set the people free," as bumper stickers proclaimed "Lee's hot, Scott's not." Once again, federal and state battle lines were drawn over desegregation, for, as Louis Barry sadly observed, "It's not the bus, it's still us."[6]

There were some who tried to restore a measure of balance to the riven community. One such was Eric Rougeau, a columnist for the local newspaper. He reminded his readers, "[Judge Scott] didn't invent busing. Congress, the Supreme Court and the Justice Department invented busing." It was the law, and Scott was sworn to uphold it. Besides, its demise was imminent. "The last Congress voted to cut out federal funds for forced busing for the sole purpose of desegregation," Rougeau went on, but President Carter had vetoed the bill. "A similar vote by the new Congress is a shoo-in. Don't expect Reagan to follow Carter's precedent." There was, therefore, no need for the community to fracture. His and other voices for moderation were lost in all the shouting, the posturing, and the singing of "The Ballad of Judge Lee."[7]

The conflict was eventually resolved in the Alexandria courthouse as black demonstrators sang "We Shall Overcome" and whites shouted defiance, waving placards proclaiming "Integration Stinks." Lee was warned that he risked a heavy fine and a possible jail term for contempt if he continued to resist the federal court, and he quickly dropped his posturing. He was at pains to deny any racial motivation in his actions. "I detest racism," he told reporters. "Some of my closest friends are black. I love 'em like brothers." Rather, he had taken his stand over "the right of one judge [Scott] to call another [Lee] a fraud." He would, he insisted, have fought equally hard for "three little black girls" to attend Buckeye High. Even his most fervent supporters had difficulty with his capitulation, and "The Ballad of Judge Lee" soon disappeared from the airwaves.[8]

The three girls were allowed to remain at Buckeye High until the end of the semester, and then they would transfer to Jones Street Junior High. They did not do so, their parents preferring to send them to a local "segregation academy," even with the loss of the semester's credit, rather than permit them to be bused. Judge Scott was ferociously reviled for a time; Georgia congressman Larry McDonald even introduced a bill for his impeachment into the House of Representatives. Scott's anxious wife wrote to her fellow Republican, for whom she had "great admiration," Senator Strom Thurmond, seeking his intervention. Nothing would come of it, the Senate's new Justice Committee chair assured her. He understood perfectly that her husband had simply been implementing the law as it stood—but, it was to be hoped, not for much longer. The new Congress would soon "effectively deal with the busing problem."[9]

The whole incident, occurring in the shadow of Reagan's inauguration, doubtless went unnoticed by the president-elect and his advisers. Yet it might have reminded them that there was unfinished business in the South and that they would soon be dealing with the same basic issues of racial justice that had occupied the national agenda since the legislative achievements of 1964 and 1965. Conversely, it might also have shown them that the southern political strategy developed in the recent campaign was working. Michelle La Borde's mother, Ina, was a union organizer, someone the Democrats would normally have counted as safely in their column—but no longer. Her daughter's predicament had seen to that. Ina La Borde and millions like her were on the way to becoming "Reagan Democrats," and the issue that drove them was race, resistance to the pace and the manner of change, with forced busing and racial quotas as the twin flashpoints. It was hardly surprising, therefore, that the Reagan transition team had filed its brief seeking to nullify the Carter administration's final affirmative action agreement.

Opening Salvos

Those who had fought against busing most fiercely certainly believed that victory was near. "It seems to me that the time has now come for Congress to put an end to one of the most aggravated forms of tyranny now being practiced upon the people of the United States . . . the forced busing of schoolchildren for integration purposes," wrote former North Carolina senator Sam Ervin to the current incumbent, Jesse Helms. Helms assured him that he planned to introduce such legislation without delay while praising his predecessor for laying the "groundwork" for the struggle against "this form of tyranny." Moreover, he was certain that "our efforts will be fruitful in the months ahead." Ervin was much encouraged, too, by the new president's first public statements about busing, commending Reagan for his "courage and intellectual honesty" in describing it "as a useless and wasteful endeavor." With its ending, relief would at last be granted to "helpless schoolchildren of both races."[10]

From the outset, the Reagan White House seemed responsive as the new team hammered out its civil rights policy. Initial discussion centered on the three great symbolic issues: busing, the use of racial quotas in the pursuit of affirmative action, and whether to support the renewal of the 1965 Voting Rights Act, due in 1982, or at the very least the removal of those punitive provisions specifically directed at the South. White southerners expected quick and favorable action on all of these. Within days of the inauguration, there were already clear signs of a shift. A spokesperson for HEW's Office for Civil Rights indicated that plans drawn up in the dying days of the previous administration to expand the monitoring of school desegregation orders were unlikely to be approved. Rather, the existing processes were to be curtailed. More ominously, an advisory panel set up by the president-elect to examine the operation of the EEOC produced a highly critical report. The panel, chaired by J. A. Parker, the African American head of the conservative Lincoln Institute, charged the commission with going far beyond the powers given it by the Civil

Rights Act of 1964 and creating "a new racism in America in which every individual is judged by race." It recommended that the EEOC's budget be cut and that it be banned from issuing new guidelines for a year, in effect, as members of the commission were quick to point out, stripping it of its role as the "lead agency interpreting and formulating equal employment policy." Despite such protests, the president indicated that he agreed with the panel's recommendations, praising especially one that required the accuser in any discrimination charge against a firm or corporation specifically "to prove intent, and not just that a firm has a lower percentage of minority workers." The chair of the EEOC since 1977, Eleanor Norton, thereupon submitted her resignation.[11]

The Parker panel's recommendations caused a massive "shuddering" among "the civil rights establishment," reported the *Washington Post* columnist William Raspberry, the more so as the extent of the president's proposed budget cuts became apparent. Many of the social programs scheduled for downsizing brought disproportionate benefits to minority communities, while the major civil rights enforcement agencies were all similarly affected. The EEOC's staff was to be slashed by 10 percent, the Office of Civil Rights in the Department of Health and Human Services (HHS) and the Labor Department's OFCC likewise. It was, thus, scarcely surprising that, in late February, NAACP director Benjamin Hooks announced the formation of a "broad-based" coalition of minority interests to fight the cuts, even as the African American economist Thomas Sowell organized conservative blacks in their support. As the historian John Hope Franklin warned during a speech to the Joint Center for Political Studies, a black think tank, there was no longer a single black community, and the civil rights movement needed to be "dramatically restructured" in order to reflect this. The issues of the 1980s were far more complex than those of the King years, and the "charismatic leadership" style that had served so well then was now a "pathetic residue of the past." The key civil rights issues henceforth would be economic, not legal, Franklin thought, and the most pressing challenge was within the black community, not with the president, namely to "bridge the gap between the black underclass and 'blacks who had made it.'" These were challenging words that did not sit happily with everyone.[12]

While the Reagan administration settled into its groove, this sense of foreboding deepened. Of particular concern was the future of the Voting Rights Act, known to be a prime target of the president's southern allies. Worryingly, Reagan refused to express himself unequivocally in favor of its renewal, fueling anguished speculation that at the very least he planned to weaken its effect in the South by extending its provisions nationwide, thus diluting its enforcement capacity. There were also fears that, in line with his southern strategy, Reagan would not oppose the removal of the act's preclearance provisions. White southerners bitterly resented their restrictions, and powerful politicians with the president's ear, like Senators Thurmond and Helms, had made their removal a priority.[13]

In the deep South, where the right to vote had been so hard and recently won, there was apprehension that bordered on despair. In Lowndes County, Alabama, with a black majority population, white control had been absolute before 1965; then the act had brought sweeping change. John Hulett, formerly a local civil rights activist, now held the symbol of the office of sheriff, "a long, thin rubber strap" that for years "had been illegally, forcefully and frequently used on the backs of black people." Blacks no longer "worried about the sheriff's whip," wrote Reginald Stuart in the *New York Times,* but feared its return if the Voting Rights Act was allowed to expire. "We'll end up with many of our positions going back to white people," worried Sheriff Hulett. In northeastern Mississippi, Tyrone Ellis, the first black legislator elected to represent three predominantly black counties for one hundred years, warned, "If the law were allowed to expire, it would set us back 100 years." Yet the president refused to commit himself, instead asking the Justice Department for a determination as to whether the act should simply be allowed to expire in 1982.[14]

If equivocation over the renewal of the Voting Rights Act was the matter of most serious concern to African Americans and their allies in the first months of 1981, there were plenty of other indications that the new administration was planning a retreat from the activism of the past decades and seeking an accommodation on a range of unfinished business. As early as March, the new secretary of education, Terrell Bell, had announced that he was considering easing the desegregation guidelines required of colleges and universities as a condition of securing financial aid, but the clearest statement of the administration's changed direction came in a speech by Attorney General William French Smith to the American Law Institute on May 22. In it, he announced two major departures from nearly fifteen years of civil rights policy: an end to the Justice Department's vigorous pursuit of mandatory busing in school desegregation suits and to department advocacy, "in the Supreme Court or anywhere else," of affirmative action plans, "which include quotas, or remedies which amount to quotas." Both busing and quotas had, in his view, proved "ineffective and unfair" and would, thus, be abandoned. The nation, he said, "must end its over reliance on remedial devices aimed solely at achieving inflexible and predetermined mathematical balance." Mandatory busing in particular "has neither produced significant educational benefits nor won the support of most Americans." "Our goal," he concluded, expressing Reagan's long-held public position, one through which the new administration consciously sought connection with Martin Luther King Jr., "must always be genuinely color-blind state action. This meant that race, color or national origin must, for purposes of government decision-making, ultimately become irrelevant." Forced busing, racial quotas in schools or workplaces, ran completely counter to this perspective.[15]

Other ominous signs of a retreat from past policies quickly followed. In June, Bell announced the impending settlement of a ten-year court fight over the desegregation of North Carolina's state colleges and universities on terms that the Carter administration had rejected. In doing so, he stated that "coercive demands for strict quotas" had been abandoned in favor of a softer approach requiring the eventual attainment of a "flexible system of goals," with a "clear understanding" that failure to meet all of these was "not automatically . . . deemed failure to comply with the agreement" as a whole. Senator Helms had played a key role in brokering the talks that had led to the settlement, one of several reasons why the NAACP viewed it with the deepest suspicion. Bell, however, praised it as a "model for other Southern states to follow."[16]

Two days later, Helms introduced another antibusing amendment into the Senate—this time attached to the bill authorizing the Justice Department's appropriation—forbidding any further expenditure on busing programs and striking down further court-ordered busing entirely. At his confirmation hearings that same week, William Bradford Reynolds, whom Reagan had nominated as assistant attorney general for civil rights, expressed his sympathy with the amendment while conceding that its attempt to restrict the independence of the federal judiciary did raise "serious constitutional issues." Reynolds also asserted his support for the recent North Carolina desegregation agreement, said that affirmative action legislation and consequent court rulings would be applied much more narrowly on his watch, and declared that controversial school desegregation suits filed in the Carter administration's final days would all be reviewed. He took no position on the extension of the Voting Rights Act. A successful corporation lawyer with minimal civil rights experience and strongly conservative views, his nomination had fueled strong fears that it was part of a plan to destroy the effectiveness of the government's main rights enforcement agency, and his responses at the confirmation hearing simply reinforced this dread. Reynolds was, declared NAACP executive director Benjamin Hooks, "a right-wing, ideological nut."[17]

There were signs too that opponents of the great legislative and social changes had become significantly emboldened by the Reagan victory. Symbolic was the southern white resistance to the strengthening drive to mark Martin Luther King's birthday as a public holiday. Cities and states outside the South had little difficulty in doing so, but, in the Old Confederacy, there were pockets of tenacious resistance. In Alabama, for example, Birmingham, under its first black mayor, Richard Arrington, closed its municipal offices for the day, but Montgomery decided to ignore the anniversary. In Virginia, where state senator Douglas Wilder had maneuvered a bill through the General Assembly declaring King's birthday a state holiday, conservatives mounted a sustained drive aimed at persuading Governor John L. Dalton to veto the measure. Dalton, a Republican, received thousands of letters urging him to act. Wilder and other black leaders were incensed when Dalton announced his veto, but Mary L. Curtis, a Fairfax housewife and mother of four, was elated. "Praise God," she declared, because King was nothing but "a tool of the Communists." The new president seemed to think the same way, at least in private. When Jesse Helms, unsurprisingly a bitter opponent of any federal action on the King holiday, asserted forcefully that he had been a Communist, Reagan did not rule it out. "We'll know in about 35 years, won't we?" was his response, alluding to the opening of the FBI files. Whatever his reasons, Reagan initially opposed any federal recognition of King's birthday, again emphasizing to black Americans that they could no longer look to the White House for sympathetic leadership.[18]

Surveying the civil rights record of the new administration after six months, the distinguished journalist Howell Raines saw little reason for optimism. The "civil rights forces had been sustaining major losses," he thought. Though Reagan's "own racial attitudes remain something of a mystery," Raines further observed, White House spokesman David Gergen had recently admitted that he did not think the president was "a crusader for civil rights." Certainly, the NAACP leadership believed that this was so. Even before they had listened to him address their annual convention in Denver, they had decided against a standing ovation at its conclusion. The tone of the occasion was decidedly chilly; NAACP chair Margaret Bush Wilson stated in her introduction that neither she nor her organization necessarily subscribed "to the views about to be expressed." Reagan's speech was similarly uncompromising. He defended his budget cuts, denied that their impact on black Americans was disproportionate, and asserted that they would soon result in "economic emancipation" for all citizens. While committing himself to guaranteeing all Americans the right to vote, the president made no like commitment on what the *New York Times* described as "the most sensitive civil rights issue he is likely to face this year," the extension of the Voting Rights Act. His speech received only perfunctory applause, and delegates left Denver in somber mood indeed, fearing what lay ahead, and wondering aloud whether they could preserve what had been won since 1965.[19]

When the NAACP convened in Washington seven years later, members were in a decidedly more upbeat mood. As the *New York Times* reported, the organization, "which had had its moments of self-doubt in recent years," was meeting "in an atmosphere of pride in recent accomplish-ments." Membership had risen, its financial troubles were safely behind it, and, above all, it was "basking in the experience of having gone through seven years of the Reagan Administration." According to the Reverend Jesse Jackson, Reagan was "the worst civil rights President we've had in recent memory," yet "most of the nation's civil rights laws [were] still intact." The cataclysm members had feared in 1981 had not occurred.[20]

The Continuing Complexities of Desegregation

There had been some battles lost along the way. Reynolds was commit-ted to a much more individualized notion of protecting civil rights, in keeping with the president's perspective that the Constitution was color-blind, and he brought into the Justice Department a team of brilliant young lawyers similarly determined "to recast the way the government and the courts approached" the issue. The most influential of these was John G. Roberts, later to become chief justice of the United States, whose "densely written" and closely argued memoranda favoring stripping the Supreme Court of its ability to hear civil rights cases on a class rather than an individual basis and challenging recent decisions upholding quota-oriented busing and affirmative action policies surfaced more than two decades later during his confirmation hearings. Yet he was but "the most influential, the most thoughtful," of a number of like-minded young men—a "band of ideological brothers" a less sympathetic col-league called them, determined to effect a "conservative political revolu-tion" in civil rights. They did not have it all their own way, and there were bitter opponents of their views within the Civil Rights Division itself, but their influence in the administration's first two years was profound.[21]

Ending compulsory busing was the issue that exercised Reynolds and his team most urgently, for ideological and political reasons. "We are under a great deal of pressure to put forth more on the subject of busing than we have in the past," a White House aide complained des-perately in late 1981. In a terse memorandum to Reynolds and the attor-ney general, the president's close friend and the White House political director Lyn Nofziger had made that abundantly clear. The American people, or "99.9 percent of them who have supported Ronald Reagan in the past," he wrote, "were at odds with mandatory school busing." If the administration was "going to change the direction of the country," therefore, it was a "good place" to start. Why, then, had so little been done, given that a swift end to busing "was what the President wanted"?[22]

Even Reynolds came in for White House criticism. He was not weed-ing out "the careerist ideologues in the Civil Rights Division" with sufficient vigor, complained one aide, and they therefore persisted in "pushing through decisions adverse to the Reagan policies." This "business as usual" attitude had to change, "in a way that will increase the likelihood of full enforcement of the President's policy." And it *was* the president's policy. The close attention he gave to the antibusing struggle, the frequency with which he addressed the issue publicly, is at variance with the insistence of many historians that, as Gil Troy put it, the "Reagan administration's assault on the civil rights agenda was more rhetorical than real."[23]

A swift end to busing, however, proved elusive, though all sorts of notions were canvassed, including a constitutional amendment prohibiting it. Department of Justice staffers provided quiet support and advice to the congressional proponents of the various antibusing amendments, and they wrote memoranda for presidential attacks. Yet, while HHS had ruled out supporting further busing plans, there was little that could be done to halt the hundreds already in operation, short of defying the courts. This was a source of continuing frustration, as Roberts's increasingly acerbic memoranda on the subject make clear. "It is passing strange," he complained to Fred Fielding in 1984, "for us to tell Congress it cannot pass a law preventing courts from ordering busing when our own Justice Department invariably urges this policy on the courts." After three years, the president's promises on busing remained largely unfulfilled.[24]

Reagan spoke constantly about his opposition to busing, usually to an enthusiastic response. Occasionally, however, he found surprising pockets of opposition. When, in 1984, he went to Charlotte, North Carolina, and gave his standard declaration that busing was a "failed social experiment that nobody wants," he must have been surprised at the response. "You Were Wrong, Mr. President," was the indignant headline in the *Charlotte Observer*. True, resistance to the court order had initially been "powerful," but it was no longer so. Indeed, the fully integrated school system was "one of the nation's finest" and "Charlotte's proudest achievement." It could not have happened without busing. In Memphis, too, city leaders of both races agreed that busing had created a fairer school system as white students slowly returned to "enriched educational programs." In general, however, the president's attacks struck a responsive chord.[25]

The Justice Department, too, hastened the end of a policy it had once vehemently advocated. Busing still had some supporters within the Civil Rights Division, in particular Ted Olsen, an assistant attorney general whose publicly expressed position, according to Morton C. Blackwell, a disgruntled fellow staffer, "could have been expected from the Justice Department during the Ford and Carter Administrations." Those who were determined to end busing, and who had worked so hard to elect Ronald Reagan, surely had "reason to expect some leadership from his Administration in their behalf." Instead, the only folk who could take any comfort from recent developments were "the professional civil rights extremists," he thought, and this would not change without a "wholesale personnel replacement at the Justice Department."[26]

Such a dramatic change did not occur; nevertheless, the tide at Justice did turn against busing. The influence of Olsen and those like him gave way to the much more restrictive perspectives of Roberts and the other conservatives. Early in 1985, *Time* asserted that the morale in the Justice Department, in particular, of the 175 career lawyers in the Civil Rights Division, was at rock bottom, "bored and idle" as recent political appointees now provided support for those who wished to restrict the rate of social change. "Everything," said one of them, "is exactly the opposite of the way it's supposed to be." In January of that year, the department, in a landmark case, urged the Fourth Circuit Court of Appeals, sitting in Richmond, Virginia, to allow the Norfolk school system to end its fourteen-year-old court-ordered busing plan. Twenty-two black plaintiffs joined to argue that to do so "could unravel the years of efforts to integrate and equalize the nation's schools" and would make resegregation much easier to achieve. Reynolds, for the department, agreed that the "case represented a major turning-point in the history of school desegregation," in that it would enable school systems that had clearly eliminated de jure segregation to discontinue forced busing and return to neighborhood schools, the first time that Justice had argued against court-ordered busing. Conceding that discrimination had clearly existed in Norfolk's schools before 1971, Reynolds asserted that the "wrong" had now been remedied, that the school system was now clearly unitary, and that to continue to punish Norfolk's children through forced busing was, therefore, immoral. The Court eventually upheld the school board's plan to end busing, despite the fact that more than 30 percent of the district's new neighborhood schools would be all black. Reynolds was delighted, for the decision set a precedent that more than 150 school districts would be eligible to follow.[27]

He was right. The use of busing as essential for real school integration was increasingly difficult to sustain, but this was due as much to larger social and demographic trends as to presidential rhetoric or Justice Department opposition. White flight, the dynamic phenomenon of the 1970s, continued into the next decade throughout the South's burgeoning urban areas. Birmingham, Richmond, and even Montgomery lost substantial numbers of their white residents to the suburbs and satellite towns, while many of those remaining moved their children from the public schools into private academies. This wholesale transfer of students often affected small communities as well as large. Southern schools were, by the mid-1980s, still the most desegregated in the nation, yet white flight nevertheless helps explain the dwindling relevance of new court-ordered busing. *Milliken* had effectively prevented busing across school district lines, while using busing in largely black city districts had little effect. There were few white students left to bus.[28]

Civil rights groups, academics, professional educators, and social commentators all deplored the Reagan administration's antibusing stance, arguing that, without it, *Brown* could not possibly be implemented. Nevertheless, a growing number of black voices could now be heard questioning its efficacy. Some, like Clarence Pendleton, whom Reagan had appointed to head a reconstituted Commission on Civil Rights, could easily be dismissed as, in the contemptuous words of Benjamin Hooks, the president's "mercenaries" and "Pollyannas of this administration . . . who lie in the face of history." Others were harder to ignore. The southern-born William Raspberry, a respected *Washington Post* columnist, and the academic Derrick Bell, then dean of the University of Oregon Law School, both argued persistently that busing wasted "black political and educational energies in return for small ambiguous gains." It obscured, stressed Raspberry, the fundamental issue of how to educate children whose parents "put little value" on what schools did. "Sending kids from one school to the next" was not the answer. Rather, the money spent on busing should be diverted to better programs for all black children, whatever the racial composition of their classrooms. Some black parents, often those of children who had been bused, were having second thoughts. Their children were being sent further and further from their neighborhoods because of white flight, sometimes having to get up as early as 5:00 A.M. to get to class on time. Was it really worth the hassle?[29]

In June 1986, the Supreme Court declined to hear an appeal by black parents to block the *Norfolk* decision, despite their impassioned plea that to end busing "was a charter for the resegregation of the public schools of the South." As Reynolds had predicted, a host of school districts throughout the nation hastened to follow Norfolk's lead. One of the first to do so was Oklahoma City, and the bitterly contested action there eventually reached the Supreme Court. In *Oklahoma City v. Dowell*, the Court, decisively reshaped during Reagan's presidency, in 1991 ruled in favor of the school board. A majority of the justices accepted the argument that, as the board had moved effectively to end the city's de jure segregated school system, admittedly through court-ordered busing, this busing plan could, nonetheless, be dropped in favor of a return to neighborhood schools, even though they would rarely be racially balanced owing to residential segregation. Where people chose to live, argued Chief Justice William Rehnquist in his majority opinion, was a private matter. The institutionalized discrimination of the past had been eliminated. Though not regarded as of particular significance at the time, the Court's decision in *Dowell,* its first concerning public schools in more than a decade, was, in fact, a landmark, with immediate application to the South. Together with *Freeman v. Pitts* in 1992, involving similar circumstances in De Kalb County, Georgia, it effectively ended court-ordered busing as a means of achieving desegregation where local school boards could show that they had eliminated the vestiges of past discrimination "to the extent practicable." The decision had particular relevance to the South and border states, where de jure dual systems had been mandated until *Brown.* "I think there's going to be a lot of pressure on school boards to go back to neighborhood schools," remarked Gwendolyn B. Gregory, deputy general counsel of the National School Boards Association.[30]

Oklahoma City v. Dowell could be seen as the culmination of the Reagan administration's attack on court-ordered busing, one that moved eventually from rhetorical support to practical and effective action. It also provides an important prism through which to view the broader story of school desegregation in the South after 1980. Obviously, it was a story of infinite variety, as commentators emphasized when noting *Brown's* thirtieth anniversary in 1984. Walter Goodman, in a long and thoughtful *New York Times* article, wrote of the "uneven results" achieved in the three decades, pointing to southern "success stories" such as Charlotte and Austin, Texas, but emphasizing that, with four hundred school districts still under court orders to integrate, there was no room for complacency as white flight continued. The "magnet schools" program, much favored by the Reagan administration—the provision, in predominantly urban black districts, of schools so resource rich that white students would be attracted back to the cities—was doing little "to significantly alter the racial makeup of school districts," said the NAACP's director of education, Dr. Beverley Cole. Only busing had done that, and it was under sustained attack.[31]

The Crisis produced a special edition to mark the *Brown* anniversary. Most contributors used the opportunity to attack the administration for its lack of leadership in furthering school desegregation and, in particular, its stand against busing. Again, Charlotte-Mecklenburg was generally hailed as an example of what could be achieved through enlightened local leadership. Without busing, "there was no other way," admitted Jay Robinson, superintendent of the Charlotte-Mecklenburg district, "to desegregate schools until neighborhoods become more integrated," but this Reynolds and his staff simply chose to ignore.[32]

Academics with expertise in desegregation issues were already sounding increasingly pessimistic about the future of integrated schools. Gary Orfield, then of the University of Chicago, first warned that "resegregation of schools is the great issue of the next generation" in 1987. He and his researchers have done so ever since. At the time, Orfield was commenting on developments at Central High, in Little Rock, Arkansas, the site of the iconic 1957 confrontation. Thirty years later, the Little Rock school district had to implement a new court-ordered plan, this time to combat resegregation. White flight throughout the 1980s had resulted in a school district now 71 percent black—in 1957, it had been 74 percent white—while the adjacent suburban districts of Pulaski County and North Little Rock were overwhelmingly white. Yet, only six years earlier, there was considerable optimism that a range of new programs and a vigorous promotional campaign by white parents who had stayed within the system was at last reversing the drift. Such optimism was misplaced. Little Rock, warned Orfield, "was an example of what is happening all over." Outside the South, and especially in the largest cities, "the public school systems are almost 90% black and integration isn't possible."[33]

Orfield, the codirector of Harvard University's Civil Rights Project for many years before moving to UCLA and long the nation's leading expert on resegregation, has continued to chart its progress publicly over the decades. But there are many others—like the Georgetown University law professor and former clerk to Justice Marshall Sheryll Cashin—who have also chronicled the retreat from, in Cashin's words, "the most massive federal intervention in the name of social justice since Reconstruction." Much of the data on which these researchers have drawn have come from cities outside the South—Boston, Philadelphia, Chicago, Detroit, Los Angeles—with large black and Latino populations that are increasingly poverty-stricken and unable to move beyond the confinement of their particular ghetto. Yet, while it is still true that southern schools remain the most integrated in the nation, resegregation is clearly on the increase in the South. Indeed, the South has the swiftest resegregation rate in the nation. The percentage of black students in majority-white schools in the South reached its peak of 43.5 in 1988, Reagan's last year as president. Since then, it has declined steadily, plummeting to 30 percent in 2002. In Mobile, Alabama, as a typical example, where the percentage of white central city students declined from just over 65 in 1980 to 49.8 in 2002, that of black and Latino students rose in exact correspondence. Throughout the South, school enrollments have followed residential patterns as white flight continues, though never with the vast disparities that exist in northern and midwestern cities. This is the reason that Orfield and John Boger called their 2005 edited collection *School Resegregation: Must the South Turn Back?* Unlike the rest of the country, they believed that the final choice was not yet made.[34]

The reasons for southern resegregation mirror those for resegregation nationwide. They include the *Dowell* decision and the consequent return to neighborhood schools, the persistence of residential segregation, continued white flight, the dramatic growth of the South's Latino population—a factor that has added further complexity to the region's racial balances—the reluctance of successive presidents from Reagan on to take the lead in favor of continued integration, and the growing disillusion of black parents, politicians, educators, and social commentators alike with integration, demanding, instead, better funding and more involvement in shaping policy and administration. As Elizabeth Eckford, one of the nine blacks who challenged segregation in Little Rock in 1957, said forty years later, "There was a time when I thought integration was one of the most desired things. . . . I appreciate blackness more than I did then."[35]

Yet such recent and real concerns over the failure of *Brown*, or the 1964 legislation, or judicial activism to end segregation in southern schools, should not diminish in any way the significance of the changes that did occur. As the historian James Patterson has aptly written, "The extent of change in many areas of the South, indeed, can scarcely be exaggerated. . . . By the late 1980s, most of the heavily black schools in the South were much better funded and much closer to having equal facilities than earlier." Black and white teachers were paid equally; they taught students of both races. Some black principals ran integrated schools. There had been problems along the way, but "in all these respects public education in many parts of the South had been revolutionized." The distinguished sociologist Orlando Patterson is similarly inclined to emphasize what *Brown*, Congress, and the courts had achieved by 1990 and finds the warnings of Orfield and his colleagues of a return to "a nineteenth century" education separatism to be "grossly exaggerate[d]." He believes that school integration will, henceforth, follow the integration of neighborhoods and welcomes the moves in this direction, however slight. Both Pattersons, then, share the view that *Brown*, the civil rights acts, and judicial activism revolutionized public education in the South and, with it, southern society.[36]

Higher Education

In April 2001, the state of Mississippi, the lead plaintiff, U.S. representative Bennie Thompson, the state's black colleges and universities, and the Department of Justice reached an agreement that ended *Ayers v. Fordice*, a case that had been before the courts since 1975. Jack Ayers, a black sharecropper acting on behalf of his son, had filed the suit, alleging that Mississippi had failed to integrate its higher education institutions fairly, in that its three formerly black universities remained vastly inferior to those that had formerly been all white. In 1992, the U.S. Supreme Court had agreed, ordering Mississippi "to reform its discriminatory spending and education policies." This was the first time the Court had ruled on desegregation in higher education, and its decision had implications for the seventeen southern or border states that had once operated de jure segregated systems. The Mississippi settlement nearly ten years later was the symbolic last act in a long struggle that had its beginning in the immediate postwar years and gained national attention in 1962 with Meredith's enrollment at the University of Mississippi.[37]

At one level, the desegregation of higher education in the South was easily achieved. After Meredith, George Wallace's humiliating attempt to prevent the integration of the University of Alabama, and the passage of the 1964 Civil Rights Act, all states adopted open-entry policies—and hoped to leave it at that. Black students soon appeared on the formerly all-white campuses, most visibly on their football and basketball teams. Not until the Carter administration did the federal government show some concern for the huge gulfs yet remaining and, in particular, the substance of *Ayers v. Fordice,* the failure to treat the formerly black and formerly white institutions equally. By this time, a number of similar suits had been filed, and central to them all was the refusal of southern state governments to address this issue. In Tennessee, there had been a decade of demonstrations and campus disruption as state and university officials, under court order to do so, tried, reluctantly and fruitlessly, to satisfy competing demands. South Carolina's traditionally all-black university was still 98.6 percent black in 1978, while the state's eleven formerly all-white institutions remained 91.4 percent white. Successive administrations had been reluctant to press higher education desegregation cases because of the difficulty of proving intent, but, eventually, Carter's Education and Justice departments decided to deal with the growing problem in various ways. They envisaged the creation of unitary systems in each state, the moving of some professional schools and faculties to the formerly black colleges, the movement of students likewise, and the merging of some black and white colleges, with duplication of faculties and courses kept to an absolute minimum. However, these plans had not moved much beyond the template state when Carter left office, though one of his final actions was to write to four southern governors advising them that their colleges and universities remained unconstitutionally segregated and that they thus risked losing federal funds. The new administration was to take a very different approach.[38]

When Secretary of Education Bell announced that the new administration and the state of North Carolina had agreed to end the conflict over integrating the state's higher education system, it was on terms very different to those on which the Carter administration would have insisted. There were to be no forced mergers, no compulsory reassignments, no shifting of programs from white to black schools. Rather, the black colleges were to be helped through the provision of significantly increased funding, some of which would be used for the creation of twenty-nine new academic programs and three graduate centers, designed to attract white students. The agreement also set "goals" of achieving 10.6 percent black enrollment at white schools and 15 percent white enrollment at black schools by 1986, but Bell insisted that these were not quotas, and there were no sanctions if the goals were not met. The agreement was welcomed with huge relief by white college educators but not by the NAACP, which eventually filed an appeal. Black educators, however, saw much good in it. North Carolina's traditionally black colleges—North Carolina A&T, Elizabeth City State College, Winston-Salem State College, Fayetteville State University, and North Carolina Central University—would all maintain separate identities; they would not be closed or merged with larger, formerly all-white institutions, as the Carter plans had assumed. These were colleges with proud traditions and histories; they had educated the state's black leaders in the long years of segregation and had provided the local captains and foot soldiers in the civil rights struggles. They stood, as the historian Adam Fairclough has written, "proud monuments to black achievement in adversity—institutional links to emancipation and all its liberating potential." They were, Fairclough continued, of crucial importance to "African-Americans' sense of community." When integration was finally enforced in the South, hundreds of black high schools, each with its own rich traditions, had became only memories, and southern black communities had no wish to see their colleges similarly "swallowed up or merged." Thus, black and white southerners came to seek similar outcomes as the North Carolina settlement became a blueprint for the region.[39]

Louisiana was the next state to settle what had been a seven-year desegregation lawsuit, along lines similar to the North Carolina settlement. The state would spend millions of dollars over the next six years improving the quality of its traditionally black institutions, scholarship programs would be expanded, blacks would have more power at the upper levels of the system's administration, and the freshman classes in all institutions would have an open admissions policy, but the separate identities of all colleges would be preserved. This the black leaders had insisted on, that Grambling University, with its famous football team, and the Southern University system, with its treasured Shreveport, Baton Rouge, and New Orleans campuses, would remain separate institutions. "The black community is terribly proud of these schools," explained Dr. Daniel C. Thompson of Dillard University. "They like to boast that these are our schools." They had no objection to some white students attending, and they certainly welcomed the money that might achieve this, he said, as long as their separateness was never compromised. Again, the wishes of white politicians and educators to lose as little as possible of the old system coincided with those of their black counterparts, despite the vocal objection of the national NAACP. The significance of the new administration's approach, Reynolds said at the agreement's signing, was that "the historical importance of the black colleges is recognized."[40]

Reynolds was not similarly appreciative of the terms on which a federal judge approved in 1984 a settlement to end segregation at historically black Tennessee State University (TSU)—and neither were its students. The events leading to his action provide a good example of the complexities and competing demands that marked the desegregation of higher education in the South. TSU had been ordered in 1977 to merge with the Nashville campus of the University of Tennessee. By 1983, it was obvious that this had not occurred. With the percentage of black freshmen at TSU standing at 90.2 in 1983, said federal judge Thomas A. Wiseman as he reopened the case, "it is obvious that the phenomenon of a black TSU is still existing," ordering that all steps be taken to make the ratio 50–50 by 1993. The Justice Department, alone among the parties to the lawsuit, opposed his decision. "Such an approach does little to solve the problems in a higher education system," angrily asserted Reynolds, "and may well in the long run do more to destroy traditional black colleges than to desegregate them." Black students at TSU seemed to agree. When they heard of Judge Wiseman's order, they marched on the federal courthouse to voice their opposition, fearing the loss of a campus "where they feel welcome," and then circulated a petition urging the Justice Department to appeal the judge's order. Whatever its reasons, the Reagan administration was right on the issue of preserving black schools, said David Charles Mills, a TSU student. TSU had long been a beacon in the black community; it had trained generations of the state's black leaders. Now, said Mills, young blacks who wished to follow them might not even gain entry. In this, he said, he agreed with Reynolds and the Reagan administration, not the NAACP. The settlement had given racially preferential treatment to whites, at the expense of black Tennesseans and black traditions.[41]

In the years following Judge Wiseman's order, the percentage of white students at TSU increased significantly, reaching 34.5 percent in 1990, many on scholarships reserved for them. White faculty numbers increased as well. It was far from easy for the white students, however. Dawn Vaden, a white nursing major, talked of "repeated slurs" from black students and admitted that she rarely felt at ease on the campus. She understood, however, the reasons for their hostility. "I don't think it will ever be 50–50," she said. "This is their school. I don't think they are going to give it up." Dr. Andrew Jackson, a black sociology professor, made the same point. "If Tennessee State desegregates by bringing more white students," he asked, "why must she surrender her cultural identity in order to create a white presence?" Traditionally white schools had never been required to do so. Black students and graduates, too, believed that the drastic integration plan was destroying the school's precious character and mission. TSU never reached the 50–50 ratio, and, in December 2000, Wiseman's order was removed, in favor of a mandate to become, as far as possible, "racially non-identifiable." As the historian Bobby Lovett concluded, TSU "remained an historically black university," but it was also the state's most "racially diversified" institution. Given the previous bitterness and division, it was a solution most could live with.[42]

The Reagan administration's noncoercive approach to the desegregation of higher education was broadly popular with the black and white education communities, for differing reasons. It was much less so with the civil rights coalition. Indeed, the NAACP considered it, alongside the curtailment of busing, to be one of the areas in which they lost most ground during the 1980s. They fought the various agreements every step of the way, claiming that they failed to desegregate the systems properly and that the black colleges remained disadvantaged. This was certainly borne out by an Education Department study completed in 1988, Secretary William Bennett admitting that six southern and border states—Delaware, Florida, Georgia, Missouri, Oklahoma, and Virginia—were still in partial violation of a 1971 court order requiring them to desegregate their public universities and colleges. Four states—Arkansas, North and South Carolina, and West Virginia—were judged to be in full compliance, while others had not yet met specific goals regarding faculty hiring and the improvement of curriculum and facilities. Bennett put the best spin he could on the report, praising the advances made under the Reagan administration. "Even in the offending states," he argued with some justice, "a black student who graduates from high school has opportunities to go to college and will find, if he has the qualifications, many institutions eager to have him." The NAACP and other civil rights groups were much less positive. "The Department has effectively excused 10 Southern states from their affirmative obligations to dismantle their racially dual systems," claimed James Byrd, an NAACP lawyer. New York congressman Ted Weiss, a liberal, believed that "it [Bennett's positive spin] fit in with the pattern of the Reagan Administration not wanting to enforce civil rights legislation."[43]

Moreover, some of the agreements reached in 1981 had already fallen apart. In 1988, a federal court ruled that the Louisiana settlement had failed, in that the commitment to upgrade the traditionally black colleges financially and to end some program duplication had not been honored. Paul Verkuil, president of the College of William and Mary, was contracted to produce a new plan. It required much more black involvement at the highest levels of administration, enhanced spending on the traditionally black colleges, especially Southern University and Grambling, and an unequivocal guarantee that no institution would be closed or merged. Not until 1994 was the Louisiana situation resolved. The Verkuil plan was the basis but with further provision for undergraduate and graduate programs to be added to both black and white schools, specifically to attract students of the other race. Again, the Reagan approach had left unfinished business for succeeding administrations.[44]

In no state, however, was the struggle to integrate higher education more prolonged, more difficult, and more divisive than in Mississippi. In 1970, state officials refused to file a desegregation plan, as required by HEW, commencing a pattern of defiance that continued for the next two decades, a defiance that Reagan's Justice Department failed to deal with, despite *Ayers v. Fordice*. The case dragged on throughout the 1980s and into the next decade as successive state administrations made little attempt to upgrade the historically black colleges, aiming rather to shut them down or merge them with formerly all-white institutions. One of those marked for closure was the struggling Mississippi Valley State University (MVSU), whose most famous alumnus was Jerry Rice, then a wide receiver for the San Francisco 49ers. It was located deep in the Delta, in Itta Bena, where white resistance to integration had been at its most vicious. Now the plan was to move all the MVSU students to nearby Delta State, a formerly white school in Cleveland, undeniably a better-staffed and better-equipped institution, but one where the Confederate flag still flew on special occasions. The resultant controversy, remarked a visiting reporter, stirred "one of the most intense racial and political and legal battles in Mississippi's history . . . one reminiscent for many people here of the emotionally charged period 30 years ago when James Meredith became the first black at the University of Mississippi." It starkly demonstrated how important these traditionally black schools were to their local communities, no matter how impoverished, which would fight tenaciously to hold on to them. Not even Governor Fordice's threat to call out the national guard if he were ordered to equalize spending between black and white institutions dampened this determination.[45]

Tamla Moore, an MVSU sophomore, explained what underpinned this commitment. She would never attend a white college, she insisted. "I just got out of high school and I don't want to go through all that racial tension again." At her school, they even had two proms, so far apart were the black and white students. There was no such tension, no such division at MVSU. Commented Franklin G. Jenifer, president of

Howard University in 1992, "In a perfect world, we may have black and white students in the same schools." But Mississippi was yet far from such perfection.[46]

Earlier that year, the Supreme Court had agreed with him. In its first ruling on a higher education issue for years, it had decisively reversed an appeals court decision that Mississippi had done all it could to desegregate its public universities. Successive judgments also ruled out plans to close or merge the black colleges, thus enabling MVSU to survive as a traditionally black institution and, with the help of the blues legend B. B. King, modestly to thrive. By 2000, it had even enrolled 103 white students. *Ayers v. Fordice* was finally settled in 2001, on terms that maintained the independence of all the colleges but guaranteed them equal funding. Thus ended the legal battles to achieve the desegregation of higher education in the state—and in the South. Some traditionally black colleges, of course, have done better than others. North Carolina Central University, in Durham, has a prestigious law school that boasts among its graduates the state's governor in 2007, Michael Easley, and a nationally recognized niche area in biotechnology. Nineteen percent of its student body in 2007 was white. South Carolina State has recently attracted "dozens of whites" to its various programs through aggressive recruiting and attractive minority scholarships. MVSU, on the other hand, despite the gains of the 2001 settlement and a successful fundraising drive headed by B. B. King and the actor Morgan Freeman, remains "predominantly a regional institution serving students whose relatives or friends have attended" earlier. But its survival is no longer in doubt, and this is mainly due to the determination of southern black communities not to accept the disappearance of the institutions that had sustained them during Jim Crow.[47]

If the civil rights community believed, as did the NAACP, that the desegregation of higher education was one area in which it had lost ground during the Reagan years, it did at least claim one specific and highly symbolic victory. From 1970, the IRS had routinely denied tax exemption to the segregated schools—often the "segregation academies" that had mushroomed throughout the South following the enforcement of *Brown*. The guidelines for so doing were strengthened in 1978, sparking bitter debate over freedom of religion, given that most of these schools claimed some Christian affiliation. The 1980 Republican platform pledged to "halt the unconstitutional regulatory vendetta launched by Mr. Carter's IRS commissioner against independent schools," and Reagan, speaking as the GOP candidate to six thousand cheering students at South Carolina's Bob Jones University, one of the schools affected, affirmed his unequivocal support. Urged on by Mississippi congressman Trent Lott, and with Bob Jones the test case, the new administration revoked the policy and abandoned its action against the university. The resultant national uproar caught it completely by surprise. In vain did the president argue that the issue was one of religious freedom. Bob Jones, the university's founder and guiding light, had stated angrily in 1965 that his institution would never "sign away its birth right for a mess of government porridge" and comply with the 1964 act, and, though the school had recently enrolled a few black students, it strictly forbade interracial dating and circumscribed black-white contact in various other ways. To African Americans, it was a clear statement of where the administration stood on civil rights. In 1983, however, the Supreme Court ruled against the government, finding that the IRS policy of denying exemptions to such schools to be justified. The NAACP rejoiced, accepting the decision as a lonely victory in those barren years.[48]

Jobs and Freedom

In a 1991 *New York Times* article, Steven Holmes warned that, should the Bush administration attack "programs that give preference to minority and female job seekers, it was tampering with a bipartisan concept that has become as familiar to American business as tally sheets and bottom lines." This had been the enduring lesson of the Reagan years, when all administration attempts to curtail such programs had been opposed "by corporate lobbyists as well as civil rights groups." Without doubt, of the range of civil rights legislation and court rulings since 1964, it was Title VII of the original Civil Rights Act that had the most immediate national ramifications, in terms of both its general application and the opportunity it gave so many other groups, most importantly women, to challenge traditional employment barriers. Nevertheless, as the historians Robert Zieger and Nancy MacLean have both recently emphasized, its effect in the South was of particular significance, in that it opened up the textile mills, where black workers had heretofore been banned from all but the most menial work. Public service positions, too, throughout the region, including its police departments, could no longer remain white, or with only token integration, once Title VII was enforced. As a black Mississippian asserted, "I wouldn't have my present job, if it weren't for that law."[49]

Those who were part of the conservative tide that swept Ronald Reagan into the White House had heard his views on affirmative action—and agreed with them. In particular, his opposition to race-based quotas in filling job vacancies, determining promotion possibilities, or deciding college admissions struck a special resonance. "I am old enough to remember when quotas existed in the U.S. for the purpose of discrimination," the new president was fond of saying, but that would certainly not be the case with his administration. The Constitution was color-blind, yet affirmative action policies denied this. Reagan's appointments to the key civil rights enforcement positions—Reynolds and Clarence Thomas at the EEOC were the most important—shared this perspective, which they articulated at every opportunity. Indeed, even Martin Luther King's "Dream" speech, with its emphasis on character content rather than skin color, was decontextualized, wrested from its historic location as part of a national movement for "Jobs and Freedom," and used to reinforce the stand against *quotas,* the administration's code word for *affirmative action.* "Opponents of affirmative action may finally have won, not in court, but at the ballot box," editorialized the *Washington Post* in March 1981, as the confident Reaganites moved to limit the reach of Title VII.[50]

A systematic unpicking of affirmative action policies, however, was not a priority of Reagan's first term. Rather, the "backlash emerged . . . not as a coordinated effort" but as "an awkward and even contradictory skirmish," waged indirectly through appointments policy and slashing the budgets of the key enforcement agencies. A protracted example of this was the determination to make the U.S. Commission on Civil Rights much more reflective of administration policy by changing its composition. Reagan replaced its chair, Arthur S. Flemming, a strong supporter of affirmative action, easily enough, appointing in his stead a black conservative, Clarence Pendleton Jr. He had much more trouble with the other commissioners. Led by Mary Francis Berry, they fought hard to retain their jobs and their independence, challenged the president's authority to remove them, and were soon backed by a large cross section of public opinion, including senators profoundly disturbed by Reagan's insistence that the commission simply reflect his administration's views. Eventually, a compromise was worked out, enlarging the commission from six to eight members, half to be appointed by the president and half by Congress, with the president selecting the chair and Congress his or her deputy. In fact, Reagan had won the battle. In 1984, the reconstituted commission issued a statement deploring the use of quotas in appointments policy, Pendleton declaring, "Such racial preferences merely constitute another form of unjustified discrimination, create a new class of victims and, when used in public employment, offend the constitutional principle of equal protection of the law for all citizens." The commission had, thus, become "a lapdog for the Administration instead of a watchdog for civil rights," declared an outraged Berry.[51]

The Justice Department, under Reynolds's influence, began to intervene in cases testing the limits of affirmative action, especially those involving police and fire departments. Most of these cases were in the South and involved temporary hiring quotas as a means of remedying long records of systematic racial discrimination. In 1984, Justice won what Reynolds described as a "monumental triumph for civil rights," one that "realizes the dream of Martin Luther King," when the Supreme Court ruled in *Firefighters Local Union 1784 v. Stott* that an affirmative action plan in Memphis that protected recently hired African American firefighters from being laid off while whites with more seniority were being let go violated Title VII of the Civil Rights Act. This "exhilarating decision," Reynolds continued, had moved the nation along "the high road of race neutrality." He thought that "no more fitting interpretation of Title VII could come in its twentieth anniversary year." For the civil rights coalition, however, it was an ominous harbinger of future struggles.[52]

Stott, despite dispute over its wider implications, did demonstrate that affirmative action could be successfully challenged in the courts. After his triumphant reelection, therefore, the president considered that the time was right for a frontal assault. Accordingly, the new attorney general, Edwin Meese, and Reynolds determined to rescind Executive Order 11246, the linchpin of affirmative action policies since Lyndon Johnson first promulgated it in 1965, which required the compliance of all federal contractors. It had set the standard for most that had followed for the past two decades. But now, said one White House official, it was time to "wipe out the effect of nearly twenty years of quota programs." This the president could do easily as the only opposition would come from "the entrenched civil rights leadership," a constituency of diminishing national significance that Reagan could safely ignore.[53]

The unnamed official, Meese and Reynolds, even the president himself, all were wrong. As expected, the NAACP reacted furiously, accusing Reagan of trying to roll back the gains of the previous two decades, but other groups soon joined the "storm of protest." Women, Latinos, educators, labor unions, all were vocal in their opposition, but so, to the administration's considerable discomfort, were representatives of its core constituency, corporate America. Many business leaders had learned to live with affirmative action; some had even come to appreciate its virtues, in that it provided them with a much wider talent pool. Moreover, they feared what fifty states might do if left to their own devices once federal regulations had been withdrawn. Congressmen, too, even those usually disposed to support the president unequivocally, became nervous as a result. When something was working, said House minority leader Bob Michel, "you don't fix it." Within the cabinet itself, Secretary of Labor William Brock led a spirited opposition group. In vain did Reagan and Meese protest that they were simply trying to create the color-blind society King had dreamed of; the opposition was so broad and so vehement that the policy of direct confrontation was abandoned in favor of a return to less obvious means of circumventing Title

VII. It was, Reynolds recollected, "getting in the way of other things that are more important," tacit admission of a grave political misjudgment. For the NAACP, it was a victory in the struggle to preserve what had been so recently and painfully won. Despite the hostility of the current racial environment, Benjamin Hooks assured delegates to its 1986 convention that "there was still reason to rejoice."[54]

Supreme Court decisions, too, gave further reason for rejoicing as they did not always turn out to be as supportive of the administration as was *Stott*. Four 1987 rulings, including one to do with the desegregation of Alabama's police forces, aroused Reynolds's particular ire. Taken together, they upheld the use of racial and gender quotas in certain specified circumstances, refuting the "Administration's contention that Title VII prohibited the use of goals and timetables in hiring." In particular, they clearly negated the victory Reynolds had claimed through *Stott*, and he reacted angrily, describing the rulings as "extremely unfortunate." He was especially savage with Justice William J. Brennan, who had written the majority opinion in all four cases. Liberals like Brennan, he told students and faculty at the University of Missouri School of Law, "would have us cast off the constitutional vestments of the Founding Fathers and substitute judicial pronouncements unhinged from the text and history of the Constitution." Brennan declined to comment. For the civil rights coalition, it was further vindication of their position. These Supreme Court rulings, Benjamin Hooks exulted, were "a significant rebuke to the Reagan Administration's pernicious effort to destroy affirmative action."[55]

Yet, in the longer term, Reagan's indirect chipping away at Title VII was effective. He never funded the enforcement agencies to the level where they could perform effectively, but, most importantly, his opportunity to appoint four new Supreme Court justices, including its chief, William H. Rehnquist, shifted its balance decidedly to the right. As Linda Greenhouse wrote in 1989, following one of the five decisions that year that cumulatively greatly reduced the ability of workers to bring employment discrimination suits under Title VII, there could no longer be "any remaining doubt about whether former President Reagan had accomplished his goal of moving the Court in a more conservative direction on civil rights." There was more to come under his successor. With the retirement of two of the Court's most liberal judges, Brennan and Thurgood Marshall, George Bush was able to solidify the conservative majority, and, though David Souter proved to be rather too liberal for some, Marshall's replacement, Clarence Thomas, who as Reagan's EEOC chair had amply demonstrated his opposition to the broad use of Title VII, was all they had hoped for. President Clinton's two appointments were insufficient to shift the court closer to the center on affirmative action. Though it was not ruled unconstitutional in the 1990s, as Justices Scalia and Thomas might have wished, successive decisions have greatly reduced Title VII's sweep.[56]

In the late 1970s and early 1980s, Title VII as applied through the courts achieved its primary aim in that it largely destroyed Jim Crow in the southern workplace. This was most obvious in the public services; whites-only and tokenist policies substantially disappeared from the region's police and fire departments, its classrooms and lecture halls, its state and municipal offices and agencies of government, and its hospitals and health services, assisted greatly by the growing influence of black politicians. Moreover, black businesses could tender for government contracts, Title VII affording them convenient protection in doing so under its set-aside provisions. There was plenty of work in the Sun Belt boom of the 1980s for black tradesmen and even women, though rarely in the best-paying jobs. Yet, as the historian David Goldfield has observed, "Affirmative action programs tended to favor the blacks who qualified for the expanding white collar segment of the southern labor market." Many did well there. Goldfield quotes an Atlanta attorney, busy making money, noting "that the only 'ism' he was interested in was capitalism." A black businessman on the Mississippi coast enthused about the "quality of life" there, compared to New York, and it is true that blacks continued to return to the South throughout the 1980s—"in their millions"—attracted by the prospect of decent jobs in the changed world. Delores Watson returned to her home town of Saluda, South Carolina, after twenty years in Los Angeles, partly to seize the chance of starting her own business, but also to give her two children a life away from the gang violence of the city's mean streets. Marshall Logan returned to Asheville, North Carolina, after an adult life spent in New Jersey, because his roots were there and it was no longer the racially divided town of his boyhood. For them all, the 1964 Civil Rights Act had realized its promise.[57]

For a time, it had worked, too, for those seeking to break the color line in the South's manufacturing industries and especially the flagship, cotton textiles. In his previous work, Timothy Minchin has demonstrated how Title VII transformed the mill workplace, creating myriad opportunities for black men and women that had not existed before 1964. Yet it was a bitter victory. As Minchin comments, "It is clear that at the very time when blacks began to enter textiles in large numbers, the industry began a serious decline." Mill closings and the movement of hundreds of thousands of jobs offshore has been the steady story of the last three decades—southern blacks won the right to good textile jobs at the time they were drying up. The same is true of the region's other manufacturing industries—and, in particular, steel—all victims of postindustrialization, globalization, and NAFTA. Neverthe-less, the effects of Title VII were profound. It transformed the southern workplace, and the dynamic advancement of the black middle class is compelling evidence of its success. Yet much of the rural South, the preindustrial South, remains in deep structural poverty, as do the unemployed in the region's cities, from which the most affluent of both races have fled. The hopelessness and helplessness of those trapped in the Ninth Ward of New Orleans during Hurricane Katrina showed the world the limits of affirmative action. So did a recent study of infant mortality in the Southeast. For decades, the rate had been falling steadily, even in the poorest rural counties, but, since 2003, it has been on the rise, most dramatically in Mississippi. Not surprising, said Dr. William Langston of the State Department of Health: "Programs take money and Mississippi is the poorest state in the nation." Cuts in wel-fare in a region where there are no longer any jobs has had a deadly effect. Jamekia Brown, of the "tired town" of Hollander, deep in the Delta, twenty-two years old and pregnant with her third child, could not even afford the gas to visit an obstetrician, let alone pay for head-stones to mark the graves of her first two babies. Title VII could not do much for her—or for her region.[58]

The Right to Vote

It was the president's equivocation about the renewal of the Voting Rights Act that caused most concern to the civil rights coalition in the Reagan administration's first few weeks. Many shared John Hulett's fear that the act had provided the underpinning for the scale of change over the past fifteen years and that to weaken it would place these gains in jeopardy. In testimony before the House Judiciary Committee early in 1981, Benjamin Hooks stressed that, though the Voting Rights Act was "the single most effective piece of legislation drafted in the last two decades," it had not yet reached its full potential and that, despite the protestations of white southerners, its provisions were still being breached. Without its continued protection, the danger of a return to some of the pre-1965 practices was real. The unstated aim of those who argued otherwise or who advocated its extension throughout the nation was the "killing of the Act by making enforcement impossible." White southerners, Hooks insisted, had not yet demonstrated beyond doubt that they supported the rights of all minorities in "exercising this most fundamental of all freedoms."[59]

Southern congressmen and senators, led by Helms and Thurmond, predictably advocated repeal of the act or wanted to render it ineffective through extending its coverage and, then, removing its crucial preclearance provisions. Reagan had said in his election campaign that preclearance "imposes unequal burdens on some parts of the nation," and the Helms/Thurmond camp was also given strong initial support by a group of conservative Republicans led by Henry Hyde of Illinois, a powerful member of the House Judiciary Committee. By the end of July, however, Hyde had changed his mind on preclearance, the Judiciary Committee had approved its extension "with no impairment of its enforcement provisions," and within a few weeks the president had said that his "inclination," too, was to support an extension. Meanwhile, the Justice Department had demonstrated its intention to continue the vigorous enforcement of the act, twice rejecting a plan to redistrict the Virginia State Senate on the grounds that it discriminated against black voters in Norfolk. It seemed, therefore, that the NAACP's fears that the administration had planned to retreat on voting were unfounded.[60]

And so it proved. The renewed act easily passed the House by a vote of 389–24, and, though Helms vowed to filibuster the Senate version "until the cows come home," it was an empty threat—all the more so once his ally Strom Thurmond withdrew from the battle. The act, which the *New York Times* described as "a strong measure," soon cleared the Senate by a vote of 85–8. Reagan signed a twenty-five-year extension into law on June 29, 1982, declaring as he did so the right to vote to be the "crown jewel" of American liberties. Despite this rhetoric, it was not a cause he had championed but rather "a bow to political reality." Commentators and historians remain puzzled by his initial reluctance to seize the higher ground.[61]

Throughout the 1980s and into the next decade, the Justice Department investigated hundreds of alleged violations of the Voting Rights Act. In 1981, for example, it threw out a North Carolina redistricting plan on the grounds that the "strangely irregular" fishhook-like shape of the new Second Congressional District, held by the powerful Democrat L. H. Fountain, seemed to have been redrawn specifically to exclude Durham County, with its large, politically active black community. As Reynolds pointed out, the district had lost nearly 7 percent of its black registered voters as a consequence. The next year, hundreds of federal observers monitored primary elections in nine Alabama counties, the first use of such examiners in seven years, "to determine whether minorities are able to vote without interference." Others were assigned to two rural Georgia counties where there had been clear interference with black voter registration. In tiny St. George, South Carolina—population 2,134, of which 41 percent was black—the department filed suit in 1983 to force new elections for the entire town council, alleging that its staggered-term system made the election of a black councillor almost impossible to achieve. In 1988, the department supported a suit, filed by

Representative Tyrone Brooks, alleging that Georgia's system of electing justices in broad judicial circuits by a majority vote rather than a simple plurality was "blatantly discriminatory" and in flagrant contravention of the Voting Rights Act. After complex legal maneuvering, it was the Justice Department that ended up the final arbiter, and, in April 1990, in "a sweeping decision" it overturned Georgia's judicial system on the grounds that "judicial races fall under the same guidelines as legislative ones." It was a decision of real significance, climaxing a decade of determined enforcement of the law.[62]

Obviously, by this time Reynolds was no longer head of the Civil Rights Division, but, in his determination to secure equal access to southern ballot boxes, he had displayed a level of commitment that surprised even his sternest critics. One such was Jesse Jackson, who in 1983 challenged Reynolds to come with him to Mississippi to see for himself how in many rural counties pre-1965 voting practices persisted. Somewhat to Jackson's surprise, Reynolds accepted, agreeing "to go down to Mississippi next week and personally look into the complaints," winning Jackson's respect as they stood arm in arm in a black church in Canton, singing "We Shall Overcome." On his return to Washington, Reynolds readily conceded that he had found serious deficiencies in registration in several counties, refused to preclear a "record number" of local redistricting plans, and sent federal registrars to the offending districts. The result of his action was an immediate increase in both voter registration and black elected officials, most dramatically, a 150 percent increase in black county supervisors throughout the state by 1988. Even Reynolds's sharpest opponents agreed that, unlike his retreat on past policies on busing and affirmative action, his determination to enforce the Voting Rights Act was exemplary and that the ethos he imbued persisted in the Justice Department after his departure. In July 1991, as one example, in what the *New York Times* described as "new vigor," Justice blocked legislative redistricting plans in both Mississippi and Alabama, on the usual grounds that they discriminated against black voters. When a curb on such departmental activism finally came, as in so many other areas of civil rights enforcement, it was through the growing conservatism of the Supreme Court, rather than any retreat from the priorities Reynolds had helped establish.[63]

Partly as a result of Justice Department intervention, there was a steady increase in black political participation in the South during the Reagan years and, with this, a corresponding increase in electoral power. By 1992, 25 percent of Mississippi's state legislators were black, as were hundreds of local officials such as sheriffs, mayors, town councillors, and county supervisors. What a contrast this was with the lily-white pre-1965 situation. Likewise, Alabama, second only to Mississippi in its determination to preserve white supremacy, had 706 elected black officials. In Albany, Georgia, Charles Sherrod, who had gone there in 1961 as an SNCC activist to work for voter registration, had been elected a city commissioner by 1976 and then mayor in 1984. The South teemed with such examples of the changed political configuration wrought by the Voting Rights Act. Much of this new influence was played out at the local level, though Goldfield and others have demonstrated that the southern black vote had become a key factor in shaping national debate on some issues as well. Most notable was the failure of Judge Robert Bork's nomination to the Supreme Court in 1987. Sixteen southern senators, none of whom had won a majority of white votes but who had received overwhelming black support, aligned themselves against Bork. And, of course, in January 1990 Douglas Wilder was sworn in as governor of Virginia, the first African American ever to hold such office. None of this could have occurred without the 1965 act. As the NAACP, in 1988, celebrated its achievements during the hostile Reagan era, its preservation was clearly, for black southerners, the most important of these.[64]

There were other, more specific victories to celebrate. One in which NAACP members took particular pride was the organization's leading role in the coalition that fought the Bork nomination. Bork, "an heroic figure" to conservatives, was profoundly disliked by liberals of all stripes. He had opposed the 1964 Civil Rights Act as unconstitutional, had denounced *Roe v. Wade* as "a serious and wholly unjustifiable judicial usurpation of state legislative authority," and as a federal appeals court judge had consistently stood strongly against judicial activism. In response, Senate liberals, themselves strongly influenced by an effective grassroots campaign against the nominee led by the NAACP and pro-choice groups, vehemently and successfully fought his nomination. On October 23, 1987, the Senate rejected Bork by a vote of 58–42, to the rejoicing of the civil rights constituency.[65]

Congress gave the NAACP cause for further rejoicing the following year, again after a grassroots campaign that the civil rights coalition had led. In March, it had passed the Civil Rights Restoration Act, aimed at reversing the effect of a 1984 Supreme Court decision, *Grove City College v. Bell,* that effectively narrowed "the scope of four major civil rights laws to prevent tax-payer financing of discrimination." Immediately, the civil rights coalition started a campaign to nullify its effect, and effectively the 1988 act, passed with overwhelming bipartisan majorities, did just that, making it clear that "all aspects of an organization must comply with civil rights requirements if any part or program of its entities receives federal funding." Reagan had vowed to veto the legislation on the grounds that it gave the federal government far too much power over state and local authorities and the private sector, "from churches and synagogues to farmers, grocery stores and businesses of all sizes." The *New York Times* described the president's decision as "foolish and wrong." It urged him to think again and "join the broad consensus for social justice." He did not do so, and Congress easily overrode his veto, dealing "the administration a severe political defeat." For the civil rights coalition, many of whom considered the act to be the most significant in twenty years, it was a precious triumph in a bleak decade.[66]

Still, the greatest and most highly symbolic victory had occurred nearly five years earlier, when, on November 3, 1983, President Reagan signed the bill establishing Martin Luther King's birthday as a federal holiday. This was an enactment he had once strongly opposed, proposing instead a scholarship scheme for black students. It became harder, however, for even the most convinced Reaganites, having decontextualized Martin Luther King's famous speech of August 28, 1963, for their own anti–affirmative action purposes, to oppose the burgeoning movement. In 1982, the King Center presented to Congress a petition with more than six million signatures on it as the legislative support grew exponentially. Though Jesse Helms remained resolute in last-ditch opposition, other former segregationist icons, uncompromising leaders of past southern defiance, eagerly queued up to sponsor the enabling federal legislation. One was the diehard Dixiecrat Strom Thurmond, who declared his intention to do so before a wildly cheering student audience at Voorhees College, a historically black school in Denmark, South Carolina. For thousands of white southerners, however, his was the ultimate betrayal. "I had always felt that there was at least one person in Washington with some convictions and that person was you," wrote a shocked John D. Boswell of North Augusta, South Carolina. "I now see that I was wrong. You also appear to have sold out to the blacks." W. T. Wiggins Jr., also of North Augusta, was similarly disgusted with the old Dixiecrat and told him so, wondering whether he had become "senile." By voting for the bill, according to David Duke of the National Association for the Advancement of White People, Thurmond and southerners like him had "proven themselves traitors to the nation": "Their names will forever live in infamy." Hundreds expressed similar views, indicative of the continuing divisive potential of King's memory. Yet, by establishing the King holiday, Reagan had drawn to a symbolic end the southern dimension of the civil rights struggle. In that sense, despite the welter of promises half realized or betrayed, despite the persistence of racism in American life, the NAACP's celebrations in 1988 were apt. There was no going back. The Second Reconstruction had been preserved.[67]

11

FROM BUSH TO BUSH

The Complexities of Civil Rights

"When the subject is civil rights," wrote the journalist Steven A. Holmes in 1991, there were "two George Bushes." There was the George Bush who told a cheering group of black supporters in town for his inauguration that King's dream of equality would be "a vision for his tenure," who talked movingly of the "moral stain of segregation" and of his determination to cleanse the nation of its last vestiges. There was the George Bush who appointed the first black chairman of the Joint Chiefs of Staff, General Colin Powell, and who donated half the proceeds of his autobiography to the United Negro College Fund.

But there was also the George Bush whose 1988 election campaign featured the blatantly racist Willie Horton advertisements, who appointed the bleakly conservative Clarence Thomas to the Supreme Court in place of the liberal icon Thurgood Marshall, and who repeatedly threatened to veto the Civil Rights Act of 1991. The act strengthened the nation's laws against job discrimination, laws that the Supreme Court had severely weakened two years earlier. George Bush, concluded Holmes, was "a man whose public and private life has included both episodes of moral courage and incidents which his opponents say demonstrate either racial insensitivity or a willingness to use the racial card for political gain." It was this dualism that characterized his attitude toward civil rights throughout his presidency. Nowhere was it more in evidence than during the long struggle to pass the 1991 Civil Rights Act.[1]

Despite Willie Horton, Bush began his presidency with a higher level of support from black Americans than any other Republican president in the modern era. He "enjoyed one major advantage," explained Eleanor Holmes Norton, the congressional delegate from Washington, DC, and that was "not being Reagan." Blacks had heeded his call for "a kinder, gentler America"; they had noted certain symbolic actions like meeting with the Congressional Black Caucus, which his predecessor had never done, and his attendance at "significant black events," again something Reagan had rarely bothered with, and had high hopes that he would again provide the moral leadership that had so characterized the early years of the civil rights era.[2]

This sense of possibility did not last long. It was severely tested in the administration's first weeks by the nomination of William Lucas as assistant attorney general and head of the Civil Rights Division. Lucas, a black conservative who supported tax exemptions for segregated private schools and vehemently opposed quotas, was scarcely the liberal successor to Reynolds that the civil rights constituency had been seeking. At his confirmation hearings, he displayed, along with a disturbing inexperience in the field of civil rights law, such a bleakly negative view of his proposed role that even Representative John Conyers of Michigan, his original sponsor, withdrew his support, as did Jesse Jackson. The NAACP had been opposed from the start. Though conservative groups rallied to his support, they could not prevent the House Judiciary Committee from rejecting the nomination on the grounds of inexperience—despite the former segregationist leader Strom Thurmond's plea to "give this black man a chance." The whole affair cost the president much of the goodwill with which the black community had regarded the new administration.[3]

President Bush's nomination problems were compounded further by his choice of Arthur A. Fletcher, a conservative black lawyer and businessman who had also served briefly as secretary of labor in the Nixon administration, as chair of the U.S. Commission on Civil Rights. Liberals had pressed for the appointment of former commissioner Arthur S. Flemming, who was also strongly supported by civil rights activists in what one of them termed "a measure of his [Bush's] commitment." Fletcher, however, a close friend of the president's who with his wife occasionally visited the White House for private dinners and movie screenings, lobbied hard for the job. His appointment, he told Bush, "will indicate that the Bush Administration hasn't blinked, nor is it back peddling [sic] on its commitment to civil rights, employment affirmative action, minority business opportunity and a higher quality of life for all of the nation's citizens." In response, the president assured him, "When the time comes to name a new chairman of the Civil Rights Commission, I'll be proud to have an old friend and loyal trooper in that important post." Fletcher's appointment was formally announced on March 5, 1990, despite the opposition of civil rights activists and some of the commission's members and the disquiet of the president's advisers, who believed he had missed an opportunity to gain political capital.[4]

The president's few remaining pockets of support were effectively squandered by his 1990 veto of Senate Bill 1204, the first attempt to redress the Supreme Court's damage to the nation's antidiscrimination laws, and then by the vicious and partisan battle over passage of the 1991 act. The issue, as it had been with Reagan, was quotas, for Bush, too, used the code word. The 1990 bill had been an attempt to reverse the impact of six Supreme Court decisions, the cumulative effect of which made it much harder for employees to prove job discrimination. Bush's veto of what he termed a "quota bill," said the historian Steven Shull, "represented the first of a major civil rights bill in the last quarter century." Moreover, the president again tried to have it both ways, expressing his deep regret at "having to take this action," and conceding that he endorsed many of its provisions. For the civil rights coalition, such equivocation smacked of hypocrisy. "George Bush has made it clear where he and his Republican Party really stand," angrily declared George Brown, the Democratic Party chair. The president had caved in to his conservative, southern white supporter base.[5]

The bill was revived in a slightly amended form in 1991, and again the debate was bitter and partisan. Again, too, the president initially opposed it as a quota bill, while John R. Dunne, his assistant attorney general for civil rights, argued that its passage "would only make quotas more pervasive." Democrats bitterly assailed the administration's opposition, especially given that blacks were currently serving in such large numbers in the Gulf War. "The nearest thing I know of to a quota is the disproportionate number of African-Americans in the armed forces in the Persian Gulf," remarked Conyers bitterly as leaders of civil rights and women's groups joined in opposition. Women, already angered by what seemed the insensitive treatment of Anita Hill during the fierce debate over Clarence Thomas's nomination, were particularly critical of Bush, causing enough wavering in Republican ranks to make it doubtful whether a second presidential veto could be sustained. After nearly a year of angry division and denials from Bush that he had "caved in over civil rights," the president nonetheless did so, signing a measure stronger in its antidiscrimination provisions than the one he had vetoed twelve months before. He had capitulated, reported the *New York Times,* "only when it became clear that if he vetoed the bill, the Senate would narrowly override it." Moreover, the vehemence of his continued denunciation of quotas, together with the gracelessness with which he conceded defeat, eroded his little remaining support in the black community. There was no difference between Reagan and Bush, Benjamin Hooks told the NAACP's annual convention in 1992. "I've had the misfortune of serving eight years under Reagan and three under Bush," he continued, and it had been a constant "fight to save what we already had." Though the storm had been weathered and what had been won since 1964 had been preserved, it had been a close-run thing. But there might be hope for progress around the corner, Hooks believed, if the Clinton-Gore ticket was successful in November. These two men, though southerners, had been changed by the civil rights struggle. "We know them," he declared.

They had "hunted and fished with black people," they had "lived with them, been in their country stores," they were men "who understand, who eat the same corn bread."[6]

It was this same sense of possibility that continued to draw black southerners and their children home. When they were interviewed, "vastly improved race relations" was always listed as a significant factor in prompting the decision to return. "There is a whole generation out there," explained Isaac Robinson, a sociologist at North Carolina Central University, "whose ideas of the South have very little to do with the lynching of blacks, segregation or the Ku Klux Klan." These were the reasons black people had once left the South in such large numbers, but they had little relevance now for the new arrivals—or even the returnees. "They know there is some racism," Robinson concluded, "but it is not the predominant thing in their minds." Much more important was a sense of "being plugged into African-American roots and family roots." There were "patterns that are very comforting here," mused Phoebe Benson, recently returned to Columbia, South Carolina, after a long absence. "It's like the smell of fresh-washed sheets and bacon frying in the morning. These are verities . . . reassuring to me." She now enjoyed them more than ever, no longer a second-class citizen in the place of her birth.[7]

From time to time, however, the old world recrudesced. Delores Watson, back home in Saluda, South Carolina, after twenty years in Los Angeles, angrily confronted an elderly white woman in a post office queue when she overheard her use a racially demeaning epithet. The woman had quickly "apologized and left." Yet even such unpleasantness had its upside, she thought. She would not have dared to speak out in such a way twenty years before. Selma, Alabama, again found itself the focus of unwelcome national attention. In 1990—a quarter of a century after the confrontation on the Edmund Pettus Bridge—an interracial struggle over school management erupted when the superintendent of schools, Norward Roussell, the first black to hold the job, clashed with the white-dominated school board over his plans to open up the honors program at Selma High School to more black students. The board refused to renew his contract, white parents withdrew their children from the school, black students staged a sit-in in support of Roussell, there was some interracial violence, and once more the state police and the Alabama National Guard were required to restore order in the city. The South may have changed remarkably in a mere two decades, yet there were still ugly reminders of its past.[8]

"Our First Black President"

African Americans had voted overwhelmingly for the Clinton-Gore ticket in 1992 and were, thus, taken somewhat by surprise when the new president's first public statement on a civil rights issue concerned gay Americans and military service. That he had chosen to do so was trenchant testimony to just how broad the concept of civil rights had become and how legislation and legal judgments originally aimed at ending a specific regional evil had become national in effect, involving much more than the web of relations between black and white Americans. A detailed report on the Clinton administration's civil rights record, *A Bridge to One America,* released in 2001 by the national watchdog the U.S. Commission on Civil Rights, dramatically emphasized this point. There were sections on the rights of Asian Americans, Pacific Islanders, non-English-speaking residents, American Indians, and prisoners, and sections condemning hate crimes and police misconduct as well as sections covering the more enduring areas of sex, race, and ethnicity. Not one section dealt with what were once considered the specifically southern problems of school segregation, denial of the franchise, and equal access to public facilities. The notion of protecting civil rights had moved far beyond the inequalities the legislation of the 1960s had been enacted to ameliorate, in some ways testimony to its success.[9]

Nevertheless, the issues of the 1960s had a habit of resurfacing as the nation moved toward the twenty-first century. Gary Orfield and his Harvard colleagues continued to chart the course of school resegregation. In 1999, a wide-ranging study showed that, while in the 1980–1981 school year just under 63 percent of black students attended schools where at least half the students were minorities, by the 1996–1997 school year nearly 69 percent did and that the situation was even worse for Latinos. Southern school systems were still the most desegregated in the nation but were, nevertheless, following the trend. The winding down of court-ordered busing and continued residential segregation were the main reasons; the developing conservative majority on the Supreme Court also played its part. One 1995 decision, in particular, bothered those who remained committed to integration. In *Missouri v. Jenkins,* in a 5–4 decision over who should bear the cost of Kansas City's magnet school program, the Court ruled that states were not required to pay for schemes designed to attract white students back to inner-city schools. If school systems wished to establish these, they should bear the full cost. In his concurring opinion, Justice Clarence Thomas expressed his strong disagreement with those who believed "that any school system that is black is inferior and that blacks cannot exist without the company of whites," a view that some black social scientists, journalists, and academics were also beginning to espouse publicly. Blacks, wrote Glenn Loury in 1997, needed better schools no matter their racial makeup. Orlando Patterson, while supporting school desegregation, continued to argue that the only true means of achieving this was through integrated neighborhoods.

Remedies such as busing had become "irrelevant." It was one thing to abandon busing, he believed, "but quite another to give up on integration." Rather, "we should turn to the underlying problem that had brought busing about," residential segregation. "By doing so, we will not only solve the educational problems of our minorities . . . but also make for a more tolerant and genuinely multi-ethnic nation."[10]

Whenever possible, the Clinton administration acted to check the trend toward resegregation. The Justice Department intervened in *Missouri v. Jenkins* on behalf of the black plaintiffs, opposing Missouri's request to have Kansas City's schools declared successfully integrated. This represented a "drastic shift from where the Justice Department ha[d] been" since 1981. In addition, Clinton's Justice Department had backed the University of Maryland in a suit that challenged its practice of reserving a number of four-year scholarships for black students only, reversing the policy of the Bush administration. The president, himself a product of a segregated southern school system, frequently used the White House podium to emphasize his support for *Brown*. "This generation faces a lot of challenges that are part of the unfinished business of helping us to live together as one people," he told students at Rev. Dr. Martin Luther King Jr. Middle School in Beltsville, Maryland, on *Brown's* fortieth anniversary, terming the decision a "miracle," and attacking "a new segregationism that is tearing us apart." He issued a similar warning three years later from the steps of Little Rock Central High School, again to mark the fortieth anniversary of one of the civil rights movement's iconic events. Praising the courage of the nine black students who had first climbed those steps, he deplored the reality that, despite "the abolition of legalized segregation," black and white Americans "remained disturbingly isolated from each other in their schools and in their everyday lives." It was Little Rock, he asserted, "that made racial equality a driving obsession" in his own life. "Like so many Americans, I can never repay my debt to these nine people. . . . They purchased more freedom for me, too, and for all white people." The president's power to reverse the reality of resegregation may have been limited, but he left no doubt as to where he stood. A son of the changing South, he had occupied the mansion from which Orville Faubus had orchestrated the events that turned the Little Rock Nine into symbols of resistance. Thirty years later, as governor, he had invited the nine to dine there and had thanked them for redeeming his state and his region. Ten years later, as president, he did so again—with equal emotion.[11]

Clinton also strongly defended the government's role in expanding equal opportunity in the workplace, also partly in reaction to increasingly restrictive Supreme Court decisions. The most significant of these was *Adarand Construction v. Pena,* when, in a 5–4 decision involving set-asides for minority contractors, the Court narrowed the scope in which these could be considered constitutional. Though it did not actually strike down any affirmative action programs, it nevertheless invited further legal challenges, adding fuel to a growing weight of opinion that such policies were all but dead. Moreover, the vengeful, Gingrich-controlled Congress had vowed to slash the EEOC's budget savagely, despite what White House counselor Stephen Warnath starkly described as "an enormous build-up of pending cases," to the extent that it could no longer "effectively carry out its law enforcement responsibilities." The mood within the agency was, thus, one of frustration and despair.[12]

Clinton's response was vigorous and one of the most effective uses of the bully pulpit afforded the president in his whole career. In a "historic speech" at the National Archives on July 19, 1995, he reinforced his administration's commitment to affirmative action, urging the nation to "mend it, not end it." The policy had "been good for America," he said. It should not "go on forever" and would "be retired when its job is done." That day would surely come. While many gaps in economic opportunity had been closed, there was still a long way to go. Black leaders were delighted with the speech, believing that it reflected both a national and congressional consensus, and credited Clinton with a major role in preventing the "imminent demise of affirmative action programs" so confidently predicted by "pack journalism." Whatever the reason, Congress did not support several anti–affirmative action proposals in 1995, much to the president's political advantage as he sought reelection the following year.[13]

In the increasingly hostile environment that Clinton faced after the 1994 congressional elections had swept the Republicans into power, however, there were limits to what executive action could achieve. The president routinely sought increased funding for the agencies of enforcement, especially the EEOC and the Justice Department's Civil Rights Division. Equally routinely, the Republican-controlled Congress ignored or rejected these requests. Nevertheless, EEOC suits increased markedly during the 1990s—the historian James Patterson described the agency as doing "a land office business"—again impressive evidence of a renewed commitment to Title VII. As with school desegregation, the Clinton administration also intervened in court cases with the aim of "mending" the system, rather than "ending" thirty years of successful endeavor. There were those who expected much more from him, those who became bitterly critical of what they judged to be his constant and politically driven search for the middle ground on the key civil rights issues, but even these critics were forced to admit that there was a different tone to his administration's voice; gone was "the malevolence that there was in the Reagan Administration or the indifference there was in the Bush Administration."[14]

Given Reagan's twenty-five-year extension of the Voting Rights Act in 1982, this was not an issue that engaged either of his successors. Yet the protection of the right of minority groups to equal political participation was still an active issue in the 1990s. One of Clinton's early legislative successes was the passage of the National Voter Registration Act of 1993—popularly known as the Motor Voter Act—the result of his determination to make registration as transparent and as accessible as possible. Its provisions included allowing the simultaneous application for both drivers' licenses and voter registration cards, while registration by mail was also permitted under certain conditions. By 1998, only Mississippi had failed to adopt the enabling legislation. There, the fiercely conservative governor, Kirk Fordice, had defiantly vetoed the bill, asserting that the motor voter law should be renamed the "welfare voter" law, but a compromise was eventually reached. Moreover, the Justice Department was active in supporting those who opposed the growing tendency of state and federal courts to disallow redistricting plans that were aimed at creating what were termed *majority-minority districts,* many of which were in the South, and were clearly permissible under the 1965 Voting Rights Act. The president again used his bully pulpit to denounce such restrictions. They represented, he asserted in 1994, "a direct attack . . . on electoral districts that contain African-American or Hispanic population majorities." The position of his administration was unequivocal. "We are committed to the gains made by minority voters through the enforcement of the Voting Rights Act," he insisted, and the Justice Department's determined involvement throughout the decade was a powerful reason why majority-minority districts survived the assaults on them. Certainly, the Commission on Civil Rights was unstinting in commending "the Clinton Administration for its efforts to uphold redistricting plans that ensure minority voting rights."[15]

Nevertheless, it was the 1965 Voting Rights Act, its perceived limits, and the need some civil rights advocates saw to go beyond its provisions that caused one of the most divisive debates of Clinton's early presidency, leaving some in the civil rights community permanently embittered. In April, the president had nominated Lani Guinier, a close personal friend of both the Clintons from their Yale Law School days, currently a professor at the University of Pennsylvania School of Law, to be assistant attorney general in charge of the Justice Department's Civil Rights Division. Conservatives, still smarting at the way liberals had savaged Bork and Clarence Thomas, saw a chance to even the score. They were particularly incensed that, during the press conference at which Clinton introduced her, she lambasted William Bradford Reynolds for leading what she contemptuously termed Reagan's "counter revolution on civil rights." Poring over her scholarly writings, they soon found plenty of ammunition to use against her: in particular, material on the inadequacies of the Voting Rights Act. Arguing that its guarantee "that blacks have an opportunity to elect blacks" was woefully insufficient, she advocated a variety of proportional voting schemes, all designed to enhance the power of black voters and lawmakers—in the code word of previous years, the use of *quotas*. Clinton's conservative opponents had a field day, attacking her as "the quota queen," assailing her unfairly as only too willing to shred the "one person, one vote" principle that had served the nation so well since 1787 in the interest of enhanced minority power. Faced with the vehemence of the campaign against Guinier and the doubts of even some of his liberal supporters as to her suitability, the president clumsily withdrew her nomination, denying her the chance to defend her record before the Senate Judiciary Committee. Civil rights stalwarts were bitter at this capitulation. Representative Kweisi Mfume, the head of the Congressional Black Caucus, said he and many like him "who had worked hard to put Bill Clinton in office . . . feel betrayed." The freshman Democrat senator Paul Wellstone vehemently expressed his "disappointment in the Senate and the President." Even some moderate Republicans regretted Clinton's seeming spinelessness. "I think President Clinton has made a mistake in withdrawing the nomination of Ms. Guinier," mused Senator Arlen Specter. "There are some fights you have to fight even if you may lose them." Eventually, Clinton regained the respect of much of the civil rights community, but it did take time.[16]

One of the reasons Clinton did regain that respect was his evenhanded appointments policy—of those nominated for federal judgeships by 1994, for example, 61 percent were women, minorities, or both. Another was his tireless use of the bully pulpit the White House gave all incumbents in the cause of racial reconciliation. Unlike his immediate predecessors, Clinton welcomed the chance to speak to predominantly black audiences, often choosing black churches or the sites of iconic civil rights struggles to do so. In 1996, he reminded a cheering crowd in Birmingham of how much had changed since the 1963 demonstrations there and asked them to build a bridge to the future "wide enough and strong enough for everybody to walk across." A few days later, he told the congregation of St. Paul's AME Church in Tampa how humbled he was in speaking from a "historic pulpit which had been graced by Martin Luther King, Thurgood Marshall, Adam Clayton Powell, Jackie Robinson." Sadly, however, there were "still too many white people who wouldn't feel as comfortable sitting in this church as I do today," he observed. "They read the same Bible as you do. They claim the same savior as you do. They ought to feel at home here. . . . And you ought to feel at home in their churches."[17]

There was, therefore, still work to be done. Here, again, his Arkansas roots gave Clinton special passion—and credibility. There was also his personal style, his essential southernness. From early childhood, Steven A. Holmes wrote in 1996, "Mr. Clinton has exhibited a comfort and an ease in his personal dealings with members of minority groups, especially blacks. He has displayed . . . his familiarity with black culture, black music and black icons." He was "at home in black churches," he knew the hymns; he knew the cadences of the preachers. Ernest Green, one of the Little Rock Nine and a friend of Clinton's, recalled Vernon Jordan, the president's closest black confidant, once remarking that he was "one of the few white people who knew by heart" all three verses of "Lift Every Voice and Sing," often called the Negro National Anthem. Green cut in. "Mr. President, I beg to differ," he said, "you are one of the three people, period, who know all three verses." African Americans, the historian Gary Gerstle has written, like the writer Toni Morrison, felt so at ease with Clinton that they privately regarded him as "the first black president." The historian Darlene Clark Hine wrote, "[The] majority of African Americans consider President Bill Clinton to have been the most beneficent occupant of the executive branch of the federal government in its history." Blacks voted overwhelmingly for Clinton in 1996 and supported him unreservedly when his personal indiscretions led to the impeachment crisis that so diminished his second term.[18]

Between January 1995 and June 1996, the South's savage recent past returned, with the deliberate burning of fifty-nine African American churches. There was widespread national attention and sympathy, to which Congress and the president responded with the passage of the Church Arson Protection Act. It specified much stricter penalties for the perpetrators of such outrages as well as a range of preventative measures, including the creation of the National Arson Task Force, headed by the assistant attorney general in the Civil Rights Division. Seven of the burnings had occurred in Mississippi, where such incidents had once been commonplace. The Mt. Zion Baptist Church in Ruleville, extensively damaged on March 21, 1996, had been burned to the ground three decades previously, an act of violent resistance to the Mississippi freedom movement. Located deep in the Delta, Ruleville was home to both the movement icon Fannie Lou Hamer and the arch-segregationist Senator James Eastland. It was a civil rights battleground then, and Mt. Zion Baptist was a site of political activity before the Klan destroyed it. Had it done so again?[19]

In July 1996, in order to bring together the black and white communities in towns where church burnings had occurred, the Mississippi Advisory Committee to the U.S. Commission on Civil Rights held a number of community forums at which the immediate impact of the incidents was thoroughly canvassed, but the forums invariably broadened into a discussion of local race relations after three decades of change. The citizens of Ruleville participated in the fourth of these, held in Cleveland, at Delta State University's Performing Arts Center on July

10–11, 1996. The proceedings provided real insight into what had altered in Ruleville and what remained the same. The most immediately obvious difference was that the town's mayor, Shirley Edwards, was black, as were three of the five aldermen. Moreover, the Reverend Dexter Brown, Mt. Zion's pastor, and Jacqueline Buckner, the director of the church choir, both stated that race relations in Ruleville were now so good that they doubted whether the burning had been racially motivated. There was no residential segregation there. People were no longer "living in Jim Crow times," Mrs. Buckner insisted. Brown agreed, stating that his church had white members and that, though some had "been chided by other whites" for their attendance, there had been "no open acts of hostility or violence" against them. Jim Friar, the FBI agent in charge of investigating the burning, was a little more hardheaded. Race was still a "central issue in Mississippi all the time," he contended, yet even he conceded that, given Ruleville's conflicted past, relations between its communities were "in better shape" than most. As for the burning, the church was located one hundred yards from a bridge that was notorious "as a party site for youth who abuse drugs and alcohol," and Friar thought that the fire was more likely to have been an act of random vandalism than a white supremacist hate crime. Attempts to hold "Klan rallies in the area have failed in the past several years," he told the meeting. Ruleville's citizens had well and truly buried their ugly racist history.[20]

Nevertheless, the past could sometimes resurface. The Reverend Brown admitted that local law enforcement officers had initially shown "little interest" in investigating the blaze and had become active only after sustained FBI and Arson Task Force pressure. Nor had the town's white churches provided him or his congregation with much assistance. Indeed, though the local chamber of commerce, the Rotary Club, and other community organizations were now fully integrated, there was still little private social interaction in the Delta. "African-Americans keep to themselves," he admitted, and so did white people. Jacqueline Morris, a Cleveland resident, thought the Delta to be "the most unchanged place since the Civil War." She had become friends with a white female coworker, and they had both received "negative reactions" for "socializing after work hours"—from both whites and blacks. It was one thing "to talk and be friends" at work, quite another "to cross the line" in their private worlds. Blacks in Cleveland mainly went to one school, whites to another—and this was by choice—while the more privileged children of both races attended integrated private academies "north of Ruleville." Without doubt, race relations in Ruleville had changed profoundly for the better since the bitter days of white supremacy. Healing had started, but it was nowhere near complete.[21]

It was primarily to further such racial healing that, on June 13,

1997, Clinton issued Executive Order 13050, presenting his Initiative on Race (also known as the One America Initiative), and appointing his Advisory Board on Race. Its task was to promote "a constructive national dialogue on challenging racial issues" and to recommend solutions to "racial problems in areas such as economic opportunity, housing, health care and the administration of justice." Chaired by the distinguished African American historian John Hope Franklin, the panel labored diligently for fifteen months, eventually producing a report that even its supporters described as "modest." While full of exhortations to "make racial reconciliation a reality," it gave little specific direction on how to do so. To civil rights activists, the board had "squandered an opportunity" to move "beyond the familiar positions of liberals and conservatives." It was simply "a list of platitudes," asserted Randall Kennedy of the Harvard Law School. Most commentators agreed with Kennedy. The president, already embroiled in personal scandal, had little to say about the report, though in 1999 he did adopt in modified form one of the principal recommendations, the establishment of a White House office for the Initiative on Race, to further the work of the advisory board. The office had scarcely begun to function, however, when Clinton left office. Those who had invested considerable optimism in the Initiative in Race, in the hope that it would lead to greater racial understanding, were left with "a palpable sense" of disappointment.[22]

Nevertheless, the advisory board's voluminous correspondence files do reveal the familiar dichotomy in the way in which Americans thought about race and racial change. Most whites wrote positively about the current state of race relations, emphasizing the dimensions of the changes since 1965, and some even feared that the current initiative could have a negative effect. "One thing that the president's Initiative on Race is sure to accomplish," Richard S. Inge, of Hammond, Louisiana, believed, was "the reopening of old wounds that were in the process of healing." Black correspondents were usually much less sanguine about the future, emphasizing, like the Reverend Michael H. Jordan, of Erwin, North Carolina, that skin color still divided Americans as "black" or "white" and that the "human challenge" of overcoming this barrier remained. Similar perspectives were expressed at the town meetings and panel discussions held as part of the board's consultative process. Even some liberal whites believed "a Clintonian conversation," no matter how well-meaning, to be superfluous, given the huge changes since 1965, including the rise of "a genuine black middle class" and its importance to the national culture. Some influential and conservative blacks, led by Ward Connerly, the champion of California's Proposition 209, which ended racial quotas in the state, even formed their own multiracial panel to serve as a "more balanced alternative" to the administration's initiative, which they described as "a liberal monologue," its face set firmly toward the past and, thus, "avoiding the hard and controversial issues" urgent to the rapidly changing present.[23]

The Franklin board held only one forum in the Deep South, at the University of Mississippi in March 1998. In preparation for the two-day meeting, community leaders throughout the state were asked to provide the names of local people who could be invited to join "the relevant dialogue groups" and help them identify common local concerns. Some black Mississippians expressed their reservations at the whole procedure. She had "had it with the talk," said Marsha Watson, a graduate student at Ole Miss. She wanted action on what she saw as the root cause of current inequalities, the linkage between "racism and economic injustice." "Racism is a useful device of people with power and money to divide people without power and money," agreed Susan M. Gilson, another black student leader. That was how it had been historically in the South, and, in that sense, little had changed. Discussion about economic inequality dominated the Mississippi forum, despite periodic attempts to shift its focus to more positive themes. Former Mississippi governor William Winter agreed with Gilson. As a white man he had enjoyed "a favored status for a long time." Now, all must "recognize that the doors of opportunity had to be open equally to everybody on the basis of ability, commitment and willingness to work, irrespective of race and gender." This had yet to happen in the South, notwithstanding the end to legal segregation. Despite the emergence of a black middle class and of a black political elite, despite all the affirmative action policies, race and economic inequality remained inextricably linked in the region. The challenge was to break this nexus.[24]

Toward the end of Clinton's first term, the Civil Rights Division of the Justice Department had reported on its accomplishments so far. Among the highlights were the vigorous enforcement of the motor voter law and the effectiveness of the *Shaw v. Reno* Task Force in defending racially fair redistricting plans in the South against claims that they were unconstitutional "racial gerrymanders." The division was proud, too, of its success rate in winning Title VII suits against state and local governments guilty of employment discrimination and remained equally committed to "eliminating the vestiges of segregation" remaining at all levels of education. In particular, it had continued "its challenges to the former separate higher education systems in Mississippi and Alabama." In Alabama, such pressure had won "for the first time the establishment of endowments for the state's historically black schools." Overall, this had been a term of "substantial accomplishments," despite financial stringencies, a record on which it would surely build should the president be reelected.[25]

Four years later, the Commission on Civil Rights also thought that the Clinton administration's civil rights policies had been positive and had "helped to end the long period of stagnation, indifference and dogged maintenance of the status quo" that had prevailed for two decades. The president had asked at least some of the right questions, he had "dramatically changed the national dialogue" on race, yet "all too often his good intentions had failed to come to fruition." Much, therefore, remained to be done before America had achieved King's "ideal of a nation where everyone is judged solely on his or her character and nothing more," and the commission exhorted the new president to take up this challenge. Clinton had already done much the same. His last message to Congress, on January 15, 2001, had as its title "The Unfinished Work of Building One America."[26]

Into a New Century

The Commission on Civil Rights did not wait, as it had done with President Clinton, until the end of his presidency before making public its views on his successor. Indeed, as early as September 2004, it had produced an interim statement, "Redefining Rights in America: The Civil Rights Record of the George W. Bush Administration, 2001–2004." It did find some matters to praise: it noted that Bush had "assembled a commendably diverse Cabinet and moderately diverse judiciary," for example, and had moved swiftly to make good on his promise to end racial profiling in federal law enforcement. Yet, while recognizing that the events of September 11, 2001, had raised new and complex civil rights issues to which there were no easy answers, the report's tone was profoundly negative. The president had neither "exhibited leadership on pressing civil rights issues" nor "taken action that matched his words." Rather, the president had "implemented policies that have retreated from long-established civil rights promises" in the areas in which "the judicial and legislative achievements of the 1960s and 1970s largely broke down the system of segregation and legal basis for discrimination—education, employment, housing, public accommodations, and the ability to vote." Furthermore, unlike his predecessor, Bush rarely spoke about civil rights issues, and, when he did, he attempted to shift the terms of the debate. *Civil rights* in his rhetoric, the commission asserted, had become synonymous with *faith-based program,* and *equal access* meant the removal of discrimination against religious organizations, not the traditional issues of race and gender or even sexual preference. After four decades of advance, the first years of the new century had been marked by stagnation and retreat. The commission itself had become split between conservatives and liberals, with meetings conducted in an atmosphere of such frigidity that consensus became almost impossible.

This situation ended abruptly after the 2004 election, when the president took advantage of the retirement of two long-term liberal members, replacing them both with conservative black Republicans, and, thus, ensuring a 6–2 conservative majority on the commission. For many liberals, this was further sad evidence of the end of the civil rights era.[27]

Certainly, Justice John Paul Stevens was in no doubt that the Supreme Court, as led by John Roberts, was in full retreat from the true meaning and spirit of *Brown*. On June 28, 2007, in a 5–4 ruling it had struck down voluntary integration programs in the Seattle and Louisville school systems, a decision that would have implications for hundreds of other school districts in the nation. Invoking *Brown* as the basis for the majority opinion, the chief justice argued that it meant that children could no longer be "told where they could not go to school on the basis of race," yet that was precisely what the Seattle and Louisville school districts were doing. "The way to stop discrimination on the basis of race is to stop discriminating on the basis of race," he wrote. Stevens was outraged. In his dissent, he stated his "firm conviction that no member of the court I joined in 1975 would have agreed with today's decision," noting the "cruel irony" of the majority's invocation of *Brown* while "robbing the landmark ruling of much of its force and spirit." The Court, Stevens believed, had rewritten "the history of one of this court's most important decisions" and, in so doing, had turned its back on its proudest moment. A *New York Times* editorial made the same point. "The citizens of Louisville and Seattle, and the rest of the nation," it concluded, "can ponder the majority's kind words about *Brown* as they get to work today making their schools, and their cities, more segregated." The decision was one the Bush administration had both sought and supported. The solicitor general had filed a brief the previous year, during the hearing, arguing that student assignment policies such as those adopted in Seattle and Louisville clearly violated both *Brown* and the Constitution. Though the Commission on Civil Rights had found some positive aspects to the centerpiece of the president's education program, "No Child Left Behind," it was, nevertheless, bitterly critical of its failure to address the escalating march toward resegregation. Now, the Justice Department's active involvement in what eventually was decided on June 28, 2007—"the most important in years on the issue of race and education," said the *Washington Post*—seemed stark evidence of the administration's willingness, having moved the Supreme Court decisively to the right, to abandon the whole ideal of racial equality in America. The *New York Times* mordantly titled its editorial on the decision "Resegregation Now." Meanwhile, in Tuscaloosa, Alabama, black parents, in despair at a new school rezoning plan that effectively resegregated the district, prepared to use the transfer provisions in "No Child

Left Behind" in a desperate attempt to undermine it. The Supreme Court had left them no other avenue.[28]

In July 2006, surrounded by "stalwarts of the civil rights movement," including Julian Bond, Jesse Jackson, and the Reverend Al Sharpton, the president signed into law a further twenty-five-year extension of the Voting Rights Act. Despite some grumbling in the House from white southerners, particularly over continuing the preclearance requirement, the measure had had an easy passage through Congress, eventually clearing the Senate 98–0. As he signed the extension, Bush spoke eloquently of his determination "to continue to build on the legal equality won by the civil rights movement to help ensure that every person enjoys the opportunity that this great land of liberty offers." Referring to his secretary of state, born in Bull Connor's Birmingham, he asserted, "Condi Rice understands what this Act has meant." Yet, two years earlier, the Commission on Civil Rights had found that, in the 2002 midterm elections, there had been significant violations of the Voting Rights Act—the routine photographing of black voters in Arkansas being a particularly troubling example—on which the Justice Department had shown a great reluctance to act.[29]

Of greatest concern to civil rights advocates, however, was Justice's decision to approve controversial, allegedly Republican-engineered redistricting plans in Texas and Georgia. Career staff attorneys and voting analysts, on examining these, were in no doubt that they hurt minority voters and, thus, contravened the Voting Rights Act, recommending, therefore, that the plans be rejected. However, senior Justice officials, all political appointees, overruled them. Earlier, a similar conflict had occurred over a proposed voter identification law in Georgia that obviously needed preclearance in terms of the 1965 act. Again, a team of department lawyers and analysts rejected it as "being likely [to work] against black voters," and, again, they were overruled. The chief of the department's Voting Rights Section, John Tanner, a Bush political appointee, told Georgia officials that their program could go forward. Such conflict within the Justice Department between career attorneys and political appointees had been previously seen during the Reagan years, with similar results—anger, frustration, and eventual departure. The Civil Rights Division lost 20 percent of its lawyers in 2005, many of whom accepted a buyout program that seemed targeted to move out "those who did not share the Administration's conservative views on civil rights laws," to be replaced by conservative political appointees with little civil rights experience. Those who remained found themselves, often unwillingly, as part of a determined administration drive to recast the government's civil rights emphasis, "aggressively pursuing religion-oriented cases, while significantly diminishing its involvement in the traditional area of race." Vigorous prosecution of suspected violations of the Voting Rights Act was a casualty of this switch, as John D. Rich implied when he stepped down in 2007 after thirty-seven years as head of the Voting Rights Section. To the civil rights community, the Bush administration had subverted the provisions and impact of the 1965 act, despite all the soaring rhetoric to the contrary.[30]

The Commission on Civil Rights's draft report described Bush's stance on affirmative action as "equivocal at best"; again, there was plenty of stirring rhetoric, but it was rarely backed up with decisive action. Moreover, on what was clearly the most significant case to be decided by the Supreme Court during his first term, *Grutter v. Bollinger,* the president had made his position crystal clear. Appearing on national television, he had announced that his administration was seeking to have the University of Michigan's affirmative action policies ruled unconstitutional owing to the consideration of race as a key factor in selecting students for its prestigious law school. In language reminiscent of his Republican predecessors, he denounced the process as being a disguised racial quota. No affirmative action case had aroused such interest in a decade, and, when the Court, in a 5–4 decision, largely upheld the university's position, most described it as a defeat for the president. Civil rights groups were jubilant, chastising Bush as "duplicitous and hypocritical," while moderate commentators like Orlando Patterson urged him to think again. "It is easy to show that the benefits of affirmative action far outweigh its social and individual costs," Patterson wrote. But the Court's most ideologically conservative justices thought otherwise, and, with Sandra Day O'Connor, who wrote the majority opinion, soon to retire, the victory could well be fleeting. In a few months, with the appointment of John Roberts as chief justice, then Samuel Alito as an associate, the president had a Court of the complexion he desired, as the Seattle and Louisville decision would show.[31]

One presidential action on civil rights, however, achieved overwhelming acclaim. On November 13, 2006, under overcast skies, President Bush joined his predecessor, members of Congress, African American celebrities, including Oprah Winfrey and Maya Angelou, and a host of the movement's former leaders on the National Mall, all gathered at a groundbreaking ceremony for the memorial to honor Dr. Martin Luther King Jr. "An assassin's bullet could not shatter his dream," the president declared. "As we break ground, we give Martin Luther King his rightful place among the many Americans honored on the National Mall. It will unite the men who declared the promise of America and defended the promise of America with the man who redeemed the promise of America." Differences were set aside for the moment, as history and memory blended.[32]

12

THE AFTERMATH

From History to Memory

When Josephine Boyd Bradley returned to Grimsley High School in Greensboro, North Carolina, on March 30, 2006, the reception she received could scarcely have been more different than that which greeted her when she had first nervously entered its doors in September 1957. Then, as the only African American in a student body of two thousand, she was the victim of constant racial slurs, physical intimidation, and studied insults from students and faculty. Forced to take her meals in the library, she endured the torment, partly, she said, owing to the support of three white students who befriended her, themselves suffering insult and ostracism as a consequence. She graduated in 1958, the first black student in the state to do so from a formerly all-white high school, and went on to a successful career in higher education. But it had cost her part of her youth. She had refused to cry "during that long-ago year," she recalled, "but now I know I can let the tears flow. I know the mission has been accomplished."[1]

In 2006, Bradley was back at Grimsley, this time as the school's honored guest, there to receive the plaudits of the student body (now 42 percent nonwhite), to witness the unveiling of her portrait (to be hung in the school's main hall), and to be formally hailed as a civil rights pioneer. In response, she said she wanted no apology for the mistreatment she had suffered; rather, she considered her presence to be a wonderful "celebration" of her small part in "a moment in history" that had profound consequences. Desegregating Grimsley High was "one of the most powerful things and meaningful things I have ever done," she told her student audience, who, though initially only dimly aware of the history she had made, perhaps now had a greater sense of its significance. "I think it takes a lot of courage to do something like that," mused the ninth-grader Tracey Canada. "I don't think I would have been able to do that."[2]

Dorothy Counts, one of the four students who integrated the Charlotte school system in September 1957 and the one whose presence at

Harding High School sparked so much violence that she had to be withdrawn after four days for her own safety, was similarly reconciliatory. She had forgotten some of what happened on her first day, she said fifty years later, "and forgiven most of the rest." But she had spent half a century thinking about the events—and looking at the photographs of the jeering, menacing crowd that had followed her into school. If you studied them the right way, she claimed, you knew that she had been the winner. "What I see is that all of these people are *behind* me. They did not have the courage to get up in my face." She had made much the same point in a press interview on September 4, 1957. The students who had so hounded her that day "didn't hurt [her]": "They only hurt themselves." Far from hating them, she felt "sorry for them," she had said then.[3]

James Lawson was invited back to his old school, too, in 2006, to Vanderbilt University in Nashville, from which he had been expelled forty-six years before for his key role in organizing the lunch counter sit-ins that heralded an expansion of the nonviolent protest movement. Lawson, who had previously studied nonviolence as a means of protest while serving as a Methodist missionary in India, was one of a handful of black students attending Vanderbilt in 1960. After his expulsion, his reputation as the movement's leading theoretician of nonviolent action grew exponentially, and, as such, he deeply influenced a whole generation of civil rights activists, including Stokely Carmichael, Marion Barry, and John Lewis. Now, aged seventy-eight, Vanderbilt had asked him to return—as a distinguished visiting professor. "It isn't often that an institution gets the chance to correct for a previous error," said the university's associate provost, Lucius Outlaw. Lawson, though surprised by the university's invitation, was delighted to accept and further agreed to donate his papers to the Vanderbilt archives. For him, as for Josephine Bradley, his return marked a positive reconnection with the past.[4]

Unlike Lawson, Bradley was a pioneer of the civil rights movement whose story was never national news, scarcely known, in fact, outside her local community. There were thousands like her throughout the South, and, as the civil rights movement passed into memory, they frequently found themselves similarly honored by these communities and, ironically, even by those who had once stood against them so fiercely. When, in early 2006, residents of Hattiesburg, Mississippi, honored the senior citizens Richard and Earline Boyd, they were both too frail to walk to the podium. Instead, they simply stood at their seats as the mixed-race audience applauded their bravery in sheltering white civil rights activists during the tumultuous events of Freedom Summer, 1964. For that, local Klansmen once firebombed their house, and each day brought its own special dangers. But the Boyds were resolute in the cause, as were the other Hattiesburg residents similarly honored that

Friday evening, with its theme "Drum Majors for Justice." "I'm just happy to be here today; it's been a long time," said Richard. Earline was more reflective and concerned that Freedom Summer and its impact had already been forgotten. "It's hard to talk to young people about what we went through because a lot of them don't care," she lamented. "Some of them do, but a lot of them don't care. Some of them will forget what happened." The event organizer, Anthony Harris, also a Freedom Summer volunteer, warned that there was still work to be done. Impressive as the accomplishments of the past decades had been, the struggle had no time limit. This is the essential message, too, of the hundreds of autobiographical accounts written by former participants in the movement, white or black, national figures or foot soldiers. Intensely proud of their part in the struggle, they knew that it was far from finished.[5]

Johnny DuPree, Hattiesburg's first black mayor, was unable to attend the ceremony for the Boyds; however, he was a featured speaker at a similar local event a few months later commemorating the work of Victoria Gray Adams, who had recently died. Along with Fanny Lou Hamer, Adams had been a founding member of the Mississippi Freedom Democratic Party. "Our world has been changed through the efforts of a few individuals," the mayor told a diverse crowd. "Victoria Gray Adams was one of those individuals." Stan Ziblusky, who had taught in Hattiesburg's freedom schools that momentous year, had journeyed from New York to pay his tribute. "Victoria was one of the keys to the whole movement here," he recollected. Her work as a founding member of the Mississippi Freedom Democratic Party led to the national publicity that helped change everything. Her granddaughter, Tujuana Frost, summed up Adams's life simply but truly. "She worked so tirelessly to pave the way for so many of us here today." A few weeks later, a large crowd gathered in White Hall, Lowndes County, Alabama, to honor the families, and the memory, of eight sharecroppers who had unsuccessfully tried to register to vote in 1965 and had been run off their land as a consequence. They had lunch in an auditorium "filled with civil rights artifacts," while listening to the recollections of those who had been involved. "The man who owned the land I lived on told me he was going to run barbed wire through my house and that I had to move," remembered Elijah Gordon. Bob Mants, once an SCLC activist, later a Lowndes County commissioner, said that he had organized the event in order to give some recognition to the forgotten foot soldiers of the movement. "I wanted to arrange a tribute to the farmers because of the important part they played in our struggle."[6]

Unsurprisingly, given the passage of time, many of these tributes took place at funerals and memorial services, some of which were great national occasions. After Rosa Parks died in October 2005, she was eulogized throughout the world as a woman who had changed history through a single act of defiance. When Nelson Mandela glimpsed her on the edge of the vast crowd gathered to welcome him in triumph to Detroit in 1990, he rushed to embrace her, shouting "Ro-sa Parks, Ro-sa Parks, Ro-sa Parks," thus symbolizing her significance to his and his people's own freedom struggle. Then, as she lay in state successively in Detroit, in Montgomery, and, finally, in Washington, the first woman, black or white, to lie in honor in the Capitol Rotunda, tens of thousands of Americans stood in line just to view her casket, as speakers extolled "the mother of the civil rights movement in life and death." Similar sentiments were expressed in the U.S. Congress. There, both the House and the Senate unanimously approved legislation making her the first African American woman to be honored permanently in the National Statuary Hall. Her likeness would stand forever, ironically, alongside Jefferson Davis and Robert E. Lee, but not the man most inspired by her simple action, Martin Luther King Jr. "She did more to build a perfect union than most of the statues in the room," was the comment of Jesse Jackson Sr.[7]

The death of Coretta Scott King was marked by similar national ceremony. Her body was carried through the streets of Atlanta by a horse-drawn carriage to the Georgia state capitol to lie there in honor, the first African American and first woman to do so. The casket was escorted into the Rotunda by her four children, Georgia's then governor Sonny Perdue, who is white, and Atlanta's African American mayor at the time, Shirley Franklin. She was "a gracious and courageous woman," extolled the governor, "absolutely an anchor of support for her husband" and "an inspiration to millions." Others contrasted the honors afforded Mrs. King with the manner in which Georgia had ignored the death of her husband in 1968. Then, Governor Lester Maddox, an outspoken segregationist, had refused to authorize any form of public tribute. It had been "a national insult to Dr. King and the King legacy and the whole civil rights movement that was sweeping across the South," declared state representative Tyrone Brooks, once a young SCLC activist. But times had changed, as Mayor Franklin acknowledged. She could not possibly have held the office if not for the Kings and those who worked with them. "I am standing on very broad shoulders," she said, as twenty-five thousand of her constituents filed past the casket.[8]

Coretta King's funeral was held in the Atlanta suburb of Lithonia, at the New Birth Missionary Church, where her daughter Bernice was a pastor. "Four Presidents, countless other dignitaries and thousands of ordinary people," wrote Maria Newman in the *New York Times,* gathered to pay tribute. President George W. Bush spoke briefly, acknowledging her as "one of the most admired Americans of our times," as did Senator Edward Kennedy, but "the biggest applause in the service" was reserved for former president Clinton, who challenged Americans to carry on the legacy the Kings had left, for the fight to advance civil rights was far from over. Ingrid Dove, an Atlanta social worker, was lucky enough to gain a seat in the balcony of the crowded church, and she spoke to a reporter after the service. So many had come, she said, like her, out of respect for the work Mrs. King had done, not only for African Americans, but for all humanity. Like Rosa Parks, she had become an international symbol of aspiration and inspiration.[9]

Much more localized, but equally pointed, were the sentiments expressed when John Hulett died in Mosses, Lowndes County, Alabama, in August 2006. Along with Stokely Carmichael, he had been one of the founders, in 1966, of the Lowndes County Freedom Association, which first took the black panther as its symbol of resistance to racist oppression. Huey P. Newton and Bobby Seale soon appropriated the emblem, moved it to California, and achieved some national exposure as a result, but Hulett had wished for no such prominence. Elected sheriff of Lowndes County—previously one of Alabama's most ferociously racist bastions—in 1970, he held the office for more than twenty years before becoming a probate judge. Unafraid of the Klan and other hate groups, Hulett was a symbol not only of resistance to segregation but also of subsequent racial reconciliation. "John Hulett did more for race relations than any man I know of in this State," commented Ted Bozeman, a white southerner and, like Hulett, a former Lowndes County judge. "He was well liked and respected in both the white and black communities."[10]

Hulett's funeral service was cut short so that mourners could honor his memory by attending the official opening of America's newest civil rights museum. This was the first of three "interpretive centers" to be built along U.S. 80, the highway between Selma and Montgomery. Tracey Larkin, a former Montgomery councilman and the chair of the ceremony, paid tribute to Hulett in his opening remarks. There was clearly a "sweet irony" in the timing of Hulett's death, he believed, "and the culmination of this great project, which seeks to memorialize all that he stood for." Never a nationally known civil rights icon, John Hulett, like Rosa Parks, exemplified the inspirational power of individual action.[11]

Memorials and museums commemorating the great events of the movement, the leaders and the foot soldiers who fought the battles, dot the American South, in the same way as do those remembering the Civil War. There are fixed-site general spaces such as the National Civil Rights Museum in Memphis, formerly the Lorraine Motel, where Martin Luther King was shot, and the Birmingham Civil Rights Institute and Museum, without doubt the most elaborately conceived and visited of these. Both these museums attempt to provide an overview of the civil rights era while at the same time emphasizing the events specific to the locality. Thus, the Memphis museum devotes a lot of exhibit space to King: his life, his leadership, and the circumstances of his death. Both museums, incidentally, have become increasingly important as heritage tourist attractions.[12]

Many memorials are specific to iconic events and locations. Selma's Voting Rights Museum celebrates the struggle for voting rights that culminated in the 1965 Selma–Montgomery march. Birmingham's Kelly Ingram Park, where Bull Connor unleashed his police dogs and trained his fire hoses on marching schoolchildren during 1963's tumultuous summer, was renovated in 1992 and dedicated as "A Place of Revolution and Reconciliation." The "Freedom Walk" that bounds it is broken up by "dark sculptures from the protests," including "snarling police dogs, jailed protesters and enormous water cannons." Commissioned sculptures of the Little Rock Nine likewise stand in the grounds of the Arkansas state capitol building, while Central High School itself has become a working memorial. The gas station across the street, from which reporters phoned in their stories in 1957, has recently been refurbished as a museum documenting the confrontation. Superbly presented and maintained, like so many others, by the National Parks Service, it also offers to the expanding number of visitors guided tours of Central High, still a working institution.

In August 2006 the Selma–Montgomery Historic Trail was opened. It, too, is developed and maintained by the National Parks Service. In Greensboro, North Carolina, the International Civil Rights Center and Museum, originally established on a modest budget in 1994 to commemorate the beginning of the sit-in movement there, opened in February 2010. Such event-specific museums have normally been strongly supported by local and state authorities, reflecting the influence of black politicians and public officials and also the realization that, through the transformation of sites of protest into tourist attractions, "memorialization of the movement has become a way to turn a stigmatized past into a commercial asset," as the historian Glen Eskew has written. According to Eskew, "The rationale of African-American heritage tourism proved too great for politicians to resist." And the opposition of "reactionary whites" was easily brushed aside. Some former movement activists have themselves become involved with the heritage tourist industry. Charles E. Cobb Jr., a field secretary for the SNCC in the Mississippi Delta during the 1960s, recently published *On the Road to Freedom,* a moving personal history of the movement, but also a guide to four hundred of its battle sites, easily accessible for those who want to revisit the ground.[13]

Many of the events of the civil rights era are commemorated annually. The forty-second anniversary of the beatings on the Edmund Pettus Bridge in 1965 brought presidential candidates Barack Obama and Hillary Rodham Clinton to Selma. Both spoke at church services on the same street, three blocks apart, both paid homage to the same civil rights leaders, and both concluded the services by locking arms with worshippers and swaying to "We Shall Overcome." They then joined former president Bill Clinton, along with black congressmen and movement veterans, as they retraced the path of the 1965 march. The symbolism of their words and actions, remarked the journalist Alvin Benn, "wasn't lost on anybody." Earlier in the year, participants in the 1961 freedom rides, joined by one hundred college students, had retraced their historic journey. Congressman John L. Lewis recalled the beating they had received in Montgomery. "It was so quiet before the mob came, almost eerie," he said. "Then all of a sudden they attacked, and left us lying there, bloody and unconscious." Gbemende Johnson, a graduate student in political science at Vanderbilt University, was deeply moved by such stories. "I can't imagine it," he admitted. "It was just incredible bravery." Reenacting these events of fifty years ago, said Shevan Evans, also from Vanderbilt, was "all about awareness" and, thus, crucially important in inspiring "people today to continue the fight against discrimination and hatred."[14]

The widespread renaming of streets after the heroes and heroines of the movement has long been a central aspect of its commemoration. By 2003, over 730 cities and towns—70 percent of them in the South—had their Martin Luther King Jr. Boulevards, Avenues, or Highways. Rosa Parks, too, has been similarly commemorated throughout the nation. Changing road names has rarely been controversial in the larger centers with significant black residential districts. In the smaller towns and counties of the South, however, it has often been a different story. Derek H. Alderman has discussed in fascinating detail the contest in Bullock County, Georgia, between black citizens and military veterans over a proposal in 1994 to name a new perimeter highway after King. The veterans preferred Veterans Memorial Parkway, and, after much dispute, they prevailed, largely owing to the vocal support of a significant number of black former soldiers. In Americus, Georgia, city officials balked at renaming part of U.S. Highway 19, until blacks threatened a boycott of city businesses. During the bitter struggle, one white public official crassly suggested that half the highway be named after King, the other half after his assassin, James Earl Ray. In liberal Chapel Hill, North Carolina, white residents of Airport Road held up its renaming until they were assured that the words "formerly Airport Road" would appear on the new street signs. Street signs bearing King's name are frequently vandalized. In Dade County, Florida, "General Robert E. Lee" was once painted over nine signs for Martin Luther King Jr. Boulevard; in other locations, King Boulevard signs are routinely shot at or otherwise defaced. Such public commemoration of King's memory and legacy remains a bitter pill for some white Southerners to swallow.[15]

Equally unpalatable to some was the designation of January 15, King's birthday, as a federal public holiday—as exemplified by a McDonalds Restaurant in Memphis that in its 1989 calendar labeled the date "National Nothing Day"—while there has often been disagreement within local black communities as to how it should best be observed, who should control it, and whether white people should participate. Conversely, to many white Americans, King "remains primarily a black man, and his birthday a black holiday for black people," one they choose not to mark in any way. Over the years, however, the holiday has lost much of its controversial nature, and most communities observe it with parades, church services, and reflections on King's leadership and legacy, a day on which white Americans genuinely and willingly participate. In 2007, the theme of the fifth annual Martin Luther King Jr. Day Parade in Durham, North Carolina, was "Rediscovering Lost Values." Onlookers cheered as marchers of all races "snaked down Fayetteville Street to the sound of drumbeats, shoe taps and cheers." They waved banners and signs declaring "No More Gang Violence" and "Keep the Dream Alive." Louise Gooche, team captain of the Durham City Divas, an interracial senior citizens cheering squad, thought that the parade represented King's ideals and that the holiday was important in that it brought the neighborhood "into community and camaraderie and togetherness." In Atlanta, Republican senator Saxby Chambliss and King's sister, Christine King Farris, held hands and prayed together at a memorial service in Ebenezer Baptist Church as thousands gathered outside to watch a live telecast. In Montgomery, dozens of young people spent part of the day picking up trash, their particular tribute to the man who "always advocated giving over receiving." Jeff Downs, a white city official, arrived with his young son and soon "began picking up everything from paper to snack packages." There was the occasional discordant note. James Lawson, speaking from the pulpit in Nashville's Gordon Memorial Baptist Church from which he once attacked segregation, took the opportunity to denounce President Bush and his colleagues. "War is hell," he shouted, quoting President Eisenhower. "Why then do we have baptized people in the White House, Condoleezza Rice, George Bush, all baptized folk, who are creating wars in Afghanistan and Iraq and thinking about Iran?" He pleaded with the president and those who advised him "to adopt the practices of King and follow the commands of Christ in loving others . . . to move us away from war to peace, from animosity to friendship." The twin themes of reconciliation and a return to nonviolence in the public and private worlds dominate the celebration of the Martin Luther King Jr. holiday. Though still seen as primarily a black holiday, it is slowly becoming a national day of recollection and renewal.[16]

Why had Hollywood ignored the civil rights movement as a theme for historical drama, queried the *Washington Post* staff writer Ann Hornaday in July 2007? "All the social, cultural and political touchstones of the baby boom generation"—World War II, the Kennedy assassinations, the Vietnam War, Watergate, feminism, gay rights, AIDS, and all manner of political scandals—have been turned into major feature films. The civil rights movement remained the exception, and this she found both puzzling and somewhat shocking. Not even the life of Martin Luther King had been the subject of a biopic—unlike his contemporaries Malcolm X and Muhammad Ali. "Here is a chapter in American life," she concluded, "whose legacy and ramifications . . . are still deeply and painfully felt, . . . filled with charismatic characters and compelling stories," yet they had largely gone untold in the nation's "dominant narrative art form." Studio executives, she believed, were just not willing to take the risk.[17]

Hornaday was only half right. Though the defining civil rights movie is yet to be made, producers and directors have tackled civil rights themes over the years, often unsuccessfully. Some of the movies have been made for television, with specific audiences in mind. Disney's *Selma, Lord, Selma,* for example, a simplistic dramatization of the events surrounding the historic Selma–Montgomery march, was aimed specifically at young people. *The Rosa Parks Story,* a highly sentimentalized biopic about the heroine of the Montgomery bus boycott, is similarly one-dimensional in its narrative and characterization. *Once upon a Time When We Were Colored*, again made for a restricted television audience, is a gentle and affectionate recollection of the strength of the black community in a Mississippi Delta town in the 1950s and 1960s, but it touches only tangentially on the civil rights movement. These are but three examples of many such films, low budget, made for television, and directed primarily at a black audience.[18]

Of the few big-budget and mainstream studio-produced films that deal with the civil rights movement, easily the best known is Alan Parker's *Mississippi Burning*. Released in 1988, and starring Gene Hackman, Willem Dafoe, and Frances McDormand, it is a fictionalized account of the murders of Mickey Schwerner, Andrew Goodman, and James Chaney in 1964 and the subsequent hunt for their killers. A box-office success, it generated controversy on its release and continues to do so. Film critics, civil rights activists, and historians of the movement have all attacked it, with considerable justice, for, as Hornaday points out, "valorizing the white investigators of the crimes rather than emphasizing the heroic stories of their nominal subjects." Civil rights activists were marginalized in *Mississippi Burning;* J. Edgar Hoover's FBI officers became the unlikely heroes. Rob Reiner's 1996 *Ghosts of Mississippi,* with Alec Baldwin as Bobby DeLaughter, the white assistant district attorney who in 1994 successfully prosecuted the murderer of Medgar Evers, the Mississippi NAACP state secretary, in 1963, has been similarly attacked for focusing "on a white character as savior" and paying little attention to Evers and his fellow activists.[19]

Another box-office success, *The Long Walk Home* (1990), with Sissy Spacek and Whoopi Goldberg, concerns the interaction between a middle-class white woman and her maid during the Montgomery bus boycott and did seek "to give equal screen time to its white and black heroines." Yet, in having Spacek's character drive in the car pools, it emphasized her bravery over that of those black drivers who daily risked danger. Not until 2000, argues Jennifer Fuller, was "a mainstream civil rights drama told from the perspective of local activists on the ground" screened. This was Turner Network Television's original movie *Freedom Song*. Starring Danny Glover, one of America's best-known black actors, who was also its coproducer, the film is the inverse of *Mississippi Burning*. Fictionalizing and amalgamating a number of incidents that occurred in Mississippi in 1961 as the SNCC began its voter registration work there, it emphasizes the local origins of the movement, the strength of the black community leadership, and the importance of young people as the movement's foot soldiers, often in defiance of their parents and other authority figures. In this story, whites have little place except as the systematic purveyors of violence. There is one sympathetic Justice Department official, played by David Strathairn, but, unlike *Mississippi Burning*'s FBI heroes, he can do little to prevent the violence and quickly retreats to Washington. The stated aim of the producers was to redress the imbalance of earlier films and "to show that the black community was on the front lines of the struggle." They succeeded brilliantly. Former SNCC chairman Chuck McDew told the *New York Times* in 2000 that *Freedom Song* was the first movie "ever made that captured the spirit and integrity of the people involved in the movement." It remains so still, not only the best film to deal with this history, but also the last, as producers and directors look outside the South, and beyond its recent past, for themes in which to explore race in America.[20]

Documentary filmmakers continue to find the civil rights movement a rich field in which to plough. Scores of films have been made, often with local people or incidents as their subjects, and with only local or regional exposure. Some are made as part of university programs in the creative arts. Tuskegee University's Department of English helped produce *Fly Away*, a film that is based on the life of Amelia Boynton Robinson, who was gassed, beaten, and left for dead on the Edmund Pettus Bridge during the Bloody Sunday march and that examines the participation of black women in the struggle. But without doubt the best-known documentary series is *Eyes on the Prize*, the first part of which covers the years between 1955 and 1965. It has had an impact far beyond the United States. Hundreds of thousands of students throughout the world continue to gain their understanding of the civil rights struggle through experiencing its dramatic power. First screened in 1987 to extraordinary acclaim, it is still shown repeatedly on cable channels throughout the globe, including on PBS in the fall of 2006; easily accessible on tape or DVD, it is without doubt the most influential single source for the civil rights era. Yet it is more than that. "[*Eyes on the Prize*] is the most powerful reminder we have of how broad the struggle was," wrote Bob Herbert in the *New York Times*, "how many people of great courage—from small children to very old men and women—signed out on it . . . and what all of us owe to all of them." It was more than a great piece of filmmaking, he concluded. "It is a national treasure, important for all the reasons that history is important." As such, it will always be one of the movement's most significant memorials.[21]

Mississippi, on which so many films have focused, was where most of the worst atrocities and miscarriages of justice occurred during the struggles. But it was Mississippi, too, that led the way in bringing those who perpetrated them to much-delayed justice. Beginning with the eventual conviction of Byron de la Beckwith in 1994, after two previous mistrials, for the slaying of Medgar Evers, state prosecutors have been successful in closing twenty-seven such cases. In 2005, one of these "atonement trials" gained sustained national and international attention. This was the prosecution of the eighty-year-old Edgar Ray Killen, accused of organizing the murders of Schwerner, Goodman, and Chaney, near Philadelphia, in Neshoba County, in June 1964, at the commencement of Freedom Summer. Their brutal execution, which sparked a manhunt involving hundreds of troops, state police, and FBI agents, remains, in the words of the historian John Dittmer, "the most depressingly familiar story of the Mississippi movement." Though seven Klansmen, including Neshoba County deputy sheriff Cecil Price and Klan leader Sam Bowers—found guilty in 1998 of killing another local black leader, Vernon Dahmer—were eventually convicted of violating the three victims' civil rights, none served more than six years in prison. Meanwhile, the memory of their actions continued to divide the local community.[22]

Killen, once a feared Klan leader but forty years on a crippled old man in a wheelchair, breathing through a tube attached to an oxygen tank, sat impassively through the trial as Mississippi attorney general Jim Hood presented a detailed compilation of the evidence against him. Much of his argument had been painstakingly drawn from forty thousand pages of material provided by the FBI. Present in the court were Schwerner's widow, Rita Schwerner Bender, and James Chaney's younger brother, Ben, who, as a grieving five-year-old clutching at his brother's coffin, provided one of the most moving television images of the civil rights years. When the jury found Killen guilty of three counts of manslaughter—having been deadlocked on the murder charges—and he had been sentenced to sixty years in prison, an elderly black man who had worked with the victims on a voter education project pushed his way to Rita Bender's side and held her in a silent embrace. Ben Chaney was not similarly lost for words. "I want to thank God," he said, "that today we saw Preacher Killen in a prison uniform taken from the courthouse to the jailhouse." His eighty-three-year-old mother was happy with the verdict, he continued. "She finally believes that the life of her son had some value to the people in this community." Many others in the courtroom, and in the larger community, had a similar sense of closure, echoing the words of Attorney General Hood that the verdict proved, finally, that "there's justice for all in Mississippi."[23]

There were some in both the county's white and its black communities, however, who were less exultant. A few unrepentant white supremacists like Harlan Majure thought the evidence against Killen to be hopelessly biased. The Klan, he claimed to reporters, was always a peaceful organization that "did a lot of good." Others made connections with the far-off ghosts of the Civil War and Reconstruction era. The whole trial, but particularly the pervasive presence of the national media, reminded many of the mythology of those years, said the local resident Deborah Posey. "It was when the North came into the South and told the South . . . you have to do this, this and this." It was still happening. Rita Bender, on the other hand, believed that the manslaughter verdict clearly showed that there were still people in the community "who choose not to see the truth" of her husband's murder. Elsie Kirksey, a local black police dispatcher, thought likewise. "One trial can't change Neshoba County," she told reporters. It was only a "starting point." Yet, 70 percent of the county's residents claimed to be glad that the case had been reopened, even those who still believed the victims to have been "outside troublemakers," for after four decades they would now be left alone. In that sense, too, Killen's atonement trial had been worth the effort. Four years later, in May 2009, Philadelphia, though a majority-white town, elected James A. Young, a black Pentecostal minister, as its mayor. He narrowly defeated the white incumbent. For many, following Killen's conviction, it was the final act of redefinition. "It will erase the thought that we're just a white racist town," said Dorothy Webb, a retired white school principal who had supported Young. In his victory speech, Young agreed. Philadelphia, "which has some of the worst history," now had "some of the best," he thought. The town had finally laid its infamous national image to rest.[24]

Furthermore, Killen's atonement trial had sparked some Mississippi officials into seeking the reopening of Mississippi's longest-running civil rights cold case, the 1955 murder of fourteen-year-old Emmett Till. In April 2006, Attorney General Hood announced that he was reviewing evidence provided by the FBI before deciding to re-present the case to a grand jury, seeking charges against seventy-three-year-old Carolyn Bryant Donham, the only known suspect in the youth's slaying who was still alive. Eventually, Leflore County's district attorney did seek a manslaughter charge against the old woman, but, in February 2007, a grand jury refused to indict her, effectively closing the books on a crime that had long become synonymous with the roots of the civil rights era. Till's name, however, lived on. The same day as the grand jury reached its decision, U.S. attorney general Alberto R. Gonzales announced the creation of an FBI unit specifically charged with investigating unsolved racial killings from the civil rights era. It was to be named after Emmett Till. The unit immediately went to work with a will, concentrating first on seven unsolved and clearly racially motivated killings that took place in Alabama between 1956 and 1964 and for which the SPLC had provided its extensive files. A few months later, Alabama formed its own Cold Case Investigative Unit, to work with the FBI. Its purpose, said State attorney general Troy King, would be "to bring the light of justice to those who have gone too long in the darkness, by making sure that justice is won and done."[25]

The killings of Schwerner, Goodman, and Chaney remain the defining event of Klan violence during Freedom Summer. But there were other murders during those dangerous months, all of black people, that got little notice at the time and whose perpetrators are mainly still unpunished and likely to remain so. There has so far been one notable exception. In that fervid summer of 1964, searchers for the bodies of the three missing civil rights workers pulled two decomposed corpses from the Mississippi River. Initially thought to be two of the missing trio, once they were identified as two local black youths with no political associations, Henry Hezekiah Dee and Charles Eddie Moore, "their deaths, like their lives, were forgotten," said the journalist Jerry Mitchell—except by their families, who fruitlessly sought justice. Justice eventually came, but more than four decades later. After a Canadian documentary team had drawn attention to the case, a seventy-one-year-old ex-Klansman, James Ford Seale, was eventually charged with the abduction and murder of the two boys. The main witness against him was his elderly coconspirator, Charles Marcus Edwards, granted immunity from prosecution in return for his testimony. Despite the efforts of the defense team to discredit Edwards and to emphasize the absence of any corroborating evidence, a mixed-race jury convicted Seale, and he was later sentenced to life imprisonment. For the families of the victims, the verdict finally brought closure. Thelma Collins, Henry Dee's sister and the same age as his murderer, had never spoken of his death to anyone, not even her children. "I wanted my children to live a happy life," she said. "I didn't want my children to come up hating nobody about nothing like that." But at last she could acknowledge her loss; as the verdict was read, her tears began to flow. Writing in the *Hattiesburg American,* one columnist, while admitting the darkness of Mississippi's racist past, nevertheless thought, "For every conviction that is gained from Mississippi's darkest hour comes a glimmer of hope. It is a hope that says while a world may never be able or willing to forgive, we can take solace that at least the good within all of us will never forget." Jerry Mitchell, the *Jackson Clarion-Ledger* reporter who had made it his life's work to investigate the crimes of the civil rights era, also welcomed Seale's trial but warned that it might be the last of such prosecutions. The potential witnesses were slipping away, and justice too long delayed would soon be justice ever denied.[26]

Alabama, too, has had its share of atonement trials. In a brilliant essay, Renee C. Romano has analyzed the reactions of Birmingham's communities to the trials of three Klansmen accused of perpetrating what she describes as "the most tragic and heinous crime of the civil rights era," the bombing of the Sixteenth Street Baptist Church on September 15, 1963, in which four young girls were killed. Robert Chambliss was found guilty of murder for his role in 1977, Thomas Edwin Blanton in 2001, and Bobby Frank Cherry in 2002. With Cherry's imprisonment, much of white Birmingham breathed a collective sigh of relief that the "shameful past," of which he was a monstrous relic, had finally been atoned for and the community redeemed. "Justice delayed is not justice denied," said U.S. attorney Doug Jones. The racism of the past had "given way to a desire to see justice done." Black citizens were less sanguine. For Myrna Jackson, vice president of the Birmingham NAACP, the guilty verdict was "an attempt to pacify blacks in the short term," as racial, economic, and education inequalities continued.[27]

Most blacks nevertheless conceded that such atonement trials had their value. In that spirit, in August 2006, Alabama governor Bob Riley, responding to pressure from the NAACP, state politicians, and surviving family members, offered a reward for information leading to the arrest and eventual conviction for murder of James Bonard Fowler, who in February 1965 had shot and killed Jimmy Lee Jackson in the racially troubled town of Marion. Fowler, then a state trooper, had never denied killing the civil rights activist but always claimed self-defense, despite the contrary statements of a host of eyewitnesses. Jackson's cousin, Calvin Hogue, praised the governor's decision. "All we want is the truth," he said. "Lots of us were there, and we know what happened that terrible night." In May 2007, a Perry County grand jury indicted Fowler for the slaying, and the following month he surrendered to authorities, was formally charged with Jackson's murder, and was released on a $250,000 bond. Hogue, now a Perry County deputy sheriff, was there to witness the surrender. Selma district attorney Michael W. Jackson, who had sought Fowler's indictment, when asked for his reaction, drew attention to the historical significance of Jackson's death. It had "led to the voting rights march," he pointed out, which in turn "helped trigger the Voting Rights Act, which helped enfranchise a lot of people." As Alabama's sole black district attorney, he was, he said, "a direct beneficiary of it."[28]

While most support the eventual bringing to justice of those who killed and maimed decades ago, there are some who see the dangers in heaping all responsibility for the violence on the bent shoulders of a few very old, somewhat demented Klansmen. Communities, argues Romano, can too easily ignore their own complicity, their silences, effectively denying the institutionalized racism that permitted these atrocities. Certainly, the conviction of Preacher Killen caused many Mississippians to hope that it symbolized "the regenerative energy of a decent people," to recognize the "value of truth and reconciliation." "We have come far," observed Susan M. Glisson, executive director of the University of Mississippi's William Winter Institute for Racial Reconciliation, in "acknowledging those dark days" and in moving beyond them. Yet there was still much work to be done before the South was fully healed. Many of the issues of the past remained not only unresolved but also "operational in current policies and daily interactions." To deny this truth was to perpetuate segregation's legacy.[29]

There was a further aspect to the belated redressing of past injustices. That was the movement to seek pardons, often posthumous, for those convicted of various offences during the long years of struggle. Most significant were those seeking to clear the name of Rosa Parks. Responding to pressure from civil rights leaders during the fiftieth anniversary celebrations of the boycott in December 2005, the Alabama state legislature passed a measure removing the convictions of those charged with violating segregation-era ordinances from the court records. Though it was the celebration of Mrs. Parks's individual action that prompted this response, it had the potential to clear retrospectively the names of hundreds of others similarly sentenced. Lillie May Bradford, who was arrested four years earlier than Parks for going to the front of the bus, welcomed the move. When her pardon came through, she said, she planned to "frame it and hang it on the wall next to her charge sheet." Reporters inquired as to what possible difference it could make after half a century. "It's important to me," was her telling response. Washington Booker, on the other hand, had no interest in being pardoned. As a schoolboy, he had been arrested in 1963 for defying Bull Connor's dogs and fire hoses and angrily refused exoneration for "demanding civil rights I should have had the day I was born." His arrest and subsequent jailing remained the proudest moment of his life. "I don't want to take it off my record," he said. He and his fellow marchers had "changed the course of human history," and he was determined to keep his involvement on the public record. So many responded similarly that surprised legislators speedily inserted a provision requiring those who wished to be pardoned to apply for it individually, though family members could do so on behalf of those who had died in the half century between. Thus, the ambivalences of those most affected were recognized.[30]

One of the most remarkable crusades to clear the name of a convicted civil rights activist occurred in Hattiesburg, Mississippi, where in the late 1950s Clyde Kennard made three attempts to enroll at all-white Mississippi Southern College, now the University of Southern Mississippi. What happened to him as a result constituted, in the historian John Dittmer's words, "the most tragic [case] of the decade." The retribution accorded the World War II veteran, according to Dittmer, affected Mississippi State NAACP secretary Medgar Evers more deeply than any of the many examples of racially motivated injustice he had to investigate. Even given the climate of violence and lawlessness that prevailed in Mississippi at the time, the state's revenge against a young man "whose only offence was a desire to attend a college near his home" was sickening in the extreme.[31]

Briefly, the facts of the case were these. After leaving the army in 1952, Kennard enrolled at the University of Chicago but was forced to return to Forrest County to help run the family farm prior to completing his degree. His decision to try and enroll at Mississippi Southern was primarily in order to finish his education, though he was given strong support by the NAACP. For that he was hounded by the Mississippi State Sovereignty Commission—"Mississippi's secret police," John Dittmer called the commission's members—and, when it was clear that neither pressure nor persuasion would deter him, Kennard was charged with stealing five bags of chicken feed, convicted on perjured testimony in a court where all semblance of impartiality was absent, and given the maximum sentence of seven years in the state's notorious Parchman prison. In 1962, as NAACP lawyers continued to work for his release, he was diagnosed with abdominal cancer. Prison authorities denied him the treatment he needed, and only when it became obvious that he would die in prison, with the consequent unfavorable publicity, did Governor Ross Barnett order his release. Kennard died in Chicago on July 4, 1963, aged only thirty-six, a tragic victim of Mississippi's racist justice system. He was buried in Forrest County, at Mary Magdalene Baptist Church, where he had once taught Sunday school and directed the youth choir.[32]

Kennard's bravery, his fraudulent conviction, and his death, though remembered by a few as part of Mississippi's dark past, were, nevertheless, a largely forgotten aspect of the state's "civil rights era lore until December 2005, when Jerry Mitchell of the *Jackson Clarion-Ledger* tracked down the key trial witness against Kennard. Not only did he readily admit to his perjury; he stated that the State Sovereignty Commission had engineered Kennard's framing, an assertion the commission's own records confirmed. This damning new evidence, when made public in the *Clarion-Ledger*, prompted widespread general interest in the case and, among some, a renewed determination to clear Kennard's name. State senators, the NAACP, prominent businessmen, lawyers, judges, educators, and students at the University of Southern Mississippi, working with the Northwestern University Center on Wrongful Convictions, all joined forces in petitioning Governor Haley Barbour for a posthumous pardon. "This is something that should have been taken care of years ago," insisted LaKeisha Bryant, president of the Afro-American Students Association at Southern Mississippi, who led the local effort. "For too long we've sat back and kept quiet about it."[33]

Governor Barbour reacted promptly. Though refusing to pardon Kennard on the ground that state law made no provision for pardoning the dead, he did in other ways make clear his belief that the young man had been the victim of a corrupt justice system. At a ceremony to honor Kennard held in the state Senate chamber, he read a proclamation stating, "Clyde Kennard, if he were living, would be entitled to have his rights restored, and were he still living, his rights would have been restored during this Administration." Barbour then declared March 30, 2006, to be "Clyde Kennard Day" and urged all citizens "to remember his legacy, the injustices he suffered, and his significant role in the history of the Civil Rights Movement in Mississippi."[34]

While Kennard's supporters were still determined to see his conviction vacated, they nevertheless recognized the symbolic significance of Barbour's action. It was a step forward, agreed nineteen-year-old Tangee Carter, a student at Southern Mississippi. "We're much closer to getting his name completely cleared." Ellie Dahmer, whose husband, Vernon, had been killed by Klansmen in 1966, was similarly positive. "He deserved every bit of it," she said. "Even though he suffered . . . he didn't hate anyone." He therefore, she thought, exemplified all that was best about the movement. But there was more work to be done, asserted LaKeisha Bryant, before Kennard's spirit was completely free. Raylawni Branch, one of the first two black students at Southern Mississippi, agreed. "I want to see justice—total exoneration of his name because he was guilty of nothing."[35]

Kennard's supporters, who now included nationally prominent figures like NAACP chairman Julian Bond and the Pulitzer Prize–winning author Taylor Branch, continued their work on a petition for filing with the Mississippi Parole Board, as John Weathers, district attorney for Forrest and Perry counties, admitted that he, too, was seeking ways to reopen the case. Both Branch and Bond contacted Governor Barbour personally, urging him "to do justice at last in the case of an upright, wrongfully persecuted stalwart for fairness and freedom." Meanwhile, Steven Drizin, legal director of the Northwestern Center, contacted the parole board directly and reported that members were anxious to receive the petition as quickly as was practical. It was duly filed on April 12, along with more than one thousand pages of supporting documents and signatures, including those of Bond, Congressman Bennie Thompson, University of Southern Mississippi president Shelby Thames, and retired state supreme court justice Reuben Anderson.[36]

The parole board, however, took its time reviewing the petition, then rejected it on the grounds that "all other legal remedies had not been exhausted." Former governor William Winter and retired federal appeals court judge Charles Pickering soon saw to that. On May 17, their names headed a petition to the Forrest County Circuit Court urging Judge Robert Helfrich "to vacate Kennard's 1960 conviction," thus rendering the guilty verdict null and void. Helfrich promptly did so. During a "solemn 20 minute hearing," he ruled that Kennard "was innocent of receiving stolen property." "Because the matter began here [the Forrest County courthouse]," he declared, "it should end here." Judge Helfrich did not consider the matter to be primarily "a black and white issue." Rather, it was "a right and wrong issue": "To correct that wrong, I am compelled to do the right thing and that is to declare Mr. Kennard innocent." After forty-six years, Clyde Kennard had received a measure of the justice denied him in 1960, the most recent of "a string of legal rulings in which," wrote Rachel Leifer of the *Hattiesburg American*, "the state of Mississippi has confronted its violent segregationist past." Ironically, in 2004, Judge Pickering had been able to take his place on the federal bench only as a recess appointment, the Senate Judiciary Committee having previously delivered President George W. Bush a sharp rebuff by rejecting his nomination. Then, he had been opposed by every civil rights group in Mississippi, on the basis of a poor civil rights record. His recess appointment, claimed the chair of the Congressional Black Caucus, was "yet one more attempt by the Bush Administration to turn back the clock on the rights and freedom that countless Americans marched and died for over the past 40 years." Yet, here he was now, spearheading the drive to clear the name of one of those who had died for the cause.[37]

Contributors to an online forum monitored by the *Hattiesburg American* generally supported Helfrich's decision, though some disagreed with his assertion that it was "not a black-white thing" but rather a matter of simply rectifying a grave miscarriage of justice. The two could not be separated, argued one correspondent. "It was about race when it happened. This is the South after all." Others congratulated Helfrich for what was still "a bold position to take in the Deep South." Only one participant ridiculed spending time and money on Kennard when there were troubling issues plaguing some local communities—increased and drug-related crime, unwed mothers and their wayward children, absentee and feckless fathers—much more deserving of attention. As for Kennard's family and friends, they rejoiced in the exoneration. "I'm happy this is over—for Clyde's name's sake" and for those who knew him as an "honorable and good man," exulted his brother-in-law, the eighty-two-year-old Reverend Willie Grant, the pastor of Hattiesburg's Martin Luther [King] Avenue Baptist Church. He was "going to go home and shout." The city's black community shouted with him. Thus, though in Kennard's case justice came far too late, it did at least bring closure.[38]

Kennard's exoneration again prompted Mississippians to revisit the state's racist past, taking heart in how much had changed in the past four decades. Judge Pickering thought that the ruling "demonstrate[d] the tremendous racial progress Mississippi had made since the 1950's and 1960's" and that there would be more healing, provided the races continued working together. Vernon Dahmer Jr., the son of the murdered civil rights leader, was similarly upbeat. "When we look at where we were pre-1960 and where we are today and the progress we've made—we had to come further than anybody else," he declared optimistically. Yet the past had an untimely way of reasserting itself. Less than a week after Judge Helfrich's decision, Richard Barrett filed a petition in the same court seeking to block Kennard's exoneration. Barrett, a Jackson attorney and the leader of the white supremacist Nationalist Movement, who had previously defended members of Mississippi's discredited State Sovereignty Commission as "patriots," believed "absolutely" in Kennard's guilt. More importantly, he argued, the judge's reasoning indicated clearly his own racism. Because the jurors who had convicted Kennard had happened to be white, Helfrich had dismissed them as "evil"—hence his petition, filed on behalf of five white "common folks" from central Mississippi. A few months earlier, Barrett had organized a "Killen Appreciation Day" to welcome the recently convicted killer back to Philadelphia, during the brief period he was out on bond. Killen's willingness to attend the function was one of the reasons the trial judge ordered him back to jail. "[This] seems to me . . . grounds to deny bond," he said. "This trial involved the death of three persons who died in a cruel, heinous and atrocious manner," emphatically not a cause for celebration. For all the progress, then, vestiges of the past were still alive and well.[39]

13

POVERTY AND PROGRESS

Four Decades of Change

No southern State government has ever seriously considered establishing a body like South Africa's Truth and Reconciliation Commission as a means of examining the crimes and injustices of the segregation years, of giving victims and their families a chance to confront those who had abused them, and of, thus, achieving a degree of surcease. Some have argued that the atonement trials served that purpose, but the comparison goes only so far. A key aspect of the South African procedure was to give those who murdered and maimed during the apartheid decades the chance to repent, to apologize directly to those they had cruelly wronged, and, through personal encounter, to enhance the prospect of forgiveness or, at the least, closure. The atonement trials contained no such provisions. None of those convicted ever confessed their guilt, let alone apologized to the families of those whose lives they had taken. Rather, most continued to profess their innocence and, like Thomas Blanton, claim that they had been framed. "I think I was cleverly set up by the government," he complained from his prison cell in 2006. Edgar Killen, too, continued to deny any involvement in the Neshoba County killings.[1]

Groups such as the Atlanta-based Committee for Truth and Reconciliation in the South and the University of Mississippi's Winter Institute strongly advocate the general application of the South African model in the South, and there have been occasional attempts to establish private truth and reconciliation–type commissions to examine particular incidents in a community's past. In Greensboro, North Carolina, a coalition of black and white liberal activists, with support from individual city councillors and the local newspaper, set up their own commission to investigate the killing of five Communist organizers in November 1979 during a "Death to the Klan" protest march. Although the shooting was filmed, six people were acquitted of murder charges in 1980. This, together with the belief that Greensboro's leaders had botched all subsequent investigations, meant that tensions in the African American community never abated, eventually prompting the formation of a group of "volunteer commissioners" to seek "restorative justice" on the South African model. The commission, which had no official standing, took two years to complete its task. It held public hearings and interviewed scores of people privately, its four-hundred-page report appearing in November 2005. Though it distributed blame for the tragedy widely, prime responsibility was laid on city officials and the police department, who, it argued, despite overwhelming evidence of the probability of violent confrontation, failed to protect the people at the site of the rally. At the very least, there should be an apology for this tragic error in judgment. Not so, was the response of Greensboro mayor Keith Holiday. Tim Bellamy, the African American police chief, refused to comment, while most city council members believed the whole enterprise to be a waste of time and money. Without a generalized community commitment to use the report's findings, to recognize that there were some in the city who still felt real pain over what had happened in 1979, and to try and ease it, the commission could achieve little, and the divide remained. Here, again, the divergence with the South African experience is clear.[2]

In 2000, North Carolina's state government did appoint a commission to inquire into one of the darkest events in its history, the bloody race massacre that had occurred in Wilmington in 1898. The riot resulted in the overthrow of the New Hanover County government in what some historians have called the nation's only recorded coup d'état and ensured the triumph of white supremacy in the state. Clearly different from the Truth and Reconciliation Commission model, for there were obviously no surviving witnesses or perpetrators, the Wilmington Riots Commission report did apportion blame and recommended economic and social compensation for the descendants of victims who could be traced. Similarly, three weeks later, the U.S. Senate formally apologized to the descendants of African Americans who had been lynched, for failing to make it a federal crime despite the requests of seven presidents to do so. Two hundred descendants of lynching victims, plus one ninety-one-year-old man thought to be the only living survivor of a lynching attempt, watched from the gallery before joining senators for a commemorative luncheon on Capitol Hill. For most of them it was, as Simeon Wright put it, "a very moving experience," though rarely had they known their relatives personally. She had heard about her uncle's murder through "whispers from neighbors," said seventy-eight-year-old Winona Puckett Padgett. Avis Thomas-Lester wrote in the *Washington Post* that the atmosphere was "like a family reunion, except that the people sharing food and fellowship were not related" but rather "bonded instead by a common history—a heritage of pain born when their ancestors were beaten, tortured, burned at the stake and hanged." Moreover, these horrible events, too, had occurred outside the reach of direct memory. Again, there could be no direct confrontation between victim and perpetrator.[3]

In the first months of 2007, the legislatures in four southern or border states—Virginia, Maryland, North Carolina, and Alabama—passed resolutions either apologizing or expressing regret for, as the North Carolina resolution put it, "the injustice, cruelty and brutality of slavery" and the subsequent legal discrimination against blacks. Though some legislators fretted that to do so might invite claims for reparations, only in Alabama was there serious opposition. There, white Republicans held the measure up for two months as they clashed repeatedly and heatedly with the black sponsors, all Democrats. Eventually, the resolution passed, with some legislators clearly moved to action more by the realization that the delay was hindering Alabama's drive to persuade the German steel giant ThyssenKrupp to locate a mill there than through any higher moral concern. Not all white Alabamians approved of their action, as the newspaper chat columns amply demonstrated. "Won't be getting an apology from anyone in my family," declared one such. "Those who passed the legislation can say what they want. . . . I wasn't involved, so I don't owe nothing." Not all black Alabamians supported the resolution either. "It's way too late for the state to say it's sorry for keeping blacks in bondage for all those years," thought the eighteen-year-old student Tasha Tolar, "so why bring it up when slavery is over and done?" Nonetheless, such resolutions, despite lacking practical implications, did at least represent some attempt to atone for the racism and injustice of the past.[4]

Much more specifically directed to the struggle for school integration was the Virginia state legislature's decision in 2004 to establish a $2 million scholarship fund to mark the fiftieth anniversary of the *Brown* decision and to acknowledge the damage done to black children during the years of massive resistance—when state authorities closed whole school systems rather than desegregate them. Most white children were able to continue their education in private academies, but thousands of blacks were forced to drop out altogether or move away from home. Aldrena Thirkell, now fifty-seven, was one such. When her school in Farmville closed for good, she and her brothers were sent away to Baltimore, forcing years of separation from her mother that still caused her pain. As one of the first sixty Virginians to receive a *Brown* scholarship, she planned to use the money to study creative writing and, thus, to share her bitter recollections of segregation's travails. "My main thing is to maybe, hopefully, provide a voice for people who didn't have a voice, to tell them it's okay to express your feelings," she reflected. Virginia's governor, Mark Warner, saw these scholarships not as "a reparations type of deal" but rather as a belated attempt to give some education to those denied it as children. For the editor of the *Farmville Herald,* which had once staunchly supported massive resistance, their purpose was broader. "I think this is a moment of redemption for the Commonwealth," he wrote. "It shows we can grow toward one another and we can heal the wounds of the past."[5]

A further striking example of time blunting the sharpest edges of southern racism occurred in the struggling Mississippi community of Stonewall. Located just south of Meridian, named after the Confederate hero Stonewall Jackson, and for more than a century a thriving textile town, it had lost its economic focus in 2002 when Burlington Industries closed its mill there for good. In 1969, unwelcome social change had come to Stonewall, in the form of an order that its only recreation center, a handsome, tiled Olympic-sized swimming pool, be desegregated forthwith. Built, owned, and maintained by the mill, the pool had been the "joyful center of town life" for generations of white residents, especially the children. Its black residents had only the local creeks in which to swim. Rather than allow blacks access, Burlington Industries closed the pool, a decision supported by local officials. "Being Southerners as we are," recalled Ardell Covington, who was mayor at the time, "people just didn't want to mingle that close." In particular, black men and white women swimming together "was a no-no." Not only was the pool closed; it was filled in "with truck-loads of red Mississippi dirt" until completely covered, one more casualty of the White South's intransigence in the face of mandated change.[6]

In 2006, more than thirty years on, a local businessman named Gilbert Carmichael decided to excavate the pool, part of a general desire to provide some focus in a town devastated by the loss of its single industry through the restoration and refurbishment of its decaying mill buildings as apartments and malls for people working in Meridian. To his surprised delight, it was still in serviceable shape and was reopened for the summer of 2007, this time for the whole community to use, poignant testimony to southern change but also to the wasted years that went before. "Look at all the years it's been buried," lamented the local resident Tom Sebring as he removed dirt from the partially exposed tiles, "and of no use at all."[7]

Such moments of redemption can easily be found in the contemporary South. It is nearly five decades since Martin Luther King enunciated his dream or since President Johnson acted on it. Legal segregation has gone; black southerners vote and sit in state legislatures, on court benches, and in board rooms. They govern most of the region's cities. They teach about the freedom struggle, often to students who find it impossible to believe that their grandparents lived in a world so cruelly circumscribed by race. It is, literally, outside their experience. In Birmingham, where Bull Connor had once run the most viciously racist of regimes, the office of police chief was held by a black woman, Annetta Nunn, from 2003 until her retirement in 2007. A life-size photograph of Connor's nemesis, Martin Luther King, hung on her wall. Farmville, Virginia, was once a center of the "massive resistance" movement. In April 2006, the state's then Republican senator, George Allen, chose it to make a speech in which he deplored the "legacy of separate and unequal schools" and the pain segregation had caused the community. At his side stood Democratic representative John L. Lewis, King's trusted bridge to the SNCC. He had learned much from Lewis, Allen freely admitted, "about cruelty and inhumanity," but also about "the power of forgiveness." When officials in Montgomery hired a design firm to reshape the city's downtown blocks, its brief was to rebuild a space that now "belongs to the whole nation because of what happened here." The twin legacies of the Civil War and the civil rights movement "would reverberate literally for centuries" through their work.[8]

But who could doubt, either, that the South's grim past lies never far below this changed surface? White city councillors in Hattiesburg, Mississippi, were both astonished and irritated at the vehemence with which their black colleagues fought to change the name of one of the city's downtown thoroughfares. What was originally called Mobile Street had had its name changed to Market Street just prior to the Second World War in order to define more distinctly the white and black areas of the city. Prior to that, as Mobile Street, it had been the center of black business and street life, a vibrant, distinctive area that annoyed, then threatened the white community, the more so as black and white servicemen from training camps nearby crowded there for the music, the liquor, and the women. There was race tension in the air, and the solution was to drive the black businesses out, then symbolically rename the district. In 2006, as part of post-Katrina rebuilding, the whole downtown was to be refurbished—including Market Street. In that context, black councillors sought to have the district's original name restored. White residents and businesspeople could see no purpose in the change, but black citizens, a few of whom could still remember it as it once was, became increasingly adamant. Mobile Street was part of their history; white folk had taken it from them. The dispute split the city council on racial lines, and an uneasy compromise—that the district be designated Market-Mobile Street for a year before any further action—satisfied no one. "As an African-American community, we've continually been told 'not now,'" complained Councilwoman Deborah Delgado. "Just because some people don't know our history and the reason for our pride in that community, we are again being told to wait." White councillors could not see her point. The change would, they thought, seriously inconvenience white businessowners, already reeling from the effects of Katrina. Market Street had been the name for nearly seventy years and should remain so. In these two communities, living in one small city but with parallel histories, the racialized past continually cast a long shadow.[9]

Commemorative events often brought such different histories into sharp conflict. Emilye Crosby calls the epilogue to her wonderful study of the civil rights struggle in Claiborne County, Mississippi, "Looking the Devil in the Eye: Who Gets to Tell the Story?" "Most of the community's history holds different meanings for blacks and whites," she writes, asserting that most whites now profess to have only the haziest of recollections of the beatings, the shootings, and the church burnings that for blacks are still the raw signposts of their freedom struggle. Crosby then described how these "divergent views on the community's history" greatly influenced the attempts by civic leaders, particularly in the county seat of Port Gibson, to try and attract tourists to the area by focusing on a celebration of its antebellum past. That type of romanticized image, with its enduring overtones of slavery and white supremacy, was anathema to black citizens, but the more recent past, with its sustained fight against segregation and white control, was one that white citizens preferred to forget. In December 1994, a permanent exhibition, "No Easy Journey," celebrating Claiborne County's civil rights movement opened, but with limited and uneasy white involvement. Crosby contrasts this with the much greater enthusiasm for an earlier exhibit built around the photographs of a local white planter, all taken early in the twentieth century, that "conveyed the community's history (and African Americans) through the eyes of a very wealthy and powerful white man." Similarly, *Cannonballs and Courage,* a book published in 2003 to celebrate Port Gibson's bicentennial and mainly financed by the local business community, was written entirely from a white perspective, to the point of caricature. A few months later, black high school students, in *Holla: Claiborne County Teenagers Have Their Say,* a dramatized depiction of their local history, offered a perspective in which the saccharine racial harmonies of *Cannonballs* gave way to a world of continuing racial division. The two communities are still far apart in an understanding of their shared histories. What has changed, concludes Crosby, "is that now African Americans, including high school students working with a cultural arts organization, can publicly assert a vision of their community at odds with the one put forth by white leaders." That is a powerful and enduring accomplishment of the civil rights years.[10]

In 1959, Robert C. Khyatt was the placekicker for the University of Mississippi's celebrated Rebels football team, kicking goals for Ole Miss to the strains of "Dixie" in a stadium swirling with Confederate flags.

Nearly forty years later, as the university's new chancellor, he called for a "campus-wide period of self-analysis" aimed at ending further use of such Confederate symbols at Ole Miss. Since James Meredith's enrollment in 1962, the university's growing number of black students had made no secret of how offensive they found them. More, the school's racist image, said the football coach, Tommy Tuberville, "was devastating for recruiting." Potential faculty members, too, had listed Ole Miss's devotion to Confederate traditions as a reason for going elsewhere. Alumni, especially, were outraged at Khyatt's action, as were some white students. "They're part of our Southern heritage," lamented Christopher Bridgewater, a senior from Memphis. But, in the post–civil rights South, such reminders of its racist past held dwindling currency, irate alumni notwithstanding. Tellingly, the campus bookstore had stopped selling the most sacred of all southern symbols, the Confederate flag, even before Khyatt's call: cheerleaders at the football games waved it no longer.[11]

Throughout the region, public display of the Confederate flag divided black and white southerners with intensifying ferocity. After the *Brown* decision and the quickening demand for black civil rights, some states of the Old Confederacy took to flying the battle flag atop their state capitols as a potent symbol of defiance, though only Alabama and South Carolina persisted with the practice for more than a few years. In 1993, Alabama's Democratic governor, James E. Folsom Jr., unexpectedly thrust into office by the abrupt removal of his predecessor, declared that the flag would no longer fly in Montgomery, leaving South Carolina as the sole holdout. There, in November 1996, Republican governor David Beasley, in a statewide television address prompted by an increasing number of flag-waving racial incidents, urged South Carolinians "to compromise on the Confederate flag, and teach our children that we can live together." He advocated the symbol's removal from the statehouse to a nearby Confederate memorial, a proposal that required legislative approval. It took four years of bitter debate and escalating violence before this was achieved. "The Confederate flag's not for sale here," Jake Knotts, a state representative from Lexington County, declared in 1999. Blacks were equally adamant that it had to go. "The flag embraces and perpetuates the ideology of white supremacy," said Carl B. Grant, a Columbia lawyer. In 1999, the NAACP called for an economic boycott of South Carolina because of the flag issue. The following year, the New York Knicks, who had been regularly using Charleston as their preseason training base, decided to locate elsewhere, announcing that they would return when the flag stopped flying. Citing the example of Alabama, where Mercedes and Honda had established plants once the state had moved "past its history," Paula Harper Bethea, the chair of the state chamber of commerce, urged South Carolina to do likewise. In a "shrinking world," she pleaded, the South could be an island unto itself no longer. "If we are going to be part of the next millennium, we have to move that flag off our Statehouse, and put it in a place of honor elsewhere."[12]

In the words of NAACP president Julian Bond, "Money talks." In May 2000, after fierce debate in which the economic damage caused by the controversy was emphasized, the South Carolina state legislature decided that, on June 30, the flag would fly above the statehouse for the last time. Though hard-liners on both sides found the outcome unacceptable, most were relieved that the controversy had ended. A crowd of three thousand gathered to watch the flag's lowering; there were some angry interchanges but no violence. Indeed, many South Carolinians of both races rather saw the event "as a signal of renewal." "It's a historic occasion, no doubt about that," reflected J. Todd Rutherford, a black member of the House of Representatives. Speaker David H. Wilkins agreed. "This is a defining moment for our state," he said, "a giant step forward."[13]

School redistricting issues still occasionally have the capacity to reignite past tensions, particularly in small southern towns and rural counties where residential separation is not a cause of de facto school resegregation, where voluntary desegregation plans are in operation, or where court orders still apply. Sometimes busing can even make an unwelcome reappearance. In 2006, the school board in Covington County, Mississippi, and the Department of Justice agreed on a plan to resolve a forty-year-old desegregation suit. A number of students from a predominantly black middle school in Hopewell would, henceforth, attend high school in Seminary, thirty miles away, rather than in nearby Mt. Olive or Collins, which were mainly black, while a smaller number of white students from Seminary would also be bused to other schools. Sending the Hopewell students to Seminary, which was 91 percent white, explained school board chair Sammy Herrin, would eventually raise its percentage of black students to around 35, thus satisfying Justice Department requirements. The solution, however, satisfied no one, not the local NAACP branch, not the Hopewell parents, who argued that it laid the main burden of integration on their children, and certainly not the white Seminary parents whose children would be sent elsewhere to make way for the Hopewell students. "To take the kids from here and truck them 20, 30 miles," said Herbert Harper, a white Hopewell businessman. "They'll have to get up before dawn. I just have a problem seeing what it's going to accomplish other than irritating both black and white folks in Covington County." The settlement had certainly done that. "I understand the history of our government and how it has coddled these rednecks down here in Mississippi for the last 300 to 400 years and has mistreated its black citizens by denying them a proper education," angrily asserted Lyndale McGee, the president of Covington County

Concerned Citizens, a local activist group with close ties to the NAACP, as he vowed to continue to fight for a fairer outcome. An online forum run by the *Hattiesburg American* starkly illustrated the continuing capacity of school desegregation issues to ignite raw racial conflict. "I strongly disagree with the comments mr. magge [*sic*] made he called us rednecks what if Ike Sanford would have called them n-word?" posted "pitbullboy." There were scores of similar attacks on McGee from outraged whites, while blacks generally supported his contention that it was the black children of Hopewell who were predominantly the victims of the suit's settlement. Mississippi's divided past had again burst the fragile veneer of racial healing.[14]

In High Point, North Carolina, where in 2006 the school board voluntarily redrew district attendance lines in order to provide for greater diversity in the city's three high schools, the debate was carried on in more temperate tones than in Covington County, but the racial divisions were similarly apparent. While black parents, though disappointed that some children would no longer attend their neighborhood school, were generally supportive of the school board's action, many white parents were much less accepting. "Diversity is fine if it happens naturally," argued Lindalyn Kakadelis. "But when you start forcing it, you're not going to achieve what you need to achieve." "Students don't like the redistricting," claimed fifteen-year-old Brittany White. The issue over diversity "doesn't make sense," she added. Students should, she thought, always be able to attend the school nearest their home. Again, in the post–civil rights South, school attendance lines still had the capacity to divide.[15]

In 2007, fifty years after "the epic desegregation struggle at Central High School," and in the wake of a federal judge's ruling that the city's schools were fully desegregated, the Little Rock, Arkansas, school district was once more sundered by race. At bitter issue were the plans of the school district superintendent, Roy Brooks, to raise test scores and improve the general quality of the schools by slashing the board's bureaucracy, cutting nonteaching jobs, and even closing some schools to check white flight. Brooks, who is black, was supported by white board members—now a minority—and most white parents but opposed by a black community increasingly determined to oust him. The dispute threatened to overshadow the symbolic overtones of the commemorative year, revealing a community still embroiled in the issues of the past. "I've never seen anything like this—the divisiveness, the hate," said the teachers' union leader, Katharine Wright Knight. The civil rights lawyer John Walker angrily accused Brooks of having no identification with the concerns of the black community. "The only thing he stands for is putting black people down," he claimed. Whites hailed the cuts, arguing that test scores were already on the improve, proof that Brooks' tough approach was working. Andre Guerrero, a white school board member, said the dispute demonstrated that the racial battle lines of 1957 still stood, just in different form. Eventually, the board had its way, Brooks's contract was not renewed, and some white parents removed their children from the public schools as a consequence.[16]

The ongoing tension was set aside temporarily in September 2007 as Little Rock commemorated the fiftieth anniversary of the struggle. Yet again, the Little Rock Nine returned to Central High, reported the *New York Times*, this time in three white stretch limousines as fans "swarmed them for autographs and pictures." Former president Bill Clinton, the presidential aspirant Senator Hillary Rodham Clinton, governors, congressmen, civil rights icons, community business leaders, all were there to welcome them back on a day of "unmitigated adulation of the nine" and in celebration of what their actions had meant. Yet, as Gary Orfield pointed out, the "high point of desegregation in the Little Rock School District" was long gone. In 1980, the average black student attended schools that were 50 percent white. In 2007, the percentage had shrunk to 20. Central High itself was 40 percent white, a better balance than in the other area schools, but also on the decline. Little Rock was "in the situation that a lot of the South is," he warned once more, and, given the Supreme Court ruling against even voluntary raced-based plans, it would become even more rapidly resegregated, a reality the anniversary celebrations could not mask.[17]

Desegregation was long gone in Wilcox County, deep in Alabama's Black Belt, by 2007. There, the struggle to enforce the civil rights laws had been ferociously resisted. Referring to Dan Barry's wry remark, Rosie Collier Shamburger, the county school superintendent and, thus, responsible for twenty-two hundred students, only ten of whom were white, said, "True integration in the county's school system lasted only as long as it takes to walk out a door." White residents established several private academies so "that their children would not have to sit beside children of another color," while the state's financing formula ensured that the public schools would be systematically shortchanged. Decades and several court battles later, the situation has much improved. Court-enforced changes to the funding system plus increasing county taxes have meant far better facilities and, with these, rising test scores. But the schools remain almost entirely black as white children have never drifted back to the system. Nor are they likely to. Fifty years after Little Rock, life in Wilcox County "remains complicated," as it does elsewhere in the rural South.[18]

Online newspaper blogs often provided sites for lingering white racism, usually under the cloak of anonymity. "They should also be taught that Blacks in Africa enslaved other Blacks and then, for the right price, sold their black slaves to white merchants who brought them to America," was one response to a story in the *Hattiesburg American* describing a course on slavery offered in a local middle school. "Why is it that everything in this country has to always be black or white?" wrote another. Surely it was high time that "sleeping dogs" were left to lie. A third wanted to know, "What makes a Honky a honky and a Cracker a cracker," implying that blacks were also inclined to use insulting terms when referring to their fellow southerners. Commemorative events of particular significance to black southerners—like Black History Month or the Martin Luther King holiday—can also be relied on to produce such responses. Ku Klux Klan rallies—of which there are now very few—have a similar potential, although, more often than not, protesters outnumber the true believers. At one such rally, in Athens, Alabama, in September 2007, several hundred people from area churches drowned out the Klan's racist rhetoric with hymn singing and chants of "Love." James Williams, of Tanner, Alabama, who is black, attended the rally with his white wife, Andrea, and three of their five children. He was not afraid "to have his young children hear the Klan message of racial hatred and separation," he said. "We believe in Jesus Christ and we are raising our children up in the church and these guys won't change their minds." Though the city had issued the Klan leaders with a parade permit, they decided it wiser not to proceed, and, indeed, only three of them dared to don their distinctive gowns and hoods.[19]

Insults, epithets, symbolic actions, and violence were all part of the mix that focused national attention on the small timber town of Jena, Louisiana, in 2007 and that, to some, showed how little the South had changed since the 1960s. In September the previous year, three nooses had appeared, tied to an oak tree on the grounds of the local high school. Traditionally, white students only had sat in its shade, but the previous day a black student had defied this convention. Race relations at the school had always been tense, reflecting those in the larger Jena community. When the predominantly white school board, dismissing the nooses as merely a youthful prank, suspended the white students responsible for three days only, these tensions escalated. There was fighting between black and white students, there was arson, and, on December 4, six black students attacked a white youth, Justin Barker, to avenge an earlier racial insult. The victim, bruised and concussed, spent a few hours in the hospital but recovered sufficiently to attend a party, where friends described him as "his usual smiling self." Nevertheless, the six black youths who had attacked him were arrested and charged with second-degree attempted murder, though the charges were later scaled back. In June 2007, the first of six to be tried was seventeen-year-old Mychal Bell, a promising football player who had been in trouble previously and was on parole at the time of the assault. Bell, who had been in jail since his arrest, was convicted by an all-white jury of aggravated battery and, thus, faced up to twenty-two years imprisonment. Jena, wrote the journalist Gary Younge, had quickly become "a national symbol of racial injustice." Civil rights groups throughout the nation took to the internet, using YouTube, Web mail, and bulk e-mail to campaign against the way the students, known collectively as the Jena Six, had been treated, in what seemed a "throwback to the worst kind of Deep South justice."[20]

In September, a Louisiana appeals court overturned Bell's conviction on the grounds that he should have been tried as a minor, given that he was only sixteen when the assault occurred. He remained in custody, however, as District Attorney Reed Walters decided whether to appeal. Consequently, organizers decided to proceed with a day of protest on September 20, the date of Bell's scheduled sentencing. Thousands of demonstrators filed through Jena's dusty streets in a spectacle reminiscent of the great marches more than four decades previously, a point not lost on either the organizers or the speakers. "That's not a prosecution, that's persecution," the Reverend Jesse Jackson told the crowd of ten thousand gathered at the La Salle Parish Courthouse. "We will not stop marching until justice runs down like water." Martin Luther King III also spoke, imploring the crowd to remember his father's message. Eric Depradine, a senior at the University of Louisiana at Lafayette, well understood the demonstration's connection with the past. "This is the first time something like this has happened for our generation," he remarked. "You always heard about it from history books and relatives. This is a chance to experience it for ourselves." The Democrat presidential aspirants Senators Hillary Clinton and Barack Obama and former senator John Edwards all issued statements urging justice in the case, as did President Bush. "All of us in America want there to be fairness when it comes to justice," Bush told reporters.[21]

In a long op-ed piece in the *New York Times*, the sociologist Orlando Patterson asked what "really attracted thousands of demonstrators to the small Louisiana town." While the opportunity to relive the civil rights era had its attractions for some, most were there for a more contemporary purpose. The protest, he thought, "was a long overdue cry of outrage at the use of the prison system as a means of controlling young black men," and Mychal Bell's conviction had been a symbol of this. "A tenth of all black men between ages 20 and 35 are in jail or prison," he pointed out, and, while this certainly reflected an unfair law enforcement system, it also pointed to "catastrophic" problems within the black social structure. The Jena miscarriage of justice, he hoped, would do more than reinforce stereotypical notions of a racist legal system. It should also focus black attention on "the simple fact that young black men commit a disproportionate number of crimes, especially violent crimes, which cannot be attributed to judicial bias, racism or economic hardship." If the African American community started to address this problem, then the Jena outrage could have a positive and lasting effect.[22]

The Jena demonstration was a peaceful one, but, as the participants left for home, they were again reminded of the South's ugly past. As they waited for their buses, a white youth drove through their ranks, "hangman's nooses dangling from the rear of his pick-up truck." Jeremiah Munsen was quickly arrested and charged on several counts, but not the one his arresting officer most wished to use. "I wish we had a charge in Louisiana for aggravated ignorance," complained police sergeant Clifford Gatlin, "because this is a classic case." Mychal Bell's fortunes, on the other hand, briefly took a turn for the better. After talks with Governor Kathleen Blanco, District Attorney Walters decided against appealing the decision to send the case to juvenile court, and, shortly after, Bell was released on $45,000 bail. He and his parents immediately left Jena temporarily for their "safety and welfare," following a series of threats to their lives. Subsequently, the town council voted unanimously "to create an interracial committee to study racial relations" in the community and identify any problems. For the town's black residents, the action was far too little and came far too late. It was a racist town, said the Jena native Casa Compton. "There's always been prejudice and bigotry here. Everyday they're throwing away a black man's life down here." True, the oak tree that had set everything in motion had been chopped down, but its roots were still there.[23]

The aftershocks continued in Jena in the weeks ahead. Mychal Bell's period of freedom was short-lived. Within a few days, he was back in jail, a state district judge having decided that the attack on Barker constituted a violation of his earlier parole, and he was sent to prison for eighteen months. Moreover, he still faced trial in juvenile court for the alleged attack. The House Judiciary Committee held a hearing on the matter with federal officials and community activists at which black members angrily attacked the first black U.S. attorney for Louisiana's western district, Donald Washington, for failing to involve the federal government in the case. "Shame on you," shouted Representative Sheila Jackson Lee, a Texas Democrat. "Why didn't you intervene?" Most ominously, nooses started appearing throughout the country—looped over a tree at the University of Maryland, in a locker at a Long Island police station, on the sports field at a North Carolina high school. "[The noose] is a symbol of America's oldest form of domestic terrorism," deplored Hilary O. Shelton, the director of the NAACP's Washington office. The events in Jena had brought it back.[24]

The Jena issue continued to simmer as Bell awaited trial in juvenile

court in December for Barker's beating. Thousands of protesters surrounded the Justice Department headquarters in mid-November,
demanding that the new attorney general, Michael B. Mukasey, intervene. In a general statement, Mukasey pointed out that, though his
agency was working with local police and civil rights groups to "investigate aggressively dozens of noose-hangings and other recent racially
and religiously motivated" crimes, he had no authority to stop Bell's
trial from proceeding. To most people's profound relief, however, Bell's
lawyers and the local prosecutor eventually negotiated a plea agreement
that avoided a second trial and limited the amount of detention time for
the teenager to around eight months. Bell agreed to plead guilty to one
charge of second-degree battery, to testify against his codefendants
should they stand trial, to pay $935 to Barker's family, to undergo coun-
seling, and to "be reintegrated into the school system." In return, the
prosecution agreed to credit the ten months he had already served
toward his eighteen-month sentence. Carol Powell Lexing, one of Bell's
lawyers, emphasized that, while the defense team was "prepared to go
forward with the trial," they had "to do what's best for the client," and
the plea bargain would enable him to get on with his life. Moreover, District Attorney Walters was hopeful that he could reach similar agreements with the remaining defendants. Though he insisted that neither
the "intense" media coverage nor the civil rights demonstrations had
influenced his decision, there could be little doubt that all Jena's citizens
hoped that they could now move on.[25]

Despite the idealized situation presented in television series such as
In the Heat of the Night, where a wise and tolerant white chief of police
(Carroll O'Connor) presided over a happily integrated workplace in the
fictional Mississippi town of Sparta, southern police departments were
often very difficult to integrate successfully. Some still remain potential
sites of racial tension, uneasy windows to the past. What occurred in
Greensboro, North Carolina, in 2006 starkly illustrates this point. In
January, after an investigation lasting several months, the city's white
police chief, David Wray, was forced to resign, the circumstances vividly
throwing into relief both the changes that had occurred and the continuities that persisted in the post–civil rights South. This investigation
showed that Wray, who had joined the department in 1981 as a patrol-
man, had deliberately targeted black officers, including his own deputy,
Tim Bellamy, for secret internal investigations by a coterie of white officers and that these had led to the deliberate planting of evidence as well
as to unfair suspension and dismissal. Wray had even kept a "black
book" containing false and racist comments about his black fellow officers. Yet it was one of these, Lieutenant James Hinson, though suspended and falsely branded by Wray as a suspected drug dealer, who had

first stood up publicly against him, thereby forcing the investigation, and it was a white official, the city manager, Mitchell Johnson, who forced Wray out of office. Wray's African American assistant, Tim Bellamy, took over on an interim basis, later to be confirmed permanently in the office, to the general approbation of his fellow officers and most of the local community. Hinson's lawyer, Joe Williams, summed up the wider meaning of Wray's ousting. "Thanks to a courageous Lieutenant Hinson, city manager and city attorney, the good old boy network is gone forever in the Greensboro Police Department," he told reporters. Wray, he implied, exemplified the persistence of racial attitudes belonging to the southern past, while Johnson and Hinson represented the South as it could become.[26]

Nevertheless, the dispute exposed simmering racial divisions on the Greensboro City Council, the more acutely after a highly confidential report into the charges against Wray had been leaked to the press. Though she vehemently denied the allegation, the flamboyant and acerbic Dianne Bellamy-Small, a black council member, was widely suspected of being the culprit. Eventually, a white council member, Florence Gatten, publicly called for her resignation, describing her as a "rogue" and a systematic abuser of power. Bellamy-Small refused to oblige; members of the black community charged Gatten with launching a "political lynching campaign," claiming that she personified "the depths of racism" still present in the town. In an atmosphere growing steadily more rancorous, Bellany-Small's opponents collected enough signatures from both whites and blacks to force Greensboro's first recall election since 1927. The poll was a triumph for Bellamy-Small, who gained 65 percent of the vote, but did little to relieve the unease in the black community. According to Wray's lawyer, Kent Keller, Greensboro had become a city where "the neutral ground" between the races was fast disappearing.[27]

Mayor Johnny Dupree's problems with the Hattiesburg Police Department were different, though stemming from the same historic roots. When he nominated two black department heads, including David Wynn as police chief, the racially polarized city council, with whites in a majority of one, insisted that they would not be confirmed. Acting on a provision giving him "a reasonable length of time" to present his nominees, the mayor installed them into office anyway. Incensed, the white council members filed suit against Dupree to force him to bring on the vote. Meanwhile, a number of white police officers left the department. The reasons they gave were various, and, though most had to do with aspects of Wynn's management style, his race, though mentioned obliquely, was always a factor. "The whole mayor/council department heads debacle has escalated into a shameful mess," angrily editorialized the local newspaper. Hattiesburg "had made such a valiant effort in the past 20 years to overcome its past," but, unlike Sparta, Hattiesburg was a real Mississippi town. That past could not be so easily overcome.[28]

Wynn, tired of the fight, eventually moved on to a position in airport security, but his departure changed little. Dupree's choice as his successor, Frazier Bolton of the Atlanta Police Department and also black, was similarly opposed by the white council members, who wished to confirm Acting Chief Frank Misenhelter in the job, on the grounds that "the time is not right to bring in a new chief." Black councillors and community leaders claimed that race was the real issue, and they were right. It was left to James Dukes, a white Hattiesburg attorney and a member of the team that had successfully prosecuted Vernon Dahmer Sr.'s murderers, to state this unequivocally. "Let's take the lid off this meeting here tonight, because you and I know what this is about," he told a crowded gathering of concerned citizens. "Don't hide behind the idea" that anything else mattered. Stella Mackabee implored all the councillors to let the past go and to come together for the good of the community. Council president Kim Bradley did heed these appeals. After the meeting, he decided to change his position to one of support for Bolton, who was confirmed the next day by a majority vote. "I am not doing this to avoid the flag of racism," he claimed during a long speech, but rather so that the community could start healing. Black community leaders applauded his change of heart. "This . . . could be a catalyst to bring healing and allow us to move forward in a positive way," thought Forrest County's NAACP branch president, Clarence Magee. Some white residents were less sanguine. "Thanks for nothing," wrote one newspaper blogger to Bradley, accusing him of showing "no guts" and of capitulating to black pressure yet again. "Hummer" could see little between Bolton and his predecessor. "I think he even looks like Wynn," he thought, "just not as dark." Racial division and distrust still determined the shape of local politics.[29]

Lowndes County, Alabama, the Black Panther Party's symbolic home, had elected a black sheriff since the 1965 Voting Rights Act and the eventual triumph of the iconic John Hulett. When his popular successor, Willie Vaughner, died suddenly in July 2007, there was a general assumption among the county's majority-black population that his longtime deputy, John A. Williams, would succeed him. Consequently, there was outrage when Governor Bob Riley chose instead a white parole officer, Charlie W. "Chip" Williams. Again, racial tensions surfaced quickly. "If this was Shelby County, Cullman County, where there is a vast majority white population, would the Governor go on a limb and appoint a black official to this position?" angrily asked Hulett's son, the county probate judge. Whites pointed out that Chip Williams had run against Vaughner in the last election, receiving more than 25 percent of the vote, and was, thus, next in line. Moreover, given the county's rising crime rate, the governor was right to "go with someone who might better get the job done." Scores of online newspaper comments demonstrated that Lowndes County's black and white citizens, too, still thought about issues in predominantly racial terms and that those connected with law enforcement were particularly divisive.[30]

These complex issues of race, class, gender, and equal justice conjoined in 2006 in an extraordinary situation that arose at one of the nation's most prestigious education institutions, Duke University, in Durham, North Carolina, one that gripped the nation for weeks and was widely reported internationally. In March 2006, a city police officer took a call from a young black woman who said that she had been invited to dance at a private house party earlier in the evening. There, she alleged, three members of Duke's elite men's lacrosse team had sexually assaulted her in the bathroom of the residence, which happened to be that of two of the team's captains. When it was revealed that she was a part-time student at historically black North Carolina Central University and that the three accused were all from economically privileged northern backgrounds, the symbolic dimensions of the incident were clear. Local blacks demanded swift retribution, as did their national leaders. The Reverend Jesse Jackson said that his Rainbow/PUSH Coalition would pay the victim's college tuition henceforth so that she would "never again . . . have to stoop that low to survive," and black and white students demonstrated nightly outside the house where her rape had allegedly taken place. For Komo Davis, "the school he had once considered a source of pride had become a source of shame and animosity." Nothing had really changed; the racism of the past had become "subversive": "It's almost covert, but it's still here." Bishop John Bennett of Durham's Church of the Apostolic Revival told a news conference that demonstrations would continue until "justice is served." The house, meanwhile, had become "a symbol of a system that caters to and protects the rich"—and white.[31]

The university's leadership reacted swiftly. President Richard Brodhead canceled the remainder of the team's season, whereupon its coach resigned. He also appointed two panels, one to investigate the team's behavior, the other to examine the university's handling of the matter. Meanwhile, Durham district attorney Mike Nifong, at the time running for reelection, announced that his office would aggressively investigate the young woman's allegations and that criminal charges were likely to be laid. In mid-April, two of the accused players, Ryan Seligmann and Collin Finnerty, were arrested and charged with first-degree forcible rape, first-degree sexual offense, and kidnapping. A third player, David Evans, was arrested and charged a few days later. President Brodhead expressed relief that the course of justice was on track and stressed that "the university and the city needed to work to restore the bonds this episode has strained." In New York, the Reverend Al Sharpton put his plans to visit the Duke campus in support of the victim on hold pending the court proceedings.[32]

Scarcely had the young men been arrested, however, than the prosecution's case started to unravel. Over the following months, it became clear that, contrary to Nifong's assertion, there was no credible DNA evidence connecting the three accused to their supposed victim or even suggesting that she had been raped at all. She, herself, constantly changed her account of what had happened and was eventually revealed to have a history of making false accusations to the police. Moreover, Nifong was shown to have deliberately withheld evidence from the defense team, to have committed several other breaches of the law, and to have otherwise behaved unethically. Eventually, he was removed from the case, all charges against the three were dropped, and the North Carolina attorney general publicly declared them to be "totally innocent" of any offenses. The university reached a financial settlement with the accused, and President Brodhead apologized for giving way to public opinion in "not demanding the presumption of innocence" for them. He, along with the Duke community, had to learn that "instant moral certainty before the facts had been established" could seriously damage human lives. Eventually, the only person to go to jail was Nifong, for contempt of court following his disbarment, his thirty-year career in tatters. Yet the demonizing of the young men did not end. Tricia Dowd, of Northport, New York, and the mother of a lacrosse team member, attended a meeting of angry students at North Carolina Central University where the prevailing sentiment was that they should still be prosecuted, "whether it happened or not," to atone for past sins and that it was time for blacks to consider "retributive correction" given that fear of such violence had long proved to be "the only deterrent to white supremacy." Mrs. Dowd admitted to extreme naïveté. "I didn't know there was so much hate in the world," she said. The whole matter had done serious damage to Duke University's reputation. It had cost the three young men a year of their lives—better than "30 years in prison for a hoax," said Ryan Seligmann, but severely "emotionally damaging" nonetheless. Most importantly, it had shown how the ugly legacy of racial distrust and hatred could still so swiftly divide even the most liberal of southern communities.[33]

When the Democratic presidential candidate John Edwards embarked on a tour designed to highlight the enduring nature of poverty in America, it was scarcely surprising that it began in the Mississippi Delta. Past presidential aspirants and incumbents had taken the same confronting path. "I found out something I never knew," declared Robert Kennedy after his visit there in 1968. "I found out that my world was not the real world." More familiar with southern poverty, President Clinton was, nevertheless, sufficiently distressed by what he saw during a 1999 visit that he immediately pledged $15 million to the Delta for community development projects. Again, in 2007, John Edwards briefly reminded America that 20 percent of Mississippians still lived below the poverty level, and television once again beamed images of homes without bathrooms, children without adequate food, and young people without hope in counties with double-digit unemployment rates. Moreover, the rural poor were disproportionately black; the great reforms and consequent social changes of the past fifty years had not altered that basic circumstance. It was their voices, "their personal stories," that Edwards hoped to share with the nation.[34]

The reasons for the persistence of southern rural poverty are many, and it is certainly not solely the residual effect of segregation. The collapse of the cotton industry at both the growing and the manufacturing levels destroyed the economic landscape that had prevailed for more than a century, while the tobacco and steel industries suffered similar structural shifts. The swift spread of Hispanics, often recent arrivals, throughout the southern states vastly complicated their racial mix and increased the competition for the diminishing number of unskilled, low-wage jobs available. Yet race always determines so much else. Of the billions of federal dollars that went in agricultural subsidies to the Delta region between 2001 and 2005, 95 percent went to large commercial farms, almost all of which were white owned.

Poverty stricken Bolivar County was illustrative. White farmers there received $200 million in crop subsidies, but, throughout the whole region, just $11 million went into Rural Development program grants "to replace the abandoned factories, decaying houses and boarded-up downtowns in dozens of dirt-poor, majority-black Delta towns." The small agricultural community of Shelby, in Bolivar County, was typical. "It's just a sad situation," lamented Judy Hall, the leader of a women's group desperately trying to save what little was left of the town. "There is no industries, no factories, no hope for the future, nothing to keep the people here." Yet Shelby was once a thriving commercial community, with "theaters, service stations and steakhouses," its prosperity firmly based on cotton and rice. Now, the stores were mostly boarded up, and the white population had fled, leaving a community 90 percent black and with a median household income of $17,798—less than half the national average. Shelby received only $106,000 from the Rural Development program, which it spent on police cars and a mower. The wide disparity between farm subsidies and Rural Development community money has done more than simply preserve the Delta's two-tiered, racially structured economy; it has widened the "economic chasm between the races, according to local residents, government officials and researchers," wrote the *Washington Post* reporters Gilbert M. Gaul and Dan Morgan. Nothing much had changed "for 200 to 300 years," said Ben Burkett, a black farmer. Whites still owned most of the land, and with that came economic control. True, the Voting Rights Act meant that black state legislators like John Mayo now represented these Delta counties, including Bolivar. The schools, though mostly black owing to white flight, were, nevertheless, better funded, but to little purpose. "We've lost entire generations of young blacks because we told them to stay in school and get a good job," Mayo said. But there were no jobs there when they graduated. The "smart kids" mainly left. Shelby and its counterparts were, thus, full of "families who have given up hope." G. Reeves Neblett, a white Shelby lawyer and agribusinessman, who had received $3 million in federal payments since 2001, agreed with Mayo. In his opinion, "the economic and education gap" between Bolivar County's whites and blacks was now far too wide ever to be bridged. "We are now to the point that it is such a culture difference between those who are privileged and who had the education that I don't know how you will close that" was his sad judgment, one he shared with Shelby's black mayor, Dorothy Grim. Social and political change had come to Bolivar County—she was proof of that—yet to little real economic effect.[35]

The superb 2000 Pulitzer Prize–winning *New York Times* series "How Race Is Lived in America" included an account of a typical working day at the Smithfield Packing Company, in Bladen County, North Carolina, that graphically illustrated the complex intersections of race relations and economic inequality in the contemporary South. Most of the supervisors in the vast hog-killing plant were white and the skilled tradespeople Lumbee Indians, leaving the hard, unskilled, dirty, low-paid slaughtering and cutting jobs to blacks and Mexicans—the latter recently arrived in Robeson County, often illegally, and prepared to work for minimal wages. Racial tensions abounded at Smithfield, between white supervisors and black workers, between the Lumbees and the whites, and increasingly between blacks and Latinos. Blacks bitterly resented the willingness of the newcomers to accept $7.70 an hour without complaint; the Hispanic workers were frightened by such aggression, which frequently spilled over into life outside the plant. The lack of a common language, too, increased these divisions. At the plant, the cafeterias and locker rooms were self-segregated: there were separate English and Spanish lines at the social security office and the county health clinics. As for the few whites working on the killing floor, the Latinos simply added a further dimension to their historical racial prejudices. "The tacos are worse than the niggers," an old white worker complained to his Indian workmate, who simply "leaned against the wall and laughed." In Robeson County, too, the half century of change had done very little to reshape the lives or outlook of the working poor, black, white, or recently arrived.[36]

Perhaps the saddest consequence of the persistence of southern poverty has been the upsurge in infant deaths. For decades, infant mortality rates had steadily declined, but, in "an ominous portent," the trend has now reversed throughout the Southeast, with Alabama, the Carolinas, Louisiana, Tennessee, and Mississippi all reporting sharp jumps in 2004 and 2005. Most striking in all states was the large racial disparity. In Mississippi, for example, where the turnaround was most acute, infant deaths among blacks rose to 17 per thousand births in 2005 from 14.2 in 2004; the rise in the white rate was from 6.1 to 6.6. Both were above the national average. Public health officials provided a litany of reasons—lack of employment opportunities, cuts to welfare and Medicaid, poor access to doctors, the growing epidemics of obesity, diabetes, and hypertension among potential mothers. All, however, could be directly linked to the persistence of poverty. "Poor mothers in general, black or white, are not as healthy," said Dr. Bouldin Marley, a Clarksdale, Mississippi, obstetrician, and increasingly they "arrive in labor having had little or no prenatal care." Lack of motivation might be a factor, but much more important was lack of means. "If you didn't have a car and had to go 60 miles to see a doctor, would you go very often?" asked Ramona Beardain, the director of Delta Health Partners, a federally funded program that targets impoverished and inexperienced pregnant teenagers and new mothers. Krystal Allen, already at seventeen a mother of two and pregnant with her third, agreed. She wanted to visit a clinic more regularly, she said, and had signed up with Medicaid to do so. But that required a trip to Greenville, thirty-six miles away, and rarely did her mother have sufficient gas in the car to take her. It was with such stories that John Edwards set out to galvanize the national conscience.[37]

Hurricane Katrina starkly reminded the nation that chronic urban poverty was not confined to the decaying industrial cities of the Northeast and Midwest and that, in the South, as elsewhere, it was disproportionately black. The images of the impoverished residents of New Orleans's Ninth Ward, unable to flee the approaching cataclysm because they lacked the means to do so, remain seared in many memories. There were those who were quick to attribute the failure of the New Orleans effort to systemic racism. There was little enthusiasm to risk money or lives to save black people, they charged. Yet, as the commentator Juan Williams has pointed out, the city's successful, black or white, had little difficulty in avoiding the storm's disastrous aftermath. "Regardless of race," he wrote, "people with cars, credit cards, bank accounts, family and friends had a way out." The poor were left behind. It seemed, said then senator Barack Obama, that the "incompetence" of the local, state, and federal governments in helping Katrina's victims "was color-blind." Studies of what is often termed the *urban underclass* have rarely been given a southern face. Rather, there has been much emphasis on stories of black southerners fleeing such tensions and returning home now that the caste system has been swept away. Yet southern cities, too, have their ghettos, their gangs, their drugs, and their violence—above all, their poverty, as Katrina showed. Deindustrialization, the drying up of unskilled jobs, as in Birmingham's steel plants, has had its bitter consequences throughout the region—and it is all the more poignant as so many of the jobs lost had but recently become accessible to blacks. As elsewhere, it is young black men who are the most disadvantaged. Southern cities now have black political, business, and administrative elites, and that is, indeed, a transformation, yet black mayors and police chiefs often preside over troubled communities, with reduced tax bases, overstretched services, inadequate schools, large-scale unemployment, and escalating crime rates.[38]

Of course, to emphasize the persistence of race-based economic inequality in the South is not to ignore the significance of the post-1965 emergence of black political and economic elites and a growing and vibrant black middle class, controlling nearly $800 billion in annual purchasing power. This could not have happened without the destruction of the caste system. When Juan Williams talks of African Americans today as being "the most highly educated and most affluent black people in world history," his words have a special resonance in the region, for it is here that this remarkable progress is most marked. Black men and women govern most of the South's larger cities and towns; they sit in the state legislatures and in the Congress of the United States. Some, like John L. Lewis, are veterans of the struggles of the 1960s, and their concerns still reflect this, but many are younger men and women, raised in the years after those battles were won. Indeed, Alabama's charismatic black congressman, Artur Davis, who aspires to become the state's first black governor, initially achieved power by seizing it from the men of the 1960s, the "Moses generation," as Gwen Ifill calls them in her recent pathbreaking book. Davis and his ilk, Ifill says, belong to the "Joshua generation," the black political leaders of the post–civil rights era. Bakari Sellers, the son of the former SNCC leader Cleveland Sellers and a South Carolina legislator, argues that the best way for him to serve his black community is through forming alliances with white and Hispanic South Carolinians—coalitions of the poor—for their basic concerns are the same. "If you are poor and black in South Carolina, or poor and white in South Carolina, you face basically the same issues," he says, "[fundamental] inequalities in health care, and education."[39]

Artur Davis's political strategies are similar, building coalitions with whites, not emphasizing past racial division. Both men point to Barack Obama's primary campaign strategy as the model to follow in the South. Obama talked about race as little as possible, in contrast with Jesse Jackson's primary campaigns of 1984 and 1988. Obama, says Davis, who was born in 1967, is, like him, clearly one of the Joshua generation; Jackson was of the older Moses vintage. But the rules in the South have changed, as they have throughout the nation. Jesse Jackson Sr. was not even asked to speak at the 2008 Democratic national convention. Instead, his son Jesse Jr.—emphatically of the "Joshua" cut—took the spotlight.[40]

Of course, black southerners do much more than practice politics; they sit on court benches, and they run police departments, school systems, and university programs. They coach the football teams at recently integrated colleges and high schools. They staff formerly whites-only hospitals, they manage branches of the same stores their parents and grandparents could shop but not eat in, and they own businesses, big and small. True, "race and poverty remain as close as red beans and rice in New Orleans," as they do less sharply in the rest of the nation; equally true, even middle-class blacks rarely have the same level of savings and investments as do white Americans. Yet, even after Katrina had exposed the brutal reality, most black Americans still believed that their position had improved in recent years and that those who were not "moving ahead" had mainly themselves to blame. In the South, more than elsewhere, the expanded access to education and the ballot box, the destruction of the barriers imposed by sanctioned racial segregation, enabled many black citizens to take control of their destiny. The overriding importance of the civil rights era, Martin Luther King said just before his death, "was what this period did to the psyche of the black man": "We straightened our backs up." That stark economic inequalities continue to exist should not mask the significance of these words or the consequential growth of the black middle class.[41]

A number of recent commentators on the transformation of the southern political economy and the consequent movement of white southerners into the Republican Party, most notably Byron E. Schafer and Richard Johnson, have deemphasized race as an explanatory factor, choosing rather to attribute this massive shift as arising from economic factors. These included the desire for lower taxes, for less government regulation, and for less welfare support for the poor, together with the individualized notion of rights so clearly articulated by the Reaganites that led them to reject the basic premises behind affirmative action policies and other collective rights-based initiatives. In so doing, they were simply part of a national trend; there was nothing uniquely southern about their behavior. Southern historians like Dan Carter, however, remain far from convinced. In a recent review article in *Dissent,* he pointed out that the levels of Republican support are far higher among white southern households of all income levels than in the rest of the nation, while the unguarded actions of men like Trent Lott in his speech supporting Strom Thurmond's Dixiecrat rebellion show that, in the politics of the contemporary South, the issue of race is still alive and well and firmly ensconced in the new southern Republicanism. When Karl Rove moved so aggressively to disenfranchise convicted felons, he did not do so in overtly racist terms, but he knew well that, in the South, doing so would deprive the Democrats of thousands of potential votes as the vast majority of those so affected were black. Similarly, in Georgia and North Carolina, Republican attempts to limit the impact of the motor voter law, and in particular the requiring of picture identification before allowing someone to vote, have been opposed for similar reasons. Such requirements, said Emmett Bondurant, a civil rights lawyer, "disproportionately affect poor, minority and elderly voters"—precisely why Republicans found them so attractive.[42]

One of the lesser-known aspects of the lives of the Little Rock Nine is that four of them have white partners. The historian Elizabeth Jacoway has noted that they never "take a group picture with their white spouses or mixed-race children," partly because they have no wish to rekindle segregationist shibboleths about mixed-race sex. Ernest Green calls it the "zipper issue." Sex and race were still "highly combustible," he claims, while Spirit Trickey, Minniejean Brown's interracial daughter, who works as a National Parks Service tour guide at the Central High memorial, says one of the questions visitors most regularly ask her is why the four crossed racial lines. Her standard response was that they "married who they fell in love with"; nevertheless, she finds the persistence of the questioning to be "telling." "Combustible" the issue still may be, but the four exemplify the fact that black-white marriages are on the rise in the South, as is, insofar as it can be measured, "dating out." In particular, black women like Toinetta Jones, of Alexandria, Virginia, are disobeying their mothers' insistence that they "never bring a white man home." For a long time, she followed this edict, she says, but now she dates "anyone who asks me out," regardless of skin color. One reason is the narrowing of the field of marriageable black men for women like Jones, who have started to scale the corporate or middle-class ladders. Black men are more than seven times more likely to be in prison than white men and more than twice as likely to be unemployed. Whatever the reasons, the number of black-wife, white-husband couples rose significantly between 2000 and 2006. Nevertheless, 75 percent of black-white unions still involve black husbands, at all socioeconomic levels, from Clarence Thomas to popular culture. In *My Name Is Earl,* a highly successful sit-com that caricatures southern lower-class life and whose plots frequently revolve around petty criminality, the show's title character maintains good relations with his strident ex-wife Joy, who now lives with Darnelle, a somewhat feckless, spaced-out black man.[43]

It is, however, impossible to quantify whether there has been any increase in close friendships and private connections between black and white southerners resulting from the end of segregation. In 2000, the *New York Times* interviewers for *How Race Is Lived in America* certainly found many folk like Gladys West, black, and Betsy Harper, white, of Grifton, North Carolina, who considered themselves best friends even though they had met only seven years previously. They had both grown up in Grifton but had had no connection before then because, said Mrs. West, "I couldn't talk to whites unless I worked for them." But the South had changed, and now the two elderly women visited each other regularly, sharing recipes, reminiscing, enjoying each other's presence. Race played no factor in their friendship, Mrs. Harper claimed. "Except when we go to church. She stays with her congregation and I stay with mine." In Decatur, Georgia, the reporter Kevin Sack found one church where whites and blacks did praise God together—the Assembly of God Tabernacle, a Pentecostal place of worship. With a membership 55 percent white, 43 percent black, and the rest Asian or mixed race, it is an oasis in a region where, as Martin Luther King once lamented, 11:00 A.M. on Sunday was still the most segregated hour of the week. The choir was "thoroughly mixed," said Sack. "Its praise and worship style music falls comfortably between the traditionally country hymns of white Pentecostalism and the thumping gospel funk of the modern black church." Moreover, mixing did not stop at the end of the service. Blacks and whites visited each other's homes, they "share rooms at retreats," and they care for each other. And in so doing, writes Sack, "these accountants and teachers, nurses and software consultants discover the common threads of their middle class lives" as well as the cultural differences they need to accommodate and the racial resentments still to be overcome.[44]

There are institutions like the Assembly of God Tabernacle scattered throughout the South, spaces where black and white southerners can get to know each other as individuals, can get past racial stereotypes. Business-oriented clubs like Rotary sometimes serve this purpose, while, in the centers of power, the elites of the two races socialize constantly at public events such as gallery openings, memorial services, football games, college ceremonials, and political fund-raisers. Nevertheless, the easy banter, the connections formed between neighbors after work or at the weekends, occurs much more rarely. The continued segregation of neighborhoods has made this very difficult, as does the legacy of the past. Even at the Assembly of God Tabernacle, history always has the potential to divide. Janice Pugh, a white member, could not comprehend "why black folks remained obsessed with race." Surely, it was time to move on. Eventually she told her black friend Rudine Hardy this. "You don't understand," Hardy snapped back. "You're not black." For her, past and present could not be so easily separated.[45]

Early in 2009, a poignant story from Montgomery County, Georgia, illustrated the uneasy fragility of contemporary southern race relations and just how difficult the separation of past and present can become. The nation had just inaugurated its first black president, yet there were two formal dances on successive nights for the fifty-four classmates who had just graduated from Montgomery County High—the first for the white students, the second the next evening for the blacks. The proms have always been separate there, as in other small southern towns. White parents continue to insist on it, despite the growing distaste of their children. Blake Conner, who is white, initially refused to attend his event, while two white sisters, Terra and Tamara Fountain, both with black boyfriends, wanted to go to the black prom but were barred from doing so. Besides, said Terra, "My mum wouldn't pay. She doesn't like me talking to black people anyway." Kera Nobles, who is black, was left "smoldering with anger" at the persistence of segregation's aftertaste. "It was the one night to see all your friends dressed up, and I'm told I have to wait . . . because of the color of my skin." She went to the white prom anyway, standing outside to support her white classmates. The next night they did the same for her. Meanwhile, the school's head, Leon Batten, made the decision to hold integrated proms in the future, despite fierce white opposition. He knew it would be hard. "But," he said, "we will persist and over time the segregation will be history."[46]

In May 2004, the *Washington Post* reporter Michael Dobbs visited the small South Carolina town of Summerton. There, nearly sixty years previously, a dispute over the provision of a bus to carry black children to their segregated and manifestly unequal schools, including Scott's Branch High, had escalated into a demand for complete school desegregation, one of the five suits that eventually became part of *Brown v. Board of Education*. Dobbs found Summerton much changed; legal segregation had long since disappeared. Scott's Branch High, rebuilt and refurbished, with "heated class rooms, a library, a gymnasium and a computer lab," bore no resemblance to the ramshackle building of 1954, with its outside toilets and cast-off text books. Its current students had no doubt that those involved in the suit had achieved their aims. They had wanted facilities for their children equal to those provided in all-white Summerton High, said one of them, Cynthia Pershia. "They achieved their goal." The school district's superintendent, Clarence Willie, agreed while at the same time confirming what had already become obvious to Dobbs. The world in which Summerton's blacks now lived had been transformed since 1954, yet, in some fundamental ways, little had changed. "The gulf between blacks and whites encompasses almost every aspect of life," he concluded. The two races still worshipped apart and socialized apart. The glistening Scott's Branch High had only six white students and two Hispanics in its total enrollment of 480. Most white children attended Clarendon Hall, a private Christian academy. The once all-white Summerton High now served as the school district's headquarters. The two communities, like those in other small southern towns, lived largely separate lives. "We can't do much about that now," mused Willie, nor did it concern him overmuch. Dolphus Weary, the president of Mission Mississippi, a Christian group actively promoting racial reconciliation through personal contact, was more optimistic. He had recently produced a cookbook, *Chit'lins to Caviar*, full of recipes from many different ethnic backgrounds. "You need to have it in your kitchen," he asserted, "so when you have a white family over for supper, you'll know what white people eat." Which vision of the region's future will prevail, Willie's or Weary's?[47]

POSTSCRIPT

The narrative in this book ends in December 2007 and, thus, does not cover the epochal presidential election campaign of 2008 or the unfolding story of Barack Obama's presidency. Yet nothing is of more significance to its narrative than his triumph. The myriad commentators who saw his accession to power as the fruition of Martin Luther King's dream were essentially correct. There were many reasons—a collapsing economy, an unpopular war, concern over the country's polarization, massive demographic change, a president who conspicuously failed to lead when it mattered most—why 2008 was a Democratic year. Nevertheless, the election of the first African American president could not have occurred without the determination to enforce the legislation of 1964 and 1965 and the committed resistance after 1980 to those who sought to dilute its effect. In that sense, Barack Obama, raised far from southern battlegrounds, was, nevertheless, the legatee of the struggles there.

This was a point not lost among the citizens of Albany, Georgia, particularly those who could remember the bitter times of the early 1960s. Rutha Mae Harris "chanted softly" a familiar refrain as she drove to the polling place that morning. "I'm going to vote like the spirit say vote," she sang.

> I'm going to vote like the spirit say vote,
> I'm going to vote like the spirit say vote,
> And if the spirit say vote, I'm going to vote,
> Oh Lord, I'm going to vote when the spirit say vote.

Rutha Mae had learned that song as a twenty-one-year-old student in 1961, "the year Barack Obama was born in Hawaii, half a universe away," and had sung it at mass meetings in Mount Zion Baptist Church. She had sung it marching to Albany's city hall as she and her fellow students demanded the right to vote. She had sung it in the city jail, once described by King as "the worst he ever inhabited." Now, as she and her fellow movement foot soldiers entered the polling booths, "some in wheelchairs, others with canes," their joy was manifest. "We marched, we sang and now it's happening," exulted eighty-year-old Mamie L. Nelson. "It's really a feeling I cannot describe." That evening, with all the networks declaring Obama the winner, Ms. Harris could not hold back the tears. "The emotions of a lifetime released in a flood." Jesse Jackson cried, too, for all the world to see as he watched Obama's victory speech; so did John L. Lewis. Both these national figures, also veterans of the movement, would surely have joined Rutha Mae as she sang "Glory, Glory, Hallelujah." For them, the connection between the marches, the beatings, the killings, the consequent legislation, its determined enforcement, and Obama's election was triumphantly clear and direct. "King made the statement that he viewed the Promised Land, won't get there, but somebody will get there," declared the Reverend Horace C. Boyd, the pastor of Albany's Shiloh Baptist Church for more than fifty years, "and that day has dawned." He was "glad" of it.[1]

Sunday services throughout the South on November 9 were festive outpourings of thanksgiving. "God has vindicated the black folk," exalted Pastor Shirley Caesar-Williams in her sermon to her flock in the Raleigh, North Carolina, Mount Calvary Word of Faith Church. "We got a new family coming in. . . . And guess what? They look like us. Amen, amen. They look like us." The Reverend J. Rayfield Vines Jr., the pastor of Richmond's Hungary Road Baptist Church and old enough to remember segregation's indignities, spoke of the past only to give those "who had not tasted the bitterness of segregation . . . an idea of why we all shouted." Last Tuesday evening, he said, "My cup runneth over. . . . My eyes have seen the glory." Nowhere "was the weight of history more palpable" than at King's old church, Ebenezer Baptist. Barack Obama had "stood against the fierce tide of history," declared the Reverend Raphael G. Warnock, and he had triumphed. King's surviving sister, Christine King Farris, then reminded the congregation of her brother's last speech. "As he predicted the night before he left us," she said, "I may not be with you, but as a people we will reach the promised land." That, she was convinced, was the meaning of Tuesday's result. "Yes, it is our promised land," she shouted, as the congregation waved American flags in affirmation.[2]

Obama's defeated opponent essentially made the same point in his gracious concession speech. "This is an historic election," John McCain declared. "I recognize the special significance it has for African-Americans and for the special pride that must be theirs tonight." America had moved a long way from "the cruel and frightful bigotry of the recent past." The repudiated George W. Bush thought likewise. "Many of our citizens thought they would never live to see [the election of an African American president]," he mused in the Rose Garden the day after. "This moment is especially uplifting for a generation of Americans who witnessed the struggle for civil rights with their own eyes, and four decades later see a dream fulfilled."[3]

Much indeed had changed in Albany, Georgia, since Rutha Mae Harris had first sung her freedom songs. In 1961, Asa D. Kelley Jr., an arch-segregationist, was mayor, and the chief of police, Laurie Pritchett, was perhaps King's most thoughtful and successful adversary. Now both offices were held by black men. Nevertheless, much has changed little. The city's neighborhoods are still segregated by race, the public schools are overwhelmingly black, and the income gap between the races remains yawning despite a vibrant, expanding black middle class. In this, Albany was no different from scores of southern cities in 2008. The pace and scale of change remained uneven.[4]

Obama's triumph underscored similar dramatic changes and historic continuities throughout the region. The newly elected president had, after all, carried both Virginia and North Carolina, thus breaking the solid Republican South. Some commentators saw in this the end of "the so-called Southern strategy of Richard Nixon," which aimed to ensure regional dominance through "co-opting Southern whites on racial issues." According to Emory University's Merle Black, an expert on southern politics, the 2008 result clearly showed that strategy's limits. The region had "moved from being the center of the political universe to being an outside player in presidential politics," agreed the Louisiana State University political scientist Wayne Parent. The "Southern strategy" was a thing of the past.[5]

Nevertheless, the past was still visible, as voting statistics clearly displayed. Less than 33 percent of white southerners supported Obama— 43 percent of whites did so nationally. In Alabama, nine out of ten whites voted for McCain; throughout the region, Obama gained about half as many white votes as had the losing Democrat, John Kerry, four years before. Race was the only explanation. She was "bothered by the idea of having a black man over me in the White House," agreed a white woman in Mississippi's Lamar County. Don Dollar, who worked at city hall, was much more forthright. Anyone not upset by Obama's victory "should seek religious forgiveness," he thought. The Lamar County businesswoman Gail McDaniel feared that there would "be outbreaks from blacks" in the days ahead. "From where I'm from, this is going to give them the right to be more aggressive." Some were more direct in their anger. Black Obama supporters in Snellville, Georgia, woke on November 5 to find that their lawns had been trashed overnight or pizza boxes filled with human waste left at their front doors. Eshe Riviears's teenage son was suspended from school in Marietta, Georgia, for wearing an Obama shirt. "Whether you like it or not, we're in the South," the principal had explained. There were "a lot of people who are not happy" with the result. As black southerners rejoiced at having reached the mountaintop, many whites, especially those over thirty and living in the region's smaller towns and rural counties, feared what lay ahead. "I believe our nation has been ruined," lamented Grant Griffen, a forty-six-year-old white Georgian, "and has been for several decades." Richard Barrett, the leader of a white supremacist group in Learned, Mississippi, thought that, when "the flag of the Republic of New Africa" was "hoisted over the White House" on Inauguration Day, many would consider it "an act of war" and react accordingly.[6]

President Obama's inauguration did little to bridge the racial divide in Paris, Texas. An agricultural community one hundred miles north of Dallas, with a population of twenty-six thousand, nearly six thousand of whom were black, residentially segregated and overwhelmingly poor, Paris was once the scene of brutal public lynchings, and some black residents maintained that the climate that had produced them had changed little. "I think we are stuck in 1930 right now," warned Brenda Cherry, the founder of Concerned Citizens for Racial Equality. "If you complain about anything, you are going to be punished." In September 2008, the death of a young black man, Brendon McClelland, run over by two whites after an argument, escalated the tensions in Paris—as its angry black citizens talked of lynching twenty-first century style. Though the arrest of the two men responsible, who were in fact friends of McClelland's and had been drinking with him the day of his death, suggested a more personal reason for their action, it did little to dampen the level of community outrage. If, to some, Obama's election signaled the end of racial politics in the South, this was clearly not evident in Paris, Texas. There were a few voices of optimism to be heard, however, most insistently from the town's older black residents, who remembered the days of Jim Crow and who, thus, knew, as the local youngsters in the New Black Panther Party did not, how much things had changed for the better. So did the town's white mayor, the long-term resident Jesse James Freelen, who reminded all that his predecessor had been black, as was his deputy. "Once we start communicating," he thought, "we will find a way out. The problems we believe we have are not as big as we think." Even Paris could change, once the will was there to do so.[7]

When William Raspberry, the longtime *Washington Post* columnist who had retired in 2005, was asked by his old paper to reflect on the wider meaning of Obama's ascendancy, he was uncertain that the mountaintop had been successfully climbed or that a "post-racial" America had arrived. It was a "hugely significant" event nonetheless, in that it showed that race was no longer "an automatic deal-breaker" in southern politics. Furthermore, it could enable black America to move beyond what he termed the "civil rights paradigm," to leave behind the politics of grievance and white injustice and reach out for a fresh model, one that acknowledges that there is more than "a racial explanation for all that goes wrong in our community," and a renewed determination to combat these ills from within. Barack Obama's "ascendancy to the most powerful position in the world," he concluded, "does not mean an end to all black problems—including the problem of racial discrimination— there would still be plenty of that about." "But," he hoped, "it may allow our children to begin to see life as a series of problems and possi- bilities, and not just a list of grievances." The president-elect had come to see clearly that black America, "active and confident," had the capac- ity to do this, as his election had so triumphantly displayed to his com- munity, to the nation, to the world—and to the future.[8]

Appropriately, let the last words in this book belong to James "Little Man" Presley, of Sledge, Mississippi, the grandson of slaves, brought up by his mother, and "so closely tied to his slave past" that he was "still farming cotton on the same land as his ancestors." He had voted for Obama with a "heap of pride," that same pride he had first felt four decades earlier as he listened to the words of Martin Luther King. "I'm a church man," Presley told a CNN reporter. "I kind of figured this here is going to be like it was with Moses with the children of Israel. On the day, when he gets to be president, we're all going to be rejoicing. . . . I never thought one would get there." Obama's election showed once and for all that anything was possible, that "the White House isn't just for white folks." In the reflections of this seventy-two-year-old black man lay the enduring purpose of the civil rights movement—and of this book.[9]

Notes

Abbreviations

AFL-CIO Civil Rights Papers — AFL-CIO Civil Rights Department, Southern Office Records, 1964–1979, Southern Labor Archives, University Library, Georgia State University

Alabama Governors' Papers — Alabama Governors' Papers, Alabama Department of Archives and History

BPL — Birmingham Public Library

Carter Library — Jimmy Carter Library

CFAC — Correspondence Files, Administrative Correspondence, PABR Files

Chambers Papers — Julius L. Chambers Papers, Special Collections Department, J. Murrey Atkins Library, University of North Carolina at Charlotte

CRDJA Papers — Civil Rights during the Johnson Administration Papers (microfilm), Borchardt Library, La Trobe University

CRDNA Papers — Civil Rights during the Nixon Administration Papers (microfilm), Baillieu Library, University of Melbourne

CRSA Papers — Civil Rights and Social Activism in the South Papers (microfilm), Borchardt Library, La Trobe University

Dent Papers — Harry Dent Papers, Strom Thurmond Institute, Clemson University

Dole Files — Elizabeth Dole Files, Ronald Reagan Presidential Library

EEOC — Equal Employment Opportunity Commission

Ervin Papers — Samuel Ervin Papers, Southern Historical Collection, Wilson Library, University of North Carolina at Chapel Hill

Ford Library — Gerald R. Ford Presidential Library

Frederick Alexander Papers — Frederick Douglas Alexander Papers, Special Collections Department, J. Murrey Atkins Library

Greensboro Civil Rights Fund Papers — Greensboro Civil Rights Fund Papers, Southern Historical Collection, Wilson Library, University of North Carolina at Chapel Hill

Hawkins Papers — Reginald A. Hawkins Papers, Special Collections Department, J. Murrey Atkins Library, University of North Carolina at Charlotte

Jonas Papers — Charles Raper Jonas Papers, Southern Historical Collection, Wilson Library, University of North Carolina at Chapel Hill

Kelly Alexander Papers	Kelly M. Alexander Papers, Special Collections Department, J. Murrey Atkins Library
LBJ Library	Lyndon Baines Johnson Presidential Library
McKissick Papers	Floyd McKissick Papers, Southern Historical Collection, Wilson Library, University of North Carolina at Chapel Hill
NAACP Papers	NAACP Papers (microfilm), Borchardt Library, La Trobe University
NARA-Atlanta	National Archives and Records Administration, Atlanta
NARA-Philadelphia	National Archives and Records Administration, Philadelphia
NPM	Richard M. Nixon Presidential Materials, National Archives and Records Administration, College Park
NSV-UNCC	New South Voices Collection, Special Collections Department, J. Murrey Atkins Library, University of North Carolina at Charlotte
PABR Files	President's Advisory Board on Race Files, William Jefferson Clinton Presidential Library
Reagan Library	Ronald Reagan Presidential Library
Russell Papers	Richard B. Russell Papers, Richard B. Russell Library for Political Research and Studies, University of Georgia
SCLC Papers	Southern Christian Leadership Conference Papers (microfilm), 1956–1970, Borchardt Library, La Trobe University
SOHP	Southern Oral History Program, Wilson Library, University of North Carolina at Chapel Hill
SRC Papers	Southern Regional Council Papers (microfilm), Special Collections Department, Robert W. Woodruff Library, Atlanta University Center
Talmadge Papers	Herman E. Talmadge Papers, Richard B. Russell Library for Political Research and Studies, University of Georgia
Thurmond Papers	Strom Thurmond Papers, Strom Thurmond Institute, Clemson University
Warnath Files	Stephen Warnath Files, William Jefferson Clinton Presidential Library

INTRODUCTION

1. Martin Luther King Jr., "Our God Is Marching On!" in *The Eyes on the Prize Civil Rights Reader: Documents, Speeches, and Firsthand Accounts of the Black Freedom Struggle, 1954–1990,* ed. Clayborne Carson et al. (New York: Penguin, 1991), 224–27 (quotations on 225, 226, 227); David J. Garrow, *Bearing the Cross: Martin Luther King, Jr., and the Southern Christian Leadership Conference* (New York: Morrow, 1986), 412–13.

2. See, e.g., Fred Powledge, *Free at Last? The Civil Rights Movement and the People Who Made It* (Boston: Little, Brown, 1991); and Juan Williams, *Eyes on the Prize: America's Civil Rights Years, 1954–1965* (New York: Penguin, 1987).

3. King, "Our God Is Marching On!" 226–27.

4. Clive Webb, "A Continuity of Conservatism: The Limitations of *Brown v. Board of Education,*" *Journal of Southern History* 70, no. 2 (May 2004): 329; Joseph Crespino, *In Search of Another Country: Mississippi and the Conservative Counterrevolution* (Princeton, NJ: Princeton University Press, 2007), 173.

5. Chandler Davidson, "The Recent Evolution of Voting Rights Law Affecting Racial and Language Minorities," in *Quiet Revolution in the South: The Impact of the Voting Rights Act, 1965–1990,* ed. Chandler Davidson and Bernard Grofman (Princeton, NJ: Princeton University Press, 1994), 30; John Doar to Nicholas de Katzenbach, July 22, 1965, pt. 1, reel 9, CRDJA Papers.

6. Testimony of Herbert Hill, January 15, 1962, U.S. Congress, House, Special Subcommittee on Labor of the Committee on Education and Labor, *Proposed Federal Legislation to Prohibit Discrimination in Employment in Certain Cases because of Race, Religion, Color, National Origin, or Sex: Hearings before the Special Subcommittee on Labor of the Committee on Education and Labor,* 87th Cong., 2nd sess., 1962, 719; Leroy Hamilton, Interview with Author (Minchin), July 25, 1997, Woodbine, GA (quotation).

7. Nick Kotz, *Judgment Days: Lyndon Baines Johnson, Martin Luther King Jr., and the Laws That Changed America* (Boston: Houghton Mifflin, 2006), xi. Kotz's book is an exploration of the relationship between Martin Luther King and Lyndon Johnson and how they worked together to pass the civil rights acts of 1964 and 1965.

8. U.S. Commission on Civil Rights, *Jobs and Civil Rights: The Role of the Federal Government in Promoting Equal Opportunity in Employment and Training* (Washington, DC: U.S. Government Printing Office, 1969), 222.

9. As we explore more fully in chapter 1, this focus on the South led southern opponents of civil rights legislation to argue that their native region was being unfairly victimized. As Georgia senator Richard Russell commented in 1964, "The [civil rights] bill is aimed at what has become the most despised and mistreated minority in the country—namely, the white people of the Southern states." *Congressional Record* 110, no. 123 (June 18, 1964): 2 (Russell quotation), copy, ser. 10, folder 3, box 8, Russell Papers.

10. Charles Evers Interview, April 3, 1974, 18 (Johnson quotation), pt. 3, reel 1, CRDJA Papers.

11. Hugh Davis Graham, *The Civil Rights Era: Origins and Development of National Policy, 1960–1972* (New York: Oxford University Press, 1990), 259; "Establishing a Nationwide School Desegregation Program under Title VI of the Civil Rights Act of 1964," March 1, 1969, reel 16, CRDNA Papers; "Jobs, Job Training, and Economic Security," December 3, 1965, pt. 1, reel 14, CRDJA Papers. The South is here considered to be the eleven former Confederate states.

12. See, e.g., Brian Ward and Tony Badger, introduction to *The Making of Martin Luther King and the Civil Rights Movement,* ed. Brian Ward and Tony Badger (Basingstoke: MacMillan, 1996), 2; Crespino, *In Search of Another Country,* 276; Adam Fairclough, "The Civil Rights Movement in Louisiana, 1939–54," in ibid., 15–20 (quotation on 19); and Stephen G. N. Tuck, *Beyond Atlanta: The Struggle for Racial Equality in Georgia, 1940–1980* (Athens: University of Georgia Press, 2001), 1–4.

13. This scholarship on the 1930s and 1940s has been heavily influenced by

Robert Korstad and Nelson Lichtenstein's pathbreaking "Opportunities Lost and Found: Labor, Radicals, and the Early Civil Rights Movement," *Journal of American History* 75 (December 1988): 786–811. For other important studies in this vein, see Beth Tompkins Bates, *Pullman Porters and the Rise of Protest Politics in Black America, 1925–1945* (Chapel Hill: University of North Carolina Press, 2001); Robert Korstad, *Civil Rights Unionism: Tobacco Workers and the Struggle for Democracy in the Mid-Twentieth-Century South* (Chapel Hill: University of North Carolina Press, 2003); Patricia Sullivan, *Days of Hope: Race and Democracy in the New Deal Era* (Chapel Hill: University of North Carolina Press, 1996); Michael K. Honey, *Southern Labor and Black Civil Rights: Organizing Memphis Workers* (Urbana: University of Illinois Press, 1993); and Merl E. Reed, *Seedtime for the Modern Civil Rights Movement: The President's Committee on Fair Employment Practice, 1941–1946* (Baton Rouge: Louisiana State University Press, 1991).

14. Michael K. Honey, *Going Down Jericho Road: The Memphis Strike, Martin Luther King's Last Campaign* (New York: Norton, 2007), xviii.

15. Crespino, *In Search of Another Country*, 276. For other case studies, see Emilye Crosby, *A Little Taste of Freedom: The Black Freedom Struggle in Claiborne County, Mississippi* (Chapel Hill: University of North Carolina Press, 2005); Cynthia Griggs Fleming, *In the Shadow of Selma: The Continuing Struggle for Civil Rights in the Rural South* (Lanham, MD: Rowman & Littlefield, 2004); Winston A. Grady-Willis, *Challenging U.S. Apartheid: Atlanta and Black Struggles for Human Rights, 1960–1977* (Durham, NC: Duke University Press, 2006); Christina Greene, *Our Separate Ways: Women and the Black Freedom Movement in Durham, North Carolina* (Chapel Hill: University of North Carolina Press, 2005); Bobby L. Lovett, *The Civil Rights Movement in Tennessee: A Narrative History* (Knoxville: University of Tennessee Press, 2005); J. Todd Moye, *Let the People Decide: Black Freedom and White Resistance in Sunflower County, Mississippi, 1945–1986* (Chapel Hill: University of North Carolina Press, 2004); and Timothy B. Tyson, *Blood Done Sign My Name: A True Story* (New York: Crown, 2004).

16. Jacquelyn Dowd Hall, "The Long Civil Rights Movement and the Political Uses of the Past," *Journal of American History* 91, no. 4 (March 2005): 1233. The only overview of southern race relations that does cover the post-1965 era in detail is David R. Goldfield, *Black, White, and Southern: Race Relations and Southern Culture, 1940 to the Present* (Baton Rouge: Louisiana State University Press, 1990). Full of helpful insights, Goldfield's book is, however, not based on archival sources. As it was published in 1990, it also fails to take the story into the 1990s or the first decade of the twenty-first century as *After the Dream* does. For a recent study that covers the momentous changes in the northern states, with some coverage of the post-1965 era, see Thomas J. Sugrue, *Sweet Land of Liberty: The Forgotten Struggle for Civil Rights in the North* (New York: Random House, 2008). For a fine recent study of civil rights during the Johnson administration, see David C. Carter, *The Music Has Gone Out of the Movement: Civil Rights and the Johnson Administration, 1965–1968* (Chapel Hill: University of North Carolina Press, 2009). In this important study, Carter notes that "the years after 1965 have attracted far less scrutiny" than the years before *Brown*, an imbalance that it is crucial to address (p. xii).

17. The struggle for fair housing is not covered here largely because this was

predominantly a northern issue. Also, the focus here is on the 1964 Civil Rights and the 1965 Voting Rights acts, neither of which addressed housing (it was covered later by the 1968 Civil Rights Act). For more on the housing issue in the North, see James R. Ralph Jr., *Northern Protest: Martin Luther King, Jr., Chicago, and the Civil Rights Movement* (Cambridge, MA: Harvard University Press, 1993).

18. "Remarks of the President at Howard University," June 4, 1965, 2, "Civil Rights Releases (White House)" folder, box 331, Fred Panzer Files, LBJ Library.

19. J. Harvie Wilkinson III, *From Brown to Bakke: The Supreme Court and School Integration, 1954–1978* (New York: Oxford University Press, 1979), 102–3; "Civil Rights Act of 1964" (Public Law 88-352), July 2, 1964, pt. 1, reel 9, CRDJA Papers.

20. Theodore Hesburgh to Richard Nixon, March 28, 1969, reel 21, CRDNA Papers. As the U.S. Commission on Civil Rights put it, the overall intent of these provisions was to "foster full minority participation in the process of self-government." U.S. Commission on Civil Rights, *The Voting Rights Act: Ten Years After* (Washington, DC: U.S. Government Printing Office, 1975), 7.

21. Ray Arsenault, *Freedom Riders: 1961 and the Struggle for Racial Justice* (Oxford: Oxford University Press, 2006), 1–10; Aldon D. Morris, *The Origins of the Civil Rights Movement: Black Communities Organizing for Change* (New York: Free Press, 1984), 195–228; Glenn T. Eskew, *But for Birmingham: The Local and National Movements in the Civil Rights Struggle* (Chapel Hill: University of North Carolina Press, 1997), 3–17; Ramsey Clark Interview, February 11, 1969, 11–13, pt. 3, reel 1, CRDJA Papers; "Public Accommodation Proposal in Rights Program Hits Slowdown," *Montgomery (AL) Advertiser,* June 25, 1963, clipping, folder 19, box 022362, Alabama Governors' Papers.

22. Robert H. Zieger, *For Jobs and Freedom: Race and Labor in America since 1865* (Lexington: University Press of Kentucky, 2007), 1–2; Honey, *Going Down Jericho Road,* 42, 48; Nancy MacLean, *Freedom Is Not Enough: The Opening of the American Workplace* (Cambridge, MA: Harvard University Press, 2006), 5; Address by Rev. Dr. Ralph David Abernathy, June 19, 1968, pt. 4, reel 26, SCLC Papers.

23. Roy Wilkins Interview, April 1, 1969, 13, pt. 3, reel 3, CRDJA Papers; Manfred Berg, *"The Ticket to Freedom": The NAACP and the Struggle for Black Political Integration* (Gainesville: University Press of Florida, 2005), 250, 264; Steven F. Lawson, *Black Ballots: Voting Rights in the South, 1944–1969* (New York: Columbia University Press, 1976); Black Lawyers' Remarks, ca. 1979 (closing quotation), "Blacks and the Carter Administration (2)" folder, box 12, Louis Martin Files, Carter Library.

24. James T. Patterson, *Brown v. Board of Education: A Civil Rights Milestone and Its Troubled Legacy* (New York: Oxford University Press, 2001), xvii; "Charles Hamilton Houston Lays Out a Legal Strategy for the NAACP, 1935," in *From Freedom to "Freedom Now," 1865–1990s,* ed. Thomas C. Holt and Elsa Barkley Brown, vol. 2 of *Major Problems in African American History* (Boston: Houghton Mifflin, 2000), 256–57.

25. Gunnar Myrdal, *An American Dilemma: The Negro Problem and Modern Democracy,* 20th anniversary ed. (New York: Harper & Row, 1962), 882; "Memorandum on School Desegregation to President Nixon from Senator

Thurmond," n.d., "Strom Thurmond" folder, box 16, President's Personal File, 1969–74, NPM.

26. "Decade of Black Struggle Has Mixed Result in South," *New York Times,* February 8, 1970, 1, 50; Allen J. Matusow, *The Unraveling of America: A History of Liberalism in the 1960s* (New York: Harper & Row, 1984), 187.

27. U.S. Commission on Civil Rights, *The Voting Rights Act: Ten Years After,* 39; Testimony of John Lewis, March 25, 1975, U.S. Congress, House, Judiciary Committee, *Extension of the Voting Rights Act: Part 1,* 94th Cong., 1st sess., 1975, 128; Adam Fairclough, *To Redeem the Soul of America: The Southern Christian Leadership Conference and Martin Luther King, Jr.* (Athens: University of Georgia Press, 1987), 398.

28. Mary Beth Norton et al., *A People and a Nation: A History of the United States,* 6th ed. (Boston: Houghton Mifflin, 2001), A57; Chandler Davidson and Bernard Grofman, introduction to Davidson and Grofman, eds., *Quiet Revolution in the South,* 3; Fairclough, *To Redeem the Soul of America,* 398.

29. For an overview of these cases, see Patterson, *Brown v. Board of Education,* 145–46, 153–59. These cases will be explored more fully in the chapters that follow, particularly chapters 4 and 5.

30. "The *Brown* Decision 25 Years Later: Indicators of Desegregation and Equal Educational Opportunity," May 17, 1979, 1, "*Brown v. Board*—Reception Lists O/A9509 (1)" folder, box 14, Louis Martin Files, Carter Library.

31. Jack E. Davis, *Race against Time: Culture and Separation in Natchez* (Baton Rouge: Louisiana State University Press, 2001), 233; "24 Years of Integration: Has Busing Really Worked?" *U.S. News and World Report,* May 8, 1978, 43–53. On the continuing importance of school desegregation, consider reaction to the Supreme Court's 2007 decision declaring that public schools in Louisville and Seattle cannot take explicit account of race in order to achieve integration. For an overview, see Jeffrey Rosen, "Can a Law Change a Society?" *New York Times,* July 1, 2007.

32. "A Report from the 56th Annual National Convention of the NAACP," June 28–July 3, 1965, folder 9, box 23, Kelly Alexander Papers; Goldfield, *Black, White, and Southern,* 246 (1980 statistic).

33. John Dumbrell, *The Carter Presidency: A Re-Evaluation,* 2nd ed. (Manchester: Manchester University Press, 1995), 91 (first Martin quotation); Louis Martin Exit Interview, 7, December 10, 1980 (other quotations), "White House Staff Exit Interviews" folder, box 5, Louis Martin Files, Carter Papers; Zieger, *For Jobs and Freedom,* 175–82.

34. George Lewis, *Massive Resistance: The White Response to the Civil Rights Movement* (London: Hodder Arnold, 2006), 5–8; Jason Sokol, *There Goes My Everything: White Southerners in the Age of Civil Rights, 1945–1975* (New York: Knopf, 2006), 9, 13 (quotation).

35. As Crespino observes in his study of Mississippi, the traditional emphasis on white resistance to black rights "reduces history to a morality tale, . . . ignores ongoing struggles for racial justice, and . . . oversimplifies white reaction to the civil rights struggle." Crespino, *In Search of Another Country,* 4. See also Kevin M. Kruse, *White Flight: Atlanta and the Making of Modern Conservatism* (Princeton, NJ: Princeton University Press, 2005); Matthew D. Lassiter, *The Silent Majority: Suburban Politics in the Sunbelt South* (Princeton, NJ: Princeton University Press, 2006); and Sokol, *There Goes My Everything.*

36. Patricia Cohen, "Interpreting Some Overlooked Stories from the South," *New York Times,* May 1, 2007.

37. Harry Fleischman, "Brown and Intergroup Relations," *The Crisis,* June/July 1979, 250; Philip G. Grose, *South Carolina at the Brink: Robert McNair and the Politics of Civil Rights* (Columbia: University of South Carolina Press, 2006), 277 (McNair quotation).

38. For an overview of the disturbances in Quincy, see "Racial Trouble Awakens Sleepy Town in Florida," *Atlanta Journal and Constitution,* October 18, 1970, 8B (both quotations). For similar protests elsewhere, see Frye Gaillard, "It's Abernathy's Dream Now," *Race Relations Reporter* 3, no. 5 (March 1972): 4–6; Tuck, *Beyond Atlanta,* 198–201.

39. Southern Regional Council, "The South and Her Children: School Desegregation, 1970–1971," March 1971, 34, reel 220, SRC Papers.

40. Terry Lynd, Interview with Author (Minchin), November 13, 2004, Satsuma, AL.

41. The problems experienced by organizations such as the SNCC and the SCLC are explored more fully in the chapters that follow, particularly chapter 3.

42. August Meier, "Epilogue: Toward a Synthesis of Civil Rights History," in *New Directions in Civil Rights Studies,* ed. Armstead L. Robinson and Patricia Sullivan (Charlottesville: University Press of Virginia, 1991), 212. The importance of the NAACP has been highlighted by the recent publication of Berg, *"The Ticket to Freedom";* Gilbert Jonas, *Freedom's Sword: The NAACP and the Struggle against Racism in America, 1909–1969* (New York: Routledge, 2005); Kevern Verney and Lee Sartain, eds., *Long Is the Way and Hard: One Hundred Years of the NAACP* (Fayetteville: University of Arkansas Press, 2009); and Patricia Sullivan, *Lift Every Voice: The NAACP and the Making of the Civil Rights Movement* (New York: New Press, 2009). None of these works, however, gives sustained coverage to the post-1965 era. For slightly older works that also emphasize the NAACP's importance, particularly prior to 1955, see Adam Fairclough, *Race and Democracy: The Civil Rights Struggle in Louisiana, 1915–1972* (Athens: University of Georgia Press, 1995), esp. xi–xxi; and Tuck, *Beyond Atlanta,* 40–73.

43. "NAACP Fall Program," *The Crisis,* October 1965, 522; Report of the 29th Annual Conference of the North Carolina Conference of the NAACP, October 12–15, 1972, folder 16, box 23, Kelly Alexander Papers.

44. Jack E. White Jr., "NAACP Restates Integration Goal," *Race Relations Reporter* 2, no. 13 (1971): 4 (1969 statistics); Stan Scott to Warren Rustand, March 24, 1975, "NAACP 1971–75" folder, box 91, Robert Orben Files, Ford Library.

45. "Let's Add 300,000 More: Region V Fair Share 75,000, 1978," folder 5, box 18, Kelly Alexander Papers. Region 5 comprised the states of Alabama, Florida, Georgia, Mississippi, North Carolina, South Carolina, and Tennessee.

46. "A Report from the 56th Annual National Convention of the NAACP," June 28–July 3, 1965, 3 (quotation), folder 9, box 23, Region V Quarterly Report, April–August 1980, folder 1, box 18, and NAACP 1980 Annual Report (Southeast Region), folder 25, box 17, all Kelly Alexander Papers.

47. James E. Ferguson II, Interview with Author (Minchin), June 14, 1996, Charlotte, NC; Herbert Hill, Interview with Author (Minchin), November 16, 1995, Madison, WI; "Steel Giants Face a Blast on Bias," *Business Week,* June

11, 1965, 81–82; Ken Bode, "Unions Divided," *New Republic,* October 15, 1977, 21.

48. NAACP Annual Report, 1974, 45–50, and NAACP Annual Report, 1976, 21–22, 38–40, 45–48, both folder 3, box 26, Kelly Alexander Papers.

49. At the time of writing, there was no organizational history of the SRC, a civil rights group that has been in continuous operation since 1944. It is given treatment only within broader studies, and these studies focus on its early years. See, e.g., John Egerton, *Speak Now against the Day: The Generation Before the Civil Rights Movement in the South* (New York: Knopf, 1994); and Morton Sosna, *In Search of the Silent South: Southern Liberals and the Race Issue* (New York: Columbia University Press, 1977).

50. John Lewis to E. T. Kehrer, May 3, 1975, folder 2, box 1592, AFL-CIO Civil Rights Papers.

51. Pat Buchanan to Ken Cole, November 26, 1971, "Commission on Civil Rights, 1/1/71–12/31/72" folder, box 1, White House Special Files (FG-90), NPM; Theodore Hesburgh Interview, February 1, 1971, 25, pt. 3, reel 2, CRDJA Papers.

52. The LDF broke away from the NAACP in 1957 after the IRS insisted that the NAACP divest itself of its tax-deductible arm. As Gilbert Jonas explains, the LDF occupied separate offices and had different boards, but its lawyers frequently represented NAACP members in cases brought to enforce civil rights legislation in the South. See Jonas, *Freedom's Sword,* 73–77, 350–51. For the LDF's involvement in Green and Swann, see Patterson, *Brown v. Board of Education,* 145, 155–56.

53. Morris Dees with Steve Fiffer, *A Season for Justice: The Life and Times of Civil Rights Leader Morris Dees* (New York: Scribner, 1991), 97; King, "Our God Is Marching On!" 224, 226, 227.

1. HISTORIC PROGRESS

1. Carter, *The Music Has Gone Out of the Movement,* 22–26, 199–200; "Crisis of Color '66," *Newsweek,* August 22, 1966, 18; Sam J. Ervin Jr. to William Tucker, February 21, 1968, folder 7570, box 170, Ervin Papers; Fred Panzer to Lyndon Johnson, June 2, 1967, pt. 1, reel 3, CRDJA Papers.

2. "Address of the President upon the Signing of the Civil Rights Act of 1964 on Nationwide Radio and Television," July 2, 1964, 3, "Civil Rights Bill Signing Broadcast" folder, box 125, Bill Moyers Files, LBJ Library.

3. Walter Hawkins Jr. to Richard B. Russell, August 18, 1967, ser. 10, folder 4, box 5, Russell Papers; John Ferguson to Herman Talmadge, July 14, 1967, and Herman Talmadge to John Ferguson, July 17, 1967, both ser. 3, folder 7, box 3, Talmadge Papers.

4. Martin Luther King Jr. to Friend, n.d. (quotation), pt. 4, reel 23, SCLC Papers; Harvard Sitkoff, *King: Pilgrimage to the Mountaintop* (New York: Hill & Wang, 2008), 219–22.

5. Carter, *The Music Has Gone Out of the Movement,* xiii–xiv, 225–33; Taylor Branch, *At Canaan's Edge: America in the King Years, 1965–68* (New York: Simon & Schuster, 2006), 705–6; Andrew Young Interview, June 18, 1970, 19 (quotation), pt. 3, reel 3, CRDJA Papers.

6. "The March on Time," *Newsweek,* September 10, 1973, 24–26 (Rustin quotation on 26).

7. Clayborne Carson, *In Struggle: SNCC and the Black Awakening of the 1960s* (Cambridge, MA: Harvard University Press, 1981), 265–66 (quotation), 287–301; "Which Way for the Negro?" *Newsweek,* May 15, 1967, 19; "Is Integration Irrelevant?" *New Republic,* June 4, 1966, 7.

8. August Meier and Elliott Rudwick, *CORE: A Study in the Civil Rights Movement, 1942–1968* (New York: Oxford University Press, 1973), 374–431; Fairclough, *To Redeem the Soul of America,* 273–307, 369–82; Sitkoff, *King,* 172–73, 227–28.

9. Carter, *The Music Has Gone Out of the Movement,* xii–xv, 22–29 (quotation on xii). For an overview of the events at the NAACP's 1968 convention, where Wilkins's leadership was briefly challenged, see "The Turbulent 59th: An Exciting Convention," *The Crisis,* August–September 1968, 226–45.

10. "Whither the Civil Rights Struggle," *The Crisis,* November 1965, 556–64 (quotations on 556, 557); Branch, *At Canaan's Edge,* 114 (Johnson quotation).

11. Sokol, *There Goes My Everything,* 183; "Floor Statement by Senator John Stennis," July 11, 1963, 1, 5, ser. 3, folder 4, box 7, Talmadge Papers.

12. *Congressional Record* 110, no. 123 (June 18, 1964): 1–2 (Russell quotation on 2), copy, ser. 10, folder 3, box 8, Russell Papers; Telegram from Toulminville (AL) Civic Club, March 25, 1964 (second quotation), "HU2/ST1—11/22/63–2/4/65" folder, box 27, White House Central Files, LBJ Library. Because most northern states had their own equal accommodations and fair employment laws, the Civil Rights Act did not affect them as much as it did southern states, which did not have such laws, because state laws took precedence. Shortly before the act was passed, e.g., thirty-two states had statutes prohibiting discrimination in public accommodations; none of them were former Confederate states. See "States Having Statutes Prohibiting Discrimination in Public Accommodations," February 1964, pt. 1, reel 12, CRDJA Papers.

13. *Congressional Record* 110, no. 123 (June 18, 1964): 1 (Russell quotation), copy, ser. 10, folder 3, box 8, Russell Papers; "Some Hard Questions about the Civil Rights Act," June 1964 (Johnson quotation), pt. 1, reel 9, CRDJA Papers.

14. EEOC, *Making a Right a Reality: An Oral History of the Early Years of the EEOC, 1965–1972* (Washington, DC: EEOC, 1990), 6 (King quotation); "Excerpt from Annual Report of Roy Wilkins," January 4, 1965, 1, "Civil Rights—Misc. 1965" folder, box 6, Lee C. White Files, LBJ Library.

15. H. F. Braselton to Richard B. Russell, June 22, 1964, Owen H. Page to Richard B. Russell, June 19, 1964, and W. H. Ragsdale to Richard B. Russell, June 22, 1964, ser. 10, folder 8, box 37, and James W. Lewis to Richard B. Russell, June 29, 1964, ser. 10, folder 4, box 37, all Russell Papers; Numan V. Bartley, *The New South, 1945–1980: The Story of the South's Modernization* (Baton Rouge: Louisiana State University Press, 1995), 388–89.

16. James A. Ruth to George Wallace, June 12, 1964 (first quotation), and Jesse T. Todd to George C. Wallace, July 10, 1964, both folder 11, box 22371, Alabama Governors' Papers.

17. These letters are contained in ser. 10, folders 1–5, box 129, Russell Papers. Specific examples are cited in the next note.

18. Emmett David Foskey Jr. to Richard Russell, August 29, 1963, and Marge Manderson to Richard B. Russell, September 17, 1963, ser. 10, folder 4,

box 129, and Richard Russell to Mrs. Helen C. Fowler, December 9, 1963, ser. 10, folder 2, box 129, all Russell Papers.

19. Richard B. Russell to Frank H. Williams, June 17, 1964, ser. 10, folder 5, box 97, Russell Papers; Carl Sanders Interview, May 13, 1969, 7–8, pt. 3, reel 3, CRDJA Papers; Allen Coley, Interview with Author (Minchin), October 13, 1997, Natchez, MS.

20. Lyndon Baines Johnson, "To the Congress of the United States," April 28, 1966, pt. 1, reel 2, CRDJA Papers; NAACP 1967 Annual Report (Southeast Region) (quotation on 46), folder 25, box 17, Kelly Alexander Papers.

21. Ad Hoc Businessmen's Group, "Status of Desegregation of Thirty-Nine Selected Southern Cities," March 1964, pt. 1, reel 13, CRDJA Papers; "Crisis of Color '66," *Newsweek*, August 22, 1966, 24.

22. Under Title II, the CRS was responsible for conciliating complaints in states that did not have their own public accommodations laws. In addition, Title X empowered the service "to provide assistance to communities and persons therein resolving disputes, disagreements or difficulties relating to discriminatory practices based on race, color or national origin." For more information, see LeRoy Collins to Lyndon Johnson, August 4, 1964, "Civil Rights—Community Relations Service" folder, box 3, Lee C. White Files, LBJ Library.

23. Lee C. White to Lyndon Johnson, September 30, 1964, and "Citizens for Progress," *McComb Enterprise-Journal*, November 17, 1964, clipping, both "HU2/ST24—7/17/64–11/30/64" folder, box 27, White House Central Files, and Harold C. Fleming to Lee C. White, November 20, 1964 (first two quotations), and Calvin Kytle to John T. Connor, December 14, 1965 (closing quotation), both "Civil Rights—Community Relations Service" folder, box 3, Lee C. White Files, all LBJ Library.

24. "Administration Seeks to Ease Way for South in Accepting New Law," *Wall Street Journal*, June 22, 1964 (quotation), clipping, folder 11, box 022371, Alabama Governors' Papers; Bureau of the Budget Memorandum, June 26, 1964, "Civil Rights Act of 1964, Title VI" folder, box 2, Lee C. White Files, LBJ Library.

25. Sokol, *There Goes My Everything*, 196 (first quotation), 197, 200; "Again the Chamber Wisely Leads toward Respect for Law in Atlanta," *Atlanta Constitution*, July 2, 1964, 4 (second quotation); "May Our Children Look Back Proudly on Our Response to Lawful Duty," *Atlanta Constitution*, July 3, 1964, 3; "Mayor Asks Restraint by Negroes," *Atlanta Constitution*, July 3, 1964, 10; Goldfield, *Black, White, and Southern*, 146.

26. Memorandum, February 11, 1964, pt. 1, reel 12, CRDJA Papers (first quotation); "Civil Rights Law at Work: South's Reaction Is Mixed," *New York Times*, January 24, 1965, 1, 39 (quotation).

27. Sokol, *There Goes My Everything*, 227–28; R. C. Larry, Interview with Author (Minchin), July 23, 1997, Port St. Joe, FL; NAACP 1967 Annual Report, 71, folder 2, box 26, Kelly Alexander Papers.

28. Luther Hodges to George Wallace, June 30, 1964, and July 2, 1964, both folder 4, box 022384, and George Wallace to Gordon M. Williams, July 7, 1964 (quotations), folder 11, box 022371, all Alabama Governors' Papers.

29. E. P. Murchison to George Wallace, folder 11, box 022371, Alabama Governors' Papers. In his papers, there is no record of a reply from Wallace.

30. George C. Wallace to Mrs. Marie Scola, August 25, 1966, Mrs. Beulah Bryson to Mr. and Mrs. Wallace, August 22, 1966, and Mrs. Marie Scola to

George Wallace, August 21, 1966, all folder 11, box 022400, Alabama Governors' Papers.

31. For a full list, see *Greater Atlanta Council on Human Relations Newsletter,* July 1963, and Atlanta Council on Human Relations, "Integrated Hotels, Motels, Restaurants, and Cafeterias," July 23, 1963, both pt. 4, reel 23, SCLC Papers.

32. "Maddox Carries Pistol, Turns Away 3 Negroes," n.d., clipping, folder 169, box 1604, AFL-CIO Civil Rights Papers; Sokol, *There Goes My Everything,* 183–87 (Maddox quotation on 186); Grady-Willis, *Challenging U.S. Apartheid,* 54.

33. George C. Wallace to Lester Maddox, August 24, 1964, folder 11, box 22371, Alabama Governors' Papers.

34. Lee C. White to Lyndon Johnson, September 8, 1964, "Civil Rights—Misc. 1964" folder, box 6, Lee C. White Files, LBJ Library; Tuck, *Beyond Atlanta,* 194; "Notes on People," *New York Times,* December 4, 1974, 49.

35. "Negroes Ready Another Wave of Demonstrations against Bias in the South," *Wall Street Journal,* February 5, 1964; Memorandum, February 11, 1964, pt. 1, reel 12, CRDJA Papers; Ad Hoc Businessmen's Group, "Status of Desegregation of Thirty-Nine Selected Southern Cities," March 1964 (Greensboro quotation), pt. 1, reel 13, CRDJA Papers.

36. Lawyers' Committee for Civil Rights under Law, "Report on the Committee Office in the South," June 2–August 6, 1965, 16 (quotation), 18–20, "Civil Rights (2)" folder, box 21, Harry McPherson Files, LBJ Library.

37. A. Z. Young to the President, July 14, 1965, "HU2/ST14-ST19" folder, box 26, White House Central Files, "Selected Racial Developments" (FBI report), March 25, 1966, "Race Relations and Related Matters, January–July 1966 4 of 4" folder, box 71B (2 of 2), Mildred Stegall Files, and "Selected Racial Developments" (FBI report), July 30, 1966, "Race Relations and Related Matters, January–July 1966 1 of 4" folder, box 71B (2 of 2), Mildred Stegall Files, all LBJ Library.

38. "John L. LeFlore: Your Friend in Need," 1975, flyer, pt. 1, reel 13, and "Documented Civil Rights Victories of the Non-Partisan Voters League and Citizens Committee, 1961–1968," pt. 2, reel 16, both CRSA Papers. For an overview of the NPVL's work, see Keith Nicholls, "The Non-Partisan Voters League of Mobile, Alabama: Its Founding and Major Accomplishments," *Gulf South Historical Review* 8, no. 2 (Spring 1993): 74–88. Nicholls's article is the only published study of the NPVL.

39. "Complaint," July 5, 1964, and Affidavit of Eddie Wallace, July 9, 1964 (quotation), both pt. 2, reel 3, CRSA Papers.

40. Affidavit of Mary Willis et al., September 5, 1967, and Affidavit of Quincy Stephens et al., September 5, 1967 (first and second quotations), pt. 2, reel 3, and "Mobile Civil Rights Achievements 1962–1968, Non-Partisan Voters League" (closing quotation), pt. 2, reel 16, all CRSA Papers.

41. Annual Report: NAACP Southeast Region, 1965, 3 (first quotation), folder 24, box 17, and Kelly M. Alexander, "A Discussion of Where Do We Go from Here" (subsequent quotations), February 6, 1965, folder 9, box 23, both Kelly Alexander Papers.

42. See, e.g., "Questionnaire on Observance of New Civil Rights Law," July 3, 1964, folder 8, box 23, "Holiday Inn–South, Greensboro, N.C.," February 6,

1965, folder 9, box 23, and Annual Report: NAACP Southeast Region, 1965, 8, folder 24, box 17, all Kelly Alexander Papers.

43. Annual Report: NAACP Southeast Region, 1965, 8 (quotation), folder 24, box 17, and NAACP 1967 Annual Report (Southeast Region), 46, folder 25, box 17, both Kelly Alexander Papers.

44. NAACP 1967 Annual Report (Georgia Branch), 5, folder 18, box 17, Kelly Alexander Papers; Tuck, *Beyond Atlanta,* 197.

45. Annual Report: NAACP Southeast Region, 1965 (first quotation on 10), folder 24, box 17, Kelly Alexander Papers; "NAACP Tests Accommodations in Hattiesburg, Mississippi," February 26, 1965, pt. 20, reel 3, NAACP Papers; NAACP 1965 Annual Report, 41–42, folder 2, box 26, Kelly Alexander Papers; Clarence Mitchell Interview, April 30, 1969, 21 (Mitchell quotation), pt. 3, reel 3, CRDJA Papers.

46. "The Negro: 'We Feel More Free,'" *Newsweek,* August 22, 1966, 21.

47. In this 1963 letter, King spoke out against the "stinging darts of segregation" and explained to a white audience that nonviolent protest against unjust Jim Crow laws was morally defensible. See "Letter from Birmingham City Jail," in Carson et al., eds., *The Eyes on the Prize Civil Rights Reader,* 153–58 (quotation on 155). For a fuller analysis of this "literary masterpiece," see Sitkoff, *King,* 95–100 (quotation on 99).

48. Alfred L. Alexander Interview, May 10, 2001, 4, and Katie Grier Interview, October 27, 2001, 7, both NSV-UNCC.

49. "Clubmanship," *Time,* January 28, 1966, 13; Annual Report: NAACP Southeast Region, 1965, 10, folder 24, box 17, Kelly Alexander Papers.

50. See, e.g., Affidavit of Gusta Ann Goodwill, August 4, 1966, and Affidavit of William Cannon, March 16, 1968, both pt. 2, reel 3, CRSA Papers.

51. "Clubmanship," *Time,* January 28, 1966, 13; "The Department of Justice during the Administration of President Lyndon B. Johnson: Civil Rights Division," January 1969, 80–83, "Civil Rights Division Narrative History 2 of 2" folder, pt. 10, box 5, Administrative Histories, LBJ Library.

52. "Selected Racial Developments" (FBI report), January 7, 1966, "Race Relations and Related Matters, January–July 1966 4 of 4" folder, box 71B (2 of 2), Mildred Stegall Files, LBJ Library; John Lewis with Michael D'Orso, *Walking with the Wind: A Memoir of the Movement* (San Diego: Harcourt Brace, 1998), 373–75.

53. For a recent discussion of the Orangeburg protests and their broader significance in southern history, see John A. Salmond, *Southern Struggles: The Southern Labor Movement and the Civil Rights Struggle* (Gainesville: University Press of Florida, 2004), 1–7, 25–28, 139–40.

54. "Curfew Imposed by Governor in Orangeburg, S.C.," *New York Times,* February 10, 1968, 23 (Brown quotation); Grose, *South Carolina at the Brink,* 227 (Sellers quotation); Jack Nelson and Jack Bass, *The Orangeburg Massacre* (Cleveland: World, 1970), 76–98, 138–46; Tom Dent, *Southern Journey: A Return to the Civil Rights Movement* (Athens: University of Georgia Press, 1997), 83, 99 (final quotation). For a recent discussion of the shooting, which is the subject of two films, see Tim Arango, "Films Revisit Overlooked Shootings on a Black Campus," *New York Times,* April 16, 2008.

55. Grose, *South Carolina at the Brink,* 226–27; Nelson and Bass, *The Orangeburg Massacre,* 229 (Clark quotation). For another example of a small

business in the small-town South evading Title II, see the case of Glenn's Frozen Custard in Burlington, NC, as discussed in Howard Glenn to Sam J. Ervin, May 15, 1969, and Jerris Leonard to Howard Glenn, May 6, 1969, both folder 8511, box 190, Ervin Papers.

56. Branch, *At Canaan's Edge,* 112–14 (Johnson quotation).

57. C. T. Vivian Interview in Henry Hampton and Steve Fayer with Sarah Flynn, *Voices of Freedom: An Oral History of the Civil Rights Movement from the 1950s through the 1980s* (New York: Bantam, 1990), 236; Branch, *At Canaan's Edge,* 114–15; Kotz, *Judgment Days,* 312 (first and second Lewis quotations); John Lewis to Lyndon B. Johnson, August 6, 1965, pt. 1, reel 9, CRDJA Papers (final quotation).

58. Branch, *At Canaan's Edge,* 114; Kotz, *Judgment Days,* 312, 319 (Russell quotation); Allen J. Ellender Interview, July 30, 1969, 11–12, pt. 3, reel 1, CRDJA Papers.

59. Strom Thurmond to E. H. Agnew, March 10, 1965 (first two quotations), Political Affairs 4, folder 1, box 20, Thurmond Papers; Strom Thurmond Interview, May 7, 1979, 8 (final quotation), pt. 3, reel 3, CRDJA Papers.

60. Branch, *At Canaan's Edge,* 112; Mrs. Percy A. Hauglie to Strom Thurmond, March 19, 1965, Political Affairs 4, folder 1, box 20, Thurmond Papers; Mrs. John Mark Temples to President Johnson, March 15, 1965, ser. 10, folder 4, box 34, Russell Papers. For other similar examples, see Dr. M. B. Nickles to Strom Thurmond, March 16, 1965, Political Affairs 4, folder 2, box 21, and Mrs. H. J. Reiland to Strom Thurmond, March 18, 1965, Political Affairs 4, folder 1, box 20, both Thurmond Papers.

61. "Remarks of the President at the Signing Ceremony of the Voting Rights Bill," August 6, 1965, 4 (Johnson quotation), "Civil Rights Releases (White House)" folder, box 331, Fred Panzer Files, LBJ Library; "A Barrier Falls: The U.S. Negro Moves to Vote," *Newsweek,* August 16, 1965, 9; John Lewis to Lyndon B. Johnson, August 6, 1965, pt. 1, reel 9, CRDJA Papers; James B. Bramlett to Strom Thurmond, August 12, 1965, Civil Rights 1, folder 3, box 2, Thurmond Papers.

62. Branch, *At Canaan's Edge,* 275; Bartley, *The New South,* 339–40.

63. Washington Research Project, *The Shameful Blight: The Survival of Racial Discrimination in Voting in the South* (Washington, DC: Washington Research Project, 1972), 49, 183; Harry E. Kinnane to George C. Wallace, March 28, 1965, folder 10, box 022395, Alabama Governors' Papers. For another example of a white writer who was supportive of the Voting Rights Bill, see Robert T. Lakebrink to George Wallace, March 17, 1965, folder 9, box 022395, Alabama Governors' Papers.

64. Justice Department Reports on Madison County, Mississippi, and Lowndes County, Alabama, both August 9, 1965, pt. 1, reel 9, CRDJA Papers; "A Barrier Falls: The U.S. Negro Moves to Vote," *Newsweek,* August 16, 1965, 9.

65. U.S. Commission on Civil Rights, *Political Participation: A Study of the Participation by Negroes in the Electoral and Political Processes in 10 Southern States since Passage of the Voting Rights Act of 1965* (Washington, DC: U.S. Government Printing Office, 1968), iii (quotation), 12–13.

66. Nicholas deB. Katzenbach to the President, August 5, 1965 (quotation), "Voting Rights 1965" folder, box 3, Lee C. White Files, and "The Department of Justice during the Administration of President Lyndon B. Johnson: Civil

Rights Division," January 1969, 6–7, "Civil Rights Division Narrative History 1 of 2" folder, pt. 10, box 5, Administrative Histories, both LBJ Library.

67. John Macy Jr. to Mr. Moyers, August 14, 1965 (quotation), and Lee C. White to the President, December 4, 1965, pt. 1, reel 9, CRDJA Papers.

68. "Statement by the President," August 6, 1966 (first quotation), pt. 1, reel 9, CRDJA Papers; U.S. Commission on Civil Rights, *Voting in Mississippi* (1965) (second quotation on 59), copy, pt. 4, reel 20, SCLC Papers.

69. "A Corner Turned," *Time,* May 13, 1966, 11 (Bolden and Mitchell quotations).

70. U.S. Commission on Civil Rights, *The Voting Rights Act: The First Months* (Washington, DC: U.S. Government Printing Office, 1965), 2; U.S. Commission on Civil Rights Press Release, December 5, 1965, 3 (quotation), pt. 4, reel 20, SCLC Papers; U.S. Commission on Civil Rights, "Extension and Expansion of the Voting Rights Act of 1965," memorandum, March 28, 1969, reel 21, CRDNA Papers.

71. U.S. Commission on Civil Rights, *Political Participation,* 17, 155 (quotation); "Who's Afraid of Those Negro Voters?" *New Republic,* October 30, 1965, 10; John W. Macy Jr. to the President, April 25, 1968, pt. 1, reel 9, CRDJA Papers.

72. "Negro Registration," *New Republic,* November 13, 1965, 7–8; U.S. Commission on Civil Rights, *Political Participation,* 17; "Voter Listing Activity," August 18, 1965, pt. 1, reel 9, CRDJA Papers.

73. U.S. Commission on Civil Rights, *The Voting Rights Act: Ten Years After,* 49–50; U.S. Commission on Civil Rights, *Political Participation,* 14–17; VEP Press Release, "What Happened in the South, 1966," December 14, 1966, pt. 4, reel 20, SCLC Papers.

74. "New Voters," *The Crisis,* October 1965, 498–501 (quotation on 498), 532.

75. NAACP 1965 Annual Report, 40, folder 2, box 26, Kelly Alexander Papers; Dr. John W. Nixon to George C. Wallace, June 23, 1965, and Cecil C. Jackson Jr. to Dr. John W. Nixon, July 8, 1965, both folder 12, box 022392, Alabama Governors' Papers. Jackson was Wallace's executive secretary and replied to Nixon on his behalf.

76. "Voter Registration Campaign Continues," *The Crisis,* June–July 1968, 202, 203; "Registration Campaign Enrolled Million Voters," *The Crisis,* February 1969, 86–87; Katie McGill Interview, November 1, 2001, 4, NSV-UNCC.

77. "Mobile Civil Rights Achievements, 1962–1968, Non-Partisan Voters League," pt. 2, reel 16, and "Registering to Vote," n.d., pt. 2, reel 11, both CRSA Papers.

78. John W. Macy to Lyndon B. Johnson, January 31, 1966, pt. 1, reel 9, CRDJA Papers; Bernard S. Lee to Hosea Williams, November 8, 1965, pt. 4, reel 19, SCLC Papers; U.S. Commission on Civil Rights, *Political Participation,* 155.

79. U.S. Commission on Civil Rights Press Release, December 5, 1965, pt. 4, reel 20, SCLC Papers; Andrew Young Interview, June 18, 1970, 27, pt. 3, reel 3, CRDJA Papers; Rev. Walter E. Fauntroy to John Doar, December 15, 1965, pt. 4, reel 6, SCLC Papers.

80. Golden A. Frinks to Nicholas Katzenbach, May 14, 1966, folder 8, box 2, and Dr. Reginald A. Hawkins to Ramsey Clark, June 11, 1968, folder 9, box 2, both Hawkins Papers.

81. U.S. Commission on Civil Rights, "Extension and Expansion of the Vot-

ing Rights Act of 1965," memorandum, March 28, 1969, 3–4, reel 21, CRDNA Papers.

82. George C. Wallace to Hugh P. King, August 9, 1965, George C. Wallace to Nettie L. Tate, August 12, 1965 (first two quotations), and George C. Wallace to Virgil Chappell, August 17, 1965 (last quotation), all folder 11, box 022395, Alabama Governors' Papers.

83. U.S. Commission on Civil Rights, "Extension and Expansion of the Voting Rights Act of 1965," memorandum, March 28, 1969, reel 21, CRDNA Papers; Statement of Mrs. Frankie Freeman, July 9, 1969, U.S. Congress, Senate, Committee on the Judiciary, *Amendments to the Voting Rights Act of 1965: Hearings before the Subcommittee on Constitutional Rights,* 91st Cong., 1st sess., 1969, and 91st Cong., 2nd sess., 1970, 47; Bernard S. Lee to Hosea Williams, November 8, 1965, pt. 4, reel 19, SCLC Papers.

84. Hubert Humphrey to Lyndon B. Johnson, February 2, 1966, pt. 1, reel 9, CRDJA Papers; "The Department of Justice during the Administration of President Lyndon B. Johnson: Civil Rights Division," January 1969, 34, "Civil Rights Division Narrative History 1 of 2" folder, pt. 10, box 5, Administrative Histories, LBJ Library.

85. U.S. Commission on Civil Rights, *Political Participation,* 115–27 (quotation on 116); Statement of Mrs. Frankie Freeman, July 9, 1969, U.S. Congress, *Amendments to the Voting Rights Act of 1965,* 46.

86. "Rationale of Program Components" (Wilcox County report), December 1965, pt. 4, reel 9, SCLC Papers; U.S. Commission on Civil Rights, *Political Participation,* 116–17, 127–28 (quotation).

87. U.S. Commission on Civil Rights, *Political Participation,* 177 (first quotation); Ramsey Clark Interview, February 11, 1969, 24, pt. 3, reel 1, CRDJA Papers.

2. "Token Beginnings"

1. F. Peter Libassi to Douglass Cater, February 2, 1967, "HU2-5 Education-Schooling 1/6/67–2/20/67" folder, box 51, White House Central Files, LBJ Library; Douglass Cater to the President, June 30, 1967, pt. 1, reel 8, CRDJA Papers.

2. "School Desegregation 1966: The Slow Undoing," December 1966, 4, reel 221, SRC Papers; "10 Years of Civil Rights—Report by the Chief Enforcer," *U.S. News and World Report,* September 23, 1974, 87.

3. Amicus Curiae Brief for the Houston Chapter, the American Jewish Committee, January 1967, *Broussard v. Houston Independent School District,* pt. 23A, sec. 3, reel 10, NAACP Papers; "May 17, 1954—Eleven Years Later," *The Crisis,* May 1965, 279.

4. Patterson, *Brown v. Board of Education,* xvii–xviii (quotation on xvii).

5. American Friends Service Committee and NAACP LDF to John W. Gardner, November 15, 1965, pt. 4, reel 2, SCLC Papers; Office of Civil Rights History, "OCR Historical Record," January 1969, 41–47 (first quotation on 46), "Administrative History of the HEW 2 of 2" folder, vol. 1, pt. 3, box 2, Administrative Histories, LBJ Library; Francis Keppel to Superintendent (sample letter), n.d. (Keppel quotation), pt. 1, reel 8, CRDJA Papers.

6. Press Conference, n.d. (Califano quotation), "School Desegregation"

folder, box 8, Joseph Califano Files, LBJ Library; U.S. Commission on Civil Rights, *Survey of School Desegregation in the Southern and Border States, 1965–66* (Washington, DC: U.S. Government Printing Office, 1966), 79–81; F. Peter Libassi to Joseph Califano, August 1, 1966, pt. 1, reel 8, CRDJA Papers; Statement by Nicholas deB. Katzenbach in Support of the Proposed Civil Rights Act of 1966, June 6, 1966, 8, pt. 1, reel 11, CRDJA Papers.

7. Francis Keppel to Joseph A. Califano Jr., August 29, 1965 (first quotation), "Education and the Civil Rights Act," September 29, 1965, Joe Califano to the President, September 10, 1965 (second quotation), and HEW Compliance Report, September 16, 1965, all pt. 1, reel 8, CRDJA Papers.

8. NAACP 1965 Annual Report (Southeast Region) (first quotation), folder 24, box 17, Kelly Alexander Papers; American Friends Service Committee and NAACP LDF to John W. Gardner, November 15, 1965 (second quotation), and Alabama Council on Human Relations, "The First Year of Desegregation under Title Six in Alabama," September 1965, both pt. 4, reel 2, SCLC Papers. The impact of opposition from southern politicians, particularly Democrats, on school desegregation policies during the Johnson administration is explored further below.

9. HEW Compliance Report, September 16, 1965, pt. 1, reel 8, CRDJA Papers.

10. Crespino, *In Search of Another Country,* 176.

11. Address by Nicholas deB. Katzenbach, June 4, 1966, pt. 1, reel 11, CRDJA Papers; "Mass Integration Is Quiet in South," *New York Times,* August 31, 1965, 1, 42 (King quotation).

12. Wilkinson, *From Brown to Bakke,* 109–10; "Possible SNCC Protest against Office of Education Desegregation Policy," n.d., and Douglass Cater to Marvin Watson, February 22, 1966, both pt. 1, reel 8, CRDJA Papers; Douglass Cater to Lyndon Johnson, March 25, 1966, "Douglass Cater: Memorandums to the President, March 1966" folder, box 14, Douglass Cater Files, LBJ Library.

13. U.S. Commission on Civil Rights, *Survey of School Desegregation,* 55–66; Douglass Cater to Marvin Watson, February 22, 1966, pt. 1, reel 8, CRDJA Papers.

14. "Desegregation: It Remains a Lagging Uphill Battle," *New York Times,* January 12, 1966, 45; John A. Hannah to Lyndon Baines Johnson, February 11, 1966 (Civil Rights Commission quotation), pt. 1, reel 8, CRDJA Papers; NAACP Southeast Region 1967 Annual Report, 5, folder 25, box 17, Kelly Alexander Papers.

15. U.S. Commission on Civil Rights, *Survey of School Desegregation,* 56–66 (quotation on 63).

16. Constance Curry, *Silver Rights: The Story of the Carter Family's Brave Decision to Send Their Children to an All-White School and Claim Their Civil Rights* (San Diego: Harcourt Brace, 1995), xix–xxvii, 1–22.

17. Marian Wright Edelman, introduction to Curry, *Silver Rights,* xi–xvii (quotations on xiv, xv).

18. "Statement by Harold Howe II, U.S. Commissioner of Education," March 7, 1966 (quotations), and Harold Howe II to Farris Bryant et al., April 13, 1966, both pt. 1, reel 8, CRDJA Papers.

19. F. Peter Libassi to Joseph Califano et al., August 8, 1966 (quotation), pt. 1, reel 8, CRDJA Papers; "Remarks of William L. Taylor, Staff Director, U.S.

Commission on Civil Rights," June 11, 1966, 1–2, "Civil Rights (4)" folder, box 22, Harry McPherson Files, LBJ Library.

20. F. Peter Libassi to Joseph Califano et al., August 10, 1966, pt. 1, reel 8, CRDJA Papers; Crespino, *In Search of Another Country,* 137–39, 176–77.

21. Douglass Cater to the President, June 30, 1967, "Douglass Cater: Memorandums to the President, June 1967 (1)" folder, box 16, Douglass Cater Files, LBJ Library.

22. "Race and Schools," *New Republic,* October 12, 1968, 7.

23. Harold Howe II to Joseph A. Califano Jr., February 9, 1966 (first quotation), and Peter Libassi to the Secretary, September 26, 1967 (second quotation), and September 29, 1967, all pt. 1, reel 8, CRDJA Papers; "Freedom of Choice" (HEW document), October 1968 (final quotation), reel 15, CRDNA Papers.

24. "Remarks of Roy Wilkins," October 20, 1966, *Braxton v. The Board of Public Instruction of Duval County, Florida,* pt. 23A, sec. 1, reel 15, NAACP Papers; "NAACP Annual Meeting," January 8, 1968, *The Crisis,* February 1968, 45–47 (quotation on 46).

25. Barbara A. Morris to Robert L. Carter, January 17, 1968, and "Statement in Support of Defendants' Motion," June 26, 1968, both *Cato v. Parham,* pt. 23A, sec. 1, reel 12, NAACP Papers.

26. Trial Testimony of Robert Cunningham, November 30, 1966, 54, and Trial Testimony of Revis Hall, December 1, 1966, 182, both *Lee v. Macon County,* pt. 23A, sec. 1, reel 9, NAACP Papers.

27. Mrs. Owen Barfield to Sam Ervin, February 14, 1968, folder 7573, and William H. Wheeler Jr. to Sam Ervin, December 15, 1967, folder 7572, both box 170, Ervin Papers.

28. Herman Talmadge Interview, July 17, 1969, 15, pt. 3, reel 3, CRDJA Papers; Crespino, *In Search of Another Country,* 175 (quotations); Sam J. Ervin Jr. to Earnest M. Watkins, July 30, 1968, folder 7578, box 170, Ervin Papers.

29. F. Peter Libassi to the Secretary, September 26, 1967, pt. 1, reel 8, CRDJA Papers; Douglass Cater to the President, May 13, 1965, and May 27, 1965, both "Douglass Cater: Memorandums to the President, May 1965" folder, box 13, Douglass Cater Files, LBJ Library.

30. Harold D. Cooley to Mr. President, September 14, 1966, and Henry H. Wilson Jr. to Lyndon Johnson, September 28, 1966, both "HU2-5 Education-Schooling 9/1/66–1/5/67" folder, box 51, White House Central Files, LBJ Library.

31. Henry H. Wilson Jr. to Joe Califano, April 5, 1966, "Civil Rights" folder, box 11, Henry Wilson Files, LBJ Library; Douglass Cater to Lyndon Johnson, February 26, 1966, and Nicholas deB. Katzenbach to Lyndon Johnson, February 10, 1966, both "Douglass Cater: Memorandums to the President, February 1966" folder, box 14, Douglass Cater Files, LBJ Library.

32. Richard B. Russell et al. to Mr. President, May 2, 1966, "HU2-5 Education-Schooling 5/4/66–8/31/66" folder, box 50, White House Central Files, LBJ Library; Lyndon B. Johnson to Richard B. Russell, May 16, 1966, ser. 10, folder 6, box 126, Russell Papers. For an example of ongoing lobbying, see B. Everett Jordan to John W. Gardner, September 12, 1966, "HU2-5 Education-Schooling 9/1/66–1/5/67" folder, box 51, White House Central Files, LBJ Library.

33. William J. Peterson Jr. to Richard B. Russell, October 24, 1966, David S. Seeley to Bobby Driggers, October 25, 1966, Charles Campbell Memo to File, October 19, 1966 (first quotation), and William J. Peterson Jr. to Richard B.

Russell, October 14, 1966 (second quotation), all ser. 10, folder 6, box 122, Russell Papers.

34. Report of Subcommittee on Tax Exemption for Segregated Schools, October 6, 1967 (quotations), and Report of the Subcommittee on Education, October 9, 1967, both pt. 1, reel 11, CRDJA Papers.

35. Junius Griffin to Dr. Martin Luther King Jr., n.d., pt. 4, reel 19, SCLC Papers; "The Natchez Agreement," *The Crisis,* January 1966, 24–26; Crosby, *A Little Taste of Freedom,* 101–17; "School Desegregation," *The Crisis,* October 1965, 524–25 (quotation).

36. "Why We Protest," October 1966, *Board of Public Instruction of Duval County, Florida v. NAACP,* pt. 23A, sec. 1, reel 15, NAACP Papers. For an overview of the NAACP's prior activism in Jacksonville, see Abel A. Bartley, "The 1960 and 1964 Jacksonville Riots: How Struggle Led to Progress," *Florida Historical Quarterly* 78, no. 1 (1999): 46–73.

37. Deposition of Wendell P. Holmes Jr., March 15, 1967, 12, and Final Judgment, April 17, 1967, 10, 12 (Waybright quotation), both *Board of Public Instruction of Duval County, Florida v. NAACP,* pt. 23A, sec. 1, reel 15, NAACP Papers; "NAACP Sets 2-Day School Boycott Here," *Florida Times-Union,* October 23, 1966; James B. Crooks, *Jacksonville: The Consolidation Story, from Civil Rights to the Jaguars* (Gainesville: University Press of Florida, 2004), 99–101.

38. U.S. Commission on Civil Rights, *The Black/White Colleges: Dismantling the Dual System of Higher Education* (Washington, DC: U.S. Government Printing Office, 1981), 7–9; F. Peter Libassi to the Secretary, June 14, 1967, pt. 1, reel 8, CRDJA Paper; Peter Wallenstein, "Afterword: Unfinished Business," in *Higher Education and the Civil Rights Movement: White Supremacy, Black Southerners, and College Campuses,* ed. Peter Wallenstein (Gainesville: University Press of Florida, 2008), 229–37 (quotation on 229).

39. Marcia G. Synnott, "African American Women Pioneers in Desegregating Higher Education," in Wallenstein, ed., *Higher Education and the Civil Rights Movement,* 204–5.

40. Douglass Cater to Lyndon Johnson, April 14, 1965, "Douglass Cater: Memorandums to the President, March–April 1965" folder, box 13, Douglass Cater Files, LBJ Library; Gertrude Samuels, "Four Years After Governor Wallace Stood in the Door—There Are 300 Negroes at the University of Alabama," *New York Times Magazine,* May 14, 1967, 32–33, 79, 80, 82, 84, 86, 88–89 (quotations on 84).

41. "May Queens and Effigies," *Newsweek,* June 5, 1967, 40–41.

42. Ernest Green, "Address Before Arkansas State AFL-CIO," June 7, 1967, folder 34, box 1595, AFL-CIO Civil Rights Papers.

43. David Johnson, Interview with Author (Minchin), July 27, 1997, Bogalusa, LA (first quotation); Lyndon B. Johnson to Franklin D. Roosevelt Jr., January 6, 1966, pt. 1, reel 8, CRDJA Papers.

44. "Administrative History of the EEOC" (Johnson administration document), November 1, 1968, 5–6, pt. 2, reel 1, CRDJA Papers; U.S. Commission on Civil Rights, *Jobs and Civil Rights,* 13–16 (quotations on 14, 16).

45. "Administrative History of the EEOC," November 1, 1968, 99–104, 203 (McClellan quotations on 99), and Franklin D. Roosevelt Jr. to Lyndon B. Johnson, October 29, 1965, both pt. 2, reel 1, CRDJA Papers; U.S. Commission on Civil Rights, *Jobs and Civil Rights,* 18.

46. MacLean, *Freedom Is Not Enough,* 70, 120–21; EEOC Second Annual Report, June 1, 1968, 6, pt. 2, reel 3, CRDJA Papers.

47. Testimony of B. Tartt Bell, January 15, 1962, U.S. Congress, *Proposed Federal Legislation to Prohibit Discrimination in Employment,* 762; Testimony of Herbert Hill, ibid., 719.

48. EEOC's Office of Research and Reports, "Negro Employment in the Textile Industries of North and South Carolina," November 21, 1966, vii (second quotation), 1 (first quotation), 25, 43–46, pt. 2, reel 2, and EEOC Second Annual Report, June 1, 1968, 22, pt. 2, reel 3, both CRDJA Papers.

49. "Plaintiffs' Proposed Findings of Fact and Conclusions of Law," March 30, 1981, 4–5, *Edgar Russell et al. v. American Tobacco Company,* and "Plaintiffs' Proposed Findings of Fact and Conclusions of Law," July 7, 1969, 3–6 (quotation on 6), *Dorothy P. Robinson et al. v. P. Lorillard,* both NARA-Atlanta.

50. Clifford L. Alexander Jr. Interview, June 4, 1973, 13–14, pt. 3, reel 1, and "Administrative History of the EEOC," November 1, 1968, 53, 122, 196–97, and Franklin D. Roosevelt Jr. to Lyndon B. Johnson, October 29, 1965, both pt. 2, reel 1, all CRDJA Papers; Remarks by Don Slaiman, January 13, 1971, 5, folder 13, box 1593, AFL-CIO Civil Rights Papers.

51. "Administrative History of the EEOC," November 1, 1968, 44–46, 58 (quotation), 111–12, and Franklin D. Roosevelt Jr. to Lyndon B. Johnson, October 29, 1965, both pt. 2, reel 1, and EEOC Second Annual Report, June 1, 1968, pt. 2, reel 3, all CRDJA Papers.

52. "Administrative History of the EEOC," November 1, 1968, 44–46, pt. 2, reel 1, and Clifford L. Alexander Jr. to Lloyd Hackler, August 31, 1967, and EEOC Second Annual Report, June 1, 1968, 21–24 (quotation on 23), both pt. 2, reel 3, all CRDJA Papers.

53. EEOC Second Annual Report, June 1, 1968, pt. 2, reel 3 (quotation), and "Administrative History of the EEOC," November 1, 1968, 119–26, pt. 2, reel 1, both CRDJA Papers.

54. NAACP Southeastern Region: 1965 Annual Report, 21–23 (quotation on 21), folder 24, box 17, Kelly Alexander Papers.

55. John W. Nixon to Lyndon Johnson, May 23, 1966, "Civil Rights (4)" folder, box 22, Harry McPherson Files, LBJ Library; Report of the 24th Convention of the NAACP North Carolina Conference of Branches, November 24–25, 1967, folder 11, box 23, Kelly Alexander Papers; "Administrative History of the EEOC," November 1, 1968, 106, pt. 2, reel 1, CRDJA Papers; EEOC, *Making a Right a Reality,* 15 (Rayburn quotation).

56. NAACP Southeastern Region: 1965 Annual Report, 21–23, folder 24, box 17, Kelly Alexander Papers.

57. "Credit," *The Crisis,* January 1966, 8; "NAACP Files Job Bias Complaints," *The Crisis,* May 1967, 211–12; "Administrative History of the EEOC," November 1, 1968, 117, pt. 2, reel 1, CRDJA Papers.

58. EEOC, *Making a Right a Reality,* 14, 15 (quotations); "Accomplishments of the Equal Employment Opportunity Commission," July–August 1967, pt. 2, reel 3, CRDJA Papers.

59. "Summary Report of Pending Complaints on Civil Rights," April 19, 1965, folder 1, box 2839, and Remarks by Don Slaiman, January 13, 1971, 5, folder 13, box 1593, both AFL-CIO Civil Rights Papers.

60. Franklin D. Roosevelt Jr. to Lyndon B. Johnson, October 29, 1965, and "Administrative History of the EEOC," November 1, 1968, 197, both pt. 2, reel 1, CRDJA Papers.

61. MacLean, *Freedom Is Not Enough,* 1–2; "Negro Leader Killed by Blast in Natchez," *New York Times,* February 28, 1967, 1, 40; "Natchez Bomber Strikes Again," *The Crisis,* April 1967, 132–37 (quotations on 133, 134).

62. Michelle Brattain, *The Politics of Whiteness: Race, Workers, and Culture in the Modern South* (Princeton, NJ: Princeton University Press, 2001), 3–17; MacLean, *Freedom Is Not Enough,* 13–34.

63. "Negro Hopes Wane as '64 Civil Rights Law Founders," *Wall Street Journal,* January 13, 1967, clipping, "Civil Rights 1967–1968" folder, box 331, Fred Panzer Files, LBJ Library.

64. EEOC's Office of Research and Reports, "Nine City Minority Group Employment Profile," August 6, 1967 (quotation), "Atlanta Standard Metropolitan Statistical Area Employment Profile," 1966, and "New Orleans Standard Metropolitan Statistical Area Employment Profile," 1966, all pt. 2, reel 2, CRDJA Papers.

65. Clifford L. Alexander Jr. Interview, November 1, 1971, 35 (first Alexander quotation), and June 4, 1973, 8 (second Alexander quotation), pt. 3, reel 1, and EEOC "Second Annual Report," June 1, 1968, 13, pt. 2, reel 3, all CRDJA Papers.

66. "Jobs, Job Training, and Economic Security—Preliminary Report," December 3, 1965, pt. 1, reel 14, CRDJA Papers; Report of the 24th Convention of the NAACP North Carolina Conference of Branches, November 24–25, 1967 (NAACP quotation), folder 11, box 23, Kelly Alexander Papers; Lyndon Johnson, "Message on Equal Justice," February 15, 1967, 12, "Civil Rights—General—1967" folder, box 7, Barefoot Sanders Files, LBJ Library.

67. Robert M. Wood to Richard B. Russell, August 18, 1967, and Richard B. Russell to Robert M. Wood, August 24, 1967, both ser. 10, folder 4, box 5, Russell Papers. For another example of employer opposition to an expanded EEOC, see John P. Baum to Richard B. Russell, March 13, 1968, ser. 10, folder 6, box 4, Russell Papers.

68. Alan Brinkley, *American History: A Survey,* vol. 2, *Since 1865* (Boston: McGraw-Hill, 2003), 819. For a good overview of black migration to the North, see the essays in Joe William Trotter Jr., ed., *The Great Migration in Historical Perspective: New Dimensions of Race, Class, and Gender* (Bloomington: Indiana University Press, 1991).

69. "Median Negro Income outside South Is $5700," *New York Times,* October 25, 1968, 50; "Final Draft: Negro Report," 1967, "Negro Statistics" folder, box 57, Harry McPherson Files, LBJ Library; "Civil Rights" (Johnson administration fact sheet), May 8, 1968, pt. 1, reel 10, CRDJA Papers; "The White House Message on Civil Rights," January 24, 1968, "Civil Rights" folder, box 17, Barefoot Sanders Files, LBJ Library.

70. "Jobs, Job Training, and Economic Security—Preliminary Report," December 3, 1965, pt. 1, reel 14, CRDJA Papers.

71. "NAACP Special Report: Starvation in America," *The Crisis,* August–September 1967, 382–86 (quotations on 382); "Aiding the Rural Poor" and "Feed Me!" *The Crisis,* May 1968, 152–55, 156–59.

72. "Black Farm Families—Hunger and Malnutrition in Rural Alabama," April 28, 1968 (quotation on 7), pt. 4, reel 20, SCLC Papers.

73. Report of the Subcommittee on Public Employment (Task Force on Civil Rights for 1968), October 6, 1967, in pt. 1, reel 11, CRDJA Papers.

74. "Atlanta SCLC to Launch 'Operation Breadbasket,'" October 23, 1962 (first quotation), Rev. Fred C. Bennette Jr., "A Report of Activities in Operation Breadbasket Department," July 19, 1965, 6–8 (quotation on 8), Andrew J. Young to Edward G. Sullivan, January 30, 1968, Rev. Fred C. Bennettte Jr. to Dr. William A. Rutherford, January 22, 1968, and Leonard R. Mitchell to Randolph T. Blackwell, February 1, 1966, all pt. 4, reel 23, SCLC Papers.

75. Branch, At Canaan's Edge, 670–73; John Dittmer, Local People: The Struggle for Civil Rights in Mississippi (Urbana: University of Illinois Press, 1995), 383 (Kennedy quotation); "Statement by Dr. Martin Luther King Jr.," December 4, 1967, 3 (King quotation), pt. 4, reel 27, SCLC Papers.

76. Branch, At Canaan's Edge, 719 (King quotation); Honey, Going Down Jericho Road, 98–127, 317–18, 418–23 (quotation on 317).

77. Carter, The Music Has Gone Out of the Movement, 201, 208.

78. "Panel on Civil Disorders Calls for Drastic Action to Avoid 2-Society Nation," New York Times, March 1, 1968, 1, 22 (quotations); "Text of Summary of Report by National Advisory Commission on Civil Disorders," New York Times, March 1, 1968, 20.

79. Roy Wilkins with Tom Mathews, Standing Fast: The Autobiography of Roy Wilkins (New York: Viking, 1982), 328.

80. Wade Murrah to Editor, March 6, 1968, ser. 10, folder 6, box 4, Russell Papers. For another similar example, see Donald E. Eberhart to Richard Russell, May 20, 1968, ser. 10, folder 4, box 4, Russell Papers.

81. "Text of Summary of Report by National Advisory Commission on Civil Disorders," New York Times, March 1, 1968, 20 (quotation); Carter, The Music Has Gone Out of the Movement, 226, 232.

82. Branch, At Canaan's Edge, 752–66; Honey, Going Down Jericho Road, 364–65.

3. A Fragmented Crusade?

1. Honey, Going Down Jericho Road, 407–8, 433–42 (quotation on 442); Branch, At Canaan's Edge, 763–64, 769–70.

2. "In the Nation's Press: The Convention," The Crisis, August–September 1970, 276–79; Robert J. Norrell, The House I Live In: Race in the American Century (New York: Oxford University Press, 2005), 263–68.

3. "A Fragmented Crusade," New York Times, April 5, 1969, 1; "Dr. King's Followers Modify His Approach in Their Continuing Pursuit of Social Change," New York Times, January 7, 1972, 9 (Abernathy quotation). For a full analysis of Abernathy's strengths and weaknesses, see Gaillard, "It's Abernathy's Dream Now."

4. Theodore Hesburgh to Len Garment, December 10, 1970, reel 3, CRDNA Papers; Carter, The Music Has Gone Out of the Movement, xii–xv.

5. Theodore Hesburgh to Len Garment, December 10, 1970, reel 3, CRDNA Papers; Thomas A. Johnson, "Decade of Change in South Gives Negroes High Hopes," New York Times, August 16, 1970, 1, 54; "Decade of Black Struggle Has Mixed Result in South," New York Times, February 8, 1970, 1, 50 (closing quotation).

6. Honey, *Going Down Jericho Road,* 445–47 (quotation on 447); "Memorandum for the President: Civil Disturbances," April 8, 1968, pt. 1, reel 4, CRDJA Papers.

7. Honey, *Going Down Jericho Road,* 447; Situation Room Information Memorandum, April 8, 1968 (Nashville quotation), pt. 1, reel 4, CRDJA Papers.

8. "900 Police, Firemen Called for Funeral," *Atlanta Constitution,* April 8, 1968, 3; "April Aftermath of the King Assassination" (Riot Data Review study), August 1968, pt. 1, reel 10, CRDJA Papers.

9. Alfred L. Alexander Interview, May 10, 2001, 11–12, NSV-UNCC; Dr. Robert Albright Interview, August 10, 1992, 7, NSV-UNCC; Larry Reni Thomas, *The True Story behind the Wilmington Ten* (Hampton, VA: U.B. & U.S. Communications, 1993), 23–33 (Hans quotation on 26).

10. GER to Lyndon Johnson, April 6, 1968, pt. 1, reel 4, CRDJA Papers. GER was, apparently, George Reedy, who was a special assistant to LBJ at this time.

11. "April Aftermath of the King Assassination" (Riot Data Review study), August 1968, pt. 1, reel 10, CRDJA Papers (quotations on 69); "Funeral Is Ignored by Whites but Some Atlanta Stores Close," *New York Times,* April 10, 1968, 33; "Maddox to Spend Day in His Office," *Atlanta Constitution,* April 9, 1968, 3. For reaction to King's death, see also "200,000 Pay Tribute to King," *Atlanta Constitution,* April 10, 1968, 1, 10.

12. Lucy T. Davis to Strom Thurmond, April 7, 1968, Civil Rights 3, folder 2, box 4, and John B. Halloran to Strom Thurmond, July 14, 1968, Civil Rights 2, folder 2, box 3, both Thurmond Papers; Sally T. Basler and Frank L. Basler to Richard B. Russell, April 8, 1968, ser. 10, folder 5, box 4, Russell Papers.

13. Lindsey Cowen et al. to Richard Russell, April 9, 1968, ser. 10, folder 5, box 4, Russell Papers; Marjorie Langdale to Strom Thurmond, April 5, 1968, Civil Rights 1, folder 3, box 3, Thurmond Papers. For another fine example of a similar letter, see Mrs. Mary Lee Hart to Richard B. Russell, May 17, 1968, ser. 10, folder 4, box 4, Russell Papers.

14. PAM Memo to File, May 24, 1968, ser. 10, folder 4, box 4, Russell Papers; Strom Thurmond to Henry S. Johnson, July 22, 1968 (quotation), Civil Rights 2, folder 3, box 4, Thurmond Papers; W. B. Outz Jr. to Richard Russell, April 15, 1968, ser. 10, folder 4, box 118, Russell Papers.

15. William H. Chafe, *The Unfinished Journey: America since World War II* (New York: Oxford University Press, 1995), 368 (first two quotations); John Morton Blum, *Years of Discord: American Politics and Society, 1961–1974* (New York: Norton, 1991), 304.

16. Albert Turner, "Weekly Progress Report," March 11, 1968, pt. 4, reel 27, SCLC Papers; Fairclough, *To Redeem the Soul of America,* 385–88.

17. Address by Rev. Dr. Ralph David Abernathy, June 19, 1968 (first Abernathy quotation), and "Statement Prepared by Dr. Ralph D. Abernathy," July 16, 1968 (other Abernathy quotations), both pt. 4, reel 26, SCLC Papers; Honey, *Going Down Jericho Road,* 500–501; Gerald D. McKnight, *The Last Crusade: Martin Luther King, Jr., the FBI, and the Poor People's Campaign* (Boulder, CO: Westview, 1998), 141–42.

18. Mary Neary to Strom Thurmond, April 20, 1968, Civil Rights 3, folder 3, box 4, Thurmond Papers.

19. Jess F. Heard to Strom Thurmond, May 7, 1968, Civil Rights 3, folder 4, box 4, Thurmond Papers; Zach C. Hayes to Richard B. Russell, June 11, 1968

(second quotation), ser. 10, folder 2, box 103, and Margaret D. Cobb to Richard B. Russell, December 8, 1967, ser. 10, folder 1, box 5, both Russell Papers; "The Leader of the Great Crusade," *Montgomery (AL) Advertiser,* May 2, 1968, clipping, pt. 4, reel 27, SCLC Papers.

20. Bartley, *The New South,* 394–97; Norrell, *The House I Live In,* 266; Norton et al., *A People and a Nation,* 876 (Nixon quotation); Harry Dent Interview, April 3, 1978, 1, 3 (quotation), box 1, A. James Reichley Interview Transcripts, Ford Library.

21. Dean J. Kotlowski, *Nixon's Civil Rights: Politics, Principle, and Policy* (Cambridge, MA: Harvard University Press, 2001), 2 (quotation), 9–10.

22. "Wilkins Assesses Nixon's '100 Days'" *The Crisis,* May 1969, 216–17.

23. "The Nomination of Judge Haynsworth" and "Guidelines Retreat Called 'Invitation to Disaster,'" *The Crisis,* August–September 1969, 270–71, 280–81 (Wilkins quotation on 281); Kotlowski, *Nixon's Civil Rights,* 77–93.

24. Richard Nixon, *RN: The Memoirs of Richard Nixon* (New York: Macmillan, 1978), 437 (Moynihan and Nixon quotations); "The 61st Annual Convention—Arousing a National Storm," *The Crisis,* August–September 1970, 255–56 (Spottswood and Garment).

25. "The March of Time," *Newsweek,* September 10, 1973, 39; Fairclough, *To Redeem the Soul of America,* 389–97; Nixon, *RN,* 436 (quotations).

26. Carson, *In Struggle,* 260–64, 287–98; "Innis Says Nixon Puts Blacks Off," *Atlanta Constitution,* September 7, 1970, 10A; Meier and Rudwick, *CORE,* 424–25 (Innis quotation on 424).

27. Fairclough, *Race and Democracy,* 381–87; Tuck, *Beyond Atlanta,* 197–201.

28. "Abernathy Pledges Support to Strikers," *Charleston News and Courier,* April 1, 1969, 1A, 7A; "Charleston Finale," *New York Times,* July 22, 1969, 38. For an excellent study of the strike, see Leon Fink and Brian Greenberg, *Upheaval in the Quiet Zone: A History of Hospital Workers' Union, Local 1199* (Urbana: University of Illinois Press, 1989).

29. J. Mills Thornton III, *Dividing Lines: Municipal Politics and the Struggle for Civil Rights in Montgomery, Birmingham, and Selma* (Tusacaloosa: University of Alabama Press, 2002), 500; "A Fragmented Crusade," *New York Times,* April 5, 1969.

30. Johnson, "Decade of Change in South," 1 (Gilmore quotation); Mary E. Mebane, "The Black and White Bus Lines," *New York Times,* January 2, 1971, 17.

31. Sokol, *There Goes My Everything,* 109 (Thompson quotations); Testimony of Clarence Mitchell, July 10, 1969, U.S. Congress, *Amendments to the Voting Rights Act of 1965,* 91; "The 'Hot' Sixtieth," *The Crisis,* August–September 1969, 275.

32. Clarke Reed to Bryce Harlow, June 30, 1970, folder 202, box 6, Dent Papers; "Pulse of the Public," *Atlanta Constitution,* February 11, 1970, 4A.

33. "Sit-Ins Birthplace Has No Marker," *Winston-Salem Journal,* February 1, 1970.

34. Johnson, "Decade of Change in South"; Samuel W. Dart to Richard Nixon, December 19, 1969, folder 15, box 022637, Alabama Governors' Papers.

35. "Five Years After, Selma Cannot Forget Historic Rights March," *New York Times,* March 22, 1970, 44 (Falkenberry quotation); Aaron Henry Interview, September 12, 1970, III-7, pt. 3, reel 2, CRDJA Papers.

36. Department of Justice Annual Report, February 3, 1970, reel 2, CRDNA Papers (quotation); Howard Glenn to Sam J. Ervin, folder 8511, box 190, Ervin Papers.

37. "Starting Out: Challenging the Status Quo," *SPLC Report,* Special Anniversary Issue, January 2006, 4. The *SPLC Report* is the modern-day successor of the *Poverty Law Report.*

38. "Seeking Justice: A Brief History of the Southern Poverty Law Center," www.splcenter.org/center/history/history.jsp (accessed September 1, 2006); Morris Dees, "A Smith Corona and a $15 Check," *SPLC Report,* Special Anniversary Issue, January 2006, 2 (quotation); "Gilmore v. Montgomery," *Poverty Law Report,* January 1976, 3.

39. U.S. Commission on Civil Rights, "Extension and Expansion of the Voting Rights Act of 1965," memorandum, March 28, 1969, reel 21, CRDNA Papers; Theodore M. Hesburgh to Charles Raper Jonas, December 8, 1969, folder 822, box 17, Jonas Papers.

40. "The Negro Vote in 1969," *The Crisis,* December 1969, 394; "Mississippi: Jubilee Day," *Newsweek,* May 26, 1969, 25; "Blacks in Politics: A Long Way to Go in Mississippi," *New Republic,* June 28, 1969, 19–21; Charles Evers Interview, April 3, 1974, 15 (Evers letter quotation), pt. 3, reel 1, CRDJA Papers.

41. "Negro Voted Mayor of Chapel Hill, N.C.," *New York Times,* May 7, 1969, 1, 31 (Lee quotation); "Elections: The Mayor of Chapel Hill," *Newsweek,* May 19, 1969, 15–16.

42. J. Stanley Pottinger to Stanley S. Scott, September 24, 1974, "Voting Rights Act Extension" folder, box 23, Stanley Scott Files, and Thomas R. Hunt to J. Stanley Pottinger, October 25, 1974, "Civil Rights—Weekly Reports (2)" folder, box 3, Geoffrey Shepard Files, both Ford Library.

43. U.S. Commission on Civil Rights, "Extension and Expansion of the Voting Rights Act of 1965," memorandum, March 28, 1969, Jerris Leonard to John Ehrlichman, June 9, 1969 (Court's decision quotation), and U.S. Supreme Court, *Gaston County, North Carolina v. United States,* June 2, 1969, 9, all reel 21, CRDNA Papers.

44. Lewis with D'Orso, *Walking with the Wind,* 434 (Lewis quotation); Testimony of Vernon E. Jordan Jr., February 25, 1970, U.S. Congress, *Amendments to the Voting Rights Act of 1965,* 445–48; VEP, "How to Conduct a Registration Campaign," May 1967 (closing quotation on 3), pt. 4, reel 20, SCLC Papers.

45. Lewis with D'Orso, *Walking with the Wind,* 436; Ella J. Baker, "Bigger Than a Hamburger," in Carson et al., eds., *The Eyes on the Prize Civil Rights Reader,* 120–22.

46. For an informative biography of Hamer, see Chana Kai Lee, *For Freedom's Sake: The Life of Fannie Lou Hamer* (Urbana: University of Illinois Press, 1999).

47. Lewis with D'Orso, *Walking with the Wind,* 435.

48. "Louisville, KY" and "Clarksville, Tenn.," *The Crisis,* April 1969, 183; "Youth Unit Leads Voter Drive," *The Crisis,* August 1971, 193.

49. Mike Monroe to Daniel P. Moynihan, June 12, 1969, reel 21, CRDNA Papers.

50. Arthur W. Stanley, "White Violence—Lamar, S.C.," *The Crisis,* May 1970, 196.

51. Testimony of Clarence Mitchell, July 10, 1969, U.S. Congress, *Amend-*

ments to the Voting Rights Act of 1965, 92, 95 (second quotation), 99–108 (first quotation on 108); Testimony of Aaron Henry, February 25, 1970, ibid., 482–88 (quotation on 488). See also Testimony of Vernon E. Jordan Jr., February 25, 1970, and Testimony of Mrs. Frankie Freeman, July 9, 1969, ibid., 28–87, 445–58.

52. U.S. Congress, *Amendments to the Voting Rights Act of 1965*, 274 (February 18, 1970; Ervin quotation); Testimony of Lester Maddox, February 24, 1970, 342, 365, and Testimony of A. F. Summer, February 24, 1970, 368, both ibid.

53. Mrs. W. T. Brightwell to Philip A. Hart, January 14, 1970, ser. 10, folder 6, box 3, Russell Papers. For another similar example, see Resolution by the Oglethorpe County (GA) Republican Party, March 7, 1970, ser. 10, folder 6, box 3, Russell Papers.

54. Mrs. Sidney Q. Janus to Richard B. Russell, March 10, 1970, ser. 10, folder 6, box 3, Russell Papers.

55. Steven F. Lawson, *In Pursuit of Power: Southern Blacks and Electoral Politics, 1965–1982* (New York: Columbia University Press, 1985), 154–57; Kotlowski, *Nixon's Civil Rights*, 71–72.

56. Minutes of the North Carolina NAACP Conference of Branches Annual Meeting, January 25, 1969, folder 13, box 23, Kelly Alexander Papers; U.S. Commission on Civil Rights, *Jobs and Civil Rights*, 6–7 (quotation on 6).

57. USIA Report, January 27, 1970 (Abernathy quotation), and William R. Hudgins et al. to Richard Nixon, February 6, 1970, both reel 2, CRDNA Papers.

58. NAACP 1970 Annual Report, 85 (first quotation), folder 2, box 26, and Minutes of the North Carolina NAACP Conference of Branches Annual Meeting, January 25, 1969 (Smith quotation), folder 13, box 23, both Kelly Alexander Papers; U.S. Commission on Civil Rights, *Jobs and Civil Rights*, 45.

59. Nicholls, "The Non-Partisan Voters League," 84; "Mobile Civil Rights Achievements 1962–1968, Non-Partisan Voters League," pt. 2, reel 16, CRSA Papers.

60. *Watkins v. United Steelworkers*, 516 F. 2d 41 (1975) at 43.

61. "Trouble in the South's First Industry: The Unions Are Coming," *New York Times Magazine*, August 5, 1973, 10; Decision of the Fourth Circuit Court in *Sledge v. J. P. Stevens*, October 4, 1978, 61, box 2, Amalgamated Clothing and Textile Workers' Union Southern Textile Regional Office Papers, Southern Labor Archives, Georgia State University; "Violence in the Factories," *Newsweek*, June 29, 1970, 45 (quotation).

62. Herbert Hill, Interview with Author (Minchin), November 16, 1995, Madison, WI; Alton Collins, Interview with Author (Minchin), February 3, 1996, Columbus, GA. For a fuller account of these changes and their significance, see Timothy J. Minchin, *Hiring the Black Worker: The Racial Integration of the Southern Textile Industry, 1960–1980* (Chapel Hill: University of North Carolina Press, 1999), esp. 1–6, 45–55.

63. Remarks of Elizabeth J. Kuck, December 3, 1969, 2, "EEOC 1969 (4 of 4)" folder, box 84, Garment Files, NPM; Deposition of Mae Crews, January 7, 1970, 37, *Adams v. Dan River Mills*, NARA-Philadelphia.

64. U.S. Commission on Civil Rights, *Jobs and Civil Rights*, 14, 19, 39. Nathan was the author of this detailed report.

65. William H. Brown III to Robert J. Brown, November 23, 1970, and "Statement of William H. Brown III," August 11, 1969, 4, 6 (first and last quotations), both "EEOC 1969 (2 of 4)" folder, box 84, Garment Files, NPM. For Brown's removal, see Kotlowski, *Nixon's Civil Rights*, 120–21.

66. "EEOC Coverage Expands July 2, 6 Million More Employees Protected by Title VII," press release, June 17, 1968, pt. 2, reel 3, CRDJA Papers; U.S. Commission on Civil Rights, *Jobs and Civil Rights,* 19.

67. Leonard Garment to Richard Nixon, August 4, 1970, "EEOC 1969 (3 of 4)" folder, box 84, Garment Files, NPM; Kotlowski, *Nixon's Civil Rights,* 118; William H. Brown III to Robert P. Mayo, December 10, 1969, "EEOC 1969 (4 of 4)" folder, box 84, Garment Files, NPM.

68. William H. Brown III to Melvin Laird, March 3, 1970, "EEOC 1969 (3 of 4)" folder, box 84, Garment Files, NPM; "Administrative History of the EEOC," November 1, 1968, 120–21, pt. 2, reel 1, CRDJA Papers; Jack Greenberg to Lyndon Johnson, February 1, 1968, "HU2-1 10/17/67–12/5/68" folder, box 44, White House Central Files, LBJ Library.

69. U.S. Commission on Civil Rights, *Jobs and Civil Rights,* 2, 87–103, 143 (quotations on 2, 143).

70. Robert Pruitt to Richard Nixon, June 21, 1970, and Noble M. Melencamp to Robert Pruitt, July 14, 1970, both reel 20, CRDNA Papers; "A Study of Patterns of Discrimination in Employment for the Equal Employment Opportunity Commission," September 1966, 1, pt. 2, reel 1, CRDJA Papers.

71. U.S. Commission on Civil Rights, *Jobs and Civil Rights,* 45 (Hill quotation).

72. Testimony of Allison L. Chapital, April 16, 1968, 30–31, 34–35, and "EEOC Decision," August 10, 1967, both *Chapital v. Chrysler Corporation,* pt. 23A, sec. 3, reel 1, NAACP Papers.

73. "EEOC Decision," May 14, 1968, and Trial Testimony of Lincoln Woods, December 13, 1971, 64, both pt. 23A, sec. 2, reel 4, and James J. Kilpatrick to William D. Wells, May 15, 1972, 2, pt. 23A, sec. 2, reel 1, all *Banks v. Lockheed-Georgia,* NAACP Papers.

74. Trial Testimony of Marion E. Franks, December 13, 1971, 80–81, and Trial Testimony of Ralph Banks, December 13, 1971, 198, both *Banks v. Lockheed-Georgia,* pt. 23A, sec. 2, reel 3, NAACP Papers.

75. For a representative snapshot of the NAACP's Title VII litigation, see Amended Complaint, August 23, 1968, *Love v. United States Steel Corporation,* pt. 23A, sec. 1, reel 9, Complaint, November 18, 1970, *Buckner v. Goodyear Tire and Rubber,* pt. 23A, sec. 1, reel 1, "Plaintiffs' Second Amended Complaint," May 1, 1970, *Parson v. Kaiser Aluminum,* pt. 23A, sec. 3, reel 3, and "Amended Complaint," n.d., *Norman v. Missouri Pacific Railroad,* pt. 23A, sec. 1, reel 14, all NAACP Papers.

76. William D. Wells to Nathaniel R. Jones, December 8, 1972, *Banks v. Lockheed-Georgia,* pt. 23A, sec. 2, reel 1, and Memorandum of Opinion and Order, March 7, 1972, 20, *Buckner v. Goodyear Tire and Rubber Company,* pt. 23A, sec. 1, reel 2, both NAACP Papers.

77. William D. Wells to Nathaniel R. Jones, December 8, 1972, *Banks v. Lockheed-Georgia,* pt. 23A, sec. 2, reel 1, and District Court Order, December 19, 1973, *Norman v. Missouri Pacific Railroad Company,* pt. 23A, sec. 1, reel 15, both NAACP Papers.

78. Alan Draper, *Conflict of Interests: Organized Labor and the Civil Rights Movement in the South, 1954–1968* (Ithaca, NY: ILR Press, 1994), 3–16; Zieger, *For Jobs and Freedom,* 175–207; MacLean, *Freedom Is Not Enough,* 90–103.

79. For an overview of the building trades controversy, see Graham, *The Civil Rights Era,* 280–87; and MacLean, *Freedom Is Not Enough,* 90–113.

80. John L. LeFlore to Fred Wilkins, August 5, 1970, pt. 2, reel 5, CRSA Papers; "The Tampa Urban League: A Proposal to Increase Minority Participation in Labor Unions' Apprenticeship Programs in Tampa, Florida" (Tampa Urban League document), n.d., and "Double Discrimination," *Tampa Tribune*, n.d., clipping, both folder 65, box 1596, AFL-CIO Civil Rights Papers.

81. E. T. Kehrer to Don Slaiman, June 8, 1871, and "Blacks Eye Militancy for Building Jobs," *New York Times*, n.d. (ca. 1971), clipping, folder 66, box 1596, AFL-CIO Civil Rights Papers.

82. "Black Capitalism: Mostly an Empty Promise," *Time*, July 9, 1973, 44; Dwight L. Chapin Memorandum to Richard Nixon, February 4, 1970, reel 2, CRDNA Papers; "Black Prosperity Image Found to Be Superficial," *New York Times*, May 31, 1976, 1.

83. Theodore Hesburgh to Richard Nixon, March 28, 1969, reel 21, CRDNA Papers.

4. DEFIANCE AND COMPLIANCE

1. Roland Crabbe to Richard M. Nixon, February 18, 1970, reel 15, CRDNA Papers.

2. The Silent Majority to Richard M. Nixon, April 10, 1970, reel 15, CRDNA Papers.

3. Both the SRC and the NEA reports are extracted in Testimony of Samuel Etheridge, May 21, 1974, U.S. Congress, House, Education and Labor Committee, *Juvenile Justice and Delinquency Prevention and Runaway Youth: Hearings before the Subcommittee on Equal Opportunities*, 93rd Cong., 2nd sess., 1974, 526–31 (quotation on 529).

4. Southern Regional Council, "The South and Her Children," 6.

5. Grose, *South Carolina at the Brink*, 277 (McNair quotation); Jack Sansone to Albert Brewster, January 21, 1970, folder 15, box 022637, Alabama Governors' Papers.

6. "Does Integration Still Matter to Blacks?" *Time*, March 9, 1970, 14 (anonymous mechanic quotation).

7. Charles E. Belie et al. to Richard Nixon, April 6, 1970, reel 6, CRDNA Papers. For another similar example, see "Remarks of Roy Wilkins," October 20, 1966, *Bradley v. the School Board of the City of Richmond*, pt. 23A, sec. 1, reel 15, NAACP Papers.

8. U.S. Commission on Civil Rights, *Five Communities: Their Search for Equal Education* (Washington, DC: U.S. Government Printing Office, 1972), 24; John Egerton, *Promise of Progress: Memphis School Desegregation, 1972–1973* (Atlanta: Southern Regional Council, 1973), 6; "Order," June 20, 1970, *Bradley v. School Board of the City of Richmond, Virginia*, pt. 23A, sec. 2, reel 15, and "Order," *Braxton v. the Board of Public Instruction of Duval County, Florida*, May 8, 1963, pt. 23A, sec. 1, reel 15, both NAACP Papers; Richard Russell to Harlow Autry, February 5, 1970 (quotation), folder 3, box 118, Russell Papers.

9. Patterson, *Brown v. Board of Education*, 145–46 (Brennan quotation on 146); Crespino, *In Search of Another Country*, 181–82; U.S. Supreme Court, "Opinion," *Green v. County School Board of New Kent County, Virginia et al.*, May 27, 1968, 9, copy, reel 15, CRDNA Papers.

10. Dan T. Carter, *The Politics of Rage: George Wallace, the Origins of the*

New Conservatism, and the Transformation of American Politics (Baton Rouge: Louisiana State University Press, 2000), 384, 471; Bartley, *The New South*, 397.

11. "Text of High Court Order," *New York Times*, October 30, 1969, 34; Kotlowski, *Nixon's Civil Rights*, 31–37; Patterson, *Brown v. Board of Education*, 154 (quotations); Wilkinson, *From Brown to Bakke*, 78–79.

12. "Liberals in South Are Elated by Court's Ruling on Schools," *New York Times*, October 31, 1969, 24 (both quotations).

13. "'All Deliberate Speed'—Good-Bye, Good Riddance," *The Crisis*, November 1969, 356–57 (quotation on 357).

14. Wilkinson, *From Brown to Bakke*, 120–21; Patterson, *Brown v. Board of Education*, 136–37.

15. Harry S. Dent to Richard Nixon, August 15, 1969, reel 9, CRDNA Papers; G. G. W. Hoover to Albert Brewer, October 30, 1969, and Billie Ruth Chambless to James Allen, November 3, 1969, both folder 14, box 022637, Alabama Governors' Papers.

16. Charles C. Bolton, *The Hardest Deal of All: The Battle over School Integration in Mississippi, 1870–1980* (Jackson: University Press of Mississippi, 2005), 170–71 (quotation). For an example of pleas for more time, see E. Lee Dear et al. to President Richard M. Nixon, September 16, 1969, reel 16, CRDNA Papers.

17. L. H. Fountain to Harry S. Dent, December 8, 1969, reel 16, CRDNA Papers; Strom Thurmond to Bryce Harlow, May 22, 1969, Civil Rights 2, folder 1, box 3, Thurmond Papers.

18. Southern Regional Council, "The South and Her Children," 17; "How White Views of the Negro Have Changed," *Newsweek*, August 22, 1966, 24; C. M. Treppendahl Jr. to Warren E. Burger, September 9, 1969, folder 14, box 022459, Alabama Governors' Papers.

19. For important work on gender and white supremacy, see Glenda Gilmore, *Gender and Jim Crow: Women and the Politics of White Supremacy in North Carolina, 1896–1920* (Chapel Hill: University of North Carolina Press, 1996), xv–xx, 91–146. For revealing insights into the links between "black political and sexual power," see also Jane Dailey, "The Limits of Liberalism in the New South: The Politics of Race, Sex, and Patronage in Virginia, 1879–1883," in *Jumpin' Jim Crow: Southern Politics from Civil War to Civil Rights*, ed. Jane Dailey, Glenda Elizabeth Gilmore, and Bryant Simon (Princeton, NJ: Princeton University Press, 2000), 88–114 (quotation on 90).

20. Mrs. Percy E. McLamb to President Richard M. Nixon, folder 8516, box 190, Ervin Papers; Georgia Edwards to Strom Thurmond, October 9, 1970, Civil Rights 2, folder 9, box 3, Thurmond Papers. For other revealing examples, see Mrs. Addie Parker to Senator Irvin (*sic*), November 6, 1969, folder 8514, box 190, Ervin Papers; and Helen P. Cooper to Albert Brewer, September 19, 1969, folder 14, box 22459, Alabama Governors' Papers.

21. Florence P. Gibbens to Strom Thurmond, September 24, 1969, Civil Rights 2, folder 6, box 4, Thurmond Papers.

22. Mrs. Ruel McLeod to Harry Dent, May 20, 1969, and Harry S. Dent to Mrs. McLeod, May 24, 1969, both reel 17, CRDNA Papers.

23. Harry Dent Interview, April 3, 1978, 2–3, box 1, A. James Reichley Interview Transcripts, Ford Library; Howard H. Callaway to Harry Dent, February 16, 1970, ser. 2, folder 1, box 7, Howard H. Callaway Papers, Richard B. Russell Library for Political Research and Studies, University of Georgia.

24. Mr. and Mrs. Hugh C. Wade to Richard Russell, October 22, 1969, ser. 10, folder 2, box 119, and Richard B. Russell to Colonel L. J. Bolton, October 28, 1969, ser. 10, folder 3, box 119, both Russell Papers. For another similar example, see Mr. and Mrs. T. H. Bailey to Richard Russell, November 4, 1969, ser. 10, folder 3, box 119, Russell Papers.

25. Mrs. G. Carroll Brown Jr. to President Nixon, July 26, 1970, reel 17, CRDNA Papers. For a similar letter addressed to Nixon's chief domestic adviser, see Mrs. Charles E. Liggon Jr. to Mr. Ehrlichman, March 3, 1970, reel 16, CRDNA Papers.

26. Mrs. Franklin McCrery to Robert H. Finch, January 15, 1969, folder 8530, box 190, Ervin Papers; Mrs. William J. Ward to Richard Nixon, January 5, 1970, reel 15, CRDNA Papers.

27. Mrs. G. T. Chappell to Richard B. Russell, February 11, 1970, and Mrs. G. T. Chappell et al. to Richard B. Russell, January 24, 1970, both ser. 10, folder 1, box 118, Russell Papers. For another example, see Mrs. J. D. Squires et al. to Strom Thurmond, September 17, 1969, Civil Rights 2, folder 6, box 4, Thurmond Papers.

28. Mrs. Roy Hughes et al. to President Nixon et al., November 1, 1969, reel 15, CRDNA Papers; Watt E. Smith to Strom Thurmond, September 29, 1970, Civil Rights 2, folder 9, box 3, Thurmond Papers.

29. "Close, Cool Off, Sandersville White Faculty Asks," *Atlanta Constitution*, February 6, 1970, 11; "Maddox Preaches Defiance of Court," *Atlanta Constitution*, February 9, 1970, 1, 9 (Maddox quotations).

30. "Integration Crisis Deepens in South: One School Closed," *New York Times*, February 6, 1970, 20; "Mississippi School Destroyed by Fire," *New York Times*, February 11, 1970, 16. For another example, see "Violence Closes Florida School," *Atlanta Constitution*, February 12, 1970, 5C.

31. Robert E. McNair to Mr. President, January 26, 1970, reel 17, CRDNA Papers.

32. Stanley, "White Violence—Lamar, S.C.," 196.

33. Ibid.; "White Parents Overturn Two School Buses in S.C.," *Raleigh (NC) News and Observer*, March 4, 1970, 3.

34. "15 Are Arrested in Attack on Buses with Negro Children in South Carolina," *New York Times*, March 5, 1970, 19 (Best quotation); "Lamar Gives Its Answer to the Courts," *New York Times*, March 8, 1970, D2.

35. "Lamar Gives Its Answer to the Courts," *New York Times*, March 8, 1970, D2.

36. Grose, *South Carolina at the Brink*, 281 (McNair quotation); "Statement by the Vice President," March 4, 1970, Civil Rights 2, folder 2, box 2, Thurmond Papers.

37. UPI Press Release, March 6, 1970 (first two quotations), and Strom Thurmond to John Mitchell, March 3, 1970, both Civil Rights 2, folder 2, box 2, Thurmond Papers.

38. Stanley, "White Violence—Lamar, S.C.," 196–202 (quotations on 199, 200, 201).

39. "Lamar Gives Its Answer to the Courts," *New York Times*, March 8, 1970, D2; Sammye H. Nance to Strom Thurmond, April 21, 1970, Civil Rights 2, folder 3, box 2, Thurmond Papers.

40. James C. Melton to Strom Thurmond, April 20, 1970, Civil Rights 2,

folder 3, box 2, Thurmond Papers; Wilkinson, *From Brown to Bakke*, 123 (Duncan quotation).

41. Mrs. Clyde C. Dutton to Strom Thurmond, March 4, 1970, Civil Rights 2, folder 2, box 2, Thurmond Papers.

42. "Troopers Protect Pupils as Lamar Schools Open," *New York Times*, March 11, 1970, 34 (quotations); James C. Melton to Strom Thurmond, April 20, 1970, Civil Rights 2, folder 3, box 2, Thurmond Papers; Wilkinson, *From Brown to Bakke*, 124.

43. "South Calm and Peaceful in Integration of Schools," *Raleigh (NC) News and Observer*, September 1, 1970, 1.

44. "Desegregation Brings Problems in South," *Raleigh (NC) News and Observer*, September 2, 1970, 12; "Dixie School Troubles Minor, Officials Say," *Atlanta Constitution*, September 4, 1970, 16A.

45. Jean Fairfax to Jack Greenberg, October 7, 1970, folder 23, box 3, Chambers Papers.

46. "Dixie School Boycotts Rise," *Atlanta Constitution*, September 3, 1970, 10A.

47. Southern Regional Council, "The South and Her Children," 11; John Roche Gould to Albert Brewer, February 4, 1970, and Albert P. Brewer to John Roche Gould, February 9, 1970, both folder 16, box 022637, Alabama Governors' Papers. For more insight into Brewer's ideas, see Albert P. Brewer to James P. Ross, February 11, 1970, folder 16, box 022637, Alabama Governors' Papers.

48. "U.S. Acts against Whites in Alabama School Sit-In," *New York Times*, September 4, 1970, 1; "Parents Sued over Alabama White Sit-Ins," *Atlanta Constitution*, September 4, 1970, 10A; "Judge Says Parents Agree to End Their Defiance," *Talladega Daily Home*, September 5, 1970, 1 (quotation), 8.

49. Mrs. June A. Gagnon et al. to the President, May 6, 1970 (quotation), and James A. Haley to Richard M. Nixon, May 21, 1970, both reel 15, CRDNA Papers.

50. Elizabeth Buchanan et al. to Richard Nixon, January 23, 1970, ser. 3, folder 1, box 4, Talmadge Papers.

51. John Stennis to Richard M. Nixon, August 24, 1970, and Fred J. Roberts Jr. et al. to Richard M. Nixon, July 15, 1970, both reel 16, CRDNA Papers.

52. "South Opens Fight to Save School Choice," *Atlanta Constitution*, February 6, 1970, 1 (quotation), 8; "School Enforcement Fight Won by Dixie," *Atlanta Constitution*, February 19, 1970, 1; Crespino, *In Search of Another Country*, 192–99.

53. Robert L. Crook to President Richard M. Nixon, March 4, 1970, and "Senate Concurrent Resolution No. 507," January 28, 1970 (quotation), both reel 16, CRDNA Papers.

54. "Plan Is Secret, Maddox Says," *Atlanta Constitution*, February 18, 1970, 1A (quotation); "Greenville, S.C., Begins Integration Peacefully," *Atlanta Constitution*, February 18, 1970, 11.

55. Bartley, *The New South*, 391–92; Lester Maddox to Richard Nixon, September 1, 1970, reel 15, CRDNA Papers; "Maddox Mails 10,000 Pleas," *Atlanta Constitution*, February 10, 1970, 3 (first two quotations); "Maddox Says Just Get Rid of the Buses," *Atlanta Constitution*, February 7, 1970, 1 (last two quotations).

56. "Schools Staying Closed," *Atlanta Constitution*, February 24, 1970, 1;

"Houston Students Switch as Ordered," *Atlanta Constitution*, February 26, 1970, 1; "Maddox Calls Judges 'Tyrants' After Fall of Anti-Busing Law," *Atlanta Constitution*, February 27, 1970, 21.

57. "Defy Federal School Order, Urges Wallace," *Atlanta Constitution*, February 9, 1970, 2 (quotations); "Wallace Elected Governor in Alabama Landslide Vote," *New York Times*, November 4, 1970, 31.

58. "Desegregation Brings Problems in South," *Raleigh (NC) News and Observer*, September 2, 1970, 12.

59. Bolton, *The Hardest Deal of All*, 173; "Desegregation 1970," *Newsweek*, July 27, 1970, 35–36; "Year of Decision for White-Only Schools," *U.S. News and World Report*, July 27, 1970, 16–17.

60. "Private Education in Alabama Growing Fast," 1971, folder 14, box 022682, Alabama Governors' Papers.

61. J. L. LeFlore to Albert Brewer, January 8, 1970, pt. 2, reel 16, CRSA Papers; Tom Jennings to Strom Thurmond, April 23, 1970, Civil Rights 2, folder 3, box 2, Thurmond Papers; W. B. Lindsey to Richard M. Nixon, September 12, 1969, folder 14, box 022459, Alabama Governors' Papers; Mrs. Roy Hughes et al. to Richard Nixon et al., November 1, 1969, reel 15, CRDNA Papers.

62. See, e.g., Strom Thurmond to Dr. Thomas G. Gibson Jr., December 12, 1969, folder 827, box 17, Jonas Papers; "Memorandum on School Desegregation to President Nixon from Strom Thurmond," n.d., "Strom Thurmond" folder, box 16, President's Personal File, 1969–74, NPM.

63. Clarke Reed to Bryce Harlow, June 30, 1970, folder 202, box 6, Dent Papers.

64. Jean Fairfax to Jack Greenberg, October 7, 1970 (LDF quotations), folder 23, box 3, Chambers Papers; "Jittery School Is Center of Race-Troubled County," *Raleigh (NC) News and Observer*, February 14, 1971, 4; Bolton, *The Hardest Deal of All*, 177.

65. Dr. R. G. Ferrell to Richard B. Russell, January 19, 1970, folder 5, box 118, ser. 10, Russell Papers. For another good example, see Professor Robert W. Brehme to Richard Nixon, August 20, 1970, reel 16, CRDNA Papers.

66. Dr. Thomas G. Gibson to Charles R. Jonas, December 5, 1969, folder 827, box 17, Jonas Papers; Dr. R. G. Ferrell to Richard B. Russell, January 19, 1970, folder 5, box 118, ser. 10, Russell Papers.

67. John L. LeFlore to Albert Brewer, January 8, 1970, pt. 2, reel 16, CRSA Papers. In LeFlore's files, there is no record of a reply from Brewer. For more information on how blacks were more likely to be drafted and killed in Vietnam, especially before 1968, see Christian G. Appy, *Working-Class War: American Combat Soldiers and Vietnam* (Chapel Hill: University of North Carolina Press, 1993), esp. 19–22.

68. Bolton, *The Hardest Deal of All*, 177–78; William E. Simon to James M. Cannon, May 17, 1975 (quotation), "HU2-1, 1/1/75–9/30/75" folder, box 5, Subject File, Ford Library.

69. Negro Principals of the Alabama Association of Secondary School Principals, "Position Paper on the Desegregation Controversy of Schools in Alabama," folder 12, box 22459, Alabama Governors' Papers; Southern Regional Council, "The South and Her Children," 9.

70. U.S. Commission on Civil Rights, *What Students Perceive: A Report of the U.S. Commission on Civil Rights* (Washington, DC: U.S. Government Print-

ing Office, 1969), 8 (first quotation); "Whites and Negroes in Daytona Beach Face Changes in Habits Too," *New York Times,* February 4, 1970, 24; Southern Regional Council, "The South and Her Children," 9 (Educational Resources Center quotation); "Mississippi Action Revealed by NEA," *Atlanta Constitution,* February 24, 1970, 14 (final two quotations).

71. Jean Fairfax to Jack Greenberg, October 7, 1970 (first, second, and sixth quotations), folder 23, box 3, Chambers Papers; "Mass Ousters of Black Students a Growing Integration Problem," *New York Times,* August 28, 1971, 1, 22 (third, fourth, and fifth quotations). The SRC provided the best definition of *pushouts,* as students who "have been expelled or suspended from school or who, because of intolerable hostility directed against them, finally quit school." Testimony of Peter E. Holmes, May 21, 1974, U.S. Congress, *Juvenile Justice and Delinquency Prevention,* 502 (SRC quotation).

72. Southern Regional Council, "The South and Her Children," 12 (first two quotations); "'Dixie' Battle: 'Old Times Am Not Forgotten,'" *Atlanta Constitution,* October 18, 1970, 9B; NEA report extracted in Testimony of Samuel Etheridge, May 21, 1974, U.S. Congress, *Juvenile Justice and Delinquency Prevention,* 530 (final quotation).

73. Dent, *Southern Journey,* 301–2.

74. "Violence Erupts in Carolina City," *New York Times,* May 18, 1969, 82 (quotation); "Grievances to Be Aired at Meeting Here Today," *Burlington Times-News,* May 15, 1969.

75. "Black Students Seek Answers," *Burlington Times-News,* May 16, 1969 (first quotation); "School Grievances Are Listed," *Burlington Times-News,* May 21, 1969 (second quotation).

76. Thomas, *The True Story behind the Wilmington Ten,* 33–37 (quotation on 36).

77. "Wilmington Toll 2; Guard Is Called Out," *Raleigh (NC) News and Observer,* February 8, 1971, 1.

78. Thomas, *The True Story Behind the Wilmington Ten,* 22; "Wilmington Race Riot Draft Report Offers Revelations," December 8, 2005, available at www.ah.dcr.state.nc.us/1898-wrrc/report/report.htm (accessed July 6, 2006); "Wilmington Toll 2; Guard Is Called Out," *Raleigh (NC) News and Observer,* February 8, 1971, 1 (Williamson quotation). For a detailed secondary account of these events, see Leon Prather Sr., *"We Have Taken a City": The Wilmington Racial Massacre and Coup of 1898* (Cranbury, NJ: Associated University Presses, 1984).

79. John L. Godwin, *Black Wilmington and the North Carolina Way: Portrait of a Community in the Era of Civil Rights Protest* (Lanham, MD: University Press of America, 2000), 236, 239; Tyson, *Blood Done Sign My Name,* 258–59. The case of the "Wilmington Ten," a major controversy arising out of the violence that occurred as the schools desegregated, is covered in chapter 8.

80. "Troops Called to Keep Curfew in North Carolina Racial Strife," *New York Times,* November 8, 1970, 73; "Jittery School Is Center of Race-Troubled County" and "School Situation Recalled," both *Raleigh (NC) News and Observer,* February 14, 1971, 4.

81. "A Small Louisiana Town Hangs on the Edge of Racial Disaster," *New York Times,* March 28, 1970, 33 (quotations); Fairclough, *Race and Democracy,* 451.

82. Southern Regional Council, "The South and Her Children," 14 (Earle case); NEA report extracted in Testimony of Samuel Etheridge, May 21, 1974, U.S. Congress, *Juvenile Justice and Delinquency Prevention,* 528–29.

83. "Lawyers' Breakfast," *The Crisis,* September 1971, 214 (first quotation); Testimony of Julius Chambers, June 5, 1971, U.S. Congress, Senate, Select Equal Educational Opportunity Committee, *Equal Education Opportunity, 1971: Part 10, Displacement and Present Status of Black School Principals in Desegregated School Districts,* 92nd Cong., 1st sess., 1971, 5397 (second quotation).

84. Southern Regional Council, "The South and Her Children," 10; "NEA Says South Cuts Black Jobs," *New York Times,* March 19, 1971, 1.

85. "The Black Principal Eliminated" (National Association of Secondary School Principals study), June 7, 1971, U.S. Congress, *Equal Education Opportunity, 1971: Part 10,* 5332–33.

86. NAACP 1970 Annual Report, 75, 88, folder 2, box 26, Kelly Alexander Papers.

87. Complaint, June 16, 1971, "Separate Answer of Warren, Arkansas, School District #1 to Complaint," July 9, 1971, and "Hearing—Travistine Alexander," August 10, 1970, 94 (quotation), all *Alexander v. Warren School District,* pt. 23A, sec. 1, reel 10, NAACP Papers.

88. "Hearing—Travistine Alexander," August 10, 1970, 99, *Alexander v. Warren School District,* pt. 23A, sec. 1, reel 10, NAACP Papers.

89. "Memorandum Opinion," November 23, 1971, and Mrs. Travistine Alexander to James Myerson, September 20, 1972, both *Alexander v. Warren School District,* pt. 23A, sec. 1, reel 11, NAACP Papers; U.S. Commission on Civil Rights, *What Students Perceive,* 13.

90. "Scott Won't Stand in School Door," *Atlanta Constitution,* February 1, 1970, 2D (Scott quotation); Lassiter, *The Silent Majority,* 263–64; Crespino, *In Search of Another Country,* 11; Southern Regional Council, "The South and Her Children," 17 (Harris survey).

91. "Dual System Ends in Many Southern Schools," *Durham (NC) Morning Herald,* September 1, 1970, 5B; "South Calm and Peaceful in Integration of Schools," *Raleigh (NC) News and Observer,* September 1, 1970, 1; Southern Regional Council, "The South and Her Children," 3.

92. "Desegregation 1970," *Newsweek,* July 27, 1970, 35–36 (quotations on 35).

93. "A Good Beginning," *Winston-Salem Journal,* September 2, 1970; "Talking Sense," *Atlanta Constitution,* February 7, 1970, 4.

94. U.S. Commission on Civil Rights, *Title IV and School Desegregation* (Washington, DC: U.S. Government Printing Office, 1973), 2, 17–19 (quotations on 19); "Survey Shows Integration Works," *Atlanta Constitution,* October 18, 1970, 2.

95. "How Greenville Integrated Its Schools," *Charlotte (NC) Observer,* February 22, 1970, 5A; "Carolina Schools Integrate Easily," *New York Times,* February 18, 1970, 26; "Greenville, S.C., Begins Integration Peacefully," *Atlanta Constitution,* February 18, 1970, 11 (Fuller quotation).

96. "Integration Comes to Mississippi," *Washington Post,* n.d. (Anderson quotation), clipping, "Desegregation—Aiding Desegregation—Title VI Techniques, 1 of 3" folder, box 63, Garment Files, NPM; W. F. Minor, "Mississippi Schools in Crisis," *New South* 25, no. 1 (Winter 1970): 35 (second quotation).

97. Minor, "Mississippi Schools in Crisis," 33–34.

98. Ibid., 31–36 (Wheeler quotation on 34); Louis Patrick Gray, "How Can This Committee Help the Development of Unitary School Systems," June 15, 1970, reel 16, CRDNA Papers.

99. Edward S. Goode to Albert Brewer, August 29, 1969, and Albert P. Brewer to Edward S. Goode, September 10, 1969, folder 14, box 022459, Alabama Governors' Papers. For the position of the Alabama Chamber of Commerce, see "Statement of the Mobile Area Chamber of Commerce," September 2, 1970, pt. 2, reel 26, CRSA Papers.

100. Parks Scott to Albert Brewer, February 6, 1970, folder 16, box 022637, Alabama Governors' Papers. For other similar examples, see Mrs. James P. Ross to Albert Brewer, February 4, 1970, folder 16, box 022637, and Mr. and Mrs. George D. Bynum to Albert Brewer, September 6, 1969, folder 14, box 022459, both Alabama Governors' Papers.

101. "School Desegregation Smooth in Durham," *Raleigh (NC) News and Observer,* September 20, 1970 (quotations); Greene, *Our Separate Ways,* 196–223.

102. "The First Day: 'It's Parents Who Are Worried,'" *Durham (NC) Morning Herald,* September 3, 1970, 1 (Stephens quotation); "School Desegregation Smooth in Durham," *Raleigh (NC) News and Observer,* September 20, 1970 (Chambers quotation).

103. Southern Regional Council, "The South and Her Children," 18, 19 (first two quotations); "Toward Equal Educational Opportunity: The Report of the Select Committee on Equal Educational Opportunity," December 31, 1972, U.S. Congress, Senate, Select Committee on Equal Educational Opportunity, *Toward Equal Educational Opportunity: Report before the Senate Select Committee on Equal Education Opportunity,* 92nd Cong., 2nd sess., 1972, 26 (final quotation).

104. Southern Regional Council, "The South and Her Children," 11; Lester Maddox to Richard M. Nixon, January 9, 1970, reel 15, CRDNA Papers.

105. Southern Regional Council, "The South and Her Children," 10; "Virginia's Holtons Say Yes," *Time,* November 15, 1971, 43; Lassiter, *The Silent Majority,* 263–64; Wilkinson, *From Brown to Bakke,* 153–54.

106. "Court Faces Tough Decisions as Arguments on Schools End," *Atlanta Constitution,* October 15, 1970, 1.

5. The Busing Years

1. "Supreme Court, 9–0, Backs Busing to Combat South's Dual Schools," *New York Times,* April 21, 1971, 1 (first quotation), 29; Davison M. Douglas, *Reading, Writing, and Race: The Desegregation of the Charlotte Schools* (Chapel Hill: University of North Carolina Press, 1995), 206–12; Patterson, *Brown v. Board of Education,* 156–57; "A Supreme Court Yes to Busing," *Time,* May 3, 1971, 13 (second quotation).

2. "Supreme Court, 9–0, Backs Busing to Combat South's Dual Schools," *New York Times,* April 21, 1971, 29 (Eastland quotation); L. D. Abernethy to Charles Jonas, April 21, 1971, folder 906, box 19, Jonas Papers.

3. Mrs. A. J. Woodle to Charles Jonas, April 22, 1971, and Charles Raper Jonas to Mrs. A. J. Woodle, May 6, 1971, both folder 906, box 19, Jonas Papers; "News of Decision Trickles Slowly through Charlotte," *Charlotte (NC) Observer,* April 21, 1971 (Sanders quotation).

4. Madge Hopkins Interview, October 17, 2000, Interview K481, SOHP; Mrs. Mary Nash Jones to Julius Chambers, April 30, 1971, folder 26, box 3, Chambers Papers; "Julius Chambers Waited a Long Time," *Charlotte (NC) Observer,* April 21, 1971.

5. Patterson, *Brown v. Board of Education,* 158; "A Supreme Court Yes to Busing," *Time,* May 3, 1971, 13 (quotation); "Busing: An American Dilemma," *Newsweek,* March 13, 1972, 24–28.

6. Leonard Garment to John Ehrlichman, October 7, 1971, and William E. Timmons to the Attorney General, September 9, 1971, both "School Desegregation" folder, box 65, John W. Dean File, NPM.

7. "Pupil Integration Paced by South," *New York Times,* January 13, 1972, 32 (quotation); HEW News, January 16, 1972, "Desegregation Statistics" folder, Bradley H. Patterson Jr. Files, White House Central Files, NPM.

8. "Toward Equal Educational Opportunity," 11 (quotation); HEW News, January 16, 1972, "Desegregation Statistics" folder, Bradley H. Patterson Jr. Files, White House Central Files, NPM.

9. "Busing Decisions Provide Leeway," *Race Relations Reporter* 2, no. 16 (September 1971): 4–6; Kotlowski, *Nixon's Civil Rights,* 39 (Nixon quotation); Harry S. Dent to the President, June 4, 1971, reel 10, CRDNA Papers.

10. Save Our Neighborhood Schools Petition, November 11, 1971 (first and second quotations), reel 18, CRDNA Papers; Testimony of John P. Green, March 15, 1972, U.S. Congress, House, Judiciary Committee, *School Busing: Part 2, Hearings before Subcommittee No. 5,* 92nd Cong., 2nd sess., 1972, 958. For another similar example, see Brenda Berry to George Wallace, September 14, 1972, folder 16, box 022675, Alabama Governors' Papers.

11. Mrs. Henry H. Parish to Richard M. Nixon, March 21, 1972, reel 18, and William A. Collins to Richard M. Nixon, April 30, 1971, reel 17, both CRDNA Papers; Wilkinson, *From Brown to Bakke,* 150.

12. David L. Gaddis to Richard Nixon, n.d., November 13, 1971, reel 10 (first quotation), William A. Collins to Richard M. Nixon, April 30, 1971, reel 17 (second quotation), and Stella Claunch to Richard M. Nixon, August 4, 1971, reel 10, all CRDNA Papers.

13. Testimony of G. Elliott Hagan, March 8, 1972, U.S. Congress, *School Busing: Part 1, Hearings before Subcommittee No. 5,* 92nd Cong., 2nd sess., 1972, 133; Remarks of Sam J. Ervin Jr., December 31, 1972, U.S. Congress, *Toward Equal Educational Opportunity,* 408; Karl E. Campbell, *Senator Sam Ervin, Last of the Founding Fathers* (Chapel Hill: University of North Carolina Press, 2007), 229.

14. "What the Gallup Poll Discovered about Busing," *Newsweek,* March 13, 1972, 28; "Busing Amendment," *New Republic,* February 26, 1972, 5; "Back to Busing," *New Republic,* December 18, 1971, 5–6 (quotation); "Bus Stop at the House," *New Republic,* November 20, 1971, 7–8.

15. "The Busing Issue Boils Over," *Time,* February 28, 1972, 22; "Busing Plan Sets Off White Boycott in Augusta, Ga.," *New York Times,* February 15, 1972, 12 (Anderson quotation); "School Boycott Fails in Most Cities," *Macon News,* February 29, 1972, 12A (final quotation).

16. Memorandum, January 5, 1972, 4, 5, 26–27, 67, *Bradley v. School Board of the City of Richmond,* pt. 23A, sec. 2, reel 15, NAACP Papers.

17. "Bumpy Road in Richmond," *Time,* February 28, 1972, 22–23 (all quo-

tations on 22); "3300 Autos Driven to Capital in Protest," *New York Times,* February 18, 1972, 1.

18. "Justices Fail to Settle Merger of Schools Issue," *Wall Street Journal,* May 22, 1973; William T. Coleman Jr. to Jack Greenberg et al., May 25, 1973, *Bradley v. School Board of the City of Richmond,* pt. 23A, sec. 2, reel 16, NAACP Papers.

19. "Florida Primary: The Real Candidate Is Named Busing," *New York Times,* February 27, 1972, 3; "Voters Favor Busing Ban by Overwhelming Margin," *New York Times,* March 15, 1972, 1, 32; Mrs. M. R. Thorpe et al. to Richard M. Nixon, January 21, 1970 (final quotation), reel 15, CRDNA Papers.

20. Jack Winfield to George C. Wallace, December 2, 1971, folder 14, box 022675, Alabama Governors' Papers.

21. "Some Parents Dodge School Integration," *New York Times,* January 4, 1972, 4; Bolton, *The Hardest Deal of All,* 190; Wilkinson, *From Brown to Bakke,* 150–51.

22. Edward L. Morgan to Richard M. Nixon, March 3, 1972 (Morgan quotations), and "Constitutional Amendment," n.d., both reel 46, and Harry S. Dent to Mrs. Henry H. Parrish, April 5, 1972, reel 18, all CRDNA Papers; Kotlowski, *Nixon's Civil Rights,* 39–40.

23. Ralph David Abernathy et al. to Richard M. Nixon, March 13, 1972 (quotation), reel 46, CRDNA Papers; Vernon Jordan et al. to Friend, September 1972, folder 21, box 15, Frederick Alexander Papers.

24. Testimony of William T. Coleman Jr., March 3, 1972, U.S. Congress, *School Busing: Part 1,* 381 (Lent quotation), 383–84; Statement of Arthur Lynch, T. M. Martin, and Walter McDaniel (read by Arthur Lynch), May 18, 1972, U.S. Congress, *School Busing: Part 3, Hearings before Subcommittee No. 5,* 92nd Cong., 2nd sess., 1972, 1691.

25. See Testimony, February 28–May 24, 1972, U.S. Congress, *School Busing: Part 1,* 201–32, 290–309, *School Busing: Part 2,* 1178–93, and *School Busing: Part 3,* 1327–39.

26. Jackie Robinson to Richard Nixon, March 21, 1972, reel 14, CRDNA Papers. For more on Robinson's criticisms of the Nixon administration, see John R. Brown III to Maurice H. Stans, January 26, 1970, reel 2, CRDNA Papers; and Kotlowski, *Nixon's Civil Rights,* 139–40.

27. "Busing: A Fraudulent Issue," *The Crisis,* June–July 1972, 185 (first quotation); Wilkins with Mathews, *Standing Fast,* 339; Testimony of Roy Wilkins, March 16, 1972, U.S. Congress, *School Busing: Part 2,* 990 (second quotation); "It All Depends on Whose Ox Is Gored," July 21, 1969, pt. 2, reel 18, CRSA Papers.

28. NAACP 1972 Annual Report, 36, folder 2, box 26, Kelly Alexander Papers; "NAACP Petition to President Richard M. Nixon," June 14, 1972, reel 17, CRDNA Papers. For another petition example, see Urquhart O. Dixon to Richard Nixon, July 15, 1972, reel 18, CRDNA Papers.

29. Sherrell Mitchell to George C. Wallace, November 15, 1971, and George C. Wallace to Sherrell Mitchell, January 11, 1972, both folder 15, box 022675, Alabama Governors' Papers. For Wallace's earlier refusal to respond to black complaints, see Carter, *The Politics of Rage,* 238.

30. "WRAL-TV Viewpoint," February 12, 1970, reel 16, CRDNA Papers;

Jack Bass and Walter DeVries, *The Transformation of Southern Politics: Social Change and Political Consequence since 1945* (New York: Basic, 1976), 222, 237–38. For further insight into Helms's views, see Jesse Helms, *Here's Where I Stand: A Memoir* (New York: Random House, 2005), 158–60.

31. "Statement by the President," August 24, 1972 (Nixon quotation), "School Desegregation" folder, box 65, John W. Dean File, NPM; Harry S. Dent to Richard Nixon, October 30, 1969, reel 9, and Harry Dent to Richard Nixon, April 21, 1971 (Dent quotation), reel 10, both CRDNA Papers.

32. Kotlowski, *Nixon's Civil Rights,* 40–41; Campbell, *Senator Sam Ervin,* 230–31; George C. Wallace to Richard M. Nixon, n.d., and Governor George Wallace Press Release, December 9, 1971, both folder 13, box 022675, Alabama Governors' Papers; Carter, *The Politics of Rage,* 418, 424.

33. "Private Schools Seem to Be the Coming Modern Day Thing," January 1972, 1–7 (quotations on 1, 4), reel 168, SRC Papers; "'White Academies' in the South—Booming Despite Obstacles," *U.S. News and World Report,* April 19, 1971, 76 (Simmons quotation).

34. James M. Tucker to George C. Wallace, July 21, 1971, folder 14, box 022682, Alabama Governors' Papers. For another example of the correspondence between the Wallaces and private school administrators, see Thos. M. Pruitt Sr. to Jack W. Wallace, July 1, 1971, folder 14, box 022682, Alabama Governors' Papers.

35. Robert M. Bowick to Virginia M. Stone, August 2, 1971 (first quotation), Wesley P. Smith to George C. Wallace, July 2, 1971 (second quotation), and George C. Wallace to Dr. Max Autrey, June 1, 1971 (final quotation), all folder 14, box 022682, Alabama Governors' Papers.

36. Wallace's role in raising funds for private schools is not mentioned by his most respected biographer, Dan T. Carter. Carter does detail well, however, how Wallace tried to moderate his racial views in early 1971 after a bruising campaign against Albert Brewer. See Carter, *The Politics of Rage,* 237, 394, 417 (quotations).

37. "The Docket," *SPLC Report,* March 1973, 4; "Supreme Court Deals Blow to Private Segregated Schools," *SPLC Report,* August 1974, 1 (quotation).

38. Responding to complaints from its branches, the NAACP, e.g., argued that the new private schools had been established "to evade public school desegregation." See "NAACP Urges IRS Tax Probe of Dixie Schools," *The Crisis,* March 1971, 66.

39. David R. Hubbard to Elliot Richardson, March 18, 1971, Civil Rights 2, folder 1, box 2, Thurmond Papers; U.S. Commission on Civil Rights, *Five Communities,* 2.

40. Kitty Terjen, "Close-Up on Segregation Academies," *New South* 27, no. 4 (Fall 1972): 50–58.

41. Mrs. Hugh M. McArn Jr. to Earl Ruth (copied to Charles Raper Jonas), November 2, 1971, folder 906, box 19, Jonas Papers.

42. "Some Parents Dodge School Integration," *New York Times,* January 4, 1972, 4 (Wooten quotation); "Nixon Renews Bus Issue; Stand Called Diversionary," *New York Times,* September 11, 1973, 39.

43. Jon Nordheimer, "'The Dream,' 1973: Blacks Move Painfully toward Full Equality," *New York Times,* August 26, 1973, 1, 44; "Toward Equal Educational Opportunity," 28 (Theodore Hesburgh testimony).

44. Egerton, *Promise of Progress,* 3, 19.

45. Mr. and Mrs. R. C. Fletcher et al. to President Nixon, February 11, 1970 (quotation), reel 16, CRDNA Papers; U.S. Commission on Civil Rights, *Five Communities,* 24–30.

46. U.S. Commission on Civil Rights, *Five Communities,* 30–33 (quotation on 30); "The Winston-Salem Journal," *Charlotte (NC) Observer,* April 23, 1971 (*Winston-Salem [NC] Journal* quotation).

47. U.S. Commission on Civil Rights, *Five Communities,* 9–15 (quotation on 15).

48. "Busing: The Issue That Will Not Go Away," *The Crisis,* December 1978, 350 (study quotation); U.S. Commission on Civil Rights, *Five Communities,* 2.

49. Douglas, *Reading, Writing, and Race,* 75; "Taking a Stand," *Charlotte (NC) Observer,* September 2, 2007, 24A. Published to commemorate the fiftieth anniversary of Counts's enrollment at Harding High, this special edition of the *Charlotte Observer* contains many other stories on the history of school desegregation in Charlotte.

50. Darius L. Swann to the Charlotte Mecklenburg Board of Education, September 2, 1964, Scott Thrower to Whom It May Concern, September 1, 1964, and J. LeVonne Chambers to Gloria Stadler, July 15, 1965, all folder 13, box 3, Chambers Papers.

51. Douglas, *Reading, Writing, and Race,* 140–41; Summary of Case in the guide to the Chambers Papers, available at http://dlib.uncc/special_collections/manuscripts/html/85.php (copy in author's possession).

52. Douglas, *Reading, Writing, and Race,* 174–77; Southern Regional Council, "The South and Her Children," 29 (first quotation); James B. McMillan to Mordecai C. Johnson, April 7, 1970, folder 19, box 3, Chambers Papers.

53. Douglas, *Reading, Writing, and Race,* 140–41; "Bus My Child? You're Dreaming," *Charlotte (NC) Observer,* May 14, 1969 (Warren quotation).

54. Lassiter, *The Silent Majority,* 3; Mrs. Geraldine T. Barris to Charles R. Jonas, June 25, 1969, folder 828, box 17, and G. Don Roberson to Charles R. Jonas, December 5, 1969, folder 827, box 17, both Jonas Papers. For an example of white fears that busing would undermine house prices, see Lenoir C. Keesler to William J. Waggoner, February 10, 1970, folder 3, box 2, William Waggoner Papers, Special Collections Department, J. Murrey Atkins Library, University of North Carolina at Charlotte.

55. Unsigned Letter to Julius Chambers, April 25, 1971, folder 26, box 3, Chambers Papers. For another example of the hate mail received by Chambers, see J. M. Wright to "Darkey Chambers," 1971, folder 27, box 3, Chambers Papers.

56. Southern Regional Council, "The South and Her Children," 21; Daisy S. Stroud Interview, June 20, 2001, 21, NSV-UNCC.

57. Douglas, *Reading, Writing, and Race,* 142 (Poe quotation); Southern Regional Council, "The South and Her Children," 23–24; Wilkinson, *From Brown to Bakke,* 137–39.

58. Douglas, *Reading, Writing, and Race,* 58–61; Stanford R. Brookshire to Dr. Reginald A. Hawkins, May 10, 1963, and R. A. Hawkins to Stanford R. Brookshire, May 11, 1963, both folder 11, box 2, Hawkins Papers.

59. J. LeVonne Chambers to Lila Bellar, February 18, 1970, folder 17, box 3, Chambers Papers.

60. Southern Regional Council, "The South and Her Children," 34–37 (quotations on 35).

61. "Supreme Court Ruling," *Charlotte (NC) Observer,* April 21, 1971; "News of Decision Trickles through Charlotte," *Charlotte (NC) Observer,* April 21, 1971 (Hoogenaker quotation).

62. Daisy S. Stroud Interview, June 20, 2001, 16, NSV-UNCC; "News of Decision Trickles through Charlotte," *Charlotte (NC) Observer,* April 21, 1971; Wilkinson, *From Brown to Bakke,* 156–57 (anonymous mother quotation).

63. U.S. Commission on Civil Rights, *Five Communities,* 36–40.

64. Douglas, *Reading, Writing, and Race,* 61–63; Complaint, October 31, 1972, *Lynch v. Snepp,* pt. 23A, sec. 2, reel 13, NAACP Papers; Kelly M. Alexander Jr., "Student Program for Desegregation," *The Crisis,* November 1973, 316 (quotation).

65. Timothy Gibbs Interview, May 27, 1998, 4, Interview K480, SOHP; Madelyn Wilson Interview, February 2, 2002, 8, 18, NSV-UNCC.

66. "Mass Ousters of Black Students a Growing Integration Problem," *New York Times,* August 28, 1971, 1, 22; Elizabeth Schmoke Randolph Interview, June 16, 1993, 15–16, NSV-UNCC; Testimony of Julius Chambers, June 15, 1971, U.S. Congress, Senate, Select Equal Educational Opportunity Committee, *Equal Education Opportunity, 1971: Part 11, Status of School Desegregation Law,* 92nd Cong., 1st sess., 1971, 5397.

67. "There Is a CRISIS in Charlotte-Mecklenburg Schools . . . and *Black Students* Are Taking the Weight," November 11, 1972, folder 4, box 3, and Reginald Smith to Bob Valder, March 20, 1973, folder 2, box 4, both Chambers Papers.

68. Patsy Rice Camp Interview, March 23, 1999, 2 of tape log, Interview K479, SOHP; "News of Decision Trickles Slowly through Charlotte," *Charlotte (NC) Observer,* April 21, 1971 (Brooks quotation).

69. Douglas, *Reading, Writing, and Race,* 246; U.S. Commission on Civil Rights, *Five Communities,* 38–39; Mrs. Grace J. Broskie to Charles Jonas, May 26, 1971, folder 906, box 19, Jonas Papers.

70. See "The Following Students Are Living in the Westchester Community but They Are Attending Schools Other Than the One They Were Assigned To," Unsigned Letter to Julius Chambers, folder 27, box 3, Chambers Papers; "Some Parents Dodge School Integration," *New York Times,* January 4, 1972, 4 (Self quotation).

71. John E. Cobb to Julius L. Chambers, March 26, 1973, and J. LeVonne Chambers to John E. Cobb, April 7, 1973, both folder 2, box 4, Chambers Papers.

72. J. LeVonne Chambers to David S. Holmes Jr., January 13, 1972, folder 1, box 4, and Julian Mason to James B. McMillan, May 21, 1973, folder 2, box 4, both Chambers Papers.

73. Lassiter, *The Silent Majority,* 206–8.

74. Ibid.; "24 Years of Integration," 47.

75. Wilkinson, *From Brown to Bakke,* 158–59; Elizabeth Schmoke Randolph Interview, June 16, 1993, 8, 11, NSV-UNCC.

76. Stanford R. Brookshire Interview, May 22, 1979, 4, NSV-UNCC; Douglas, *Reading, Writing, and Race,* 251; Daisy S. Stroud Interview, June 20, 2001, 19, 21, 25, NSV-UNCC. For more insights into how busing was recalled by the

two races, see "School Busing: How Far Has It Come?" *Los Angeles Times,* December 15, 1975, 1, 17.

6. HOME HAS CHANGED

1. "Black Politics: New Way to Overcome," *Newsweek,* June 7, 1971, 26–31 (quotation on 30).

2. "2 Cities, North and South, Show Progress by Blacks," *New York Times,* August 28, 1973, 1, 26.

3. "Back Home in Tifton," *New York Times Magazine,* December 2, 1973, 36–37, 90 (quotation), 92, 94 (quotation), 98, 100, 102, 104.

4. Paul Delaney, "Era of Routine Violence against Blacks by Whites in the South's Black Belt Appears Ended," *New York Times,* September 19, 1973, 33.

5. "2 Cities, North and South, Show Progress by Blacks," *New York Times,* August 28, 1973, 1, 26; "Back Home in Tifton," *New York Times Magazine,* December 2, 1973, 98, 104.

6. Affidavit of Jessie Kyles, December 5, 1971, pt. 2, reel 4, CRSA Papers. For other similar complaints, see John L. LeFlore to Jerris Leonard, December 7, 1970, and Affidavit of Jenkins Abrams Jr., December 7, 1970, both pt. 2, reel 4, CRSA Papers.

7. Jack Greenberg to John L. LeFlore, September 21, 1971, pt. 2, reel 14, CRSA Papers; "Why More Blacks Are Moving South," *U.S. News and World Report,* February 26, 1973, 53; "And Blacks Go South Again," *New York Times,* July 4, 1972, 17 (Mebane quotation).

8. "Why More Blacks Are Moving South," *U.S. News and World Report,* February 26, 1973, 53–55.

9. For a fine account of the Ole Miss crisis, see Charles W. Eagles, *The Price of Defiance: James Meredith and the Integration of Ole Miss* (Chapel Hill: University of North Carolina Press, 2009). For a good summary, see Dittmer, *Local People,* 139–42.

10. "Meredith Moves Back to Mississippi," *New York Times,* June 28, 1971, 12.

11. Washington Research Project, *The Shameful Blight,* 3–4; "Black Politics: New Way to Overcome," *Newsweek,* June 7, 1971, 26, 30.

12. "Gains for Blacks in Politics," *U.S. News and World Report,* June 11, 1973, 76; "Black Power Enclave," *New Republic,* January 16, 1971, 11; "Black Politics: New Way to Overcome," *Newsweek,* June 7, 1971, 26, 30.

13. Charles V. Hamilton, "Finding a Reason to Vote," *The Nation,* December 16, 1978, 668–71 (Jackson quotation on 671).

14. Maynard Jackson Interview in Hampton and Fayer with Flynn, *Voices of Freedom,* 623; Tom Eden to John L. LeFlore, June 3, 1974, and "Vote John LeFlore," n.d., flyer, both in pt. 1, reel 13, CRSA Papers; Ralph Abernathy to SCLC Contributor, December 1973, folder 170, box 1604, AFL-CIO Civil Rights Papers.

15. "Atlanta Elects a Black Mayor, First in a Major Southern City," *New York Times,* October 17, 1973, 1, 69; Maynard Jackson Interview in Hampton and Fayer with Flynn, *Voices of Freedom,* 629.

16. Kruse, *White Flight,* 240.

17. Mayor Maynard Jackson, "Inaugural Address" and "Can Atlanta Suc-

ceed Where America Has Failed?" both in Carson et al., eds., *The Eyes on the Prize Civil Rights Reader,* 614–18, 618–24 (quotation on 614); Maynard Jackson Interview in Hampton and Fayer with Flynn, *Voices of Freedom* (quotation on 630).

18. "Brief on Motion for Preliminary Injunction," February 24, 1970 (quotations on 2 and 7), and "Legal Memorandum in Support of Plaintiffs' Motion for a Preliminary Injunction," February 1970, 6 (final quotation), both *Nixon v. Brewer,* pt. 23A, sec. 1, reel 10, NAACP Papers; Dees with Fiffer, *A Season for Justice,* 133 (Dees quotation).

19. "Order and Decree," January 3, 1972, 400 (quotation), and Nathaniel R. Jones to Morris Dees, January 13, 1972, both *Sims v. Amos,* pt. 23A, sec. 1, reel 10, NAACP Papers; "Martin Luther King's Dream Coming True," *Poverty Law Report,* January 1974, 2; "Nixon v. Brewer," *Poverty Law Report,* January 1976, 4.

20. "Montgomery County 'At-Large' Plan Voided," *Poverty Law Report,* January/February 1979, 1; NAACP 1972 Annual Report, 38, folder 2, box 26, Kelly Alexander Papers.

21. Davidson and Grofman, introduction to *Quiet Revolution in the South,* 7.

22. Complaint, January 11, 1972 (first two quotations), and Plaintiffs' Brief, March 14, 1972, 7 (Perry quotation), both *Stevenson v. West,* and "Order," June 17, 1976, *South Carolina Conferences of Branches, NAACP v. John C. West,* all pt. 23A, sec. 2, reel 14, NAACP Papers.

23. Orville Vernon Burton et al., "South Carolina," in Davidson and Grofman, eds., *Quiet Revolution in the South,* 211–16 (quotation on 214).

24. Complaint, n.d., 1, 6 (quotation), and "Trial Memorandum of Plaintiffs," December 10, 1971, both *Bacote v. Carter,* pt. 23A, sec. 2, reel 1, NAACP Papers; Laughlin McDonald et al., "Georgia," in Davidson and Grofman, eds., *Quiet Revolution in the South,* 87–88.

25. Lewis with D'Orso, *Walking with the Wind,* 436; Mike Monroe to Daniel P. Moynihan, June 12, 1969, reel 21, CRDNA Papers.

26. Andrew Young, *An Easy Burden: The Civil Rights Movement and the Transformation of America* (New York: Harper Collins, 1996), 517–21 (quotation on 521).

27. J. Stanley Pottinger to Stanley S. Scott, September 24, 1974 (quotations), "Voting Rights Act Extension" folder, box 23, and Congressional Black Caucus Position Statement, August 21, 1974, 17, "Black Caucus—Meeting with the President, August 1974: Position Statements" folder, box 4, both Stanley Scott Files, Ford Library.

28. William B. Saxbe to Gerald R. Ford, December 6, 1974, "HU2-4 Voting" folder, box 9, White House Subject Files, Ford Library; Richard L. Engstrom et al., "Louisiana," in Davidson and Grofman, eds., *Quiet Revolution in the South,* 111.

29. For an overview of these events, see John A. Salmond, *"My Mind Set on Freedom": A History of the Civil Rights Movement, 1954–1968* (Chicago: Dee, 1997), 67–72.

30. Williams, *Eyes on the Prize,* 290; "Former Albany, Ga., Police Chief Builds a New Reputation in a New Town," *New York Times,* March 21, 1971, 55 (quotations).

31. "Eugene 'Bull' Connor Dies at 75," *New York Times,* March 11, 1973, 61.

32. Sokol, *There Goes My Everything*, 247–48; "Ex-Sheriff Is Sentenced to 2 Years," *New York Times*, December 2, 1978, 12.

33. "Blacks Elected in Selma," *New York Times*, August 9, 1972, 16; "Blacks Press for Control in Selma Election Today," *New York Times*, July 10, 1984, 12.

34. "Day Set in Honor of Medgar Evers," *New York Times*, June 12, 1973, 22. Although the evidence against him was compelling, de la Beckwith was not convicted of the murder until 1994. See Crespino, *In Search of Another Country*, 270.

35. "Most Major Cities Will Ignore Birthday of Dr. King on Friday," *New York Times*, January 11, 1971, 19.

36. The WRP's history is available at http://www.childrensdefense.org/about-us/our-history/washington-research-project.html (accessed September 20, 2010; copy in author's possession); Washington Research Project, *The Shameful Blight*, 4–5.

37. Washington Research Project, *The Shameful Blight*, iv, 5 (quotations), 20–24.

38. Ibid., 18.

39. Ibid., 24–29 (quotation on 28).

40. "Black Power Enclave," *New Republic*, January 16, 1971, 12.

41. "Aid Cutbacks Stun Black Mayors," *Christian Science Monitor*, February 12, 1973, 2; Southern Conference of Black Mayors, "Overview," n.d. (quotations), folder 2, box 1592, AFL-CIO Civil Rights Papers; Timothy L. Jenkins to James E. Bostic Jr., May 13, 1974, "Southern Conference of Black Mayors (1)" folder, box 20, Stanley Scott Files, Ford Library.

42. "America's Black Mayors: Are They Saving the Cities?" *Saturday Review World*, May 4, 1974, 11.

43. Testimony of John Lewis, June 10, 1971, U.S. Congress, House, Judiciary Committee, *Enforcement of the Voting Rights Act: Hearings before Subcommittee No. 4*, 92nd Cong., 1st sess., 1971, 241 (quotations), 243.

44. "The March of Time," *Newsweek*, September 10, 1973, 38–40 (quotation on 39). For an overview of the Liuzzo murder, see Lewis with D'Orso, *Walking with the Wind*, 362.

45. "The March of Time," *Newsweek*, September 10, 1973, 38–40 (quotations on 39, 40).

46. "Statement of Affirmative Action for Equal Employment Opportunities by the United States Commission on Civil Rights," November 17, 1972, 1, 3, 4, reel 19, CRDNA Papers.

47. Congressional Black Caucus Position Statement, August 21, 1974, "Black Caucus—Meeting with the President, August 1974: Position Statements" folder, box 4, Stanley Scott Files, Ford Library; Ben J. Wattenberg and Richard M. Scammon, "Black Progress and Liberal Rhetoric," *Commentary 55*, no. 4 (April 1973): 36; "Statement of Affirmative Action for Equal Employment Opportunities by the United States Commission on Civil Rights," November 17, 1972, 1, 3, 4 (income statistics), reel 19, CRDNA Papers.

48. Remarks of Raymond L. Telles, June 5–7, 1972, 2–3, "EEOC, 1971–74" folder, White House Central Files, Subject Files (Confidential Files), box 23, NPM; NAACP 1972 Annual Report, 37, folder 2, box 26, Kelly Alexander Papers.

49. Black Caucus of Telephone Workers Petition, September 14, 1972, folder 3, box 2839, AFL-CIO Civil Rights Papers.

50. BEAD Negotiating Committee to J. W. Cleveland, December 7, 1980, folder 5, box 2839, AFL-CIO Civil Rights Papers.

51. Trial Testimony of Elmo Myers, December 2–5, 1974, 244, 273–74, and BAM Petition, May 5, 1970, both *Myers v. Gilman Paper,* NARA-Atlanta.

52. Stephen C. Schlesinger, "Black Caucus in the Unions," *The Nation,* February 2, 1974, 142–44; Remarks of William E. Pollard, March 10, 1976, 6, folder 2, box 1592, AFL-CIO Civil Rights Papers.

53. "Statement of Affirmative Action for Equal Employment Opportunities by the United States Commission on Civil Rights," November 17, 1972, 2 (first quotation), reel 19, CRDNA Papers; Prepared Statement of William H. Brown III, October 4, 1971, 49–50, Prepared Statement of Clarence Mitchell, October 6, 1971, 210–11, and Testimony of Joseph L. Rauh Jr., October 6, 1971, 227, all U.S. Congress, Senate, Labor and Public Welfare Committee, *Equal Employment Opportunities Enforcement Act of 1971: Hearings before the Subcommittee on Labor.* 92nd Cong., 1st sess., 1971.

54. Kotlowski, *Nixon's Civil Rights,* 118–20; Ronald R. Frost to Richard B. Russell, May 29, 1970, ser. 10, folder 6, box 3, and W. L. Nicoll to Richard B. Russell, November 6, 1969 (first quotation), ser. 10, folder 7, box 3, both Russell Papers; Campbell, *Senator Sam Ervin,* 231 (second quotation).

55. "John L. LeFlore: Your Friend in Need," 1975, flyer, pt. 1, reel 13, John L. LeFlore to Joe A. Bailey, June 20, 1970, pt. 2, reel 5, and "Accomplishments," n.d., pt. 2, reel 16, all CRSA Papers; Nicholls, "The Non-Partisan Voters League," 82.

56. Zieger, *For Jobs and Freedom,* 176–77, 181 (quotation); "Sears Roebuck—Atlanta," n.d., "EEOC Papers: Minority Employment Reports" folder, box 3, Thomas G. Cody Files, Ford Library.

57. Zieger, *For Jobs and Freedom,* 177–79, 216 (quotation on 177).

58. Minchin, *Hiring the Black Worker,* 3; Zieger, *For Jobs and Freedom,* 179.

59. "Getting It Together in Jobs," *The Crisis,* September 1971, 212.

60. Wattenberg and Scammon, "Black Progress and Liberal Rhetoric," 35–44 (quotation on 42); John A. Morsell, "Black Progress or Illiberal Rhetoric," *The Crisis,* June–July 1973, 200–203.

61. Morsell, "Black Progress or Illiberal Rhetoric."

62. Ibid., 201 (Henderson quotation); R. D. Morrison to Stanley S. Scott, October 11, 1973, "Black Colleges, 1972–75 (2)" folder, box 4, Stanley Scott Files, Ford Library. Morrison's data referred to people under eighteen years of age.

63. Goldfield, *Black, White, and Southern,* 209 (Ayers and Morris quotations); Untitled Speech, n.d., 1 (first McKissick quotation), folder 7487, box 337, and "Speech by F. B. McKissick, Snr.," June 23, 1978, folder 7481b, box 337, 10, 15 (second and third McKissick quotations), both McKissick Papers.

7. Paving the Way for Full Participation

1. "Text of Remarks by the President to Be Delivered to the 66th Annual Convention of the NAACP," July 1, 1975 (Ford quotations), "SP3-130 NAACP Convention, Washington D.C." folder, box 61, White House Central Files (Subject File), Ford Library; "NAACP 66th Annual Convention—'You Gotta Belong!'" *The Crisis,* October 1975, 267–78.

2. "NAACP 66th Annual Convention—'You Gotta Belong!'" *The Crisis,* October 1975, 267.

3. "Meeting with Key Black Civil Rights Leaders," October 23, 1974, "Presidential Meeting with Black Civil Rights Leaders" folder, box 18, Stanley Scott Files, Ford Library; White House Press Release, July 1, 1975, "SP3-130 NAACP Convention, Washington D.C." folder, box 61, White House Central Files (Subject File), Ford Library.

4. Stan Scott to Herb Klein, July 9, 1971 (Wilkins quotation), "NAACP 1971–75 (1)" folder, and Clarence Mitchell to Gerald R. Ford, November 1, 1974 (Mitchell quotation), "NAACP, 1971–75 (3)" folder, both box 14, Stanley Scott Files, and "Remarks of the President at the Los Angeles Press Club Breakfast," May 26, 1976, "Busing" folder, box H35, President Ford's Committee Papers, 1975–76, all Ford Library.

5. "Remarks of the President at the Los Angeles Press Club Breakfast," May 26, 1976, "Busing" folder, box H35, President Ford's Committee Papers, 1975–76, Ford Library.

6. Jim Connor to Bob Goldwin, October 6, 1975, and "A Former Teacher on Busing," October 1, 1975, both "Human Rights—Equality: Education" folder, box 24, Presidential Handwriting File, and "Wilkins Critical of Ford," *Milwaukee Journal,* November 18, 1974, clipping, "HU2-1 Education-Schooling 8/9/74–12/31/74" folder, box 5, White House Central Files (Subject File), all Ford Library.

7. Chafe, *The Unfinished Journey,* 445–48.

8. NAACP Annual Report, 1974, 45, folder 3, box 26, Kelly Alexander Papers.

9. Gerald R. Ford Interview, March 8, 1978, 1, box 1, A. James Reichley Interview Transcripts, Ford Library; "Black Americans," April 10, 1976 (Ford quotation), "Civil Rights" folder, box H35, President Ford's Campaign Committee Papers, Ford Library.

10. Patterson, *Brown v. Board of Education,* 181; Art Quern and Allen Moore to Jim Cannon, June 3, 1976, "June 2–9, 1976" folder, box 5, James M. Cannon Files, Ford Library.

11. "For Blacks: Big Strides in a New South," *U.S. News and World Report,* February 25, 1974, 56, 59; "Lawsuits May Alter Job Practices in South," *New York Times,* February 2, 1974, and "Toward Equal Job Opportunity," *Christian Science Monitor,* April 23, 1974, clippings, "Affirmative Action" folder, box 103, Noel Sterrett Clipping File, Carter Library.

12. Dumbrell, *The Carter Presidency,* 89.

13. Remarks of William E. Pollard, Director, Department of Civil Rights, AFL-CIO, March 10, 1976, folder 2, box 1592, AFL-CIO Civil Rights Papers; "Impact of Early Suit Felt in Local Programs," *Poverty Law Report,* November/December 1976, 8.

14. "Segregation Remembered," *Time,* September 27, 1976, 42–43 (quotation on 43).

15. "For Blacks: Big Strides in a New South," *U.S. News and World Report,* February 25, 1974, 56, 59 (quotations on 56).

16. "10 Years of Civil Rights—Report by the Chief Enforcer," *U.S. News and World Report,* September 23, 1974, 87–88.

17. Weekly Reports of Thomas R. Hunt, August 30, October 4, and October 11, 1974, all "Civil Rights—Weekly Reports (1)" folder, box 3, Geoffrey Shepard Files, Ford Library.

18. Weekly Reports of Thomas R. Hunt, August 30 and October 4, 1974, "Civil Rights—Weekly Reports (1)" folder, box 3, Geoffrey Shepard Files, Ford Library.

19. "Notes on People," *New York Times*, December 4, 1974, 49; Department of Justice Report, February 3, 1970, reel 2, CRDNA Papers.

20. "The Races: Going Back to Dixie," *Newsweek*, March 25, 1974, 37.

21. Ibid.; "Blacks Return to South in a Reverse Migration," *New York Times*, June 18, 1974, 1, 49 (quotations).

22. Bob Blauner, *Black Lives, White Lives: Three Decades of Race Relations in America* (Berkeley and Los Angeles: University of California Press, 1989), 175 (Spence quotation). For another similar example, see the interview with Herbert Williams in "The South Today," *Time*, September 27, 1976, 44.

23. Harris Survey, October 2, 1975, "June 11–14, 1976" folder, box 5, James M. Cannon Files, Ford Library; Ronald P. Formisano, *Boston against Busing: Race, Class, and Ethnicity in the 1960s and 1970s* (Chapel Hill: University of North Carolina Press, 1991), 1–21, 66–76 (quotation on 1).

24. LeRoy Brown to Patricia Lord, September 26, 1974, folder 17, box 022675, Alabama Governors' Papers.

25. Travis Smith to Strom Thurmond, September 13, 1976, folder 27, box 3 (Correspondence Files), Thurmond Papers; "Petition against Court Ordered Forced Busing," October 21, 1975, "Louisville Petitions (1)" folder, box 14, Bobbie Kilburg Files, Ford Library.

26. "24 Years of Integration: Has Busing Really Worked?" *U.S. News and World Report*, May 8, 1978, 46; Kathleen M. Troth to Strom Thurmond, February 3, 1976, folder 27, box 3 (Correspondence Files), Thurmond Papers.

27. Michael Albritton to President Ford, September 21, 1976, "Administrative Office: Correspondence Topical File" folder, box B74, President Ford Committee Records, Ford Library. For another similar example, see Save Our Community Schools Petition to President Gerald Ford, June 19, 1976, "Administrative Office: Correspondence Topical File" folder, box B74, President Ford Committee Records, Ford Library.

28. Dick Parsons to Jim Cannon and Phil Buchen, October 23, 1975, and Edward H. Levi to James M. Cannon, March 29, 1976, both "Busing (1)" folder, box 1, and White House Fact Sheet, June 24, 1976 (quotation), "Busing (4)" folder, box 1, all Arthur F. Quern Files, Ford Library.

29. For an example of these letters, see Mr. and Mrs. Alan Taylor Pidgern to Strom Thurmond, April 10, 1976, Civil Rights 2, folder 1, box 2, Thurmond Papers. For insight into the close relationship between Helms and Thurmond, see Helms, *Here's Where I Stand*, 54–55.

30. Quotation in "Crippling the Civil Rights Act," *Washington Post*, December 4, 1974, clipping, "Civil Rights—General" folder, Geoffrey Shepard Files, Ford Library; "Limits on Rights Enforcement Fought," *Washington Star-News*, December 3, 1974; Strom Thurmond to Ms. Jean Walden, June 8, 1976, folder 27, box 3 (Correspondence Files), and Strom Thurmond to Donald R. Kelly, April 15, 1976, Civil Rights 2, folder 1, box 2, both Thurmond Papers.

31. Strom Thurmond to Gerald R. Ford, July 18, 1975, "Affirmative Action" folder, box 6, Patricia Lindh and Jeanne Holm Files, Ford Library.

32. Harris Survey, October 2, 1975, "June 11–14, 1976" folder, box 5, James M. Cannon Files, Ford Library; LeRoy Brown to Jerry McWhorter, May

6, 1974, folder 17, box 022675, Alabama Governors' Papers; Bass and DeVries, *The Transformation of Southern Politics,* 406, 407 (Carter quotation).

33. Bass and DeVries, *The Transformation of Southern Politics,* 406 (quotation); Fleischman, "Brown and Intergroup Relations," 250 (summary of commission study).

34. David Matthews to Gerald Ford, March 29, 1976, "Busing (1)" folder, box 1, Arthur F. Quern Files, Ford Library.

35. "NAACP Special Fund Receives $50,000," *The Crisis,* December 1974, 352; Patterson, *Brown v. Board of Education,* 178–82 (first quotation on 180); NAACP 1974 Annual Report, 32 (Marshall quotation), folder 3, box 26, Kelly Alexander Papers. For an informed overview of the entire *Milliken* case, see Sugrue, *Sweet Land of Liberty,* 449–92.

36. "10 Years of Civil Rights—Report by the Chief Enforcer," *U.S. News and World Report,* September 23, 1974, 87–88; Thomas R. Hunt to J. Stanley Pottinger, November 15, 1974 (quotation), "Civil Rights—Weekly Reports (2)" folder, box 3, Geoffrey Shepherd Files, Ford Library.

37. John Caughey, "*Brown:* 'The Noblest Decision,'" *The Nation,* May 18, 1974, 614–15 (quotation on 615); "*Brown*—20 Years Later," *The Crisis,* May 1974, 152 (second quotation), 154 (first quotation).

38. NAACP 1976 Annual Report, 45 (quotation), folder 3, box 26, Kelly Alexander Papers; Joseph Featherstone, "Children Out of School," *New Republic,* March 29, 1975, 13–14 (HEW study); NAACP 1976 Annual Report, 46, folder 3 box 26, Kelly Alexander Papers; "Chapman v. Thomasville Board of Education," *Poverty Law Report,* August 1974, 4.

39. Testimony of Peter E. Holmes, May 21, 1974, and Testimony of Samuel Etheridge, May 21, 1974, both U.S. Congress, *Juvenile Justice and Delinquency Prevention,* 487, 501, 520, 526 (quotation).

40. "Testing . . . Grouping: The New Segregation in Southern Schools?" 1976, 4–5, 46–47, report held at the SRC's headquarters, Atlanta (copy in author's possession).

41. U.S. Commission on Civil Rights, *The Black/White Colleges,* 9; "Statement of Affirmative Action for Equal Employment Opportunities by the United States Commission on Civil Rights," 1972, reel 19, CRDNA Papers; "HEW Cold to Regents' Desegregation Plans," *Atlanta Constitution,* May 19, 1970, 1.

42. Lewis with D'Orso, *Walking with the Wind,* 199; Richard D. Trent, "The Reciprocal Impact of the *Brown* Decision on Higher Education," *The Crisis,* June/July 1979, 226–29 (data on 229); J. Stanley Pottinger, "10 Years of Civil Rights—Report by the Chief Enforcer," *U.S. News and World Report,* September 23, 1974, 87.

43. U.S. Commission on Civil Rights, *The Black/White Colleges,* 9–10; Jim Cannon, "Affirmative Action Meeting," September 10, 1975 (quotation), "Affirmative Action, August 1975–June 1976" folder, box 1, Richard D. Parsons Files, Ford Library; Caspar W. Weinberger to Gerald R. Ford, March 4, 1975, "Higher Education: Affirmative Action (2)" folder, box 5, David H. Lissy Files, Ford Library.

44. "Black Colleges Held Endangered," *New York Times,* June 27, 1971, 33.

45. M. K. Nelson to Stanley S. Scott, October 9, 1973, and R. D. Morrison to Stanley S. Scott, October 11, 1973, both "Black Colleges, 1972–75 (2)" folder, box 4, Stanley Scott Files, Ford Library.

46. Congressional Black Caucus, "Position Statements Presented to the President of the United States," August 21, 1974, "Black Caucus—Meeting with the President, August 1974: Position Statements" folder, and Joseph A. Gore to Stanley S. Scott, October 11, 1973, "Black Colleges, 1972–75 (2)" folder, both box 4, Stanley Scott Files, Ford Library; Kotlowski, *Nixon's Civil Rights,* 151–55 (data on 154).

47. "CBO Details Income Disparities of Black and White Americans," *Daily Labor Report,* January 4, 1978, A11.

48. For a fine overview of the media's discovery of the Sun Belt, which dated to a series of *New York Times* articles in February 1976, see Bartley, *The New South,* 431–32.

49. U.S. Comptroller General, "The Equal Employment Opportunity Commission Has Made Limited Progress in Eliminating Employment Discrimination," September 28, 1976 (quotation on 40), "Comptroller General Report on EEOC" folder, box 1, Thomas G. Cody Files, Ford Library; "Who Gets the Pink Slip?" *Time,* February 3, 1975, 58.

50. Remarks of William E. Pollard, March 10, 1976, and E. T. Kehrer to William Pollard, April 30, 1975 (second quotation), both folder 2, box 1592, AFL-CIO Civil Rights Papers.

51. E. T. Kehrer to William Pollard, March 18, 1975, folder 2, box 1592, AFL-CIO Civil Rights Papers.

52. John Calhoun, "Watergate and Black America," June 12, 1974, "Watergate and Black America" folder, box 23, Stanley Scott Files, Ford Library; Morsell, "Black Progress or Illiberal Rhetoric," 203 (*Crisis* quotation). For a useful summary of Watergate, see Chafe, *The Unfinished Journey,* 420–27.

53. Dorothy Height et al. to the President, September 23, 1974 (quotations), and NAACP Press Release, October 25, 1974, both "Human Rights—Equality (1)" folder, box 24, Presidential Handwriting File, Ford Library.

54. Charles B. Rangel to Friend, May 5, 1975 ("front-line victim"), and Statement by Vernon E. Jordan Jr., July 27, 1975, both "Blacks—Voter Background (3)" folder, box A12, President Ford's Committee Papers, 1975–76 Files, Ford Library.

55. "King's Legacy," *Time,* January 27, 1975, 22; "Thousands Mark '65 March in Selma, Ala.," *New York Times,* March 9, 1975, 50 (King quotation).

56. Mrs. Martin Luther King to George Meany Jr., November 18, 1975, folder 171, box 1604, AFL-CIO Civil Rights Papers; "Mrs. Coretta Scott King Biography," available at http://www.thekingcenter.org/MrsCSKing/ (accessed September 20, 2010; copy in author's possession); Statement of Mrs. Coretta Scott King, March 15, 1976, House Committee, Equal Opportunity and Full Employment, Part 5, 224.

57. "Commemorating Dr. King's 45th Birthday Anniversary," January 14, 1974, folder 170, Mrs. Martin Luther King Jr. to Sponsor, December 1975, folder 171, and Coretta Scott King to Friends of the Center, n.d., folder 173, all box 1604, AFL-CIO Civil Rights Papers.

58. Annual Report of the 29th Conference of the North Carolina NAACP, October 12–15, 1972, folder 16, box 23, Kelly Alexander Papers; "10 Years of Civil Rights—Report by the Chief Enforcer," *U.S. News and World Report,* September 23, 1974, 87–88.

59. "Mississippi's Federal Agencies: A Paper Tiger Approach to Black Employment," August 1974, 3 (first quotation), 4 (second quotation), "Minor-

ity Employment in Federal Agencies in Mississippi" folder, box 14, Stanley Scott Files, Ford Library.

60. NAACP 1974 Annual Report, 34 (first quotation), folder 3, box 26, and Speech of J. Francis Polhaus, November 8, 1975, folder 19, box 23, both in Kelly Alexander Papers.

61. U.S. Comptroller General, "The Equal Employment Opportunity Commission Has Made Limited Progress in Eliminating Employment Discrimination," September 28, 1976 (quotations on 2, 62), "Comptroller General Report on EEOC" folder, box 1, Thomas G. Cody Files, Ford Library.

62. Ethel Bent Walsh to Elmer B. Staats, June 11, 1976, "Comptroller General Report on EEOC" folder, box 1, Thomas G. Cody Files, Ford Library; "The Anti-Bias Bottleneck," *Wall Street Journal*, October 22, 1974, clipping, "Civil Rights—General" folder, box 3, Geoffrey Shepherd Files, Ford Library.

63. Statement of John H. Powell Jr., September 17, 1974, U.S. Congress, House, Education and Labor Committee, *Equal Employment Opportunity Commission: Hearings before the Subcommittee on Equal Opportunities*, 93rd Cong, 2nd sess., 1974, 5–6, 25 (quotation).

64. Statement of Michael Markowitz, September 17, 1974, U.S. Congress, *Equal Employment Opportunity Commission*, 180–83 (quotation on 183); Statement of Homer L. Deakins, September 17, 1974, U.S. Congress, *Equal Employment Opportunity Commission*, 186.

65. Statement of Arthur S. Flemming, September 25, 1975, U.S. Congress, House, Education and Labor Committee, *Oversight Hearings on Federal Enforcement of Equal Employment Opportunity Laws: Part 2*, 94th Cong., 1st sess., 1975, 49–58.

66. "U.S. Wins Georgia Bias Case," *Washington Post*, February 1, 1974, clipping, "Affirmative Action" folder, box 103, Noel Sterrett Clipping File, Carter Library.

67. Complaint, April 12, 1974, 5, 7, *U.S. et al. v. Allegheny-Ludlam Industries et al.*, unprocessed case records, BPL.

68. Affidavit of J. Bruce Johnston, December 9, 1975 (quotation on 3), *U.S. et al. v. Allegheny-Ludlam Industries et al.*, BPL; NAACP Annual Report, 1974, 49, folder 3, box 26, Kelly Alexander Papers.

69. Jonas, *Freedom's Sword*, 298; Statement of Gary A. Myers, September 22, 1975, U.S. Congress, *Oversight Hearings on Federal Enforcement of Equal Employment Opportunity Laws*, 36–38; Zieger, *For Jobs and Freedom*, 210.

70. "Court Upholds Back Pay in Job Bias Case," *Washington Post*, June 26, 1975, A1; Deposition of Joseph P. Moody, November 9, 1966, *Moody v. Albermarle Paper*, NARA-Atlanta; Joe McCullough, Interview with Author (Minchin), October 3, 1997, Savannah, GA.

71. Bass and DeVries, *The Transformation of Southern Politics*, 405.

72. U.S. Commission on Civil Rights, *The Voting Rights Act* (quotation in letter of transmittal); Testimony of John Lewis, March 25, 1975, U.S. Congress, *Extension of the Voting Rights Act: Part 1*, 128; Bryant Rollins, "Black Passage: From Civil Rights to the Ballot Box," *New York Times*, November 14, 1976, D4.

73. U.S. Commission on Civil Rights, *The Voting Rights Act*, 40–42.

74. Remarks of William E. Pollard, March 10, 1976, folder 2, box 1592, AFL-CIO Civil Rights Papers; NAACP 1974 Annual Report, 18 (first quotation), folder 3, box 26, Kelly Alexander Papers; Testimony of John Lewis,

March 25, 1975, U.S. Congress, *Extension of the Voting Rights Act: Part 1,* 129; U.S. Commission on Civil Rights, *The Voting Rights Act,* 49–52 (quotation on 52).

75. William B. Saxbe to Gerald R. Ford, December 6, 1974, "HU2-4 Voting" folder, box 9, White House Central Files (Subject File), Ford Library.

76. See House Committee, February 25, March 14 and 25, 1975, U.S. Congress, *Extension of the Voting Rights Act: Part 1,* 17–60, 62–74, 127–29, 548–75, 901–3 (Lewis quotation on 128–29).

77. Statement of Clarence Mitchell, March 25, 1975, U.S. Congress, *Extension of the Voting Rights Act: Part 1,* 888; Testimony of Dr. Aaron E. Henry, March 25, 1975, ibid., 667–69 (quotation on 669).

78. Statement of Walter Flowers, March 3, 1975, U.S. Congress, *Extension of the Voting Rights Act: Part 1,* 140; Testimony of Albioun F. Summer, March 25, 1975, ibid., 678; Testimony of Daniel R. McLeod, March 14, 1975, ibid., 539.

79. Testimony of Daniel R. McLeod, March 14, 1975, ibid., 555, 563.

80. Lewis with D'Orso, *Walking with the Wind,* 440–45.

81. "Politics: Out of a Cocoon," *Time,* September 27, 1976, 28; U.S. Commission on Civil Rights, *The Voting Rights Act,* 60–62; Testimony of John Lewis, March 25, 1975, U.S. Congress, *Extension of the Voting Rights Act: Part 1,* 129.

82. U.S. Commission on Civil Rights, *The Voting Rights Act,* 81–82, 186.

83. Thomas R. Hunt to J. Stanley Pottinger, October 18, 1974 (quotation), and Thomas R. Hunt to J. Stanley Pottinger, November 22, 1974, both "Civil Rights—Weekly Reports (2)" folder, box 3, Geoffrey Shepard Files, Ford Library.

84. Lawson, *In Pursuit of Power,* 224–53 (quotations on 228 [Treen], 253 [Lawson]); "10 Years of Civil Rights—Report by the Chief Enforcer," *U.S. News and World Report,* September 23, 1974, 88.

85. "Statement upon Signing of Voting Rights Bill," August 6, 1975, and "Invitees: Voting Rights Act Extension Signing Ceremony," August 6, 1975, both "HU2-4 Voting" folder, box 9, White House Central Files (Subject File), Ford Library.

86. Lawson, *In Pursuit of Power,* 244; Speech of J. Francis Polhaus, November 8, 1975, folder 19, box 23, Kelly Alexander Papers.

87. "Fact Sheet: Amendments to the Voting Rights Act," August 6, 1975 (first quotation), "Voting Rights, July 18–August 6, 1975" folder, box 39, James M. Cannon Files, Ford Library; "Black Clubbed in Selma Assails Blacks Aiding Wallace," *New York Times,* April 24, 1974, 22; "Black Paper Backs Wallace Saying He Has 'Softened,'" *New York Times,* April 26, 1974, 33; "The South Today," *Time,* September 27, 1976, 37–38 (Wallace quotations on 38); Jack Bass and Marilyn W. Thompson, *Strom: The Complicated Personal and Political Life of Strom Thurmond* (New York: PublicAffairs, 2005), ix–x, 33–35, 259.

88. "Black Passage: From Civil Rights to the Ballot Box," *New York Times,* November 14, 1976, D4; "The Black Vote: Balance of Power," *The Crisis,* December 1976, 337–38; "Blacks Elected Carter!" n.d. (quotation), "Blacks and the Carter Administration (1)" folder, box 12, Louis Martin Files, Carter Library; Dumbrell, *The Carter Presidency,* 88.

89. Dumbrell, *The Carter Presidency,* 100; King, "Our God Is Marching On!" 226.

8. Mixed Outcomes

1. "Black Newsmen Question President on Africa Policy, Job and Urban Programs," April 6, 1978 (first quotation), "Black Media 9/76–4/78" folder, box 2, Martha (Bunny) Mitchell Files, Carter Library; "Civil Rights/Campaign" (quotation file), April 14, 1976 (second and third quotations), "Civil Rights" folder, box H23, President Ford's Campaign Committee Records, Ford Library.

2. Coretta Scott King to "Our Friends Everywhere," November 14, 1977, folder 4, box 1592, AFL-CIO Civil Rights Papers; Region V Quarterly Report, April–August 1980, 1, folder 1, box 18, Kelly Alexander Papers.

3. For insight into the problem of rising black expectations, see Vincent Harding, "So Much History, So Much Future: Martin Luther King, Jr., and the Second Coming of America," in *Have We Overcome? Race Relations since Brown,* ed. Michael V. Namorato (Jackson: University of Mississippi Press, 1979), 35.

4. "Governing Georgia," *Newsweek,* September 13, 1976, 32–34 (quotation on 33); "Carter on Busing," n.d., "Debate Background—Busing" folder, box 15, David Gergen Files, Ford Library; Norrell, *The House I Live In,* 287; Peter G. Bourne, *Jimmy Carter: A Comprehensive Biography from Plains to Postpresidency* (New York: Scribner, 1997), 146–47.

5. "New Governor of Georgia Urges End of Racial Bias," *New York Times,* January 13, 1971, 1 (first quotation); "Governing Georgia," *Newsweek,* September 13, 1976, 32–34; "Carter on Busing," n.d. (second quotation), "Debate Background—Busing" folder, box 15, David Gergen Files, Ford Library.

6. "Debate Questions: Busing," n.d. (quotation), "Busing" folder, box 31, Sam Bleicher Files, Carter Library.

7. "The Black Vote: The Balance of Power," *The Crisis,* December 1976, 337–38; Harry S. Dent to Richard Cheney, November 10, 1976, folder 562, box 26, Dent Papers.

8. "The Black Vote: Balance of Power," *The Crisis,* December 1976, 337–38; Lewis with D'Orso, *Walking with the Wind,* 438, 439.

9. "Coretta King Uneasy over the Selections for Carter Cabinet," *New York Times,* January 13, 1977, 15; Dumbrell, *The Carter Presidency,* 89.

10. "Ambassador Young's Offense," *New York Times,* n.d. (quotation), clipping, "Young, Andrew, Departure from UN (1)" folder, box 109, Louis Martin Files, Carter Library. For a summary of the controversy over Young's resignation and black reaction to it, see "Andrew Young's Transgression," *Washington Post,* August 16, 1979, and "Statement of Black Leadership Forum," August 16, 1979, both "Young, Andrew, Departure from UN (1)" folder, box 109, Louis Martin Files, Carter Library.

11. Louis Martin Exit Interview, December 10, 1980, "White House Staff Exit Interviews" file, box 5, and Louis Martin, "The First Two Years," December 21, 1978, "Blacks and the Carter Administration (1)" folder, box 12, both Louis Martin Files, and "Remarks by Drew S. Days III," February 17, 1978, "Discrimination-Employment" folder, box 15, Annie Gutierrez Files, all Carter Library.

12. "King's Legacy," *The New Republic,* April 8, 1978, 8; Louis Martin to Black Mayors List, October 7, 1978, "Black Mayors" folder, box 9, Louis Martin Files, Carter Library; David J. Garrow, *Protest at Selma: Martin Luther*

King, Jr., and the Voting Rights Act of 1965 (New Haven, CT: Yale University Press, 1978), 1.

13. NAACP 1980 Annual Report (Southeast Region), 11–13, folder 25, box 17, Kelly Alexander Papers; Dittmer, *Local People*, 120–23.

14. "Center Attorney Challenges Unrepresentative Governments," *Poverty Law Report*, November/December 1979, 4; "Mobile: A Great Leap Backward," *Poverty Law Report*, June/July 1980, 2.

15. "The Bolden Decision Stonewalls Black Aspirations," *Southern Changes*, July–August 1980, 12; Consent Decree, February 4, 1983, *Mobile v. Bolden*, pt. 2, reel 1, CRSA Papers.

16. "Mobile: A Great Leap Backward," *Poverty Law Report*, June/July 1980, 2; Peyton McCrary, Jerome A. Gray, Edward Still, and Huey L. Perry, "Alabama," in Davidson and Grofman, eds., *Quiet Revolution in the South*, 51–52; Nicholls, "The Non-Partisan Voters League," 85–86.

17. Dent, *Southern Journey*, 210; Charles Sherrod, "Organizing in Albany, Georgia" and "Student Nonviolent Coordinating Committee Statement of Purpose," both in Carson et al., eds., *The Eyes on the Prize Civil Rights Reader*, 119–20, 138–39.

18. Jimmie Lewis Franklin, *Back to Birmingham: Richard Arrington, Jr., and His Times* (Tuscaloosa: University of Alabama Press, 1989), 116–80 (quotation on 180).

19. Franklin, *Back to Birmingham*, 181 (first quotation), 209, 245 (second quotation); Christopher MacGregor Scribner, *Renewing Birmingham: Federal Funding and the Promise of Change* (Athens: University of Georgia Press, 2002), 138, 140.

20. Charles V. Hamilton, "Finding a Reason to Vote," *The Nation*, December 16, 1978, 668–71.

21. Kruse, *White Flight*, 241; "The Black Middle Class: Making It," *New York Times Magazine*, December 3, 1978, 34–36, 138, 140, 144, 146, 148, 150, 152, 154, 155–57; Maynard Jackson and Dillard Munford Interviews in Hampton and Fayer with Flynn, *Voices of Freedom*, 631–40 (quotations on 631, 634, 640).

22. "Montgomery Relaxes as Racism Recedes," *New York Times*, April 4, 1978, 16 (quotation); Frye Gaillard, *Cradle of Freedom: Alabama and the Movement That Changed America* (Tuscaloosa: University of Alabama Press, 2004), 343–44; "Fond Salute to 'Mother' of Civil Rights," *New York Times*, January 15, 1980, 16.

23. Anne Schraff, *Coretta Scott King: Striving for Civil Rights* (Berkeley Heights, NJ: Enslow, 1997), 92–94, 103–5; "The King Holiday: A Chronology," available at http://www.thekingcenter.org/kingholiday/chronology.aspx (accessed September 20, 2010; copy in author's files).

24. "Congressional Black Caucus Legislative Agenda," n.d. (quotation), "Congressional Black Caucus 7/77–9/78" folder, box 6, Martha Mitchell Files, Carter Library; "President, in Atlanta, Asks Congress to Vote Holiday for Dr. King," *New York Times*, January 15, 1979, 1; Louis Martin to Bobby Jackson, May 5, 1980, "Correspondence File, Ja–Jo. 1979–81" folder, box 28, Louis Martin Files, Carter Library.

25. "Interview with the President," January 10, 1979 (first quotation), "Blacks and the Carter Administration (1)" folder, box 12, and "Remarks of the President at Cheyney State College Commencement Ceremony," May 20, 1979, "Presidential Speeches" folder, box 80, both Louis Martin Files, Carter Library.

26. "Pressure Rises for Day in Georgia Hailing Dr. King," *New York Times*, January 10, 1979, 12 (Scott quotation); "Kennedy to Seek a Holiday Marking Dr. King Birthday," *New York Times*, January 13, 1979, 8 (SCLC quotation).

27. "President, in Atlanta, Asks Congress to Vote Holiday for Dr. King," *New York Times*, January 15, 1979, 1, 15.

28. "House Sets Back a Plan to Make Dr. King's Birthday U.S. Holiday," *New York Times*, December 6, 1979, 1, B23; Helms, *Here's Where I Stand*, 163 (Helms quotation); William H. Wiggins Jr., "O Freedom! Afro-American Emancipation Celebrations," in *Martin Luther King, Jr. and the Civil Rights Movement*, ed. John A. Kirk (Basingstoke: Palgrave Macmillan, 2007), 224 (McDonald quotation).

29. J. E. Malone to Strom Thurmond et al., n.d., CMS Series 1981, folder 27, box 3, Thurmond Papers; Wiggins, "O Freedom!" 223–31; Matthew Dennis, *Red, White, and Blue Letter Days: An American Calendar* (Ithaca, NY: Cornell University Press, 2002), 275 (King quotation).

30. Harry S. Dent to Strom Thurmond, June 25, 1979, and December 22, 1980, both folder 616, box 30, Dent Papers.

31. Bass and Thompson, *Strom*, 301; "Wooing the Black Vote," *Time*, January 30, 1978, 17; "South Carolina," *New Republic*, November 4, 1978, 28–30 (quotation on 29).

32. "On Capitol Hill," *Washington Post*, December 7, 1979, A4 (Conyers quotation); "The King Holiday: A Chronology," available at http://www .thekingcenter.org/kingholiday/chronology.aspx (accessed September 20, 2010); Stevie Wonder, "Happy Birthday," 1980, lyrics available at http://www .lyricsfreak.com/s/stevie+wonder/happy+birthday_20131794.html (accessed September 20, 2010; copy in author's possession); "On Capitol Hill," *Washington Post*, December 7, 1979, A4.

33. "The *Brown* Decision 25 Years Later: Indicators of Desegregation and Equal Educational Opportunity," May 17, 1979, 1, and Gordon Stewart to Jimmy Carter, May 16, 1979, both "*Brown v. Board*—Reception Lists O/A9509 (1)" folder, box 14, Louis Martin Files, Carter Library.

34. "A New Racial Poll," *Newsweek*, February 26, 1979, 39–40; "Busing: The Issue That Will Not Go Away," *The Crisis*, December 1978, 350–52 (Orfield quotation on 350); "24 Years of Integration," 44–45, 47.

35. "Busing: The Issue That Will Not Go Away," *The Crisis*, December 1978, 350; Norton et al., *A People and a Nation*, 919–21, 924; Mrs. Robert Keys to Strom Thurmond, July 24, 1979, folder 13, box 2 (Correspondence Files), Thurmond Papers.

36. Strom Thurmond to Jack Richards, January 15, 1980 (quotation), folder 11, box 2 (Correspondence Files), and Strom Thurmond to Michael F. Warth, June 3, 1977, Civil Rights 2, folder 16, box 2, both Thurmond Papers; Helms, *Here's Where I Stand*, 160.

37. "Back to Busing—Again," *Time*, September 12, 1977, 44; James P. Turner to John M. Harmon, June 30, 1977 (closing quotations), "Busing 6–7/77" folder, box 120, Margaret McKenna Files, Carter Library.

38. "24 Years of Integration," 44, 46.

39. Greene, *Our Separate Ways*, 212; Dorothy Craig Interview, November 15, 2004, 12, 13, Interview U-37, SOHP.

40. "NAACP Suspends Atlanta Unit: Repudiates School Agreement," *The*

Crisis, May 1973, 168–69; Lassiter, *The Silent Majority*, 107–14; Kruse, *White Flight*, 5 (quotation).

41. "24 Years of Integration," 45 (Minor quotation); "Atlanta Ads Seek Students for Schools," *New York Times*, March 17, 1980, 12.

42. "'White Academies' in the South—Booming Despite Obstacles," *U.S. News and World Report*, April 19, 1971, 75–76; Dan Barry, "Legacy of School Segregation Endures Separate but Legal," *New York Times*, September 30, 2007; Moye, *Let the People Decide*, 206.

43. "Scene of an Early 'Victory': Schools Are Still Segregated," *New York Times*, May 18, 1979, 14 (Briggs and Fleming quotations); Patterson, *Brown v. Board of Education*, 206–7; Raymond Wolters, *The Burden of Brown: Thirty Years of School Desegregation* (Knoxville: University of Tennessee Press, 1984), 129–74.

44. "Blacks and Equality of Educational Opportunity," *The Crisis*, May 1977, 183; U.S. Commission on Civil Rights, *Statement on Metropolitan School Desegregation: A Report of the United States Commission on Civil Rights* (Washington, DC: U.S. Government Printing Office, 1977), 1–6, 112–18 (quotations on 7, 112).

45. Christine H. Rossell, "School Desegregation and White Flight," *Political Science Quarterly* 90, no. 4 (Winter 1975–76): 675–95. For a fine summary of the debate about the links between busing and white flight, see Patterson, *Brown v. Board of Education*, 174–77.

46. "24 Years of Integration," 45.

47. "Forced Busing and White Flight," *Time*, September 25, 1978, 61. For a much more recent study that links massive white flight to desegregation, see Kruse, *White Flight*.

48. Richard A. Pride and J. David Woodard, *The Burden of Busing: The Politics of Desegregation in Nashville, Tennessee* (Knoxville: University of Tennessee Press, 1985), 126–31, 137–43 (quotations on 131, 142).

49. "Subsidizing Segregation," *New Republic*, December 23, 30, 1978, 11–13.

50. "Subsidizing Segregation," *New Republic*, December 23, 30, 1978, 12, 13; Crespino, *In Search of Another Country*, 12–13, 237–40, 276.

51. "Your Skin Is Your Uniform in Tupelo's Latest Warfare," *Atlanta Journal*, September 28, 1978 (Robinson quotation); Samuel L. Banks, "Blacks and Equality of Educational Opportunity: Twenty-Three Years After Brown," *The Crisis*, May 1977, 182.

52. "The Other Side of the New South (II)," *New Republic*, April 1, 1978, 18–19 (Cooper quotation on 19).

53. NAACP 1980 Annual Report (Southeast Region), 6 (quotation), folder 25, box 17, and NAACP 1980 Annual Report, 6–8, folder 3, box 26, both Kelly Alexander Papers.

54. U.S. Commission on Civil Rights, *The Black/White Colleges*, 2, 9, 23, 24; "Revised Criteria Specifying the Ingredients of Acceptable Plans to Desegregate State Systems of Public Higher Education," April 14, 1978, folder 6, box 23401, Alabama Governors' Papers.

55. U.S. Commission on Civil Rights, *The Black/White Colleges*, 26–34.

56. "More Blacks in Colleges," *U.S. News and World Report*, July 18, 1977, 69 (Silard quotation); U.S. Commission on Civil Rights, *The Black/White Colleges*, 43, 45.

57. Lerone Bennett Jr., "Have We Overcome?" in Namorato, ed., *Have We*

Overcome? 190 (final two quotations), 191 (first quotation). For similar points, see also Harding, "So Much History," 31–35.

58. Thomas R. Hunt to J. Stanley Pottinger, October 11, 1974, "Civil Rights—Weekly Reports (1)" folder, box 3, Geoffrey Shepard Files, Ford Library; Lovett, *The Civil Rights Movement in Tennessee,* 364–77; U.S. Commission on Civil Rights, *The Black/White Colleges,* 17–18 (quotation on 18).

59. Hon. Joseph Addabbo et al. to Jimmy Carter, September 8, 1978, "Wilmington 10 (1)" folder, box 107, Louis Martin Files, and "Decision on the Ten," *Newsweek,* February 6, 1978, 40, clipping, "Wilmington 10" folder, box 35, Annie Gutierrez's Files, both Carter Library.

60. Rev. Ben Chavis to President Carter, May 28, 1977, "Wilmington 10 Petitions (3)" folder, box 43, Ed Smith Files, Carter Library.

61. Margaret Costanza to Jimmy Carter, February 10, 1978 (statistics), and Ms. Imani Kazana to Midge Costanza, January 31, 1978, "Wilmington 10 (North Carolina Civil Rights 1/78–2/78)" folder, box 35, Seymour Wishman Files, and Louis Martin to Governor Hunt, September 20, 1978, "Wilmington 10 (1)" folder, box 107, Louis Martin Files, all Carter Library.

62. "The Ideological Temptation," *National Review,* February 17, 1978, 199 (Amnesty International quotation); Lennox S. Hinds to Robert Malson, March 14, 1978, "Wilmington 10 (North Carolina Civil Rights, 1/78–2/78" folder, box 35, Seymour Wishman Files, and *Financial Times,* June 9, 1977, clipping, "Wilmington 10 (2)" folder, box 107, Louis Martin Files, both Carter Library.

63. Louis Martin to Anne Wexler, September 13, 1978 (quotation), and "History of the Wilmington N.C. Ten," January 1978, both "Wilmington 10 (1)" folder, box 107, Louis Martin Files, "Confidential Note," January 9, 1978, and Lennox S. Hinds to Robert Malson, March 14, 1978, both "Wilmington 10 (North Carolina Civil Rights 1/78–2/78)" folder, box 35, Seymour Wishman Files, all Carter Library.

64. Black Lawyers' Remarks, ca. 1979, 2–3, "Blacks and the Carter Administration (2)" folder, box 12, Louis Martin Files, Carter Library.

65. For more on the *closed society* label, see James W. Silver's classic *Mississippi: The Closed Society* (London: Gollancz, 1964); and Crespino, *In Search of Another Country,* 5–6.

66. "Progress and Poverty in Two Cities," *U.S. News and World Report,* May 14, 1979, 54. The essays from the University of Mississippi conference were published as Namorato, ed., *Have We Overcome?*

67. "Greensboro, 1980," *New Republic,* February 16, 1980, 10–11; "Greensboro Welcomes 4 Heroes Home," *Washington Post,* February 2, 1980, A6 (quotation); "Twenty Years Later, a Lunch Counter Revisited," *Washington Post,* February 1, 1980, A2.

68. "Blacks Returning to Southern Cities," *New York Times,* July 5, 1981, 1; "The Black Middle Class: Making It," *New York Times Magazine,* December 3, 1978, 34–36, 138, 140, 144, 146, 148, 150, 152, 154, 155–57.

69. "Montgomery Relaxes as Racism Recedes," *New York Times,* April 4, 1978, 16.

70. "Twenty Years Later, a Lunch Counter Revisited," *Washington Post,* February 1, 1980, A2.

71. Dumbrell, *The Carter Presidency,* 90 (Rustin quotation); White House

Press Release, April 6, 1978, and "Interview with the President," April 5, 1978, both "Black Media 9/76–4/78" folder, box 2, Martha Mitchell Files, Carter Library.

9. "No Substantial Progress"

1. Statement by Vernon E. Jordan Jr., January 17, 1969, 3 (quotation), "Blacks and the Carter Administration (1)" folder, box 12, Louis Martin Files, Carter Library; Dumbrell, *The Carter Presidency*, 100–102.

2. "Few Economic Gains Seen for Blacks in the South," *New York Times,* April 27, 1980, 22 (SRC report summary); "President, in Atlanta, Asks Congress to Vote Holiday for Dr. King," *New York Times,* January 15, 1979, 1 (Carter quotation); "I Feel So Helpless, So Hopeless," *Time,* June 16, 1980, 30 (Irons quotation).

3. "Winds of Change," *New York Times,* November 5, 1979, 1 (Bond quotation).

4. "Urban League Leader Calls 1979 a 'Year of Crisis' for U.S. Blacks," *New York Times,* January 18, 1979, 1; Statement by Vernon E. Jordan Jr., January 17, 1979, "Blacks and the Carter Administration (1)" folder, box 12, Louis Martin Files, Carter Library (quotations on 1, 4).

5. Jimmy Carter, "NAACP Speech," July 4, 1980, "Speeches (1)" folder, box 94, Louis Martin Files, Carter Library (quotation on 10–11); "Reagan Campaigns at Mississippi Fair," *New York Times,* August 4, 1980, A11.

6. "The Social and Economic Status of Negroes in North Carolina," November 2, 1977, folder 21, box 23, Kelly Alexander Papers.

7. "America's Rising Black Middle Class," *Time,* June 17, 1974, 35; "Black Youth: A Lost Generation," *Newsweek,* August 14, 1978, 27 (Callahan quotation).

8. Zieger, *For Jobs and Freedom,* 204–6 (King quotation on 206).

9. Bartley, *The New South,* 431–32; Goldfield, *Black, White, and Southern,* 209–10 (quotation on 209); Bruce J. Schulman, *From Cotton Belt to Sunbelt: Federal Policy, Economic Development, and the Transformation of the South, 1938–1980* (New York: Oxford University Press, 1991), 174–83.

10. Nick Kotz, "The Other Side of the New South (1)," *New Republic,* March 25, 1978, 16–19 (quotation on 16).

11. "Floyd B. McKissick," n.d., brochure, folder 1753, box 81, McKissick Papers. For more detail on Soul City and the problems that it encountered, see Christopher Strain, "Soul City, North Carolina: Black Power, Utopia, and the African American Dream," *Journal of African American History* 89, no. 1 (Winter 2004): 57–74.

12. "Basic Fact Sheet on Soul City, North Carolina," n.d., 2 (quotation), folder 1750, and "General Description of Soul City," n.d., 46, folder 1746a, both box 80, McKissick Papers.

13. Donald F. Johnson to Charles Allen, October 22, 1974, folder 2125, box 99, Industrial Marketing Report, n.d., folder 2131, box 100, and HUD Press Release, February 17, 1979, folder 1813, box 83, all McKissick Papers.

14. "Recommendations on Changing the Name of Soul City," January 24, 1978, 1, folder 528, box 28, McKissick Papers.

15. "Warren Industrial Park: Marketing Strategy Recommendations for

1979," December 19, 1978, 4–5, folder 1753, box 81, and "A Factual Presentation Relating to Site Selection," n.d., 14–15, folder 2130, box 99, both McKissick Papers; Schlesinger, "Black Caucus in the Unions," 143; "Remarks by Don Slaiman," January 13, 1971, 5, folder 13, box 1593, AFL-CIO Civil Rights Papers.

16. U.S. Commission on Civil Rights, *The Decline of Black Farming in America: A Report of the United States Commission on Civil Rights* (Washington, DC: U.S. Government Printing Office, 1982), iv (quotation), 2–5.

17. U.S. Commission on Civil Rights, *The Decline of Black Farming,* 89–92, 176 (quotation); North Carolina Advisory Committee to the U.S. Commission on Civil Rights, *Where Mules Outrate Men: Migrant and Seasonal Farmworkers in North Carolina* (Washington, DC: U.S. Government Printing Office, 1979), 1–17.

18. "Affirmative Inaction: Public Employment in the Rural Black Belt" (Special Report of the Southern Regional Council), February 1980 (quotations on cover page and 2), held at the Southern Regional Council's headquarters, Atlanta. A copy of this report is in the authors' possession.

19. "Paving the Way for Fair Treatment" (Dees quotation), www.splcenter.org/legal/landmark/employ.jsp (accessed September 1, 2006; copy in author's possession); Carter, *The Politics of Rage,* 109.

20. Dees with Fiffer, *A Season for Justice,* 14 (Dees quotation); "Black Alabama State Trooper Hiring Lags," *Poverty Law Report,* January 1974, 1 (final quotation).

21. "Black Alabama State Trooper Hiring Lags," *Poverty Law Report,* January 1974, 1; "Alabama Continues Trooper Discrimination," *Poverty Law Report,* November/December 1977, 1 (quotations).

22. "Troopers Skirt Trial, Settle Out of Court," *Poverty Law Report,* April/May 1979, 1, 4; "First Woman Is Employed as Alabama State Trooper," *Poverty Law Report,* July/August 1979, 3.

23. "Bias toward Blacks Persists in Trooper Unit," *Poverty Law Report,* February 1984, 4. For a fine summary of this case, see Jack Bass, *Taming the Storm: The Life and Times of Judge Frank M. Johnson, Jr. and the South's Fight over Civil Rights* (New York: Doubleday, 1993), 373–82.

24. "Consent Decree on EEOC Directed to Arkansas State Police Force," *Daily Labor Report,* February 13, 1978, A5; "Justice Files EEO Lawsuit against Government Units in Texas, Virginia," *Daily Labor Report,* December 26, 1978, A9.

25. "The AFL-CIO and Civil Rights: 1978," 6–7, folder 6, box 1592, AFL-CIO Civil Rights Papers.

26. U.S. Commission on Civil Rights, *Promises and Perceptions: Federal Efforts to Eliminate Employment Discrimination through Affirmative Action,* Report of Thirteen State Advisory Committees to the U.S. Commission on Civil Rights (Washington, DC: U.S. Government Printing Office, 1981), 1–3, 15, 25 (quotation).

27. U.S. Commission on Civil Rights, *The Federal Civil Rights Enforcement Effort, 1977: To Eliminate Employment Discrimination: A Sequel* (Washington, DC: U.S. Government Printing Office, 1977), v–xi, 329–35 (quotations on 330, 335).

28. "Congressional Black Caucus Legislative Agenda," n.d., "Congressional Black Caucus 7/77–9/78" folder, box 6, Martha Mitchell Files, Carter Library; "Rights Group Urges Marches in U.S. and State Capitols," *New York Times,* August 12, 1980, 14 (SCLC quotations).

29. E. T. Kehrer to Atlanta Area Unions, January 6, 1977, folder 173, box

1604, AFL-CIO Civil Rights Papers; "Dr. King's 48th Birthday Is Celebrated at Church Where He Was Co-Pastor," *New York Times,* January 16, 1977, 18.

30. Coretta Scott King to "Our Friends Everywhere," November 14, 1977 (quotation), folder 4, box 1592, and Mrs. Martin Luther King Jr. to E. T. Kehrer, March 31, 1977, folder 173, box 1604, both AFL-CIO Civil Rights Papers.

31. "Statement of Southeastern Region V NAACP on Employment," March 19, 1977, 3 (Hurley quotation), folder 11, box 18, and Region V Quarterly Report, April–August 1980, folder 1, box 18, both Kelly Alexander Papers.

32. Dumbrell, *The Carter Presidency,* 100–102 (quotations on 101, 102); Statement from the King Center on the Death of Mrs. Coretta Scott King, February 1, 2006, available at http://www.thekingcenter.org/MrsCSKing (accessed July 30, 2010).

33. "How to Woo Blacks," *New Republic,* February 4, 1978, 2 (poll); Black Lawyers' Remarks, ca. 1979, 3, "Blacks and the Carter Administration (2)" folder, box 12, Louis Martin Files, Carter Library.

34. "Government's Industry-Wide EEO Trucking Agreement Threatened by Recent Decisions," *Daily Labor Report,* January 9, 1978, C1–C5 (first quotation on C2); "Civil Rights Commission Says 1977 Was Bad Year for Job Status of Women and Minorities," *Daily Labor Report,* February 13, 1978, A3–A5 (second quotation on A3).

35. "UPIU Defendants Post-Trial Memorandum," June 9, 1980, *Myers et al. v. Gilman Paper Company,* 1, 30–31, NARA-Atlanta; Findings of Fact and Conclusions of Law, December 16, 1982, *Myers et al. v. Gilman Paper Company,* in ser. 3, folder 8, box 9, United Paperworkers International Union Local 446 Papers, Southern Labor Archives, Georgia State University, Atlanta.

36. "Plaintiffs' Proposed Findings of Fact and Conclusions of Law," March 30, 1981, 1–3, and EEOC Charge of James Watlington et al., August 3, 1966 (quotation), both *Russell et al. v. American Tobacco Company,* NARA-Atlanta.

37. "Plaintiffs' Proposed Findings of Fact and Conclusions of Law," March 30, 1981, 1–4, Memorandum Opinion, July 10, 1981, and Consent Decree, March 14, 1983, all *Russell et al. v. American Tobacco Company,* NARA-Atlanta.

38. "EEOC Decision," n.d., 3–4, *Love v. United States Steel,* pt. 23A, sec. 1, reel 9, NAACP Papers; Decision, February 22, 1972, 3–4, *US v. St. Louis–San Francisco Railway Company,* and "Plaintiffs' Pretrial Findings of Fact and Conclusions of Law," May 22, 1972, 5, *Norman v. Missouri Pacific Railroad Company,* both pt. 23A, sec. 1, reel 14, NAACP Papers; Timothy J. Minchin, *Don't Sleep with Stevens! The J. P. Stevens Campaign and the Struggle to Organize the South, 1963–80* (Gainesville: University Press of Florida, 2005), 179.

39. "The Supreme Court and DeFunis," *Christian Science Monitor,* April 25, 1974, clipping, "Affirmative Action" folder, box 103, Noel Sterrett Clipping File, Carter Library; "Bakke Wins, Quotas Lose," *Time,* July 10, 1978, 30–31, 40. For the broader importance of *Bakke,* see Howard Ball, *The Bakke Case: Race, Education, and Affirmative Action* (Lawrence: University Press of Kansas, 2000), 200–211.

40. Eleanor Holmes Norton to Jimmy Carter, September 9, 1977, "Bakke Case 5/77–7/78" folder, box 2, Martha Mitchell Files, and Annie Gutierrez to Stu Eizenstat, February 28, 1977, "Bakke Case—February" folder, box 149,

Stuart Eizenstat Subject Files, both Carter Library; "The Landmark *Bakke* Ruling," *Newsweek*, July 10, 1978, 28.

41. "What the Weber Ruling Does," *Time*, July 9, 1979, 48; MacLean, *Freedom Is Not Enough*, 251 (Carter quotation).

42. MacLean, *Freedom Is Not Enough*, 249–51 (Weber quotation on 250); Zieger, *For Jobs and Freedom*, 181–82.

43. MacLean, *Freedom Is Not Enough*, 254 (quotations); Steven V. Roberts, "The *Bakke* Case Moves to the Factory," *New York Times Magazine*, February 25, 1979, 37–38, 84–85, 100.

44. "What the Weber Ruling Does," *Time*, July 9, 1979, 48–49.

45. Complaint, May 25, 1979, and Affidavit of Norman Youngblood, June 29, 1979, both *Youngblood v. Rock Hill Printing and Finishing Company*, NARA-Atlanta; "Racism Rebounds in Part of South," *New York Times*, July 5, 1979, 1, 12.

46. "Klan Fights Leftists and Nazis at Its Exhibit," *New York Times*, February 27, 1979, 12 (first quotation); "Blacks and the Klan Clash Again in Selma, After Decade of Peace," *New York Times*, April 15, 1979, 16; "More Racial Unrest in Birmingham," *New York Times*, July 7, 1979, 6.

47. "The Great White Hope," *Newsweek*, November 14, 1977, 28 (Grosser quotations); "Klan Leader Debates Racial Bias with Ralph Abernathy at Campus," *New York Times*, October 5, 1979, 26.

48. "The KKK Tries to Rise Again," *Newsweek*, June 18, 1979, 42; "The KKK Goes Military," *Newsweek*, October 6, 1980, 35 (second quotation); "Violent Klan Group Gaining Members," *New York Times*, March 15, 1979, 18; "SPLC Defends Black in Klan Shooting," *Poverty Law Report*, September/October 1979, 3 (sheriff quotation); "Racism Rebounds in Part of South," *New York Times*, July 5, 1979, 1, 12 (final quotation). For more information on the Scottsboro case, see Dan T. Carter, *Scottsboro: A Tragedy of the American South* (Baton Rouge: Louisiana State University Press, 1969).

49. "Klansmen Begin a White-Rights March in Alabama," *New York Times*, August 10, 1979, 9; "Klan Reenacts King March," *Poverty Law Report*, September/October 1979, 3 (quotation).

50. "Klan Fights Leftists and Nazis at Its Exhibit," *New York Times*, February 27, 1979, 12; "Klanwatch," *Poverty Law Report*, November/December 1980, 4 (quotation); "A History of Seeking Justice," *SPLC Report*, Special Anniversary Issue, January 2006, 1.

51. "Reaction Mixed to TRC Report," *Greensboro (NC) News and Record*, May 27, 2006; Greensboro Truth and Reconciliation Commission Report, May 25, 2006, 1–3, available at http://www.news-record.com (copy in author's possession); Elizabeth Wheaton, *Codename Greenkil: The 1979 Greensboro Killings* (Athens: University of Georgia Press, 1987), 9 (Dawson quotation).

52. "Black White Perceptions: Race Relations in Greensboro," November 1980, iii, iv, 50, folder 513, box 15, Greensboro Civil Rights Fund Papers.

53. "Black White Perceptions: Race Relations in Greensboro," November 1980, 3–5, 7 (Melvin quotation), 8–10, 13 (Simkins quotation), 33–36, folder 513, box 15, Greensboro Civil Rights Fund Papers.

54. "A New Racial Poll," *Newsweek*, February 26, 1979, 39–40 (quotations); Fleischman, "Brown and Intergroup Relations," 251.

55. Stu Eizenstat to Jimmy Carter, May 16, 1979, "Brown v. Board O/A

9509" folder, and White House Press Release, May 17, 1979 (Califano quotation), and Jimmy Carter Statement, May 17, 1979, both *"Brown v. Board—Reception Lists O/A9509 (1)"* folder, all box 14, Louis Martin Files, Carter Library.

56. Jimmy Carter Statement, May 17, 1979, *"Brown v. Board—Reception Lists O/A9509 (1)"* folder, box 14, Louis Martin Files, Carter Library; Fleischman, "Brown and Intergroup Relations," 250; Estelle W. Taylor, "Revised Treatment of Black Americans in Publications After *Brown*," *The Crisis,* June/July 1979, 253 (quotations); Broadus N. Butler, "The Alienation Syndrome," *The Crisis,* June/July 1979, 263–72.

57. "Whither the Civil Rights Movement?" *New York Times,* April 9, 1979, 18; "Economic Issues in the Black Community," May 4, 1978, folder 7482, box 337, McKissick Papers.

58. Beth Abramowitz to Louie Martin et al., March 28, 1979, *"Brown v. Board* Reception O/A 9509 (1)" folder, box 14, Louis Martin Files, Carter Library; Fairclough, *To Redeem the Soul of America,* 397; Jonas, *Freedom's Sword,* 365–66.

59. Crosby, *A Little Taste of Freedom,* 111–13, 237–40; "Mississippi Whites Seek $3.5 Million from NAACP," *The Crisis,* January 1974, 29 (quotation).

60. "Increase in Membership Fees," *The Crisis,* December 1976, 13; Earl T. Shinoster to Kelly Alexander, May 13, 1981, folder 5, box 17, and NAACP 1980 Annual Report (Southeast Region), folder 25, box 17, both Kelly Alexander Papers.

61. NAACP 1980 Annual Report (Southeast Region), folder 25, box 17, Kelly Alexander Papers (quotation on 17; statistics). For an overview of the disturbances, see "Miami Riot Continues; 18 Killed," *Washington Post,* May 19, 1980, A1, A10.

62. "Miami's Racial Trouble Points to Gap in City's Leadership," *New York Times,* May 23, 1980, B4.

63. John O. Brown Interview in Hampton and Fayer with Flynn, *Voices of Freedom,* 654; Marvin Dunn, "Death Watch," in Carson et al., eds., *The Eyes on the Prize Civil Rights Reader,* 666–87 (quotation on 674).

64. U.S. Commission on Civil Rights, "Confronting Racial Isolation in Miami," in Carson et al., *The Eyes on the Prize Civil Rights Reader,* 683, 684 (quotation); Hampton and Fayer with Flynn, *Voices of Freedom,* 653.

65. "Miami's Concerned Black Organizations for Justice Issues a Manifesto of 'Collective Needs,'" in Holt and Brown, eds., *From Freedom to "Freedom Now,"* 323; "NAACP Head Asks Effort to Reduce Blacks' Anger," *New York Times,* May 30, 1980, 10; NAACP 1980 Annual Report (Southeast Region) (closing quotation on 22), folder 25, box 17, Kelly Alexander Papers.

66. NAACP 1980 Annual Report (Southeast Region), 16–17 (quotation), 22–25, folder 25, box 17, Kelly Alexander Papers; "Schools in Georgia Reopen, but Race Tension Persists," *New York Times,* April 11, 1980, 10; Robert Dallek, *Ronald Reagan: The Politics of Symbolism* (Cambridge, MA: Harvard University Press, 1984), 56–57, 64.

67. Dumbrell, *The Carter Presidency,* 98; Louis Martin to Jimmy Carter, November 7, 1980, "11/11/80" folder, box 212, Presidential Handwriting File, Carter Papers.

68. Louis Martin to Jimmy Carter, "3/14/79" folder, box 122, Presidential

Handwriting File, Carter Library; "Reagan Urges Blacks to Look Past Labels and to Vote for Him," *New York Times,* August 6, 1980, A1 (Reagan quotation); "Reagan Is Endorsed by 2 Black Leaders," *New York Times,* October 17, 1980, A1.

69. "Reagan Signs Bill to Limit Busing," *Atlanta Constitution,* September 15, 1970, 2A; "White House Repudiates Andrew Young Remarks," *New York Times,* October 16, 1980, B6 (Young quotation); "Race Issue in Campaign: A Chain Reaction," *New York Times,* September 27, 1980, 1, 8.

70. Bourne, *Jimmy Carter,* 463, 472; Bartley, *The New South,* 455; "Mrs. King Calls the Klan 'Comfortable' with Reagan," *New York Times,* September 30, 1980, 20 (King quotation).

10. THE REAGAN COUNTERREVOLUTION

1. Harry Dent to Ms. Esther Mahaffey, December 1, 1980, folder 572, box 27, Dent Papers.

2. *Washington Post,* January 23, March 4, 1981.

3. *Washington Post,* January 8, 17, 1981.

4. *Washington Post,* January 13, 14, 15, 1981.

5. *Washington Post,* January 16, 1981.

6. *Washington Post,* January 16, 1981.

7. Eric Rougeau, "Restraint in Buckeye Case," *Shreveport Journal,* January 25, 1981, clipping, CMS Series 1981, folder 27, box 3, Thurmond Papers.

8. *Washington Post,* January 16, 1981.

9. *Washington Post,* January 16, 17, 20, 1981; Mrs. Nauman Steele Scott to Strom Thurmond, February 5, 1981; Strom Thurmond to Mrs. Scott, March 3, 1981, CMS Series 1981, folder 27, box 3, Thurmond Papers.

10. Sam J. Ervin Jr. to Senator Jesse Helms, March 16, 1981, Sam J. Ervin Jr. to President Reagan, March 20, 1981, and Senator Jesse Helms to Sam J. Ervin Jr., March 30, 1981, all Subgroup B: Private Papers, box 70, File 355, Ervin Papers.

11. *Washington Post,* January 23, 26, 30, 1981.

12. *Washington Post,* February 6, 13, 28, March 4, 12, 1981.

13. *Washington Post,* May 9, June 8, 16, 1981.

14. Reginald Stuart, "Alabama Blacks Fear Losing the Voting Rights Act," *New York Times,* April 14, 1981.

15. "Address of the Honorable William French Smith, Attorney General of the United States, Before the American Law Institute," Friday, May 22, 1981, "Busing, 1982 Desegregation" folder, box 16, Subject Files, 1981–83, Elizabeth Dole Files, Reagan Library; *Washington Post,* March 5, May 22, 23, 1981.

16. *Washington Post,* June 21, 1981.

17. Michael S. Serrill, "Uncivil Times at 'Justless,'" *Time,* May 13, 1985; *Washington Post,* June 23, 25 (quotations), 1981. For a much more sympathetic view of Reynolds and his tenure in office, see Raymond Wolters, *Right Turn: William Bradford Reynolds, the Reagan Administration and Black Civil Rights* (New Brunswick, NJ: Transaction, 1996).

18. *Washington Post,* January 7, March 20, 24 (Curtis quotation), 1981; *Boston Globe,* January 15, 2007 (Reagan quotation); Edward P. Morgan, "The Good, the Bad, and the Forgotten: Media Culture and the Public Memory of the Civil

Rights Movement," in *The Civil Rights Movement in American Memory*, ed. Renee C. Romano and Leigh Raiford (Athens: University of Georgia Press, 2006), 143.

19. *Washington Post*, June 30, 1981; *New York Times*, June 30 (Wilson quotation), July 16 (Raines remarks, Gergen quotation), 1981.

20. *New York Times*, July 12, 1988 (other quotations), January 15, 1989 (Jackson quotation).

21. R. Jeffrey Smith, Amy Goldstein, and Jo Becker, "A Charter Member of the Reagan Vanguard," *Washington Post*, August 1, 2005 (all quotations); John G. Roberts to Fred F. Fielding, February 15, 1984, "Civil Rights (1)" folder, box 12658, John G. Roberts Files, Reagan Library.

22. Lyn Nofziger to Ed Meese, Brad Reynolds, Ed Schultz, and William French Smith, August 24, 1981, "Busing" folder, OA box 10555, Fred Fielding Files, and Red Cavaney to Richard Hauser, November 14, 1981, Elizabeth Dole Files, both Reagan Library.

23. Craig Fuller to Kenneth Cribb, July 23, 1981, "Civil Rights Policy" folder, OA box 9448, Edward Meese Files, Reagan Library; Gil Troy, *Morning in America: How Ronald Reagan Invented the 1980s* (Princeton, NJ: Princeton University Press, 2005), 97.

24. See D. L. Cuddy File, and Smith (*sic*) to Strom Thurmond, May 6, 1982, "Busing (1)–(3)" folder, box 11313, both Stephen Galebach Files, and John G. Roberts to Fred Fielding, February 15, 1984, "Civil Rights (1)" folder, box 12658, John G. Roberts Files, all Reagan Library.

25. Lee A. Daniel, "In Defense of Busing," *New York Times*, April 17, 1983 (all quotations); Tom Wicker, "Fighting the Last War," *New York Times*, June 7, 1985; "NAACP Deplores Passage of Senate Anti-Busing Amendments," *The Crisis*, February 1982, 24; "Then and Now in Charlotte (N.C.)," *The Crisis*, May 1984, 5.

26. Morton C. Blackwell to Elizabeth Dole, July 22, 1982, box 16, Elizabeth Dole Files, Reagan Library. Olsen would later become solicitor general and would earn the fierce enmity of most Democrats for his defense of George W. Bush's position in the disputed election of 2000. At the time, however, his position on busing was regarded by his colleagues as far too liberal.

27. Serrill, "Uncivil Times" (first two quotations); *Washington Post*, January 9, 1985 (other quotations), February 16, 1986.

28. U.S. Commission on Civil Rights, *New Evidence on School Desegregation*, Clearinghouse Publication 92 (Washington, DC: U.S. Commission on Civil Rights, 1987), passim; Patterson, *Brown v. Board of Education*, 189. On white flight, see Kruse, *White Flight*; and Lassiter, *The Silent Majority*.

29. Lee A. Daniel, "In Defense of Busing," *New York Times*, April 17, 1983 (Hooks quotations); *Washington Post*, June 30, 1985 (other quotations); Lena Williams, "Controversy Awakens as Districts End Busing," *New York Times*, March 25, 1986; Patterson, *Brown v. Board of Education*, 180, 188.

30. *Washington Post*, January 16, 1991 (Gregory quotation); Patterson, *Brown v. Board of Education*, 195–99; Peter Irons, *Jim Crow's Children: The Broken Promise of the Brown Decision* (New York: Penguin, 2002), 259–78.

31. Walter Goodman, "*Brown v. Board of Education*: Uneven Results 30 Years Later," *New York Times*, May 17, 1984 (Goodman and Cole quotations).

32. Marian Clayton, "Desegregating America's Public Schools," *The Crisis*, May 1984, 20–21 (Robinson quotation on 21).

33. *New York Times,* September 13, 1981, September 27, 1987 (Orfield quotations).

34. Sheryll Cashin, *The Failures of Integration: How Race and Class Are Undermining the American Dream* (New York: PublicAffairs, 2004), 207, 218; John Charles Boger and Gary Orfield, eds., *School Resegregation: Must the South Turn Back?* (Chapel Hill: University of North Carolina Press, 2005), 54, 168, 170.

35. Patterson, *Brown v. Board of Education,* 208; Boger and Orfield, eds., *School Resegregation,* passim. For an overview, see Gary Orfield, "The Southern Dilemma: Losing *Brown,* Fearing *Plessy,*" introduction to Boger and Orfield, eds., *School Resegregation,* 1–25. For residential segregation, see Erica Frankenberg, "The Impact of School Segregation on Residential Housing Patterns: Mobile, Alabama, and Charlotte, North Carolina," in ibid., 164–84. For the effect of court decisions in the 1990s, see Erwin Chemerinsky, "The Segregation and Resegregation of American Public Education: The Courts' Role," in ibid., 30–47.

36. Patterson, *Brown v. Board of Education,* 186; Orlando Patterson, *The Ordeal of Integration: Progress and Resentment in America's Racial Crisis* (New York: Basic, 1997), 188–92.

37. *Washington Post,* November 17, 1992 (quotation); *New York Times,* April 24, 2001. For Meredith, see Salmond, *"My Mind Set on Freedom,"* 41–45; and Bolton, *The Hardest Deal of All,* 94.

38. An excellent study of the desegregation of a major Southern university is Robert A. Pratt, *We Shall Not Be Moved: The Desegregation of the University of Georgia* (Athens: University of Georgia Press, 2002). See also Lovett, *The Civil Rights Movement in Tennessee,* 335–49, 355–70; and *New York Times,* January 8, July 21, August 30, 1981.

39. Adam Fairclough, *A Class of Their Own: Black Teachers in the Segregated South* (Cambridge, MA: Harvard University Press, 2007), 418–20; *New York Times,* June 21, July 11, August 26, 1981.

40. *New York Times,* August 23 (Thompson quotation), 26, 30 (Reynolds quotation), 1981.

41. *New York Times,* September 26 (Wiseman and Reynolds quotations), October 14 (black students' comments), 1984; Lovett, *The Civil Rights Movement in Tennessee,* 380–84.

42. *New York Times,* May 29, 1991; Lovett, *The Civil Rights Movement in Tennessee,* 395–400.

43. *New York Times,* February 11, 1988.

44. *New York Times,* June 4, 1989, November 7, 1994.

45. *New York Times,* February 11, 1991; *Washington Post,* November 17, 1992 (quotation).

46. *Washington Post,* November 17, 1992 (quotations); *New York Times,* May 9, 1994.

47. *New York Times,* June 27, 1992, May 9, 1994, April 9, 2000, April 24, 2001, May 1, 2006, May 29, 2007 (quotations).

48. Crespino, *In Search of Another Country,* 257–63; Troy, *Morning in America,* 95–98; John P. Diggins, *Ronald Reagan: Fate, Freedom, and the Making of History* (New York: Norton, 2007), 311; Wolters, *Right Turn,* 465–86 (Republican platform pledge on 475); Bob Jones to William L. Taylor, U.S. Commission on Civil Rights, April 3, 1965 (Jones quotation), file F1/B022384,

Alabama Governors' Papers; Memorandum for Files, "Implications of Bob Jones Decision" (other quotations), "Civil Rights: Bob Jones Decision" folder, box 9441, Michael Uhlman Files, Reagan Library.

49. Zieger, *For Jobs and Freedom*, 216–17 (black Mississippian's assertion on 216); *New York Times*, November 22, 1991 (other quotations); MacLean, *Freedom Is Not Enough*, 314–20. We are indebted to Zieger's and MacLean's fine studies, along with Terry H. Anderson's excellent *The Pursuit of Fairness: A History of Affirmative Action* (New York: Oxford University Press, 2004), for much of what follows.

50. *Washington Post*, March 27, 1981 (quotations); Zieger, *For Jobs and Freedom*, 210–12; McLean, *Freedom Is Not Enough*, 328, 340; Thomas E. Jackson, *From Civil Rights to Human Rights: Martin Luther King Jr. and the Struggle for Economic Justice* (Philadelphia: University of Pennsylvania Press, 2007), 360.

51. *New York Times*, June 1, 1983, January 18, 1984; Michael H. Sussman, "A Sorry Story . . . Reagan's Record of Civil Rights Retrenchment," *The Crisis*, April 1984, 28–37 (first two quotations); Anderson, *Pursuit of Fairness*, 176–77 (last quotation); MacLean, *Freedom Is Not Enough*, 312–13.

52. *Washington Post*, June 15, 1984; *Washington Post*, June 14, 1984; *New York Times*, June 14, 1984; Draft of Op-Ed Piece by [William] Reynolds, "Civil Rights (1)" folder, box 12658, John G. Roberts Files, Reagan Library. See also "Civil Rights—Affirmative Action" folder, box 11298, Stephen Galebach Files, Reagan Library; and Anderson, *Pursuit of Fairness*, 180–82.

53. MacLean, *Freedom Is Not Enough*, 300–301.

54. *New York Times*, May 3, June 24, 1985, June 30, 1986 (NAACP and Hooks quotations); Anderson, *Pursuit of Fairness*, 185–89 (Michel quotation on 188, Reynolds quotation on 189); MacLean, *Freedom Is Not Enough*, 304–13; Hugh Davis Graham, "Civil Rights Policy," in *The Reagan Presidency: Pragmatic Conservatism and Its Legacies*, ed. W. Elliot Brownlie and Hugh Davis Graham (Lawrence: University Press of Kansas, 2003), 283–92.

55. *New York Times*, July 3 (first quotation), September 13 (Reynolds quotations), 1986; Anderson, *Pursuit of Fairness*, 189–92 (Hooks quotation on 192).

56. *New York Times*, June 7, 1989 (Greenhouse quotation); Anderson, *Pursuit of Fairness*, 201–9, 240–43; MacLean, *Freedom Is Not Enough*, 338.

57. Goldfield, *Black, White, and Southern*, 219–21 (all quotations); *New York Times,* July 5, 1981, September 23, 1991.

58. Erik Eckholm, "In Turnabout, Infant Deaths Climb in the South," *New York Times*, April 22, 2007 (Langston and Brown quotations); Goldfield, *Black, White, and Southern*, 220–21; Minchin, *Hiring the Black Worker*, 270–71; Zieger, *For Jobs and Freedom*, 217–18.

59. Benjamin L. Hooks, "Extend the Voting Rights Act—the Need Is Still Great," *The Crisis*, July 1981, 266–67, 307, 310.

60. *Washington Post*, June 16 (first quotation), 19, 29, July 18–19, 26, 31 (second quotation), August 5 (last quotation), 7, 1981. In particular, see Dorothy Gilliam, "Now They're After the Voting Rights Act, the Big Daddy," *Washington Post*, June 8, 1981; and *New York Times*, July 2, 1981.

61. Diggins, *Ronald Reagan*, 311; *New York Times*, April 13 (first quotation), June 13, 29 (second quotation), July 4 (last two quotations), 1982; Voting Rights Timeline, ACLU Web site, http://www.aclu.org/voting-rights/voting-rights-act-timeline.

62. *New York Times,* December 13, 1981 (first quotation), September 4, 1982 (second quotation), April 27, 1990 (other quotations); *Washington Post,* July 23, 1983.

63. *Washington Post,* July 11, 1983 (first two quotations); *New York Times,* July 3, 1991 (last quotation); Wolters, *Right Turn,* 72–73; J. Morgan Kousser, *Colorblind Injustice: Minority Voting Rights and the Undoing of the Second Reconstruction* (Chapel Hill: University of North Carolina Press, 1999), passim (but see 243–76).

64. Goldfield, *Black, White, and Southern,* 233–44; *New York Times,* February 8, 1984, January 14, 1990, January 31, August 9, 1992.

65. John Ehrman, *The Eighties: America in the Age of Reagan* (New Haven, CT: Yale University Press, 2005), 144–47; Troy, *Morning in America,* 290–94; Diggins, *Ronald Reagan,* 316–17.

66. *New York Times,* March 7, 1988 (first five quotations); Steven A. Shull, *American Civil Rights Policy from Truman to Clinton: The Role of Presidential Leadership* (Armonk, NY: Sharpe, 1999), 93–96 (last quotation on 94).

67. John D. Boswell to Strom Thurmond, September 18, 1983, W. T. Wiggins Jr. to Strom Thurmond, September 20, 1983, and David Duke to Strom Thurmond, October 13, 1983, all Volume Mail Series, folder 217, box 11, Thurmond Papers; Dennis, *Red, White and Blue Letter Days,* 261–63; Bass and Thompson, *Strom,* 301; Diggins, *Ronald Reagan,* 311–12.

11. FROM BUSH TO BUSH

1. *New York Times,* January 17, 1989, June 9, 1991 (quotation). In an attempt to depict Bush's 1988 Democratic opponent, Massachusetts governor Michael Dukakis, as being soft on crime, the Republican campaign team had produced a series of television ads featuring Willie Horton, a convicted first-degree murderer who was black and who had killed a white man and repeatedly raped his fiancée while on furlough from prison. See James T. Patterson, *Restless Giant: The United States from Watergate to Bush v. Gore* (New York: Oxford University Press, 2005), 223.

2. Shull, *Civil Rights Policy,* 4–5; *New York Times,* June 9, 1991 (all quotations).

3. Shull, *Civil Rights Policy,* 131–34; *New York Times,* February 25, April 18 (quotation), July 1, August 2, 1989.

4. Arthur A. Fletcher to President George Bush, February 10, 1989 (Fletcher quotation), President George Bush to Arthur A. Fletcher, n.d. (Bush quotation), President George Bush to Chase Untermeyer, April 18, 1989, and Chase Untermeyer to President George Bush, March 2, 1990 ("measure of . . . commitment"), all Presidential Records of George Herbert Walker Bush, Record Group FG 093, Commission on Civil Rights, boxes 408–9, George Herbert Walker Bush Presidential Library and Museum; Shull, *Civil Rights Policy,* 133–34; *Washington Post,* July 14, 2005. Fletcher soon became a trenchant critic of the president's restrictive policies on affirmative action, somewhat to Bush's displeasure. See President George Bush to Arthur A. Fletcher, October 24, 1990.

5. Shull, *Civil Rights Policy,* 96–99; *New York Times,* October 23, 1990 (Brown quotation).

6. Shull, *Civil Rights Policy,* 98–100; *New York Times,* January 4, February

8 (first and second quotations), March 13, June 4, October 27 (third quotation), November 18, 22 (fourth quotation), 1991, July 13, 1992 (Hooks quotations).

7. Ronald Smothers, "South's New Blacks Find Comfort Laced with Strain," *New York Times,* September 23, 1991.

8. Ibid. (Watson quotation). For Selma, see Patterson, *Brown v. Board of Education,* 191–92.

9. Shull, *Civil Rights Policy,* 67–68; U.S. Commission on Civil Rights, *A Bridge to One America: The Civil Rights Performance of the Clinton Administration* (Washington, DC: U.S. Government Printing Office, 2001).

10. Orlando Patterson, "What to Do When Busing Becomes Irrelevant," *New York Times,* July 18, 1999; Patterson, *Brown v. Board of Education,* 200–203 (Lowry quotation on 201, Thomas quotation on 200–201).

11. *New York Times,* October 27, 1993 (first quotation), May 18 (first Clinton quotation), November 24, 1994, September 26, 1997 (second Clinton quotation).

12. Stephen Warnath, Memo to Staff, n.d., folder 1, box 4, Warnath Files.

13. Warnath Memorandum on Presidential Directive to Ensure Affirmative Action, May 1996 (last two quotations), folder 3, box 1, both Warnath Files, and Press Release by Richard Womack, Acting Executive Director, Leadership Conference on Civil Rights, October 20, 1995 (other quotations), folder 1, box 1.

14. Patterson, *Restless Giant,* 242 (Patterson quotation); *New York Times,* October 20, 1996 (other quotations), September 7, 1997, March 1, 1998; Shull, *Civil Rights Policy,* 259–60.

15. U.S. Commission on Civil Rights, *A Bridge to One America,* 53–55 (all quotations); Shull, *Civil Rights Policy,* 69; Kevin Sack, "Pride and Prejudice; The South's History Rises, Again and Again," *New York Times,* March 22, 1998.

16. *New York Times,* May 9 (first and second quotations), June 4, 5 (Mfume, Wellstone, and Specter quotations), 1993; Shull, *Civil Rights Policy,* 134–38 (third quotation).

17. *New York Times,* May 18, 1994; "Remarks of the President to the People of Birmingham, Alabama," October 24, 1996, and "Remarks of the President to the Congregation of St. Paul's AME Church, Tampa, Florida," November 3, 1996, both http://www.clinton6.nara.gov/1996 (copy in author's possession).

18. *New York Times,* May 18, 1994; Steven A. Holmes, "On Civil Rights, Clinton Steers a Bumpy Course between Right and Left," *New York Times,* October, 20, 1996; Gary Gerstle, *American Crucible: Race and Nation in the Twentieth Century* (Princeton, NJ: Princeton University Press, 2001), 367; Darlene Clark Hine, "African Americans and the Clinton Presidency: Reckoning with Race, 1992–2000," in *The Clinton Riddle: Perspectives on the Forty-second President,* ed. Todd G. Shields, Jeannie M. Whayne, and Donald R. Kelley (Fayetteville: University of Arkansas Press, 2004), 80.

19. See U.S. Commission on Civil Rights, *A Bridge to One America,* 76; U.S. Commission on Civil Rights, *Burning of African-American Churches in Mississippi and Perceptions of Race Relations,* Community Forum Executive Summary (Washington, DC: U.S. Commission on Civil Rights, 2004), 1–4, 11.

20. U.S. Commission on Civil Rights, *Burning of African-American Churches,* 5–15.

21. Ibid., 11, 14–18.

22. U.S. Commission on Civil Rights, *A Bridge to One America,* 63–65;

New York Times, September 18, 1998 (all quotations). The full report, "One America in the 21st Century: Forging a New Future," can be downloaded from the Clinton Library Web site.

23. Richard S. Inge to President's Initiative on Race, October 12, 1997, folder 2, Rev. Michael Jordan to President's Initiative on Race, March 30, 1998, folder 6, and Kendra Kirby, Chair, Human Relations Commission, Durham, NC, to John Hope Franklin, July 21, 1997 (third and fourth quotations), folder 8, all box 30, CFAC, PABR Files; *New York Times,* April 30, 1998 (last three quotations); *Washington Post,* April 30, 1998.

24. Susan M. Gilson to John Hope Franklin, November 6, 1997, A. J. Mull, "Race Initiative to Propose Solutions," *Daily Mississippian,* March 6, 1998, clipping, and William Winter, Statement to Forum and to *Jackson (MS) Clarion-Ledger,* n.d., all "Mississippi Town Hall Info." file, folder 10, box 112, Correspondence Files—Miscellaneous, PABR Files.

25. "Accomplishments of the Civil Rights Division in the Clinton Administration," internal memorandum, May 1996, folder 1, box 4, Warnath Files.

26. U.S. Commission on Civil Rights, *A Bridge to One America,* viii, 173.

27. U.S. Commission on Civil Rights, *Redefining Rights in America: The Civil Rights Record of the George W. Bush Administration, 2001–2004,* Draft Report for the Commissioners' Review (Washington, DC: U.S. Commission on Civil Rights, 2004), Executive Summary; Darryl Fears, "Civil Rights Commission Prepares for a New Era," *Washington Post,* December 9, 2004.

28. Linda Greenhouse, "In Steps Big and Small, Supreme Court Has Moved Right," *New York Times,* July 1, 2007; *New York Times,* June 5, 2006, June 28, 29 (Roberts, Stevens, and *Times* editorial quotations), September 17, 2007; *Washington Post,* June 5, September 4, 2006, June 28, 29 (*Post* quotation), 2007; *Durham (NC) Herald-Sun,* June 5, 2006; U.S. Commission on Civil Rights, *Redefining Rights in America,* 45–50.

29. U.S. Commission on Civil Rights, *Redefining Rights in America,* 36–39; *Washington Post,* July 21, 28 (quotation), 2006. In January 2009, the Supreme Court agreed to decide whether Congress had "overstepped its constitutional authority" by extending the preclearance requirement in 2006. *New York Times,* January 10, 2009.

30. *Washington Post,* November 13 (second quotation), 17 (first quotation), December 2, 10, 2005; *Boston Globe,* July 3, 2006; *New York Times,* June 14, 2007 (last quotation). The Georgia law was later struck down by a federal court as discriminatory, and the beleaguered Tanner was eventually transferred to another job. See *Washington Post,* December 15, 2007.

31. U.S. Commission on Civil Rights, *Redefining Rights in America,* 58–60 (first two quotations on 60); Linda Greenhouse, "Affirmative Action Reaffirmed," *New York Times News Service,* reprinted in *Salt Lake City Deseret News,* June 24, 2003; Orlando Patterson, "Affirmative Action: The Sequel," *New York Times,* June 22, 2003; "The Last Race Problem," *New York Times,* December 30, 2006; *Washington Post,* August 1, 2005.

32. *New York Times,* November 13, 2006.

12. THE AFTERMATH

1. *Greensboro (NC) News and Record,* March 31, April 1 (quotation), 2006. For a fuller account of Bradley's year at Grimsley, see William H. Chafe,

Civilities and Civil Rights: Greensboro, North Carolina, and the Black Struggle for Freedom (New York: Oxford University Press, 1980), 72–74.

2. *Greensboro (NC) News and Record,* March 29, 30, 31 (quotations), 2006.

3. *Charlotte (NC) Observer,* September 2, 2007.

4. *New York Times,* October 4, 2006.

5. *Hattiesburg (MS) American,* January 28, 2006. A very good example of a participant memoir is Lewis with D'Orso, *Walking with the Wind.* See also Constance Curry et al., *Deep in Our Hearts: Nine White Women in the Freedom Movement* (Athens: University of Georgia Press, 2000).

6. *Hattiesburg (MS) American,* August 15 (first two quotations), September 10 (third quotation), 2006; *Montgomery (AL) Advertiser,* September 3, 2006 (other quotations).

7. *New York Times,* October 25, 2005; *Washington Post,* November 19, 2005 (Jackson quotation); *Guardian Weekly,* November 4–10, 2005 (other quotations).

8. *Washington Post,* February 4 (first two quotations), 5 (last quotation), 2006.

9. *Washington Post,* February 7, 8, 2006; *New York Times,* February 7, 8 (quotations), 2006.

10. *Montgomery (AL) Advertiser,* August 22 (quotation), 23, 2006.

11. *Montgomery (AL) Advertiser,* August 27, 2006.

12. For detailed discussion of the complex and controversial politics behind the building of these museums, see Glenn Eskew, "The Birmingham Civil Rights Institute and the New Ideology of Tolerance," in Romano and Raiford, eds., *The Civil Rights Movement,* 28–66; and Derek H. Alderman, "Street Names as Memorial Arenas," in ibid., 70–75. For a comparative overview, see Kevin Sack, "Museums of a Movement," *New York Times,* June 28, 1998; Owen J. Dwyer and Derek H. Alderman, *Civil Rights Memorials and the Geography of Memory* (Chicago: Center for American Places at Columbia College, 2008); and Scott Vogel, "Trailing History," *Washington Post,* February 22, 2009.

13. Eskew, "Birmingham Civil Rights Institute," 29; Owen J. Dwyer, "Interpreting the Civil Rights Movement: Contradiction, Confirmation and the Cultural Landscape," in Romano and Raiford, eds., *The Civil Rights Movement,* 7–8, 19, 29; Dwyer and Alderman, *Civil Rights Memorials,* 33–35; Elizabeth Jacoway, *Turn Away Thy Son: Little Rock, the Crisis That Shocked the Nation* (New York: Free Press, 2007), 356; *Montgomery (AL) Advertiser,* August 27, 2006; *Greensboro (NC) News and Record,* October 1, 2006; *New York Times,* February 1, 2010; Charles E. Cobb Jr., *On the Road to Freedom: A Guided Tour of the Civil Rights Trail* (Chapel Hill, NC: Algonquin, 2008), passim.

14. *Montgomery (AL) Advertiser,* January 27 (all quotations), March 3–5, 2007; *New York Times, Washington Post,* March 4–5, 2007.

15. *Durham (NC) Herald-Sun,* December 12, 2006; Alderman, "Street Names," 67–95. A good account of another controversial but ultimately successful bid to name a street in the small Georgia town of Eatonton after King is Derek H. Alderman, "Street Names and the Scaling of Memory: The Politics of Commemorating Martin Luther King within the African American Community," in Kirk, ed., *Martin Luther King, Jr.,* 232–44. For Martin Luther King Day, see *Nashville Tennessean,* January 15, 2007; *New York Times,* January 15,

2007; *Montgomery (AL) Advertiser,* January 14, 2007; *Durham (NC) Herald-Sun,* January 13, 2007; and Dennis, *Red, White, and Blue Letter Days,* 266.

16. *Montgomery (AL) Advertiser,* January 14, 2007 ("picking up everything"); *Nashville Tennessean,* January 15, 2007 (Lawson quotation); *Durham (NC) Herald-Sun,* January 13, 2007 (other quotations).

17. Ann Hornaday, "Waiting for Action! Instead of Making Films about the Civil Rights Era, Hollywood Has Made Excuses," *Washington Post,* July 10, 2007.

18. *Selma, Lord, Selma* (Disney, 2004); *The Rosa Parks Story* (Xenon Pictures, 2002); *Once upon a Time When We Were Colored* (Republic Pictures, 1995).

19. *Mississippi Burning* (MGM, 1988); *Ghosts of Mississippi* (Castle Rock, 1996); Hornaday, "Waiting for Action!" Jennifer Fuller, "Debating the Present through the Past: Representations of the Civil Rights Movement in the 1990s," in Romano and Raiford, eds., *The Civil Rights Movement,* 185–86.

20. *The Long Walk Home* (Miramax Films, 1990); *Freedom Song* (TNT Originals, 2000); Fuller, "Debating the Present," 179, 187–89.

21. *Eyes on the Prize* (Blackside Production Co., 1987); *Montgomery (AL) Advertiser,* October 2, 2006; Bob Herbert, "A Story of Struggle and Hope," *New York Times,* November 16, 2006.

22. Jonathan Steele, "The Price of Freedom," *Guardian Weekly,* July 16–22, 1964; *New York Times,* June 20, 2005; Dittmer, *Local People,* 247–51, 418. For a concise account of Killen's trial, see Howard Ball, *Justice in Mississippi: The Murder Trial of Edgar Ray Killen* (Lawrence: University Press of Kansas, 2006).

23. *New York Times,* June 20, 21 (quotations), 22, 23, 2005; *Washington Post,* June 20–23, 2005. In August, Killen was released briefly on bail pending the hearing on his appeal, partly on the grounds of his precarious health, but was returned to prison the next month following reports that he had been observed walking about town unaided and filling his car at the local gas station. Ball, *Justice in Mississippi,* 192–93.

24. *New York Times,* June 21, 2005. For Young's election, see Robbie Brown, "Mississippi City Known for Klan Killings Elects Its First Black Mayor," *New York Times,* May 22, 2009; and Chris McGreal, "Mississippi Burning Town Elects Black Mayor," *The Age* (Melbourne), May 24, 2009.

25. For the Till probe and its aftermath, see *Jackson (MS) Clarion-Ledger,* March 17, 2006; *Hattiesburg (MS) American,* February 27, March 1, 2007; *Washington Post,* February, 28, 2007; and *Montgomery (AL) Advertiser,* July 26, 29 (quotation), 2007.

26. *Jackson (MS) Clarion-Ledger,* May 27 (first quotation), June 14, 15 (second quotation), July 21, 2007; *Hattiesburg (MS) American,* June 17, 2007 (third quotation).

27. Renee C. Romano, "Narratives of Redemption: The Birmingham Bombing Trials and the Construction of Civil Rights Memory," in Romano and Raiford, eds., *The Civil Rights Movement,* 96–133 (quotations on 96, 120, 124).

28. *Montgomery (AL) Advertiser,* August 26 (first quotation), 29, 2006, May 9, 11, June 28, 2007; *Jackson (MS) Clarion-Ledger,* May 10, 2007; *New York Times,* May 10, 2007 (second quotation).

29. Renee C. Romano, remarks at Plenary Session 1 of "The Little Rock

Desegregation Crisis: Fifty Years Later, an International Conference," Little Rock, AR, September 6–8, 2007; Ball, *Justice in Mississippi,* 24–26 (Glisson quotations on 25).

30. *Raleigh (NC) News and Observer,* March 21, 2006; Julian Borger, "Civil Rights Heroes May Get Pardons," *Guardian,* April 4, 2006 (all quotations).

31. Dittmer, *Local People,* 79–83.

32. Ibid.; *Hattiesburg (MS) American,* March 30, May 18, 2006. For a full account of the Kennard case, see Timothy J. Minchin and John A. Salmond, "'The Saddest Story of the Whole Movement': The Clyde Kennard Case and the Search for Racial Reconciliation in Mississippi, 1955–2007," *Journal of Mississippi History* 71, no. 3 (Fall 2009): 191–234.

33. *Hattiesburg (MS) American,* March 30, 2006.

34. *Hattiesburg (MS) American,* March 30, 2006.

35. *Hattiesburg (MS) American,* March 31, 2006.

36. *Hattiesburg (MS) American,* April 7, 14, 2006.

37. U.S. Commission on Civil Rights, *Redefining Rights in America,* 18–19 (Congressional Black Caucus quotation); *Hattiesburg (MS) American,* May 17, 18 (other quotations), 2006.

38. *Hattiesburg (MS) American,* May 18, 20, 2006.

39. *Hattiesburg (MS) American,* May 22 (first quotation), 23 (second quotation and Barrett petition and quotations), 2006; Sack, "Pride and Prejudice"; Ball, *Justice in Mississippi,* 192–93 (trial judge quotation on 192).

13. Poverty and Progress

1. *New York Times,* June 12, 2005; *Montgomery (AL) Advertiser,* May 17, 2006 (Blanton quotation); Romano, "Narratives of Redemption," 124.

2. *Greensboro (NC) News and Record,* May 25, 28, 31, June 1–2, 2006; Ball, *Justice in Mississippi,* 25.

3. *Durham (NC) Herald-Sun,* June 1, 2006; *Charlotte (NC) Observer,* June 8, 2006; *Washington Post,* June 13 (last quotation), 23 (first two quotations), 2006; *New York Times,* June 14, 2006.

4. *Montgomery (AL) Advertiser,* April 12, 16, 25 (other chat column quotations), 26 (Tolar quotation), May 26, 2007; *Greensboro (NC) News and Record,* April 12, 2007 (North Carolina resolution); Jonathan Capehart, "Contrition for America's Curse," *Washington Post,* April 12, 2007.

5. *Washington Post,* June 26, 2005.

6. Adam Nossiter, "Unearthing a Town Pool, and Not for Whites Only," *New York Times,* September 18, 2006.

7. Ibid.

8. *Washington Post,* May 1, 2006 (Allen quotations); *Montgomery (AL) Advertiser,* August 21, September 9 (last two quotations), 2006. Allen lost his bid for reelection. Nunn now is a well-known gospel singer and recording artist.

9. *Hattiesburg (MS) American,* March 17, 18, 22, April 2, 5 (Delgado quotation), 9, 2006.

10. Crosby, *A Little Taste of Freedom,* 269–82 (quotations on 269, 274, 282).

11. Kevin Sack, "Old South's Symbols Stir a Campus," *New York Times,* March 11, 1997.

12. Ronald Smothers, "Governor Finds Down Follows Up in Alabama,"

New York Times, August 25, 1993; Rick Bragg, "Time to Lower the Rebel Flag, a Southern Governor Says," *New York Times,* November 27, 1996 (first quotation); David Firestone, "Bastion of the Confederacy Finds Its Future May Hinge on Rejecting the Past," *New York Times,* December 5, 1999 (Knotts, Grant, and Bethea quotation); Steve Popper, "Knicks Won't Train in South Carolina," *New York Times,* February 23, 2000.

13. *New York Times,* May 11, June 2, 2000.

14. *Hattiesburg (MS) American,* March 8, 9 (McGee quotation), 10 (Harper quotation), 17, 21 (last quotation), 2006.

15. *Greensboro (NC) News and Record,* January 20, February 22–23, March 12 (quotations), 2006.

16. Adam Nossiter, "Fifty Years Later, Little Rock Can't Escape Race," *New York Times,* May 8, 2007.

17. *Washington Post,* September 25, 26 (quotations), 2007; *Jackson (MS) Clarion-Ledger,* September 23, 2007.

18. Dan Barry, "Legacy of School Segregation Endures, Separate but Legal," *New York Times,* September 30, 2007. For the civil rights struggle in Wilcox County, see Fleming, *In the Shadow of Selma.*

19. *Hattiesburg (MS) American,* February 1, 2007 (blog quotations); *Montgomery (AL) Advertiser,* September 17, 2007 (Williams quotation).

20. Gary Younge, "Black and White of American Justice," *Guardian Weekly,* September 21, 28, 2007; *New York Times,* September 18, 2007.

21. *New York Times,* September 20, 21 (quotations), 2007; *Washington Post,* September 21, 2007.

22. Orlando Patterson, "Jena, O.J. and the Jailing of Black America," *New York Times,* September 30, 2007.

23. Younge, "Black and White of American Justice" (first and second quotations in September 21 installment, third quotation in September 28 installment); *New York Times,* September 19, 27–28, 2007; *Washington Post,* October 6, 2007; Casa Compton Interview in Richard G. Jones, "In Louisiana, a Tree, a Fight and a Question of Justice," *New York Times,* September 19, 2007.

24. *Washington Post,* October 12, 16 (first quotation), 20 (second quotation), 2007.

25. *Washington Post,* November 17 (first quotation), December 2, 4, 2007, June 27, 2009; *New York Times,* December 4, 2007 (other quotations).

26. *Greensboro (NC) News and Record,* January 10–14, 2006 (both quotations from January 12 edition).

27. *Greensboro (NC) News and Record,* February 26, 27 (Gatten quotation), March 1, 3, 17, 22, April 19, August 22, September 17, 19, 22, 23 (Keller quotation), 2007.

28. *Hattiesburg (MS) American,* May 3 (first quotation), 6, June 1 (second quotation), 2006.

29. *Hattiesburg (MS) American,* October 16, 17 (other quotations), 18 (Magee, unidentified blogger, and "Hummer" quotations), 2007.

30. *Montgomery (AL) Advertiser,* July 14, August 2 (quotations), 2007.

31. *Durham (NC) Herald-Sun,* April 9 (other quotations), 16 (first quotation), 2006; *New York Times,* March 20, April 5, 2006.

32. *Washington Post,* April 18, 2006; *New York Times,* April 18, 2006; *Durham (NC) Herald-Sun,* April 13, 2006, September 29, 2007 (quotation).

33. *Durham (NC) Herald-Sun,* May 1, June 16–18, August 6, September 29 (Brodhead quotations), 2007; Peter Applebome, "After Duke Prosecution Began to Collapse, Demonizing Continued," *New York Times,* April 15, 2007 (Dowd quotations); *Washington Post,* April 11, 2007 (first quotation and Seligmann quotation).

34. *Jackson (MS) Clarion-Ledger,* July 23, 2007; *Washington Post,* July 16 (Edwards quotation), 17, 2007; Dean Talbot, *Brothers: The Hidden History of the Kennedy Years* (New York: Free Press, 2007), frontispiece (Kennedy quotation).

35. Gilbert M. Gaul and Dan Morgan, "A Slow Demise in the Delta; U.S. Farm Subsidies Favor Big over Small, White over Black," *Washington Post,* June 20, 2007.

36. Charlie Le Duff, "At a Slaughterhouse, Some Things Never Die," in *How Race Is Lived in America: Pulling Together, Pulling Apart,* with an introduction by Joseph Lelyveld (New York: Holt, 2001), 97–115. This, like the other articles in *How Race Is Lived in America,* was originally published as a fifteen-week series in the *New York Times.*

37. Eckholm, "In Turnabout, Infant Deaths Climb."

38. *Montgomery (AL) Advertiser,* August 21, 2006; Erik Eckholm, "Plight Deepens for Black Men, Studies Warn," *New York Times,* March 20, 2006; Peter Whoriskey, "Katrina Hits Blacks Harder Than Whites," *Washington Post,* May 10, 2007; Juan Williams, *Enough* (New York: Three Rivers, 2006), 170–78 (Williams quotation on 170, Obama quotation on 178). See also Douglas S. Massey and Nancy A. Denton, *American Apartheid, Segregation and the Making of the Underclass* (Cambridge, MA: Harvard University Press, 1993), 71–72, 86–87, 222–23; Andrew Hacker, *Two Nations: Black and White, Separate, Hostile, Unequal* (New York: Scribner, 1992), passim; Godfrey Hodgson, *More Equal Than Others: America from Nixon to the New Century* (Princeton, NJ: Princeton University Press, 2004), 172–202; Norrell, *The House I Live In,* 312–20.

39. Williams, *Enough,* 6, 40–41, 172–74; Gwen Ifill, *The Breakthrough: Politics and Race in the Age of Obama* (New York: Doubleday, 2009), 58–59, 89–109, 216–18 (Sellers quotation on 216).

40. Ifill, *Breakthrough,* 94–95, 106–9, 111–14.

41. Hacker, *Two Nations,* 113–15, 125–33; Eugene Robinson, "Which Black America?" *Washington Post,* October 9, 2007; Williams, *Enough,* 41 (King quotation), 170 ("race and poverty . . .").

42. Dan Carter, "Is There Still a South and Does It Matter," *Dissent,* Summer 2007, 92–96. Carter points out that, of households with an annual income of between $30,000 and $100,000, 74 percent in the South vote Republican. The figure for the rest of the nation is 52 percent. Of low-income whites, i.e., those earning less than $30,000 annually, the only major group John Kerry won in 2004, in the South 57 percent nevertheless stayed with the GOP. Byron E. Schafer and Richard Johnston, *The End of Southern Exceptionalism: Class, Race, and Partisan Change in the Postwar South* (Cambridge, MA: Harvard University Press, 2006); *Greensboro (NC) News and Record,* May 31, 2006.

43. Juan Williams, "A Little Rock Reminder," *Washington Post,* September 25, 2007 (Green and Trickey quotations); Dionne Walker, "More Black Women Consider Dating Out," *Durham (NC) Herald-Sun,* August 5, 2007 (Jones quotations); Jacoway, *Turn Away Thy Son,* 354.

44. *How Race Is Lived in America,* 1–21, 292–93.

45. Ibid., 16–18; *Hattiesburg (MS) American,* July 1, 2007.

46. Leonard Doyle, "America Has Obama yet Deep South Prom Teens Still Have but a Dream," *The Age* (Melbourne), June 22, 2009.

47. *Hattiesburg (MS) American,* September 25, 2006 (Weary quotation); Michael Dobbs, "Southern Town Still Divided by Race," *Guardian Weekly,* May 20–26, 2004 (other quotations).

Postscript

1. Kevin Sack, "A Time to Reap for Foot Soldiers of Civil Rights," *New York Times,* November 4, 2008.

2. "Black Churchgoers Celebrate, Give Thanks for Obama's Win," CNN. com, November 9, 2008, www.cnn.com/2008/POLITICS/11/9/obama.churches/ap/index.html (copy in author's possession).

3. Robert G. Kaiser, "A Moment for the Ages, Many Years in the Making; Forces Great and Small Led to Historic Election," *Washington Post,* November 10, 2008.

4. Sack, "A Time to Reap."

5. Adam Nossiter, "For South, a Waning Hold on National Politics," *New York Times,* November 11, 2008.

6. Ibid. See also "Election Spurs 'Hundreds' of Race Threats, Crimes," *New York Times,* November 15, 2008; Howard Witt, "White Extremists Lash Out over Election of First Black President," *Los Angeles Times,* November 23, 2008; and Ifill, *Breakthrough,* 244. Such incidents were by no means confined to the South. Throughout the nation, there were cross burnings, assassination threats, and other racist manifestations in the days following Obama's victory.

7. James C. McKinley Jr., "Killing Stirs Racial Unease in Texas," *New York Times,* February 15, 2009.

8. William Raspberry, "Beyond Civil Rights," *Washington Post,* November 11, 2008.

9. Wayne Dash, "Grandson of Slaves: Obama Is Our Moses," CNN.com, January 13, 2009, www.cnn.com/2009/US/01/12/grandson.of.slaves/index/html (copy in author's possession).

BIBLIOGRAPHY

MANUSCRIPTS

Alabama Department of Archives and History, Montgomery, AL
Alabama Governors' Papers.

Baillieu Library, University of Melbourne, Melbourne
Civil Rights during the Nixon Administration Papers (microfilmed from the Nixon Presidential Materials collection at the National Archives, College Park).
FBI Files on the Reverend Jesse Jackson (microfilm).

Birmingham Public Library, Birmingham, AL
United States of America et al. v. Allegheny-Ludlam Industries (United States District Court for the Northern District of Alabama, 1974).

Borchardt Library, La Trobe University, Melbourne
Civil Rights and Social Activism in the South Papers (microfilmed from the holdings of the University of South Alabama Archives, Mobile, Alabama).
Civil Rights during the Johnson Administration Papers (microfilmed from the Lyndon Baines Johnson Library, Austin, Texas).
NAACP Papers, Part 20: White Resistance and Reprisals, 1956–1965 (microfilmed from the Manuscript Division of the Library of Congress, Washington, DC).
NAACP Papers, Supplement to Part 23, Series A: Legal Department Case Files, 1960–1972 (microfilmed from the Manuscript Division of the Library of Congress, Washington, DC).
Southern Christian Leadership Conference Papers, 1954–70 (microfilmed from the Martin Luther King Jr. Library and Archive, Martin Luther King, Jr. Center for Nonviolent Social Change, Atlanta, GA).

George Herbert Walker Bush Presidential Library, College Station, TX
Records of the United States Commission on Civil Rights.

Jimmy Carter Library, Atlanta
Sam Bleicher Files.

Stuart Eizenstat Files.
Annie Gutierrez Files.
Louis Martin Files (Special Assistant for Black Affairs).
Margaret McKenna Files.
Martha "Bunny" Mitchell Files.
Presidential Handwriting File.
Ed Smith Files.
Noel Sterrett Clipping File.
Seymour Wishman Files.

William Jefferson Clinton Presidential Library, Little Rock, AR
President's Advisory Board on Race Files.
Stephen Warnath Files.

Gerald R. Ford Presidential Library, Ann Arbor, MI
James M. Cannon Files.
Thomas G. Cody Files.
David Gergen Files.
Judith R. Hope Files.
Bobbie Kilburg Files.
Patricia Lindh and Jeanne Holm Files.
David H. Lissy Files.
Robert Orben Files.
Richard D. Parsons Files.
President Ford Committee Records.
Presidential Handwriting File.
Arthur F. Quern Files.
A. James Reichley Interview Transcripts.
Stanley Scott Files.
Geoffrey Shepard Files.
Vice Presidential Papers.
White House Central Files—HU (Human Rights) and Name File.

Lyndon Baines Johnson Presidential Library, Austin, TX
Administrative Histories.
Joseph Califano Files.
Douglass Cater Files.
Harry McPherson Files.
Bill Moyers Files.
Frederick Panzer Files.
Barefoot Sanders Files.
Mildred Stegall Files.
Lee C. White Files.
White House Central Files (HU2).
Henry Wilson Files.

National Archives and Records Administration, Atlanta

Dorothy P. Robinson et al. v. P. Lorillard Company (United States District Court for the Middle District of North Carolina, 1966).

Edgar Russell et al. v. American Tobacco Company (United States District Court for the Middle District of North Carolina, 1968).

Edward Gilley et al. v. Hudson Pulp and Paper Company (United States District Court for the Middle District of Florida, 1976).

Elmo V. Myers et al. v. Gilman Paper Company (United States District Court for the Southern District of Georgia, 1972).

Fred Roberts et al. v. St. Regis Paper Company (United States District Court for the Middle District of Florida, 1970).

Joseph P. Moody et al. v. Albemarle Paper Company (United States District Court for the Eastern District of North Carolina, 1966).

Norman Youngblood v. Rock Hill Printing and Finishing Company (United States District Court, District of South Carolina, 1979).

National Archives and Records Administration, College Park, MD
Confidential Files.
John W. Dean Files.
Harry S. Dent Jr. Files.
John D. Ehrlichman Files.
Leonard Garment Files.
Richard M. Nixon Presidential Materials.
Bradley H. Patterson Jr. Files.
President's Personal File, 1969–74.
White House Central Files.
White House Special Files (FG90).

National Archives and Records Administration, Philadelphia
Julious Adams et al. v. Dan River Mills (United States District Court, Western District of Virginia, 1969).

Ronald Reagan Presidential Library, Simi Valley, CA
Elizabeth Dole Files.
Fred Fielding Files.
Stephen Galebach Files.
John G. Roberts Files.
Michael Uhlman Files.

Richard B. Russell Library for Political Research and Studies, Athens, GA
Howard H. Callaway Papers.
Richard B. Russell Papers.
Herman E. Talmadge Papers.

Southern Historical Collection, Wilson Library, University of North Carolina at Chapel Hill
Samuel Ervin Papers.
Greensboro Civil Rights Fund Papers.
Charles Raper Jonas Papers.
Floyd B. McKissick Papers.

Southern Labor Archives, University Library, Georgia State University, Atlanta
AFL-CIO Civil Rights Department, Southern Office Records, 1964–1979.
Amalgamated Clothing and Textile Workers' Union Southern Textile Regional Office Papers.
United Paperworkers International Union, Local 446 Papers.
United Steelworkers of America Papers.

Southern Regional Council, West Peachtree Street, Atlanta
Southern Regional Council Papers (unprocessed post-1968 material).

Special Collections Department, J. Murrey Atkins Library, University of North Carolina at Charlotte
Frederick Douglas Alexander Papers.
Kelly M. Alexander Papers.
Julius L. Chambers Papers.
Reginald A. Hawkins Papers.
William Waggoner Papers.

Special Collections Department, Robert W. Woodruff Library, Atlanta University Center
Southern Regional Council Papers (microfilm).

Strom Thurmond Institute, Clemson University, Clemson, SC
Harry Dent Papers.
Strom Thurmond Papers.

GOVERNMENT DOCUMENTS

Equal Employment Opportunity Commission. *Making a Right a Reality: An Oral History of the Early Years of the EEOC, 1965–1972.* Washington, DC: Equal Employment Opportunity Commission, 1990.
U.S. Commission on Civil Rights. *The Voting Rights Act: The First Months.* Washington DC: U.S. Government Printing Office, 1965.
———. *Survey of School Desegregation in the Southern and Border States, 1965–66.* Washington, DC: U.S. Government Printing Office, 1966.
———. *Political Participation: A Study of the Participation by Negroes in the Electoral and Political Processes in 10 Southern States since Passage of the*

Voting Rights Act of 1965. Washington, DC: U.S. Government Printing Office, 1968.

———. *Jobs and Civil Rights: The Role of the Federal Government in Promoting Equal Opportunity in Employment and Training.* Washington, DC: U.S. Government Printing Office, 1969.

———. *What Students Perceive: A Report of the U.S. Commission on Civil Rights.* Washington, DC: U.S. Government Printing Office, 1969.

———. *Five Communities: Their Search for Equal Education.* Washington, DC: U.S. Government Printing Office, 1972.

———. *Title IV and School Desegregation.* Washington, DC: U.S. Government Printing Office, 1973.

———. *The Voting Rights Act: Ten Years After.* Washington, DC: U.S. Government Printing Office, 1975.

———. *The Federal Civil Rights Enforcement Effort, 1977: To Eliminate Employment Discrimination: A Sequel.* Washington, DC: U.S. Government Printing Office, 1977.

———. *Statement on Metropolitan School Desegregation: A Report of the United States Commission on Civil Rights.* Washington, DC: U.S. Government Printing Office, 1977.

———. *Where Mules Outrate Men: Migrant and Seasonal Farmworkers in North Carolina.* Report of the North Carolina Advisory Committee to the U.S. Commission on Civil Rights. Washington, DC: U.S. Government Printing Office, 1979.

———. *The Black/White Colleges: Dismantling the Dual System of Higher Education.* Washington, DC: U.S. Government Printing Office, 1981.

———. *Promises and Perceptions: Federal Efforts to Eliminate Employment Discrimination through Affirmative Action.* Report of Thirteen State Advisory Committees to the U.S. Commission on Civil Rights. Washington, DC: U.S. Government Printing Office, 1981.

———. *The Decline of Black Farming in America: A Report of the United States Commission on Civil Rights.* Washington, DC: U.S. Government Printing Office, 1982.

———. *New Evidence on School Desegregation.* Clearinghouse Publication 92. Washington, DC: U.S. Commission on Civil Rights, 1987.

———. *Burning of African-American Churches in Mississippi and Perceptions of Race Relations.* Community Forum Executive Summary. Washington, DC: U.S. Commission on Civil Rights, 1996.

———. *A Bridge to One America: The Civil Rights Performance of the Clinton Administration.* Washington, DC: U.S. Government Printing Office, 2001.

———. *Redefining Rights in America: The Civil Rights Record of the George W. Bush Administration, 2001–2004.* Draft Report for the Commissioners' Review. Washington, DC: U.S. Commission on Civil Rights, 2004.

U.S. Congress. House. Education and Labor Committee. *Equal Employment Opportunity Commission: Hearings before the Subcommittee on Equal Opportunities.* 93rd Cong, 2nd sess., 1974.

————. Education and Labor Committee. *Juvenile Justice and Delinquency Prevention and Runaway Youth: Hearings before the Subcommittee on Equal Opportunities*. 93rd Cong., 2nd sess., 1974.

————. Education and Labor Committee. *Oversight Hearings on Federal Enforcement of Equal Employment Opportunity Laws: Part 2*. 94th Cong., 1st sess., 1975.

————. Education and Labor Committee. *Equal Opportunity and Full Employment: Part 5, Hearings before the Subcommittee on Equal Opportunities*. 94th Cong., 2nd sess., 1976.

————. Judiciary Committee. *Enforcement of the Voting Rights Act: Hearings before Subcommittee No. 4*. 92nd Cong., 1st sess., 1971.

————. Judiciary Committee. *School Busing: Part 1, Hearings before Subcommittee No. 5*. 92nd Cong., 2nd sess., 1972.

————. Judiciary Committee. *School Busing: Part 2, Hearings before Subcommittee No. 5*. 92nd Cong., 2nd sess., 1972.

————. Judiciary Committee. *School Busing: Part 3, Hearings before Subcommittee No. 5*. 92nd Cong., 2nd sess., 1972.

————. Judiciary Committee. *Extension of the Voting Rights Act: Part 1*. 94th Cong., 1st sess., 1975.

————. Judiciary Committee. *Extension of the Voting Rights Act: Part 2*. 94th Cong., 1st sess., 1975.

————. Special Subcommittee on Labor of the Committee on Education and Labor. *Proposed Federal Legislation to Prohibit Discrimination in Employment in Certain Cases because of Race, Religion, Color, National Origin, or Sex: Hearings before the Special Subcommittee on Labor of the Committee on Education and Labor*. 87th Cong., 2nd sess., 1962.

U.S. Congress. Senate. Committee on the Judiciary. *Amendments to the Voting Rights Act of 1965: Hearings before the Subcommittee on Constitutional Rights*. 91st Cong., 1st sess., 1969, and 91st Cong., 2nd sess., 1970.

————. Labor and Public Welfare Committee. *Equal Employment Opportunities Enforcement Act of 1971: Hearings before the Subcommittee on Labor*. 92nd Cong., 1st sess., 1971.

————. Select Equal Educational Opportunity Committee. *Equal Education Opportunity, 1971: Part 10, Displacement and Present Status of Black School Principals in Desegregated School Districts*. 92nd Cong., 1st sess., 1971.

————. Select Equal Educational Opportunity Committee. *Equal Education Opportunity, 1971: Part 11, Status of School Desegregation Law*. 92nd Cong., 1st sess., 1971.

————. Select Equal Educational Opportunity Committee. *Toward Equal Educational Opportunity: Report before the Senate Select Committee on Equal Education Opportunity*. 92nd Cong., 2nd sess., 1972.

AUTHORS' INTERVIEWS

Chambers, Julius. June 28, 1996, Durham, NC.
Coley, Allen. October 13, 1997, Natchez, MS.
Collins, Alton. February 3, 1996, Columbus, GA.
Ferguson, James E., II. June 14, 1996, Charlotte, NC.
Hamilton, Leroy. July 25, 1997, Woodbine, GA.
Hill, Herbert. November 16, 1995, Madison, WI.
Johnson, David. July 22, 1997, Bogalusa, LA.
Larry, R. C. July 23, 1997, Port St. Joe, FL.
Lynd, Terry. November 13, 2004, Satsuma, AL.
McCullough, Joe. October 3, 1997, Savannah, GA.
Moody, Joseph P. March 12, 1996, Roanoke Rapids, NC.

ARCHIVED INTERVIEWS

New South Voices Collection, Special Collections Department, J. Murrey Atkins Library, University of North Carolina at Charlotte
Albright, Robert. August 10, 1992.
Alexander, Alfred L. May 10, 2001.
Brookshire, Stanford R. May 22, 1979.
Dunlap, Daisy. October 27, 2001.
Grier, Katie. October 27, 2001.
McGill, Katie. November 1, 2001.
Randolph, Elizabeth Schmoke. June 16, 1993.
Stroud, Daisy S. June 20, 2001.
Wilson, Madelyn Joyce S. February 2, 2002.

Southern Oral History Program, Wilson Library, University of North Carolina at Chapel Hill
Camp, Patsy Rice. March 23, 1999.
Craig, Dorothy. November 15, 2004.
Gibbs, Timothy. May 27, 1998.
Hopkins, Madge. October 17, 2000.

BOOKS, ARTICLES, AND DISSERTATIONS

Anderson, Terry. *The Pursuit of Fairness: A History of Affirmative Action*. New York: Oxford University Press, 2004.
Appy, Christian G. *Working-Class War: American Combat Soldiers and Vietnam*. Chapel Hill: University of North Carolina Press, 1993.
Arsenault, Ray. *Freedom Riders: 1961 and the Struggle for Racial Justice*. Oxford: Oxford University Press, 2006.
Ball, Howard. *The Bakke Case: Race, Education, and Affirmative Action*. Lawrence: University Press of Kansas, 2000.

———. *Justice in Mississippi: The Murder Trial of Edgar Ray Killen.* Lawrence: University Press of Kansas, 2006.

Bartley, Abel A. "The 1960 and 1964 Jacksonville Riots: How Struggle Led to Progress." *Florida Historical Quarterly* 78, no. 1 (1999): 46–73.

———. *Keeping the Faith: Race, Politics, and Social Development in Jacksonville, Florida, 1940–1970.* Westport, CT: Greenwood, 2000.

Bartley, Numan V. *The New South, 1945–1980: The Story of the South's Modernization.* Baton Rouge: Louisiana State University Press, 1995.

Bass, Jack. *Taming the Storm: The Life and Times of Judge Frank M. Johnson, Jr. and the South's Fight over Civil Rights.* New York: Doubleday, 1993.

Bass, Jack, and Walter DeVries. *The Transformation of Southern Politics: Social Change and Political Consequence since 1945.* New York: Basic, 1976.

Bass, Jack, and Jack Nelson. *The Orangeburg Massacre.* New York: World, 1970.

Bass, Jack, and Marilyn W. Thompson. *Strom: The Complicated Personal and Political Life of Strom Thurmond.* New York: PublicAffairs, 2005.

Bates, Beth Tompkins. *Pullman Porters and the Rise of Protest Politics in Black America, 1925–1945.* Chapel Hill: University of North Carolina Press, 2001.

Berg, Manfred. *"The Ticket to Freedom": The NAACP and the Struggle for Black Political Integration.* Gainesville: University Press of Florida, 2005.

Blauner, Bob. *Black Lives, White Lives: Three Decades of Race Relations in America.* Berkeley and Los Angeles: University of California Press, 1989.

Blum, John Morton. *Years of Discord: American Politics and Society, 1961–1974.* New York: Norton, 1991.

Boger, John Charles, and Gary Orfield, eds. *School Resegregation: Must the South Turn Back?* Chapel Hill: University of North Carolina Press, 2005.

Bolton, Charles C. *The Hardest Deal of All: The Battle over School Integration in Mississippi, 1870–1980.* Jackson: University Press of Mississippi, 2005.

Bourne, Peter G. *Jimmy Carter: A Comprehensive Biography from Plains to Postpresidency.* New York: Scribner, 1997.

Branch, Taylor. *Pillar of Fire: America in the King Years, 1963–65.* New York: Simon & Schuster, 1998.

———. *At Canaan's Edge: America in the King Years, 1965–68.* New York: Simon & Schuster, 2006.

Brattain, Michelle. *The Politics of Whiteness: Race, Workers, and Culture in the Modern South.* Princeton, NJ: Princeton University Press, 2001.

Brinkley, Alan. *American History: A Survey.* Vol. 2, *Since 1865.* 11th ed. Boston: McGraw-Hill, 2003.

Brownlie, W. Elliot, and Hugh Davis Graham, eds. *The Reagan Presidency: Pragmatic Conservatism and Its Legacies.* Lawrence: University Press of Kansas, 2002.

Button, James W. *Blacks and Social Change: Impact of the Civil Rights Movement in Southern Communities.* Princeton, NJ: Princeton University Press, 1989.

Byerly, Victoria. *Hard Times Cotton Mill Girls: Personal Stories of Womanhood and Poverty in the South*. Ithaca, NY: ILR Press, 1986.

Campbell, Karl E. *Senator Sam Ervin, Last of the Founding Fathers*. Chapel Hill: University of North Carolina Press, 2007.

Carson, Clayborne. *In Struggle: SNCC and the Black Awakening of the 1960s*. Cambridge, MA: Harvard University Press, 1981.

Carson, Clayborne, David J. Garrow, Gerald Gill, Vincent Harding, and Darlene Clark Hine, eds. *The Eyes on the Prize Civil Rights Reader: Documents, Speeches, and Firsthand Accounts from the Black Freedom Struggle, 1954–1990*. New York: Penguin, 1991.

Carter, Dan T. *Scottsboro: A Tragedy of the American South*. Baton Rouge: Louisiana State University Press, 1969.

———. *The Politics of Rage: George Wallace, the Origins of the New Conservatism, and the Transformation of American Politics*. 2nd ed. Baton Rouge: Louisiana State University Press, 2000.

———. "Is There Still a South and Does It Matter?" *Dissent*, Summer 2007, 92–96.

Carter, David C. *The Music Has Gone Out of the Movement: Civil Rights and the Johnson Administration, 1965–1968*. Chapel Hill: University of North Carolina Press, 2009.

Cashin, Sheryll. *The Failure of Integration: How Race and Class Are Undermining the American Dream*. New York: PublicAffairs, 2004.

Chafe, William H. *Civilities and Civil Rights: Greensboro, North Carolina and the Black Struggle for Freedom*. New York: Oxford University Press, 1980.

———. *The Unfinished Journey: America since World War II*. 3rd ed. New York: Oxford University Press, 1995.

Cobb, Charles E., Jr. *On the Road to Freedom: A Guided Tour of the Civil Rights Trail*. Chapel Hill, NC: Algonquin, 2008.

Colburn, David. *Racial Change and Community Crisis: St. Augustine, Florida, 1877–1980*. New York: Columbia University Press, 1985.

Crespino, Joseph. *In Search of Another Country: Mississippi and the Conservative Counterrevolution*. Princeton, NJ: Princeton University Press, 2007.

Crooks, James B. *Jacksonville: The Consolidation Story, from Civil Rights to the Jaguars*. Gainesville: University Press of Florida, 2004.

Crosby, Emilye. *A Little Taste of Freedom: The Black Freedom Struggle in Claiborne County, Mississippi*. Chapel Hill: University of North Carolina Press, 2005.

Curry, Constance. *Silver Rights: The Story of the Carter Family's Brave Decision to Send Their Children to an All-White School and Claim Their Civil Rights*. San Diego: Harcourt Brace, 1995.

Curry, Constance, et al. *Deep in Our Heart: Nine White Women in the Freedom Movement*. Athens: University of Georgia Press, 2000.

Dailey, Jane. "The Limits of Liberalism in the New South: The Politics of Race, Sex, and Patronage in Virginia, 1879–1883." In *Jumpin' Jim Crow: Southern Politics from Civil War to Civil Rights*, ed. Jane Dailey, Glenda Elizabeth Gilmore, and Bryant Simon, 88–114. Princeton, NJ: Princeton University Press, 2000.

Dallek, Robert. *Ronald Reagan: The Politics of Symbolism.* Cambridge, MA: Harvard University Press, 1984.

Davidson, Chandler, and Bernard Grofman, eds. *Quiet Revolution in the South: The Impact of the Voting Rights Act, 1965–1990.* Princeton, NJ: Princeton University Press, 1994.

Davis, Jack. *Race against Time: Culture and Separation in Natchez.* Baton Rouge: Louisiana State University Press, 2001.

Dees, Morris, with Steve Fiffer. *A Season for Justice: The Life and Times of Civil Rights Lawyer Morris Dees.* New York: Scribner, 1991.

Dennis, Matthew. *Red, White, and Blue Letter Days: An American Calendar.* Ithaca, NY: Cornell University Press, 2002.

Dent, Tom. *Southern Journey: A Return to the Civil Rights Movement.* Athens: University of Georgia Press, 1997.

Diggins, John P. *Ronald Reagan: Fate, Freedom and the Making of History.* New York: Norton, 2007.

Dittmer, John. *Local People: The Struggle for Civil Rights in Mississippi.* Urbana: University of Illinois Press, 1995.

Douglas, Davison M. *Reading, Writing, and Race: The Desegregation of the Charlotte Schools.* Chapel Hill: University of North Carolina Press, 1995.

Draper, Alan. *Conflict of Interests: Organized Labor and the Civil Rights Movement in the South, 1954–1968.* Ithaca, NY: ILR Press, 1994.

Dumbrell, John. *The Carter Presidency: A Re-Evaluation.* 2nd ed. Manchester: Manchester University Press, 1995.

Dwyer, Owen J., and Derek H. Alderman. *Civil Rights Memorials and the Geography of Memory.* Chicago: Center for American Places at Columbia College, 2008.

Eagles, Charles W. *The Price of Defiance: James Meredith and the Integration of Ole Miss.* Chapel Hill: University of North Carolina Press, 2009.

Egerton, John. *Promise of Progress: Memphis School Desegregation, 1972–1973.* Atlanta: Southern Regional Council, 1973.

———. *Speak Now against the Day: The Generation Before the Civil Rights Movement in the South.* New York: Knopf, 1994.

Ehrman, John. *The Eighties: America in the Age of Reagan.* New Haven, CT: Yale University Press, 2005.

Eskew, Glenn T. *But for Birmingham: The Local and National Movements in the Civil Rights Struggle.* Chapel Hill: University of North Carolina Press, 1997.

Fairclough, Adam. *To Redeem the Soul of America: The Southern Christian Leadership Conference and Martin Luther King, Jr.* Athens: University of Georgia Press, 1987.

———. *Race and Democracy: The Civil Rights Struggle in Louisiana, 1915–1972.* Athens: University of Georgia Press, 1995.

———. *A Class of Their Own. Black Teachers in the Segregated South.* Cambridge, MA: Harvard University Press, 2007.

Fink, Leon, and Brian Greenberg. *Upheaval in the Quiet Zone: A History of Hospital Workers' Union, Local 1199.* Urbana: University of Illinois Press, 1989.

Fleming, Cynthia Griggs. *In the Shadow of Selma: The Continuing Struggle for Civil Rights in the Rural South.* Lanham, MD: Rowman & Littlefield, 2004.

Formisano, Ronald P. *Boston against Busing: Race, Class, and Ethnicity in the 1960s and 1970s.* Chapel Hill: University of North Carolina Press, 1991.

Franklin, Jimmie Lewis. *Back to Birmingham: Richard Arrington, Jr., and His Times.* Tuscaloosa: University of Alabama Press, 1989.

Gaillard, Frye. *Cradle of Freedom: Alabama and the Movement That Changed America.* Tuscaloosa: University of Alabama Press, 2004.

Garrow, David J. *Protest at Selma: Martin Luther King, Jr., and the Voting Rights Act of 1965.* New Haven, CT: Yale University Press, 1978.

———. *Bearing the Cross: Martin Luther King, Jr., and the Southern Christian Leadership Conference.* New York: Morrow, 1986.

Gerstle, Gary. *American Crucible: Race and Nation in the Twentieth Century.* Princeton, NJ: Princeton University Press, 2001.

Gilmore, Glenda Elizabeth. *Gender and Jim Crow: Women and the Politics of White Supremacy in North Carolina, 1896–1920.* Chapel Hill: University of North Carolina Press, 1996.

Godwin, John L. *Black Wilmington and the North Carolina Way: Portrait of a Community in the Era of Civil Rights Protest.* Lanham, MD: University Press of America, 2000.

Goldfield, David R. *Black, White, and Southern: Race Relations and Southern Culture, 1940 to the Present.* Baton Rouge: Louisiana State University Press, 1990.

Grady-Willis, Winston A. *Challenging U.S. Apartheid: Atlanta and Black Struggles for Human Rights, 1960–1977.* Durham, NC: Duke University Press, 2006.

Graham, Hugh Davis. *The Civil Rights Era: Origins and Development of National Policy, 1960–1972.* New York: Oxford University Press, 1990.

Greene, Christina. *Our Separate Ways: Women and the Black Freedom Movement in Durham, North Carolina.* Chapel Hill: University of North Carolina Press, 2005.

Greene, John Robert. *The Presidency of Gerald R. Ford.* Lawrence: University Press of Kansas, 1995.

Grose, Philip G. *South Carolina at the Brink: Robert McNair and the Politics of Civil Rights.* Columbia: University of South Carolina Press, 2006.

Hacker, Andrew. *Two Nations, Black and White: Separate, Hostile, Unequal.* New York: Scribner, 1992.

Hall, Jacquelyn Dowd. "The Long Civil Rights Movement and the Political Uses of the Past." *Journal of American History* 91, no. 4 (March 2005): 1233–63.

Hampton, Henry, and Steve Fayer, with Sarah Flynn. *Voices of Freedom: An Oral History of the Civil Rights Movement from the 1950s through the 1980s.* New York: Bantam, 1990.

Helms, Jesse. *Here's Where I Stand: A Memoir.* New York: Random House, 2005.

Hodgson, Godfrey. *More Equal Than Others: America from Nixon to the New Century.* Princeton, NJ: Princeton University Press, 2004.

Holt, Thomas C., and Elsa Barkley Brown, eds. *From Freedom to "Freedom Now," 1865–1990s.* Vol. 2 of *Major Problems in African-American History.* Boston: Houghton Mifflin, 2000.

Honey, Michael K. *Southern Labor and Black Civil Rights: Organizing Memphis Workers.* Urbana: University of Illinois Press, 1993.

———. *Going Down Jericho Road: The Memphis Strike, Martin Luther King's Last Campaign.* New York: Norton, 2007.

Ifill, Gwen. *The Breakthrough: Politics and Race in the Age of Obama.* New York: Doubleday, 2009.

Irons, Peter. *Jim Crow's Children: The Broken Promise of the Brown Decision.* New York: Penguin, 2002.

Jackson, Thomas E. *From Civil Rights to Human Rights: Martin Luther King Jr. and the Struggle for Economic Justice.* Philadelphia: University of Pennsylvania Press, 2007.

Jacoway, Elizabeth. *Turn Away Thy Son: Little Rock, the Crisis That Shocked a Nation.* New York: Free Press, 2007.

Jonas, Gilbert. *Freedom's Sword: The NAACP and the Struggle against Racism in America, 1909–1969.* New York: Routledge, 2005.

Kirk, John A., ed. *Martin Luther King, Jr. and the Civil Rights Movement.* Basingstoke: Palgrave Macmillan, 2007.

Korstad, Robert. *Civil Rights Unionism: Tobacco Workers and the Struggle for Democracy in the Mid-Twentieth-Century South.* Chapel Hill: University of North Carolina Press, 2003.

Korstad, Robert, and Nelson Lichtenstein. "Opportunities Lost and Found: Labor, Radicals and the Early Civil Rights Movement." *Journal of American History* 75 (December 1988): 786–811.

Kotlowski, Dean J. *Nixon's Civil Rights: Politics, Principle, and Policy.* Cambridge, MA: Harvard University Press, 2001.

Kotz, Nick. *Judgment Days: Lyndon Baines Johnson, Martin Luther King Jr., and the Laws That Changed America.* Boston: Houghton Mifflin, 2006.

Kousser, J. Morgan. *Colorblind Injustice: Minority Rights and the Undoing of the Second Reconstruction.* Chapel Hill: University of North Carolina Press, 1999.

Kruse, Kevin M. *White Flight: Atlanta and the Making of Modern Conservatism.* Princeton, NJ: Princeton University Press, 2005.

Lassiter, Matthew D. *The Silent Majority: Suburban Politics in the Sunbelt South.* Princeton, NJ: Princeton University Press, 2006.

Lawson, Steven F. *Black Ballots: Voting Rights in the South, 1944–1969.* New York: Columbia University Press, 1976.

———. *In Pursuit of Power: Southern Blacks and Electoral Politics, 1965–1982.* New York: Columbia University Press, 1985.

————. *Running for Freedom: Civil Rights and Black Politics in America since 1941.* 2nd ed. New York: McGraw-Hill, 1997.

Lee, Chana Kai. *For Freedom's Sake: The Life of Fannie Lou Hamer.* Urbana: University of Illinois Press, 1999.

Lelyveld, Joseph. *How Race Is Lived in America: Pulling Together, Pulling Apart.* New York: Holt, 2001.

Lewis, George. *Massive Resistance: The White Response to the Civil Rights Movement.* London: Hodder Arnold, 2006.

Lewis, John, with Michael D'Orso. *Walking with the Wind: A Memoir of the Movement.* San Diego: Harcourt Brace, 1998.

Lovett, Bobby L. *The Civil Rights Movement in Tennessee: A Narrative History.* Knoxville: University of Tennessee Press, 2005.

MacLean, Nancy. *Freedom Is Not Enough: The Opening of the American Workplace.* Cambridge, MA: Harvard University Press, 2006.

Massey, Douglas S., and Nancy A. Denton. *American Apartheid: Segregation and the Making of the Underclass.* Cambridge, MA: Harvard University Press, 1993.

Matusow, Allen J. *The Unraveling of America: A History of Liberalism in the 1960s.* New York: Harper & Row, 1984.

McKnight, Gerald D. *The Last Crusade: Martin Luther King, Jr., the FBI, and the Poor People's Campaign.* Boulder, CO: Westview, 1998.

Meier, August, and Elliott Rudwick. *CORE: A Study in the Civil Rights Movement, 1942–1968.* New York: Oxford University Press, 1973.

Minchin, Timothy J. *Hiring the Black Worker: The Racial Integration of the Southern Textile Industry, 1960–1980.* Chapel Hill: University of North Carolina Press, 1999.

————. *"Don't Sleep with Stevens!": The J. P. Stevens Campaign and the Struggle to Organize the South, 1963–80.* Gainesville: University Press of Florida, 2005.

Minchin, Timothy J., and John A. Salmond. "'The Saddest Story of the Whole Movement': The Clyde Kennard Case and the Search for Racial Reconciliation in Mississippi, 1955–2007." *Journal of Mississippi History* 71, no. 3 (Fall 2009): 191–234.

Morris, Aldon D. *The Origins of the Civil Rights Movement: Black Communities Organizing for Change.* New York: Free Press, 1984.

Moye, J. Todd. *Let the People Decide: Black Freedom and White Resistance in Sunflower County, Mississippi, 1945–1986.* Chapel Hill: University of North Carolina Press, 2004.

Myrdal, Gunnar. *An American Dilemma: The Negro Problem and Modern Democracy.* 20th anniversary ed. New York: Harper & Row, 1962.

Namorato, Michael V., ed. *Have We Overcome? Race Relations since Brown.* Jackson: University Press of Mississippi, 1979.

Nelson, Jack, and Jack Bass. *The Orangeburg Massacre.* Cleveland, OH: World, 1970.

Nicholls, Keith. "The Non-Partisan Voters League of Mobile, Alabama: Its

Founding and Major Accomplishments." *Gulf South Historical Review* 8, no. 2 (Spring 1993): 74–88.

Nixon, Richard. *RN: The Memoirs of Richard Nixon.* New York: Macmillan, 1978.

Norrell, Robert J. *The House I Live In: Race in the American Century.* New York: Oxford University Press, 2005.

Norton, Mary Beth, et al. *A People and a Nation: A History of the United States.* 6th ed. Boston: Houghton Mifflin, 2001.

Patterson, James T. *Brown v. Board of Education: A Civil Rights Milestone and Its Troubled Legacy.* New York: Oxford University Press, 2001.

———. *Restless Giant: The United States from Watergate to* Bush v. Gore. New York: Oxford University Press. 2005.

Patterson, Orlando. *The Ordeal of Integration: Progress and Resentment in America's Racial Crisis.* New York: Basic, 1997.

Powledge, Fred. *Free at Last? The Civil Rights Movement and the People Who Made It.* Boston: Little, Brown, 1991.

Prather, Leon, Sr. *"We Have Taken a City": The Wilmington Racial Massacre and Coup of 1898.* Cranbury, NJ: Associated University Presses, 1984.

Pratt, Robert A. *We Shall Not Be Moved: The Desegregation of the University of Georgia.* Athens: University of Georgia Press, 2006.

Pride, Richard A., and J. David Woodard. *The Burden of Busing: The Politics of Desegregation in Nashville, Tennessee.* Knoxville: University of Tennessee Press, 1985.

Ralph, James R., Jr. *Northern Protest: Martin Luther King, Jr., Chicago, and the Civil Rights Movement.* Cambridge, MA: Harvard University Press, 1993.

Reed, Merl E. *Seedtime for the Modern Civil Rights Movement: The President's Committee on Fair Employment Practice, 1941–1946.* Baton Rouge: Louisiana State University Press, 1991.

Robinson, Armstead L., and Patricia Sullivan, eds. *New Directions in Civil Rights Studies.* Charlottesville: University Press of Virginia, 1991.

Romano, Renee C., and Leigh Raiford, eds. *The Civil Rights Movement in American Memory.* Athens: University of Georgia Press, 2006.

Rossell, Christine H. "School Desegregation and White Flight." *Political Science Quarterly* 90, no. 4 (Winter 1975–1976): 675–95.

Salmond, John A. *"My Mind Set on Freedom": A History of the Civil Rights Movement, 1954–1968.* Chicago: Dee, 1997.

———. *Southern Struggles: The Southern Labor Movement and the Civil Rights Struggle.* Gainesville: University Press of Florida, 2004.

Schafer, Byron E., and Richard Johnston. *The End of Southern Exceptionalism: Class, Race and Partisan Change in the Postwar South.* Cambridge, MA: Harvard University Press, 2006.

Schraff, Anne. *Coretta Scott King: Striving for Civil Rights.* Berkeley Heights, NJ: Enslow, 1997.

Schulman, Bruce J. *From Cotton Belt to Sunbelt: Federal Policy, Economic*

Development, and the Transformation of the South, 1938–1980. New York: Oxford University Press, 1991.

Scribner, Christopher MacGregor. *Renewing Birmingham: Federal Funding and the Promise of Change, 1929–1979*. Athens: University of Georgia Press, 2002.

Shields, Todd G., Jeannie M. Whayne, and Donald R. Kelley, eds. *The Clinton Riddle: Perspectives on the Forty-Second President*. Fayetteville: University of Arkansas Press, 2004.

Shklar, Judith. *American Citizenship: The Quest for Inclusion*. Cambridge, MA: Harvard University Press, 1991.

Shull, Stephen A. *American Civil Rights Policy from Truman to Clinton: The Role of Presidential Leadership*. Armonk, NY: Sharpe, 1999.

Silver, James W. *Mississippi: The Closed Society*. London: Gollancz, 1964.

Sitkoff, Harvard. *King: Pilgrimage to the Mountaintop*. New York: Hill & Wang, 2008.

Sokol, Jason. *There Goes My Everything: White Southerners in the Age of Civil Rights, 1945–1975*. New York: Knopf, 2006.

Sosna, Morton. *In Search of the Silent South: Southern Liberals and the Race Issue*. New York: Columbia University Press, 1977.

Strain, Christopher. "Soul City, North Carolina: Black Power, Utopia, and the African American Dream." *Journal of African American History* 89, no. 1 (Winter 2004): 57–74.

Sugrue, Thomas J. *Sweet Land of Liberty: The Forgotten Struggle for Civil Rights in the North*. New York: Random House, 2008.

Sullivan, Patricia. *Days of Hope: Race and Democracy in the New Deal Era*. Chapel Hill: University of North Carolina Press, 1996.

———. *Lift Every Voice: The NAACP and the Making of the Civil Rights Movement*. New York: New Press, 2009.

Synnott, Marcia G. "African American Women Pioneers in Desegregating Higher Education." In *Higher Education and the Civil Rights Movement: White Supremacy, Black Southerners, and College Campuses*, ed. Peter Wallenstein, 199–228. Gainesville: University Press of Florida, 2008.

Talbot, David. *Brothers: The Hidden History of the Kennedy Years*. New York: Free Press, 2007.

Thomas, Larry Reni. *The True Story behind the Wilmington Ten*. Hampton, VA: U.B. and U.S. Communications, 1993.

Thornton, J. Mills, III. *Dividing Lines: Municipal Politics and the Struggle for Civil Rights in Montgomery, Birmingham, and Selma*. Tusacaloosa: University of Alabama Press, 2002.

Trotter, Joe William, Jr., ed. *The Great Migration in Historical Perspective: New Dimensions of Race, Class, and Gender*. Bloomington: Indiana University Press, 1991.

Troy, Gil. *Morning in America: How Ronald Reagan Invented the 1980s*. Princeton, NJ: Princeton University Press, 2005.

Tuck, Stephen G. N. *Beyond Atlanta: The Struggle for Racial Equality in Georgia, 1940–1980*. Athens: University of Georgia Press, 2001.

Tyson, Timothy B. *Blood Done Sign My Name: A True Story*. New York: Crown, 2004.

Verney, Kevern, and Lee Sartain, eds. *Long Is the Way and Hard: One Hundred Years of the NAACP.* Fayetteville: University of Arkansas Press, 2009.

Wallenstein, Peter, ed. *Higher Education and the Civil Rights Movement: White Supremacy, Black Southerners, and College Campuses.* Gainesville: University Press of Florida, 2008.

Ward, Brian, and Tony Badger, eds. *The Making of Martin Luther King and the Civil Rights Movement.* Basingstoke: Macmillan, 1996.

Washington Research Project. *The Shameful Blight: The Survival of Racial Discrimination in Voting in the South.* Washington, DC: Washington Research Project, 1972.

Webb, Clive. "A Continuity of Conservatism: The Limitations of *Brown v. Board of Education.*" *Journal of Southern History* 70, no. 2 (May 2004): 327–336.

Wheaton, Elizabeth. *Codename Greenkil: The 1979 Greensboro Killings.* Athens: University of Georgia Press, 1987.

Wiebe, Robert H. "White Attitudes and Black Rights from *Brown* to *Bakke.*" In *Have We Overcome? Race Relations since Brown,* ed. Michael V. Namorato, 147–71. Jackson: University Press of Mississippi, 1979.

Wilkins, Roy, with Tom Mathews. *Standing Fast: The Autobiography of Roy Wilkins.* New York: Viking, 1982.

Wilkinson, J. Harvie, III. *From Brown to Bakke: The Supreme Court and School Integration, 1954–1978.* New York: Oxford University Press, 1979.

Williams, Juan. *Eyes on the Prize: America's Civil Rights Years, 1954–1965.* New York: Penguin, 1987.

———. *Enough.* New York: Three Rivers, 2006.

Wolters, Raymond. *The Burden of Brown: Thirty Years of School Desegregation.* Knoxville: University of Tennessee Press, 1984.

———. *Right Turn: William Bradford Reynolds, the Reagan Administration and Black Civil Rights.* New Brunswick, NJ: Transaction, 1996.

Young, Andrew. *An Easy Burden: The Civil Rights Movement and the Transformation of America.* New York: Harper Collins, 1996.

Zieger, Robert H. *For Jobs and Freedom: Race and Labor in America since 1865.* Lexington: University Press of Kentucky, 2007.

FILMS AND TELEVISION SERIES

Eyes on the Prize. Blackside Production Company, 1987.

Freedom Song. TNT Originals, 2000.

Ghosts of Mississippi. Castle Rock, 1996.

In the Heat of the Night. NBC, 1988–1994.

The Long Walk Home. Mirimax Films, 1990.

Mississippi Burning. MGM, 1988.

My Name is Earl. NBC, 2005–.

Once upon a Time When We Were Colored. Republic Pictures, 1995.

The Rosa Parks Story. Xenon Pictures, 2002.

Selma, Lord, Selma. Disney, 2004.

INDEX